The Underside of History

St. Louis and His Wife Marguerite (Helmut Peter Buchen)

The Underside of History
A View of Women through Time

Elise Boulding

Westview Press
Boulder, Colorado

Illustrated by Helen Barchilon Redman

Copyright 1976 by Westview Press, Inc.

Published 1976 in the United States of America by
     Westview Press, Inc.
     1898 Flatiron Court
     Boulder, Colorado   80301
     Frederick A. Praeger, Publisher and Editorial Director

Library of Congress Cataloging in Publication Data

Boulding, Elise.
     The underside of history: a view of women through time
     Bibliography
     Includes index.
     1. Women—History.   I. Title.
HQ1127.B68   301.41'2'09   75-30558
ISBN 0-89158-009-3

Printed and bound in the United States of America

To all the women,
of every time and space,
who are this book

Contents

Part 1
Setting the Stage

Part 2
Women as Civilizers

Part 3
The Emergence of Women from the Renaissance: 1450 to 1900

Part 4
Epilogue

A section of photographs appears
following page 413

List of Tables

List of Figures

Preface

This book was started during a year of retreat spent in my hermitage in the mountains near Boulder. It was a year of reading, reflection, withdrawal, a year needed to develop a deeper sense of connectedness after a very crowded life. This is the kind of book that can
only be written in solitude. Like all macrohistory, it is autobiographical—the story of the author's search for meaning in human existence.
The underside theme came naturally. A woman activist in the twentieth century cannot avoid identity struggles because society gives
her little ground to stand on. Because I am a sociologist as well as an
activist, I saw that struggle in historical terms. Women have for millennia had to work for the public good from privatized spaces. Why?
    The tension between the activist, the sociologist, and the inwardly-
inclined Quaker, in the process of trying to answer that question in
this book, has been almost unbearable. On the one hand there was
the problem of establishing an adequate knowledge base for writing
a macrohistory. The awareness of my lack of training as a historian,
and of the hit-and-miss quality of my scholarship, has been so acute
that I have repeatedly decided to give up the project because of my
incompetence to do it—only to be driven back to it by some more
powerful counterforce. It is necessary for women to be willing to

stick out their necks when an unprecedented task presents itself. Perhaps the hardest problem of all was to justify to myself attempting to write a scholarly book at a time when I felt called to an inward, spiritual journey. Bending the mind to a major analytic task when the spirit is attuned to prayer is a very special discipline. I held to the discipline for the two years required to finish the book.

The entire book was written at the hermitage, a little one-room cabin in the woods above our family cabin. I carried every one of the hundreds of books used for the work up the steep hill on my back, so I have a physical as well as mental sense of the weight of history. After my university leave was over and I returned to teaching, I came out each weekend to continue work on the book. The hermitage was the only place where there was mental space enough to lay out all the chronologies and all the maps of civilizations I needed to unroll in my head in order to write the history. It was the only place where there was room enough to unreel before the inward eye all the dramas of the past that the books evoked. For two years, the hermitage was bursting with images. Images of the overside of history, images of the underside, and always images of women. So many women—half the human race—and so magnificent. How could I capture and portray what I saw?

The book itself is a failure—a travesty of the history I wanted to record. But it is a necessary failure, because there has to be a first attempt. In reading it, others will see what needs to be done to recover the underside of the human experience, and particularly to recover women as part of history.

If I were to begin this book now, with what I know after two years of work, I would write it differently and, I think, better. I would be able to give a better balance to the presentations of the life situation of women in different social classes, especially to the situation of laboring women, slaves, prostitutes, and laboring children. I have not been able to convey the human suffering of the underside adequately. There have been times when it has almost overwhelmed me. The elites have invariably had more than their share of attention in the book. They too have suffered, however, and again I have failed to portray the heavy burdens of their lives. It seemed so important to point to their accomplishments.

If suffering has been underrecorded, so has joy. In such a book as this, a macrohistory, how do you capture the laughter of young working girls on holiday, the joy of sunrise for a solitary old woman glad to be alive? How do you capture the sound of children playing in the street, the rhythm of kitchen work by busy mothers to the music of clicking pots and pans on feast days, the contentment of the grandmother by the fireside with her granddaughter on her knee? The frontispiece picture of the sculpture of St. Louis and Marguerite of Provence captures something of the joy of the underside. The expression of delight on Marguerite's face as she looks up at her husband cannot be attributed to the trappings of authority of church and state that he bears, dressed in Crusaders' garb, holding a model of the Holy Sepulchre in his right hand and the shield of France in his left. Her expression springs from another source; authority can neither command nor quell it.

I never wanted to write a "big-name" history, but it is relatively easy to dig out the names of the great women achievers, names which are often missing from the standard histories. Thus I found myself continually slipping into big-name history, in spite of myself. Those names had to be put back in the record!

There are wild imbalances in the book in terms of macrohistorical perspective. The major one is the excessive attention to Western history. I could not master the necessary scholarship, in the time I had, to write the world history I originally intended. Also, the nineteenth century gets far more attention than it should have. Yet it seemed right to present the nineteenth century as I did, because the twentieth century activities of women make little sense without a knowledge of their nineteenth century roots. As a sociologist I could not resist a somewhat lengthy discussion of nineteenth century women social scientists, since my profession has no image of its own underside.

The breathless summary of a thousand years of third world history in chapter 12 should perhaps not have been attempted, but I could not be content to enter the last chapter without it.

I have become increasingly aware in recent months of the number of historians who are now doing in-depth studies of particular historical periods, the kind of studies that I so keenly felt the lack of while writing this book. Where their work has come to my attention I have mentioned them, but there is much more work going on than I have been able to uncover. Every specialist will find that the period she or he knows best has been badly treated here, and will find much to criticize. I regret this, but had I been a period specialist I would never have dared to write this book. The justification for macrohistory is supposed to be that it has a validity of its own, independent of individual historical facts. I rejoice that there will be not only one but many successors to this work, each with new facts and new insights about the underside.

As with every historian, my own commitments and beliefs have shaped the emphases I have given to history. I have given more weight to religious currents as a crucial force in the development of the human potential than others might give. Militarism has been treated as pathology, and the development of the sequence "urbanism/societal differentiation/hierarchy/centralization" as one among several possible patterns of human development. I have presented no "grand theory" of history. I have not even fully "explained" the role of women in history. Rather I have tried to develop a perspective, a way of thinking about these roles, that can help us all to connect better with the new developments that are unfolding as we move into the twenty-first century.

The fact that the book has been completed during International Women's Year gives me particular satisfaction. It is a rare experience for a nonconformist to have one's inner agenda coincide with an agenda set by the world. During the 1975 activities I have become increasingly aware of the quality of leadership that United Nations Assistant Secretary General Helvi Sipila has given to the women's year. Her leadership gives me hope that the United Nations itself will help to open up for women the futures that I have seen glimpses of while writing this book.

The book is long, but the material commanded the length. Those who prefer to read the book as a story may skip the first two chapters and go right to chapter 3, where the tale of *Mulier sapiens* begins. Those who wish to understand the frame of reference within which the history was conceived, however, will want to read the first two chapters. Those who wish to study more deeply a particular topic or period may check the references listed at the back of the chapters to which they apply.

Now I would like to celebrate the people who have made this book possible. Kenneth Boulding's role has been a very special one. He learned the skills of the homemaker in his sixties in order to take over the bulk of household responsibilities while I lived at the hermitage. He cheered me on when I got discouraged, and was always willing to listen when I needed to think out loud about difficult points. He read and commented on each chapter as I wrote it. The fact that we disagree on many things in the interpretation of history made these sessions especially valuable.

The thirty-four-year partnership that Kenneth and I have had has given me many opportunities to know the vitality of the underside of life, and to see how it intersects with the overside. In 1942-1943, when Kenneth was teaching at Fisk University in Nashville, Tennessee,

I discovered the black underside of American society. I had splendid teachers, and the most outstanding among them, then and later, were husband-wife partnerships. Clara and Robert Park and Marie and Charles Johnsen were among my teachers at Fisk. It was they who led me into sociology. Later, in the Parks' apartment in Chicago, I first met Helen and Everett Hughes. They had then just finished a study of the French underside of Canada. Still later, Evey and David Riesman taught me about the underside of the individual in the lonely crowd. Marion and Reuben Hill showed me the connectedness of the family underside with the study of public policy after I became Reuben's student at Iowa State College at Ames, and the Bouldings and Hills began a lifelong family friendship. Another major early teaching for me about adaptation from the underside came from Robert Angell's book on family adjustments to the depression, though it was not until some years later that I had the delight of knowing Esther and Robert Angell at the University of Michigan. All the wives I have mentioned belonged in some sense to the underside while their husbands became well-known in wider circles (with the exception of Helen Hughes), yet they were writers, artists, scholars, teachers, and community leaders, as well as wives and mothers. I know their extraordinary creativity at first hand.

They were not simply "expressing themselves through their husbands." They were expressing *themselves.* The public arena lacks the flavor it might otherwise have had because of the relative invisibility of their work and that of the countless other women whose creativity has flourished in private spaces.

My own launching out from the underside came in 1954, the year I began translating Fred Polak's *Image of the Future* from the Dutch. The power of his interpretation of history as an unfolding of visions of the future, and his personal encouragement to me to do my own visioning in that year when he and Louisa Polak Moor, the gifted Dutch poet, lived with our familiy, effected the launching.

Because there was another baby on the way, the launching took a while. Three important transition activities bridged the time gap in the late fifties and the sixties: 1) my years of work with the Women's International League for Peace and Freedom, 2) my work with the newly established Center for Research on Conflict Resolution at Michigan, and 3) the editing of the Newsletter which led to the founding of the International Peace Research Association in Europe. In these settings I learned overside skills while still on the underside.

My returning to school at the University of Michigan in 1965 to take a doctorate when our fifth and youngest reached fourth grade was the visible manifestation of that launching. Kenneth and all five children participated in it. The companionship of our children has been as important in my personal and intellectual development as any other influence in my life. They too have helped make the book possible: Russell, Mark, Christine, Philip, and William; three new daughters, Bonnie, Susan, and Cyndi; and two grandchildren, Bjorn and Abram.

My own Norwegian immigrant parents, no longer living, shaped my perception of the human possibility many years ago. I owe to my ever-eager, ever-curious mother, Birgit Marianna Johnsen, the assurance that it is all right to want to know, to explore, to experiment. I owe to my gentle father, Josef Biorn-Hansen, a basic experience of acceptance that provided the security from which exploration could take place. Together they taught me that the giving and receiving of love and tenderness is not sex-differentiated. My sisters, Sylvia and Vera, because they were so much younger than I, kept the child's-eye view of the world alive and precious for me in a way that directly contributed to my continuing delight in the underside of creation.

Once launched as a middle-aged graduate student at the University of Michigan, I was grateful for the supportive attitudes of members of the sociology department who were then coping as best they knew how with the first wave of "Older Women Returning to Graduate School." Charles Moskos was my first advisor. I sometimes think that it is because he always heard what I was saying, even before I had the vocabulary to say it, that I gained the courage to go on with the exploration of women's roles that led to this book.

All the women I have ever known in the women's movement have helped me prepare for undertaking this macrohistory of women: my sisters in the Women's International League for Peace and Freedom, and the international groups the League introduced me to; the women I came to know in the year we lived in Japan, and the year we lived in Jamaica; the women I have known in Latin America, Korea, India, and in all the countries of Europe, East and West, including especially the women of my own native land, Norway. The women I have known as neighbors in every community where we have lived, and the women I have worked with in local political and community action programs, and the many Quaker women I have known, have also each in their way helped prepare this book. My professional colleagues in the social sciences, including the associates who served with me on the American Sociological Association Committee on the Status of Women in the Profession, and the women who have worked with me in the International Sociological Association's Research Committee on Sex Roles in Society, all helped me to reflect in new ways on a lifetime of experience of the underside, and to develop the vocabulary to write about it.

The person who has been my closest associate in my new professional life, and who has done the most to help in the long-run preparation of this book, is my friend and administrative assistant, Dorothy Carson. The work of organizing all the multitudinous tasks of scholarly documentation, of supervising the computerizing of the United Nations data on women, of producing handsome and readable charts and tables, and of supervising the actual putting together of the final manuscript has all been done by her. She has also provided valuable continous critical feedback. Without her, there would be no book. Since this has been a two-year job for her as well as for me, and has involved many "overtime hours," there are no words with which I can adequately express my gratitude for what ohe hao done.

Another associate who has worked with me continously on the book for the entire two-year period is Anita Cochran, the Institute of Behavioral Science librarian, who gave many hours to book searches, sometimes with only the slightest of clues to what was needed. She contributed that type of creative librarianship which reduces the pain and enhances the joy of scholarly work.

I am grateful to the University of Colorado Committee on Creative Research for the award of a Faculty Fellowship for the fall of 1974, and to the Institute of Behavioral Science for the facilities available to me for research. I want to express particular gratitude to the University of Colorado libraries for the speed and efficiency of their interlibrary loan service. I am further grateful to the United Nations for the timely award of a contract to convert all United Nations data on women into a form more usable both for scholars and activists, in connection with preparations for International Women's Year. Gloria Scott, of the Social Development and Humanitarian Affairs division, has immeasurably helped our work by performing as a sensitive and facilitating communications link between her division at the United Nations and our program at the Institute of Behavioral Science.

In the early stages of the book, I discussed historical perspectives on women's roles with a number of people; their encouragement helped me to go on with the project. I particularly want to thank Margaret Mead, Jessie Bernard, Berenice Carroll, Saul Mendlovitz, and Johan Galtung for listening and being supportive at that stage, though none of them bear any responsibility for the way the book later developed.

Much of my reading about religious women in history was done in the library of the Benedictine Monastery of Our Lady of the Resurrection near Cold Spring, New York. I am particularly grateful to Brother Victor Antonio of the monastery for his insights about the role of women in the Christian church, and for his help in finding books on women religious. My discussions and retreats with Brother Victor and with sisters of various contemplative and apostolic orders have greatly deepened my understanding of the importance of monastic life in releasing the creativity of women.

Just two months before the completion of the manuscript I was fortunate to discover the Boulder artist, Helen Barchilon Redman, who brought a whole new dimension to the book by becoming both art consultant and illustrator. She prepared for the outward eye many of the images I have seen with the inward eye—sometimes discovering pictures that gave historical verification to phenomena I had only imagined and hypothesized about. I am also grateful to Kathy Hamilton of Boulder Graphics who took a number of difficult problems of schematic representations of maps, drawings, and diagrams and produced beautifully readable graphics as needed. I take particular pleasure in the fact that Bonnie Boulding rendered the drawings for the village layouts in chapter 4. I owe a special debt to Judy Fukuhara, who typed version after version of each chapter of this book with speed, accuracy, and loving care, always finding the time to work on this apparently never-ending project no matter how much else she had to do.

The contribution of the readers of the manuscript has been invaluable. They set me straight when I had the history wrong. They helped me get a better perspective on the whole book. Sheila Johansson's critique as a demographically trained historian was invaluable, and I only regret that, because time was running out, I could not respond more completely to her criticism. Professor Susan Armitage of the University of Colorado history department, librarian Anita Cochran of the Institute of Behavioral Science, and sociologist Suzanne Tessler were the other readers who went through the entire manuscript to critique accuracy, coherence, and perspective. Without their comments I could never have reshaped the original unwieldy and excessively moralizing manuscript into the somewhat more readable version that finally went to the publisher. I am grateful to the period specialists who also went over specific chapters and gave invaluable comments: Professors William Proctor and E. H. Hallgren, medievalists, and Joy King, classicist. My thanks also go to anthropologically trained editor Sharon Bryan who read the first five chapters; to a young family friend and potter, Brian Giffen, who read the entire manuscript and commented on its content and readability from the perspective of the craftsman; and to my sister Vera Larson, who read chapter 2, one of the hardest and most rewritten chapters in the book, and whose perspectives as a family therapist helped me over a specially difficult part.

My research associates who have worked on the global data bank used in chapter 13, Shirley Nuss, Robert Passmore, and Michael Greenstein, have made an important contribution to the book. Shirley Nuss' creative work on women's roles will become increasingly evident in her own published work in the future, and in the collective publication in 1976 of an international women's data handbook by Nuss, Carson, Greenstein, and myself.

The eighty students in the Social History of Women class I taught in the fall of 1975 have played a special part in the final preparation of this book, through the insights generated in our semester-long dialogue about life on the underside. Some of the historical research done by individual students during the semester has been footnoted or inserted in the book at the last minute, and I am grateful for the willingness of these students to share their work with me.

The burden of the last great rush of manuscript preparation was greatly lightened by the work of Alanna Preussner of the University of Colorado English department, who did a mammoth reference-checking and editorial job. Mario Holguín, Maureen Mee, and Holly Hollingsworth also gave great help in the final stages of the manuscript preparation. I was lucky to have in Westview's Lynne Rienner a most careful and discerning copy editor.

To all these people, and to the many others I have not mentioned by name, but who have also helped in various ways not always easy to specify, I say thank you!

Elise Boulding
University of Colorado
December 26, 1975

Part 1
Setting the Stage

1
Sampling the Invisible

History is a problem in sampling. Depending on the point in time at which one considers that one's ancestors became fully human, there have been somewhere between sixty and seventy-seven billion of us around, women and men, weaving an infinite variety of gossamer social webs to girdle the planet. We are an interesting lot, we humans. Yet the most informed of the four billion of us alive today know precious little about our story. We know little enough about our contemporary family, and when we start probing back through history we find huge blank spaces relieved here and there by fragmentary images of kings, pyramids, temples, and battlefields. If we try to go back much beyond five thousand years, our imaginations give out entirely. Yet we and the immediate ancestors to the human race, *Homo* and *Mulier erectus,* have been around for about two million years.[1] Anyone wandering in the bookstores of Stockholm, Brussels, Frankfurt, or Chicago looking for history books will find hundreds on the history of Western civilization, and only dozens on the history of the rest of the world. Yet most of the human beings who have walked through history have lived elsewhere. They have lived all over the planet, of course, but most have lived in Asia. The sampling of human experience in our history books is, in short, very poor.

It would not matter so much that those of us who live in the West focus on our own recent corner of history if we kept it in the proper perspective. But of course we do not. We have created a myth called the "Evolution of Mankind" from our fragments. One of the many strange things about this myth is that it does not include woman. The history of humankind has been written as if it were the history of Western man. An otherwise excellent world history widely used in college courses, McNeill's *The Rise of the West* (1963), contains two mentions of women in a thousand pages.

The elimination of most of the human race from the historical record shrinks our human identity. We don't know fully who we are. We know even less what we might become. Obviously this book cannot answer these broad questions, but it will deal with some specific questions of the role of women in history. In failing to see what was happening to women we have misunderstood the story of the rise of cities and empires, the thrust of "social progress." I propose an attempt to recover some of the wholeness of the human identity by going back to sample the underside, the invisible side, of history, and bring its women to life.

This is not intended to be an exercise in polemics, though polemical elements will inevitably creep in. The history of polemics about the role of women is a long one, and this book is written in the context of the twentieth century version of an old battle. The last round of polemics previous to our own time began about a hundred years ago, when Bachofen wrote *Das Mutterrecht* to show that society had once been a matriarchy and that humankind had once lived under the rule of women. The flurry this book and others caused died down when it was demonstrated that the evidence had been misinterpreted. Women, briefly regarded with suspicious awe, could safely be allowed to lapse into invisibility again. Now we have more complete anthropological data on contemporary tribal societies, including "Stone Age type" hunting and gathering bands. We have archaeological reconstructions of ancient Paleolithic campsites, of the first agrovillages of the Near East, of the first cities of the Mediterranean.

We also have new studies of the literature of antiquity, of ancient laws, and of the political structures of city-states, kingdoms, and empires. A whole new light has been thrown on the European Middle Ages through studies of parish records. Medieval writings in praise of women, as well as denunciations, have been uncovered. The history of the industrial revolution has been rewritten. Out of all this a very different picture of the role of women emerges than the one reflected in the polemics of the nineteenth century or the new polemics of the twentieth. Yet when we turn to standard contemporary histories, women disappear from sight. Queens and courtesans are the most likely female characters to survive the historians' sorting process.

When Cora Castle undertook in 1910 a statistical study of eminent women in history, on the basis of names that appeared in any three out of six major European encyclopedias, she was able only to come up with 868 women, given all of history to draw on. The categories of women treated as most eminent by the encyclopedias, in terms of numbers of lines of biography, were, in rank order: 1) queens, 2) politicians (mostly French salon women of the 1600s), 3) mothers, 4) mistresses, 5) beauties, 6) women religious, 7) women of tragic fate, and 8) women important only through marriage. Substantive achievements of women as the basis for mention trailed in the last seven categories (Castle, 1913).

This kind of treatment of women in history is now outmoded, and yet strangely persistent. The view of Western history as an evolutionary unfolding from the time of the first post-Roman "barbarian" kingdoms led to compelling conceptions of individualism in the nineteenth century, but they were applied to men of the middle and upper classes only. In the twentieth century these conceptions reappear as leftover agenda items for populations excluded from nineteenth century developments, particularly women, the working classes, the poor, and colonized peoples. The excluded folk are now applying these conceptions to themselves. The nineteenth century was the century of the celebration of individualism, but the twentieth century is the century of the celebration of the individuality of all human beings, including women.

The celebration of the individuality of women has taken diverse forms. There have been social science analyses of the occupational segregation and the status inequalities that characterize women's roles everywhere, throwing light on the dynamics of inequality.[2] There has been reconsideration of the theories of the golden age of matriarchy, some more ideological than scholarly, as in Diner's *Mothers and Amazons* (1965) and Davis' *The First Sex* (1971). Reed's *Woman's Evolution from Matriarchal Clan to Patriarchal Family* (1975), also ideological, attempts to synthesize earlier materials into a new statement about matriarchy. Other books in a more polemical style and focusing on the "woman as victim" theme are as varied as Millet's *Sexual Politics* (1973) and Firestone's *Dialectic of Sex* (1970).

In between are a variety of efforts to understand the meanings for women of equality, of participation, and of liberation, in the context of the human condition in the twentieth century. It has been the accumulated work of my contemporaries in the decades between the close of World War I and the onset of the women's liberation era, providing a fresh unclouded look at women, that has made this book possible. Margaret Mead, Alva Myrdal, Viola Klein, Mary Beard, Jessie Bernard, Athena Theodore, Mirra Komarovsky, Barbara E. Ward, Harriet Holter, Evelyn Sullerot, and Ester Boserup are among the leading social scientists of Euro-North America who contributed to the ways of thinking that this book represents. The book has been written out of a Western tradition of thought, but looks to a future when all the major cultural traditions of the planet will be drawn on to delineate the shapes of women's roles in human society.

Margaret Mead was a pioneer in drawing attention to the processes that shaped male and female roles, through cross-cultural analysis. Mead was also among the first to spell out the character of role transition in the modernization process, both for women and for men (Mead, 1950, 1955, 1968, 1970).

Alva Myrdal did a pioneering analysis of the structural constraints that shaped women's roles, first in a policy-oriented study of Sweden (1945) and then, jointly with Viola Klein (Myrdal and Klein, 1968), in a cross-cultural analysis of women's double role as homemaker and producer. Myrdal and Klein were the first to see the large-scale entry of women into the labor force in this century as a return to a former economic productivity, as the "recovering of women's lost territory" (1956: 1-2).

Mary Beard (1946) was the first of the mid-twentieth century historians to utilize the best of modern techniques of documentation and analysis to portray women as significant actors in the public arena throughout history. Documenting the role women played in public affairs in Egyptian, Greco-Roman, and successive European eras from the early Middle Ages to the present, she also drew a picture of successive openings and closings of roles to women.

Jessie Bernard (1975) uncovered and described the underlife—the socially hidden activity and movement—of academic women and has gone on to uncover the underlife of women in their twentieth century roles. Athena Theodore did the same for professional women (1971), and Mirra Komarovsky provided an early sociological analysis of sex roles in terms of cultural contradictions (1946). Barbara E. Ward (1963) forcefully drew the attention of Westerners to what modernization was doing to women in those civilizations of Asia that had traditionally given a more egalitarian status to women than Western values permitted. The essays she assembled from Asian women scholars showed among other things how women were being forced out of independent economic roles and relegated to wife-hostess roles by Westerners accustomed only to dealing with men in public decision-making spheres.

Sullerot (1968), initially examining contemporary occupational data on women in France, was led to an examination of earlier occupational roles of women in Europe and opened up the old, long-forgotten subject of times when women held more equal participatory and decision-making roles than they do now.

Holter (1970) was the first to do a systematic analysis of how practices of stratification lead to power discrepancies between men and women; Boserup (1970) was the first to document in detail, from a precise analysis of agricultural practices, the "how" of early sex-based division of labor leading to that stratification and loss of power. The 1958 International Institute of Differing Civilization Conference on Women's Role in the Development of Tropical and Subtropical Countries (Carr-Sanders, 1959) laid the foundation for a general understanding of the effect of modernization on women's roles, and a series of United Nations conferences and associated research on the status of women over the last two decades demonstrate that the problems continue.

The women scholars so briefly mentioned in this roster represent only the most visible top rank of a large body of women who have during this century laid the basis for a reconceptualization of the roles of women and men in society.

The reader will note that all the scholars I have cited are women. While their perspectives are very different one from the other, their work collectively does represent a special stream of thought in mid-twentieth century sociology. One name that I would add here because of the importance of the global perspective he introduced is William Goode. In looking at the sweep of changes on the entire planet from the perspective of the family, he has made a significant contribution to the understanding of the underside (Goode, 1963). While his analysis has been confined to the past half-century, the depth of his historical insight gives his work a macrohistorical dimension. It took courage for Goode to write his book, and his achievement helped give me courage to write this one.

Uncertainty about the whole phenomenon of role differentiation based on sex, compounded by uncertainties engendered by continuing economic and environmental crises, makes the women's liberation era a time of considerable tension in male-female relationships. As we move toward the twenty-first century we need new perspectives on society, on history, on the human identity. It is a good time to view

the historical process as experienced by women and men. The problems of sampling will continue to dog us: the very invisibility of
women in the historical record makes the effort to include them in a
resurvey of the past problematic. The fact of that invisibility tends to
pull us toward the women-as-victim position on women in history.
The meager reporting on women in the documents we turn to compounds the conviction that they have been excluded from decision
making, recognition, and reward, and left to do the dirty work of society. The middle position, however, between the victim theory and
the decline-from-golden-age-of-matriarchy theory, is the one that
best fits the materials assembled in this book.[3] It is the position eloquently put forward by Beard (1946). In antiquity and in the Middle
Ages there were women who took leadership roles and were involved
in public affairs. Events associated with the developments of the industrial revolution and postmedieval political and legal institutions
reduced the leadership roles of elite women.

The thrust of the present book is different from that of Beard in
several important respects, however. In examining leadership roles of
elite women, there is more emphasis on the structural constraints
that shaped their roles. There is also a continuing emphasis on the
contrast between the predominantly human-welfare orientation of
women's activities, in all social classes, and the predominantly con-
quest-and-dominance orientation of men's activities. That contrast
remains essentially unchanged once city life becomes a focal point of
human existence. In the twentieth century, as in the Mediterranean
civilizations of 2000 B.C., there are no women in the national security
councils of any country, no women in top-level military commands,[4]
no women among the top ecclesiastical authorities (who have historically also had armies at their disposal) of any major religion. Women
heads of state, then as now, can be counted on the fingers of one
hand, with several fingers left over. Even at local levels, few women
will be found in any historical period in positions of responsibility in
any of these centralized hierarchies. The visible world continues to
be male. There is a continuing effort throughout this book to look at
what women *have* been doing in all classes of society, not just among
the elite, and to document the range and variety of their occupations
in the hidden underlife. Finally, there is a commitment to viewing
women's roles in the context of the total time span of human experience, going back before the appearance of our own species to the
two or three million years when *Mulier* and *Homo erectus* explored
the earth, and bringing the exploration up to the threshold of the
twenty-first century.

Some of the perspectives that went into the making of this book are not directly rooted in any of the recognized traditions of the study of women, stemming rather from the other major involvements of my own life. The concern with victimization, oppression, and violence as human problems, and the concern with the extension of the concept of human community from the tribe to the world as a whole, with all the social and political ramifications of that extension, come out of my work as a peace researcher and social activist. The concern for the spiritual dimension in human development comes out of my struggles to integrate the intellectual, spiritual, and activist dimensions in my own life as a homemaker, mother, scholar, teacher, and activist. Finally, the concern to understand the sweep of history comes out of my own profound conviction that the present is intolerable unless understood in the context of the long slow processes of human development on the planet.

It seems appropriate to bring all these concerns together in a book about women because the status of women, as many scholars have now noted, is indeed a useful indicator of how society is doing in its historical enterprise of making humans more humane. When we look at the imbalances regarding women both in the social record and in society itself, we are getting clues about general social imbalances, not just about the status of women. Women's biological attributes do not affect the generalizability of the discoveries we make. With what we know now, it can be said that the social invisibility of women is a cultural artifact rather than a biological necessity. It is also in part a conceptual artifact, due to an underestimation of the role of the household in society dating perhaps from the first empires of antiquity. The faulty conceptualization has made understandings of and policies about sex-based roles peculiarly resistant to those processes of social change that reshape other social roles.

The household unit in society through the first millennium A.D. was responsible for about 90 percent of the total production of the city-states and empires.[5] If we define as *household production* all that is produced inside and adjacent to the home, including courtyard and kitchen garden, family workshop and farm fields (workshop and fields are psychologically adjacent to the household, but may be geographically distant and require long walks for women to their "household" worksites), then we may say that women have at the very least been equal partners in production through most of history. Not infrequently, and particularly in wartime, they have been the major contributors to that production. As long as the household was also the major work base for men, the equal partnership concept would hold. Long before the industrial revolution, however, a substantial amount of craft production was being carried on by both women and men in village and city workshops owned by others. In work outside the household site, women were always disadvantaged.

It happens that many studies of the industrial revolution have focused on the textile industry, which happened in its preindustrial phase to be a family industry carried out in the home as workshop. This has led scholars mistakenly to conclude that the majority of men and all women were carrying out their productive activities within their own households up to the time of the industrial revolution. See, for example, Smelser's (1959) analysis of the impact on families of the shift from home to factory worksites in the British cotton industry. Even Myrdal and Klein make the same mistake (1968). This issue will be further explored in chapters 10 and 13.

In household-based production, then, women have historically probably been an equal and sometimes dominant partner in terms of productivity and decisions about resource allocation. It was the 10 percent of production carried on outside the household, increasing in proportion from A.D. 1000 to the time of the industrial revolution, that placed women at a disadvantage and in menial roles. As we shall see, women of the elite were much less disadvantaged beyond the household.

Women's economic partnership roles throughout history deserve more attention. Recent research indicates that the capital available to women in their domestic partner role, through dowry, inheritance, and management of production activities, was considerably larger than hitherto realized (Goitein, 1967; Jennings, 1975; Herlihy, 1962). Their use of this capital in civic projects also has not been recognized. With the industrial revolution and the shrinking of domestic productivity down to one-fourth to one-fifth or less of the total productivity of a society, capital available to women also shrank and nondomestic worksites became more important. That shrinkage was accompanied by political changes that abolished the public roles of elite women, compounding economic deprivation with political deprivation at the very time when new ideals of political participation were developing. The old household partnership model could no longer serve, and industrialization seemed to spell disaster for women.

An Alternative "Development Story"

The old nineteenth century theme of inevitable progress through industrialization has worn thin. Though enthusiasm can still be found for the view that there is one basic upward path for human societies, with clearly marked stages on the way, prophecies of the decline of the West have moderated this enthusiasm.[6] We are also more knowledgeable about alternative ways of entering modernity stemming from different cultural traditions, with China as the most notable example. This has brought into favor the more modest concept of the multilinearity of social evolution. Other ways of conceptualizing the historical process that sidestep the "onward and upward" issue have been developed by the demographer and the ecologist.

According to the ecological view of history,[7] *Homo erectus* lived for two or three million years in a state of equilibrium in relation to available environmental resources, in a condition of zero population growth. Two factors contributed to population limitation: 1) babies in hunting and gathering bands must be carried in movements from campsite to campsite and in the daily search for food; and 2) bands seem to operate on a principle of limiting the population to a number that can be comfortably cared for and supported by gathering the most desirable and readily available plant and animal foods. This means that there is always more food in the environment than a given band uses, and in times of drought there are ample resources to fall back on. (Farmers are more apt to starve during droughts than food gatherers.) Population control mechanisms among humans (techniques for abortion and contraception are known in most if not all tribal societies) are apparently suspended, or at least practiced more selectively, once nomadic existence has been replaced by a settled agricultural way of life.[8] Children become an asset rather than a handicap. The change in attitudes regarding childbearing that took place about 10,000 B.C. seems to be very difficult to reverse now that environmental constraints once more require limitation of population.

Significant population expansion began about 10,000 B.C. But because there was plenty of room to spread out, and the initial number of settled agriculturalists engaged in this new enterprise of actively breeding children was small, it took a long time to create the kind of population densities that laid the basis for urban civilizations, census-taking, and a decline in the status of women.

Ever since this great transition from the Paleolithic to the Neolithic we have been dealing with increasing problems of scale. From nomadic campsite to agricultural village, from village to trading town, trading town to city, city to city-state, city-state to empire, and empire to nation-state, from raw nationalism to the modified nationalism of a United Nations system, each step represents an increase in population concentration and in the complexity of the sex- and class-segregated patterns of organizing that concentration.

Resource shortages continually developed as societies outgrew their ecological niches. These shortages might come from population growth, but they might also come from the development of structural inequalities in a society that created a nonproductive, overconsuming sector that could not continue to be supported by the existing resource base. Either way, there was pressure for the development of new production technologies.

Shifts in production technology have usually squeezed women out of formerly central roles. Thus, women were the cultivators under the old slash-and-burn agricultural system, but when higher yields required the invention of the plow, men took over[9] and assigned auxiliary tasks to women. Women are the builders when housing involves twig shelters, skin tents, and woven grass huts; they may hang on through the making of adobe houses; but when it comes to fired bricks and processed materials, men take over.[10]

The shift in roles comes about each time because more hands are needed. In the process of inventing productivity-enhancing technologies, auxiliary tasks requiring less skill than the former production role are generated, and if the new technology displaces women, it is women who perform these auxiliary tasks.

Problems of Scale and Dominance Traps for Women

Repeatedly in history, humans were pushed to the threshold of necessary innovations—pushed by socially and biologically created wants in the face of environmental constraints. From the time of the earliest agricultural settlements, women carried a heavy double load of providing a continuing supply of babies throughout their reproductive years—as contrasted with careful spacing in the nomadic state—while participating in the full productive work of society on the farm, in the cottage industry of the home, or in workshops outside the home. As long as the household was the main worksite, technological change did not disadvantage women too seriously; they still retained control of some capital. But, as we will see in chapter 4, I am suggesting that they never had sufficient leisure in the early agrovillages to grasp adequately the new problems of scale that were created in village settings. Hence, inventions to deal with problems of scale became a male task, and women were simply left with new work residues.

In the egalitarian band society, and in what Fried (1967) calls the ranked societies— tribal societies with special prestige roles which involve responsibility for redistribution of goods, but not personal access to more goods—no individuals, women or men, are removed from the primary producer roles. Kinship structures form the infrastructure of society, and most political roles are embedded in kinship roles. It is in the shift from the ranked to the stratified society that some individuals are removed from primary producer roles, with the consequence that differential access to resources develops. In the stratified society the individuals who cease to be primary producers control the labor, and the products, of their fellows. A class society has come into existence. Neither the ecological model, in which population concentration forces that shift, nor the Engels-Marx model, in which domination by men over women in the monogamous household patterns all later stratification and differentiation of access to resources, really accounts for the dynamics of dominance, nor for the fact that one of the forms dominance takes is male control over the female's access to some of her means of production.

In the next chapter we will be exploring the determinants of male dominance as seen by the sociobiologist. For the purposes of this discussion it is enough to point out that hunting-gathering bands are generally monogamous and sex-egalitarian. The domination of female by male stems from other sources than physique and monogamy, and its later forms are linked in complex ways to accumulation and the reward system. Undoubtedly domination of the female has been a powerful reenforcer of all other dominance systems.

In this chapter we are looking at the historical situation of women primarily in terms of social structure. Social historians have pointed out the special role that urbanism has played in the development of stratification systems. Sullerot (1968) sees urbanism as providing the opportunity for "thinker males" to free themselves from producer roles by lumping breeder and producer functions together for cattle, slaves, and females. This in turn gave the major impetus to stratification processes in general and to the domination of the woman by the man in particular.

I suggest that the accumulation of the power to dominate may be a push-pull process involving both pressure from above and from below. The stratification system that emerges from this push-pull process is one in which women are found to be marginal in terms of command roles. A loose stratification of tribes into have and have-more groups could have set in motion a dynamic that led to heavier work loads within households for women than for men. As we will see in chapters 3 and 4, the male hunting role played a special part in the tilting of work loads toward women. Hunting was arduous work while in process, but much more sporadic than women's work. This dynamic resulted in women becoming a special category that has persisted as a social phenomenon through ten thousand years of history. The biological breeder-feeder role of women very likely reenforced other tendencies to place extra work loads on women.

Ceremonials, ranking, and stratification all in their way helped the societies that evolved them in dealing with problems of scale. In stratified societies only elite women participated publicly in policy planning and decision making. They used their male-derived status for a parallel, if secondary, exercise of power. Ceremonies and rituals are interesting because they have the unique property of being relevant techniques of social organization at every level of community. Women play an important role in the ceremonial life of every society, and much Paleolithic and early Neolithic ceremonial was probably created by women in their priestess roles.

Each increment of size and complexity of social organization has its implications for women's roles, including the twentieth century rediscovery of the Paleolithic dictum that population must be held in balance with environmental resources. I sometimes wonder if our motto today does not need to be: "Forward to the Paleolithic!" The folk of the Neolithic, with their cozy farm communities, working like dogs and breeding like rabbits, have little that is useful to say to us. And while I am not prepared to join Richard Lee and Irven De Vore's (1968) bushmen, or Colin Turnbull's (1968) forest people, bands like these have sometimes been called the only leisure societies left on the planet. They have had population control and (relative) abundance, leisure time, a rich ceremonial life, and relative peace, throughout the entire period that Eurasia has fought to ever higher levels of struggle.

On the other hand, we cannot simply write off the experience of the last twelve thousand years. However we evaluate the achievements of these millennia, they are in fact the products of the human experience. Empire and military glory have undoubtedly been valued too highly, but they do belong somewhere in the story. Revaluing our own creativity as we look at a fuller record of human history, in order to gain an understanding of how to nurture the best of the human potentials in the future, is a task not to be ignored. As we understand better what women were actually doing century by century through recorded time, we will have a better comprehension of our own behavioral repertoire, and of the social inventions at our disposal.

The Approach of This Book

The Long Look

The reconstruction and revaluing of women's roles undertaken in this book necessitate a long walk through history, from the time of our earliest primate ancestors onward. We will move through the hundred-thousand-year wanderings of the Paleolithic; on into the great transition from hunting and gathering to herding and planting; on to life inside city walls and life outside it for the nomads and the forest dwellers; to the great primary civilizations of the Middle East and Asia, and the feudal civilizations on its fringes; on to the most recent sweep of culture from the Greco-Romanic-Islamic empires to "European Enlightenment"; and finally to the last two centuries of gradual industrialization-urbanization of large parts of the planet. It was originally intended to keep this a world history right up to the twentieth century. The impossibility of covering developments in Asia, Africa, and Latin America with the limited research time available has led me, reluctantly, to focus on "the West" after the fall of Rome. A sweeping historical survey of the third world is included as chapter 12, before the final chapter, in order to bring that whole sector of underlife experience of third world women into focus before launching into a discussion of the future.

The immediate stimulus for this work came from a study in the middle sixties of the current participation of women in the economic, educational, and civic sectors on four continents (E. Boulding, 1969). It was finding an enormous variation in traditional participation patterns in Africa and Asia, compared to a narrow range of participation in modernized societies, that led me to the questions I am asking here, and to the historical survey which this book represents.

I found that women's traditional roles were the most autonomous and participatory in countries that entered modernization from the essentially preurban kingdoms of Africa and the outpost empires of Asia, and from tribal societies. Women in the central empire countries from the anciently urbanized Syriac-Palestinian area had the least individuated roles.

While for Western countries the "floor" of participation is higher than for preindustrial societies—that is, there is a participatory level below which women do not fall in the West—the ceiling is also lower; women do not rise to the heights of participation that they do in some traditional African and Asian countries. This means that the theories that equate societal differentiation with increased autonomy and participation are inadequate. Nevertheless, since social structures pattern individual participation, attention must be paid to the differentiation process.[11]

An important feature of structural differentiation is the relative independence of the various systems within the society. In the simplest societies, economic, political, legal, religious, and educational systems are all embedded in the kinship structure. The idea of the completely differentiated society assumes that each sector operates to a degree independently in terms of definition of tasks and responsibilities, and that each individual operates on the basis of universalistic principles rather than from special interest. In fact, of course, such terms as *military-industrial complex* and *power elite* indicate that both embeddedness and particularism continue into the present.

On the one hand, the old view of "primitive societies" as ones in which all human activities, all value judgments, and all loyalties refer back to family groups, and of "modern societies" as ones in which every individual regardless of sex, race, or class carries out specialized functions with an objective and sophisticated commitment to the universal good, is gradually breaking down. On the other hand, we continue to define—and experience—differentiation and centralization as leading to a higher, more all-encompassing social good and to progress. We certainly conceptualize these phenomena as progress in our social theories. Have differentiation and centralization meant progress for women?

Sampling by Means of the Random Walk

Initially, I had developed a societal-complexity profile and a women's-participation profile to measure the extent of differentiation of societal and of women's roles in each society through history. This plan had to be abandoned for two reasons. First, it would require a social historian knowledgeable enough to make proper judgments about societal complexity in different historical eras. Second, I found that information on women in the easily available history books in every period of history was so spotty, so like chance eruptions of hot springs in areas where thermal waters run close to the earth's surface, that it was impossible to do the systematic codification I had hoped to do. A number of women historians are now working with primary sources to correct this situation, and in another ten years we will have much more adequate data on women through time than were available to me. It is not my purpose to try to do badly what the trained historian can do well, but to develop a new way of thinking about women in the historical process. I hope this rough preliminary survey of the terrain has some usefulness as an interim statement while the researches of trained historians are being carried out. An adequate macrohistory of women's roles lies in the future.[12]

Instead of a sophisticated historical study of societal differentiation and women's roles, then, I offer my personal "sociological" walk through history and accounts of the activities of the women I have seen there. Whatever their social class, they have invariably been more productive and more overworked than would be suspected from an examination of the male diatribes against them that can be found in every historical era from Sumerian times on. Each one described should be taken as illustrative of countless of her sisters who remain invisible.

Although I do not present a systematic macrohistorical analysis of societal differentiation, I have given some attention to the structural features and cultural uniqueness of each society studied through time. Since both women's and men's roles are shaped by social structures and cultural patterning, it may be useful to list the kinds of societies we will be studying as we move through history. These do not necessarily represent an evolutionary sequence, and in fact some variant of each major type of society still exists in some form somewhere today. Hunting-gathering societies are found on all continents. Remnants of "forest civilizations" are found in Africa. Singapore is a city-state. Southeast Asia still contains remnants of centralized empires, as in Thailand. Table 1-1 lists the societal types considered here, and table 1-2 indicates the chronology of the appearance of each new type. Each of these new types develops a characteristic social technology. Each set of new social inventions represents adaptations to increasing size and the need for a new scale of activities. These inventions will be referred to as appropriate in each chapter as we discuss women's adaptations to new levels of complexity.

Women and "Underlife" Structures

In this section I will share some of my thinking about the meaning of underlife structures for women, and how these structures have shaped women's lives and behaviors.[13] The underlife concept implies an overlife as well, which consists of overtly articulated role structures--the visible terrain of society. Woman's sex-designated position, resistant to social changes that alter other parts of the social structure, tends to keep her in the underlife sector. From time to time there is a further contraction of roles formally designated for women, and then the feminine half of society reorganizes and readapts to carry out its functions under new cultural constraints. The role of

women in societies where these constraints have been particularly
harsh can be likened to that of the inmates in what Erving Goffman
(1961) calls the "total institutions"—such as prisons, mental hospitals, or army barracks. The temptation to treat the household,
wherever one meets it in history, as a total institution imprisoning
women and children is, however, one that must be resisted. There
will be wide variations in the amount of capital and resources for
production available to women in the household, depending both on
the socioeconomic status of the family and on the time and place in
history. Except among the very poor and the slaves, women householders are never resourceless. Normally, they are both producers
and traders. Yet it is also true that women in most societies are *to a
degree* stripped of identity, autonomy, and privacy as Goffman describes that stripping for inmates of total institutions. With some variation, women in every part of the world are treated in part as prisoners,

Table 1-1.

Societal Types

1. Band or Tribal

   a. Hunting and gathering, egalitarian
   b. Hunting and gathering, horticulture base, ranked

2. Preurban

   a. Agriculture base, "forest civilizations," ranked
      transitional
   b. Nomadic, herding, no agriculture, ranked

3. City-based State

   a. City-state, agriculture, craft industries, urban
      administration, stratified
   b. Feudal kingdom, same as city-state, but with weaker
      urban administration

4. Centralized Bureaucratic Empire

   Agriculture, large-scale industries, trade, strong
   central administration, diplomatic relations with
   other societies, stratified

5. Modern Industrialized, or Transitional

   Mass production, communications infrastructure permitting
   some local autonomy coordinated to varying degrees of
   strong, central planning; stratified, agricultural
   activity involves as little as five percent of the labor
   force

Table 1-2

Chronology of the Emergence of Societal Types,
50,000 B.C. to Present

Time Period	Type of Society
50,000 B.C.-- 10,000 B.C.	Hunting and Gathering
10,000 B.C.-- 6000 B.C.	Settled Agricultural
6000 B.C.--	Trading Town
3500 B.C.--	City
2500 B.C.-- 1500 A.D.	City-State (Most city-states come to an end by time of Roman Empire; another series of city-states in Europe in Middle Ages)
2000 B.C.-- 500 B.C.	Empire Type A. Archaic empires (Hittite, Assyrian)
500 B.C.-- 400 A.D.	Empire Type B. Early empires (Persian, Hellenic, Roman)
400 A.D.-- 1000 A.D.	Empire Type C. Late Roman, Christian, Byzantine, Moslem, and Chinese
1000 A.D.-- 1500 A.D.	Empire Type D. Medieval feudal
1500 A. D.-- 1800 A.D.	Empire Type E. Mercantilist colonialism
1800 A. D.-- Present	Nation States and the New Imperialism

Note: Since every type that has ever existed in history still exists somewhere today, this table is only meant to indicate approximately when each new type first emerged. The dates for the city-state and the empires overlap because of different stages of development in different societies.

mental patients, and dependent children. Their names come from their fathers or their husbands. Their obligations to provide twenty-four-hour domestic service to their fathers, husbands, and children leave them perpetually on call at any time of day or night. There are substantial limitations on their rights to transact business and get credit in their own names, and they have limited rights in courts of law. They will not be found in large numbers among the bureaucrats and administrators of any society, nor in many of its public spaces.

Yet there is an interface between the private, household-centered life of women and the public life of every society, and that interface is in the law court. While law codes place restrictions on women, they also establish rights. We shall see women of substance entering the law courts to fight for their rights of property and freedom of person and freedom to do business even in societies that apparently have secluded women completely. They could do this in ancient Greece, in the Moslem world, in Byzantium, and in Europe. This interface between the women's underlife and the overlife of society, available chiefly to the wealthy, acts in every age to mitigate the severity of victimization or restraint of women.

The underlife itself, which exists in societies as different as urban Turkey and suburban America, is enormously varied and often harbors a rich unrecorded culture. That underlife has been recognized in various ways, but takes its conceptual origin from what Sullerot calls the *dedans* and the *dehors*—the within and the without. She cites Xenophon's classic justification for the servitude of women:

> The gods created the woman for the indoors functions, the man for all others. The gods put woman inside because she has less endurance for cold, heat, and war. For woman, it is honest to remain indoors and dishonest to gad about. For the man it is shameful to remain shut up at home and not to occupy himself with affairs outside (1968: 31-32).[14]

The *dedans* concept is simply descriptive to the extent that women's major workplace is in the household. What turns the *dedans* into a victimage concept is the notion of confining women to the home at all times, and denying her other worksites. This application of the *dedans* concept is indeed suggested by Xenophon in the passage quoted, although it was never practiced by more than a small group of urban middle-class women, even in Xenophon's time.

Another way to think of the underlife/overlife, within/without dichotomy is in terms of private versus public spaces. The kitchen and the courtyard, society's service areas, are for women. The agora, where the public interest is defined and acted on, is for men. Whether we call it the underlife, the within, or the private space, the basic concept tends to carry connotations of the clandestine. To the extent that the males of a society consider women's activities and thought trivial and inconsequential, there is a clandestine quality about the accompanying women's culture. The implication is that this underlife is not serious and consequential for the overlife of the society.

The presentation in literature of the women's world as inconsequential alternates with depictions of women as the source of evil. Various compilations listing all the nasty things men have said about women strongly reenforce the image of women as "outlaws" and the underlife as clandestine. Much energy has been expended on psychological analyses of the tendency of men to fear women and ascribe evil to them. H. R. Hay's *The Dangerous Sex* (1964) summarizes much of this analytic material. What really has to be explained, however, is not why there is an antiwomen literature, but why the majority of writers who deal with these matters focus exclusively on the negative references to women. As Sheila Johansson points out, from any cultural or religious tradition or set of laws it would be equally easy to compile "praise books," consisting of all the admiring and appreciative things that men have said about women. From the "praise books," including Ashley-Montagu's *Natural Superiority of Women* (1953), one could construct a very different image of the underlife, showing it as the source of human strength and copability.

There is in fact nothing inherently clandestine or superior about underlife as a concept; it has to do with spatial differentiations. To the extent that women are forcibly confined to these spaces, however, connotations of the clandestine are appropriate. Since differentiation between men's and women's spaces are found in all societies, the underlife concept becomes crucial to an analysis of women's roles. Ignorance of it has been a major factor in failures in development planning and aid schemes. Some examples follow.

Occasionally the underlife erupts into public view with large-scale actions by women, which are invariably treated as utterly mysterious phenomena. In Nigeria in December 1929, apparently peaceable, home-loving Ibo village women changed overnight,

> into a frenzied mob of thousands who attacked administration authorities while their men stood passively by. This uprising, precipitated by an unfounded (sic) rumour that Ibo women were to be taxed by the government, arose from uneasiness on the part of the women concerning

their economic position, which had already suffered from the world depression, and which they envisioned as being further threatened, as well as from other non-economic grievances (Ottenberg, 1959: 205).

In 1948, when the first mass-education teams were starting work in Ghana, they wanted to begin by organizing courses in the rural areas for the educated few, who could then teach their illiterate compatriots. Although publicity about this program was carefully aimed at educated women, three hundred illiterate women turned up at the first course, held at Peki-Blenko, and demanded instruction. Wherever the education teams went in Ghana they were confronted with the same situation: appealing for educated women to train, they were overwhelmed by hundreds of illiterate women who demanded education (Prosser, 1963). Stories of other types of public gatherings of women for a variety of purposes abound. For example,

> in January of 1964, the Tanganyikan army mutinied. On the morning of February 3, women assembled by the thousands outside the United Women of Tanganyika headquarters, bearing banners from Morogoro, Kisaraw, Bagamoyo, and a hundred other towns.
> The capital had never seen anything like it. For three and a half hours a procession of more than a mile of women marched from their headquarters in the south part of town, along Independence Avenue, through the business district, and around the water front to the government office area. The drums beat. The song of TANU (Nyerere's political party) was sung in powerful chorus. Placards flashed in the sun: Down with Violence, Mutiny and Treason!... the great UNY procession halted outside the State House and waited for the President. When Nyerere appeared at the door a mighty shout arose, mingled with the wierd half-whistle with which tribal women acclaimed their warriors (McDonald, 1966: 187-188).

How did the "submissive and downtrodden women of Africa" come to engage in such actions? The answer in each case lies in the existence of traditional women's councils that were organized into communications networks covering great geographical distances. These organizations existed long before colonial powers appeared on the scene and have made all kinds of interesting adaptations to modernization. West Africa is covered with these networks. Very occasionally a Western woman has had the opportunity of seeing one of the meeting places traditionally used by African women—nothing but a clearing in an otherwise dense bush—to which they come when summoned by drums. Messages by drumbeat, addressed to the women only, carried the word from village to village among the Ibo women in 1929; among the Akan, Transvoltan, and Ashanti women of Ghana in 1948; among the Tanganyikan women (who included the rugged women of the Masai warrior tribe) in 1964.

One particularly invisible counterpart to these all-women's councils is the woman-headed household. A persisting feature of underlife structures that we will be encountering from time to time is the phenomenon of households without men. Since the traces history leaves us concerning women almost always involve their identification as the daughter of X, the wife of Y, or the mother of Z, it is easy to overlook the fact that a certain number of these women were, and are, heading their own households and carrying out both the work of economic production and family nurturance without benefit of a male partner. While there were wealthy widows among them, most of them belonged to the working class. Their capacity to maintain households and rear children alone is another reminder of the extent of resource-management by women, and of the importance of their producer roles. In chapter 14 the figures on the percentage of women around the world who were unmarried, widowed, separated, or divorced as of 1968 are given. Comparable figures are of course not available for other historical periods, but the following estimates on widowhood for women in nonindustrialized countries today give some clues on the number of women who have headed households as widows in the past (Ridley, 1968: 21). These estimates are based on the simplified assumptions that the life expectancy at birth is forty-three, that all women marry at twenty, that all husbands are five years older than their wives, and that conditions are "normal"—i.e., famine or war conditions do not obtain.

Age of Married Women	Percentage Becoming Widowed
20-29	8.4
30-39	10.7
40-49	16.6
50-59	27.1
60-69	43.6
70-79	57.8

Since in both famine and war more women survive than men (Mayer, 1975: 572), rates of widowhood may have been higher in times past than is estimated in this table. On the other hand, life expectancies of women have been shorter than those of men at some periods of history, depending on the mortality rates for women in childbirth as compared to mortality rates for men in battle, and on the character of other societal risks for males and females (J. Lawrence Angel, as discussed in Pomeroy, 1975: 45). In any case, the widow appears often in history. While widows sometimes remarried, the evidence from the historical record is that they frequently chose to remain unpartnered in the face of great pressure to remarry, and they were often protected by law in their right to do so. A systematic historical study of this phenomenon must await the skills of the demographic historian, but readers of this book are alerted to look for the evidences of unpartnered women householders as they appear from time to time, peeking out from the underside of their times.

To account for the roles that women play in a society, we must identify the overlife and underlife structures in terms of the social spaces women can move in and the kinds of social learning that take place in them. *Social space* in this book is used in the full ecological sense of niche space available to a species. The term *social learning* is used rather than *socialization* because it emphasizes the active role of the individual rather than treating the individual as an object of the social process. The term *cultural conditioning* will be used in the next chapter to refer to the more mechanical aspects of the actions of a culture on its members.

As we move through different periods of history, we will see the ways in which structural differentiation enlarges or constricts the social learning spaces for women, and how and when constraints have been transcended.

Related to a structural differentiation is the extent of dominance relations in a society. While a great deal has been written about authoritarian versus democratic political structures, very little of it touches on the issue of the role of women in society. The Marxist critique of capitalism addresses itself directly to the situation of women, but still misses some key aspects of the woman problem by relying too much on what the public sector can do for families.[15] Neither the United States nor the United Kingdom, often pointed to as models of the democratic society in the capitalist camp, nor the Soviet Union, considered a model in the socialist camp, have avoided sex stereotyping and serious inequalities of opportunity for women. Neither has Sweden, another model country, avoided the sex dominance trap. Women are in a special way the "victims" of dominance structures in most societies.

Because of the special importance of conceptions of dominance in the analysis of women's roles, chapter 2 will be devoted to an analysis of dominance systems in the animal world and an examination of biological, environmental, and cultural determinants of human dominance systems. After a concluding examination of the potentials of alternatives to dominance and hierarchy in social organizations and human relationships, we can begin our walk through history.

Appendix 1-1
How and Where Women Learn

The factors associated with social learning for young women growing up in any society can be divided into: 1) the genetic substrate; 2) developmental sequences of physiological, emotional, intuitive, and cognitive maturation and the associated accumulation of the social knowledge stock; 3) specific learning processes—cognitive construction, trial and error (social reinforcement), modeling, and intuition; and 4) the social spaces within which learning takes place—home, community, specialized settings such as schools, church, place of work, and others.[16]

There is some genetic and developmental variation between the two sexes, but the variation is also wide within each sex. The overlap between the sexes is great. It is reasonable to conclude that given adequate social-learning opportunities women can learn to fill any social roles available in a society. Historical accounts of great women hunters, warriors, queens, poets, artists, and scientists support this view of the potential performance capacities of women.

To know how a woman will actually perform in a given society, we must know something of her opportunities for training, what kinds of social reinforcement she is getting for specific kinds of behavior, and who her role models are. We must also know in what social spaces the learning goes on. Is she confined to the private space of the home? If not, what public spaces are accessible to her? For large parts of human history the church has been the primary public space accessible to women, which accounts for the important role women have played in the great religions even when they have had positions of political power in them. If women and men share the same public spaces, women will have a broader kind of training, more varied social reinforcements, and a wider range of role models than if the spaces of women are restricted.

If marriage acts to limit social space for women, then age at marriage will be of crucial importance in determining their opportunities for social learning. Societies with child marriage usually—though not always—limit drastically women's opportunities for learning. Marriage is not necessarily a limiter of social space, however, and in some cultures it is marriage itself which frees a woman into the larger society (or, in some Moslem societies, the second marriage, which the woman may arrange for herself). In a stratified society the social spaces for the wealthy elite, for the group with the middle range of skill and material resources, and for the poor are very different for both sexes, but vary more for women than for men. As we shall see, social space and learning opportunities are relatively more restricted for women of the middle group than for either the rich or poor, though poverty places its own kinds of restrictions on learning opportunities.

The emphasis in the above discussion on access to social spaces and kinds of learning opportunities should not obscure a very important point: all human beings have more or less active minds. Everyone engages in cognitive construction, in the "creative imitation" we call modeling, and in intuitive, nonverbal formulations of reality. The interior mental work of mapping social reality and creating new social roles out of raw materials of observed behaviors of others and one's own values and preferences is unique to every woman and man. Settings and training sequences can trigger this interior creative work, but can never determine the product. In one sense, then, all social roles are created by the individuals who perform them, as social psychologists have long pointed out. This means that there are always significant degrees of freedom for women (and men), over and beyond their training and opportunities, in every society. The rags-to-riches, and slave-to-king, and prostitute-to-queen stories found in every stratified society testify to this omnipresent possibility.

Having said this, we must nevertheless return to a recognition of the constraining effect of limited social space on the learning of women. Figure 1-1 presents diagrammatically the shifting social spaces in which development takes place over time in the life of a maturing female. While the relative size and appropriate labels for various

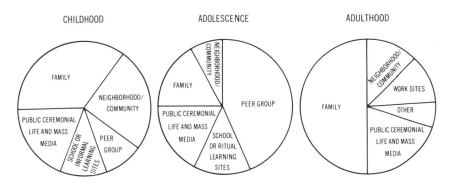

Figure 1-1. *The Context of Social Learning for Women.*

spaces will vary from society to society, one constraint is the relative importance of the family space in the life of a woman. Also, she has some kind of "ceremonial space" in every society, no matter how limited she is in respect to other spaces. If we were to do a comparable diagram for men, the family slice would be smaller, the neighborhood/community, worksites, and "other" would be larger. "Other" represents everything beyond the local community.

Notes

[1] The latest report from the Leakeys, as this manuscript is being readied for the press, is that new *erectus* finds have been uncovered dating back three and one-half million years! ("The Oldest Man," *Time* (Nov. 10, 1975:93)).

[2] We have, for example, from the economists, the papers from the "Workshop Conference on Occupational Segregation: Past, Present, and Future," Wellesley College, May 1975 (to be published in *Signs: Journal of Women in Culture and Society*, 1, no. 1(Spring 1976), supplement; also Hilda Kahne's "Economic Perspectives on the Role of Women in the American Economy," *Journal of Economic Literature* 13 (December), 1975; from the anthropologists, *Woman, Culture and Society* (Rosaldo and Lamphere, 1974); and *Women and Men: An Anthropologist's View*, (Friedl, 1975); from the historians, *Liberating Women's History: Theoretical and Critical Essays* (Carroll, 1976); and *Clio's Consciousness Raised: New Perspectives on the History of Women* (Hartman and Banner, 1974); from the sociologists, *Academic Women on the Move* (Rossi and Calderwood, 1973); and *Changing Women in a Changing Society* (Huber, 1973); and from the field of comparative and cross-cultural studies, *Our Many Sisters: Women in Cross-Cultural Perspective* (Matthiasson, 1974); *Cross-Cultural Perspectives on the Women's Movement and Women's Status* (Leavitt, forthcoming; *Women and Work: An International Comparison* (Galenson, 1973); *Women and Work in Developing Societies* (Youssef, 1973); and *Women in Perspective: A Guide for Cross-Cultural Studies* (Jacobs, 1974, a bibliography by region and by topic).

[3] I am indebted to Sheila Johansson for pointing out to me the underlying contradiction that is never fully resolved in this book: the victim theory is indeed stated and invoked from time to time, yet most of the data describe women as creative actors. Since the social reality concerning women's roles is also full of contradictions, the best I can do now is acknowledge the inconsistencies and let them stand.

[4] In the U.S. Army, the recent promotion of Jean Holm to the position of brigadier general provides the "token" exception to this. She has no responsibility for combat operations. (The woman admiral in the U.S. Navy is in charge of the Division of Nursing.)

5The only alternative production sites were palace and temple workshops and state-owned mines and public construction enterprises.

6The progress optimism of Comte (1974) was countered by Spengler, who cried doom in 1922 in his *Decline of the West* (English ed., 1926-1928). Nevertheless Weber's great works in the sociology of history, and particularly *The Protestant Ethic and the Spirit of Capitalism* (1930), remain classical sociological statements of development theory. Parsons' "Evolutionary Universals in Society" (1964) is a further development of Weberian theory. Eisenstadt, who has also worked in this tradition, has provided in his recently edited book of essays by third world scholars (1972) a searching examination of classical development theory from the perspective of change agents utilizing traditional institutions on behalf of change. Polak, in *The Image of the Future* (1961), questions the development potential in the Western self-image of the twentieth century. Nisbet (1969) provides a searching examination of what he calls the metaphor of growth in his study of Western theories of development.

7The exposition of the ecological view draws in part on Wilkinson (1973).

8The shift from zero population growth with the end of the nomadic way of life continues today as formerly nomadic bands go sedentary. A very dramatic description of the change in fertility behavior among the Kung people as they shifted from nomadism to agriculture as recently as in the decade of the 1960s appeared in *Science* (Kolata, 1974).

9Boserup, in *Women's Role in Economic Development* (1970), discusses in detail the exclusion of women from the productive process at the point of technological innovation in agriculture.

10Cole, in *From Tipi to Skyscraper* (1973), documents women's gradual loss of construction roles concurrent with technological development.

11It is by no means easy to get a picture of the progressive structural differentiation of societies as they deal with their ever-changing, ever-the-same problems of subsistence. The work of Eisenstadt (1963) in political sociology and Fried (1967) in political anthropology has been very helpful in developing a framework for observation of the historical process. Fried's work helped make clear the early transitions from egalitarian bands to ranked tribal groups to stratified societies. Eisenstadt's study of thirty-two societies that could be categorized as developed political systems has clarified the subsequent development process.

Etzioni's concept of epigenesis (1965), an alternative approach to the analysis of progressive social complexification, has not been utilized in this book although it offers a very useful additional model for historical development. I would agree with Etzioni that some structural changes are preformist, some epigenetic, and regret that my own need to keep the analysis as simple as possible kept me from introducing these distinctions.

12Sheila Johansson (1975) has developed a women's-role analysis instrument, which has just come to my attention, suitable for the macrohistorian. It contains many of the features of my own discarded instrument, but is a more sophisticated tool. As of this writing, the future of "herstory," as Johansson calls it, looks promising.

13While in this book I am looking particularly at the underlife of women, there are other groups who also live on the underside of history: peasants, the urban poor, slaves, and oppressed minorities. They too are finding their chroniclers in current decades.

[14]My translation of Xenophon from the French.

[15]The following correction to the above statement is offered by a reader: "A Marxist critique does not deal with isolated elements of a structure. It does not 'address itself directly to the situation of women' because women are not seen as an analytical category of oppression. Rather they are members of a class which in part comprises the entire structure of a capitalist system" (Tessler, 1975).

[16]For a fuller discussion of learning models, see E. Boulding (1974).

References

Ashley-Montagu, M. F.
   1953   Natural Superiority of Women. Rev. ed. New York: Macmillan.

Beard, Mary R.
   1946   Woman as Force in History: A Study in Traditions and Realities. New York: Macmillan.

Bernard, Jessie
   1975   Women, Wives, Mothers: Values and Options. Chicago: Aldine.
   1964   Academic Women. University Park: Pennsylvania State University Press.

Boserup, Ester
   1970   Women's Role in Economic Development. New York: St. Martin's Press.

Boulding, Elise
   1974   "The child and non-violent social change." Pp. 101-132 in Christoph Wulf (ed.), Handbook on Peace Education. Oslo: International Peace Research Association. (Originally written for Israel Charny ed., Design for Nonviolent Change.)
   1969   "The Effects of Industrialization on the Participation of Woman in Society." Ann Arbor: University of Michigan. Ph.D. dissertation.

Boulding, Kenneth
   1976   Comment on "The Social Institutions of Occupational Segregation." Signs: Journal of Women in Culture and Society 1, supplement (Spring). Forthcoming.

Carr-Sanders, Sir Alexander
1959 "Economic Aspects of Woman's Role in the Development of Tropical and Subtropical Countries." Women's Role in the Development of Tropical and Subtropical Countries. Report of the 31st Meeting of the International Institute of Differing Civilizations, Brussels.

Carroll, Berenice A. (ed.)
1976 Liberating Women's History: Theoretical and Critical Essays. Urbana: University of Illinois Press. Forthcoming.

Castle, Cora
1913 "A statistical study of eminent women." Archives of Psychology 7 (August).

Cole, Doris
1973 From Tipi to Skyscraper: A History of Women in Architecture. Boston: I Press.

Comte, Auguste
1974 Positive Philosophy. Tr. by Harriet Martineau. New York: AMS Press. (First published 1855.)

Davis, Elizabeth G.
1971 The First Sex. New York: Putnam.

Diner, Helen
1965 Mothers and Amazons. Tr. by John Philip Lundin. New York: Julian Press. (First published 1932.)

Eisenstadt, S. N.
1972 Post-Traditional Societies. New York: W. W. Norton.
1963 The Political Systems of Empires. New York: Free Press.

Etzioni, Amitai
1965 Political Unification: A Comparative Study of Leaders and Forces. New York: Holt, Rinehart, and Winston.

Firestone, Shulamith
1970 Dialectic of Sex: The Case for Feminist Revolution. New York: Morrow.

Fried, Morton H.
1967 The Evolution of Political Society: An Essay in Political Anthropology. New York: Random House.

Friedl, Ernestine
1975 Women and Men: An Anthropologist's View. New York: Holt, Rinehart, and Winston.

Gallenson, Marjorie
1973 Women and Work: An International Comparison. New York: Cornell University Press.

Goffman, Erving
1961 Asylums: Essays on the Social Situation of Mental Patients and Other Inmates. Chicago: Aldine.

Goitein, Solomon D.
1967- A Mediterranean Society: The Jewish Communities of the Arab World

1971   As Portrayed in the Documents of the Cairo Geniza. 2 vols. Berkeley: University of California Press.

Goode, William J.
1963   World Revolution and Family Patterns. New York: Free Press.

Hartman, Mary and Lois Banner (eds.)
1974   Clio's Consciousness Raised: New Perspectives on the History of Women. New York: Harper and Row.

Hays, H. R.
1964   The Dangerous Sex. New York: Putnam.

Herlihy, David
1962   "Land, family and women in continental Europe, 701-1200." Traditio 18:89-120.

Holter, Harriet
1970   Sex Roles and Social Structure. Oslo: Universitetsforlaget.

Huber, Joan (ed.)
1973   Changing Women in a Changing Society. Chicago: University of Chicago Press.

Jacobs, Sue E.
1974   Women in Perspective: A Guide for Cross-Cultural Studies. Chicago: University of Illinois Press.

Jennings, Ronald C.
1975   "Women in early 17th century Ottoman judicial records—The Sharia court of Anatolian Kayseri." Journal of Economic and Social History of the Orient 8, part 1: 53-114.

Johansson, Sheila
1975   Seattle, Wash.: Historian, personal communication.

Kahne, Hilda
1975   "Economic perspectives on the role of women in the American economy." Journal of Economic Literature 13(December): 1249-1292.

Kolata, Gina Bari
1974   "Kung hunter-gatherers: Feminism, diet, and birth control." Science 185: 932-934.

Komarovsky, Mirra
1946   Blue-Collar Marriage. New York: Random House.

Leavitt, Ruby R. (ed.)
1976   Cross-Cultural Perspectives on the Women's Movement and Women's Status. The Hague: Mouton. Forthcoming.

Lee, Richard B. and Irven De Vore (eds.)
1968   Man the Hunter. Chicago: Aldine.

Mathiasson, C. (ed.)
1974   Our Many Sisters: Women in Cross-Cultural Perspectives. New York: Free Press.

Mayer, J.
1975   "Management of famine relief." Science 188 (May):571-577.

McDonald, Alexander
  1966   Tanzania: Young Nation in a Hurry. New York: Hawthorne Books.

McNeill, William H.
  1963   The Rise of the West: A History of the Human Community. Chicago: University of Chicago Press.

Mead, Margaret
  1970   Culture and Commitment. Garden City, N. Y.: Natural History Press.
  1955   Cultural Patterns and Technical Change. A manual prepared by the World Federation for Mental Health, UNESCO. New York: Mentor Books.
  1950   Sex and Temperament in Three Primitive Societies. New York: New American Library.
  1949   Male and Female. San Diego: Morrow.

Millet, Kate
  1970   Sexual Politics. Garden City, N. Y.: Doubleday.

Myrdal, Alva
  1945   Nation and Family: The Swedish Experiment in Democratic Family and Population Policy. Cambridge, Mass.: MIT Press

Myrdal, Alva and Viola Klein
  1968   Women's Two Roles: Home and Work. 2nd ed. London: Routledge and Kegan Paul.

Nisbet, Robert A.
  1969   Social Change and History: Aspects of the Western Theory of Development. Oxford: Oxford University Press.

Ottenberg, Phoebe V.
  1959   "The changing economic position of women among the African Ibo." Pp. 205-233 in W. R. Bascom and M. J. Herskovits (eds.), Continuity and Change in African Cultures. Chicago: Phoenix Books.

Parsons, Talcott
  1964   "Evolutionary universals in society." American Sociological Review 29 (June): 339-357.

Polak, Fred L.
  1961   The Image of the Future. 2 vols. Tr. by Elise Boulding. New York: Oceana Press. (1973 ed., abridged by Elise Boulding, San Francisco: Jossey Bass/Elsevier.)

Pomeroy, Sarah B.
  1975   Goddesses, Whores, Wives, and Slaves: Women in Classical Antiquity. New York: Schocken Books.

Prosser, U. R.
  1963   "The role in community development, with particular response to West and East Africa." International Social Service Review 9 (April): 46-53.

Reed, Evelyn
  1975   Woman's Evolution from Matriarchal Clan to Patriarchal Family. New York: Pathfinder Press.

Ridley, Jeanne Clare
 1968   "Demographic change and the roles and status of women." Annals of
        the American Academy of Political and Social Science 371 (January):
        15-25.

Rosaldo, Michel Z. and Louise Lamphere (eds.)
 1974   Woman, Culture and Society. Stanford: Stanford University Press.

Rossi, Alice and Ann Calderwood (eds.)
 1973   Academic Women on the Move. Menlo Park, Calif.: Russell Sage.

Smelser, Neil J.
 1959   Social Change in the Industrial Revolution: An Application of Theory
        to the British Cotton Industry. Chicago: University of Chicago Press.

Spengler, Oswald
 1926- Decline of the West. Tr. by Charles Atkinson. New York: Alfred A.
 1928   Knopf.

Sullerot, Evelyne
 1968   Histoire et Sociologie du Travail Féminin. Paris: Societé Nouvelle des
        Editions Gonthier.

Theodore, Athena
 1971   The Professional Woman. Cambridge, Mass.: Schenkman.

Turnbull, Colin
 1968   The Forest People. New York: Simon and Schuster.

Ward, Barbara E. (ed.)
 1963   Women in the New Asia: The Changing Social Roles of Men and
        Women in South and South-East Asia. Paris: UNESCO.

Weber, Max
 1930   The Protestant Ethic and the Spirit of Capitalism. Tr. by Talcott Par-
        sons. London: Allen Unwin. (First published 1904-1905.)

Wilkinson, Richard B.
 1973   Poverty and Progress: An Ecological Model of Economic Development.
        London: Methuen.

Youssef, Nadia
 1973   Women and Work in Developing Societies. Population Monograph
        Series no. 15. Berkeley: University of California Institute of Interna-
        tional Studies.

2
Dominance, Dimorphism, and Sex Roles

The question of why women are everywhere the "subordinate sex" has never failed to interest both women and men, and many interpretations have been advanced to explain the phenomenon, including the interpretation that women are not really subordinate at all. It will be useful to review the evidence for the subordination of the female from the points of view of sociobiology, archaeology, and anthropology before beginning the journey through human history. Evidence about the status of the female from the mammalian world in general, from our near "relations" among the primates, and from present hunting and gathering societies, added to archaeological evidence about the kinds of tools the protohominids used, by no means leads to one simple, clear picture of the situation of the earliest human female. The facts of dominance and subordination in the human experience can still be interpreted differently. Since sexual dominance and dominance systems in general are so closely intertwined, this chapter deals with both.

The construct of social dominance represents an ideology as well as a set of behaviors and social structures, an ideology reflecting basic value judgments about the nature of the social order and of sex differentiation. In this chapter we will therefore also explore briefly the alternative construct of egalitarianism as an ideology, and as a set

35

of behaviors and social structures having implications for sex differentiation.

Since there are significant social roles in every society that stand outside dominance structures and yet relate to them, these are explored also, under the label of interstitial (in-the-cracks) roles. Both family and community roles are examined for their interstitial qualities. Finally, the symbol systems that support ascription of weakness and submissiveness to women are examined, along with the physiological bases for the pervasive symbolism of the dominance-submission dichotomy. This chapter is an attempt, in short, to examine some of the contributions from the social sciences, from sociobiology, and from folklore to conceptions about the subjugation of women.

The Politics of Subordination

In discussing sex-role dominance, people tend easily to extremes. From one side embattled champions of the downtrodden sex put forward the enslavement concept, which evokes the image of the helpless food-gathering child-breeding-feeding female in the hunting and gathering society who is both protected and victimized by the brute strength of the male; who gains a brief respite as mother-goddess and matriarch after her invention of agriculture in a world of dwindling animal prey; who then loses all claims to power and status as man invents the plow and takes over farming, the gods, and the descent-reckoning system, letting his woman work for him as slave-helper-breeder.

From the other side, champions of serene womanhood put forward the concept of the gentle queen who in an unobtrusive way rules the mighty world of men through the power of love. Reality cuts across all theories. To the extent that women do indeed help shape human destinies, enslavement theories are absurd. To the extent that women do find themselves in both *de facto* and *de jure* situations of subordination in most societies known to us, the queen theory is equally absurd. Detached perceptions of the geography of power as it relates to the status of women are rare. The drive to plead the cause of feminism has increasingly overwhelmed analysis.

In the fourteenth century, "feminist" Christine de Pisan asked simply to be accepted as a human being, free to do the things that humans do. The nineteenth century suffragette said we are political animals, like men, and must participate in decision making; give us the vote. In the twentieth century some feminists are saying we have been subjugated by men and must learn to exercise power; we don't want it as a gift—we will take it as a right.

Power is taken here simply to mean the ability to achieve desires in the face of opposition or obstacles: the power to "get what one wants." We will be concerned with that aspect of power known as dominance, a concept that has both structural and behavioral components. Both components are relevant to discussions of the subjugation of women, but must be kept conceptually distinct. The widespread practice in many cultures, including the Western European, of beating women to discipline them—best symbolized by the whip said to hang over the Russian peasant's bed in the days of the czars—is an example of the behavioral aspect of dominance. Behavioral dominance may be as crude as "beating someone up," or as refined as "staring someone down." It does not necessarily involve physical aggression, but it implies it as a potential in the situation. An example of the structural aspects of dominance is the limited personhood of women in the courts, which limits their rights to transact business and administer property in their own names.[1] No individual actor can be identified as the source of this type of domination. The former is personal and immediate in its effect, the latter impersonal and indirect, but all-pervasive. *Conscienticization* is a term used to refer to the process of awakening, on the part of a subjugated group, to a consciousness of the facts of structural dominance.

When women have been conscienticized and talk about taking power as a right, questions inevitably arise about their intended relationship to existing dominance structures. History asks the same question of all revolutionaries: will you destroy the old structures and behaviors of dominance and replace them with new models for human relationships, or will you introduce new personnel into old dominance systems?

The conscienticization of women is a particularly complex process, however, since women have never been simply a subjugated people. They have always participated in a secondary way in the prevailing dominance structures of society, from the times of the earliest incipient social stratification. The tribal chief had a queen-wife and their daughters were princesses.

In a stratified society members have control over their own lives and control of resources generated by others according to the status assigned to them by birth or skill and achievement. There are other criteria used to assign control of resources, however. Therefore, at each level of social rank, power is differentially distributed to men, women, old people, children, and racial, ethnic, and religious minorities. The fact that some women have traditionally had high social status as the wives of their husbands and daughters of their fathers and lower status in terms of their own achievements has usually been discussed under the heading of status incongruities. While status incongruities are both painful and unjust, they tend to mask the underlying phenomenon that women too have slots in the dominance structures of society (as do the various minority groups). An upper-class woman may not have as much power as her husband, but she has a lot more power, in the sense of control of her own life and of social and economic resources, than the middle-class woman. Whether she uses it or not is another matter. There is always an element of achievement in the use of power, whether acquired by birth or not, since the effective exercise of power requires skill.

What we see throughout history is a series of class or status alliances between women and men to dominate and exploit lower-status social groups. This is not necessarily conscious exploitation. How could the lady bountiful of the medieval manor or the Victorian household, hurrying on her errands of mercy, be said to exploit the poor she worked so hard to help? Her exploitation lay in supporting the dependency structures that created the helplessness of "her poor," dependency structures that provided her life with meaning. We will see many examples in the chapters to follow of women who have contributed in important ways to the shaping of society through their use of the structures of dominance available to them. They have frequently created service-oriented social institutions.

Structures of dominance are ordinarily hierarchical. When the work of a number of people needs to be coordinated, hierarchical organization with successive levels of overview of the social scene eliminates a lot of explaining and teaching. If people do what they are told, "aboveness-belowness" works well. We have had ten thousand years of experience with progressive centralization of social organization. Few social scientists, let alone laypersons, could imagine doing without it. Centralization generates the power which "is the resource that makes it possible to direct and coordinate the activities of men" (Blau, 1964: 99).

Besides being efficient, and pervasive throughout recorded history, is hierarchical dominance also a biologically determined feature of human relationships? The question can be divided into two parts: 1) are humans generally programmed to enter into dominance-subordination relations—regardless of sex; and 2) are males programmed to dominate females?

Dimorphism and Dominance

Possibly such questions arise only with the genetic diversity that accompanies the development of dimorphic life forms. It is hard to visualize amoeba-like creatures dominating each other. A study of dimorphics, the new discipline recently proposed by Kenneth Boulding (1976), may throw some light on the relationship between two-formedness and dominance behaviors. Does the extent of sexual dimorphism and the intrasex variability dimorphism has produced affect subjugation efforts? Is there a linear relationship between differentiation and dominance?

Sociobiologists say yes, finding that anatomical and behavioral dimorphism covary among nonhuman primates. What we find among these primates is a striking range of variation in dimorphism and the accompanying extent of dominance behavior. Gibbons, hardly distinguishable as to sex and with no easily detectable ranking systems, are at one end of the scale. At the other end are the highly sex-differentiated baboons with a highly visible dominance structure both among males and females (Martin and Voorhies, 1975: 123-133). The picture is more complicated than that, however. The extent of sexual dimorphism is also related to the extent of danger in the environment. The look-alike gibbons live in a friendly arboreal environment with few predators. The baboons, with males almost twice the size and weight of females, live in the dangerous savanna, full of enemies to their kind. Chimpanzees, halfway between gibbons and baboons in extent of sexual dimorphism, are half arboreal, half-terrestrial in their habits. They have a dominance system, but are fairly casual about it. Following Wilson's (1975:13) arguments that behavior is the pacemaker for evolution, it appears that the need to be able to defend their kind operated as a powerful selector for increased size and weight among the baboons.

There is considerable difficulty, however, in going from these primate cousins to humans. Compared to baboons, we are minimally differentiated in size and weight. Without observation of secondary sex characteristics it is sometimes hard to tell male and female humans apart. We are more like gibbons than we are like baboons. Yet the primate behavioral model put before us by writers like Tiger (1969) is based on the baboon, not the gibbon. Our choice of a primate role model is clearly culturally determined. Who wants to be like the unaggressive, vegetarian, food-sharing gibbons, where father is as much involved in child rearing as mother is, and where everyone lives in small family groups, with little aggregation beyond that? Much better to match the baboons, who live in large, tightly-knit groups carefully closed against outsider baboons, where everyone knows who is in charge, and where mother looks after the babies while father is out hunting and fighting.[2]

The chimpanzees, our closest cousins anatomically, will not do as primate role models in spite of their brains and skill with tools, because they are too casual about their sex life. They can take it or leave it. Humans could not conceivably be that casual about sex.

The issue is of course not one of the appropriateness of role models, but of the facts of environmental challenges and protohominids' response to them. Martin and Voorhies (1975: 175) quote Jolly's findings about Lower Pleistocene tools being primarily hand axes and simple flakes, associated with scouring and processing vegetable matter rather than with processing meat. "We" may have been vegetarians for hundreds of thousands of years before hunting was adopted. Food gathering is not a dominance-oriented activity, and points us right back to the gibbon. Even when the shift to hunting took place, probably as a result of environmental challenges, there is no proof, as Wilson points out, that women were not also hunters side by side with men. Among the lions, "the females are the providers, often working in groups and with cubs in tow, while the males usually hold back" (Wilson, 1975: 567). Among the African wild dogs, males and females hunt side by side.

However hunting began, at some long-ago point in human history it became a male specialization. The effect of that specialization on hunting and gathering societies, as we will see shortly, was distinct but possibly minimal. Hunting and gathering societies do not have generalized dominance structures, but rather give recognition to special skill as it appears in various occupations (Martin and Voorhies, 1975: 190).

We must draw on Wilson's principles of the "multiplier effect" and "social drift" for an explanation of why the hunting specialization developed such complex and divergent ramifications in most societies over time. The multiplier effect is a process by which

> a small evolutionary change in the behavior pattern of individuals can be amplified into a major social effect by the expanding upward distribution of the effect into multiple facets of social life (Wilson, 1975: 11).

Social drift is the "random divergence in the behavior and mode of organization of societies or groups of societies" (Wilson, 1975:13). An example of social drift is found in the phenomenon, described by Wilson, of vastly differing social structures, owing to differing sexual habits, arising among two closely related and interbreeding subspecies of baboons. This type of divergence is paralleled in the ethnographic literature by Douglas' study (1965: 183-213) of the Lele and the Bushong in Africa who live in very similar habitats. One is a poverty-stricken society which heavily overworks its women, and the other is more affluent and gives a higher status to its women. When such divergences occur in basically similar settings, it is easy to understand how the shift in activity patterns from food gathering to a combination of hunting and gathering could trigger great role variations between women and men.

The simplest determinants of dominance orders in those animal societies where they exist are size, age, androgen-determined levels of aggression, and luck (Wilson, 1975: 251-254). With animals of greater intelligence and more durable group formations, other factors quickly come into play. Notable among these are childhood history, mother's rank, peer group alliances, and special ability (Wilson, 1975: 291). Luck triggers the multiplier effect, as one animal's "bad day" sends its status spiraling downward, another's "good day" sends its status spiraling upward (Chase, quoted in Wilson, 1975: 295). It is clear that females are not simply passive supporters of male-defined dominance systems, as Maclay and Knipe (1972) would have us believe, but develop their own complementary systems, which are in varying degrees independent of the male systems. Top females are usually coupled with top males, but their status may have been independently derived, going back to their childhood and the status of their mothers, as well as to their own ability (Wilson, 1975: 291-294). Dominant females breed leaders, both among their daughters and among their sons. Low-status females do badly all around. They seem to be less well nourished, and they do a poor job of mothering (based on Fraser's observations of sheep and reindeer, in Wilson, 1975:288).

Rowell's dissenting reports on baboon troops without dominance hierarchies must be mentioned here, since they call some of the above observations into question; her work may trigger a whole new set of field studies. Much of the dominance behavior reported to date, particularly in the case of baboons, where the male is twice the size of the female, may be a report of what observers expected to see, or it may represent observations on stressed troops. Rowell suggests that "hierarchy may be a 'pathological response' to stressful conditions" (1973: 602). This is an extreme but interesting position, and deserves further exploration, both in primate and human societies.

This discussion began with the question of whether there was a relationship between dimorphism and dominance. We have found that dominance patterns exist within each of the sexes as well as between sexes. For all that luck, mother's status, and ability contribute to an individual's dominance status, the simple fact of greater size seems to play a continuing role. Height is an advantage to both females and males in human dominance systems (Maclay and Knipe, 1972: 42-45). As far back as 1915 it was found that bishops were taller than clergymen, university presidents taller than college presidents. The intangible of self-confidence, pointed out by Maslow (he equates self-confidence with dominance; see Maclay and Knipe, 1972: 30), is bolstered by being able to look down on the world. Women have grown taller in the twentieth century (in the United States they have gained two inches since 1900; Bois, 1969:9), but so have men, so the physiological supports for social equality continue to elude the female sex.[3]

Reproductive Behavior and Dominance

We have seen that determinants of the extent of dominance systems are partly genetic and partly environmental, and that the extent of sexual dimorphism determines the range of potential dominance behavior both within and between sexes.

The basic fact that females give birth to and feed infants seems to establish the initial social patterning for animal societies. Among many mammals there is no male involvement with offspring or family groups. See table 2-1 for a summary of data showing that among the smaller mammalian orders the male often has no continuing involvement with the female in the breeding-nurturing process. Wilson points out that the

> key to the sociobiology of mammals is milk. Because young animals depend on their mothers during a substantial part of their early development, the mother-offspring group is the universal nuclear unit of mammalian societies. Even the so-called solitary species, which display no social behavior beyond courtship and maternal care, are characterized by elaborate and relatively prolonged interactions between the mother and offspring. From this single conservative feature flow the main general features of the more advanced societies, including such otherwise diverse assemblages as the prides of lions and the troops of chimpanzees. . . . when bonding occurs across generations beyond the time of weaning, it is usually matrilineal (1975: 456).

The first helpers and defenders of the mother are thus adolescent and young-adult sons and daughters.

Among primates the pattern varies considerably, but it is fairly common to find both adolescent offspring and adult male partners as

Table 2-1

Family Patterns of Smaller Mammals

Sociobiological Patterns	Order Monotremata & Marsupalia (opossums, etc.)	Order Insectivora (hedgehogs, moles, etc.)	Order Rodentia (beavers, squirrels, etc.)	Others[*]
Solitary, no male participation	8	6	7	2
Diverse (solitary or aggregates), occasional male participation	2	1	8	6
Solitary or pair-bonded, variable, may be male participation			1	1
Familial groups (male participation)			4	
Harem (male dominance)			1	
Social groupings (male participation)				11
Totals	10	7	21	20

SOURCE: Tabulations in Wilson (1975: 457-65).

*Includes darmopters, chiropters, edentata, pholidota, lagomorpha, mysticeti, odonto-ceti, pinnipedia, tubulidentata, hyracoidea, and sirenia.

helpers and defenders to breeding females. A number of sociobiol-ogists, including Crook and Gartlan and Eisenberg (Wilson, 1975: 523-525) have argued that there is an evolutionary development among primates toward increased involvement of the male in the society. For our purposes, this and other formulations are inadequate because they do not bother to spell out the changing role of the female in the evolutionary sequence; it is considered enough to spell out the role of the males. It is clear, however, that the larger the social aggregate, the more the adult male offspring are integrated into the group in the double role of offspring and mates to adult females. Unpredictability of food supply and an increasing number of pred-ators in the environment appear to be among the factors that en-courage larger aggregations and the more complex integration of males into the aggregates. The extent of dominance by males of the females is not, however, related in any obvious way to the extent of male involvement in the society. Among the chimpanzees, where there is a clear dominance system among the males, this has no influence whatsoever on the access to females (Wilson, 1975: 546). When chimpanzee bands meet, both single females and females with offspring may move from one band to another. The males have nothing to do with this movement at all (Wilson, 1975: 539).

That the special responsibility of females for the young is associated with gender-specific behavior is not surprising. Sex-linked behaviors have been identified in Vervet monkeys that give clear evidence of sex-role differentiation in group bonding behavior. Nurturance comes from females, defense from males, vigilance from both (Wilson, 1975: 300).

There is considerable debate about the extent to which the attempt should be made to trace human behavior from primate behavior. Similar debate exists about the relevance of information about contemporary hunting and gathering bands to the behavior of early human groups. Wilson has tabulated behaviors associated with such contemporary human bands, indicating the extent of variability of comparable behavior traits among nonhuman primates. On the basis of these tabulations he has made cautious estimates about the possibility of the presence of each set of behavior traits in early humans. His table is reproduced here as table 2-2. It will be noted that the only traits he concludes can be very reliably assigned to early humans are play behavior, prolonged maternal care, and extended relationships between mothers and children.

All the evidence seems to point to the development of different behavioral repertoires for males and females at some point in hominid development, along the lines of female specialization in the care of the young and male specialization in defense. Whether the male defender role and the male as dominator of the female developed together, in response to environmental threats, or whether the male as dominator of the female was more dependent on accidents of time and place, it is hard to say.

Wilson presents some very interesting material on dominance behavior of the female, but he does not develop it in terms of dominance theory in general. He describes the conflict between mother and offspring at the point where the mother is trying to force the offspring to independence while the offspring is trying to stay with the mother. Although infant urges to explore are a well-known component of the development of autonomy, Wilson quotes observations that all point to the fact that, for monkeys, the "release from maternal bondage was achieved in considerable part by responses of punishment and rejection" (1975: 341). Weaning conflict and

Table 2-2

Social Traits of Living Hunter-Gatherer Groups and the Likelihood That
They Were Also Possessed by Early Man

Traits That Occur Generally in Living Hunter-Gatherer Societies	Variability of Trait Category Among Nonhuman Primates	Reliability of Concluding Early Man Had the Same Trait Through Homology
Local group size: Mostly 100 or less	Highly variable but within range of 3-100	Very probably 100 or less but otherwise not reliable
Family as the nuclear unit	Highly variable	Not reliable
Sexual division of labor:		
Women gather, men hunt	Limited to man among living primates	Not reliable
Males dominant over females	Widespread although not universal	Reliable
Long-term sexual bonding (marriage) nearly universal; polygyny general	Highly variable	Not reliable
Exogamy universal, abetted by marriage rules	Limited to man among living primates	Not reliable
Subgroup composition changes often (fission-fusion principle)	Highly variable	Not reliable
Territoriality general, especially marked in rich gathering areas	Occurs widely, but variable in pattern	Probably occurred, pattern unknown
Game playing, especially games that entail physical skill but not strategy	Occurs generally, at least in elementary form	Very reliable
Prolonged maternal care; pronounced socialization of young; extended relationships between mother and children, especially mothers and daughters	Occurs generally in higher cercopithecoids	Very reliable

SOURCE: Table 27-5 in Wilson (1975: 568).

territorial expulsion exists among many mammals. Since males are generally the ones expelled, while female offspring are kept as helpers for the next brood of offspring, it is males who get the experience of fighting for resources, and it is their mothers they fight. Later, the young males are accepted back in the home territory as helpers, but only after they have learned to forage for themselves. Female offspring have to learn to forage too, but their experience may be less traumatic than that of the young male.

This expulsion-from-the-nest behavior of mothers, while obviously adaptive, needs to be more fully analyzed in terms of female dominance behavior. It is related to, but separate from, the fathers' expulsion-from-the-nest behavior. The latter occurs when male offspring are near or at maturity. It is sometimes associated with the barring of young males from access to mature females by the dominant males in a troop. It may also be related to a limited food supply. Not enough attention has been given to the fact that male offspring usually have to "fight" their mothers before they have to fight their fathers. It may well be that mother-son conflicts over the right to nurturance are equally as important in the development of dominance behaviors on the part of the male as environmental threat and adult sexuality. From this perspective, increasing male involvement in social groupings would represent a gradual diminution of ingroup aggression between mothers and offspring. With the introduction of the male there is the new phenomenon of father-offspring aggression, which presumably also diminishes with time. The evolutionary development, then, would point in the direction of increasing peaceable involvement of both females and males in the continuing life of their offspring.[4]

The three evolutionary models of dominance behavior we have been examining are suggestive in both their congruences and their differences. They all indicate increasing male participation in society, but differ in interpretations of the role of dominance and aggression in social development. The Martin and Voorhies and the Wilson models imply that the only evolutionary development that takes place is in the male. The role of the female does not evolve, but remains static. If there is a theoretical possibility that the female as well as the male roles have evolved toward increasing peaceable involvement in the continuing life of their offspring, then this component would need to be added both to the Martin and Voorhies and the Wilson conceptions of increasing involvement of males with their offspring. The remaining issue, as to whether evolutionary development has been in the direction of dedifferentiation and lowered levels of aggression (the Martin and Voorhies position), or in the direction of continuing differentiation and continuing genetic selection of male ability to aggress and fight the enemy, cannot be settled by the evidence presented here.

What the data do suggest is that the range of behavioral alternatives available to humans is very wide indeed and that behavioral dominance is not a genetically specified feature either of male-female relations or of same-sex relations. Behavioral dominance may have been produced via social drift and the multiplier effect, by any one of a series of environmental constraints, or by interaction sequences involving temporary periods of female helplessness due to childbearing. The female role as provider of milk for both male and female young can act both to modify and to enhance male dominance tendencies. Similar basic sequences were bound to recur in a wide variety of settings, giving rise to the cultural variations we recognize in male-female relationships.

Dominance as a Cultural Requirement

Although we have seen that many animal societies have far more complex social patterns than they have generally been given credit for, they are very simple in comparison with human society. Given the human talent for cultural elaboration, is there something in the elaboration process itself that might inevitably lead to generalized male dominance among humans? It is by no means clear that there is such a generalized dominance of the male over the female in hunting and gathering bands. There is, in fact, cultural variability in the presence and extent of male dominance among such bands. Partly this variability may have to do with the predispositions of the ethnographer. Martin and Voorhies (1975) would argue that shifting dominance is the more common pattern, and that dominance in any particular instance tends to be situational, related not to sex but to activity and skill.

Can more complex societies exist without well-defined dominance structures? The popular conception of history as the story of a succession of conquest states would suggest that the answer is no. Evolutionary views of historical development offer contradictory insights on this subject, and simple evolutionary theories of development, as suggested in the last chapter, are inadequate to explain twentieth century realities.[5]

Dominance systems organize most of our political and economic life. Furthermore, since they are also primarily male dominance systems, they cast an extra shadow over the life of women, both in the public and domestic spheres. Men and women alike, but men more than women, are used to being rewarded for doing what society values by being given a "dominance" bank account. The growth of exchange relationships does not necessarily change this, although exchange has strong egalitarian elements because exchanges can also take place within dominance systems.[6] People of very unequal status can exchange goods or services that lead both to feeling richer than they were before without changing the inequality. Nor is cooperation incompatible with dominance. In fact, one of the notable historical features of oppression is that the downtrodden comply in their own oppression. The discovery by the oppressed that they have power is the discovery that they can gain a kind of dominance through the withdrawal of compliance. This is the power of the women's liberation movement, and of all other liberation movements. Noncompliance is by no means an insignificant technique in human history. A recent compilation of the historical uses of noncompliance gives numerous examples of an important tool in lessening social violence while still working to remove injustice (Sharp, 1973).

The use of noncompliance merely to gain social power, however, leaves us where we were before: facing a society that operates by the manipulation of dominance systems. The fact that there are sets of social interactions that operate outside dominance systems lets us know that hierarchical relations are not an across-the-board requirement for social organization. Let us look at the alternative modes of relating, and how they affect the generalized submissive stance considered culturally appropriate to women.

Alternatives to Dominance Systems

Egalitarianism

The most obvious alternative to the dominance-submission relationship is the relationship of equality. For any two people—any dyad—to remain in a relationship of complete equality for even a short stretch of time is extraordinarily difficult, as Simmel has vividly described (Wolff, 1950). Through the entire gamut of relationships that any married couple faces, for example, an exact tit-for-tat in mutual services would require an extraordinary degree of calculation and rationality. Marriages can become mutual nonaggression pacts having many of the characteristics of a cold war. What makes interpersonal relationships bearable, especially intimate ones, is that each partner from time to time throws a little bit "extra" into the relationship, and that neither keeps an account book. This is what Gouldner

(1960) calls the reciprocity multiplier, what Blau (1964) calls accumulating a capital of willing compliance, and what Fried (1967) calls generalized reciprocity. Kenneth Boulding (1973) adds to this the concept of serial reciprocity—passing on the extra to a third party.[7]

No dominance system could operate without at least small amounts of generalized reciprocity. Egalitarian systems need very large reciprocity multipliers in order to work. Stable egalitarian systems are in fact very fluid systems of alternating dominance, with each partner "taking command" when the available resources lie more fully within her or his domain, without prejudicing the participation pattern for the next situation. When we move from the dyad to the triad we move from the interpersonal to the social, but Simmel points out that an egalitarian system of three partners has the same difficulties that inhere in the two-partner system. Most triads resolve themselves into dyads, with the third party either teaming up with one of the others or exploiting them both (Wolff, 1950: 118-174).

The principle of social drift discussed earlier explains why equality is such an unstable relationship. Small situation-specific changes in behavior between partners in an egalitarian relationship may be amplified into substantial shifts in participation patterns, resulting in the development of unanticipated dominance roles.

Some recent research, such as Winch's work (1972) on complementarity in the marital relationship, has pointed to the possibility of sustaining shifting patterns of dominance. At the societal level, Robert Bales' research technique of interaction analysis, which identified "task leaders" and "emotional support" leaders in problem-solving groups, pinpoints such complementarities (Bales et al., 1965). Some techniques of group dynamics involve teaching participants to avoid dominance behavior, though "overthrowing the leader" is also a standard group-dynamics routine. The very scarcity of examples demonstrates clearly enough that dominance-submission relations are the easiest pattern for any dyad, triad, or group to fall into when faced with tasks or problems.

Altruism

There is a third mode of relating, distinct from both dominance-submission and equality: the mode of altruism. In fact, although it is not usually described in that way, altruism and egalitarianism may be thought of as lying at opposite ends of the dominance-behavioral spectrum, with submission merely a midpoint on the continuum.

Like dominance, altruism is an active mode of relating and is evoked by environmental challenge. It is the obverse of dominance in that it involves using one's own resources to better the condition of another, rather than doing something at the expense of another to better one's own condition. In the language of the sociobiologist, it is increasing "the fitness of another at the expense of one's own fitness" (Wilson, 1975: 117). Wilson discusses the genesis of altruism among animals, where it has been clearly identified, in terms of the phenomenon of kin selection. He imagines a network of blood relatives who

> cooperate or bestow altruistic favors on one another in a way that increases the average genetic fitness of the members of the network as a whole, even when this behavior reduces the individual fitnesses of certain members of the group. The members may live together or be scattered throughout the population. The essential condition is that they jointly behave in a way that benefits the group as a whole, while remaining in relatively close contact with the remainder of the population. This enhancement of kin-network welfare in the midst of a population is called kin selection (1975:117).

While the mathematics of altruism is too complex to discuss here, this line of reasoning is attractive in offering an explanation of apparently antisurvival behavior on the part of individuals. Natural selection operates to reenforce predispositions to behavior in the phylogenetic substrate that optimize group rather than individual survival. It is not sex-linked. Both females and males have capacities for altruism. In Wilson's presentation, emphasis is put on altruism as displayed by the male. However, it is also clear from his discussions that foodsharing, alloparenting (caring for offspring not one's own), and a variety of helping behaviors between parents and offspring, and among adults, are included as altruistic behavior. Helping behavior can apparently be triggered by a variety of circumstances, according to cultural conditioning.

In the stressful environments created by complex high-density human societies, altruism is presumably a response option just as dominance is. We already know that altruistic behavior, of which the reciprocity multiplier is a mild form—acts as a modifier in an otherwise unbearable world. Altruists range all the way from the totally life-spending St. Francis, or the kidney donor who faces the rest of her life at risk, to the helpful person in the office downstairs. Altruism in women and other disadvantaged groups is sometimes hard to distinguish from oppression-coerced behavior, as in the pseudo-altruism of the downtrodden, submissive wife, but the distinction can be made. Altruism arises from some inner surplus of resources. The behavior can be described physiologically, but among humans it may have other, nonphysiological components that are not well understood. While the goal of altruism is often equal status in the future for the one being helped, it does not necessarily lead to equality, any more than dominance behavior on behalf of social justice necessarily leads to equality.

Egalitarianism, Altruism, and Natural Selection

The relationship of equality of give and take, finely tuned to the respective capacities and resources of individuals or groups, is the hardest kind of social relationship to establish. It is much harder than dominating, and it is also harder than simply helping. Yet, as De Tocqueville pointed out in 1848,

> The gradual development of the principle of equality is . . . a providential fact . . . it is universal, it is lasting, it constantly eludes all human interference. . . . all men have aided it by their exertions, both those who have intentionally labored in its cause, and those who have served it unwittingly . . . (De Tocqueville, 1944).

Could natural selection operate on behalf of a "passion for equality that incites [men] to wish all to be powerful and honored"? Or is natural selection operating on behalf of a depraved taste "which impels the weak to attempt to lower the powerful to their own level" (De Tocqueville, 1944: 56)? Both are ways of conceptualizing equality. The first has an altruistic cast, the second in an inverted approach to domination. Is the social force we know as egalitarianism something which is emerging from these two preexisting dispositions?

The need to understand what it is like to be inside the skin of another, in order to make appropriate responses in social interactions, was identified as sympathy by Adam Smith in *The Theory of Moral Sentiments* (1966). Smith considered that sympathy is the basis for all society; it certainly lays the basis for the possibility of egalitarianism. Darwin saw in the need for animals to "understand each other's expressions, sounds, and signed movements" (Gruber, 1974: 97) the basis for that same sympathy. He puzzled over the process, for it could be as often painful as pleasurable to recognize another's condition. It was also clear to him, however, that communities having "the greatest number of the most sympathetic members, would flourish best, and rear the greatest number of offspring" (Gruber, 1974: 318).

If the passion for equality is the significant evolutionary force De

Tocqueville believed it to be, it nevertheless had to contend with equally significant drives for domination. As an emergent capacity among humans, its future will depend on the social values and enabling structures that come to prevail in the next few centuries.

To summarize what has been said about the alternatives to dominance relationships in the social order, they point at most to *possibilities.* Altruism appears to be as much genetically determined as aggression, which means that it is part of a possible behavior range subject to cultural modification. Neither trait is sex-linked, though behavioral emphases for the two sexes may be different. The capacity for egalitarianism is at best emergent. To the extent that various types of cooperative movements and community experiments in different parts of the world develop viable egalitarian patterns, future developments in that direction will be enhanced.

Women have, for the most part, adapted themselves to existing dominance structures. When possible, they have used their own positions in the dominance structure—linked to that of the males in their family though with fewer resources—as a power base. Women are highly skilled at converting the power they do have—deriving from the important personal services they render to men—into influence, a special and privatized "underside" power that gives women more leverage than a formal analysis of their authority roles would suggest. The theme of the power base from which women operate will be explored in each historical period in the chapters that follow, and alternative modes of operation—when they can be identified—will also be described.

Family Roles and Roles "In the Cracks"

Marriage Bonding

In some ways the family stands outside the dominance structures of the larger society, and in other ways it mirrors these structures. There are few dominance patterns within hunting and gathering type families and in the matrilocal villages of simple subsistence farming communities. But once women began to leave the villages of their mothers to marry, and had to enter the villages of their husbands' fathers (patrilocality), the fluidity of earlier relationships disappeared and the practice of male dominance began. (Male dominance of the female in the household was, of course, never complete, because both altruistic and egalitarian modes were always present in the behavior potentials. What kinds of environmental constraints and inter-band relationships made patrilocality a more adaptive solution than matrilocality to the problem of household formation will be discussed in chapter 4.) The development of patriarchal dominance was accompanied by the maintenance of a maternal "subdominance" over children. There would be the occasional situational dominance of the wife over the husband, when circumstances permitted (all societies have some stories of wives beating husbands). This entire dominance system was modified by the range of helping behaviors required of both males and females in the family unit. "Bachelor" males and females (also found in animal societies) sometimes roved as loners, sometimes attached themselves to family units as helpers/defenders.[8] Multigenerational dominance along patriarchal lines with appropriate subdominant roles for women framed the household dominance system.

With the establishment of patrilocality and male dominance, women developed a special set of interstitial or in-between roles that lie outside dominance structures and are not hierarchically ordered. These in-between roles play a special part in social bonding, conflict resolution, and crisis management within and between social groups. Women have played a historically unique role in the creation of alliance structures at all levels, from interfamilial to international. Many examples will be given of this in the chapters to follow.

Women's bonding roles operate at two levels. The first level is local and represents the type of bonding that occurs through ordinary marriage procedures, when two kin groups become allied through the marriage agreement. The woman plays a dual role here. First, she bonds the two groups as daughter of one and wife of the other. Later, as a mother herself, she extends the bonding process as parental agent on behalf of her offspring in search of mates. The second level is international and takes place when a woman is sent as "wife-diplomat" to the court of a chief, king, or emperor who poses a threat to the sending group. This too has the same double aspect: woman bonding as daughter and wife, and woman bonding as parental agent on behalf of offspring.

The absurdity of the treatment of bonding as a male specialty, as in Lionel Tiger and Maclay and Knipe, has been widely exposed in recent feminist writing, but even so there is a tendency to underestimate the significance of women's bonding roles in contemporary society. This is partly because there are many other institutional mechanisms for bonding in the twentieth century besides marriage.

Historically, however, marriage has been the major alliance mechanism of every society, and little girls are trained for roles as intervillage family diplomats. Except in cases of matrilocal residence

(husband coming to live in wife's village), the married woman strad-
dles two kin networks, two villages, sometimes two cultures. In traditional societies, in a social world framed by patrilocality, women experience an uprooting in the teen years that men do not generally undergo. During this time their capacities to engage in new learning and
adaptive behavior may well be at the maximum. Having been thoroughly trained by the women (and men) of their home village in
necessary productive skills and required social behavior, they are
then very frequently removed from the environment they were
trained to function in and taught new social behaviors. They also
often shift social roles overnight from that of loved and protected
daughter to "on-trial," sternly disciplined daughter-in-law. Men in
patrilocal societies do not undergo such a drastic family-role shift,
nor do they have to adapt to the mores of a new village after marriage. Sterling describes the woman's situation in his *Turkish Village*:

> Thus any set of women who meet daily and share their tasks, their
> child-minding and their gossip will include some who are neither kin nor
> childhood neighbors to each other. Such a set will change its composi-
> tion fairly steadily over time, by marriages in and out, and divorces, as
> well as deaths and the growing up of daughters.
>
> The women explicitly recognize this situation. One group told my
> wife that *akrabalike*, kinship, did not count for women as it did for
> men. What mattered to women was neighborliness, *komsaluk*. They did
> not mean that kinship does not count at all. Ties with kin are kept up
> by occasional visits, by gossip and news, by children going back and
> forth (1965: 173-174).

The visiting back and forth between childhood home and nuptial home means that women are in a position to engage in an intellectual synthesis of two sets of mores and two sets of lifestyles,
which gives them a perspective that their one-village husbands may
lack. While one may assume that men also get acquainted with more
than one village in a lifetime, they do not do so with the degree of
intensity, and under the conditions of divided loyalties, that women
necessarily experience. When this results in the valuing of a capacity for neighborliness independently of the kin relationship (as Sterling described above), one has the ingredients for a wider range of expectations and tolerance for social behavior. The social skill a woman
develops in learning first to *receive* neighborliness in a new setting
and then in turn to give it to later comers than herself, and the skills
of cross-cultural analysis she develops as she compares ways of doing
things in her natal with those in her nuptial village, are both vital to

the development of expertise in social networks.

This network expertise becomes particularly important in negotiating marriages for the next generation. It is the women who have the most relevant knowledge about problems between villages and how best to place marriageable offspring in relation to those problems. Whether their role is publicly acknowledged or not, women play an important part in decisions about marriage alliances in every society from tribal to imperial.

Marriages that are essentially diplomatic alliances are a much more complex affair. When a young bride is shipped from the refined and elegant court of twelfth century China to be the wife of the nomadic chieftain who has been pillaging one of the provinces of her father's kingdom, her role is a delicate one indeed. This will be explored in detail as we build up documentation of "negotiation by marriage" in the period of the primary civilizations and later among the kingdoms of Europe.

To say that women shipped off to villages or palaces are being treated as objects is nonsense. In diplomatic marriages, women have been highly educated as an investment in diplomacy. The whole image of the "woman as pawn" in marriage is misleading and uninformed. As a potential partner she is indeed manipulated, but so is her young spouse. When she in turn becomes the mother of marriageable offspring, she is herself among the manipulators. While it can be argued that the whole marriage process takes place on behalf of male-dominated systems, interesting insights emerge when marriage systems are looked at from the point of view of female interests. Martin and Voorhies have "rewritten" the ethnographic account of marriage among the Tiwi from the female perspective, paralleling the traditional male perspective (1975: 203-210), and it is clear that the same overt behaviors can be interpreted in ways that give a much higher status to women in relation to men—with much more emphasis on shifting dominance and actual egalitarianism—than ethnographers sometimes depict.

In general, marriage alliances are systems of redistribution of resources and represent institutionalized sharing behavior (Service, 1962), as well as techniques for conflict reduction, within and between communities. The role of women in relation to all these functions is an active, not simply a passive, one. Variations in the scope of activity open to women after marriage stem from cultural patterns in localities; they are not necessarily inherent in the marriage negotiation process.

The conflict specialization role for women as a consideration in marriage alliances is particularly important. Mair (1972) describes situations where tribes deliberately marry their daughters into the tribes (or villages) with whom they fight. Tyler makes the same point more dramatically in explaining the origin of the incest taboo: "Again and again in the world's history, savage tribes must have had plainly before their minds the simple practical alternative between marrying-out and being killed out" (as quoted in Farb, 1968: 26). Farb points out that the levirate (the rule that a man must marry his brother's widow) and the sororate (the rule that a woman must marry her deceased sister's husband) are institutions that function to preserve marriage alliances after the death of one of the partners (1968:27).

Women in traditional societies often have other highly specific conflict-related responsibilities. The formal function of deciding when war is justified, and of adjudicating a conflict if it can be adjudicated, was a woman's role among the Germanic tribes of Europe in Roman times and continues in some contemporary African and native American tribes. As a woman's role, adjudication does not usually survive urbanization for long.

Paid and Unpaid Work Roles

Another important in-between role for women is as unspecialized labor able to fill a variety of slots in times of crisis. We have seen this most recently during the twentieth century wars, and in the social aftermath of a high male death rate in war. When conferences on women's role in development refer to women's historical role as "an extra pair of hands" (Carr-Sanders, 1959), the emphasis is usually on the demeaning aspects for women of belonging to a reserve labor force, perpetually subject to call on short notice. This, however, side-steps the difficult problem of how a society is to generate needed labor in times of shortage and stress, and it also minimizes the opportunities for structural change in labor force composition that times of crisis afford.[9]

Interstitial roles do not generally confer status in themselves, though they may at times be highly valued for their contribution to the maintenance of dominance systems. Since the time of the Renaissance, feminists have been coming around gradually to the position that they should not undertake work that does not confer status— that does not, in other words, give them clear access to some kind of of valued social power. When income from paid jobs became the generally accepted status indicator, feminists focused on the position of women in the job market.

This was an important development. It provided for the first time an objective measure of how women were doing in their drive to participate as equals with men. Women who worked as volunteers in the community always suffered from the equivocal and ambiguous character of their status and never knew when they would be taken seriously, or have the door shut in their faces. The use of wages as the criterion in determining whether work should be done at all—the local consequence of focusing on wage-sector status—has presented some problems, however. By abolishing the voluntary sector we abolish most household and child-rearing tasks, many community services, many religious and cultural activities, and much of the process of social and technological invention.

The question then becomes, should interstitial roles be abolished in the reconstruction of society, or should all paid jobs be stripped of conventional measures of worth? To place all work in the public sector, or at the least to see to it that all productive labor is remunerated by wages, would require a vast reconstruction of society. Of course, such a reconstruction would not necessarily ensure the equality of wages, as the experience in some socialist countries with large wage inequalities has demonstrated. Essentially, it would abolish all interstitial roles and give society the job of officially allocating status and monetary worth to everyone. The opposite approach would be to abolish the wage sector and give all work an interstitial character. In modified form, this is what Scott Burns (1975) suggests. He proposes an alternative approach to the economic system, an approach that focuses on the household[10] and the volunteer sector as the most significant productive sectors and replaces monetary measures of worth with "units of time spent." This would produce something like the world that Martin and Voorhies foresee, since it would lead to decreased differentiation of sex roles and more time spent on nurture by both males and females.

Women and the Left Hand: Further Thoughts on Dimorphism and Dominance

We have examined the sociobiology of sexual dimorphism and concluded that the extent of behavioral differentiation found in most human societies has to be environmentally and culturally explained, since both sexes have wide behavior ranges available to them in relation to dominance and aggression. Small differences in ability to cope with rapidly changing and hostile environments on the part of female hominids with offspring could set in motion the multiplier effect that would create substantial behavioral amplifications of apparently insignificant adaptations. Social drift could carry these amplifications in the direction of the various patriarchal dominance patterns we find in the later stages of agriculture and with the development of trade.

Every society patterns all creation anew and develops symbol systems that support the order they impute to the cosmos. We would therefore expect a strong tendency for societies to rationalize the *de facto* subordination of the female by building into their symbol systems images of women as weak, helpless, and passive. We do indeed find this, and find it built into a system of dimorphic thinking that calls for a review of the significance of dimorphism in the evolutionary process. Dimorphic sexual selection, it will be remembered, expands the gene pools and increases fitness for survival. Dual classification systems confront the diversity resulting from the expanded gene pool and find ways to weave that diversity into the pattern of the social order. Hertz (1973) suggests that these dual systems arose out of the primitive pattern of social organization based on dividing a tribe into two moieties or halves.

Originally this would be a reversible dualism; what is in my moiety is good and sacred—what is in yours is not. The Chinese concepts of yin and yang reflect this reversible dualism. There is no imputation of good or evil, superiority or inferiority, per se, to either half of the duality. The reversibility is, however, evidently unstable:

> The evolution of society replaces this reversible dualism with a rigid hierarchical structure: instead of separate and equivalent clans there appear classes or castes, of which one, at the summit, is essentially sacred, noble, and devoted to superior works, while another at the bottom, is profane or unclean and engaged in base tasks. The principle by which men are assigned rank and function remains the same: social polarity is still a reflection and a consequence of religious polarity (Hertz, 1973: 8).

The point at which reversible dualism shifted to irreversible dualism is the point at which women became symbolically pegged as weak and bad. In his study of dual classification systems Hertz notes the great frequency with which they are based on the right and left hand, across a variety of societies.[11] The basic system goes as follows:

right	left
strong	weak
day	night
male	female

life	death
good	bad
high	low
sacred	profane

At some point during the Paleolithic our previously ambidextrous forebears shifted to right-handedness, a posture that evidently had survival value for hunters. As a result the capacities of the right hemisphere, governing the left hand, began to be underexercised, and consequently undervalued, a long time ago. These capacities include the capacity for spatial and temporal orientation and for the kind of instantaneous comprehension of complex wholes involved in analogic and intuitive thinking. It is possible that the slower, verbal-analytic (left-hemisphere) approach to problem solving was necessary to build up the neural circuitry that could later be utilized for analogic purposes. In any case, the possible role played by the experience of right-hand dominance in shaping our interpretation of the dominance-submission relationship as part of the cosmic order should not be overlooked (Ornstein, 1973; Walters, 1953).

It would appear that the symbolic classification system—right-left, male-female, strong-weak—has in effect powerfully reenforced small adaptive behavioral differences that probably go back to the beginning of hunting, and has acted to amplify these differences in ways that affect almost every type of activity in which women engage. How long it took for the new behavior pattern of right-handedness to predominate among the protohominids is anyone's guess. Presumably, in one millennium it didn't matter which hand was used. By the next millennium, it did. There must have been, as indicated earlier, some evolutionary advantage (at least in the short run) in this dominance, and it may well have aided the development of speech. Learning to talk with both hemispheres of the brain actively involved may be a much more complicated process—it would perhaps be like conducting two simultaneous conversations at all times. As it is, our second conversation is relatively nonverbal and easier to cope with. We turn over our spatial judgments and analogic intuitive thinking to our "spare brain."

In the West, the dominance of the right hand, i.e., of verbal-analytic thinking, is for the first time being seriously examined instead of assumed. It is presumably this dominance which has led both to the success of the industrial revolution and to the ecological disasters that have followed. Educators are increasingly giving attention to training the intuitive faculties along with the cognitive.[12]

A new journal[13] is devoted entirely to the integration of the two spheres. The human potential movement in a sense represents a "declaration of independence" for the right hemisphere of the brain, and therefore for the left hand. Are we witnessing a revolution against the right hand?

To the extent that this movement simply results in inverted dominance patterns, valuing the left *over* the right, it is self-defeating. In terms of the women's movement, neither elevation of feminity nor a women-can-do-everything-men-can-do approach really carries us out of the present impasse. The subordination of women historically has not done society much good. The deification of women and courtly love in the Middle Ages fitted easily into an overall pattern that included the bloody Crusades. Robert Graves' poetical pursuit of the *White Goddess* (1966) through the ages pretty much leaves women and men right where they are now—to the satisfaction of neither. And while some readers may glory in thoughts of a matriarchal age as they read Briffault's *Mothers,* or thrill to the smell of women all hot with battle as they read Diner's *Mothers and Amazons,* these attempts at the reconstruction of human experience leave the concept of dominance untouched.

Meanwhile, another concept—that of social ambidexterity—gets short shrift. A certain amount of philosophic deference is paid to the idea of a society in which women and men both have their analytic and intuitive sides equally developed—what Margaret Mead (1967) called the androgynous society—but people are generally unenthusiastic about this. Someone always calls out *"vive la différence!"* And we do tend to think of sex-role equality as a lessening of differentiation. This is not at all, however, an inevitable outcome.

In our examination of dominance and dimorphism as it affects human sex roles, many related concepts have been introduced. Some will recur later in this book, some will not. Readers are invited to make use of these concepts in whatever ways seem useful, in pondering the chapters that follow. All of the concepts will contribute something to our understanding of why women are found in both subordinate and in dominant roles throughout history. They will also help us to understand why it is necessary to look on the underside of history to find out what most women are doing.

Appendix 2-1
New Concepts in Dominance Theory

Sociobiologists are increasingly replacing old concepts of dominance with more sophisticated conceptualizations, as earlier terminology fails to describe what observers see. One group of scholars (K. R. L. Hall, I. S. Bernstein, Thelma Rowell, J. S. Gartlan, and others, in Wilson, 1975: 282) has begun working with the concept of *control animal:* one who intervenes and manages conflict, but does not exercise personal dominance. Control animals have been identified among monkeys having no clearcut dominance order. Dominance potential is used much more to keep order, to keep others from fighting, than was earlier realized.

Another nonaggressive set of behaviors earlier associated with dominance fall into related categories of *greeting behavior*—signalling the gang when one has found something good, showing off, and play. Chimpanzees engage in a good deal of noisy chest beating and arm waving, particularly when two bands meet, but these behaviors seem to be a form of greeting ritual; while they may also establish relative dominance positions of males, no aggression is involved. There is a whole range of showy behavior among chimpanzees, and it is not always clear when it is simply play, or when it is performing other functions. Play, itself, a special characteristic of higher species who do much of their exploration and invention, as well as anticipatory socialization, through play, is distinct from aggression and efforts to dominate and yet has some of the characteristics of dominance behavior. We have all watched what began as rough and tumble play, both between animals and between humans, turn into a real fight. Undoubtedly, excess androgen is discharged through play, and a comparative study of male and female play behavior in animals might throw light on the distinction between play as manipulation[14] for fun and play as an exploration of dominance possibilities.

If Martin and Voorhies (1975: 168) are right, females have less time to play than males. Apparently, even among the primates, the female has the typically longer working hours we find widely prevailing in the human experience. The female is busy feeding and caring for the young, and she must also find time for grooming the males; the males have time on their hands, and they play. Adolescent males play more than adult males, and they often play roughly, though it usually stays at "play." Is this anticipatory socialization of the young male for dominance?

The fact that the same species in different environments exhibit different degrees of aggressiveness has led sociobiologists to introduce another concept into their treatment of behavioral dominance. When baboons move out of the savanna and into the forest, they become more peaceable. Not as peaceable as the gibbon, but more peaceable than they were in the savanna. *Behavioral scaling* is the explanatory concept utilized to deal with this phenomenon:

> Behavioral scaling is variation in the magnitude or in the qualitative
> state of a behavior which is correlated with stages of the life cycle,
> population density, or certain parameters of the environment (Wilson,
> 1975: 20).

The potential for aggressive behavior is adaptive to the range of needs of the individual. The entire behavioral scale, not isolated points on it, is what is genetically fixed.

Humans too have their genetically fixed behavioral scales and can perform at one end or the other, depending on the circumstances. What they cannot do is "go over the top" or "under the floor" of their particular behavioral scale (Maslow, summarized in Maclay and Knipe, 1972: 30-31). Human males, with generally higher androgen levels than females, have higher ceilings on the average. However, cultural conditioning and social learning can shift the behavior of individuals of either sex toward the top or the bottom of their scales. Mead's *Sex and Temperament* (1967) is a classic illustration of the consequences of this conditioning for individuals in societies with different values about acceptable levels of aggression. Individuals who are forced by their society to move too near the top or bottom of their particular behavioral scales become misfits.

Territoriality is another concept that goes beyond simple dominance. It is an interesting discovery of sociobiologists that crowding elicits increased aggression and a stronger dominance order in any animal species. When species have more space they organize their relationships around territoriality, and aggressive behavior is seen only infrequently—and then chiefly at "public" sites such as waterholes. Among humans the sequence, nomadic-agrarian-urban, has on the whole been accompanied by rapidly accelerating elaborations of dominance structures and aggressive behavior.

Notes

[1]While the courts provide the arena in which some women can defend what rights they have, the courts also set the limits to their rights.

[2]New information on baboons from Rowell's field studies in Uganda call into question generalizations about baboons based on other studies. Rowell finds that "adult females serve as a focus of the group's social activity, and that they 'lead' the group in the sense of selecting the direction for the day's march; adult males change groups frequently, and the stable core of a group is the subset of adult females; the adult males of the Ishasha troops were not arranged in dominance hierarchies; and adult males failed to defend the troop against external threat, choosing rather to lead the retreat" (1973: 602).

[3]For a discussion of some new concepts in dominance theory that go beyond what is discussed in this section, see the Appendix to this chapter.

[4]This means, among other things, the development of a capacity to teach self-help skills and foster autonomy in the young without engaging in rejection behavior. It can be argued that human parenting is still in a fairly primitive stage in this regard.

[5]The utopian anarcho-socialist version of development theory, foreseeing the withering away of hierarchical organization and the development of local self-organized modes of production and sharing, has had little confirmation in the experience of the last 100 years. Nevertheless, the cooperative movement that developed out of utopian socialism embodies a continuing nonhierarchical tradition. The writings of Melman (1969) and McGregor (1960) on nonhierarchical systems in contemporary enterprises, including kibbutzim, provide continuing

evidence of the workability of the egalitarian ideal under certain conditions. So do accounts of anarchist socialism during the civil war in Spain (Dolgoff, 1974).

6Blau's *Exchange and Power* (1964) deals with some of these same issues, in a somewhat different context. Blau would argue that all social interaction creates power imbalances. See especially his chapter 5 on "Differentiation of Power" and chapter 12 on "Dialectical Forces."

7These are all specialized meanings for reciprocity. In one sense all human interactions are reciprocal, in "that each partner has a part in permitting a transaction to take place," as in victimage (Vera Larsen, 1975, private communication).

8See Wilson's very interesting discussion on alloparenting, referring to assistance given by other members of a society in the care of offspring. This phenomenon is chiefly found among the more advanced animal societies. (1975: 349-352).

9Arthur Marwich (1965) is his history of Britain during World War I builds a strong case for the *permanent* changes in participation levels of women in the labor force made possible by wartime upheavals.

10Burns estimates that the household economy is one-third the size of the total market economy. This figure is probably much too high for a highly industrialized country like the United States, though it might apply in some European countries. His main point is, however, substantially correct: while the forms of household craft have changed over the centuries, skilled and semiskilled labor in the household is a surprisingly persistent feature of the human economy.

11The dual classification system has nothing to do with left-handedness in women, but operates at the symbolic level only.

12Jerome Bruner (1965) was one of the first to make this academically respectable, with the publication of his *On Knowing.*

13*SYNTHESIS, The Realization of the Self,* 104 Dogerty Way, Redwood City, California.

14Wilson (1975: 165) emphasizes the manipulative character of play, defining it as movement of the body and manipulation of known objects and environments in novel ways.

References

Bales, Robert, et al. (eds.)
1965 Small Groups: Studies in Social Interaction. New York: Alfred A. Knopf.

Blau, Peter M.
1964 Exchange and Power in Social Life. New York: Wiley.

Bois, J. Samuel
1969 Breeds of Men: Toward the Adulthood of Humankind. New York: Harper and Row.

Boulding, Kenneth
1976 Comment on "The social institutions of occupational segregation." Signs: Journal of Women in Culture and Society 1, supplement (Spring). Forthcoming.
1973 Economy of Love and Fear. Belmont, Calif.: Wadsworth.

Bruner, Jerome
1965 On Knowing: Essays for the Left Hand. New York: Atheneum.

Burns, Scott
1975 Home, Inc.: The Hidden Wealth and Power of the American Household. Garden City, N. Y.: Doubleday.

Carr-Sanders, Sir Alexander
1959 "Economic aspects of woman's role in the development of tropical and subtropical countries." Women's Role in the Development of Tropical and Subtropical Countries. Report of the 31st Meeting of the International Institute of Differing Civilizations, Brussels.

De Tocqueville, Alexis
1944 Democracy in America. Tr. by Phillipps Bradley. New York: Alfred A. Knopf.

Douglas, Mary
1965 "The Lele—Resistance to Change." Pp. 183-213 in Paul Bohannan and George Dalton (eds.), Markets in Africa: Eight Subsistence Economies in Transition. Garden City, N. Y.: Doubleday.

Dolgoff, Sam (ed.)
  1974   The Anarchist Collectives: Workers' Self-Management in the Spanish
         Revolution 1936-1939. New York: Free Life Editions.

Farb, Peter
  1968   Man's Rise to Civilization: As Shown by the Indians of North America
         from Primeval Times to the Coming of the Industrial State. New York:
         E. P. Dutton.

Fried, Morton H.
  1967   The Evolution of Political Society: An Essay in Political Anthropology.
         New York: Random House.

Gandhi, M. K.
  1962   Village Swaraj. Comp. by H. M. Vyas. Ahmedabad, India: Navajivan
         Publishing House.

Gouldner, Alvin
  1960   "The norm of reciprocity: A preliminary statement." American Socio-
         logical Review 25 (April): 161-178.

Graves, Robert
  1966   White Goddess: A Historical Grammar of Poetic Myth. New York: Far-
         rar, Straus and Giroux.

Gruber, Howard E.
  1974   Darwin on Man: A Psychological Study of Scientific Creativity;
         Together with Darwin's Early and Unpublished Notebooks edited by
         Paul H. Barrett. New York: E. P. Dutton.

Hertz, Robert
  1973   "The pre-eminence of the right hand: A study in religious polarity."
         Pp. 3-31 in Rodney Needham (ed.), Right and Left: Essays on Dual
         Symbolic Classification. Chicago: University of Chicago Press.

Larsen, Vera
  1975   La Grange, Ill.: Family therapist, personal communication.

Maclay, George and Humphry Knipe
  1972   The Dominant Man: The Pecking Order in Human Society. New York:
         Delacorte.

Martin, M. Kay and Barbara Voorhies
  1975   Female of the Species. New York: Columbia University Press.

Marwich, Arthur
  1965   The Deluge: British Society and the First World War. Boston: Little
         Brown.

McGregor, Douglas
  1960   The Human Side of Enterprise. New York: McGraw-Hill.

Mead, Margaret
  1967   "The life cycle and its variation: The division of roles." Daedalus 96
         (Summer): 871-875.

Melman, Seymour
  1969   "Industrial efficiency under managerial vs. cooperative decision
         making: A comparative study of manufacturing enterprises in Israel."

Studies in Comparative Economic Development. Beverly Hills, Calif.: Russell Sage.

Narayan, Shirman
  1970 Relevance of Gandhian Economics. Ahmedabad, India: Navjivan Publishing House.

Needham, Rodney (ed.)
  1973 Right and Left: Essays on Dual Symbolic Classification. Chicago: University of Chicago Press.

Ornstein, Jack
  1972 The Mind and the Brain: A Multi-Aspect Interpretation. New York: Humanities Press.

Papanek, Hanna
  1976 "Women in cities: Problems and perspectives." Washington, D. C.: American Association for the Advancement of Science. Forthcoming.

Rowell, Thelma
  1973 The Social Behavior of Monkeys. Baltimore: Penguin. (As reviewed in Science 180 (May 11): 602-603, by James Loy.)

Schumacher, E. E.
  1973 Small Is Beautiful: A Study of Economics As If People Mattered. New York: Harper and Row.

Service, Elman R.
  1962 Primitive Social Organization. New York: Random House.

Sharp, Gene
  1973 Politics of Non-violent Action. Boston: Porter Sargent.

Smith, Adam
  1966 The Theory of Moral Sentiments. New York: Augustus M. Kelley. (First published 1759.)

Sterling, Paul
  1965 Turkish Village. New York: Wiley.

Tessler, Suzanne
  1975 Boulder: University of Colorado, Department of Sociology, personal communication.

Tiger, Lionel
  1969 Men in Groups. New York: Random House.

Walters, W. Grey
  1953 The Living Brain. New York: W. W. Norton.

Wilson, Edward O.
  1975 Sociobiology: The New Synthesis. Cambridge: Belknap Press of Harvard University Press.

Winch, Robert F.
  1972 Mate Selection: A Study of Complementary Needs. Ed. by Ann Greer. Dubuque, Iowa: William C. Brown.

Wolff, Kurt H.
  1950 The Sociology of Georg Simmel. London: Free Press of Glencoe.

3

The Paleolithic:
The Evolution of Home Base
and Sex-Role Differentiation

Hominids Make Themselves at Home

We are in the Great Rift Valley of East Africa, 350 miles from Kilimanjaro. Runoff streams from the mountains have made a brackish lake; the grasslands of the savanna creep up to the edge of the rift, and if we were standing up above we would see herds of wildebeests, small baboon troops, and other savanna animals moving about. We are in the valley, and the sun has just set. The year is 2,000,000 B.C. An eighteen-year-old *Australopithecus* male is hauling a freshly killed animal toward an area blocked off by a semicircular stone wall, where two females are sitting on the ground feeding babies and several small children are running about. The females shake their heads as the boy approaches and point over to an area where three males and some youngsters are busy smashing bones with rocks. "Into the kitchen, not here!" is the message. The males

---

Since this chapter covers nearly two million years, the reader is urged to study the chronology in the Appendix to the chapter. The new Leakey data, which pushes hominid existence back another million and one-half years, unfortunately did not become available until after the chapter was in production.

69

growl with pleasure as they see more meat arriving. They were getting the last bits of marrow out of yesterday's bones, since today had not been a good hunting day. The females, as soon as they have finished feeding the infants, bring the small children and join the males to get their share of meat—it has been saved for them. The bulbs and tubers gathered earlier during the day have long since been eaten, in the foraging places where they were gathered. Only the meat is carried back to camp, because the best chopping tools are here. One of the females puts a hand on the boy's shoulder. She remembers how sickly and weak he was during the bad droughts when he was little, and how he nearly died. Now he is able to bring home meat.

We can't call this little band—about twelve individuals in all—human. But they look like our second cousins, at least. They are hominids, early representatives of the human species. The particular band we have been watching really did camp on the shores of the lake in what is now Olduvai Gorge. The remains of its members, including the eighteen-year-old who had several times nearly died of malnutrition as a small child, have been dug up and examined by the Leakey family, a remarkable two-generation archaeological team (Pfeiffer, 1969: 72-92). Three hundred feet of volcanic ash had been covering that site for millennia. It was a mere fifty thousand years ago that the Rift Valley, part of the great geological fault that winds in almost continuous fissures around the planet and back on itself again, heaved and cracked once more, and exposed part of the ancient site where this hominid band had camped.

The total site is a 3,400-square-foot living floor. One area contains a rough semicircle of rocks, perhaps a windbreak (and protected place for little ones to be left?); an area about fifteen feet in diameter, "thick with shattered pieces of rock and bone and choppers" (the kitchen); and a few feet away, a place containing larger bone fragments and unshattered bones (the "dining room"). Eleven different kinds of stone implements have been found among the four thousand artifacts and fossils at this one living area. Fifty known sites remain to be excavated in the valley.

Tools, Diet, and Development

These tools are a million years older than prehistorians were prepared for.[1] "It is almost as if one opened up a musty vault in the Great Pyramid of Egypt and found vacuum cleaners and television sets," writes Pfeiffer (1969: 79). For our purposes, this site throws unexpected light on the way of life of protohuman familistic groupings.

Like some of their primate cousins, the hominids moved about in small bands. The Olduvai site was not a permanent settlement, but a camping site returned to over and over again in the course of millennia; perhaps it was a favored "home base."

Because hominid infants did not have the ability of other primates to cling to their mothers, they had to be carried. This means that mothers, just as their hands were freed by walking upright, found those hands fully occupied with babies. This was not too much of a problem in early hominid days, when males may well have carried the babies too, as some other primate males did. Moving around through the grasslands by day, there were many opportunities to set infants down while gathering roots and tubers. In these early millennia, the hominids were primarily vegetarians. Once in a while a hominid—male or female—would either come upon a newly dead small animal and try eating it out of curiosity, or, almost accidentally, actually kill a rabbit or other small creature. An account of baboons killing and eating meat in Royal Nairobi National Park is suggestive about the development of this new behavior pattern:

> Suddenly we saw directly ahead a large male baboon with a freshly killed hare in its mouth, a noteworthy event in itself since meat eating is rarely observed. But there was more to come. A whole troop was crossing the stream, and a few seconds later another large male passed with another hare, and not long after that a third male carrying the remains of a small antelope.
>
> . . . The whole troop seemed excited, jittery. Since baboons eat small animals in a matter of minutes, these animals must all have been killed recently and almost simultaneously. Perhaps one baboon came upon a hare lying in the grass and picked it up casually, and the sight of the act aroused other baboons to go after hares and other small game in the vicinity. In other words, it might have been a spontaneous flurry of activity . . . (Pfeiffer, 1969: 108).

De Vore, who was on this expedition, suggests that meat eating can be established by several recurring incidents like this as a new cultural tradition in a baboon troop.

More was involved in the development of hunting than an accidentally acquired culture trait, however. Droughts that drastically reduced usual food supplies helped turn hominids to hunting. Their first easy pickings would be the crippled and weak animals around them who could cope with the drought even less well than they. Studies of hunting and gathering societies in Africa and Australia today indicate that many miles are run per pound of meat caught.

Richard Lee (1968) reports four days of hunting for each animal caught. Phyllis Kaberry (1939) writes of the kind of physical endurance required for hunting. She tried twice to accompany men on hunting trips, and each time had to give up because she could not maintain their speed. We do not know whether the women members of the bands she studied could have kept up if they tried. We do know, however, that they rarely participate in these trips; they confine their hunting activities to hares and other small animals found near the campsite. It is interesting to note that, when women do hunt, they usually do so without weapons, relying on their knowledge of animal habits to catch an animal with their bare hands. Or, like the Tiwi women, they may hunt with dogs (Goodale, in Martin and Voorhies, 1975: 197-198).

In the Pleistocene, female hominids were being slowed down as the pelvis, enlarging to accommodate their brainier, larger-headed hominid offspring, was widening their hips and reducing their running speed.

The combination of drought-induced shortages of vegetable foods, biological accomodations of the female to hominid evolution, and the need for babies to be carried as they lost their grasping facility limited the females' freedom of movement at the same time that it expanded the males'. The female continued to hunt for tubers, but also depended on what the male could bring back. Herein lies the importance of the invention of the home base: a place to put babies down, and a place to share the meat. The home base introduced another revolutionary possibility: a place for the sick and injured to recover. In a troop constantly on the move, minor illnesses could be fatal because a sick member must either keep up or be left behind to become some predator's dinner. "It is the home base that changes sprained ankles and fevers from fatal diseases to minor ailments" (Washburn and De Vore, 1961: 101). It also gave the female a new role: that of nurse.

The shift to hunting also encouraged food sharing. Meat was hard to tear into with the vegetarian-type teeth hominids were equipped with. Tools were needed for cutting, and for crushing. Females and males both became adept at making tools from pebbles, bones, and shells,[2] and developed increasingly cooperative habits of food and equipment sharing in the small bands in which they lived and moved.

The emergence of campsites would not necessarily have to relate to hunting. In fact, there is evidence that much of the activity that went on at the campsite related to the preparation of vegetable foods. Hominids were very inventive about converting the environment into food, and were accomplished seed eaters before they were meat eaters. Foraging bands in North America, at a much later time, are estimated to have utilized two thousand different plant foods (Farb, 1969:10). Many of the plants could not be easily chewed or digested without pounding and scraping, and many of the hominid's stone tools were used for this purpose (Jolly, in Martin and Voorhies, 1975: 172).

Hominid bands, like hunting and gathering bands today, ranged from twelve to twenty-five individuals. Today, at times of severest drought, both baboons and Kalahari bushmen divide into small groupings to search for food. They recombine into larger bands when conditions are better. Similarly, food pressure probably caused the hominid bands from time to time to divide into small groups of female plus male plus children. Individualization of male-female relationships was happening at the same time. While the first bands may have consisted of females and adult offspring, at some time during these very early hominid wanderings females began stable pairing with an adult male from another band. There is no way to know whether pairing was linked to an increased dependency on animal food, increased protection needs, or both.

With the disappearance of estrus ("heat") in the female, neither males nor females were any longer propelled by a totally automatic sex drive. A milder state of continuous receptivity on the part of the female made it possible for choice to enter into the sexual relationship—choice for both the female and for the male.[3] The nurturant activities possible in the home base also added more dimensions to the male-female relationship.

The sex-based division of labor in food getting, the institution of home bases, and a pattern of social organization based on familistic groupings of male-female-children (sometimes in bands, sometimes separately), must all have evolved early in the hominid experience and long before the arrival of *Mulier* and *Homo sapiens* on the scene.

Territorial Expansion and Takeoff

Australopithecus family bands slowly started moving out of Africa. Compared to their primitive relatives, they were already "cosmopolitans," moving over a hunting territory of about five hundred miles, while baboons usually travel over a fifteen-square-mile territory. This tendency to cover vast areas in their foraging for food, instead of adapting to microenvironments, was one of the factors that led to the very rapid evolution of those early hominids into the brainy human species that succeeded them. It appeared they were always out exploring, always looking for new problems to solve.

In the course of another million years, these cerebrating hominids had circled the Mediterranean and found their way to China, always taking the valley routes, avoiding mountains, and leaving sites to be discovered millennia later by twentieth century archaeologists. Toralba in north central Spain and Terra Amata near present-day Nice in France are two four-hundred-thousand-year-old sites that give us a glimpse of the continuing evolution of the hominids.

By this time hunting has grown in importance as a human activity. Males have become very skilled at it, and can now bring down the largest animals in their environment—elephants and rhinoceros—as sites in Spain show. They have developed all kinds of hunting strategies, including working in coordinated hunting parties, and have continued to improve their tools. Cleavers, axes, borers, scrapers, and a bewildering variety of implements of stone and bone appear. While they are not marked "his" and "hers," we can infer that many of the improvements in tools during this period were also made by women. For all the variety, they still bear the marks of the basic Olduvai pattern—variations on a two-million-year-old tool kit. Significant tool complexes appear that are labeled Acheulean and Abbevillian. Homebase camps now have huts that may be up to fifty feet long, made of long branches bent to interlock at the top. Food gathering remains a major activity for women, but now they also scrape hides and perhaps build the new twig houses. House building becomes an increasingly frequent activity for them.[4]

What has been happening to *Homo* and *Mulier erectus* over the past one million years, apart from their spread through the temperate zone? The size of their brains is in the process of doubling. While the Bible tells us that we cannot add a cubit to our stature by thinking, apparently the evolutionary process has involved adding cubits to the brain size by thinking—or rather has rewarded thinking, and "selected" for cranial capacity.

Somehow a deviation-amplifying feedback system[5] became effective early for our particular primate ancestors, leading to their ever sharper judgmental capacities. Every new adventure the far-ranging hominids experienced expanded their survival capacities. They kept discovering new things to eat, new places to take shelter, new ways to make tools. Each discovery equipped them for the next one. If we go back to very early developments in the prehominid line, we may consider with Pfeiffer the special evolutionary possibilities that life in the trees offered (1969: 21-34). While early primates may have been forced into the trees because they could not compete successfully on the ground, once up there they had to deal with a new dimension: treetop living. This kind of life involved so many gaps, discontinuities, and uncertainties that a species to survive had to develop extraordinary flexibility and skill in lightning-quick spatial judgments:

> Regarded from a ground-dwellers point of view, it is roughly equivalent to moving too rapidly to stop through tall dense grasses without being able to see more than a few feet ahead. At any moment, one may suddenly come upon a deep hole directly in the path, too wide to step across. Such hazards may be numerous and scattered at random over the terrain. Frequent swift decisions are required about how far to jump and in what direction. To live in trees is to be confronted continually with analogous emergencies, analogous "holes" in the form of gaps between branches (Pfeiffer, 1969: 10).

Research on learning in human infants emphasizes the importance of optimum discontinuities in triggering learning. Using representations of a human face from very conventional to wildly distorted, it has been shown that an infant glances quickly away from both the very familiar and the unrecognizably distorted faces, and is held longest by representations that are suggestive of a face that needs "mental work" to fill in the gaps (Kagan, 1967, 1971). Our primate ancestors, then, lived from moment to moment by figuring out, literally, how to bridge gaps.

Not all who took to trees became *erectus*, however. When competition got heavy in the trees, grasping and swinging skills alone were not enough. With changing climatic and environmental conditions, the premium came first on size, then on ability to survive in two environments: both in the trees and on the ground. Some primates became hominids in the process, thriving on the double set of discontinuities of tree and ground living. At each point in this long development new neural pathways were developing, "the cerebral expression of new possibilities":

> The possible routes along which nerve signals may pass from sense organs to muscles increased enormously. The cortex is in part an organ of analysis, a dense feltwork of billions of nerve cells which lie between stimulus mechanisms and response mechanisms, between experience and action. Its complexity reflected the new complexity of the apes' world (Pfeiffer, 1969: 35).

The additional complexes neural pathways set up, once the hand was freed from the necessity of the grosser grasping movements of treetop swinging for the finer hand-wrist-finger movements of a slower-paced exploration of the ground, must in themselves have enormously expanded the cortex. Our hands literally helped develop our brains. So while the female hominid paid a high price for the loss of the more general grasping reflex in her infants, in terms of her own increased responsibility for toting them around, she gained in the long run, right along with her mate. The hand that grasped the tree limb, and clutched its mother's fur,[6] could never have wielded the bone sewing needle.

Hunting versus Gathering, and a New Division of Labor

The deviation-amplifying feedback process of challenge-response-new challenge went on as hominids began to explore the planet. Male and female were in this together. The process of mapping new environments, identifying dangers and resources, was a shared one. Because the females were often carrying babies, they may have developed somewhat different scanning skills than the males, but the cortical enrichment would have been the same. As long as hunting was confined to the pursuit of small game, caught not far from home base, role differentiation would be minimal.

We can make some guesses about what daily life was like on the basis of observations made by anthropologists who have lived with any one of the dozens of small hunting-gathering tribes found today in Africa, Australia, and South America.[7] Women in the Australian desert will walk a maximum of ten miles a day, water bowl balanced on head, nursing child on hip and small children following, in search of food: five miles out from camp, five miles back. They are quite clear about their physiological limits. They have such intimate knowledge of an area, of say five hundred square miles, that they know where each special water-bearing plant, each nut-bearing tree, edible root, and bulb are growing in that area. Careful conservationists, they leave certain emergency-type rations like the water-bearing plants "for next time."

The difference between male and female knowledge stocks in these bands is probably not large. Since the women supply up to 80 percent of the diet by weight, they must know a good deal about environmental resources (Lee, 1968: 33). Both women and men are skilled ecologists, but women may know the names and properties of more plants and bushes than men do. What the men know was taught them when they were little by the women, before they were old enough to join their fathers on hunting expeditions. It has been said that hunting is a high-risk, low-yield activity, and that food gathering is a low-risk, high-yield activity (Lee, 1968: 40). In times of drought in Africa, people who can attach themselves to desert nomad peoples do so, for desert food gatherers rarely die of starvation in droughts. The women have a wide reserve knowledge of edible plants which are not normally used (being tough to chew, less tasty, and so on), but which see them through prolonged shortages of other foods (Lee, 1968: 40). The "low-risk activity" has high survival value.

While hunting and gathering tribes of today have a million years more evolution behind them than the early hominid bands, it is nevertheless probably true that, then as now, there were women's rituals and men's rituals, based on different ways of spending the day. The rituals are a source of mutual challenge as well as of mutual pleasure; neither set of rituals is "better." Old women as well as old men play the role of tribal elders.

In short, the cognitive-analytic, the symbolic-aesthetic, and the social-bonding talents of both women and men are fully developed and fully exercised in this type of society.

At some point in the million-year spreading-out over the planet, hominids moved from small-game to large-game hunting. The Toralban and Terra Amata sites, with their huge piles of animal bones signifying large-scale kills, represent the large-game era and provide the materials for societies' favorite myth, about the brawny hunter who drags his women by the hair into his cave to do his will. A great deal of attention has been given to the analytic and coordination skills, both individual and social, which developed in the course of big-game hunting. There is no doubt that both the behavioral learning "in the field," and the considered program of training which the males in hunting societies develop to educate their young boys, involve a major evolutionary advance in capacity to deal simultaneously with large numbers of items of information, to achieve high levels of mental synthesis, and to integrate behaviors and cognitions with subtlety and speed. However, to infer from this that hunting was the "master integrating pattern of our species" (Laughlin, 1968) is to forget the other set of capacities to deal simultaneously with large numbers of items of information, to achieve high levels of mental synthesis, and to integrate behaviors and cognitions with subtlety and speed, involved with the gathering activities of the females.

Deets (1968: 281-282) points out the absurdity of considering hunting as the master pattern for human activity, given the wide range of activities early hominids engaged in. Why not, says Deetz, consider "Man the Gatherer" and "Woman the Potter"? The problem of how to use *man* in the generic sense, while imaging both women and men in our heads as we use it, compounds the difficulty of identifying particular activity patterns as crucial in human development.

The major impact of large-scale hunting was that it helped establish an asymmetrical division of labor that replaced the essentially symmetrical sharing found in gathering societies. The biological givens of childbirth and nursing then reenforced this new separation of men's work from women's work.

By 400,000 B.C., there may have been about forty thousand bands of hunter-gatherers scattered across Africa, Asia, and Europe, each with its own home base. There were haves and have-nots then, as now, since some bands found the richest grassland areas with the largest animal herds, and others managed in less fertile regions with a relative scarcity of food. It was hardly a situation of perfect competition, in the economist's terms, since most bands had no idea that there were alternative environments available to them. Some were just lucky. Over time, however, more and more bands found out about the good hunting and gathering to be had in Spain and France near the Mediterranean, and that region became an early area of population concentration.

When we see the remains of the Toralban and Terra Amata sites with their extensive building and tool remains, complex yet still stamped with the sameness of the Olduvai, we are seeing hominids already launched in the "development" process. They are about to reap the rewards of the accumulated experience and rapidly expanding brain size which, coupled with higher population density and more opportunity for social interaction, have brought them to a new phase of social evolution. The Swanscombe site near present-day London presents us with almost modern-looking women and men, nearly *sapiens.* [8] Their tools, including the two new types, Clactonian and Tayacian, are still modifications of very old patterns. The double-edged hand axe and a more sophisticated type of flint (Levallois technique) indicate, however, that they are using their brains to improve their tools. Postholes and other evidence suggest that women were building both animal-hide and twig huts. While many shelters were built in the open, evidence of tents of skin erected inside caves, probably to keep out the cold, are also found as far back as the Middle Paleolithic. Digging sticks with fire-hardened points indicate women had figured out that putting pointed sticks into the fire to dry and harden provided them with more efficient tools for food gathering.[9] Men got the idea of using the sticks to spear animals.

Neanderthals and New Skills

Fully modern woman, *Mulier neanderthalensis,* and her mate took another three hundred thousand years to evolve. (Fully modern may be a slight exaggeration, but it is generally agreed that a well-groomed and tastefully dressed Neanderthaler would not stand out as unusual in a New York subway.) By this time her brain size had fully evolved, and if she had an oversized jaw, this would be corrected by an improvement in her cooking techniques. Emerging during an inter-glacial period, she was to face during the next ice age, from 75,000 to 50,000 B.C., the greatest challenges her evolving species had yet met. One reason that she and her mate survived the cold was because of the superior stone tools they developed, known as Mousterian and Levallois; sixty different kinds of these tools have been identified, all a substantial advance over the two-million-year-old Olduvai tool models (Constable, 1973: 54).

Adventurous, *Mulier neanderthalensis* moved with her mate into a whole new set of habitats across the plains of what is now the Soviet Union and across forbidding mountain chains toward southern Asia to open up the area that was to become the birthplace of civilization. Her ecological knowledge would have been crucial in these move-ments. Without her sharp eye for new environmental features and her ability to make good judgments about the unfamiliar on the basis of what earlier had been familiar, her bands would have starved to death. Meat was sometimes abundant, sometimes not. Roots and tubers and nuts and berries were always needed.

Judging from her tool kits, she became a highly skilled dressmaker, preparing a great variety of animal skins for garments as well as for shelters.[10] As heavier and heavier winters descended on the Euro-pean Neanderthalers, her skill in finding and storing plant food was pushed to its utmost. The most important development in this period, however, was woman's learning to tame fire. This extraordi-nary achievement set her off from all animals, who feared fire, and it gave her and her children both protection against wild animals while the men were away hunting and warmth in winter. It made cave dwelling possible, since with fire it was for the first time feasible to drive animals out of the caves (they liked shelter too), and keep them out, so that hominid families could move in. Who knows what com-plex threads of thought and imagery were spun on her mental loom to enable her not to fear that which had surely burnt and hurt some members of her band, if not herself?

[S] he watched it carefully, calculatingly; [s] he accepted the odds and sought to improve them in favor of escaping fresh hurt. [S] he was learning which end of the stick [s] he could grasp with impunity. . . . the taming and use of fire raised [wo] man indeed to Promethean heights, [mistress] not of a tool but of a force (Walters, 1953: 38).

The taming of fire is usually ascribed to men, but it seems far more likely that women, the keepers of home base and protectors of the young from wild animals, would be the ones whose need for it would overcome the fear of it. Men's controlled use of fire in hunting may, however, have developed simultaneously with women's use of it at the home base. The hearth fire was for a long time "collected" from found fires and carefully saved and moved from site to site, as it is done today among the Congo pygmies described by Turnbull (1968). Learning to kindle fire was a much later development (Oakley, 1961).

With a fire burning on the hearth, and animals brought in by the men to supply food and warm skins, some Neanderthal bands survived a thirty-thousand-year ice age. Death came often. A hunter injured and frozen to death in the snow could mean a whole band wiped out. Children died of malnutrition, women died in childbirth. Each new birth would be a stern time of silent weighing of possibilities. Should this child be allowed to live? Could they feed it? As with the Australian aborigines today (Pfeiffer, 1969: 517), this decision might be primarily the mother's. She will know what the food prospects are, how much is left of last summer's plant-food store, what the weekly take-home pay in animal meat has been lately. And knowing that girl babies will be destined to be further producers of offspring, she is less likely to let girl babies live than boy babies, in the leanest times. She has learned to look ahead, to be practical.

The extent to which cannibalism was practiced to extend the food supply during hard times among the Neanderthals is not clear. Probably infants that were not to be reared were eaten, a practice that has continued to this century among some foraging people in times of drought and great hardship (Hogg, 1966: 168). Bashed human skulls and charred human bones at various cave sites leave a double trail of evidence. Sometimes fellow hominids were used for food, sometimes brains alone were consumed in a special kind of communion ritual (Constable, 1973: 104-105). We will see shortly that the ritual use of skulls, both animal and human, is one of the early culture traits of the protohumans. On the whole, the Neanderthals appear to have been a peaceable folk. Evidence for raiding parties and interpersonal violence are infrequent; most of the archaeological records tell a pacific story.

The Flowering of Neanderthal Culture

By 100,000 B.C., then, the human species has had a long experience behind it of making increasingly sophisticated adaptations to an environment it is coming to know better and better. The capacity to symbolize and record experience is beginning to emerge. The startling and still controversial work of Alexander Marshack (*Roots of Civilization*, 1972) points straight back to this Neanderthal culture as the time when the first systematic observations of lunar time periods were made and the basis for later calendrical developments established. On the strength of the fact that his work has had a surprising degree of acceptance among those scholars most involved with calendrical research, and because his line of analysis fits so well with the kind of picture I am trying to develop here, I am going to elaborate on the Marshack thesis. It should be understood that this is an imaginative reconstruction that will have to be modified when more research data are available.

Marshack's basic thesis is that *patterning events over time*—what he calls "time-factoring"—and *creating stories around repeated human experiences* that become the basis for complex ritual enactments, are capacities that developed in the Neanderthal culture and came to full flowering in Magdalenian systems of notation and of symbolic representation in painting and sculpture and in associated rituals which made use of the notations and representations. His demonstrations, based on painstaking microscopic analysis of apparently chance scratches or decorative markings on paintings and engravings, evoke calendrical overtones and suggest lunar cycles. A whole new interpretation of Neanderthal culture is emerging from his work. (See also Marshack, 1972b, 1975, and 1976.)

With the human brain now fully evolved, is it so strange to imagine the Neanderthals beginning to conceptualize lunar and solar cycles and to relate them to changing seasons? All human experience in nonurban settings is framed by the risings and settings of the sun by day and the moon by night, by the movement of the seasons and the associated ripening, harvesting, and "dead time" of plant foods. Animals as well as humans respond to these cycles, so Neanderthals had two sets of teachers—the cyclic events in nature itself, and the animal responses to these events. Side by side with these environmentally determined cycles are the biosocially determined cycles of the human lifetime: birth, puberty, pairing, death. Many other cycles develop out of the interrelationship between humans and their environment, and out of their relationships with each other in dyads, familistic groups, and bands. It is the conceptualization of all these cycles that Marshack refers to as "storying." The acting out of these conceptualizations gives an in-depth quality to the human experience, provides social support and nurture, a sense of identity, courage to face the unknown.

Most of our knowledge of the Neanderthals comes from their burials, and quite a number of Neanderthal burials have been uncovered. They all give evidence of ceremonies having been performed at the time of the burial and of preparations for burial implying a set of beliefs about death. Flint, stone, and bone tools were buried with bodies, and in at least one case (Shanidar cave burial) the body was set on a mound of wild flowers and covered with more flowers (Constable, 1973: 25). At another site, six pairs of goat horns, still attached to skulls, form a circular arrangement around a grave. A child's grave at La Ferrassie contains a piece of stone (see figure 3-1) "intentionally engraved with linear sequences" comparable to calendrical notations found much later, in the cave-art era (Marshack, 1972: 349). Careful removal of the base of the skull, or *foramen magnum,* seen in some skeletons indicates the possibility of ritual cannibalism of the kind practiced in Bronze Age Germany and, until recently, by nomadic subsistence peoples in various places (Marshack, 1972: 121; Hogg, 1966).

Fig. 3-1. *Line Rendition of an Intentionally Engraved Stone Found at La Ferrassie.*

Cave sites also give evidence of ritual use of red and yellow ochre and of a fairly elaborate bear cult. A cave containing a stone chest with seven bear skulls, and niches with six more bear skulls carefully arranged, and a second cave with a larger chest and even more bear remains, point to large-scale ritual preparations. While bear-cult remains are relatively specific, some imagination is needed to figure out how the ochre was used. It has been suggested by Constable and others that men painted their skins with ritual patterns in ceremonial preparations for hunting. This would certainly fit with observations of present-day hunting and gathering cultures, where such ritual painting is found. In fact, painting the body with ritual symbols may be the earliest form of "written communication" as well as an early art form. Frobenius (1974), examining the elaborate tattooing of the Maori, sees this ritual adornment as having become record keeping as well as communication, since each tattoo mark on a woman or man indicates parentage, status, and so on.

The appearance of ornaments in burials (for example, animal-tooth and seashell necklaces) almost as early as that of tools indicates that the impulse to decorate is about as old as the impulse to create artifacts. Frobenius (1974) suggests that all human labor is a consequence of the desire to have materials for decoration. That seems too extreme a position, but we certainly cannot ignore the fact that humans from Neanderthal on have decorated surfaces (their own bodies, tools, cave walls) in ways that did not add "utility" in the sense of economic productivity.

Join all this speculation to the evidence that Neanderthals sometimes allowed crippled babies to live and sometimes cared for helpless old people,[11] at least during periods when there were no serious food shortages, and we must realize that we are dealing with a complex culture.

The fact that Neanderthals met at special times and places to perform burial rites associated with gathering food and hunting cannot be directly related to more sophisticated calendar consciousness except through the one marked stone buried with a child, but it does lead directly to the various lunar and lunar-solar markings that come in the Aurignacian-Magdalenian times to follow. Calendar consciousness may have developed in women first, since every woman has a "body calendar"—her monthly menstrual period. She would be the first to note the relationship between her own body cycle and the lunar cycle.[12] Urban women are much less likely to notice or be affected by the phases of the moon, so that particular calendrical potential is much less obvious in modern times. This calendaring by women will be further discussed later on. The marking of seasons was equally important for women, the food gatherers, and men, the hunters, so the development of a combination lunar-solar calendar was probably a joint enterprise. (Death rituals, since they are often for infants in the first year of life (many infant burials have been found), would fall perhaps more in the women's sphere than in the men's.) The two sets of rituals that we have evidence for among the Neanderthals, then, those associated with food gathering and those associated with death, are likely to have been fully participated in by both women and men. Since they suggest elaborate advance preparations and patterned ceremonials repeated over and over, probably both women and men spent part of their work days in preparation for ceremonials.

The burden of all this discussion is that conceptualization and ritualization of social life happened very gradually, over a long period of time, and that females were fully involved in that process throughout "prehistory." The roots of ritual in the experience of death and bereavement may go back to the nonhuman primates. Mother baboons give evidence of considerable grief when their babies die, and male baboons also seem to be aware of the death of infants as a puzzling discontinuity (Altmann and Altmann, 1970: 178). It is not so strange that over a twenty-million-year period, from our primate ancestors until the Neanderthal era, *Mulier* and *Homo sapiens* evolved from feeling a baboon-like grief over the death of an infant to perceiving a time-patterned quality in death and in birth. In addition to the three sets of teachers I mentioned earlier, the cyclic events in nature, the responses of animals to them, and the biosocial cycles evinced most clearly in the woman, they had something else of crucial importance—the "home-base" setting in which to organize their perceptions night after night.

The long, slow evolution of home base must have been very basic to the development of a sense of the relatedness of the seen and the unseen in the face of the discontinuities of everyday life. When fire-lit caves became home base, and the dangers of death by freezing were added to the dangers of death by starvation, injury from hostile animals, and other perils, a new quality must have entered into both the solitude and the togetherness of the small bands. In the hardest times, bands probably rarely exceeded twelve persons. Neither large bands nor "nuclear families" could have survived.

Househunting in the Paleolithic for caves to live in, especially at the height of the ice age, was not exactly easy. The range of choice was limited. Archaeologists have estimated that a cave for a Paleolithic hunting band would need to be about two hundred and fifty square meters, allowing ten square meters per person for an average band of twenty-five. In fact this seems to be the average cave size in sites in France. In South German and Yugoslavian sites, the same number of people (judged by concentration of tools) squeezed into ten square meters as their total space. It would appear that the first housing shortages developed in the last ice age. The alternation of experiences of ranging over great spaces and being crowded into small caves was probably very important in developing the special social characteristics that were to produce *Homo* and *Mulier sapiens*.

For survival, at least two adult males and two adult females would be needed in each band. What kind of communing went on among them? Many anthropologists have given accounts of how small hunting and gathering bands sit in silence around a campfire in desert or forest. Some extraordinarily beautiful photographs of the tiny Tasaday band living in a cave on the slope of a jungle mountain on Mindanao in the Philippines (White, 1973: 137ff.) show pensive faces by firelight. The Neanderthals had limited voice box equipment and therefore a limited speech capacity. Their performance, however, shows that their intelligence was as keen as ours. Did they have better nonverbal communication modes than we? Very likely. Their culture, however, was not to last. (See Marshack [1976: 141-145] for a discussion of the origins of language.)

A New Development in the Near East: The Cro-Magnons

The Neanderthals reached their peak and then "disappeared" from history. Some of them remained in Europe and coped with the severities of the ice age, but by 50,000 B.C. many of them had moved to the Near East. Genetic isolation for the series of bands that stayed behind in Europe, as contrasted with the great intermingling in the Near East, inevitably made the Cro-Magnons of the Near East look like a different species. They did not have the oversized jaw, not having to eat so much undercooked meat in the warmer, more resource-filled environment. While a lot of their large-jawed cousins probably did die out because of environmental hardship, the ones who were left apparently intermarried with their relatives from the Near East when these trickled back to Europe, some thousands of years later. The older Neanderthals may sometimes have been hunted as "wild men" by returning Cro-Magnons, but on the whole, with their superior intelligence, they probably found a way to adapt. It was only the oversized jaw that died out.

The Near East corridor became the focal point of the next evolutionary development. While the ice age was still on, hunting was at its very best here, since this was the retreat site of the herds. "Transitional type" humans are found here in places like the Mt. Carmel rock shelter, along with successive layers of tool kits from Neanderthal to "modern" (Cro-Magnon). The experience of higher population density and intensive big-game hunting had evolved a whole new set of tools, and new patterns of social organization. When the Neanderthals' culture was at its peak of development in Europe, the species probably numbered about one million on the entire planet. In the favorable environment of the Near East the population expanded rapidly, so that by the time the new people were spreading back into Europe, humankind had tripled in size, to over three million by 35,000 B.C.[13]

With open land and a few forests in the new terrain, bands met one another much more frequently. This is the time, Hawkes suggests (Hawkes and Woolley, 1963), that alliances between bands became tribal-type associations. We can imagine that the already elaborate ceremonies the immigrant Neanderthals brought with them from Europe became much more elaborate in the friendlier climate. They would become the occasion of the coming together of a number of bands. The habit of females changing groups at the time of interband encounters, already noted in chapter 2 as a practice among chimpanzees, would by now have been developed into interband alliances. While it is not possible to reconstruct Neanderthal "family life," the evidence from cave sites and campsites is not inconsistent with the possibility that monogamous lifetime pairing had developed. At first there would be spontaneous movement of young unpaired females from their birth band to another, and a similar movement of young males, resulting in a random pairing of "eligibles." Once speech had developed, it does not seem like such a great step to go from random pairing to interband discussion about that pairing. Once coupling became a matter for interband agreement, it would be another short step to the development of interband pairing rituals.

Contemporary hunting-gathering bands have had fifty thousand years since Neanderthal times to elaborate marriage alliance patterns. Yet it is interesting to note that polygamy is rare, and where found it does not account for more than 5 percent of marriages in a band (Gardner, 1968: 210). Polygamy is also commonly associated with serial marriages for both women and men, in what Gardner calls "gerontogamy"—older males marrying younger females or vice versa. The first marriage then becomes a kind of adoptive parent-child relationship, to be succeeded for the child by other marriages. In the Paleolithic, in small bands with short life expectancies, this might well have been adaptive behavior at times.

The fact remains that stable monogamous pairing is nearly universal among hunters and gatherers today, as the two major reviews of studies of hunting-gathering societies indicate (Lee and De Vore, 1968; Bicchieri, 1972). The fact that in some of these tribes the children call all the adults mother and father does not at all mean that there is a group marriage practice, as Lewis Henry Morgan (1963) erroneously thought when he studied the Iroquois.[14]

Considerable affection between spouses is often described by observers of hunting and gathering bands. Spouse exchange between men takes place, if at all, under very well defined conditions. Marriage rituals may in themselves be simple, but the process of two families within a band, or two bands, exchanging women (or men) to set up new household units is one that always receives a lot of attention. Each hunter needs a partner, just as each gatherer needs a partner, and bands are careful that a new marriage does not leave one family short of the necessary personnel to carry on their subsistence activities. We could say that the women exchange men, or that the men exchange women, though the latter is the usual statement of the process. However one phrases the personnel exchange, the underlying fact remains that marriage is indeed an affair of the entire band. Turnbull (1968) has described with humor and sympathy how that personnel exchange goes on. The wishes of the young people are probably taken more into account in these small bands than in more urban settings. The very fluidity of the hunting band, with groups splitting off at various times of the year for various specialized types of hunting, coming together at other times, and continually recombining in various ways, makes the fact that the married pair remains stable through these changes all the more noteworthy.

With the help of the clear skies of the Near East, the early sky calendars of the Neanderthals must have become elaborated beyond the simpler European forms. But because of the nature of the campsites, there is no archaeological evidence for this. All kinds of notations may have been made on unbaked clay tablets and on hides, none of which would survive the centuries. It is only when we pick up the thread of the art and ritual practices once these peoples are back in Europe, circa 35,000 B.C., that we can interpolate back to what must have been happening in the Near East in the interim.

Back in Europe with the Cro-Magnons

It is hard to keep straight the rapid sequences and the clusters of simultaneous events which exploded on the European scene when the ebullient Cro-Magnons returned at the close of the ice age that originally drove them out. Two separate cultures, the Perigordians and the Aurignacians, apparently trickled in simultaneously about 35,000 B.C., coexisted peacefully for about fifteen thousand years, and then blended with a transitional European culture, the Chatelperronian. The Perigordians had roomy cave homes with public hearths out front, with stone wall dividers and a longhouse built at the back for comfortable group living quarters. Their tools and living patterns are easily identified, but they turn out not to be "mainstream people." The Aurignacians were somewhat different. Their tools were more elaborate and specialized; their settlement patterns involved a large central living site and satellite quarters for specialized activities. It is in their caves that we find the first cave art. In caveless regions, such as Czechoslovakia, southern Russia, and Siberia (Gravettion culture), they erected substantial longhouses and left many evidences of a rich ceremonial life. Similar evidence is found in the rare cave sites of those who stayed behind in the Near East, such as the Shanidar cave. From 20,000 to 17,000 B.C. there was a brief resurgence of glacial cold, and during this period a people labeled the Solutreans emerged with tools that were beautiful elaborations of the earlier Neanderthal tools, including the breathtaking laurel-leaf blade that in its most elaborate form could never be used as an implement. Were these people hide-out Neanderthals? Finally there was the Magdalenian culture, lasting from 17,000 to 12,000 B.C. and bringing cave art to its greatest heights at a time when many of the animals depicted were disappearing from Europe. The Magdalenians represented the peak of the population explosion that began after the last glaciation. As ice caps receded, there was more food, both on land and sea, and more social technologies to exploit them than *erectus* or Neanderthal had had.

What part did women play in this explosion? I suggested earlier that women's ecological skill was crucial in making the trek eastward and in making the successful settlements in new environments possible. Once migrating bands connected with the great animal herds roaming the mideastern corridor, however, band life styles must have changed considerably. There was no longer the same dependence on plant food, and less reason to practice infanticide; there was enough food for any number of babies. *Erectus* bands had first begun to cluster in France and Spain three hundred thousand years before, but they saw each other relatively rarely. In the Mideast they learned to live together, to develop interband relationships. While men were organizing communal hunts, women were exercising their building skills in developing new kinds of shelters with wood, stone, and skins and in making new kinds of tools to work the animal skins the men were bringing home. (See figure 3-2 for an imaginative reconstruction of women's activities.)

During this period it is likely that a further development of women's interband bonding skills took place. High-density living made increasingly important the question of how children of mating age should pair. In isolated bands, or bands that at most had contact with one or two other bands, there was little choice. With more bands in contact, there was more choice.

The habit of thinking of children in terms of interband alliances, which I have suggested might have begun as far back as 50,000 B.C.,

Figure 3-2. *Reconstruction of Cave Dwelling Life, Neanderthal.*

Top left: woman painting cave wall; foreground: girl caring for baby, woman making stone utensils, woman scraping with antler tool, older woman tending fire and infant; middleground: cleaning hide, assembling hide into garment; farground: foraging for food, woman and boy catching fish, woman gathering plants.

would now be reenforced by the expanded alliance opportunities. Since many of the work settings for women in food-gathering societies are communal settings (especially for food preparation and child care), women had if anything more time for discussion of alliance possibilities than did the men, who were away tracking down bears.

The women might discuss the relative hunting skills and strategies used by men in different bands, particularly in regard to their effectiveness in bringing back meat to the campsites. Making alliances with the best hunting bands through exchange of children ready for pairing would be an obvious strategy to evolve. Another characteristic to look for in a band would be the skill of its women in food gathering and in the preparation of skins for clothing and shelter. Then, finally, there were the skills of the individual young people ready for pairing. There were many things to take into account, and what the women discussed during the day would be talked over with the men around the campfire at night.

The interaction of women became more complex as environmental pressures lessened. It has already been mentioned that with ample food supplies there was less pressure to practice infanticide and more babies to care for. We can imagine a period of some thousands of years in which women worked in small groups up and down the valleys of Europe, sharing new knowledge about what was edible in the environment and how to prepare it, learning from each other how to make new kinds of scrapers and bone implements as they prepared meats and hides together. As they worked, they would discuss seasonal changes in plant and animal food supplies. They would also discuss babies. It is hardly possible that menstrual cycles and their relation to birth, lactation, and weaning were not thoroughly explored in these thousands of years by women working in communal groups; it was too obvious a part of their lives to be ignored. The more primitive awareness of Neanderthal women would now be replaced by a gradually dawning comprehension not only of the fact of cycles, but of their function. The lore of sun and moon and stars developed during the millennia of living in the Near East was now woven together with the recognition of menstrual cycles into a complex whole that made it possible on the one hand to predict seasonal changes in food supplies, and on the other to predict the time of birth of a new infant from the time of cessation of menstruation. It was obviously useful to be able to predict both sets of events. We know that men developed the habit of making notches and lines on bones (archaeologists call them batons) to count sequences of lunar changes which related to seasons and to significant ritual events.15 (Also interesting is the lunar phase decipherment made of the notations on one such bone by Marshack [1972: 89].)

Why on bones?

> A bone slate is small and long-lasting, it can take exceedingly fine scratching better than wood. Being relatively small, a bone slate can be carried in pocket or pouch more easily than one carries a large wooden stick, and in a culture of high mobility, where a [person] could not carry too many belongings, the small slate would be the more practical (Marshack, 1972: 90).

How would the bone slate be used? Partly for ceremonies.

> But in a culture that counted "moons" there may also have been other persons keeping a notation for other purposes: perhaps for a voyage, visit, or march, or for a menstrual or pregnancy record, or for a private period of initiation (Marshack, 1972: 90).

If the baton tradition was primarily masculine, we must look elsewhere for the women's notations, and we find them on highly abstracted female images as old as the earliest batons and animal images, scattered across Europe all the way from Spain to Siberia. Marshack has studied some of these figures under a microscope and reports that they give evidence of having been marked repeatedly by different tool points, presumably at different times. The periodic markings would appear to be "evidence of a female symbol system or a form of record keeping, very likely by adult women. The markings seem to indicate a knowedge and use of symbols to document human processes and activity" (Marshack, 1975: 84). Some of the female images shown in figure 3-4 very probably had record-keeping as well as ritual functions, but I do not have the information to substantiate such a statement.

To what extent men taught boys a "masculine" system of record keeping and women taught girls a "feminine" one we cannot know. Since both sexes were working on the basis of the same lunar cycle, and had to cooperate closely in utilization of the environment for survival, there was probably a substantial common knowledge stock passed on by both women and men to the children of a band. It is not improbable that there were special teaching ceremonies connected with puberty rites for both girls and boys. It would be at puberty that girls would be taught to keep calendars, possibly in ways not very different from those used in tribal societies today. Marshack tells us that among Siberian people of today,

women calculate child-birth by the phases of the moon. . . . Pregnancy
has a duration of ten lunar months, and the woman keeps a sort of
lunar calendar (it was always the woman who was the custodian of the
lunar calendar among these nationalities) (Frolov, 1965).

Also,

women among the Yurok Indians had menstrual calendars and could
predict birth within a day, and . . . the Yuroks also had other tally systems. The women apparently kept a menstrual count by dropping a
stick each day into a basket and kept a pregnancy count by dropping a
"month" stick each lunar month into a second basket until they
reached a count of ten (Piltina in Marshack, 1972: 337).

Calendar keeping and the design of ever more elaborated rituals
around life cycle and seasonal events seem logical activities for the
women, who spent so much more time at the campsites than the men
did.

I am not suggesting, however, that women were the sole designers
of ceremonies. Men, deeply involved in hunting, would be more
familiar with the appearances of animals on the move. When the ceremonies included painting these animals on cave walls, men may have
painted the animals and women the calendrical notations, or the
women may have instructed the men in how to make them.

Cave art was a part of ceremonial activities, ritually repeated over
and over again at the same site. Many caves have been discovered in
France containing well-hidden ceremonial sites. The evidence that
the animals on the nearly inaccessible walls have been painted and re-
painted, sketched and resketched, many times, and that children and
adults have performed special walks or dances before the pictures, all
makes it clear that these are ceremonial rather than living centers. Because of the size of handprints and heelprints, and the occasional
presence in paintings of "animal-headed" women as well as men—
i.e., shamans dressed to perform their rituals—it seems clear that
women, men, and children were all involved.

These cave painting ceremonies were not simple hunting magic,
since they appeared to involve so many different elements of symbolism and ritual, as well as references to food gathering. There are
plants, fish, and birds included in the paintings, all portrayed in relation to certain seasonal concurrences. For example, spawning salmon,
foaling horses, and growing grain are placed side by side. The symbol-

ism is complex and the notation itself sometimes approaches looking like hieroglyphics. Figure 3-3 shows the range of symbols (from Marshack, 1972: 198). They are simpler in the Aurignacian period, more complex in the Magdalenian, but there are similarities that point to some common tradition being evolved over large areas over a long span of time. The symbols represent a higher order of abstract intellectual conceptions of cycles in relation to environmental resources, as well as skillful observations and recordings of environmental detail. Since plant food and fish as well as animals are all involved in the record, I suggest that there were women recorders as well as men. Observation of plant life was women's specialty, and we may find the foundations of their later development of agriculture in these paintings, symbolic notations, and calendric markings. Because so many of these paintings and engravings are so beautiful, we have tended to think of them as individual artistic creations. Once we think of them as reflecting the emergence of art, science, philosophy, and religion in a delicate synchronization of recorded observation and ceremonial life which unfolded over many centuries, it gives us quite another sense of the quality and complexity of life of the Upper Paleolithic peoples.

Not only was there cave art and its associated ceremonial life, there was also "home art," or rather, "campsite art," and its associated ceremonial life.

Most of the calendar bones belong to home art, as do animal and fertility figurines and engraved stone slabs. If we keep in mind the users of these ritual objects, then it seems at least likely that the men might make the animal figurines and engravings, and the women the fertility figurines.[16] Marshack has made a very interesting photographic collection of these figurines, which makes it possible for the first time for the lay person to see the range of styles and possible uses for them. Prior to the Marshack analysis, the sheer diversity in the figurines, as well as their ubiquity all over Europe, was puzzling. Now it is possible to suggest some themes and functions for the figurines.

Table 3-1 presents all the different kinds of figurines, grouping them thematically rather than chronologically and listing them in order of completeness of representation.[17] Some of the figurines are pendants, meant to be worn around the neck. Some are "disposables," made perhaps by a woman as a prayer for a successful pregnancy and then thrown away.[18] Others are clearly ritual objects to be held in the hand during ceremonies, and they bear evidence of

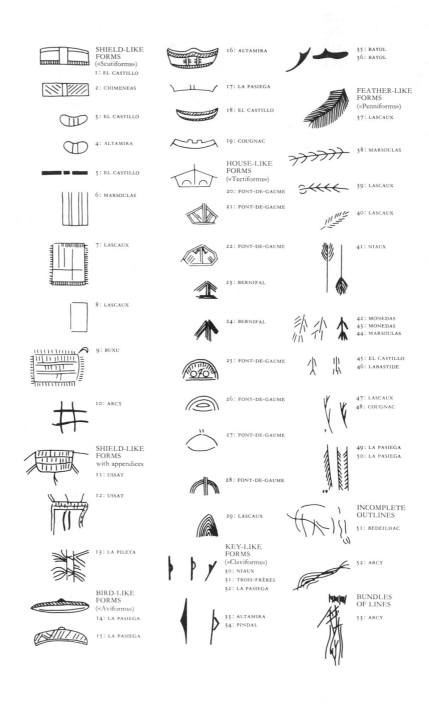

Figure 3-3. *Cave Painting Symbols.*

Table 3-1

Female Figurines from Periods Ranging from Aurignacian through
Magdalenian, Listed in Order of Completeness of Representation

	Type	Use	Period
a.	faceless, otherwise realistic pregnancy figure	rock-shelter bas relief	Upper Perigorian
b.	abstract full figure	for ritual placement	East Gravettian
c.	abstract full figure	"baton" for holding during ritual observation	Magdalenian
d.	geometric female figure	calendar bone	Upper Magdalenian
e.	abstract full figure	pendant	Upper Magdalenian
f.	abstract full figure	"disposable" for once-only use	Magdalenian
g.	double breast	pendant	East Gravettian
h.	forked image with vulva	pendant	East Gravettian
i.	forked image with vulva	pendant	Middle Magdalenian
j.	buttocks silhouette	cave wall painting, stone slab engravings	From Aurignacian to Magdalenian
k.	ritual vulval disc	"charm"	Aurignacian through Magdalenian
k.	hand (praying female?)	on bone batons, cave walls	Aurignacian to Magdalenian

SOURCE: Marshack (1972).

much handling. Still others were evidently placed on some kind of stand for ritual display and/or veneration. Figure 3-4 consists of a series of sketches and line drawings of the figurines listed.

Some of the earliest and some of the latest figurines have similar styles, so no particular thematic evolution emerges here, though it well might if I had fuller information. In addition to the classification by type of use—pendant, statuary object of veneration, disposable prayer, charm—there is probably an implication of different ritual meanings in the different aspects of the female emphasized—breast, vulva, buttocks, hands, full figure. At present, however, there is no way to interpret these. It is useful to be aware of a probable wide range of meanings so that we do not underestimate the extent of ceremonial observances associated with female figurines. At the time, the functional and impersonal quality of these figurines should be appreciated. There is no hint of the existence of an "adoration of women" in these faceless and variously styled figures. The whole mother-goddess phenomenon and the accompanying complex of male-female attitudes and relationships comes later. The one exception to this is the very first figurine (a) listed in figure 3-4; it comes from early Perigordian times, yet has many of the attributes of the much later agricultural mother-goddess; the half-moon (or horn) which she holds in her hand becomes part of the rich symbolism associated later with mother-goddesses. Because this figurine is so early, it would be a mistake to associate later symbolic meanings with it, but we see the early signs, perhaps, of the mother-goddess idea here.

We will probably never know how many of these figurines were made by males, how many by females, and to what extent females rather than males presided over the ceremonies associated with their use. It seems reasonable to infer, however, based on other evidence mentioned of women's participation in ritual, that some of them were made by women and some of the ceremonies presided over by women.

The cave art, the bone records, and the figurines all point to a highly developed capacity for both abstract thought and imagery in the late Paleolithic. A great deal has been written, particularly by Jungian "human potential" theorists, about the superior capacity for imagery of early humans. McCully (1971) suggests that the development of verbal thinking overlaid the imaging capacity, but that it is possible for persons to be in touch with the deep psychic structures that generate archetypal forms and patternings for contemporary experience. These forms are generic to the human observer-responder from ancient days. McCully (1971) draws heavily on the work of André Leroi-Gourhan in interpreting cave paintings to suggest the omnipresence of archetypal forms in the paintings, to the exclusion of any recognition of abstract, notational representations.

Without in the least minimizing the importance of archetypal forms, which may very well reflect basic psychic structures found in all humans of every culture and time period, I suggest that an exclusive focus on archetypal imagery in the analysis of cave art is a disservice both to Cro-Magnon and to modern woman and man. If the human race "dreamed before it thought," dreams soon taught thinking. The sheer growth in the area of the cortex of the ancestral brain assured the evolution of a new series of processes: observation, memory, comparison, evaluation, and selection (Walters, 1953: 38). Humans, interacting with their environment in ways discussed earlier in this chapter, equipped with the remarkable scanning, storing, retrieving, and synthesizing mechanisms of these new brains, were thinking essentially as we think. Their powers of observation and recording were the product of capacity, social need, and training. If our contemporary educational techniques leave some of these capacities untouched, that is our problem, and a remediable one. In short, we should neither romanticize the imaging capacity of Paleolithic peoples, nor downgrade their intellection capacities. We are recognizably the same family, in terms of mental functioning.

Along with the evidence of the development of an increasingly rich culture from Aurignacian to Magdalenian times, we also find that by the time of the Magdalenians weapons were being used not only against animals but also against humans. By 12,000 B.C. the Magdalenians were occupying three to four times more sites than their predecessors ever had, taking up land that had never had human settlements before.[19] The extraordinary thing is not that we begin to find evidence of interband hostilities, but that we find it so late in human history. It is certainly true that bands did not meet each other often. Estimates of territorial ranges for contemporary hunting and gathering bands are from a low of one person per three hundred square miles up to three persons per one square mile (Fried, 1967: 55). Even though territories can be identified, there is seldom exclusive use of them (Fried, 1967: 60, 67). There are always conditions under which other bands may hunt on one's territory. Our notions about the importance of territoriality have little basis either in primate or human history. Most primates have overlapping

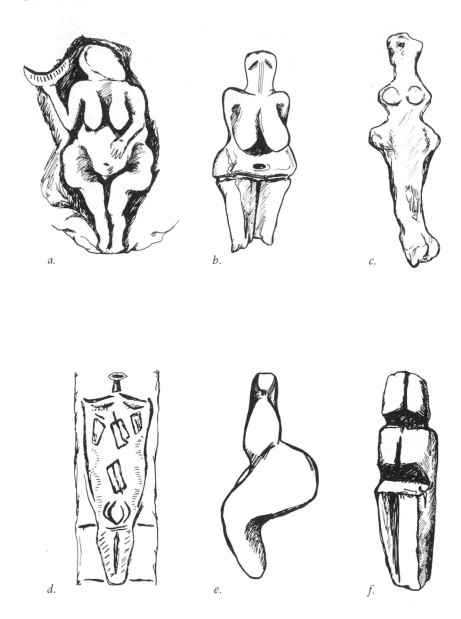

Figure 3-4. *Female Figurines.*
a. faceless female in bas relief; b. buxom female image, fired clay; c. pregnant female, reindeer antler; d. female with tiny head on calendar bone; e; stylized female, polished coal pendant; f. crude female figurine, coal.

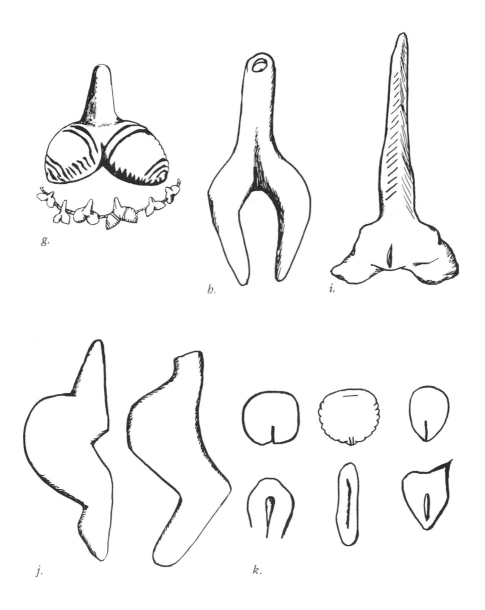

g. ivory bead double breast pendant; h. forked image with vulva, ivory pendant; i. forked image with vulva, baton; j. sculpted female buttocks; k. ritual vulva disks.

territories, sometimes even overlapping central cores, just as human bands do (Fried, 1967: 45-49).

Evidence from existing hunting and gathering bands supports the archaeological finding of peaceableness in the Paleolithic. Hostilities would be confined to raiding parties with very limited objectives, probably a consequence of interband ceremonial observances as societies developed ranking and ceremonial specialists and came to notice each other's rudimentary surpluses. Larger aggregations of bands—tribal and prestate associations—were much more the consequence of interband ceremonial gatherings than of competitive interaction or conquest. Fried (1967) points out that the organizing potential of ceremonial occasions is far greater than the organizing potential of warfare. War is irregular, brief. Ceremonials are regular, frequently lasting for weeks, and require a lot of preparation. Berndt (1962) reports a pig festival in an Australian New Guinea tribe that requires six years of preparation. The war leader, a temporary figure, would have far less status than the ceremonial leader, who would always have lots to do in preparation for the next intercommunity ceremonial. Since the work of women is important in ceremonial preparations, this suggests active participation of women in Paleolithic "public life."

We can think of Magdalenian times, then, as an era in which there was a great increase in interband ceremonial occasions with increasing population density and interband contact. The larger caves became more and more important, not only as a setting for ceremonies and the elaboration of ritual art, but for all kinds of public uses. Pfeiffer suggests that

> the caves represent protoinstitutional sites before the coming of separate specialized institutions; from time to time they probably served as prehistoric archives, shrines, offices, schools, vigil places, theaters. Indeed, for limited periods at least some of them may have been as bustling for those times as downtown business and cultural centers are today (1969: 236).

Some of these caves were very large indeed. Howell (1968: 288) mentions an occupation site in Spain, covering over four thousand square meters and opening into another, adjacent occupation site. It is not hard to imagine a complex social life in such a setting. Something happened to the Magdalenian culture, however, and it died out. Perhaps it was too specialized, and failed to adapt when certain of the resources it had counted on too heavily were depleted. Whatever the cause, the "petered-out" Magdalenian was replaced by a less advanced culture, the Azilian.

The Magdalenian period, however, saw a very significant shift in the hunting-gathering way of life that was to pave the way for the agricultural revolution both in the Middle East and in Europe. Binford (1968) identifies the lever for change in the rapid development toward the end of the Paleolithic of *facilities* as contrasted to *tools*. The first breakthrough for hominids in the development process came with the mastery of tool making, which facilitates energy transfer (spears, digging sticks, and so on) (Binford, 1968: 272). The second breakthrough involved the construction of facilities that conserve energy: fish weirs, nets, pottery. Containers, and the storage principle they embody, developed *before* agriculture.

One important aspect of the container revolution was the discovery, presumably by the women foragers, of seeds as food. Seeds are nutritious, abundant, and store easily, but only if one has containers. Also, seeds are hard to digest without grinding and boiling. Grindstones and containers for storing and boiling food appear in Europe and the Middle East well before the discovery of agriculture. Washburn and Lancaster suggest that the grinding-boiling technologies spread along the Arctic route to the New World, "setting the stage for nearly simultaneous discovery of agriculture in both the New and Old Worlds" (1968: 295).

In this view, it is the seed-using technology developed by women which paves the way for agriculture. The seed-using technology is not the whole story, of course, but is part of the great worldwide explosion in food technology that leads to the use of river and sea food and a whole range of nuts as well as seeds. Boats, which made water a resource instead of a barrier, were constructed for the first time during the late Paleolithic. This is also the time when dogs were first domesticated and used for hunting. The first bows appeared also. Everything points to a severe pressure of existing population on a dwindling supply of game. If game shortages led to these discoveries, the vast increase in food supplies that the new technology made possible immediately led to higher population densities in many areas. This cycle of increasing food supplies and increasing population densities was particularly dependent on the discoveries, skill, and ingenuity of women as food gatherers and processors. The old vegetarian diet could be eaten by foragers on the very spot where it was gathered. The new vegetarian diet needed preparation to be made digestible. Unlike meat, which could be simply roasted whole, grains had to be processed before they could be cooked.

It would be absurd to say that all these new developments stemmed from the increasing interaction of the women in the bands all up and down the valleys of Europe. Some part of the developments did happen there, however, and we have the records of the evolution of the new preagricultural knowledge stock on the walls of the caves of France, with their detailed notations of plants, animals, and fish, and the seasons of seeding and harvest for each. Some part of the developments happened, too, in the hunting expeditions in those valleys, as many braved frightening waters to find food when game gave out.

What was the status of women toward the end of the Magdalenian? It may well have been a time of sex-egalitarianism, since both sexes were being noticeably inventive. Women may have had more time for the development of ceremonials than they did formerly, as their new seed technologies led to more time spent on food processing as compared to gathering, thus increasing the amount of time spent at the home base. With food supplies abundant, and with the possibility of storage against future scarcity, children would be valued more. Accordingly, female fertility would also be valued. The fertility figurines hint at the importance of fertility for both women and men, and at the continued elaboration of ceremonial status for women as well as men.

It must be confessed that the evidence for the patterning of women's roles in relation to men from early hominid times down through the Paleolithic is scanty to the extreme. Readers will have noted this for themselves. Most of the evidence is about the band's way of life, not about the presence or absence of sex-based division of labor. This chapter has thus largely been a work of imaginative reconstruction, relating as far as possible to the available archaeological evidence. The full participation of the female in discovering environmental resources and inventing tools with which to utilize those resources has been emphasized at every turn, as has her participation in the creation and elaboration of social bonds and ceremonials. While an egalitarian society has been depicted, these millennia should hardly be thought of as a utopian era in human history. Droughts, ice ages, and danger from powerful animal predators framed a very uncomfortable and insecure existence. Bands sometimes turned on each other in violence, though not often. Infanticide was a necessary feature of responsible parenthood, and cannibalism a consequence of food shortage. The extraordinary message that comes through the evidence of camp and cave homesites, and from cave paintings and stone and bone carvings, is that hominids were continually finding new ways to respond to their changing environments. The early emergence of homesites shows the conserving, protecting side of hominid evolution, and the long treks over every continent show the adventurous side. Since male and female hominids maintained homesites together, and trekked together, one can hardly argue that either the inclination to conserve or to adventure is sex-linked. Both are basic traits of the human species.

We have come now to the threshold of the Neolithic, and we are ready to examine the special roles that emerged for women with the development of the first settled societies.

Appendix 3-1
Simplified Chronology of Archaeological
Ages and Cultures
(Focus on Europe)

Geologic Age	Archaeological Age	Number of Years Ago	Species	
Lower Pleistocene	Lower Paleolithic	2,000,000	Erectus	Oldowan, Acheulian, Abbevillian, Clactonian, Tayacian
Middle Pleistocene				
Upper Pleistocene	Middle Paleolithic	1,000,000	Neanderthal	Levallois, Mousterian
Holocene		70,000		
	Upper Paleolithic	35,000– 18,000	Cro-Magnon to Sapiens	Chateperronian, Perogordian, Aurignacian, Gravettian
LAST ICE AGE		20,000– 17,000	Sapiens	Solutrean
		17,000– 12,000	Sapiens	Magdalenian
	Mesolithic	12,000– 9,000	Sapiens	Azilian

Note: This chronology includes only cultures mentioned in this chapter, and is by no means complete. It is based on discussion in *Prehistory and the Beginnings of Civilization* (Hawkes and Woolley, 1963) and *The Neanderthals* (Constable, 1973), and has not been altered to include the additional one and one-half million years prior to 2,000,000 B.C. that the new Leakey findings now ascribe to *erectus* existence.

Notes

[1]Note that since this was written the prehistory of *Erectus* has been pushed back another million and a half years.

[2]There is a consistent tendency to underestimate the female as toolmaker, whether in archaeological or ethnographic investigation. Since she was a tool user from the start, this is rather absurd. Seashells as kitchen tools, found in the earliest sites, were certainly being used by both sexes and may as well have been "invented" by women as by men. O. T. Mason, writing in the 1890s, was very conscious of the woman as toolmaker:

> [She] will be seen in the role of potter, butcher, cook, beast of burden, fire maker and tender, miller, stonecutter (stone griddle maker), most delicate and ingenious weaver, engineer (devising a mechanical press and sieve in one woven bag and using a lever, baker, and preserver of food. Add to this her function of brewer, and you have no mean collection of primitive industries performed by one little body (1894: 40).

[3]If Rowell (1973) is correct, estrus is not that clear-cut a phenomenon in monkey troops either, which means that the evolution of the female-male relationship has been even slower and more gradual than we thought.

[4]Although we do not normally think of house building as a female activity today, there are many references to house building by women in the ethnographic literature: Aberle (1962); Sterling (1965); Sullerot (1968); Mason (1894); Briffault (1959); Fraser (1968); Turnbull (1968). Most of these references describe contemporary (nineteenth and twentieth century) house-building activities of women. Others refer to the Middle Ages and to ancient times. Cole (1973) has written the most comprehensive study to date on women as builders and architects, but most of her material is drawn from North America.

[5]This is a concept developed by Magorah Maruyama (1963).

[6]The question of how the hominids got rid of their fur I am not prepared to deal with. The aquatic-period theory of Sir Alistair Hardy, described in Elaine Morgan's

105

Descent of Woman (1972), is interesting, but we need a good deal more evidence before putting our early ancestors into the ocean for a prolonged period.

[7]The possibilities and limitations of use of ethnological data on contemporary hunting and gathering societies to make inferences about the life of early hominid bands were repeatedly discussed by both ethnologists and archaeologists at the 1966 Man the Hunter Symposium held at the University of Chicago (see especially Clark, 1968: 276-280). Since each existing society is the product of as long a period of evolution as any other contemporary society of the twentieth century, there are no simple generalizations about ancient foragers that can be made from modern ones. Yet knowledge about technologies, the use of resources and space, among current foragers can be combined with archaeological findings on such sites as Olduvai and Terra Amata to make possible some imaginative reconstructions of daily life. These images may turn out to be wrong when further information is available, but they are the best we can do at present.

[8]Information on the Swanscombe site is from Pfeiffer (1969) and Constable (1973).

[9]Since the digging stick is a primary tool for women in subsistence societies today, both for food gathering and for horticulture, it seems reasonable to suggest that they discovered the fire-hardening process on their own.

[10]Sally Binford (1968: 108) has written in some detail about the tools made and used by women for the preparation of skins.

[11]A forty-year-old skeleton at the Shanidar site indicated that a Neanderthal band had allowed a boy baby with a serious birth defect of right arm and shoulder to live, and nurtured him to a relatively ripe old age.

[12]Dr. Jock Cobb (1974), of the University of Colorado Medical Center, reports that women living near the equator apparently have a marked tendency to ovulate during the full moon. If a biological regularity occurred in identical cycles with a large number of women, this would soon create a sense of social cycle. Some of the rapidly accumulating body of research on the control of ovulation by light is summarized by Gay Luce. According to Luce (1971), the city woman with irregular menstrual periods can simulate the effect of the full moon on ovulation by keeping a light on all night for the period when ovulation should normally be taking place—and thus become perfectly regular.

[13]Estimates by E. S. Deevey (1960).

[14]It was Morgan's misinterpretation of Iroquois practices that gave rise to Engels' view of marriage as introducing the domination of females by males after an earlier group marriage situation. Ceremonial interband pairing antedates any kind of economic surplus or seizure of political power (see Engels, 1942).

[15]Marshack has expressed himself strongly on this point in a communication to the author, and there seems to be no reason to question the careful linking of evidence and intuition that stands behind his statement that the baton tradition must be regarded as a masculine one.

[16]An alternative interpretation of the use of the fertility figurines is that they were not ritual objects at all but simply dolls for children to play with. It seems not unlikely that some of the figurines served as dolls, but until there is more

evidence about play activities I prefer to follow the domestic ritual-object line of reasoning. The figurines could have served double duty for mother and daughter as fertility charm and doll. See the work of M. I. Finley (1971) for a different interpretation of all female figures and of the role of women in prehistory.

17This organization of the figurines is my own, and I take full responsibility for any possible misinterpretations.

18These it seems to me are the ones most likely to have been used as dolls in children's play.

19There were then nearly five million humans, according to E. S. Deevey's (1960) calculations.

References

Aberle, David F.
   1962   "Matrilineal descent in crosscultural perspectives." Pp. 655-730 in David M. Schneider and Kathleen Gough (eds.), Matrilineal Kinship. Berkeley: University of California Press.

Altmann, Stuart A. and Jeanne Altmann
   1970   Baboon Ecology: African Field Research. Chicago: University of Chicago Press.

Berndt, Ronald M.
   1962   Excess and Restraint: Social Control among a New Guinea Mountain People. Chicago: University of Chicago Press.

Bicchieri, M.
   1972   Hunters and Gatherers Today. New York: Holt, Rinehart and Winston.

Binford, Sally R.
   1968   "Early upper Pleistocene adaptations in Levant." American Anthropologist 70 (August): 708.

Briffault, Robert
   1959   Mothers: A Study of the Origins of Sentiments and Institutions. New York: Humanities Press. (First published 1927.)

Clark, J. Desmond
  1968   "Studies of hunters and gatherers as an aid to the interpretation of pre-historic societies." Pp. 276-280 in Richard B. Lee and Irven De Vore (eds.), Man the Hunter. Chicago: Aldine.

Cobb, Dr. Jock
  1974   Denver: University of Colorado Medical Center, Department of Preventative Medicine, personal communication.

Cole, Doris
  1973   From Tipi to Skyscraper: A History of Women in Architecture. Boston: I Press.

Constable, George
  1973   The Neanderthals. New York: Time-Life Books.

Deetz, James F.
  1968   "Hunters in archeological perspective." (Discussions, part 6.) Pp. 281-285 in Richard B. Lee and Irven De Vore (eds.), Man the Hunter. Chicago: Aldine.

Deevey, E. S.
  1960   "Human population." Scientific American (September): 195-196.

Engels, Frederich
  1942   The Origin of the Family, Private Property, and the State. New York: International Publishers. (First published 1884.)

Farb, Peter
  1968   Man's Rise to Civilization: As Shown by the Indians of North America from Primeval Times to the Coming of the Industrial State. New York: E. P. Dutton.

Finley, M. I.
  1971   "Archeology and history." Daedalus 100: 168-186.

Fried, Morton H.
  1967   The Evolution of Political Society: An Essay in Political Anthropology. New York: Random House.

Fraser, Douglas
  1968   Village Planning in the Primitive World. New York: George Braziller.

Frobenius, Leo
  1974   Childhood of Man. Magnolia, Mass.: Peter Smith.

Frolov, Boris
  1965   "Stone age astronomers." Moscow News, September 4.

Gardner, Peter M.
  1968   Discussant in Richard B. Lee and Irven De Vore (eds.), Man the Hunter. Chicago: Aldine.

Hawkes, Jacquetta and Sir Leonard Woolley
  1963   Prehistory and the Beginnings of Civilization. History of Mankind, vol. 1. New York: Harper and Row.

Hogg, Garry
  1966   Cannibalism and Human Sacrifice. New York: Citadel Press.

Howell, F. Clark
1968 "The use of ethnography in reconstructing the past." (Discussions, part 6.) Pp. 287-289 in Richard B. Lee and Irven De Vore (eds.), Man the Hunter. Chicago: Aldine.

Kagan, Jerome
1971 Change and Continuity in Infancy. New York: Wiley.

Kagan, Jerome (ed.)
1967 Creativity and Learning. Boston: Houghton Mifflin.

Kaberry, Phyllis
1939 Aboriginal Woman: Sacred and Profane. London: Routledge.

Laughlin, William S.
1968 "Hunting: An integrating biobehavior system and its evolutionary importance." Pp. 304-320 in Richard B. Lee and Irven De Vore (eds.), Man the Hunter. Chicago: Aldine.

Lee, Richard B.
1968 "What hunters do for a living, or, How to make out on scarce resources." Pp. 30-48 in Richard B. Lee and Irven De Vore (eds.), Man the Hunter. Chicago: Aldine.

Lee, Richard B. and Irven De Vore (eds.)
1968 Man the Hunter. Chicago: Aldine.

Luce, Gay
1971 Body Time: Psychological Rhythms and Social Stress. New York: Pantheon.

Marshack, Alexander
1976 "Implications of the Paleolithic symbolic evidence for the origin of language." American Scientist 64: 136-145.
1975 "Exploring the mind of Ice Age man." National Geographic 147: 62-89.
1972a The Roots of Civilization. New York: McGraw-Hill.
1972b "Upper Paleolithic notation and symbol." Science 178: 817-828.

Martin, M. Kay and Barbara Voorhies
1975 Female of the Species. New York: Columbia University Press.

Maruyama, Magoroh
1963 "The second cybernetics—Deviatio—Amplifying mutual causal processes." American Scientist 51: 164-179, 250-256.

Mason, O. T.
1894 Woman's Share in Primitive Culture. Ann Arbor, Mich.: Finch Press.

McCulley, Robert S.
1971 Rorschach Theory and Symbolism. Baltimore: William and Wilkins.

Morgan, Elaine
1972 Descent of Woman. New York: Stein and Day.

Morgan, Lewis Henry
1963 Ancient Society. Ed. by Eleanor Burke Leacock. New York: World. (First published 1877.)

Oakley, Kenneth P.
  1961 "On man's use of fire, with comments on tool-making and hunting."
        Pp. 176-193 in Sherwood Washburn (ed.), Social Life of Early Man.
        Chicago: Aldine.

Pfeiffer, John E.
  1969 The Emergence of Man. New York: Harper and Row.

Rowell, Thelma
  1973 The Social Behavior of Monkeys. Baltimore: Penguin. (As reviewed by
        James Loy in Science 180 (May 11): 602-603.

Sterling, Paul
  1965 Turkish Village. New York: Wiley.

Sullerot, Evelyne
  1968 Histoire et Sociologie du Travail Féminin. Paris: Société Nouvelle des
        Editions Gonthier.

Turnbull, Colin
  1968 The Forest People. New York: Simon and Schuster.

Walters, W. Grey
  1953 The Living Brain. New York: W. W. Norton.

Washburn, Sherwood L. and Irven De Vore
  1961 "Social life of baboon and early man." Pp. 91-105 in Sherwood L.
        Washburn (ed.), Social Life of Early Man. Chicago: Aldine.
Washburn, Sherwood L. and C. S. Lancaster
  1968 "The evolution of hunting." Pp. 293-303 in Richard B. Lee and Irven
        De Vore (eds), Man the Hunter. Chicago: Aldine.

White, Edmund
  1973 The First Men. New York: Time-Life Books.

4

From Gatherers to Planters: Women's Moment in History

The transition described in this chapter, from the hunting and gathering way of life to the agricultural settled way of life, ostensibly began about 12,000 B.C. In fact, the process really began at least ten thousand years earlier, as described in the last chapter. On the one hand, Neanderthal's and Cro-Magnon's improved hunting techniques led to a vigorous onslaught on the dwindling herds of large animals that roamed the warmer lands fringing the glacier country. On the other hand, women were developing the new seed-processing technology. While behaviors changed very slowly, there certainly were some "aha!" experiences preceding the development of agriculture. How excited the first person must have been who realized that seed spilled by chance near a campsite the year before had now sprouted into wheat. And the first baby lamb that missed the usual fate of being eaten when its wild mother was roasted must certainly have caused a flash in someone's mind as it tottered uncertainly after its new "mother" as camp broke: we don't have to hunt meat, we can raise it.

Nevertheless, the change in ways of procuring food moved as slowly as the glaciers themselves. We usually do what we know how

111

to do best, and earlier humans knew gathering and hunting best. We can watch their slowly changing diet through the changing character of the debris that archaeologists have unearthed from ancient sites. Flannery describes how after 20,000 B.C. in the Taurus-Zagros region (parts of modern Turkey and Iraq) large animal remains were increasingly supplemented by "traces of smaller, humbler creatures: turtles, land snails, fish, fresh-water crabs and mollusks, partridges and migratory water birds" (Leonard, 1973: 21). An increasing variety of nuts and seeds would also be found in such layer-by-layer analysis. When the ten-thousand-year transition was over, women and men stood in a different relationship to one another. The earliest development of agriculture, and the settlements around which it was pursued, were women's special work. The challenge of dealing for the first time in human history with continuing residence in a small area, with clear rules of access to land and the development of food-storage techniques and facilities, led to what might be thought of as women's brief period of "dominance" in history: the matrilocal period[1] in which the women of a village exchanged men with other villages.

In the previous chapter we saw the Cro-Magnons living in clusters of up to a hundred people. But those who moved on to Europe and those who stayed behind in the Middle East continued this clustering process even while they remained nomads, and the cave settlements described in Europe were matched by the caves of Shanidar in Iraq and of Belt and Hotu on the Caspian. Hunting and gathering bands were spread out all around the famous fertile crescent, the arc that inscribes the Arabian desert, curving northward from the Syrian coastal hills, east across the low hills that border the great Anatolian plain, and back down the foothills of the Zagreb Mountains. There, streams from the higher mountains, and a light rainfall, provide just enough moisture for a good grass cover without irrigation, but not enough for forests.

Life was good for these people. The composition of their diet was changing, but there were plenty of grains, nuts, roots, and fruits to supplement the meat and fish. Archaeological evidence continues to point to a relatively peaceable way of life. Human violence against other humans occasionally shows up in bashed skulls, but infrequently. Alland (1962:2), writing about a much later period, describes occasions of peaceful interpenetration of tribes in the African forests: newcomers may settle in the "empty spaces" of another tribe's territory, amicably working out with that tribe who has the right to what resources in the area. If this could be true in times of greater population density, it is not hard to visualize a similar process of peaceful accommodation among the nomadic bands of Europe and the Middle East.

Declining supplies of game meant that women had to provide increasing amounts of plant food. Women would be very aware that the men were staying away longer at a time, even while coming back with less meat.

Women and men had different kinds of teachers, and therefore were learning different kinds of things. The plants taught the women; the animals taught the men. The men knew things about speed and strategy, and also about persevering. A man can wear out any animal he hunts because he can persist longer than the animal being chased, even though the man is slower moving. So when animals became harder to find, more perseverance was required. Also, men killed everything they found. Women found that if they left some of the plants and roots in the soil when they were gathering, they would grow again in the same abundance as before for picking on a return visit. They were learning to practice conservation.

The fact that meat was getting more scarce put greater pressure on the supply of plant foods that grew near home base. What was needed was for more things to grow—more plants, more animals. The problem was *fertility*. The Cro-Magnons and their Neanderthal cousins had both been pondering fertility a long time as we saw in the last chapter. Who knows how the first thoughts about fertility came? Perhaps initially through the impact of human experiences, rather than animal and plant observation: puzzling over the death of a woman, the death of a child, moving from the sorrow of bereavement to the thought of a woman's womb, source of new life. Certainly burial rituals already showed very complex human ponderings about meanings beyond the immediate present. The fertility of women may have been inseparable from that of animals in the minds of the early hunters, since they depended so very much on both. We find such a possible linkage in a discovery from the Gravettian period. A site containing a kiln and the remains of a round earth-and-twig hut produced broken pieces of animal figures mingled with parts of figures of women. Might this have been the quarters of a Paleolithic medicine man (Hawkes and Woolley, 1963: 135)? While animal and human figurines are sometimes found together, the female figurines are often found alone. These figurines were examined in chapter 3, where we assumed that, in addition to shamans specializing in cave art and figures, there were women who made these figures for their own use. The practice of making clay figurines (usually unbaked) came with hunting bands to the Middle East, where the custom flourished. We find these figurines everywhere, still primarily as depersonalized special-purpose objects, although occasionally a beautiful "Venus" type statuette appears.

All this pondering about fertility sooner or later led to thinking about the procreative powers of female animals in a new way. If hunters captured a female with a baby, they could bring both home, and *raise* meat, instead of killing it on the spot. It does not matter whether the thought came first to the men, or to the women. Though it meant more work, it also meant more food.

Large animals would not be very convenient to bring home, but there were wild sheep and goats and pigs in the fertile crescent. Caring for sheep is a woman's job at present in some parts of Asia, and in New Guinea women breast-feed piglets when necessary (Leonard, 1973: 79). It is likely that the women of the late Paleolithic were in charge of the first domestic animals. Whatever the sequence of events, goats and sheep began to be kept near the home base, and from then on it became more complicated to leave and move everything to a new home base.

There is some disagreement about whether the domestication of animals or plants came first. In fact, both were probably happening at the same time. There is evidence from campfire remains as long ago as 20,000 B.C. that women had discovered the food value of einkorn, a kind of wild wheat that grows all through the fertile crescent. An enterprising Oklahoma agronomist, Professor Jack Harlan of the University of Oklahoma (Leonard, 1973: 22-24), noticed several years ago, on an expedition to eastern Turkey, how thick these stands of wild einkorn grew. He tried harvesting some, and once he had resorted to a nine-thousand-year-old flint sickle blade set in a new wooden handle (he tried to use his bare hands first, with disastrous results), he was able to come away with an excellent harvest. After weighing what he had reaped, he estimated that a single good stand of einkorn would feed a family for a whole year. He also found that the grains had 50 percent more protein than the wheat we now use in North America for bread flour. Einkorn grains are found everywhere on the ancient home-base sites of the fertile crescent, either as roasted hulls in cooking hearths, or as imprints in the mud-and-straw walls of the earliest preagriculture huts.

It would be inevitable that grains from sheaves of einkorn carried in from a distant field would drop in well-trodden soil just outside the home base, or perhaps in a nearby pile of refuse. When the band returned the following year to this campsite—perhaps a favorite one, since not all campsites were revisited—there would be a fine stand of einkorn waiting for them right at their doorstep. We might say that the plants taught the women how to cultivate them. Planting, however, was quite a step beyond just leaving some stalks at the site where they were picked, to seed themselves for the next year. There was less reason for deliberate planting as long as bands were primarily nomadic and there was plenty of game to follow. But in time there was a premium on campsites that would have abundant grain and fruit and nuts nearby, and then there was point in scattering extra grain on the ground near the campsite for the next year. Because of the construction of the seed, einkorn easily plants itself, so it was a good plant for initiating humans into agriculture.[2]

Gradually, bands lengthened their stays at their more productive home bases, harvesting what had been "planted" more or less intentionally, and letting the few sheep they had raised from infancy graze on nearby hills. One year there would be such a fine stand of wheat at their favorite home base, and so many sheep ambling about, that a band would decide just to stay for a while, not to move on that year.

If any one band of nomads could have anticipated what lay in store for humankind as a result of that fateful decision (made separately by thousands of little bands over the next ten thousand years), would they after all have moved on? While it may have been a relief not to be on the move, they in fact exchanged a life of relative ease, with enough to eat and few possessions, for a life of hard work, enough to eat, and economic surplus. As Childe says, "a mild acquisitiveness could now take its place among human desires" (Childe, 1963: 265).

Successful nomads have a much easier life than do farmers. Among the Kung bushmen today, the men hunt about four days a week and the women only need to work two-and-a-half days at gathering to feed their families amply for a week. (At that, meat is a luxury item, and most of the nourishment comes from nuts and roots.) The rest of their time is leisure, to be enjoyed in visiting, creating and carrying out rituals, and just "being" (Lee and De Vore, 1968).[3]

The First Settlements

For better or worse, the women and the men settled down. They settled in the caves of Belt and Hotu to a prosperous life of farming and herding on the Caspian. They settled in Eynan, Jericho, Jarmo, Beidha, Catal Huyuk, Hacilar, Arpachiyah, and Kherokitia in Cyprus, and in uncounted villages that no archaeologist's shovel has touched.

These places were home-base sites first, some going back thousands of years. Figure 4-1 shows the major Neolithic settlement sites in Southwest Asia and Europe. By 10,000 B.C. Eynan had fifty houses,

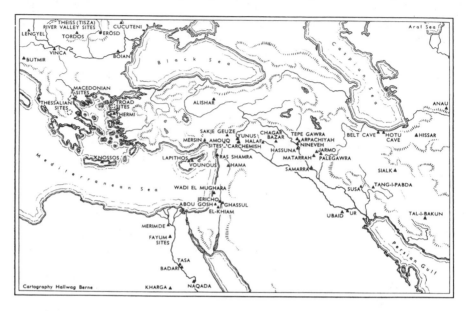

Figure 4-1. *Neolithic Settlement Sites in Southwest Asia and East Europe.*

small stone domes, seven meters in diameter, around a central area with storage pits. This was probably preagricultural, still a hunting and gathering band, but a settled one. The village covered two thousand square meters. Each hut had a hearth, and child and infant burials were found under some of the floors. Three successive layers of fifty stone houses have been found at the same site, so it must have been a remarkably stable site for a settlement.

What was life like, once bands settled down? This was almost from the start a woman's world. She would mark out the fields for planting, because she knew where the grain grew best, and would probably work in the fields together with the other women of the band. There would not be separate fields at first, but as the former nomads shifted from each sleeping in individual huts to building houses for family groups of mother, father, and children, a separate family feeling must have developed and women may have divided the fields by family groups.

Their fire-hardened pointed digging sticks, formerly used in gathering, now became a multipurpose implement for planting and cultivating the soil. At harvest time everyone, including the children, would help bring in the grain. The women also continued to gather fruit and nuts, again with the help of the children. The children watched the sheep and goats, but the women did the milking and cheese making. Ethnologists who have studied both foraging and agricultural societies comment on the change in the way of life for children that comes with agriculture. Whereas in foraging societies they have no responsibilities beyond feeding themselves and learning the hunting and foraging skills they will need, and therefore they have much leisure, it is very common in agricultural societies to put children to work at the age of three, chasing birds from the food plots. Older children watch the animals, and keep them out of the planted areas (Whiting, 1968: 337; United Nations, 1974).

I am assuming that the pressure of needing more hands that is felt by agricultural societies today was a pressure that began to be felt early among the newly settled horticulturalists, and that children were enlisted as auxiliary labor from the beginning. In the discussion that follows on the heavy work load that fell on farming women, it should be remembered that children too shared this work load. Whiting suggests that the more punitive child rearing that develops concurrently with giving serious responsibility to children for fields and animals accounts in part "for the reluctance of hunters and gatherers to change their ways and become part of the modern world" (Whiting, 1968: 337).

Space does not permit adequate attention to the changing situation of children through time. Since children move in their mothers' life spaces up to the first ten years or so of their lives, however, restriction in life space for the one is usually also restriction in space for the other. We will see how confinement, beginning with the mild confinement of the agrovillage, both increases the punitive quality of mother-child interaction and at the same time creates new opportunities for understanding human *growth* as human *development* as mothers watch children grow up. De Mause (1974), who takes a grim view of adult-child relations through most of history, suggests that the relationship mode in antiquity was primarily *infanticidal and abusive;* that this gave way in the fourth to thirteenth centuries A.D. to the *abandonment mode,* when children were primarily turned over to servants and there was much heavy beating; that the fourteenth to seventeenth centuries represent the *ambivalent mode,* when parents became aware that children could be shaped but did most of it by beating. From the eighteenth century on he sees the *intrusive mode,* involving control of children's minds, the *socialization mode,* involving training instead of conquering, and finally the *helping mode,* with parental empathy as the key to that helpfulness.

In my view, all six of these modes have coexisted from the time of the earliest agrovillages. The proportions, however, have changed over time. To the extent that women are confined with their children to very limited spaces, the abusive and abandonment modes will be present. All the same, loving children, playing with them for the sheer joy of it, and comforting them in distress, are traits to be found in the mammal world and are never absent in the human world.[4] I have gone into this amount of detail here because it is in the agrovillages that the more complex and ambivalent modes of mother-child relationship began to develop. With settled life, motherhood becomes a different phenomenon for women.

The agriculture practiced by these first women farmers and their children, producing enough food for subsistence only, must be distinguished from that agriculture which developed out of subsistence farming and which produced surpluses and fed nonfarming populations in towns. The first type is commonly called horticulture and is carried out with hand tools only. The second is agriculture proper, and involves intensive cultivation with the use of plow and (where necessary) irrigation. In areas like the hilly flanks of the fertile crescent of the Middle East, horticulture moved fairly rapidly into agriculture as it spread to the fertile plains. As we shall see, trading centers grew into towns and cities needing food from the countryside. Women and children could not unaided produce the necessary surpluses, and by the time the digging stick had turned into an animal-drawn plow, they were no longer the primary workers of the fields.

The simpler form of farming continued in areas where the soil was less fertile, and particularly in the tropical forest areas of Africa. Here soils were quickly exhausted, and each year the village women would enlist the men in helping to clear new fields which were then burned over in the slash-and-burn pattern which helped reconstitute the soils for planting again. The slash-and-burn pattern of horticulture has continued into this century, since it is a highly adaptive technique for meager tropical soils. Where the simple horticultural methods continued to be used, women continued as the primary farmers, always with their children as helpers. In a few of these societies women continued also in the positions of power described for the first agriculturalists in the pages that follow; these are usually the tribes labeled by ethnologists as matrilocal. Not many tribes have survived into the twentieth century with a matrilocal pattern, however, though traces of matrilineal descent reckoning are not infrequent.

The first women farmers in the Zagreb foothills were very busy.

Not only did they tend the fields and do the other chores mentioned above, they also probably built the round stone or mud-brick houses in the first villages. The frequency with which women construct shelters in foraging societies has already been cited.5

Women also began to spend more time on making tools and containers. No longer needing to hold the family possessions down to what they could carry, women could luxuriate in being able to choose larger and heavier grinding stones that crushed grain more efficiently. They could make containers to hold food stores that would never have to go on the road. They ground fine stone bowls, made rough baskets, and in the process of lining their baskets with mud accidentally discovered that a mudlined basket placed in the hearth would come out hardened—the first pottery. Sonja Cole (1963) suggests that pottery was invented in Khartoum in Africa about 8000 B.C., spreading northwest to the Mediterranean, but the same process probably happened over and over again as people became more sedentary.

The evidence from food remains in these early villages, 10,000 to 6000 B.C., indicates that men were still hunting, to supplement the agriculture and modest domestic herds. This means that they were not around very much. When they were, they probably shared in some of the home-base tasks.

Evidence from some of the earliest village layouts suggests that adults lived in individual huts, women keeping the children with them. Marriage agreements apparently did not at first entail shared living quarters. As the agricultural productivity of the women increased, and the shift was made to dwellings for family units, husband-wife interaction probably became more frequent and family living patterns more complex.

With the accumulation of property, decisions about how it was to be allocated had to be made. The nature of these agreements is hardly to be found in the archaeological record, so we must extrapolate from what we know of the "purest" matrilineal tribes of the recent past.

The senior woman of a family and her daughters and sons formed the property-holding unit for the family. The senior woman's *brother* would be the administrator of the properties. His power, whether over property or in political decision making, would be derivative from his status as brother (usually but not always the oldest) to the senior woman in a family. This role of the brother, so important in present-day matrilineal societies, may not have been very important in the period we are now considering, between 12,000 and 8000 B.C.

Ascribing in imagination to these ancient times the more extreme forms of more recently observed matrilinies (see pp. 148-149 of this chapter), I suggest the following scenario, assuming both matrilineality and matrilocality: When a new household was to be formed, a young woman would build her home, and a young man would come to live there somewhat on sufferance, bringing gifts. He could easily be sent away if he didn't please his wife, or his wife's mother. Older men (and sometimes young men) would have a thin time if their

Table 4-1

The Sizes of Ancient Settlements

Site	District	Area	Population	Date B.C.	Author	Stage*
Eynan		2,000 square meters	200	10,000	Mellaart	1
Wadi Fallah	Mount Carmel			8,000–7,000	Kenyon, Mellaart	1 $2b_1$
Jarmo	Kurdistan	3.5 acres	150	6,700	Braidwood	2a
Beidha				7,000 6,800 6,600	Mellaart	1 $2b_1$ $2b_2$
Catal Huyuk	Cappadocia	32 acres	2,000	6,000	Mellaart	$2b_1$
Hacilar			100	5,700	Mellaart	2a
Arpachiyah				5,288	Mellaart	$2b_1$
Kherokitia	Cyprus	15 acres	2,000	5,500	Mellaart	$2b_2$

SOURCE: Pattern for this chart has been taken from Darlington (1969) with additions from Mellaart (1965), Kenyon (1970), and Braidwood (in Leonard, 1973).

*These stages are as follows: 1, the communal village, undifferentiated functions; 2, the household and craft village, differentiated functions; 2a, local craft only; $2b_1$, unstratified; and $2b_2$, with administrative center and social stratification.

wives sent them away and they could not persuade any other woman to take them in.

To visualize more concretely the kind of society that emerged in these first villages, it may help to picture actual village layouts, some of which are reproduced in this chapter. The layouts indicate that village development can be roughly divided into two stages, the second with several subdivisions:

Stage 1. The communal village, undifferentiated functions
Stage 2. The household and craft-shop village, differentiated functions
    a. local craft only
    b. "town" with craft shops and trading activities
        1) unstratified
        2) with administrative center and social stratification

I suggest that women reached their maximum of differentiated social participation in the local craft-shop village, and possibly began to lose ground in the villages where extensive trading developed. What follows is a survey of "life styles" in these different kinds of villages. Table 4-1 provides an enumeration of the villages under study.

The Communal Village

If we study the diagrams for Eynan, Wadi Fallah, and Stage 1 of Beidha (figures 4-2a, 4-2b, and 4-2c), we see they are remarkably similar: very small round huts around a common center (which may contain a storage center or living hut). The huts are big enough for at

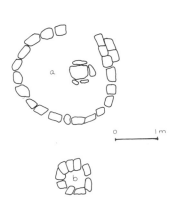

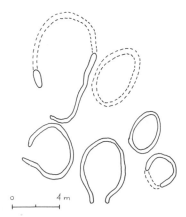

Figure 4-2a. *Natufian Village of Eynan,* *10,000 B.C.*
a. house with central hearth; b. storage pit.

Figure 4-2b. *Settlement at Wadi Fallah.* Of the same type and period as early Jericho, 8000 B.C. Round houses built on terraces.

Figure 4-2c. *Beidha, 7000 B.C., Level VI.*
a. dwellings; b. storage area.

most an adult and a child or two, not for family groupings. The village probably represents an extended family or clan group with a senior woman as head and husbands and wives living in separate huts. This pattern is still found in some parts of Africa today (Leonard, 1973: 96), as may be seen in Cameroon (figure 4-2d). Wives may or may not have cooked for husbands. Common activities and common food storage took place in the center of the circle. This type of village organization would be very efficient if the men were away a lot, hunting. There was a substantial increase in the number of personal possessions in a village like this, over what is found in nomadic base camps.

Women now had a variety of food processing equipment and all kinds of containers of stone, shells, reeds, and unbaked clay. They were also acquiring a store of ornaments, and making clay figurines. Ochre, in use for burial sites since Neanderthal times, was an important part of the early "cosmetic industry."

The circular area in which women were spending much of their time when they were not in the fields or milking sheep and goats would lend itself to a great deal of cooperative and joint activity in the processing of food and in craft activities, as well as in the care and teaching of children. It would also allow for joint planning of agricultural work, arranging marriage agreements for daughters and sons, allocating space for new houses, and deciding on distribution of property at marriage; for burials, decisions on what goods should be buried with the deceased would take place there. Ceremonial life may have been somewhat streamlined compared to Magdalenian times in Europe, because of the pressure of subsistence activities.

It is interesting that the oldest village, Eynan, shows signs of social stratification that we shall not see again until we find the more highly developed trading villages of Stage 2. At Eynan a chief and his wife were buried in ceremonial gear in the center hut (facing the snowy peaks of Mt. Hermon—were they "homesick" for their

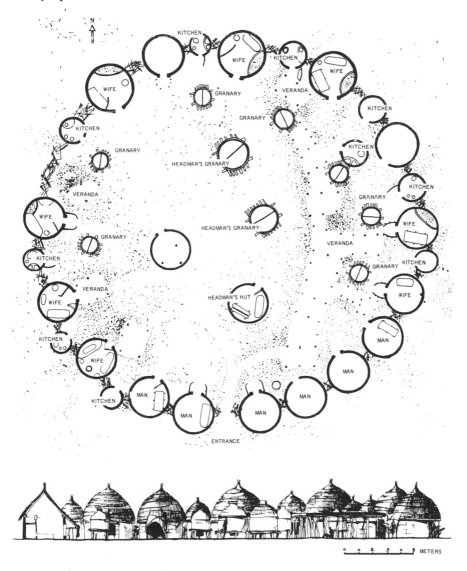

Figure 4-2d. *Plan of Massan Homestead, Twentieth Century, Yagoua, Cameroon, Africa.*

previous nomadic existence?) Wadi Fallah's circular huts (figure 4-2b) all have stone-lined fireplaces and show signs of the "mixed economy" transition from nomadism to farming; both agricultural and hunting implements and advanced polished-stone crafts are present. Jericho, for which I do not have housing drawings, was rather similar to Wadi Fallah in 8000 B.C., before the thick stone walls and towers went up around the former.[6] Jericho was an old nomadic campsite because of its ever-fresh spring. A stone shrine stood near the spring, long predating the village. Jericho gives evidence of having anciently been a main trading center for obsidian. Its circular huts all have goddess figurines, and at later levels a "trinity" of mother, father, and child appear in the figurines. Beidha (figure 4-2c), like Jericho, has a shrine outside the town; in this case, a figureless monolith—a slab of stone. All four of these villages give evidence of specialist activities from earliest layers: the ceremonial function of "chiefing" in the central hut at Eynan, a "stone and bone" polishing hut at Beidha, and obsidian trade in Jericho.

The Local Household and Craft-Shop Village and the Trading Center

Stage 2 includes two kinds of villages: the individual household and craft-shop village which made things for local consumption only, and the trading-center village. Jarmo and Hacilar are in the first category. Later levels of Jericho and Beidha, and Catal Huyuk, Arpachiyah, and Kherokitia are in the second category. They all have certain things in common. Round huts were replaced by rectangular (often two-storied) houses large enough to shelter entire families, and there were individual courtyards opening into communal spaces, with hearths and ovens usually in the courtyards or communal spaces. There were specialty work areas for the manufacture of different products, generally pottery and baskets in the least differentiated villages. There were also shrines, and often cult center buildings. Beyond this, the differences were considerable. Hacilar (figure 4-2e) and Jarmo (figure 4-2f), small villages with populations of from one hundred to one hundred and fifty, obviously provided great scope for both individual and group activities. Women had extensive pottery and basket-making areas. With these new crafts, and perhaps improved agriculture and larger herds of goats and sheep, economic surpluses would be larger. Ceremonials would become more important again, in contrast to the very simplified life of the first villages, and more attention would be given to property exchanges through marriage agreements. Fields might be further away from the village, and larger. Milking,

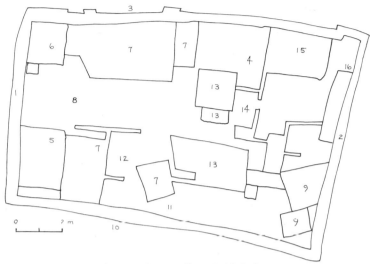

Figure 4-2e. *Hacilar, 5700 B.C.*
1. west wall; 2. east wall; 3. northwest gate; 4. north courtyard; 5. parching oven; 6. granary; 7. house; 8. small courtyard; 9. kitchen; 10. south gate; 11. south courtyard; 12. basket weaving area, 13. pottery workshop; 14. pottery courtyard; 15. shrine; 16. well.

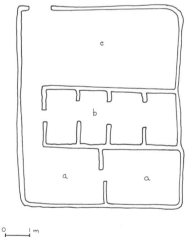

Figure 4-2f. *Jarmo House, 6700 B.C.*
a. living and sleeping quarters; b. four storage rooms; c. open courtyard. (The village had about 25 such houses with alleys or courtyards between them.)

cheese making, and butchering took more time with the larger herds. Older children would have more responsibility for the younger ones, for herding, and for nut and berry gathering, as the women became busier. Special attention would be given to the making of figurines to be placed in the cult center building, and time would be spent caring for that building. Women also made figurines for their own homes.

Men continued to hunt and were also learning to tame the fearsome wild ox, the aurochs. The bull aurochs began around this time to take its place alongside the mother-goddess in religious rites. Village herds of sheep and goats were growing larger, and it was probably the men who captured and tamed cattle. Cattle herds were looked after by the men from the very beginning.[7] Women were so busy at that time that they could not possibly have done so.

The trading towns like Jericho (not shown) had a different flavor from that of the craft villages. In Jericho quarrying and trading brought in substantial surpluses, in addition to the agricultural and craft wealth produced by the women. The new rectangular houses that overlay the old round huts were made of cigar-shaped bricks— men's or women's activity now? The new houses were extensively decorated, and the women wove circular mats for their floors, per- haps in recollection of the old round houses of long ago. Walls and floors were painted, both in plain colors and in basket-weave designs. Pottery came late in Jericho—the women had made fine limestone bowls and plates for a long time, and continued to do so while pot- tery was already being made elsewhere. Their agriculture and sheep- herding practices were similar to those of other settlements.

Life for men in Jericho was more varied than it was for women. It was based on quarrying and trading, going to the Dead Sea for salt, bitumen, and sulphur, dealing in obsidian from Anatolia, turquoise from Sinai, and cowries from the Red Sea. All these activities, like the taming of wild bulls and cows, were by-products of hunting days —discoveries made by men while tracking animals. Dealing in these products became more lucrative than continuing to track animals.

Beidha (figure 4-2g) moved, in five hundred years, from circu- lar huts to rectangular houses in a pattern that indicates fantastically rapid economic and social development, complete with social stratifi- cation:

> Three large rectangular houses measuring 16 by 20 feet displayed in- teriors finely finished in plaster, equipped with hearths bordered by plastered sills. Set into the sills were stone bowls; food could have been boiled in the bowls by filling them with water and then dropping hot stones into them. These houses faced a large open space, like the central plaza of a Latin American town. Around them and across the plaza were much smaller rectangular houses (Leonard, 1973: 103).

If the big houses belonged to those who had grown rich by trading, the smaller houses would contain the craftworkers' homes and work- shops. The women in the poorer homes presumably did more agricul- ture and less crafts.

The fact that trading towns develop a character very different from that of agricultural towns with subsistence craft activities is further evidenced by Catal Huyuk (figure 4-2h), which is in fact the largest Neolithic site in the Near East (Mellaart, 1965). One entire acre of a "priestly quarters" has been excavated, and the cult of the bull as companion to the mother-goddess is everywhere in evidence. Homes are roomy one-story buildings with hearth and oven indoors:

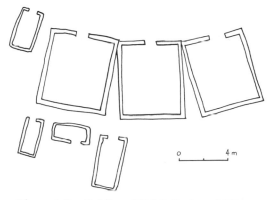

Figure 4-2g. *Beidha, 6800 B.C., Level IV.* Large fine houses and many smaller houses around a plaza.

> Each room was provided with at least two platforms of which the main one was framed by wooden posts, plastered over and painted red. A raised bench was placed at the far end of the main platform. These [platforms] served as divans for sitting, working and sleeping and below them the dead were buried (Mellaart, 1965: 82).

Darlington says,

> In Catal Huyuk . . . we are shown a society in which women are the masters. They even have larger beds (Darlington, 1969: 79).

If he is correct in his statement,[8] then the priestly quarters are probably priestess quarters. Reconstructions of cultic scenes by Mellaart (1965) also show priestesses conducting funerary rites. The preponderance of the evi-

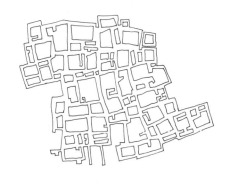

Figure 4-2h. *Catal Huyuk, 6000 B.C., Building Level IV B.*

dence points to an all-female priestly class. There is much more to learn when more parts of the town have been uncovered.

Certainly this was already a rich society. Next to two active volcanoes, both rich sources of obsidian, Catal Huyuk showed a wider variety of both import and export goods than any other town, and also a wider range of foodstuffs:

> The standard of agriculture is amazing: emmer, einkorn bread wheat, naked barley, peas, vetch and bitter vetch. . . . vegetable oil was obtained from crucifers and from almonds, acorn and pistachio. Hackberry seeds occur in great quantities suggesting the producing of hackberry wine, praised by Pliny . . . (Mellaart, 1965: 84).

The agriculture would be women's work. The standards of technology, except for pottery, were far beyond other Near East centers of the time, and Mellaart (1965) describes in eloquent detail the tools, stoneware, jewelry, woodwork, and textiles of Catal Huyuk. Wooden and stone vessels were executed with far greater mastery than the pottery.

More is known about the religion of Catal Huyuk than any other settlement because forty-nine shrines or sanctuaries have been excavated. They were built similar to the houses, but were more elaborately decorated. The familiar human and animal fertility figurines were found only *outside* the shrines. Inside were the cult statues:

> The principal deity was a goddess who is shown in her three aspects, as a young woman, a mother giving birth, or as an old woman, in one case accompanied by a bird of prey, probably a vulture. Simpler and more terrifying aspects show her semi-iconic as a stalactite or concretion with a human head which probably emphasizes her chthonic aspects related to caves and underworld (Mellaart, 1965: 92).

A male deity appeared as a boy, son-lover of the goddess, or as an older god portrayed as a bull. Here, in 6000 B.C., were the most concrete evidences of the double life-and-death aspects of the mother-goddess that made her the terror and hope of the human race during the agricultural era and far into the age of the first great civilizations. There are also indications of a more assertive male identity, in the evidences of trade and cattle breeding.

Arpachiyah (figure 4-2i), a much smaller town, perhaps settled from Catal Huyuk, tells the same story of both agricultural and trade wealth, fine arts and crafts, a highly developed religious cult life, and distinctive, elaborate houses.

There is really no way to tell how much of the craft activity in these trading towns was carried on by the women. It seems likely that cultic activity was under their control. The tensions between the male and female may well have begun sharpening in these towns, with so many non-agricultural activities competing for attention, many of them by-products of the former hunting way of life. These activities were producing a substantial surplus of both goods and food, but the only evidence (as yet) of a stratified society is in Beidha. Apparently everyone lived well in Catal Huyuk. And while administrative centers and houses of the rich may be revealed by further excavation, there was apparently no centralized planning and resource allocation. The cultic centers do not show evidence of being organized for or by administrative centers. In the absence of more information, we can only assume that women and men participated in the

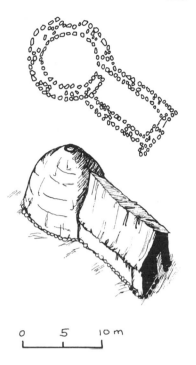

Figure 4-2i. *Plan of a "Tholos" at Arpachiyah.*
Halaf culture, Middle Chalcolithic period.

production and consumption of a variety of new kinds of goods, and that the social and ceremonial life of these people, while dominated by women, was fairly fluid.

In the last Neolithic level of Beidha (figure 4-2j) we find the "houses of the rich" were gone, and in their place was

> a house 23 by 50 feet, whose single large room was finished inside with burnished white plaster. . . . outside this rather imposing structure stretched open courtyards, and beyond them an array of rectangular buildings in even rows. Each consisted of thick stone walls enclosing six small, cubicle-like rooms and a central corridor. Some of the cubicles may have been storerooms, but others were obviously workshops. . . . To judge from articles left in them, some of their proprietors were specialists in different kinds of stone, bone or horn work. One was a jeweler who made stone beads; another cut beads out of hollow bones. One shop with many animal bones and horned skulls may have housed a butcher, or possibly a supplier of bones and horns to other workers (Leonard, 1973: 103).

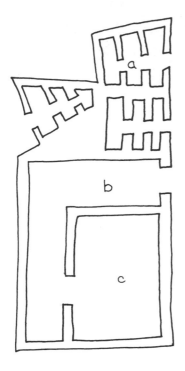

Figure 4-2j. *Beidha, 6600 B.C., Level II.*
a. shops; b. courtyard; c. meeting house. Living quarters were apparently on second stories.

Families evidently lived in quarters above the workshops, which were apparently two-storied.

Beidha had become a rural industrial center,

> supplying other villages with goods of its own manufacture and dominated by a management group whose headquarters may have been the large building with its red-banded walls and floor (Leonard, 1973: 103).

There is no evidence that the "administrative center" was lived in. The workshops do not reflect typically female crafts or even shared crafts, so it is possible that the women were specialized in agriculture only.

Our second example of an administrative center is Khirokitia (figure 4-2k), on Cyprus. While this town is more recent than any of the others described, culturally it is back in the round-house stage, perhaps because of prolonged isolation from other areas. It was near a major trade route from the Anatolian plateau to the Mediterranean, on a peninsula jutting out to the sea, and because the people had seafaring skills they were not totally isolated. The town was a trading center of a particular kind, accessible only to others with seafaring skills.

It is estimated that Khirokitia may have contained a thousand houses, and therefore a population of several thousand. The houses were comfortably furnished for complete families. There were paved stone roads, and houses ranged in size from three to eight meters in diameter. Some were dwellings, some workshops, and given the size of the settlement, it may have had an administrative center in one of the larger domed houses. The organization of the town, with paved streets, roofed corridors, and ramps from the houses to the streets, reflects some type of planning. There is not much evidence of stratification; the differences in house size may reflect different uses rather than individual wealth. Larger and smaller houses are standing side by side.

The people specialized in beautiful- ly polished stoneware, weaving, and jewelry, and raised grain, sheep, and goats. There are schematized figurines with no sex indications, and apparent- ly there were no cult centers.[9] Burials were inside the houses, and the rich burial gifts to women and men alike suggest that women and men were of equal status in this society. This town, while of a size that would need some organizing, seems to have the fluid characteristics of the villages like Hacilar and Jarmo. Khirokitia suggests that high population density, craft

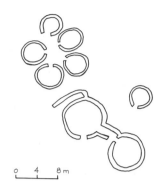

Figure 4-2k. *Khirokitia in Cyprus, 5500 B.C.* Houses and workshops are domed.

specialization, and trade do not necessarily lead to social stratifica- tion, or to a male or female priestly class.

We have spent a long time on these villages. It has been necessary to try to lay the most concrete data base possible for the discussions to follow on women's roles in the supposedly "golden age of matri- archy" during the early agricultural, precivilizational era in human history. If women ever "ruled," it was at this time. The task of out- lining the basic structure of daily life for the period is not made easier by the assumption by most archaeologists that all the activi- ties they uncover evidence of, except cooking (and sometimes pot- tery), were carried out by men. To achieve anything at all here, the evidence must be approached with an open mind and a lively imagination.[10]

I will pass over Stage 1 villages, where the egalitarian hunter- gatherer relationship between women and men translated into living separately in individual huts with minimal differentiation of activi- ties, and sharing was confined to providing for needs of children and ceremonial activities. It is in villages belonging to Stage 2a that the special cultural elaborations of the agricultural way of life developed. There was enough surplus to make differentiated activities possible, but not so much that status differentials become important (with ex- ceptions such as Beidha). The craft activities described above for women do not convey the variety of products actually made. A read- ing of the sections describing the technological achievements of the Neolithic in volume 1 of *A History of Technology* (Singer et al., 1954) is a corrective to the general tendency to assume that these early village products are rather crude. Woman's tendency to remain "Jane of all trades," to not specialize (to be discussed later), works against developing the high skill levels of specialist craftworkers. The range of tools and equipment she creates is nevertheless impressive.

While the archaeological record is fragmentary at best, whatever it is possible to know about women in this era we will discover from these records. Stage 2b towns (see table 4-1), with more differentiated skills, greater productivity, and larger surpluses, underline the nature of the challenges which new levels of productivity present. These trading towns provide clues about the transitional stage between town and urban center, but most of our information about the transition in terms of women's roles will have to come from the urban settlements themselves—discussed in the next chapter. Now to the life of the villager.

The Daily Life of the Women Villagers

Women's activities can be described as falling into three spheres, the *hearth,* the *courtyard,* and the *fields.* 1) Hearth activities included cooking, feeding, and care of small infants. 2) Courtyard activities involved both *production processes—*a) food, processing of foods to be cooked (sometimes cooking and baking also done in courtyard, combining items 1 and 2a), b) *crafts,* sewing, weaving, basket and pottery making, stoneware and implement making, jewelry, production of cosmetics, and c) *building activities,* houses, cult centers, etc.—and *social organization—*council meetings, ritual and ceremony preparations, teaching, general administration of the village. 3) Field activities included a) gathering and collecting of fruit and nuts, b) clearing, planting, cultivating, and harvesting food, c) caring for sheep and goats, d) collecting fuel for hearth fires, and e) collecting material for building.

One very distinctive feature of the women's culture is the omnipresence of children and the continuing nature of responsibility for infants and very small children. There is no moment of the day or night when this responsibility wholly lapses, although children may in fact receive highly variable amounts of care from one society to another. Additionally, pregnancy is a twenty-four-hour-a-day "activity," and ought properly to be thought of as an activity, as the term childbearing suggests, since it requires energy and resources from the mother's body. Pregnancy merges imperceptibly into the continuing responsibility for infants after birth, a responsibility that really stretches from the moment of conception until the age of three or four. The breast-feeding that begins after birth merges imperceptibly into the activity of preparing and serving food to children that extends for women to the activity of feeding all adult males in her household. There has never been a human society, to the knowledge of the anthropologist, archaeologist, or historian, where men have regularly performed the feeding role. The breeder-feeder responsibilities then form the backdrop for all other activities of women.

The activities that are hardest for us to visualize are the courtyard activities. We can extrapolate from twentieth century kitchens to the hearth without difficulty, and we have all seen pictures of women working in fields. The courtyard, however, where women even today in many parts of the world spend most of their time, eludes us. This is where the special qualities of women's culture develop. Men's work, whether hunting, trading, stonework, or (after the plough is developed) agriculture, does not keep them in these open courtyards except in the evenings after the day's work is over.[11] For the Neolithic woman, however, the courtyard is the master-integrator of all other activities. The courtyard is her administrative base as well as the scene of much of her productive activity. Here is where the older women organize work routines for the community and teach or organize the teaching of the girls, and of the boys under ten years of age.[12]

What is taught? Geneologies, songs, dances, herbal medicine lore, and tribal rituals, as well as the domestic crafts pursued in that village and some of the agricultural knowledge required in the field. Most, but not all, of the latter, is probably taught in the field. It is during daytime courtyard sessions that new dances and songs are invented, later to be performed for ceremonial occasions.

> Such institutions [i.e., the courtyard] tend to develop women leaders whose authority often extends into the larger life of the community. As queen, chieftainess, priestess, prophetess, seeress, oracle, shamaness, magician, musician, and even as old wife who has experienced life, woman exercises a natural control over members of her society. If and when women celebrate jointly with men at religious ceremonies and games, they perform as an independent unit with their own leaders (Drinker, 1948: 9).

This description hardly fits all village societies, but it summarizes rather nicely the possibilities of courtyard life in those first villages of the Middle East.

Music is an important part of women's communal life, and has been for a long time: instruments were found in the caves of the Cro-Magnons in Europe. How soon women started singing we shall never know, since archaeology can provide no evidence for it. Women's choirs will be found, however—at worship, at work, and during all the ritual occasions of village life such as childbirth, puberty rites, weddings, and the reentry of a woman into society after childbirth—a long way back in history. (See the dancing women with flautist in figure 4-3.) Drinker mentions archaic Greek figurines showing women bakers led by a woman flautist, as a fairly sophisticated example of women singing at work (figure 4-4). Tribal women have songs for every kind of rhythmic work, and a common saying is "a good singer is a good worker."

Singing has historically been a type of public participation of

Figure 4-3. *Women in Round Dance with Flautist in Center,*
Boetian, 6th Century B.C.

women. In addition to choirs, there have been individual wailers, historians, and singing storytellers, praise singers (in Africa today you can still pay a woman to do praise singing about you in public if your ego needs boosting), and party singers, who went through a village singing about a party someone was giving as a way of announcing it. A somewhat sharper use of song has been social criticism: women still have the custom of singing their opinions of men in many societies. Wailing is a distinct art, separate from singing, and used on special ritual occasions.

If ever there was a time in human history when women had free rein to develop their talents for singing, it was in these early agricultural villages. The association of women with the supernatural would give them a special role in the creation of music. Drinker (1948) points out that when leadership roles in musical creation are assigned to men, women lose their creativity and become more stereotyped in their expression. She feels that it is only in women's groups unhindered by men that women fully express their musical genius, and that the later male domination of all civilized societies "drove" women out of a field that had once been theirs. Unfortunately, there is no way we can recreate the religious music created by women in prehistory.

Women as Ritual Leaders

If the Neolithic woman was a priestess, what kind of goddess did she serve? The debate among scholars about mother-goddesses, and the

Figure 4-4. *Women Bakers Led by Flautist, Archaic Greece.*

relationship of fertility figures to mother-goddess cults, rages on.[13] We know from our examination of fertility figures in the last chapter that they were widespread and had many specialized purposes, including possibly serving as toys. There was no generalized woman-goddess figure. The figures were always faceless. Some were beautiful, suggestive of Venus to our modern eyes, others were caricatures of pregnancy and the process of giving birth. The goddess figurines were rarely associated directly with animal figures until later. Early anthropomorphic figures related to the animal world were usually male. Catal Huyuk provides the first evidence of identification of women with animals in a cultic setting.

136

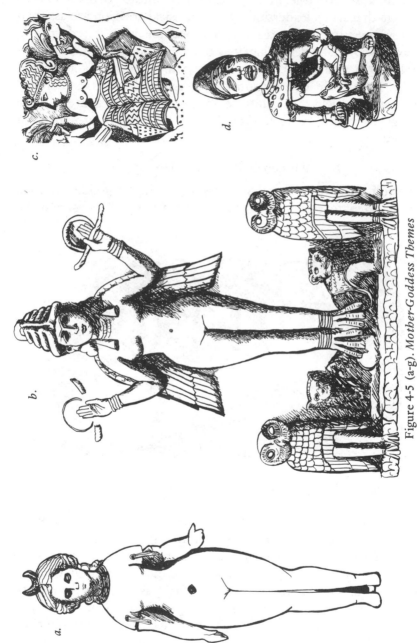

Figure 4-5 (a-g). *Mother-Goddess Themes*

a. Parthian goddess, 1st-2nd century A.D.; b. Lileth, goddess of death, Sumer, 2000 B.C.; c. Syrian fertility goddess, 8th century B.C.; d. Belgian Congo mother and child.

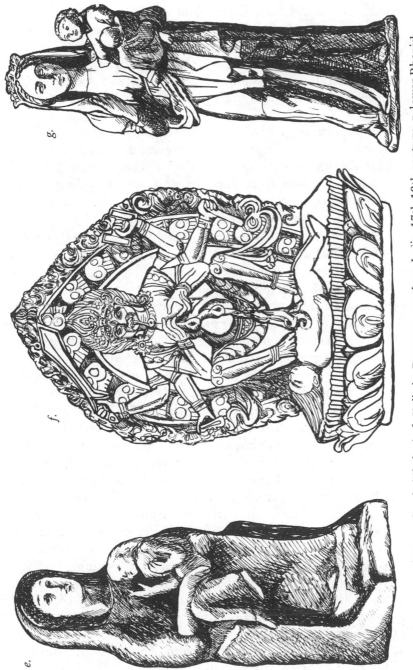

e. Demeter and Kore, Greek (Thebes); f. Kali the Devourer, northern India, 17th-18th century; g. lower Rhenish or Mosan virgin and child, 14th century.

The cult statues in later villages begin to combine the female with a son-lover and to show her three faces—of youth (sexual attractiveness), life (giving birth), and death (the vulture nearby). The more terrifying semiiconic versions suggest that once the figurines changed from impersonal fertility symbols to representations of a goddess with female attributes, the resulting goddess was both beautiful and frightening.

Our one glimpse of the woman as priestess comes from the reconstruction of a funerary rite with priestesses disguised as vultures, from Catal Huyuk. Using this as a clue, we can imagine that these priestesses presided over three types of rites, corresponding with the three aspects of the goddess in the Catal Huyuk cult rooms: 1) the rite of marriage, in her aspect of goddess of youth and beauty; 2) the rite of giving birth, in her aspect of goddess of life—this would include two kinds of rituals, one in the village itself, focused on human procreation, and one partly in the village and partly in the fields, focused on fertility of the soil and planting rituals; and 3) the funerary rites, already mentioned, in her aspect of goddess of death.

The number of cultic objects, paintings, shrines, and so on, indicates that a substantial amount of ritual activity was going on and that the priestess possibly had a full-time occupation. If this is so, it is the first evidence of a specialized role for women in the Neolithic. Their daily activities were highly differentiated in the sense that they did many different things in the course of a day, but not specialized in the sense that each woman carried out certain tasks for everyone and benefited in turn from the specialties of other women. As far as we can tell, until the time of the active development of trade when there was a demand for the specialty role associated with elaborately decorated pottery, each woman did all the tasks assigned to women. The priestess role is the one exception; the amount of training women would need to carry out the range of ritual activities suggested would preclude their carrying a normal daily work load.

We do not know the belief systems that accompanied the ritual use of the goddess figures and the associated animal representations in the Neolithic. Many archaic religious myths, both of the ancient Mediterranean world and of contemporary tribal peoples, postulate a chaos figure, essentially neutral, who produces a mother-goddess who produces the world. Sometimes the chaos figure is female, but often not. While the mother-goddess is quickly surrounded by male gods in all the traditions of the Mediterranean, scholars generally agree that the goddess was top figure first, and that her son-lover (as in Catal Huyuk) only appeared later, gradually usurping her position. There has been some inclination to romanticize the goddess, with the suggestion that women taught the "pure" high god religion in the early Neolithic. According to this view there was a later power struggle between women and men in which the goddess was dethroned and a whole galaxy of males took over; finally the monotheistic religions of Judaism, Christianity, and Islam announced the victory of one top male god over all the other gods. It is perhaps more realistic to interpret the mother-goddess as an important early attempt at conceptualizing divinity, part of a long evolutionary process. In Christianity the feminine element of the deity remains in the Virgin Mary—so there was no simple victory of god over goddess.

The trouble with romanticizing the "white goddess" or the "triple goddess," as Graves (1966) alternately calls her, is that she has so many grim aspects. Campbell makes the point that representations of men in the earliest prehistoric art are always clothed, while female figurines are naked, unadorned:

> The woman is immediately mythic in herself and is experienced as such.
> . . . the mother is experienced as the power of nature (1972: 31).

The positive side of this is the mother, giver of birth. The negative side relates to the myth found in all ancient cultures of the Mediterranean, of the god who yields his body to be slain, cut up, and buried, thus providing for a good harvest:

> In the rites of human sacrifice common to all planting cultures, this primal mythological scene is imitated literally—ad nauseum; for, as in the vegetable world, life is seen to spring from death and fresh green sprouts from decay, so too it must be in the human. The dead are buried to be born again, and the cycles of the plant world become models for the myths and rituals of mankind (Campbell, 1972:55).

That women as priestesses and representatives of the mother-goddess presided over human sacrifice of young men and children, culminating in the grisly mass sacrifices of the Phoenicians some millennia later, is indisputable. Just as we found scattered evidence for human sacrifice in the Paleolithic, so do we find traces of the same practice in the Neolithic, although the interpretation of findings of groups of skulls can never be clear. The group of baby skulls found under a basin-like structure in the earliest layer of Jericho (Mellaart, 1965: 32) probably represents human sacrifice. The fact that such findings are infrequent suggests that the practice was not widespread and not a major religious theme. Systematically organized sacrifice is the product of "higher" civilizations.

The monster women associated in mythology with goddesses, who devour their children after giving birth to them, or suck them back up into the belly, or otherwise mutilate them, may have some basis in darkly remembered ancient ritual. Fontenrose's *Python: A Story of the Delphic Myth and Its Origins* (1959) gives a sample of the horror women have inspired in their priestess-goddess roles. In fact, the asides in Graves' *The White Goddess* (1966), apparently a panegyric to the mother-goddess, have a nightmarish quality.

The theme of women as a source of terror is widespread enough both in ancient myths and in recurring bursts of anti-woman hysteria such as the witch craze of the Middle Ages to give the historian pause. Shades of the old hysteria are detectable in the outbursts of men against women in the current feminist struggle, not least in discussions on the issue of legalized abortion. The image of woman as sacrificer of children becomes linked sometimes with the image of woman as sex fiend. One ingenious theory about the fear men have of women suggests that primitive women were so highly sexed that they wore the men out completely, and that the latter finally conquered and permanently suppressed them in self-defense (Sherfey, 1972). This does not quite fit with the picture of village life we have just finished painting. The women were too busy to be sex fiends! Neither does the sex-war concept fit the earlier picture of cave life in the Paleolithic.

It is highly unlikely that there ever was a sex war or an overthrow of women. The infliction of savage constraints on sexuality, whether the constraint of the extremes of satiation or of abstinence, is probably a later phenomenon and associated with the strains of urbanization.

The Character of Matriliny

However we interpret the archaeological and mythic evidence, it does seem likely that women had a position of power in early Neolithic villages, and they probably frightened the men at least some of the time. This may seem like a far-fetched interpretation of data that on the whole point to a fairly egalitarian society. Let us back up a step from our question about women's roles as priestesses, and look at their general economic and social position. During Stages 1 and 2 of the Neolithic village, as here characterized (see table 4-1), could the villages be called matriarchal? Since they give no evidence of having chiefs, male or female (except Eynan), and since *matriarchy* means "rule by women,"[14] this makes no sense. It would make sense, however, to think of them as matrilineal, as *tracing descent* through the mother's side of the family. With the emphasis on women's fertility, in a society organized primarily on the basis of access to land for farming, control over farm land, farm products, and sheep and goats, as well as control over house, tools, and equipment used by the women, might naturally be passed on through the women. Land ownership is not in question at this stage in social development, but rather rights to use of land.[15] In the picture I am building here, it makes sense to suggest that these rights were controlled by women. It must be remembered, however, that the extent to which any of the patterns described here actually existed, including a system of matrilineal descent reckoning, is in dispute. There is no definitive evidence either way.

In villages where men did not develop trading activities, what did they do? They would have hunting and marginal farm work to do, tool making, and probably jewelry making. Women developed the pottery, weaving, and basketry, as well as managed the food processing and cared for sheep and goats. When building needed to be done, men may have helped, as they would help at harvest time. When there were attackers, the men were the defenders, but in non-trading towns this was rare. Nomadic bands were usually content to trade peacefully with the villages. If the imbalance between women's and men's activities seems implausible, here is a list of Navajo occupations from a study by Aberle (1962a):

Males	*Females*
1. Cattle	1. Sheep
2. Agriculture	2. Agriculture
3. Silversmithing	3. Weaving
4. Ceremonial practice	4. Pottery
5. House building	5. Silversmithing
6. (there were hunting	6. Cooking
and warfare, earlier,	7. Child care
but now discontinued)	8. House building

Even more dramatic evidence of the imbalance of women's and men's activities in subsistence agricultural societies has become available from recent studies undertaken for the Economic Commission for Africa (United Nations, 1974) on relative inputs of women and men to daily agricultural work in Africa. Table 4-2 describes the results of the Africa study, showing work input in terms of the amount of women's work as a percentage of the total work done in a specific category. This is known as unit-of-participation analysis. According to Boserup (1970), this type of work imbalance is to be found in all subsistence agricultural societies that follow the "slash-and-burn" practice. The traditional role of the men in these societies is hunting.

Table 4-2

Participation by Women in the Traditional Rural and Modernizing
Economy in Africa

Responsibility	Unit of Participation[*]
A. Production/Supply/Distribution	
1. Food Production	0.70
2. Domestic Food Storage	0.50
3. Food Processing	1.00
4. Animal Husbandry	0.50
5. Marketing	0.60
6. Brewing	0.90
7. Water Supply	0.90
8. Fuel Supply	0.80
B. Household/Community	
1. Household:	
(a) Bearing, rearing, initial education of children	1.00
(b) Cooking for husband, children, elders	1.00
(c) Cleaning, washing, etc.	1.00
(d) Housebuilding	0.30
(e) House Repair	0.50
2. Community:	
Self-help projects	0.70

SOURCE: The Changing and Contemporary Role of Women in African Development, UNECA, 1974; Country Reports on Vocational and Technical Training for Girls and Women, UNECA, 1972-4; studies, mission reports, discussions (United Nations, 1974).

*Unit of participation is women's work as a percentage of the total work done in each category.

To return to the Neolithic agrovillage: except when out hunting, the men were probably together less and made a relatively smaller contribution than the women to the ritual life of the village. They did not have the equivalent of the courtyard for planning group activities during the day. Hunting expeditions were probably the occasions when they felt most important, and if they could not find meat even this activity would be more punishing than rewarding.

The society appears to have been essentially non-hierarchical. The older women may have acted as organizers, but they did not exert strong authority nor withhold community resources to get special services performed. If they had, this probably would have shown up in different standards of housing and living styles. The resentments of the men may therefore have been rather diffuse. To speak of role deprivation on the part of the men is perhaps to say too much, since in order to feel deprived the men would have to have had some standard of comparison according to which their personal status was too low. However, legends from the days of the great hunts may have provided such a standard of reference.

Men may especially have resented the relatively casual attitudes of women toward marriage. Marriage is never as central to the organization of economic and social life in a matrilineal society as it is in a patrilineal one. Though actual patterns of matriliny vary a great deal around the world, the house of the woman and her daughters tends to be an important stabilizing element. In the "pure" form (as opposed to the transitional form of matriliny, called avunculocal, in which a married woman may live with her mother's brother, and men dominate through their sisters), the marriage bond is often weak, and divorce frequent. It is often remarked by anthropologists describing matrilineal societies that these are high-tension societies. Some examples of tension in matrilineal societies, which may throw light on the family situation in Neolithic society, are provided below. All of the studies surveyed were undertaken in the twentieth century (Schneider and Gough, 1962).

Man-Woman Relationships in Some Matrilineal Societies

Colson's Study of the Plateau Tonga

In a household census of two villages, it was found that of 245 households, 32 contained no adult males and 31 percent of males and 26 percent of females were divorced. A divorcee or widow may

prefer not to remarry, but can retain her own household and property. In former times she could be "headman," but no longer. There
are stories of "amazons" who rid themselves of unwanted husbands,
pairing up with daughters who have done the same, to live in all-
female hamlets with some low-status male relatives around.

> Old women chuckle happily at their independence; old men try desper-
> ately to find wives through whom they can once more establish a
> household unit catering to their wishes and giving them prestige and
> ritual potency (Colson, 1962: 68).

Aberle's Study of the Navajo

Two-thirds of the families followed a matrilocal residence pattern in
the 1930s, when Aberle's study took place. There are few rules or
ceremonies for marriage, and a deemphasis of the "bride price,"
which is not always given. "Marriage frees both partners for all subsequent marriages, in case of divorce" (Aberle, 1962a: 126). Two females out of three are divorced, three males out of four.

Fathauer's Study of the Trobrianders

This is a tribe with matrilineal descent but male rule, in the avunculocal pattern. Husband and wife work together in agriculture, but
each owns tools separately. The husband is important in child care,
but has no "rights" in the child. Divorce is "not infrequent." In marriage, women confer status on men, but not the reverse (Fathauer,
1962).

Basehart's Study of the Ashanti

This is a matrilineal system with male chiefs nominated by a queen
mother. Only 26 percent of the women were living with their husbands in one sample. Married women live with their mothers and sisters in matrilocal houses, and may bring food to a husband in his
house (his own or that of women in his family). There is little joint
activity between husband and wife; each has an equal chance to be
head of household, but men can usually obtain their own house at a
younger age than can women. Husbands and wives work and produce separately; every adult earns her or his own living. There is a
high divorce rate (Basehart, 1962).

The Akan people of Ghana, of whom the Ashanti are one, have
been referred to by Meyer Fortes, in the introduction to Oppong's
Marriage Among a Matrilineal Elite, as follows:

Traditionally marriage was (and in village communities still is) the frailest of bonds and is secondary to the matrilineal kinship ties focused in the unbreakable natal bonds of brother and sister, and symbolised by the laws of "nephew inheritance." Spouses often resided apart, with their close maternal kin, on whom they had everlasting claims (Fortes, 1974: x).

Gough's Study of the Nayar

There is hostility among brothers in the matrilineal clan, and between men of different generations. Men's affection goes into relationships with mother, and with mother's sisters. Women live in their mother's home and unsatisfactory husbands can be ordered dismissed by the mother. There is a first ritual marriage before puberty, then a series of "visiting husbands," with no limit on number though the range is usually between three and twelve. There are casual unions besides. All "husbands" visit their wives after supper, leave before breakfast, and never eat in the wife's home. The husband-wife relationship is very weak. The nuclear family—husband, wife, and their children—does not exist in Nayar society: no man has rights in one woman, or one child, and no woman has legal rights in one man, but in a group of men (Gough, 1962a, 1962b).

I do not know of a systematic comparative study of divorce rates in matrilineal and patrilineal societies, but Mair's (1972) examination of the subject leads her to conclude that there is more divorce in matrilineal than in patrilineal societies. At the societal level, rather than at the level of individual families, Murdock's (1949) finding that societies move from matrilineal to patrilineal, but never the other way, can be taken as one more piece of evidence both for the instability of matrilineal family organization and for the instability of matrilineality as a form of social organization.

The instability of matriliny in the latter sense appears to be related to a pattern of small-scale social organization characteristic of early agrovillage life. This pattern is not sufficiently flexible to allow further differentiation, particularly in the nonagricultural sector, for its marginal (male) population.

A review of the conditions under which matriliny arises and the conditions under which it is likely to disappear, as outlined by Aberle (1962b) in his major study of the phenomenon, suggests that matriliny arises in situations where there are all-women work groups and where women control the residence bases. This is precisely the situation that I am suggesting obtains in the Neolithic agricultural village. Aberle describes matriliny as

> a special adaptation to certain production conditions, capable of surviving under other, but by no means all other, conditions. Matriliny itself is not a level of organization, but on the contrary, various levels of organization occur among matrilineal, patrilineal and bilateral systems. Its association with certain production systems, its incompatibility with others, and its incompatibility with extensive bureaucratization, imply that matriliny is largely limited to a certain range of productivity and a certain range of centralization—ranges narrower than those of either patrilineal or bilateral systems. Matriliny . . . cannot be viewed as a "stage" or "level" or generation of evolutionary development (Aberle, 1962b: 702).

The instability of matrilineal systems can be explained entirely in structural terms. Had women given more attention to spin-off activities with which they were not directly concerned, and adapted their communication patterns to encompass a wider range of happenings, matriliny might have adapted to a new scale of social operation. The fact that women did not do so should not be put in primarily biological terms, although their triple producer-breeder-feeder role may have put them at a disadvantage. An inspection of their daily work load compared with that of the earlier hunting-and-gathering era suggests that they were probably suffering from work overload and information overload, and did not stand back to get the larger picture.[16]

In the discussion on the priestess role I commented that this was evidently the only specialist role for women in the Neolithic village until much later, when a demand for elaborately decorated pottery in the trading villages finally produced a cadre of specialist women potters. Why didn't women specialize sooner? Men had begun to specialize much earlier, probably because they had more time to do so. Why didn't women reduce their own work loads substantially, giving themselves more time to think about that "larger picture"? They had the "power" to allocate their own time differently, and presumably the men's time too. "Why didn't they . . . ?" is an old question in history. New social perceptions are slow to form, and we can only say that the women did not shift to the necessary new perceptions of their activities and of the total organization of village life soon enough to prevent loss of "political power."

Some readers might be inclined to argue the "traditional" conservatism of women as the reason for their failure to perceive the necessity for a new scale of social organization. An interesting study on the "Sociology of Pottery" (Foster, 1968) suggests that conservatism is a trait that arises from an occupational basis rather than being associated with gender. Based on his own field work in pottery villages in Mexico, and on his examination of data from other Latin American countries and from Tibet, India, Tunis, and Spain, Foster concludes that potters, whether male or female,

> are more conservative in basic personality structure than are their non-potter villagers. . . . as a class, potters are more resistant to innovation of all kinds than are non-potters (1968: 321).

Drawing up a list of simple innovations in the Mexican villages and listing the names of the villagers associated with the innovations, Foster found practically no potters included although they comprised 60 percent of the population. He suggests why:

> The reason lies in the nature of the productive process itself which places a premium on strict adherence to tried and proven ways as a means of avoiding economic catastrophe. Pottery-making is a tricky business at best, and there are literally hundreds of points at which a slight variation in materials or processes will adversely affect the result. . . . economic security lies in duplicating to the best of the potter's ability the materials and processes he knows from experience are least likely to lead to failure. . . . this breeds a basic conservatism, a caution about all new things that carries over into the potter's outlook on life itself (1968: 323).

Apart from the fact that as far as we know most early Near East pottery was done by women, the general situation of little margin for error leading to conservatism might apply to the whole range of activities carried out by women. Because they had so much to do, slight variations in care of farm or dairy products or pottery could lead to food spoilage, production failure, and a consequent increase in already heavy burdens. Care of children does not admit of much variation, particularly in feeding. Hunting activities, on the other hand, are often most successful for the risk-takers.

Risk-takers or not, the men certainly were the "free-floating resources"[17] of this society. As the "extra pair of hands" in the situation, they responded to the asymmetry in responsibility by inventing new patterns of social organization. The actual change process was of course far more complicated than this statement implies, and could be the subject of an entire book in itself. For now it is perhaps enough to make this suggestive application of Aberle's thesis to the Neolithic matrilineal village.

From Egalitarian to Ranked to Stratified Society

The new scale of social organization moved Neolithic society very rapidly from egalitarian to ranked to stratified society, in Fried's (1967) terminology. The egalitarian society "is one in which there are as many positions of prestige in any given age- [and sex-] grade as there are persons capable of filling them" (Fried, 1967: 33). Ranking implies that there are fewer positions of valued status than there are persons capable of filling them, but ranks do not necessarily have economic implications. The early priestly functions did not, according to Fried, carry economic advantage (1967: 140-141), for example. In those early village "rank" societies everyone, including those with prestige status, participated to some degree in maintenance activities. Control over redistribution by prestige persons did not give them any personal advantage. With larger population densities and the growth of trade there was a gradual withdrawal of high-status persons from basic maintenance activities, and these persons gained superior right of access to basic resources through administrative roles. Ranking, in short, is the "skeleton on which the musculature of stratification can grow" (Fried, 1967: 178). Since women were not among those entering the redistribution roles, the narrowing of access rights to resources immediately began to diminish women's status and opportunities. The "ancient managerial revolution" that made the great hydraulic works of antiquity possible took place with women standing on the outside, even though their own lands were involved.

What did this mean for woman? In the ranked society her place was still secure, for the ranked society is still built around the kinship system. Prestige derives from one's position in that system, and material resources are equally available to all. The stratified society, however, commands resources beyond the resources of any individual kinship system. Power holders in stratified societies use kinship-derived ceremonial bonds to develop a new resource distribution system,[18] and in the process they develop centralized power. Women, according to our interpretation, were losing out in chances for administrative roles in the newly developed upper strata, at the same time that their new status ensured their withdrawal from earlier productive roles. This left a newly created class with an increasing number of ceremonial and bonding functions and little power. For the ingenious woman, ceremonial roles could always be translated into administrative and decision-making roles, but it did not happen automatically. One might say that women were left behind in a ranked-society enclave within the new stratified society: they had prestige, but diminished command over resources.

Now that the decline of matriliny has been explained on structural grounds, what happens to the mother-goddess? Is it a phantom specter that can be exorcised, or does the mythology reflect a historical problem situation? I suggest that there was a problem situation, and that it is one of the unlucky coincidences of history that the organizational failure of matriliny happened to coincide with the beginnings of nuclear family intimacy. (The Neolithic village provides the first evidence we have of mother-father-child dwellings.) Women's failure at that time to provide adequate role-differentiation opportunities for men, when the women were in a position of dominance due to the temporary primacy of their productivity skills, may have led to family tensions that were played out symbolically in the mythic and religious life of the community, but never dealt with realistically at their source. The gradual shift from the more impersonal female symbols of the Upper Paleolithic to the naturalistically female mother-goddess of the early agricultural peoples, served by women in priestess roles and linked to the fertility of the soil, came, it could be argued, at a very bad time psychologically for the human race. According to this line of reasoning the worship of the mother-goddess as the source of life flourished at the very moment, historically speaking, when women were also a source of role-deprivation.

This proposition will not be explored in depth here, but the interested reader is urged to study Slater's *The Glory of Hera* (1968), which traces just such a connection in Greek society, at a later stage in evolution. Slater argues that Greek women were in fact dominant in the family, and that the subsequent low status of women and the male terror of women were a vicious cycle set in motion by that dominance. The Greek boy lived in a female-dominated world until the age of seven, and was then thrown into the male world. The Greek father was an outsider in his house, unable to penetrate the domestic fortress ruled by his wife. The main thrust of the argument is that under special conditions maternal dominance produces male narcissism, which is a double time bomb in that it makes men unsatisfactory husbands and fathers and leaves the next generation of boys exposed to the dominance of frustrated mothers, ad infinitum. It also produces a high achievement need in the boys, along with self-doubt, libidinal repressiveness, and a tendency to prefer tomorrow's rewards to today's. This achievement drive is the motor for economic development, as is well documented by McClelland (1961) and McClelland and Winter (1969).

The type of dominance Slater describes is rather different from the dominance described for the Neolithic village. In the village it stemmed from the nature of women's productive roles in the economy. In the Greek setting it represented a subversion of an overt male dominance. Furthermore, the Greeks already had an army of gods on their side to protect them against women. Neolithic men only had one bull god, and he was invented rather late.

The Neolithic dominance of women, if that word is appropriate, was hardly conscious and intentional. Men may have sometimes been harmed through exclusion from needed resources. On the other hand, the structural framework supporting any possible maldistribution of resources would have been minimal and weak. The scales were soon tipping in the other direction.

The Neolithic in Africa, Southeast Asia, and Europe

Africa and Southeast Asia

In order to simplify the examination of women's roles in the Neolithic I have discussed only the village life in the area known as the cradle of agriculture, the fertile crescent in the Near East. Agriculture probably began along the Nile at about the same time or soon afterward, and also in what is now upper Kenya, on the shores of the Rift Valley lakes. The character of these villages would have been somewhat different from that of the fertile crescent villages, since the African villages bordered on lakes and rivers and fishing continued as an important supplement to agriculture (S. Cole, 1963). It is usually assumed that women and men fished here during the Paleolithic, and that therefore the transition to agrovillages would not involve the kind of role separation experienced in the Near East; women and men could continue to fish side by side after agriculture developed. This shared activity would make the "you hunt, I farm" division less sharp, although hunting certainly continued. There are hints of the importance of the "village goddess" as village life became more elaborated along the Nile, and a specialized priestess class to serve cult centers would certainly have developed. We see the evidence of this at the time when the first kingdoms of the Nile were consolidated, because each village goddess had to be formally assimilated into the "national" pantheon. This will be discussed more fully in the next chapter, but it is important to note that the basis for this pantheon was laid in the Neolithic villages.

By the time of the earliest political unification there was probably a well-developed village life along the Nile, and fine craftwork. The women were pottery specialists as well as priestesses, and they may have been chiefs also. The roots of the woman-as-ruler and woman-as-administrator traditions of Egypt must lie in the Neolithic. Unfortunately, remains from this era are scantier along the Nile than elsewhere. Villages shifted sites frequently, and every Pharaoh built his own new capital on virgin land. We have little archaeological evidence on which to base inferences, and must rely on the traces of earlier social usage in later practices. A scenario about the origins of agriculture alternative to the one offered in this chapter has been developed by Loeb (1960). He places it in the tropical forest setting, but he also proposes women as the inventors of agriculture and the matrilineal form of social organization as the cultural context. According to Loeb, "agriculture started in the tropical rainforests along the banks of small rivers, specifically along those flowing into the Bay of Bengal" (1960: 303), fanning to East and West from there. This was a root-planting, rather than a seed-planting, technology. Seeds came later:

the early root-planting culture was essentially a woman's world, since it was the women who performed the main work. A reconstruction of the culture on the basis of such evidence as is available indicates that the people lived on the banks of small rivers and lakes in elongated plank houses set on piles, each family having its own room in a communal house and its own fireplace for cooking. The inhabitants of a house were a matrilineal lineage, and several such houses formed a mother-right clan. The oldest woman in a house was the matron, but her eldest brother together with the other mature men of the house formed the village council. A mother, her brother or brothers, and her children, all inhabiting one room and using a single fireplace, made up the nucleus of the family. A man's nephews, not his sons, inherited his personal possessions, such as weapons and boats. Daughters inherited household goods from their mothers. Husbands came secretly at night to visit wives, and frequently wives changed husbands without ceremony. This form of society and manner of living are believed to have been decisive in the history of mankind. Except for the outrigger canoe and the blow-gun, women were responsible for most of the inventions of the period including the use of bamboo utensils for cooking and holding liquids, the steeping and beating of tapa to make cloth, the cultivaion of root plants, and above all, the domestication of small animals as household pets. Early in the period the children caught young wild dogs and pigs and brought them home to the women to be nursed. Chickens and

other fowl were added later to the list of household animals. Eventually
chickens were used in divination and also in sports as fighting cocks
(1960: 303-304).

Evidence for matrilineality is given through archaeological evidence of the existence of matrilineal longhouses and by references to
the continued use into the recent past of such matrilineal longhouses
in Malaysia, Indonesia, the Malabar Coast of India, Japan, and in the
American Northwest (Loeb and Broeck, 1948: 419; and Sauer as
quoted in Loeb, 1960: 313). Loeb goes on to establish a connection
between the matrilineal culture with its longhouses and the use of
narcotics and intoxicants. While he does not suggest that women
evolved the use of narcotics, he presents a variety of evidence in support of the position that they invented wine and beer in the Neolithic (1960: 305-311). The importance of his work lies primarily in
the fact that he points out two different lines of agricultural development, both of which involved women: seed-planting culture, and
root-planting culture.

The penetration of agriculture into tropical forest lands in Africa,
and a similar penetration into the forests of Asia and Oceania after
the independent development of agriculture in Southeast Asia, were
sometimes peaceful and sometimes not. Vayda (1961) suggests that
peaceful expansion depends on the terrain, population density, and
skills of social organization and exploration of the tribes in question.
Since all tropical agriculture is of the slash-and-burn variety, only
skillful exploration and land use can avoid constant warfare. Warring
tribes are a well-documented phenomenon in all tropical forest lands,
but Vayda suggests that competition for resources is the primary triggering factor. The existence of headhunting in some matrilineal
forest tribes would then be associated with poor alternative technologies for exploration and expansion, rather than with some uniquely
bloodthirsty attributes of matrilineality.

Europe

Agriculture moved slowly into Europe. It took about a thousand
years for Neolithic agrovillages to spread into Italy, France, and
Spain. Crete, Sicily, and parts of Greece were the first stopping
points for migrants from the Near East. Crete in particular, with conditions most similar to those in the fertile crescent, developed a
flourishing agriculture and went on quickly to develop a high village
culture which laid the foundation for the later Cretan empire. As we
will see in chapter 6, it was in Crete that the axe cult, associated with

a mother-goddess and priestess attendants, was born. Crete became known in the ancient world for the high status of women there, after this status had eroded for women elsewhere.

The conditions for the development of the new agricultural way of life in Europe, Africa, and Asia were very different from those of the Near East. Climatic differences were great; forests had to be cleared; different kinds of crops had to be experimented with. Perhaps most important of all, Neolithic immigrants were moving into already inhabited territory. Earlier inhabitants often continued a hunting and gathering way of life for centuries after their farmer neighbors settled in, adopting elements of the new economy but continuing their own system (Hawkes and Woolley, 1963: 240).

The settlements northward into western Europe had a different character from those in southern Europe. The Danubian loess lands were so fertile, naturally well drained, and lightly forested, that they made an obvious site for primitive agricultural methods. Soil exhaustion was an important factor in the continual migrations of the farmers and their spread throughout Europe. "Always virgin soil lay ahead" (Hawkes and Woolley, 1963: 243). It has been estimated that a village moved about every quarter of a century, sometimes sooner. Hunting and fishing receded in importance, and agriculture and cattle received a major share of the working time of the village. "Lack of chief's houses or rich graves suggests an egalitarian society, and the Danubians are generally assumed to have been a peaceable folk" (Hawkes and Woolley, 1963: 244). The reconstruction of a Danubian village (figure 4-6) gives some feeling for the different life style the climate fosters. There is less emphasis on open-air work spaces, more on adequate sheltered places. The mother-goddess has traveled with these settlers, along with the new Cretan religion, the axe cult. The axe cult must have had properties particularly helpful to migrating farmers, since it spread all over Europe. It seems to be associated with an egalitarian society and with equal status for women and men.

Engels (1942) pictured a dramatic shift from matrilineal to patrilineal descent with the "overthrow of the mother right [as] the world historical defeat of the female sex." What he did not know was that what he conceived as the patriarchal "Great Family Community," or the extended family village, which he thought succeeded group marriage, was in fact a matrilineal community in many parts of the world. While none of the evidence presented in this chapter is conclusive, much of it seems to point in the same direction. The evidence does not, however, warrant establishing a "matrilineal" stage as an inevitable stage in social evolution. Other scenarios, involving different relationships between male hunters and female gatherers in the agricultural transition, could be imagined. The role of accidental factors, whether of the environment or of individual human personalities, or the vagaries of social drift in patterning social organization, could produce many variants of the transition I have described here from nomadism to settled life. The most tenable position to take is that, in some substantial number of tribal groups, women played a key role in the transition to agriculture. This key role was often associated with the reckoning of descent through the mother and with the allocation of land through the matrikin. We may remember here Wilson's statement, quoted in chapter 2: "The key to sociobiology . . . is milk" (1975: 456).

We can also say that this transition involved the development of village life: the foraging band became the village. In all centuries the most frequent pattern for human settlement has involved men and women living in villages and going out each day to farm surrounding lands. If a village got too crowded, a group of people might leave to start a new settlement, but rarely did a single nuclear family leave. Isolated homesteading requires very special social and environmental

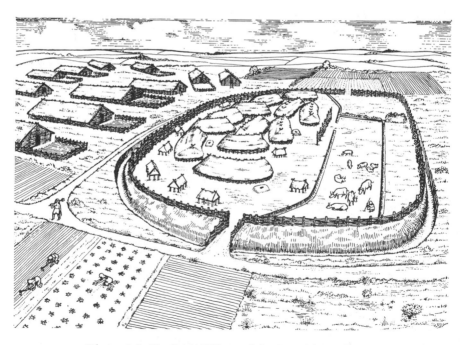

Figure 4-6. *Neolithic Village of the Danubian Culture:*
Köln-Lindenthal (Reconstruction).

conditions. The clan-based pattern of village organization has in many parts of the world remained intact in spite of the rise and fall of surrounding empires. Nevertheless, change takes place with the development of trade routes and the passing through of groups and individual adventurers who eventually create new types of settlements or transform the character of old ones. The erosion of matrilineal organization within the clan-patterned villages is one of the consequences of this contact-and-transformation sequence. We will trace out the dynamics of that process in the next chapter.

Notes

[1]The following glossary is offered to aid the reader unfamiliar with kin-reckoning terminology:

matrilineal— reckoning descent through the mother
matrilocal— married couple lives with wife's family
matriarchy— sometimes used to denote the political rule of women, which is more properly called gynocracy
matrikin— all kin reckoned through the mother
patrilineal— reckoning descent through the father
patrilocal— married couple lives with husband's family
patriarchy— political rule of men
patrikin— all kin reckoned through the father
avunculocal— married couple lives with wife's uncle (associated with matrilineal descent reckoning)

It is important to note that choice of residence after marriage and system of descent reckoning are two separate and distinct sets of traits, and may be combined in various ways; e.g., matrilineal descent may accompany patrilocal residence.

[2]The connection between good stands of wild grain and other plant food and the earliest agricultural villages was first made through some brilliant theoretical work by the archaeologist Robert Braidwood of the University of Chicago. His theories took him to the fertile crescent to dig for the first villages, and he did indeed find them where he had expected to (Leonard, 1973).

[3]Not all nomads live in environments that require such short working hours.

[4]See the comparative photographic studies undertaken by Hans Hass (1970) and Eibl-Eibesfeldt (1972) for illustrations of the universality of tenderness and helping modes in relation to children.

[5]See Doris Cole (1973). Women still build adobe houses in the Southwest of the United States today.

[6]Descriptions of Jericho are from Mellaart (1965: 31-42).

[7]Margaret Mead sees the beginnings of patriarchy in this herding activity of men. They saw what one bull could do for a herd of cows!

[8]He does not state the basis of his conclusion.

[9]It is difficult to be sure about the presence or absence of cult centers from archaeological evidence. As Hawkes makes clear in her discussion of archaeological remains from the late Paleolithic and early Neolithic (Hawkes and Woolley, 1963), one cannot always tell a kiln from an oven from a tomb from a cult center.

[10]At the same time, anthropologist Peggy Sanday's warnings about the difficulty of predicting women's contribution to subsistence in the absence of knowledge of women's tribal organization must be borne in mind (Sanday, 1973).

[11]Tool making, unlike pottery making, leads very quickly to enclosed workshops.

[12]To get some of the flavor of women's culture I am drawing on the work of Sophia Drinker, whose study *Music and Women* (1948) brings out aspects of tribal women's activities which are often not mentioned.

[13]See Pomeroy, *Goddesses, Whores, Wives, and Slaves* (1975), for some of this debate.

[14]The correct term for rule by women is gynocracy, but matriarchy is often used in this sense.

[15]Land as property is a by-product of city-state development. The king becomes holder of all state land in the name of the state god. To reward army leaders and merchant backers who help him in conquest and defense enterprises, he makes gifts of state land to them, which then become family rather than state property.

[16]Reasons for the decline of matrilineal societies in the nineteenth and twentieth centuries are somewhat different than, though related to, the reasons for the early decline of matriliny in the transition from subsistence to surplus-generating agriculture. During colonization, there was pressure from the West, from both civil and religious authorities, to conform to patriarchal European patterns of social organization. At the same time, matrilineal organization represented a sharing ethic that interfered with the dynamics of modernization, which depended on accumulation by the male head of household for his own nuclear family to the exclusion in part of all other kin (see Oppong, 1974, for an analysis of this).

[17]A key explanatory concept used by Eisenstadt in his *Political Systems of Empires* (1963).

[18]This could not happen, of course, unless the society was also becoming increasingly productive.

References

Aberle, David F.
  1962a "Navaho." Pp. 96-201 in David M. Schneider and Kathleen Gough (eds.), Matrilineal Kinship. Berkeley: University of California Press.
  1962b "Matrilineal descent in crosscultural perspectives." Pp. 655-730 in David M. Schneider and Kathleen Gough (eds.), Matrilineal Kinship. Berkeley: University of California Press.

Alland, Alexander
  1962 The Human Imperative. New York: Columbia University Press.

Basehart, Harry W.
  1962 "Ashanti." Pp. 270-297 in David M. Schneider and Kathleen Gough (eds.), Matrilineal Kinship. Berkeley: University of California Press.

Boserup, Ester
  1970 Women's Role in Economic Development. New York: St. Martin's Press.

Campbell, Joseph
  1972 Myths to Live By. New York: Viking.

Childe, Gordon
  1963 Social Evolution. New York: Meridian Press.

Cole, Doris
  1973 From Tipi to Skyscraper: A History of Women in Architecture. Boston: I Press.

Cole, Sonja
  1963 The Prehistory of East Africa. New York: Macmillan.

Colson, Elizabeth
  1962 "Plateau tonga." Pp. 36-95 in David M. Schneider and Kathleen Gough (eds.), Matrilineal Kinship. Berkeley: University of California Press.

Darlington, C. D.
  1969 The Evolution of Man and Society. New York: Simon and Schuster.

de Mause, Lloyd
   1974   "The evolution of childhood." Pp. 1-74 in Lloyd de Mause (ed.), The
          History of Childhood. New York: Psychohistory Press.

Drinker, Sophie
   1948   Music and Women: The Story of Women in Their Relation to Music.
          New York: Coward-McCann.

Eibl-Eibesfeldt, Irenäus
   1972   Love and Hate. Tr. by Geoffrey Strachan. New York: Holt, Rinehart
          and Winston.

Eisenstadt, S. N.
   1972   Post-traditional Societies. New York: W. W. Norton.
   1963   The Political Systems of Empires. New York: Free Press.

Engels, Frederich
   1942   The Origin of the Family, Private Property, and the State. New York:
          International Publishers. (First published 1884.)

Fathauer. George H.
   1962   "Trobriand." Pp. 234-269 in David M. Schneider and Kathleen Gough
          (eds.), Matrilineal Kinship. Berkeley: University of California Press.

Fontenrose, Joseph
   1959   Python: A Story of the Delphic Myth and Its Origins. New York: Biblo
          and Tannen.

Fortes, Meyer
   1974   Foreword. Pp. ix-xii in Christine Oppong, Marriage among a Matrilineal   .
          Elite. Cambridge: Cambridge University Press.

Foster, George M.
   1968   "Sociology of pottery." Pp. 317-328 in Yehudi Cohen (ed.), Man in
          Adaptation: The Biosocial Background. Chicago: Aldine.

Fried, Morton H.
   1967   The Evolution of Political Society: An Essay in Political Anthropology.
          New York: Random House.

Gough, Kathleen
   1962a "Nayar: Central Kerala." Pp. 298-384 in David Schneider and Kathleen
          Gough (eds.), Matrilineal Kinship. Berkeley: University of California
          Press.
   1962b "Nayar: North Kerala." Pp. 385-404 in David Schneider and Kathleen
          Gough (eds.), Matrilineal Kinship. Berkeley: University of California
          Press.

Graves, Robert
   1966   White Goddess: A Historical Grammar of Poetic Myth. New York:
          Farrar, Straus and Giroux.

Hass, Hans
   1970   Human Animal: The Mystery of Man's Behavior. New York: Putnam.

Hawkes, Jacquetta and Sir Leonard Woolley
   1963   Prehistory and the Beginnings of Civilization. History of Mankind, vol.
          1. New York: Harper and Row.

Kenyon, Kathleen
  1970   Archaeology in the Holy Land. 3rd ed. New York: Praeger.

Lee, Richard B. and Irven De Vore (eds.)
  1968   Man the Hunter. Chicago: Aldine.

Leonard, Jonathon Norton
  1973   The First Farmers. New York: Time-Life Books.

Loeb, Edwin M.
  1960   "Wine, women and song: Root planting and head-hunting in southeast Asia." Pp. 302-316 in Stanley Diamond (ed.), Culture and History: Essays in Honor of Paul Raden. New York: Columbia University Press.

Loeb, Edwin M. and J. Broek
  1947   "Social organization and the long house in southeast Asia." American Anthropologist 49: 414-425.

Mair, Lucy
  1972   Marriage. New York: Universe.

McClelland, David C.
  1961   The Achieving Society. Princeton, N.J.: D. Van Nostrand.

McClelland, David C. and David G. Winter
  1969   Motivating Economic Achievement. New York: Free Press.

Mellaart, James
  1965   Earliest Civilizations of the Near East. New York: McGraw-Hill.

Murdock, George
  1949   Social Structure. New York: Macmillan.

Oppong, Christine
  1974   Marriage Among a Matrilineal Elite: A Family Study of Ghanaian Senior Civil Servants. Cambridge Studies in Social Anthropology, 8. Cambridge: Cambridge University Press.

Pomeroy, Sarah B.
  1975   Goddesses, Whores, Wives, and Slaves: Women in Classical Antiquity. New York: Schocken Books.

Sanday, Peggy R.
  1973   "Toward a theory of the status of women." American Anthropologist 75: 1682-1700.

Schneider, David M. and Kathleen Gough (eds.)
  1962   Matrilineal Kinship. Berkeley: University of California Press.

Sherfey, Mary Jane
  1972   The Nature and Evolution of Female Sexuality. New York: Random House.

Singer, Charles, E. J. Holmyard, and A. R. Hall
  1954   A History of Technology: From Early Times to the Fall of Ancient Rome. Vol. 1. New York: Oxford University Press.

Slater, Philip E.
  1968   The Glory of Hera: Greek Mythology and the Greek Family. Boston: Beacon Press.

United Nations
  1974   "The data base for discussion on the interrelations between the inte-
         gration of women in development, their situation and population fac-
         tors in Africa." Regional Seminar on the Integration of Women in
         Development, with Special Reference to Population Factors. Economic
         Commission for Africa, United Nations Economic and Social Council,
         Addis Ababa, May (mimeo).

Vayda, Andrew P.
  1961   "Expansion and warfare among Swidden agriculturalists." American
         Anthropologist 63: 346-358.

Whiting, John W. M.
  1968   Discussant in Richard B. Lee and Irven De Vore (eds.), Man the Hunter:
         336-339. Chicago: Aldine.

Wilson, Edward O.
  1975   Sociobiology: The New Synthesis. Cambridge: Belknap Press of
         Harvard University Press.

5
Megaliths and Metallurgy:
The Walls Close in on Women

In this chapter, covering roughly the period from 6000 to 2000 B.C., we will consider the consequences for women of two types of development that accompanied the transition from the nomadic to the settled life: the evolution of new skills of social organization, and the discovery of the use of metals for weaponry as well as for tools. In tracing the history of this period, we will follow two migrant streams from the Near East to Europe, and look at the peoples who remained behind in the Near East and moved from village and town to city life during these four millennia. The monument builders of Europe, who erected the massive assemblages such as Stonehenge, and the townspeople of the Near East represent very different kinds of cultures. Each group invented significant technologies of social organization during this four-thousand-year period: the monument builders managed large-scale enterprises with a nonhierarchical, nonurban form of society, and the Near East townspeople developed the stratified city-state. Both groups were profoundly affected by the coming of metals and weaponry.

Traces of the matrilineal social order described in the last chapter remain, but the requirements of trade, territorial expansion, and warfare shift the focus away from the matrikin. Urban administrations devise new forms of land allotment, and old clan rights disappear. Because the transformations of scale are central to the process of erosion of the status of women, considerable attention will be given to the process, slow and gradual in its day-to-day impact on the folk of village and town, by which clan self-rule of women and men is replaced by the rule of chiefs, kings, and priests, assisted on the side by queens, princesses, and priestesses.

There are many archaeological remains for this period, but few recorded legends concerning its peoples. The religious and social practices of the European megalith builders, in particular, remain hidden, making it difficult to do even a speculative reconstruction of women's roles for the megalith people. What is particularly intriguing is that the highly advanced skills of the megalith culture evidently developed in a minimally stratified and peaceful society. Metalsmiths and traders arrived among these semiagrarian village monument builders with something they had not had before: weapons designed specifically for fighting humans. With this new type of tool available, monument building petered out and wars increasingly absorbed the energies of women and men. Tribal organization continued to be strong, however; for the inhabitants of Europe, cities were still in the future.

In the Near East, which already had a head start on agriculture, social patterns changed more rapidly. The metalsmiths had introduced their wares here first. Increasingly mobile and numerous, nomad traders pushed populations from the northern hills of the fertile crescent down to the river banks of the Tigris and the Euphrates. It was here that the large trading towns developed, and the first city-states. Temples, canals, walls, and military skills developed apace in the new cities, as people, monuments, and wealth accumulated and had to be defended. By this time the future belonged to the specialists: to those who could produce monuments and artifacts, to those who could administer their use, and to those who could organize the countryside as a granary for the city.

Agriculture was also becoming more specialized. The plow was first used in the Near East about 3000 B.C., and shortly afterward in Europe.[1] With the pressure of increasing food needs brought about by the growth of towns, there was a premium on increasing production. Men, already specialized as the traders of the villages, would be the first to recognize the advantages of increased production. Since they also had the cattle in their charge, it is logical that the men should be the ones who figured out that if they had an ox drag a hoe through the fields, the ground could be prepared a lot quicker

(Jacobsen, 1960: 53). Design improvements produced the plow, and soil preparation was taken over by men working ever larger fields.

The shift in the status of the woman farmer may have happened quite rapidly, once there were two male specializations relating to agriculture: plowing and the care of cattle. This situation left women with all the subsidiary tasks, including weeding and carrying water to the fields. The new fields were larger, so women had to work just as many hours as they did before, but now they worked at more secondary tasks. Separation from preparing the ground for sowing was also separation from the age-old planting rite on which both the religious and social structures were based. This would contribute further to the erosion of the status of women.

In what follows, we shall see what happened to women in Europe and the Near East as the new metal-using, production, and trade-oriented societies developed. To aid the reader in keeping time sequences straight, a chronology of the societies discussed in this chapter is provided in Appendix 5-1. A world map is also provided showing the location of the first world civilizations in relation to the development of agriculture.

The Megalith Builders

The limited productivity of fields and pasturages and the increase in population density in the Near East meant that every couple of generations some families would move on from an overpopulated parent village. By 6000 B.C. families were moving along the shores of the Mediterranean and up European rivers either by boat or on foot. We know that they could move by water, for a wooden dugout dating from 6000 B.C. has been found in a bog in Holland (Edey, 1972: 37). Much more sophisticated longboats with oars would also be plying the Mediterranean by this time. Women, men, children, cattle, seeds, and tools all moved together through the inviting forests of Europe as the damp and cold that were the still-lingering residue of the last ice age finally evaporated. The first villages the farmers built were unprotected by ramparts of any kind, so the migrants apparently mingled freely with the hunting-gathering peoples, the Azilians, who had stayed on in Europe after the petering out of the dynamic Magdalenian culture. The newly introduced farmers' tools and the traditional European hunter-gatherers' tools are found together in village sites. Figure 5-1 shows the distribution of a series of four peasant cultures in Europe, each from a different region of the Mediterranean, in relation to food-gathering cultures and the early Copper Age sites.

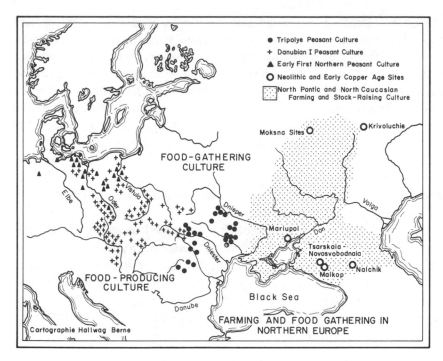

Figure 5-1. *Farming and Food Gathering in Northern Europe.*

As noted in the preceding chapter, free-standing, not wall-to-wall, housing suggests a greater emphasis on individual family units in the society. The character of these villages was very different from that of the Near East villages. The dense forests everywhere meant heavy work in clearing land and building houses. It is likely that women and men cleared, built, and planted together.

With plenty of land and wood available, these villages achieved a comfortable standard of living very quickly, as archaeological remains indicate. The groups that crossed the channel to the British Isles and those that settled in France found themselves near valuable quarries and developed sophisticated flint-mining operations. They also built great earthworks, called causewayed camps, which were apparently sites for large-scale communal celebrations. They were not fortifications (Wernick, 1973: 87-90; Hawkins, 1965: 35). We know that the monument builders, as they are sometimes called, had houses that were extremely comfortable and well furnished. This knowledge comes from the accidental uncovering of the small village of Skara Brae in the Orkneys, a third millennium B.C. village of this megalith culture. With no earth or wood on the island, everything was made of stone, including built-in furniture, beds, "dressers," tables, and so on. So well designed and efficient were the houses, by twentieth century standards, that a local woman hired by the archaeologists at the site to work for them "moved into one of the prehistoric houses and lived there quite comfortably" (Wernick, 1973: 81-82).

Musical instruments have also been found in megalith villages: clay drums of varying sizes for different pitch levels, cow horns with holes in the sides that sound like trumpets, and several types of flutes (Wernick, 1973: 83).

It is tantalizing to think of how little we know about the kind of society that produced these villages, built the great earth mounds, and then finally the great stone structures.[2] Stonehenge is the best known, though perhaps not the most remarkable, architectural achievement. The monuments of stone that were being built in France, Spain, the British Isles, and Malta between 4800 and 1800 B.C. required a degree of engineering skill beyond any known in the world at the time (figure 5-2). Although these stone structures range in size and complexity from simple free-standing stones (menhirs) from two to seventy feet in height to the towering forty-menhir alignments of Stonehenge, they have enough in common to be labeled as products of a megalith culture distinctively different from any other culture of that three-millennia period.

Many of the stone structures are associated with burials. The bulk of the burial evidence reflects egalitarian societies, with women, men, and children buried in group graves bearing

Figure 5-2. *Megalithic Architecture in Europe.*

no rank distinctions. Toward the end of this era, however, some individual tombs were constructed for prestigious people.

Since the menhir alignments are not themselves burial mounds, there have been many speculations about the possible religious significance of the monuments. Taking the measurements of Stonehenge is as popular a twentieth century activity as taking the measurements of the great pyramid was in the nineteenth century. Engineer Alexander Thom of Oxford University and astronomer Gerald Hawkins of Boston University have brought the trained scientific eye and the computer to the problem. Thom makes it clear that the megalith builders worked out many of the concepts attributed to Pythagoras and geometricians of much later dates. They also developed a unit Thom calls the megalithic yard. Hawkins presents convincing evidence that Stonehenge was used for advanced astronomical observations (Hawkins, 1965).

If Stonehenge is in fact designed around sun-moon alignments that make it possible to "capture" eclipses, equinoxes, and other celestial phenomena, this points to a complex knowledge of calendars and cycles that must have continued to accumulate from the time of the Magdalenian record keeping we noted in the last chapter. Some of it must have developed in the Near East, and some of it may have been picked up in fragments from local Azilians by the more sophisticated newcomers. One can imagine that the women of the two intermingling cultures shared their knowledge with each other, and it is perfectly possible that the immigrant women "rediscovered" some lost knowledge that the Azilian women had kept in folklore and rituals.

The newcomers might have grasped meanings that their local teachers did not know they were conveying. In any case, the kind of knowledge that went into the building of Stonehenge, about 2775 B.C., had been accumulating for a very long time. The monument builders themselves, while they had a comfortable life, had neither the amount of leisure time, the degree of specialization, nor the kind of population density that could have produced Stonehenge and other monuments in a sudden cultural explosion out of "nothing," as has sometimes been depicted.

In fact the kind of large-scale assemblies implied by the megaliths and the causeways before them were a new social phenomenon. It has been calculated that the Avebury monument could have seated an audience of two hundred and fifty thousand (Wernick, 1973: 11). In Malta a megalithic catacomb tomb contained seven thousand bodies. The practice of periodically opening a community tomb and adding new bodies contributed to the large graveyard population. Since the villages themselves were small, there must have been a communications system and a priesthood of some kind that brought people together in large numbers for special occasions, such as summer and winter solstices.

Some relatively large-scale ceremonial gatherings, which developed the community of potential builders, must have been taking place over a long period of time before the megaliths themselves were built. Since it has been estimated that a thousand strong men (or women) would be needed to transport a single fifty-ton stone, and Stonehenge was built and rebuilt over a twelve-hundred-year period, the populations of many villages must have cooperated in the building. The process would be something like the cathedral building in Europe in the Middle Ages, where entire communities turned out to participate in the hauling of materials and in the building process. The architect-priest-coordinators must have had many skills at their command.

It is hard for us to visualize large-scale nonurban social agglomerations engaging in sustained long-term cooperative activity at high skill levels, but this is precisely what was happening in the megalithic societies.[3] The fact that we do not (before the coming of the Beaker people) find evidence of accumulation of personal wealth and power in tombs or houses suggests that the priests, architects, engineers, and overseers were not in a class apart from the ordinary villagers.

What part did women play in the building activities, the ceremonies, and the daily life of the megalithic societies? We do not know for sure. But in chapter 3 we gave the evidence for both ancient and modern participation of women in construction work. They would hardly have been excluded at this particular moment in history. Certainly they farmed, fished, made tools and pottery. They probably worked in the flint mines, at crushing rock and separating ore. Figure 5-3, a rendering of a drawing from the Middle Ages in Europe, shows a woman at work at a mine. Toward the end of the megalithic era, in Egypt, women worked as captives and slaves in the gold mines of Nubia (Knauth, 1974: 12). Women may have made the small boats of sewn skins stretched over a wooden frame used before the era of the larger trading vessels. They might have made musical instruments, and certainly they worked at monument construction. Assuming there was a specialized priestess role, then the women would have developed engineering skills also. If they continued the observations and record-keeping activities we ascribed to them in the Paleolithic, they would certainly have been able to make

Figure 5-3. *Woman Washing Ore, A.D. 1556.*

the astronomical computations required to determine the placement of the stones at Stonehenge.

We know nothing of the nature of the religion the megaliths honored, except that both sun and moon played a central role in it. Ceremonials involving thousands of people gathered to greet the rising sun at the winter solstice must have created powerful and moving occasions, and suggest the possibility of a highly evolved sense of the cosmic, as well as a strong sense of community. The human sacrifices found associated with so many of the religions of the Near East are not found in the megalithic cultures.[4] Evidences of a mother-goddess are present, but sporadically. Stylized representations of the female figure, in the tradition of the fertility figurines of Stone Age Europe, are found at some European megalithic sites. The mother-goddess cult is much more strongly evidenced in Malta. In the Maltese temple monuments, the mother-goddess becomes the central cultic figure, as reflected in the statuary and arrangement of shrines (Wernick, 1973: 21-22, 36-37). Meandering lines and hitherto undecipherable curves and tracings, similar to those studied by Marshack (1972) for the European Paleolithic, are found in many megalithic tombs. It is not known whether they refer to a mother-goddess. No cult objects are found in private homes, suggesting that worship was a communal rather than a private activity.

We do not have the same evidence here for a matrilineal society that we had in the villages of the Near East, but there are arguments by analogy from twentieth century matrilinies as described in chapter 4. If the society was in fact as fluid and egalitarian as I am interpreting it to be, then descent might have been traced through both mother and father. It seems reasonable to think that older fertility-ritual traditions remained as a background to new social developments.

The European megalithic culture appears to have been totally unique in human history, in its development of large-scale social enterprises with a minimum of evidence of social stratification and no clear evidence of military struggle. The nature of the transition to a more warlike society is not clear. There are scholars who maintain that the peoples already in Europe created battle-axes out of the stone hammers and axes they used as tools. There are others who maintain that the battle-axe peoples represented a different culture, coming with more recent migrants from the East (Hawkes and Woolley, 1963: 253-254, 317-319, 322). In either case, the peaceful egalitarian society we have just described could not hold its shape in the face of an arms race heavily assisted by traders and metalsmiths from the Balkans and the Caucasus. It was not destroyed; it simply armed itself and stopped building megaliths. Whether its ancient secrets were in fact taken into custody and perpetuated by the druidic priesthood that came later we shall never know, since we know almost as little about the later druids as we know about the megalithic religion. Shadows of the mother-goddess flit in and out of this later religion too, as we shall see shortly.

The Metallurgists

From the Alps to the Persian Gulf, by the year 6000 B.C., folk were scrambling on their hands and knees to find metal—gold, silver, copper, iron—in mines, in river valleys, in whatever terrain had been recognized as yielding the new kind of wealth. They were also to be found sweating and stinking in front of hot fires which gradually evolved into smelting furnaces.

Gold and silver were always for the rich. But copper and iron, used first for jewelry and ornamentation, showed their usefulness for knives and axes. The demand first for copper and then (after 3000 B.C.) for iron was immediate and widespread. Metal sickles harvested grain much faster than stone ones. Metal knives cut cleaner and faster than stone ones. Metal axes chopped trees faster, and so on.

Women have found their way into metalsmithing from Assyrian times onward. Not many, however! Women's tendency not to specialize would historically have kept most of them out of metallurgy. Yet it might have been otherwise. They stayed with pottery, and eventually became pottery specialists, and the difference between pottery kiln and ore furnace was not so great in the earliest period. In fact, the smelting furnace evolved from the pottery kiln. But metallurgy has long been considered a man's work. A sixteenth century Sienese writer warned:

> No one should practice it unless he is accustomed to the sweat and many discomforts which it brings. He must suffer the great natural heats of summer as well as those excessive and continuous ones from the enormous fires that are used in this art. . . .
>
> He who wishes to practice this art must not be of a weak nature, either from age or constitution, but must be strong, young, and vigorous. . . . the founder is always like a chimney sweep, covered with charcoal and distasteful sooty smoke. To this is added the fact that for this work a violent and continuous straining of all a man's strength is required, which brings great harm to his body and holds many definite dangers to his life (Knauth, 1974: 22).

The author was not trying to dissuade women from the field (he would not even have thought of women, probably); he was warning men that only the brawniest of them would make it.

Metal ornaments are found in Turkey from as early as 9500 B.C. (in the already familiar caves of Shanidar) and appear intermittently for the next couple of thousand years. Between 6500 and 5200 B.C., metal objects and tools spread all over the Middle East, far from points of origin in local metal mines. The metalsmith was the first specialist whose profession determined a whole new way of life. Because of the tremendous demand for metal objects, and the scarcity of metal and metalworkers, the wandering metalsmith who set up a little furnace wherever he found metal, and produced tools and jewelry that no villager could produce, became a common figure in the Near East, Europe, and Asia within a few centuries. Twentieth century gypsies are the last of a social phenomenon that is eight thousand years old. The metalsmith's wife developed a special set of craft skills of her own to complement her husband's, and the nomadic bands had their own kind of egalitarianism, as we will see in chapter 7.

More was involved than wandering metalsmiths, however. The keen demand for metal reorganized the utilization of labor in the Mediterranean. Towns organized large-scale mining and smelting operations, and soon there was a great demand for slaves to work the mines. Metal adorned, and metal enslaved. The first dagger appeared soon after the first earring, and shortly, much of Europe and Asia was armed. The extent of that arming process, however, is quite possibly exaggerated because of our attachment to the warrior tradition in history. Scholars tend to emphasize the connection between arms and metallurgy very strongly.

The Bell Beaker people (1800-1500 B.C.) were the first European metalworkers.[5] They settled among the northern Europeans, taught them their arts, and developed trading networks. They did make knives, but they were also peaceable folk and the emphasis on weaponry came later. The next migrants were metalworker-farmers, who settled in the Carpathian Mountains, learned to make bronze, and further developed an international trade network. The graves of these and successive migrating groups, all skilled metalworkers, show increased social stratification and sometimes the practice of burying wife and children with an important chief. Above all, the dead were no longer buried with tools, but with weapons. The Urnfield people (labeled from their practice of urn burials), pre-Celtic, seem to have spread by 1250 B.C. all over Europe with their weapons and superb bronze tools, and to have used the former extensively. Did they fight to gain land, to conquer peoples they considered stupid and backward, or just for the fun of fighting? This was a new experience for the Europeans—the monument builders, and all the others too. They bought plowshares and swords from the colorful newcomers—and used the plowshares to improve their farming and the swords to defend their farms from these quarrelsome people. Knauth writes admiringly of the

> tremendous slashing sword that was the pinnacle of the Urnfield bronzesmith's art. Heavily bladed, solidly anchored in its haft, the Urnfield slashing sword turned peasants into heroes for bards to sing about (1974: 72).

Since horses were being tamed in Central Asia by 2500 B.C., men on horseback, brandishing swords and spears and wearing helmets and armor, were also a part of the scene.

Now the idea was abroad in Europe of seizing wealth rather than creating it. This meant that every village had to build walls and learn to defend itself. Given the egalitarian society that existed in Europe, both among the monument builders and the still transitional hunting and gathering peoples, women must certainly have owned and learned to use weapons. Burials do *not* reflect this, however, since only men were buried with their weapons.[6] The chief evidence that women were trained in the art of defense is the wide range of tales that existed by Roman times of tribal women fighting side by side with men on the battlefield, and the early Celtic legends of women who conducted "military academies" where they trained men in the art of fighting. These materials will be discussed later.

The building of village walls and the new focus on defense meant a constriction of activity for both women and men, but more for women, who spent more time inside the walls. There is no evidence for the *confinement* of women, however, as is supposed to have happened in India after the Aryan invasions. In fact, we can assume that women sat in village councils as men did, and continued their religious ceremonial roles, since in the time of the Caesars they were still doing these things.

Much of what has been said about the megalithic and postmegalithic woman has been inference, since the evidence is so sparse. Now we are moving toward the historical eras, particularly in Asia and North Africa, although we will still have to turn a great deal to archaeological evidence. History and legend will also have to be disentangled, and this is not easy.

Near East Towns and Walls

The familiar picture of the development of the first cities in the Near East—through the seizure of power by a priest or king (or priest-king), who emerges as top dog in a previously tribal society (e.g., in Mumfcrd, 1961)—appears to be oversimplified. The first fact that we have to face is that the agricultural village-trading town combinations we described in the last chapter were *not* the sites of the first cities. These towns were evidently an abortive urbanism. The first cities developed farther south on the banks of the Tigris and the Euphrates and on the Persian Gulf. Presumably, nomadic peoples north and east of the first agricultural settlements pushed the settlers south as a result of pressures from the steppe lands. Population pressure on the river banks pushed the development of canals so that more food could be grown to feed more people, just as it pushed the development of the plow. Apparently agriculture, trade, canal building,[7] and the erection of temples all developed more or less concurrently.

It makes little sense to argue as to which element is most important in the development of a city: location on a key trade route, agricultural surplus, population density, new technology, skills of social organization. If any of these by itself could produce a city, Jericho and Catal Huyuk would have been among the first cities, since they were once important trade centers. Or the monument builders would have produced cities, since they had both skills of social organization and some significant population densities on which to draw.

What we are talking about in this chapter is not so much final, or "definitive" urbanization, as "primordial urbanization," to use Lampard's phrase (in Hauser and Schnore, 1965: chapt. 14). Primordial urbanization refers to the coming together of diverse subcultures and subenvironments in such a way that symbiotic interaction eventually leads to "more productive modes of collective adaptation to physical and social environment." Peoples, skills, and resources came together in the region that was later known as Sumer.

The very notion of a symbiosis of subcultures implies a greater heterogeneity than was found in the first simple trading towns. The later towns became the meeting places of many cultures. Those who came to settle, came for the most part in groups, during the early urbanization. Both the town-magnetized nomads and the agriculturalists in search of new land usually moved in extended-family groupings.

The towns grew in other ways too, since they were on the trade routes between Egypt and Arabia, or between Palestine-Syria and Mesopotamia. The trade routes were already ancient by 2000 B.C.:

> Bedouins or merchants, messengers and mendicants, armies and refugees passed through the Negev, some staying permanently as peasants or soldiers or pilgrims or miners, striking roots in the soil, and together with their families and kinfolk building up civilizations which maintained relations with the places and cultures of their origins (Glueck, 1960: 48-49).

The new towns of antiquity, created at points on the trade routes, were, therefore, complex from the beginning. Older towns, growing more slowly, became more complex with time. These older towns were not simple tribal settlements, or great family communities, though clan groupings must have been important. They probably represented interclan alliances from the start.

It was probably during this phase of town development that the shift from the matrilineal extended-family residences described in the last chapter to patrilineal extended-family residences took place.

While Blumberg and Winch's study (1972) of contemporary ethnographic materials led those researchers to suggest that the conditions for development of large family systems sharing common residences would be in agricultural societies with towns having populations under five thousand, in the period we are describing many of these towns might still be matrilineal. With expanding population and the development of several levels of political hierarchy, another predisposing factor Blumberg and Winch propose, we are moving into patrilineal conditions and the likelihood of male-headed extended families. In any case, the number of families actually living together in extended-family households was probably small. Wherever we have records of such living arrangements, with some exceptions to be noted later, extended-family households tend to be associated with the upper classes and with the presence of women slaves as helpers. The phenomenon of generalized sexual availability of domestic slaves to the men of a household must have begun with this earliest urban slavery, adding one more push to the set of forces that were combining to lower the status of women in the city. The general expectation on the part of men that women in service roles were to be sexually available long outlasted slavery and continues into the twentieth century.[8]

The process of establishing rules to handle interclan transactions within the community and with seminomadic herders from the surrounding countryside would have been part of town development from the outset. In the Bau community of early dynastic Lagash, for example, out of a population of 1,200, there were 100 fishermen, 125 sailors, pilots, and longshoremen, and 100 herdsmen. The seminomadic herdsmen were especially important to the town's textile industry. They stayed free of urban roots, but worshipped the shepherd god Dumuzi in temples erected for them in the town (Adams, 1966: 49). These temples also held supplemental grain stocks for the use of the cattle, and became administrative centers for the exchange of goods both for herders and fishermen (Adams, 1960: 30). The equilibrium between herders and townspeople was never an easy one, and as the towns grew, herdsmen were given special roles in early administrative hierarchies, to try to keep relationships smooth.

In those early days, one of the major jobs of the town administrator was to see to the plowing of the lands belonging to the town. It was done by *corvée* (a labor tax), and *ensik,* the term for the head of the city-state, originally denoted "the administrator who was in charge of plowed land." Originally this position could well have been filled by a woman, or by a man designated by a council of matrons.

Students of the first urbanization, such as Adams, Jacobsen, and their associates, emphasize strongly that these first towns-to-become-cities grew organically. In the early days there were assemblies of townspeople, women and men, to deal with problems as they arose (Jacobsen, 1960). Temporary officers would be elected to carry out decisions. When conflicts arose with other towns, as specialization in trade introduced rivalries or as hostile nomads began raiding the town or its surrounding fields, temporary "kings" would be appointed to lead in attack or defense. This kind of temporary war-king has been known in tribal areas the world over. Only as the town grew in size and wealth, extending hegemony over an ever wider agricultural area including nearby villages, would the "king" take on more permanent powers—partly through his own ambition, partly through the disinclination of townspeople to spend so much time traveling to assemblies and making decisions. "Thus," as Jacobsen points out, "the expansion had the effect of overextending and breaking the pattern of primitive democracy on the top political level and replacing it with a new type of pattern: monarchy" (1960: 66).

The gradual differentiation in economic and political roles associated with increasing productivity and affluence, and the need to defend that affluence from others, created two new social phenomena that had not existed before: social distance, and expectations of certain kinds of assistance. People who stopped going to assemblies saw the king acting on their behalf, raising armies, defending them. The same process that put distance between the people and their king operated first to put distance between the people and their priestesses and priests. Religious awe fostered the climate in which political combativeness developed. Since full-time priesthoods existed before full-time kingships, the temples in the growing towns were built first. Early administrative systems evolved there; palaces came later. The skills of the priest were only indirectly of use on the battlefield, however, and the independent power of the king grew from the battlefield, not the temple. Nevertheless, the town assemblies never forgot the old days before they had kings.

The process that produces power differentials, centralization, and stratification is a complex one. Our attention is more often drawn to the seizure of power than to the giving over of power. Yet there is a good deal of evidence that historically much power has been relinquished rather than seized, in situations of early surplus or in the face of new needs for social coordination. The Book of Samuel gives a dramatic instance of such relinquishing of power, in a period just after the one we are discussing in this chapter. Some Israelites, impatient with their democratic system of tribal councils and judges in the face of complex military requirements as they tried to establish themselves in Canaan, went to their judge Samuel and said, "Now make us a king to judge us like all the nations." Jehovah advised Samuel:

> So Samuel told the people what the Lord had said: If you insist on having a king, he will conscript your sons and make them run before his chariots; some will be made to lead his troops into battle, while others will be slave laborers; they will be forced to plow on the royal fields, and harvest his crops without pay; and make his weapons and chariot equipment. He will take your daughters from you and force them to cook and bake and make perfumes for him. He will take away the best of your fields and vineyards and olive groves and give them to his friends. He will take a tenth of your harvest and distribute it to his favorites. He will demand your slaves and the finest of your youth and will use your animals for his personal gain. He will demand a tenth of your flocks, and you shall be his slaves. You will shed bitter tears because of this king you are demanding, but the Lord will not help you.
>
> But the people refused to listen to Samuel's warning. "Even so, we still want a king," they said, "for we want to be like the nations around us. He will govern us and lead us to battle" (1 Sam. 8: 5-20, *Living Bible*).

The principle of the giving over of power works in many different kinds of settings. It has been noted in Iraq today that, once the government has placed an engineer in an area to be in charge of a specific task such as irrigation works, the villagers will come to him with many other unrelated problems and give him a decision-making authority that he has not asked for (Fernea, in Kraeling and Adams, 1960: 35-37). The widespread practice in the Arab world of seeking an outside mediator rather than the local sheikh when there is a serious controversy is an example of a largely unintentional giving over of power. The mediator is supposed to be disinterested, but may of course utilize his position to further her or his own ends.

What this suggests is that the most elemental differentiation in authority, if it continues long enough to create social distance between locals and the one wielding authority and if the need for authority is great enough, gives other kinds of authority to the power holder because she or he is seen as having superior problem-solving skill. This process creates two new kinds of power: political and religious.

The rise of cities thus presents to us a mindboggling interplay of forces, as the original town assemblies alternately give and try to retract power, as kings and priests alternately seize or are handed power, each needing the other, yet each fighting to protect their separate privileges. The temple-palace administrations characteristic of Sumerian cities by 2000 B.C. were, then, secondary developments grafted onto the original towns. Memories of an ideal "town and temple" system stayed alive all through Mesopotamian history, according to Jacobsen (1960), and civic pride made it surface every time a ruling king violated ancient rights. Where royal decrees were recorded stating that the citizens of such-and-such a town did not have to pay taxes or contribute soldiers to the king's army, this was probably restitution to an aroused citizenry that had been wronged in some way. Over and over kings appear to have been forced to the wall by rebellious civic assemblies. The founding of entirely new capital cities, as we find in Sumerian times, was often a king's desperate response to the noncooperation of his subjects. In a new town of his own founding, with no ancient rights to take account of, he could tax and conscript as he pleased. Recruits would come to live there through a combination of bribery and forced resettlement.

The very concept of the development of social distance involved in this "organic" model of the rise of cities lies at the heart of the problem of women's roles in the emerging urban scene. In one sense all social bonds are distance bridging, whether they are kin ties or political ties. The distance bridging involved in kinship labeling, however, has a special immediacy about it that is associated both with the feelings about the kinship group as a solidary group and with feelings about the mother role as a key aspect of the solidarity. It is probably no accident, as Borgese points out, that collective nouns tend to be feminine, and that

> the typical, the generic, the non-individual, these are associated in our minds, and therefore in our languages, with the feminine, no less than the collective (1963: 76-77).

The feminine is associated with the aspect of the family that is dedifferentiating. The dedifferentiating aspect of kinship can particularly be noticed in such customs as adoption and blood brother ceremonies, through which the stranger is made one with the group.

The distance of the *majestas,* the ruler, the lord, from his subjects is at least in part a distance which is first created, *then* bridged. Those who do best at administration and ruling have to have distance-creating skills as well as bonding skills. Distancing is necessary both to develop perspectives on the working of all parts of the system one deals with and to deal impersonally with conflicting wants and needs of persons inside the system. The claims of kinship or any other ties are not supposed to sway one's judgment about just allocation of resources in the polity.

A woman can perfectly well learn these skills, and we will see that she often has done so. There is, nevertheless, a set of situational determinants that work against women's development of distancing skills, related to their biological role. (The matrilineal society resolved this by creating a certain amount of distance in the mother-goddess role.) As long as women are operating within the land-linked clan structures, their administrative skills operate without deterrence, since little specialization is required. Women's problems arise at the point where clan structures begin to recede in importance while the public sphere, which by definition lies outside clan structures, expands. Once social differentiation has reached the point where political bonding must supplement and extend beyond kin bonding, a woman's nonspecialist position becomes a real handicap.

An example from the hypothesized development of the urban center of Susa in the Uruk culture of the Susiana Plain of Iran in the period 3500-3150 B.C. will make the woman's problem clear (Johnson, 1975: 294-306). By the middle Uruk period there were fifty-two settlements in the Susiana Plain, consisting of villages and small towns ranging in site size from one to eight hectares, and two urban centers, one of ten and one of twenty-five hectares (Choga Mish and Susa, respectively). Archaeological excavations have shown that pottery made at each settlement had its own distinctive characteristics. It has therefore been possible to study the distribution of each pottery type and thus identify a distribution network and emergent administrative system for the entire area, centered in Susa. While details of the interpretation of the data have been questioned (Adams, 1966: 158-159), the main outlines are believable. Any kind of communications system linking one large urban center with fifty-one smaller ones would be operating with channels that cross-cut kinship channels.[9] The skill to "work the system" would be a specialized skill standing outside the array of clan specialties. This was the kind of specialization that matrilinies did not develop.

Sumer

What we will see happening to women in the towns of Sumer and elsewhere is a progressive lessening of their participation in significant decision making as clan-based roles recede in importance. Their roles continue to have some visibility, but decreasingly so. While women's failure to specialize left them behind as trade and crafts became more important, they continued to have important public roles because of their traditional responsibility for allocating and working the land and for serving in the temples of the religious cults. When the development of the plow, as outlined earlier, put more of the agricultural process in the hands of men, women began to be faced with an increasingly difficult situation as regards control over resources and production processes. Not only were they being elbowed aside in regard to decisions about land, but in some areas they were also being pushed out of pottery making too. This process was hardly a kindly effort to relieve overburdened women, but was the beginning of a very long-term trend involving relegation of all unskilled and miscellaneous tasks to women. Though we have no records describing the struggles that must have gone on as women resisted having valued roles taken away from them, we should not imagine that they quietly laid down their digging sticks and let men take over. Many centuries later, when the men of London forced the women out of one of their major occupations, brewing, we know that the women fought hard and bitterly against the loss of their occupation. But protests, petitions, and pitched battles were to no avail. And so it must have been in the Middle East, several thousand years ago.

Still, the force of custom and the need for their knowledge and experience must have kept women on the town councils for a time after this process started.[10] Certainly they held on to land rights as best they could, and to matrilineal descent reckoning. So while materials from early dynastic Lagash, a city of the Sumerian culture, make it clear that the descent of the elites was usually recorded in government records through the male, sometimes a woman is named and descent traced through her. Women sometimes appear in land deeds as heads of households and as donors and recipients of ritualized food offerings. They are recorded as doing long-distance trading under their own names, and they sometimes held administrative posts as wives of ruling husbands, as in the case of Baranamtarra, wife of the ruler Lugalanda (Adams, 1966: 82).

Women's strongest position was in relation to the temples. In general, a female priesthood served the male gods, and a male priesthood served the female gods. The names of nearly all the high priestesses are recorded from the time of King Sargon on. Harris, in her study of clay tablets recording business and legal affairs of the city of Sippar, has found the names of 10 women scribes out of a total of 185 scribes listed between 1850 and 1550 B.C. (in Claiborne, 1973:

101). We do not know whether these women scribes were trained in regular scribal schools with men, or whether they were taught inside the women's temple organizations. It is possible that women, like men, could choose between secular and religious training. In any case, many women would be needed to administer the large temple complexes.

Sumer had essentially three major centers of economic and political power: the palace, the temple, and private clan holdings (Diakonoff, 1959: 77). Women participated in temple and clan administration, but rather rarely in palace administration. The title "lasting ladyship" may refer to palace-conferred titles, but such titles are rare (Kramer, 1963). The fact that the king of Sumer ritually married a representative of the goddess Inanna once every year helped sustain the power of the priestesses for a time at least.

In the earlier, more democratic era of Sumer, women carried out a variety of business activities and freely used the "street scribes" available to everyone. As the society became more stratified and specialized, the street scribes disappeared (Kramer, 1963). Women workers lost their independent status. When we see them later in the textile factories in teams of three, spinning and weaving, it is not clear whether they were simply unmarried women, or slaves, or war captives.

Farming was increasingly in the hands of the men. A "farm manual" recently translated (Kramer, 1963: 105-108) is written as from a father to his son, with no mention of female agricultural activities at all. Since we can be sure that women were actually working in the fields, the lack of mention of this fact in the manual is an indication of the rapid erosion of women's status as farm labor. Lists of herbal remedies from a "pharmocòpeia" (Kramer, 1963: 93-97) may originally have been prepared by women herbalists for male doctors, as we know was the case later in Europe, but there is no hint of the fact in the existing records.

The various cities of Sumer differed from one another, of course. Erech, which was overrun by conquering nomad war bands in 3500 B.C., had a more patriarchal cast than Lagash; there seems to have been a complete absence of participation of women in public affairs in Erech. However, the same basic pattern of palace and temple, schools, a system of "law and order," and written records were found in all towns. Stratification was increasingly rigid. The temple roster in Erech lists the following categories of persons in 2500 B.C.: upper-class scribes, ordinary scribes, teachers, city fathers, ambassadors, temple administrators, military officers, sea captains, tax officials, priests, managers, supervisors, foremen, archivists, accountants. No women are mentioned at all.

The nomadic warlord tradition imposed on Erech contrasts markedly with the Lagash tradition, which developed locally. Warlordism led to a degree of stratification not found in communities that did not have to absorb these alien elements. Old rights and privileges resisted erosion everywhere, however. The fact that Hammurabi's code in 1751 B.C. contained sixty-eight sections on family and women, fifty on land and territory, and seven on priestesses indicates that women and clan rights were still a very important part of the Sumerian polity more than a thousand years after the time we are discussing.

As Sumerian cities developed in the pre-Hammurabic millennia, the long process of redefining matrilineal clan rights to suit a newly evolving patrilineal descent system took place. As increasing stratification left all but elite women in privatized roles of domestic production, the battle to defend ancient rights on the part of women of the middle classes who still retained interests in agricultural land must have shifted from town council to palace courtyard. Kings emerge very early as administrators of justice. For some reason women were never barred from the king's court of justice, although they were excluded from other public spaces. In all the ancient civilizations, and up to modern times, we will find women in the courts claiming their rights. While these rights have been severely reduced at times, it appears that the ruling class has to some extent always recognized the importance of the producer role of women and provided them with whatever protection the prevailing law allowed. The phenomenon of the court as the interface between the privatized life spaces of women and the public spheres of society must be considered in assessing the status of women in any period of history. An adequate understanding of the role of law in determining the participation of women in producer roles must await a systematic comparative study of all codifications of law, ancient and modern, with respect to provisions regarding women's marital status, inheritance rights, and rights to land and to capital for the transaction of business.

Codes of law were not initially the most conspicuous feature of new urban developments, however. The most visible aspects of developments in Lagash, Erech, and Ur centered around the emergence of complex temple-palace ceremonial centers and a powerful priesthood. Successive archaeological layers of these cities show an expanding *temenos*—the walled religious citadel within the town containing temples, palaces, and government buildings (Morris, 1974:

7-11). Located on desert as well as water trade routes to Syria, Egypt, and India, these communities provided ample opportunities for king and priest to accumulate economic and political power. (In Ur at one period the high priest and king were brothers, and continually struggled with each other for dominance.) When surpluses made armies possible, between harvest and seed time, nearby towns and villages were captured. Finally there was intercity warfare, and a series of "empires" depending on which city-state had most recently conquered its neighbors in war. The plum of governorship of a conquered town evidently was sometimes handed to a woman. King Dungi of Ur (2459-2401 B.C.), for example, made his daughter "lady" (apparently ruler) of Markhashi in the district of Elam. There was more monument building than warring, however, and in between warrior kings there were also peaceable ones. King Urukagina curbed the extortions of priests at funerals; prevented them from stripping the gardens of the common people of their fruit, "for taxes"; dismantled the army; and gave slaves "rights."

There is an amusing debate between the two Sumerologists, Kramer (1956, 1963) and Jacobsen (1960), about what the Sumerians were really like. Kramer sees them as contentious, ambitious people always on the make, while Jacobsen sees them as relatively peaceable, family-loving, moral, and socially conscious people. They were surely both. The two-edged character of the *polis* as a people-shaping force, observed and commented on so frequently through history, is as evident at the birth of the city as in its later evolution.

After two thousand years of intercity jockeying and warring, Sumer declined as the civilization-building dynamic shifted to Babylonia. What we can see of the remains of the eighty-nine-hectare walled city of Ur, population thirty-five thousand, gives us a taste, however, of the cities to come and of the life for the women in them. Figure 5-4, a drawing from an aerial photograph of Erbil (ancient Arbela), is of a city very much as Ur would have been; the patterns have not changed since the fourth millennium B.C. We get a strong sense of crowding, of lack of space. Children must have played in those narrow alleys; the earliest references to cities describe children playing in the streets, as in Zachariah, Chapter 8: "and the streets of the city shall be full of boys and girls playing in the streets thereof." The women, however, saw little of the streets. The enclosed courtyard pattern that characterizes the Middle Eastern city pushed women of the middle classes out of public life. The village houses of preurban Hacilar had courtyards, but they opened into one another. Women were able to gather together and carry out many of

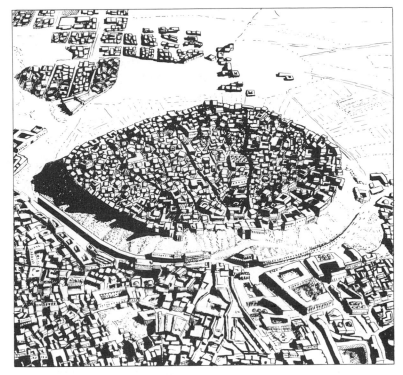

Figure 5-4. *Arbela, Today Much As It Was in the 5th Millennium B.C.*

their activities communally. In the new cities they were walled off from one another. With few public roles and few public gathering places, the walls were indeed closing in for women. Working women and domestic slaves continued to move about freely, as did the farm women outside the city walls, but there are no records of their lives. Among the elite women, there would be continued administration of family holdings outside of the city, as reflected in Hammurabic Code. Rural holdings would continue to be important for women's roles in the upper classes right up to the industrial era. We do not know how important the priestesses were who administered the women's temple buildings excavated in Ur, but they had a substantial area inside the *temenos.* Here was their public arena, close to the center of power.

Clearly Sumerian society had become increasingly stratified, and women lost ground even as their nice new center-courtyard houses were being built up around them. Nevertheless, as the center of power shifted from temple to palace, and the social dynamic shifted from peace to war, women held on to what they could. The shadow of the old egalitarian society did not totally disappear.

Egypt

Egypt, in all the long history of its classical period, never developed an urban infrastructure separate from the temple administration ruling the country on behalf of its Pharaoh.[11] In predynastic times every village had its own deity, and these were frequently female. None of these original goddesses were "spouse" goddesses, but were divinities in their own right. Later, gods and goddesses came to be listed in "companies," with complementary male and female divinities listed together. This later pairing, which linked the fate of the female divinity with that of the male, could not, however, take away from the fact that in early times female deities operated autonomously. The fortunes of a local goddess were intimately bound up with the fortunes of her village; when the village prospered, her rank and dignity kept pace; in times of defeat, she was abused. The total number of deities was gradually reduced as deities of certain villages gained special fame and were adopted by other villages. In the later process of selection from which the "great gods" of Egypt emerged, the cards were stacked by political maneuverings of priests. By the time the god Amon-Ra had become top god, his priests had seized for him the attributes of all the other gods and goddesses (Budge, 1904). But local memories were stronger than priestly maneuvers, and reflections of earlier matrilineal orientations on the fertile-crescent pattern are found everywhere.

Priests at the major temples consolidated their power by

Figure 5-5. *King Mycerinus between Hathor and Kynopolis (Giza, Egypt).*

bringing village deities and their attendants to the "capital city"—which changed from Pharaoh to Pharaoh over the centuries. The continuance of the priestess role during this time in the face of deterioration of other aspects of women's roles can be attributed in part to the continuing power of the goddesses the women served. Neith, the great goddess of Sais, was one such powerful goddess. She was originally a local Libyan delta goddess, the uncreated source of all being. Traits belonging to Neith turn up in nearly all other goddesses, including Isis and Hathor. She was also a *theotokos,* mother of god, and produced a son by parthenogenesis. Statues of Neith-Isis-Hathor, with an infant at her breast, have been taken in the Christian era for the Christian virgin and child (figure 5-6).

During the Old Kingdom epoch, all twenty-two of the Neith priesthoods were held by women (Murray, 1908). During these centuries priestesses performed a whole range of duties, from mummifying bodies, preparing funeral papyri, and serving as mourners (figure 5-7), to maintaining temple buildings, copying manuscripts, and providing religious education for the community. Later they were only allowed to sing and dance in temple choirs. Designating a woman as high priestess in early dynastic periods meant she functioned as a high priestess. In later periods, it was a purely honorific title with no duties.

Wenig's (1970) study of women's roles in ancient Egypt as portrayed in its art points to evidence from prehistoric times of a long-existing equality of rights between women and men. Women had their own separate tombs, as well furnished as men's, from earliest times; they had their own statues and tombstones when these became part of funerary custom. Social class, not sex, determined the quality of the tombs. Queens, princesses, court ladies, wives of administrators, and wives of workers all had tombs appropriate to their rank. Later, however, by the time of the great age of pyramids, queens' tombs were dwarfed by those of the Pharaohs.

Old and Middle Kingdom references in later papyri indicate that the women had full competence and rights in law and business. A woman could

> dispose of private property, such as land, servants, and slaves, money or materials, and administrate it according to her own free and independent will. She could conclude any kind of settlement, appear as contracting partner in marriage contracts, execute testaments, free slaves, make adoptions, or officiate as a witness of records. . . . she was even entitled to sue at law . . . (Wenig, 1970: 12).

Figure 5-6. *Isis with Horus,*
c. 2040-1700 B.C.

So independent was she in marriage that she could lend her husband money and charge him a stiff rate of interest. She could exclude her own children from her inheritance if she wished.

Queens and princesses and some upper-class women knew how to write, and there are mentions of women scribes. Nevertheless, while peasant- and artisan-class women worked, upper-class women, apart from priestesses, had few public roles. What roles they did have were in a typically feminine sphere—a woman might be headmistress of the wig or weaving workshop, or of the women singers, all associated with the temple or the women's section of the palace.

We can see outlined in Egyptian history the dual status of the woman of the elite, as we shall see it again and again in later periods. Stemming from an earlier, probably matrilineal, agricultural era when she did indeed exercise full decision-making power in her village council and in the village temple, her role in the rich, highly stratified society of Pharaonic Egypt kept, at the very highest level, some of the characteristics of that earlier time. She was educated and she was honored, and her "rights" were fully elaborated—but like her Sumerian sister she was gradually removed from significant decision making and exercise of power.[12] Reflections of that earlier status for women are seen in later Egyptian society to the extent that the fairly elaborate provisions for contractual relationships found in temple records continued to be applied to all who were educated enough to make use of them. (Then as now, of course, a poor, uneducated woman such as the corngrinder in figure 5-8 would scarcely know how to make use of her "rights.") We will see in the next chapter how that basic level of elite education made possible occasional dramatic eruptions of powerful women on the public scene in Egypt.

India

India appears to have gone through a Near East-type sequence of scattered, self-sufficient agricultural villages in hill country followed by a shift to the Indus Valley and irrigated agriculture and the rise of larger, centralized towns and trading centers that dominated surrounding villages (Fairservis, 1971, chapts. 4, 5). The archae-

Figure 5-7. *Chorus of Professional Egyptian Mourners*.

ological record gives evidence of a considerable degree of social stratification in these central villages, in terms of type of housing, administrative centers, and cult buildings. There were craft specialists and priesthoods in these towns, and cultic remains of "goggle-eyed mother-goddesses." Imposing "planned cities" of thirty-five thousand to forty thousand people of the Harappan civilization flour-

Figure 5-8. *Girl Grinding Corn, 5th Dynasty (Egypt)*.

ished from 2300 to 1500 B.C. These urban centers owed at least as much to local developments as to the Sumerian traders, of whom evidence is everywhere in the major cities of this civilization (Fairservis, 1971, chapts. 6, 7). The Harappan civilization is a voiceless one, however. Apart from as yet undecipherable seal inscriptions, no system of writing appears to have developed. The huge buildings inside the walled towns could be for baths, cultic worship, food storage, or palace administration—there is no way to tell from the remains. Since there is no record of the life of the men, there is certainly none of the life of the women.

It appears to have been a static civilization, never developing beyond the very earliest stage of the comparable Sumerian cities. It slowly petered out into a succession of smaller towns whose elaborate paved stone roads, monumental buildings in a raised central area of town, and megaliths erected in various arrangements between towns belied the apparent simplicity of the subsequent way of life (Fairservis, 1971, chapt. 9).

The invading Aryans, nomads from the Asian steppes who supposedly stormed the walls of Harappa (Wheeler, in Fairservis, 1971: 310-311) and then settled down in India, gave rise to the literature of the Vedic age. It is from this epic literature that we know something about the women of India. The Vedas are variously dated as being first composed as early as 2500 B.C. or as late as 1000 B.C., but they were certainly not written down until well on in the first millennium B.C., or even later. Since this body of literature was first handed down through oral tradition, the "facts" so recorded do not have the same weight as those recorded in historical eras. On the other hand, they contain history as well as myth, and deserve at least as careful attention as the much-studied later Homeric legends.

Since the Vedas were composed after the Aryans had attacked the cities, we must suppose that the poetic tradition from which the Vedas sprang developed in these post-Harappan towns with their contradictory evidence of complex ceremonial observances and relatively simple, nonurban living. Were these towns the origins of the Panchayat tradition, the famous Indian village republics? Or does that tradition reach back to the centralized villages of pre-Harappan times? Fairservis (1971) does not mention the Panchayat, but he does speak of clan councils ruling the villages and of evidence that the pre-Harappan villages were all linked administratively to the centralized stratified villages. The Panchayat tradition may then go back to 3000 B.C., or further. A student of the tax records for the pre-British Indian villages has uncovered systematic evidence that local village councils in various regions administered themselves most of the taxes they collected, sending only 20 percent on to the rajah or king and making all kinds of disbursements to villagers for both practical and ceremonial services to the community.[13] But the British reversed the direction of flow of funds, leaving only 20 percent in local coffers, and as a consequence the picture of active village councils in the Panchayat tradition has been discounted by many contemporary scholars.

For our purposes the existence of the Panchayat tradition is important, because the women participated in it. Scholars by no means agree on women's roles in the Panchayat, but the position taken in Barbara Ward's *Women of the New Asia* (1963), of a gradual decline in women's status from Vedic times until near the end of the first millennium B.C., is the one followed here. A. S. Altekar's (1956) research on women's roles in India will be utilized in this section. (Of course, a more complete study would need to draw on many different sources.) Altekar writes:

> There were democratic assemblies in the Vedic age. The marriage hymn expresses the hope that the bride would be able to speak with composure and success in these public assemblies in her old age (1956: 190).

Later women were forbidden to attend these assemblies.

It appears that there was a very substantial deterioration in the status of women—which may have begun in the Vedic Age itself—from an earlier era of full participation in the public life of the village. The Vedas reflect this higher status. At the time of the Vedas the women of the upper strata in the towns married at the age of sixteen and apparently spent considerable time in Vedic studies before marriage:

> In prehistoric times lady poets themselves were composing hymns, some of which were destined to be included even in the Vedic samhitas. According to the orthodox tradition itself as recorded in the Sarvanukramanika, there are as many as twenty women among the "seers" or authors of Rigveda. Some of these may have been mythical personages; but internal evidence shows that Lopamudra, Visvavara, Sikata Nivavari and Ghosha, the authors of the Rigveda 1.179, V. 28, VIII. 91, IX. 81. 11-20 and X. 39 and 40 respectively, were women in flesh and blood who once lived in Hindu society (Altekar, 1956: 10).

> Women students were divided into two classes, Brahmavadinis and Sadyodvahas. The former were life-long students of theology; the

latter used to prosecute their studies until their marriage at the age of fifteen or sixteen [N.B.: this would already be in a later era]. During the eight or nine years that were thus available to them for study, they used to learn by heart the Vedic hymns prescribed for the daily and periodical prayers and for those rituals and sacraments in which they had to take an active part after their marriage. . . . when writing came into general vogue, girls were initiated into the three R's as a matter of course (1956: 11).

Women scholars who specialized in a theological work called Kasakritsni

were designated as Kasakritsnas. If lady scholars in such a technical branch of study were so numerous as to necessitate the coining of a special term to designate them, is it not reasonable to conclude that the number of women, who used to receive general education, must have been fairly large?

Education was mostly centered in the family; brothers, sisters and cousins probably studied together under the family elders (Altekar, 1956: 11).

And, finally, my favorite item of information from the Vedic age:

We find one of the early Upanishads recommending a certain ritual to a householder for ensuring the birth of a scholarly daughter. Brih. Up. IV. 4. 18 (Altekar, 1956: 3).

These paragons of scholarship were also active in a variety of occupations. They farmed, wove and dyed cloth, embroidered, and followed the teaching profession. Artisan women made weapons including bows and arrows. Lower-class women traded, though upper-class women did not. Every upper-class woman was also expected to carry out the ordinary domestic and hostessing duties and to perform the Vedic rituals side by side with her husband, if married.

Whatever the proportions of myth and history in these references, this is an interesting conception of a woman's life for 2000 B.C.! That there is something unusual in the Indian tradition will come out later when we look at Indian women warriors.

China

Not very much can be said about China in this period since the earliest archaeological evidence of town life to date comes from the Shang Dynasty in 1500 B.C. That evidence points to an already ancient culture, but apart from Neolithic villages at the stage discussed in the last chapter, nothing has been found. We can suggest one thing about the role of women in this period, however. In emerging village and town life, women must have had important shamaness roles. In later centuries there were frequent efforts to stamp out the Bronze Age shamaness tradition. It nevertheless cropped up repeatedly in historical eras in times of crisis. For example, an eighth century drought impelled a high government minister to send shamanesses out to all parts of the realm to perform religious rites. They must have been around all along or he could never have found them. His successor, an unbeliever, had the shamanesses jailed or executed (Schafer, 1967: 65). There is also a tradition that the divine legitimation of ancient legendary kings of China derived from their mating with a beautiful "raingoddess." A ritual mating of the king with a high priestess-shamaness is thought to have continued down to Chou times (Schafer, 1967). We noted this type of ritual mating of king and priestess in Sumer. This may have been a common practice in many early monarchies, giving evidence of earlier matrilineal days.

Women's Roles in Fact and Myth

It seems clear that urbanization in many ways "encloses" women. Mumford (1961) speaks of the city as the container; it contains all kinds of material possessions, and it *contains* women—but it seems to *launch* men. Social class moderates the containment. Among the elite, politically minded priestesses probably had a very interesting life, and the male workers, peasants, and soldiers probably were no freer than their spouses. Few women's voices were heard in councils of state, however. The palace complex was the terrain of the princess and the high priestess only.

The privatization of women's roles has begun. In the earlier, open-courtyard village, child care was much more of a community undertaking. Women worked in groups on a variety of tasks. For the lower classes this was still true to some extent, with urbanization, but the work was so hard that there was no margin for leisure or reflection, certainly not for more than reactive thinking about the state of the *polis.* Furthermore, the successive cramping and contraction of living space for the poor in the newly walled towns and cities cut down even further on the possibility that they might make constructive use of free hours. In a book like the *History of Urban Form* (Morris, 1974) one can trace this gradual contraction and deterioration of living space for the urban poor from prehistory to the Renaissance, and the history is a grim one.

The life of elite women was never privatized, but it was gradually delimited. The increasing militarism of society diminished their palace roles and left them with increasingly ceremonial, nonpolitical functions. Settled agricultural societies have no traditions of military training for women. Some of the nomadics were to develop this, but it scarcely affected urban societies. A whole new set of cultural prescriptions for woman as a householder was about to develop, and we will follow this in the next chapter.

At the very moment that her roles were in fact being privatized, however, myth was at work in the opposite direction, creating a public image of woman as the creator of culture to an extent beyond what had ever (in all likelihood) existed in fact. We can deal with this at two levels. At one level, these myths are what Campbell calls facts of the mind (1972: 11), a way of ordering our own inward understanding of the nature of reality. At that level, these myths tell us about a profound reverence that men have for women. They are the "praise books" consciously produced by one sex for the other. At another level, they often present an elaboration, however fantastic, of certain historical facts. The effort to ground mythic figures in real-life persons cannot simply be dismissed by labeling it euhemerism. In fact, the practice of deification of ancestors was widely practiced in all the early civilizations. It was particularly applied to queens and kings who achieved special fame in their lifetimes. So, while we know perfectly well that Juno, Ceres, Minerva, Venus, Isis, and Europa are goddesses, maybe Boccaccio was not entirely wrong when in his delightful *De Claris Mulieribus (Concerning Famous Women)* in A.D. 1359 he gave biographies of Queen Ceres of Sicily, inventor of many things associated with agriculture; of Queen Minerva of Lemnos and Cyprus, who discovered the use of oil, and invented spinning, armor, and numbers; of Queen Isis, daughter of the first king of the Argives, who fled to Egypt, civilized that country, gave it laws and an alphabet; or when he described Queen Juno as a native of Samos who married King Jupiter, Queen Venus as a native of Lemnos who married King Vulcan, and Queen Europa of Crete as the mother of King Minos.[14]

In any case, a variety of goddesses, some of whom may have been based on flesh-and-blood queens, are recorded as having done useful things for humankind in the past. They have also been considered useful in the present for things as varied as childbirth and war. Beard comments on how often the early empires transformed one of their goddesses into a war goddess:

How commonly she was so transformed may be seen in a study of that attribute of her potency which is elaborated in the first volumes of the *Cambridge Ancient History* dealing with the rise and fortunes of great historic states (1946: 287).

Diner (1965), from a less scholarly stance, points out that a female deity is also frequently associated with the administration of justice—a role which, if it ever was hers, certainly did not translate into city life:

> Demeter, Themis, Nike, Poine, Nemesis, Erinys, and Justitia are the bearers of an ancient order, never completely replaced by the later, man-made law (1965: 18).

A third realm frequently associated with the woman-goddess is, interestingly enough, the alphabet. There is a whole series of woman-as-alphabet-giver legends, and since these are less well known than those associating women with agriculture, war, and justice, I will mention a few here, culled from Graves' fantasy-rich *The White God-dess* (1966) and other sources. Colleges of women priestesses are frequently associated with these legends, as well as queens and goddesses.

Carmenta, in one version a Syballine priestess who presided over a college of maidens at a place also called Carmenta, is supposed to have created a Latin alphabet from the Greek. In another version, Carmenta is replaced by Queen Nicostrata of Arcadia, who helped found Rome. She is also known as a goddess, and sometimes as an alternate form of Minerva, the goddess of wisdom.

Medusa of the Gorgons, a beautiful Libyan warrior queen whom Perseus, King of Argives, decapitated in battle, and who was later identified with the Libyan snake-goddess Lamia, is involved in giving the alphabet to Hercules; the Gorgon thus has the typical dual role in mythology of being both helper and fiend.

Queen Isis, already mentioned as a refugee from Greece in Egypt and giver of the alphabet to the Egyptians, is in the Archbishop of Seville's version of history (A.D. 636) credited with bringing the alphabet back from Egypt to Greece.

Bloodeuwedd is another priestess with a college of maidens, identified with Athena, goddess of wisdom. Her gift of wisdom was displaced by the new order of Apollo, so her fifty maidens jumped in the lake rather than be ruled by Apollo.

Samothea, a Briton, invented letters, astronomy, and science. According to some stories she also ran the Hyperborean University in Cornwall where Pythagoras is rumored to have studied. Pythagoras is also said to have learned the ancient alphabets from priestesses at a Minoan-Cretan college. These priestesses turned the older hieroglyphics into an alphabet-syllabary. There is also the legend of a Vedic college where the priestess-goddess Kali invented the Sanskrit alphabet. The Egyptian goddess Safekh-Aabut was sometimes recorded as the source of the alphabet in Egypt, alternately with Isis, and had the role of "recording angel"; she was also in charge of literature and libraries. Sumer, too, has its legends about gifts of knowledge from women. Inanna, goddess of Erech, makes an adventurous trip to Eridu to the god of wisdom and tricks him into giving her the "100 or more divine decrees" which she brings back to Erech for her people against great odds. Nidaba is the Sumerian goddess of the alphabet and of accounts (Kramer, 1963). And the list of legends goes on.

How is one to interpret these legends? We know that women did have a hand in the development of agriculture. Did they participate, as well, in the administration of tribal justice, in a priestess or prophetess role? There is ample evidence for this, as we will see in the next chapter. Did they contribute to the development of the alphabet? The status of women in the period of the first systematic record keeping that we know of, in Sumerian temples, does not forbid such an interpretation, but neither does it support it. And while we will see a number of warrior queens, the likelihood of women having played a key role in the initial development of the martial arts is almost nil. In fact, the general shift of power away from priestess-run temples to palace and male priesthood that seems to have taken place with the rise of militarism would be enough to put the alphabet into the hands of the men, if the women indeed had "had it first." The stories of mass drownings of colleges of priestesses hint at dramatic takeovers by the men. Endless speculations are possible, but unfortunately there are few facts.[15]

The invocation of woman as patron-and/or-inventor in spheres of major human activity over the next three millennia, precisely during the era when women are becoming less visible to the public eye, is certainly interesting. If the myths are not to be taken as having specific historical import, they at least point to the significance of women as the agents of symbolic reality-construction in four major human activities: agriculture, war, peace (justice, order), and letters. While some of the myths originate as late as the first millennium B.C., the time period to which they refer lies somewhere in the third and fourth millennia, or earlier. The use of the goddess as a legitimating authority for human enterprises as late as Greek and Roman times might be considered one kind of lingering evidence of an earlier, more public, role for women.

It is interesting to contrast this line of analysis, which focuses on the analytic-cognitive contributions of women to cultural development, with the Jungian analysis, which emphasizes that women's chief contribution has been through "moon thinking," i.e., non-rational thought. Esther Harding, a gifted and articulate student of Jung, has described this kind of thinking, which relates to Sophia, or divine wisdom,

> the wisdom of that inner spark which speaks and functions of itself, quite apart from our conscious control. This wisdom was called the Divine Sophia. The Greek word sophos means wisdom and Sophia is a personification of wisdom, the Lady Wisdom or the Goddess Wisdom. She is the highest incarnation of the feminine principle, the Moon Goddess in her function of spirit, divine knowledge. . . . (1971: 232-233).

Unquestionably "moon thinking" refers to a profoundly important intuitive capacity that western rationalistic traditions have shunted to one side. It is doubtful, however, that the best way to redress the balance is to now elevate this capacity as something peculiarly feminine in the human condition. Jung and Harding use masculine and feminine in a more technical sense than does the lay person, to connote bundles of capacities that lie in each of us, but the danger is that more simplistic associations will be made. It is important to look at the full range of human capacities available to women and to men, and to note and deal with the imbalances as they appear. This, in fact, is the goal of Jungian analysis.

We stand now at the threshold of the great primary civilizations, and the process has already begun of relegating women to the minor elite and interstitial roles in the urban areas where these civilizations are arising. The earlier fluidity of roles has gone, and the status of woman as householder, with all its strengths and all its limitations, is being consolidated. The stratification of urban society has produced the middle classes, that group of men and women who belong neither to the elite with its large landed estates, nor to the workers, whose only capital is in their bodies. It is the women of these classes who experience the most restriction with urbanization, as we shall see more clearly in the next chapter. Their household sphere has been vastly restricted and they have not the freedom of movement of richer and poorer women. They struggle to protect the resources at their disposal and use the courts to this end. It is the husbands of these women who fill the middling jobs of officialdom (such as those listed in the Erech roster of 2500 B.C., noted earlier in this chapter). These men are essentially the scribal class, and they bear the full brunt of the insecurities of their in-between roles. Hoffer (1964) has written forcefully about the alienation and insecurity of the scribal class through history. The wives of the scribal class have suffered doubly, through the insecurity of their husbands, and through the far more severe constriction of their own social space.[16] This social group is tiny numerically, but looms large in terms of pent-up social dissatisfaction.

The primary civilizations with their new middle classes are only one part of the unfolding social drama, however. While life in the cities was going one way, something quite different was happening in nomadic societies, and in the nonurban forest civilizations. In the next two chapters we will look at the situation of women in both types of settings.

Appendix 5-1
Chronology of Societies,
4500 B.C. to the Christian Era

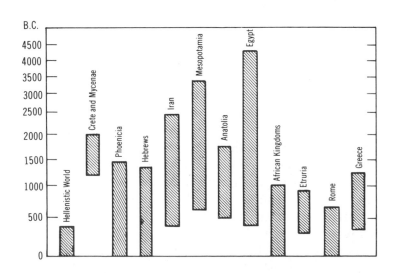

Appendix 5-2
Location of First Civilizations

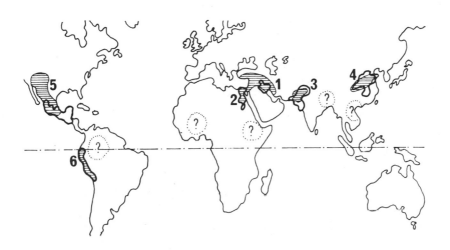

Appendix 5-2. *Location of First Civilizations (in heavy outline).*
Related to the location of the earliest known agricultural communities (the hatched areas) and other early agricultural centers. Key: 1) Southern Mesopotamia (Sumerian Civilization); 2) Nile Valley (Egyptian); 3) Indus Valley (Harappan); 4) Yellow River (Shang); 5) Mesoamerica (Aztec and Maya); 6) Peru (Inca).

Notes

[1]The first evidence in Europe, found in Sweden, is a rock painting including a plow, from about 1500 B.C. (Hawkes and Woolley, 1963: 515-516).

[2]It used to be thought that the Egyptian pyramid builders brought their skills to England. But the greatest of these monuments predate the pyramids.

[3]Kaplan, in an analysis of monument building and political systems in pre-Hispanic Mesoamerica, concludes: "We have greatly underestimated the ability of many stateless societies, particularly chiefdoms, to engage in communal production on a fairly large scale, the notion apparently being that such production requires the direction of a powerful, centralized, coercive state" (1963: 407). He also adds supporting evidence for monument building in Oceania.

[4]Or, rather, the evidence for it is very slight and highly controversial.

[5]Since the spread of the brewing of beer coincides with that of the Beaker people, it is suggested that they taught this as well as metalwork and carried their beakers with them everywhere, including to the grave, so they could always have a draught of beer handy.

[6]The only mention I have discovered of burying women with weapons is a reference in Childe to the practice of burying Siberian women with their bows (1963: 84).

[7]Wittvogels' thesis that irrigation works were the prelude to higher forms of social organization and provided a training ground in new skills has been superseded by the view that irrigation came afterward, in response to new needs (Adams, 1960).

[8]It will be noted that I am not offering a "grand theory" about the shift to patriarchy. I am rather suggesting, as in the discussion of agrovillages and matriliny in chapter 4, that a very gradual shift in the balance of power took place as a result of changing social arrangements, with the superior trade-network knowledge of the male, the process of population concentration and the attendant development of political hierarchy, and the institution of slavery as key factors in the shift.

[9]Clan organizations have in fact often served as the political infrastructure of both ancient and recent empires, most notably in China, but this could only work because interclan specialist roles were developed. This specialization came after the shift to patriarchy in China and elsewhere.

[10]Mason Hammond (1972), in *Cities of the Ancient World,* is the only writer I have come across who specifically refers to women on the town councils.

[11]At least, the evidences have never been found, though Egyptologists looking at the Sumerian sequence are beginning to wonder if there are not as yet undiscovered (or undiscoverable) town and city traces in Egypt.

[12]Exactly how much power Egyptian women had in earlier times, and how much they lost or gained through time, is a matter of dispute among scholars. An assessment of the relevant literature is not possible here, so what has been presented is the once-strong-but-now-fading-matriliny view.

[13]This is from my notes of interviews with Indian scholars in Delhi in 1970. I regret that the name of the scholar has been lost.

[14]Another practice that causes confusion for scholars is that of a famous person having the same name as the place from which she comes—a practice common in tribal societies, as noted by Colson in Fried (1967: 177).

[15]Alice and Polly Perlman (1975) have done an interesting analysis of goddesses as models of the exercise of social power, withholding interpretive comments. The classical scholar Sarah Pomeroy, in a new study of the women of antiquity, suggests that all roles assigned to goddesses in Greek and Roman mythology are "archetypal images of human females as envisioned by males" rather than reflections of any historical traces (1975: 8). I prefer not to rule out the possibility that myth is the shadow, however distorted, of ancient social structures.

[16]I am indebted to Sheila Johansson for pointing out the special constraints that wives of the scribal class would be living under in urban society. She suggests that much of the hate literature about women comes from frustrated male scribes who feared the competition of their discontented wives (personal communication, 1975).

References

Adams, Robert McCormick
  1966   The Evolution of Urban Society: Early Mesopotamia and Prehispanic Mexico. Chicago: Aldine.
  1960   Discussion, pp. 24-34 in Carl H. Kraeling and Robert M. Adams (eds.), City Invincible. Chicago: University of Chicago Press.

Altekar, A. S.
  1956   The Position of Women in Hindu Civilisation. Banaras, India: Motilal Banarsidass.

Beard, Mary R.
  1946   Women as Force in History: A Study in Traditions and Realities. New York: Macmillan.

Blumberg, Rae Lesser and Robert F. Winch
  1972   "Societal complexity and familial complexity: Evidence for the curvilinear hypothesis." American Journal of Sociology 77 (March): 898-920.

Boccaccio, Giovanni
  1963   Concerning Famous Women. Tr. by Guido A. Guarino. New Brunswick, N. J.: Rutgers University Press.

Borgese, Elisabeth Mann
  1963   Ascent of Women. London: McKibbon and Kee.

Budge, Ernest Alfred Wallis
  1904   The Gods of the Egyptians. London: Methuen.

Campbell, Joseph
  1972   Myths to Live By. New York: Viking.

Childe, Gordon
  1963   Social Evolution. New York: Meridian Press.

Claiborne, Robert
  1973   The First Americans. New York: Time-Life Books.

Diakonoff, N. M.
1959 Sumer: Society and State in Ancient Mesopotamia. Moscow: Academy of Sciences.

Diner, Helen
1965 Mothers and Amazons. Tr. by John Philip Lundin. New York: Julian Press. (First published 1932.)

Edey, Maitland
1972 The Missing Link. New York: Time-Life Books.

Fairservis, Walter A., Jr.
1971 The Roots of Ancient India: The Archaeology of Early Indian Civilization. New York: Macmillan.

Fried, Morton H.
1967 The Evolution of Political Society: An Essay in Political Anthropology. New York: Random House.

Glueck, Nelson
1960 Discussion, pp. 24-34 in Carl H. Kraeling and Robert M. Adams (eds.), City Invincible. Chicago: University of Chicago Press.

Graves, Robert
1966 White Goddess: A Historical Grammar of Poetic Myth. New York: Farrar, Straus and Giroux.

Hammond, Mason
1972 The City in the Ancient World. Cambridge, Mass.: Harvard University Press.

Harding, M. Esther
1971 Woman's Mysteries, Ancient and Modern. Revised ed. New York: Putnam.

Hauser, Philip M. and L. F. Schnore
1965 Study of Urbanization. New York: Wiley.

Hawkes, Jacquetta and Sir Leonard Woolley
1963 Prehistory and the Beginnings of Civilization. History of Mankind, vol. 1. New York: Harper and Row.

Hawkins, Gerald S., in collaboration with John B. White
1965 Stonehenge Decoded. Garden City, N. Y.: Doubleday.

Hoffer, Eric
1964 The Ordeal of Change. New York: Harper and Row.

Jacobsen, Thorkild
1960 Discussion, pp. 24-34 in Carl H. Kraeling and Robert M. Adams (eds.), City Invincible. Chicago: University of Chicago Press.

Johansson, Sheila
1975 Seattle, Wash.: Historian, personal communication.

Johnson, Gregory A.
1975 "Locational analysis and the investigation of Urok local exchange systems." Pp. 285-339 in Jeremy A. Saboloff and C. C. Lamberg-Karlovsky (eds.), Ancient Civilization and Trade. Albuquerque: University of New Mexico Press.

Kaplan, David
  1963   "Men, monuments, and political systems." Southwestern Journal of
         Anthropology 19: 397-410.

Knauth, Percy
  1974   The Metalsmiths. New York: Time-Life Books.

Kraeling, Carl H. and Robert M. Adams (eds.)
  1960   City Invincible. A Symposium on Urbanization and Cultural Develop-
         ment in the Ancient Near East held at the Oriental Institute of the Uni-
         versity of Chicago, December 4-7, 1958. Chicago: University of Chicago
         Press.

Kramer, Samuel Noah
  1963   The Sumerians: Their History, Culture, and Character. Chicago: Univer-
         sity of Chicago Press.
  1956   From the Tablets of Sumer; Twenty-five Firsts in Man's Recorded
         History. Indian Hills, Colo.: Falcon's Wing Press.

Marshack, Alexander
  1972   The Roots of Civilization. New York: McGraw-Hill.

Morris, E. J.
  1974   History of Urban Form: Prehistory to the Renaissance. New York:
         Wiley.

Mumford, Lewis
  1961   City in History: Its Origins, Its Transformations, and Its Prospects. New
         York: Harcourt Brace Jovanovich.

Murray, Margaret Alice
  1908   Priesthoods of Women in Egypt. Pp. 22-224 in vol. 1, International
         Congress of History and Religions. Oxford: Oxford University Press.

Perlman, Alice and Polly Perlman
  1975   "Women's power in the ancient world." Women's Caucus-Religious
         Studies 3 (Summer): 4-6.

Pomeroy, Sarah B.
  1975   Goddesses, Whores, Wives, and Slaves: Women in Classical Antiquity.
         New York: Schocken Books.

Schafer, Edward H. and the Editors of Time-Life Books
  1967   Ancient China. New York: Time-Life Books.

Ward, Barbara E. (ed.)
  1963   Women in the New Asia: The Changing Social Roles of Men and
         Women in South and South-East Asia. Paris: UNESCO.

Wenig, Steffan
  1970   Women in Egyptian Art. New York: McGraw-Hill.

Wernick, Robert
  1973   The Monument Builders. New York: Time-Life Books.

Part 2
Women as Civilizers

6

The Powerful
and the Powerless: Women
in Early Civilizations,
2000 to 200 B.C.

THE NEW URBANITES

In this chapter we are moving toward the historical "present." By 2000 B.C. Egypt is already old, King Sargon has created a united kingdom in Sumer, Byblos on the coast of Canaan is a great trading center, the Minoans are building the great palace of Knossos in Crete, and the nomad Sarai and her band are setting out for Palestine from the edge of Arabia. During the first few hundred years of our time span, as the new urban centers of civilization develop and expand, women are still fairly visible in each of the civilizations described. By the end of this period, the elite remain visible but the educated urban women of the middle classes find themselves hidden in cities not designed for public mingling of women and men.

That part of the world which centers on the Mediterranean was seething with political activity and trade in 2000 B.C. In the Indus Valley, the Harappan civilization, already tied into the Mediterranean trading system, was at its height. The Shang kingdom in China, however, was still five hundred years away. In all the wide spaces between the city-states, kingdoms, and empires of the Near Eastern world there was movement. Nomadic tribes moved in from the

Arabian peninsula, from the Iranian plains, and from the Asian steppes. About 2500 B.C. the herdsmen of the steppes learned to tame horses, so they moved in and out of settlements with increasing swiftness when they came to the fertile crescent. Some came to make their own settlements; others "moved in on" prosperous city-states and set up their own warrior aristocracy government, as in the case of Lagash in Sumeria; others came to plunder, and—later—discovered the benefits of trade.

The so-called Aryans—the Mitanni, the Hittites, the Scythians, the Hurrians—swarming in from between the Danube and the Don at the beginning of the second millennium,

> retained for over a thousand years a remarkable similarity of character. Whether we think of the Homeric heroes in Greece, the heroic kings in Ireland or India, or the early patricians in Rome, there appears the same pattern of warlike masculine Gods, military prowess and patriarchal government (Darlington, 1969: 141-142).[1]

They set up their own empires, of which the Hittite is the best known.

The tribal-nomadic, tribal-settled, city-state, and nation-state—usually also a conquest state—sequence is best seen in the Syriac-Palestinian region, where it evolved after Mesopotamia and Egypt were already empires. In one common pattern, the trading town grows into the city-state—a kind of territorial state where the common bond is simply shared territory. Already an ethnic mixture from centuries of trading activities and gradual absorption of incoming nomads, these towns evolve slowly from town-council government with temporary leaders to wealthy city-states with hereditary kingship, still subject to the city council of elders (who may now be called nobles). This is the Tyre and Sidon pattern. In the pattern of Israel, an ethnic nomadic group moves in and keeps its ethnic identity; as it grows in wealth and power it creates a nation-state which is not primarily territorial. We observed a similar double pattern in old Sumeria, in the contrast between the organically evolved city-state and the nomadic-conquest state. Women seem to do somewhat better in the organically evolved states.

By 1250 B.C. many of these city-states were well developed, and the Mediterranean world seemed relatively peaceful. It was true that Cretan civilizations had gone up in flames, but the Myceneans had taken over from the Cretans. The Canaanite port cities, including Tyre and Sidon, had developed into prosperous city-states with an active international trade. Egypt, Babylonia, the Hittite empire, and the Syrian city-states all had dynasties linked by political marriages: the king of Ugarit was married to an Egyptian princess; the daughter of the king of the Hittites was married to the Pharaoh Ramses II; a second daughter of the Hittite king was married to a prince of Amurru (Hawkes and Woolley, 1963). There was a great deal of visiting back and forth between these states, and they all had multilingual and multinational diplomats. International law and royal treaties secured rights for traders. For example a Hittite queen paid compensation for the sinking of a Ugarit vessel. In general there was a condition of mutual tolerance, with no rulers wanting war. Except for slaves, there was, in general, opportunity for economic and geographic mobility, and considerable security of contract. To what extent this was true for women we shall see shortly.

The year 1200 B.C. was the end of an era. By 1194 B.C. the migrations of the "Peoples of the Sea" set everybody moving again and the cozy little international club of the Mediterranean fell apart. The earlier nomadic groups were by now well settled, and suffered as much as the older peoples of the Near East in the new turmoil of movement. No one is exactly sure who the "sea peoples" were; nor is it clear who were invaders, who were only refugees from invaders, moving frantically to supposedly safer territory. It is only agreed that the sea peoples came from the north.

If there ever was a period in history when the "domino theory" of international relations applied, it was this, but unfortunately nobody knows who pushed over the first domino, or even which way they were falling. The first to be displaced by the invaders were the Anatolians: Danaans from Cilicia, Lycians, and Philistines. Here is an account of the newcomers:

> This was not an army but a congeries of peoples; some came by sea, skirting the coast; others marched overland with their womenfolk and children, traveling in heavy two-wheeled oxcarts, prepared to settle down in the conquered land; wherever they came they ravaged and burned and slew, and those that escaped the sword were enrolled in their ranks to the numbers of fighting men (Hawkes and Woolley, 1963: 394-395).

Some settled in Syria and Palestine; some, known as Etruscans, invaded Italy; others, known as Dorians, invaded Greece. Even Egypt was invaded, both by sea peoples and neighboring Libyans.

Assyria, successor to Babylon, and the Phoenician city-states survived best: Assyria by adopting the technology of the invaders, Phoenicia by buying them off. In the middle of all the turmoil, the Israelites managed to set up a kingdom for one hundred years, from 1020 to 930 B.C. At the end of the dark period the Greek city-states emerged, about 750 B.C. Two hundred years after that, Cyrus the Persian established the first "world empire." Still another two hundred years later Alexander founded another, larger, "world empire," which eventually petered out in a take-over by Rome. By this time the Mauryan empire was strong in India, and the Han in China. Olmec, Mayan, and Peruvian civilizations were developing in the new world.

This rather breathtaking romp through the history of the last two millennia before the Christian era has been necessary in order to provide the background for an analysis of women's roles. We have moved away from that simpler world of the temple-palace trading partnerships of third millennium Sumer and Egypt, a world in which traditional town councils still played a role, slavery and militarism were just beginning, and a relative social egalitarianism still prevailed. By 200 B.C. we are confronted with urban civilizations based on substantial concentrations of economic and political power, with complex diplomatic relations between centers of power, and with sharp differences between social classes. Figure 6-1 is a chronology for the societies discussed in this chapter, to help readers keep track of where we are.

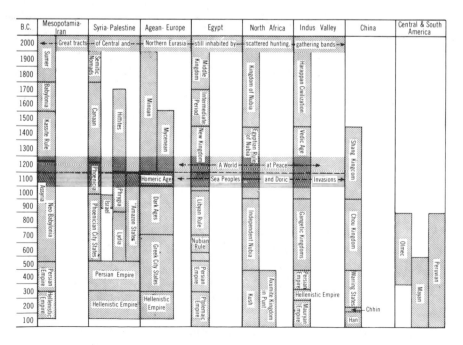

Figure 6-1. *Chronology for Societies, 2000-200 B.C.*

Urbanization, the Rise of the State, and
the New Conditions for Women

If there is something in the phenomenon "urbanism" that creates special constraints for women, it is important to understand exactly what urbanism is.

Students of early cities have given a good deal of attention to the problem of defining the concept "urban." When do we have a true city, or definitive urbanization, rather than the primordial urbanization described in the last chapter? Kluckhohn's definition is the simplest: there must be a population of at least five thousand, there must be a written language, and there must be ceremonial centers (Hauser, 1965: chapt. 14).

Conceivably some rather simple population aggregations might slip into the category "urban" under that definition, since there is no mention of diversity of population or specialization. Sjoberg (1960) adds the concepts of density of residence and the existence of a variety of nonagricultural specialists and a literate elite. Morris (1974) further adds that there must be a form of record keeping, evidence of social organization, and technical expertise. Adams includes the existence of class stratification, different degrees of ownership, and control of the sources of production; political and religious hierarchies; and a division of labor that includes craftsmen, servants, soldiers, and administrators of peasants (Morris, 1974: 7; see also Adams, 1966). Finally, Mumford would add the rise of secrecy accompanying the concentrations of power in the city along with the increasing segregation of the communication channels of temple and palace from the populace (Mumford, 1961: 64). Here we have the beginnings of the "in" network that has through the centuries excluded all but the top elite, and most women.

Women's fate in the cities lies at the intersection, one might say, of the systems of stratification and specialization. The failure of women to specialize when agricultural villages began to add new craft skills and trading activities to food production has already been discussed. As long as the society was an egalitarian one, women held their own in village and town councils. Their one major specialization, the priestess role, would help in this. Once significant differentials in control of resources emerged through the development of mining and metallurgy and associated crafts, through the expansion of accompanying trading activities, and particularly through trade in war captives, the whole situation was different for women. I have already suggested in chapter 5 that as administrative roles and centralized control over resources develop for men, the marital partnership takes on a special significance among the elite. The increased resources of the successful trader, and of the increasingly permanent warrior king-temple administrator alliance, are in some significant way shared with the spouse. In general, she receives an increasing share of the ceremonial functions, but not of the decision-making ones, so that she remains behind in a microcosm of the earlier rank society while her spouse moves ahead into the new centralized power society.[2]

Ability could lead to an extension of a woman's role, however. Thus we sometimes find queens in the Near East civilizations acting as governesses of provinces their husbands have conquered and serving as high priestesses of the major temples, essentially a papal-type role. We find other women of the royal family and of families rewarded by the king for special service similarly playing prominent roles in temple culture, in the erection of public monuments, and in the international political life of the times. The roles are nearly always second-rung roles. Only in some tribal societies, which are still essentially rank societies, and in the exceptional interregnums of empires, do we meet reigning queens who do not derive their power from the positions of their husbands.

The urbanization, or resource-centralization, of the trading town led directly to the development of the city-state in this period, so urbanization and the autonomous city-state were almost synonymous. The city-state extended wider and wider hegemony over surrounding agricultural villages, and more and more decisions about village resources and agricultural and other activities of the villagers were made in the city-state. Thus the village women, along with their spouses, lost out in decision making, while the upper strata of city women gained the ceremonial part of the power of their spouses, along with whatever else their ingenuity contrived.

It should be noted that women of the upper classes in Mesopotamia, Egypt, and India all received through private family tutors whatever education the men in the family received, and by virtue of their social position they spent some part of their time in the public arena from adolescence on. They were prepared for responsibility, and they were expected to take responsibility. When women of the royal family didn't like the way the king was handling things, they might conspire to overthrow him and put the man of their choice in power, or more rarely, seize power themselves. We shall see this phenomenon frequently in subsequent history. They were also in touch with the international scene, since some women of each royal family married kings and princes abroad. We know from Egyptian papyri that the overseas women visited and corresponded with the family back home, so the women had an excellent private communication system.

The nonroyal elite, favored with gifts of land from the king, admitted women to a share in their power to a degree worth noticing. Royal gifts of land were often administered by women. The tradition of the matron ruling the country estate while also maintaining a household in the city can be followed from Mesopotamia and Egypt in 2000 B.C. right on through Greek and Roman times, through the "age of barbarism" in Europe, through the feudal era, and up to the time of the industrial revolution. Her role was not confined to management of household consumption; she supervised agriculture, manufacturing, and the trade in estate products. She had to be as good an accountant as the average temple administrator.

What I have been describing is certainly not "equality" for women. Military action became increasingly important throughout the second millennium, and each new arms levy, each new conscription of soldiers, and each new round of booty brought home from a successful war, would enhance the power differential between women and men of the elite. The women's access to the new resources was far more limited than that of men. Power was shared, but not shared equally.

Below the level of royalty and the elite, urbanism was a very different experience. We will look at the situation of the middle classes, the skilled and unskilled working classes, and the slaves. The two groups who suffered physically the most from urbanism were 1) the unskilled workers who did the maintenance work of the city and lived in dirty, crowded quarters with inadequate food, at a standard of living far below their hunter and farmer forebears, and 2) the slaves. Suffering was not sex-linked for these folk. Among the very poor, then as now, women were neither veiled nor secluded, but worked at the same range of unskilled jobs that men did. They would be found among the construction workers, the porters and haulers, and the petty traders.

Slavery became increasingly probable for women, as for men, during this period, chiefly due to the increase in warfare and to the demand for women slaves in temples, workshops, and private homes. There were more female slaves than male, due to the frequent practice of killing male prisoners of war and taking females as booty. Slavery itself antedated wars of conquests, however. One of the earliest cargoes that moved along the trade routes was *moventia*—slaves and cattle—mainly from nomadic raiding activities. The demand for slaves was a function of economic surplus and unused resources. Male slaves were particularly useful in mines, and wherever there were large-scale construction enterprises, they could also be useful. Women could increase craft productivity. Slave women and men also worked together on a variety of maintenance tasks, as we can see from Nippur tablets showing both sexes at work together.

In ancient empires, the slave status was a highly fluid one. Today's princess could be tomorrow's slave. Skilled and highborn women were often given work commensurate with their background, though by no means always. In general, the woman slave was expected to render sexual services, whatever her other duties were, which made her situation different, though not necessarily harder, than that of the male slave. There would be an enormous difference between the living conditions of a woman who sold herself or her daughter into slavery through sheer destitution and those of the ex-princess. The term *slave woman* therefore cannot be considered to refer to any one simple status. Furthermore, every society stipulated certain conditions under which slaves could buy or be given their freedom. They frequently earned wages and could marry. Slavery was not, per se, associated with ethnic or racial characteristics.

The skilled free workers represented a class above the slaves and the unskilled workers. In this artisan class the women often contributed craft skills to the production process in the domestic workshops, side by side with their spouses, or in the government workshops. We rarely read about this early form of craft-guild activity for women, but we see pictures of such women in antiquity plying skilled trades at home and abroad. These women would share the freedom of movement of the women of the unskilled classes, but also probably the social limitations of that class. Schools were becoming increasingly widespread in the cities of the Mediterranean toward the end of the last millennium B.C., but the children of the artisan class, particularly girl children, would not be free to attend them.

The class for which status differentials for women and men showed up most sharply in the city of 2000 B.C. is precisely the class where they show up the most sharply today: at the level of the petty merchants, scribes, and lower-level administrators—the Near East equivalent of the middle class. It was the women of these groups whose lives were privatized by urbanism. The boys of this class were sent to the new city schools, but the girls were not. Neither were there family tutors to prepare the girls at home for public roles, or landed estates outside the city for the women to administer. These women did not need to go out to work, as poorer women did.

The challenge of administering a shrinking household enterprise, hemmed in by high walls and cut off from public spaces, first came to middle-class city women about this time. Mesopotamia, like any modern city, had bakeries and restaurants and sold cloth and every type of domestic article. The women no longer *needed* to bake or weave or sew (Morris, 1974). It is hard to evoke an image of these women in 2000 B.C., in their own homes. To what extent did they continue with their domestic craftwork? References to women baking and weaving at home in urban settings continue for many more centuries. Then who purchased the ready-made products available in shops? Possibly the bakeries, inns, and cloth shops were primarily for the working poor, who had no time for their own domestic work.3 But even if middle-class women wove and baked at home, their work load would be much lighter than that of working-class women. Information we have about family size (de Mause, 1974: 25) indicates that families were small and more than two children was a rarity. The average middle-class housewife also would have several slaves to help her with domestic work. Supervising and teaching slaves seems to have been an important activity for these women (Xenophon, in O'Faolain and Martines, 1973: 21-23).

One area of expanded activity that can be imagined is the rearing of the children, however few in number. I have already suggested that with urbanization women spend more time with children. The preparation of little boys for the increasingly complex life outside the home would inevitably fall in part to the mother, since boys spent much time in the women's quarters at least until ten years of age.4 Possibly Mediterranean women of 500 B.C., by the time elementary schools were common, got some of their learning through rehearsing their sons in their lessons, just as Japanese women have done in the twentieth century (Boulding, 1966). One way or another, they surely knew more about the world outside the *gynaeceum* than custom acknowledged. These years of mother-child interaction would foster a new concept of motherhood as an important role involving more than physical care for the child. In an imagined dialogue with his wife, Isomachus, as described by Xenophon, speaks of having chosen her to help make a home and raise children:

> Now, if God sends us children, we shall think about how best to raise them, for we share an interest in securing the best allies and support for our old age (O'Faolain and Martines, 1973: 21).

It would be impossible for little girls not to benefit from the increased amount of guidance given to little boys, since they shared the same domestic space. Also, the more elaborated the concepts of wife and motherhood became, the more teaching the girls themselves would receive. Sometimes there were educated slaves in the home who could supplement the education given by parents and school. Thus we find the phenomenon of increased literacy among women even though few of them were attending schools.

One of the interesting external evidences for the increasing standards of care given by mothers to children is found in the gradual development of attitudes condemning infanticide and the sexual and physical abuse of children, phenomena apparently widespread in all urban societies of these millennia. The public evidence for the change in attitude does not come until Roman times (de Mause, 1974: 42), but the beginnings of this shift are surely found in the new sets of shared experiences for mothers and children in the home spaces of increasingly self-aware societies. The double potential of those home spaces will be traced up to the twentieth century. On the one hand, to the extent that women were able to make creative use of their household resources and those spaces in the city that remained open to them (for example, cult associations), they were providing an enriched environment and education for young children. On the other hand, to the extent that women felt frustrated and cut off from society, they relieved their tensions by inflicting physical as well as psychological abuse on children. The latter situation could produce the power struggle described by Slater in *The Glory of Hera* (1968).

In any case, the fraction of the population represented by these middle-class mothers was very small indeed. Ninety-five to 98 percent of the total population was agrarian. Of the 5 percent or less of women living in the cities, by far the largest number were working women and slaves. So less than 1 percent of the women could potentially experience the frustration of confinement of the middle-class housewife. Yet one may fantasy a historical continuity from 2000 B.C. to the present, and see the frustrated urban middle-class housewife generating periodic protest movements. Like her nineteenth and twentieth century counterparts she dressed well, wore jewelry, went to shows, and was often bored. The tending of the sacred domestic hearth, which Fustel de Coulanges makes so much of in his *Ancient City* (1956), comes well after 1000 B.C., and it comes in Greece. There were no sacred hearths to tend in the homes of the Near East. Attending temple rituals in the local shrines and temples distributed throughout the urban quarters for the householders' use was in the early days of cities the only "club life" and entertainment a housewife could find (Mumford, 1961: 74).

Freedom of movement even for middle-class women varied considerably from one region and epoch to another, so the generalizations made previously must be modified. Two thousand B.C. was very different from 200 B.C., and even in 200 B.C. the situation for women in the cities of the Near East differed from that in the Greek city-states, which in turn differed among city-states. Some degree of confinement was common to all. It is one of the penalties of trying to write a macrohistory that one must frequently collapse time and space in order to draw the larger picture. As much as possible, I will try to draw attention to the differences among states in regard to the status of women.

Did the middle-class women of the second millennium develop an underlife, as I have suggested would happen in the absence of public roles? They did, and it was related to the various types of religious forms, associations, and cults developing in the urban areas from the late second millennium on. These associations were essentially of two types, the secret societies and the mystery religious cults. Secret societies form around needs which are not being met by existing religious or secular institutions; Wach (1944) calls them an undeveloped form of a specifically urban form of association. They do play a special role in adaptation to urban life. We know the early urban form best from Greece, where the *orgeones* were associations of individuals devoted to a cult of special deities, and the *thiasos* were clan associations to further common clan interests in the city. A third type of association includes many special-purpose variants of 1) the craft and professional type of association, under the protection of a special deity, and 2) mutual aid societies to assist members with births, marriages, and deaths. These latter would be of special importance to women, who always have some responsibility for arranging the marriages of the next generation, as well as the funerals of all family members. Some of the craft associations were for men only, some for families, and some for women only. Some probably had secret women's branches. These associations had the double function of dealing with problems of relationship on a new scale in the urban setting and of giving expression to creative new insights in the religious domain that went beyond traditional experience. They therefore made a logical vehicle for women's participation in the new dimensions of social existence the city brought into being.

We know very little about women's participation in the secret societies, but we know that they participated actively in the mystery religion cults. It was a common complaint of the Greek husband that his wife was off at the temple, engaged in mysterious cultic activities. Since in some cities that was practically the *only* place a middle-class

Greek housewife was supposed to be, outside of the women's quarters in her own home, we can imagine she made the most of it. The mystery religion performs many of the functions of a secret society. It is found only in complex societies and represents more advanced concepts and doctrine, more elaborate ritual, and a stronger bond of solidarity between group members than were found in earlier cults. It invariably springs up in societies whose traditional religious base is weakening, and frequently fulfills important political or economic functions. It also, however, represents an upwelling of religious impulses, of intuitions and understandings, that are reaching toward a new synthesis of the forces and counterforces experienced in the crosscurrents of the city of antiquity. The Eleusinian, Sibylline, and Mithraic cults originated in Asia Minor and Persia, and the Orphic probably in Greece itself. The full flowering of these cults came in Greece, Alexandrian Egypt, and Rome, toward the end of the period covered in this chapter.

Perhaps the real significance for women of the mystery cults, as of the world religions, is that the cults provided them with a powerful lever for wrenching themselves loose from exclusively household-centered ties. The cultic identity, like the identities provided by the world religions that followed, crosscut all other identities of sex, kin, and social class. The cult setting was the only one in which a woman could experience her full humanness. That cultic experiences could become pathological in no way detracts from the validity of this universalizing function. Cults also provided for some minimal amount of fluidity of role structure in an otherwise rigid society.

In general, role fluidity was reduced for women in the city. What fluidity remained, outside the cultic settings, was chiefly for the elite. The poor woman experienced the rigidity of poverty as did the poor man. The middle-class woman experienced the role rigidity consequent on the shrinking of the household productive enterprise and separation from economic and civic activities outside the home. The elite woman experienced the role rigidity related to almost total exclusion from military leadership. The relative contributions to the plight of the female of militarism and of her own failure to specialize during the transitional era between the agrovillage and the city are difficult to assess.

We will turn now to an examination of the actual situation of women in each of the major civilizations of the two-millennia period.

Mesopotamia

Peaceful Sumeria, culturally ambitious Babylonia, and militaristic Assyria succeed one another in the same general territory throughout these two millennia. The clay tablets from Sumer are philosophical and reflective; from Babylonia come ornamental stelae recounting the building of great monuments; from Assyria stele upon massive stele records bloody victories. How did women function in this era of unfolding disaster? They began peacefully, and with self-assurance, in the earlier Sumerian tradition of extensive temple activity by women.

Although the temple is often woman's only public space and political platform, this does not mean that outward temple activities are not also reflective of that process of profound inner ordering of perceptions of self and cosmos that we first observed in the caves of Paleolithic Europe. The more complex the social universe becomes, the more urgent is that ordering process. To do justice to that inner ordering would take a different kind of book than the present one, so an examination of the belief structure of ancient religions will not be included here.

Bearing in mind the range of meanings of temple activity, let us now examine the activity of Mesopotamian priestesses. An important part of that activity involved performing ceremonial music for special public occasions:

> There was elaborate music by women, under the direction of the queen and princesses as priestesses. Queen Shu-bad of Ur made music on harp and tambourine with her ladies in waiting or with professional musicians. . . . the word nartu, meaning "chanter," is feminine. . . . Lipushiau, the granddaughter of King Naram-Sin, was appointed player of the balag-di drum in the moon god's temple at Ur. . . . We can fancy this girl of 2380 BC drumming and making incantations to hasten the rebirth of the moons and then dancing and singing with her companions in the palace. . . . In Ishtar's temple at Erech, troops of dancing priestesses chanted their laments in a dialect used only when a female deity was supposed to be reciting (Drinker, 1948: 81).

Sargon's daughter, Princess Enheduanna, was high priestess of the moon god in the 2200s B.C., and a person of considerable consequence in her time. Her famous poem, "Exaltation of Inanna," has survived the millennia. Under her leadership, temple activities must have been lively indeed.

It should be remembered that there was a continuous influx of nomadic warrior elites into Mesopotamian ruling structures. Sometimes it was peaceful, sometimes it was violent. The process by which this happened will be discussed in more detail in the next chapter. The presence of new nomadic traditions of the participation of women in the old courts of Mesopotamia is sometimes important in explaining

Figure 6-2. *Goddess Ishtar Receiving an Offering, 18th Century B.C.*

how a few individual women played very outstanding roles when most women were lost to view. King Sargon and his daughter Enheduanna were from such a formerly nomadic aristocracy.[5]

Some of the ex-nomadic women played innovative roles in their adopted society. The high priestess Nina may have been one of these: she seems to have been an important counselor to King Gudea, Sargon's successor. We find her interpreting to him the meaning of his dream about a temple in a time of drought. He is to build a temple, Nina tells him: here is how he is to build it, and this is where he is to order materials from. Specifics follow. Presumably she draws the plans and supervises the erection of the temple. Later we run into a reference to schools for girls (for nuns?) beginning with a palace school in 1800 B.C., a private house in Ur in 1780 B.C., and a temple school which operates continuously from 1400 to 539 B.C. It was presumably within these schools that the Eme-sal literary language, spoken by women to women, developed (Diner, 1965). We infer from these references that women of the elite were well educated and produced literature, and that the talented ones participated in the major building programs of the Babylonian era. See figure 6-3 for reproductions of aristocratic Assyrian women in their headdresses. They suggest very self-assured women indeed. (Note how similar the goddess in figure 6-4 is to the women in figure 6-3.)

It is very possible that the sibyl role developed out of a combina-

Figure 6-3. *Assyrian Women in Headdresses, 3000-2500 B.C.*

tion of the Sumerian women's temple culture and the influx of prophetesses from settlements of earlier nomadic elites. The role of the prophetess exists in all nomadic societies and in many settled societies. In the millennia we are now examining, there were prophetesses in Arabia and among the early Israelites. The Sibyl was a semilegendary seeress of unknown antiquity who gave her name to a whole tradition of prophecy and triggered a major intellectual tradition set in a religious context. Sibyls were at the height of their political power in the eighth to sixth centuries B.C., especially in the Greek colonies of Asia Minor, but there are persistent references to earlier Iranian origins. All the evidence points to a well-established communication network between sibyls at different locations. The development of a trained sisterhood across Asia Minor could best have been done out of Mesopotamia. Nomadic sibyls may somehow have connected with the city sisterhoods, or with rebel members of the city sisterhoods who were looking for alternate power bases. This is sheer speculation, but the role of the sibyls as international figures advising kings and emperors at a time when few women were publicly visible invites some speculation.

Not only did the sibyls give rise to a new social role and tradition, but to a whole literature and system of interpreting history: the sibylline books. Sibyls and sibylline books continued to thrive right through the Middle Ages in Christian

Figure 6-4. *Water-dispensing Goddess from Mari, c. 2040-1870 B.C.*

Europe (Hennecke, 1963). In addition to the public political rule of sibyls, many sibylline mystery cults developed. I have already mentioned how these cults, along with the Eleusinian mysteries that originated in the Aegean, contributed to the underlife for women of urban Greek, Roman, and early Christian society.

I hope I have adequately indicated that the priestess role was a versatile one in Mesopotamia. Some strange things are written about priestesses, and they are often lumped together with temple prostitutes. The twentieth century eye has difficulty in appreciating a complex temple hierarchy of women. In the Mesopotamian temple system there apparently were a high priestess and associated priestesses of elevated rank who only married under certain conditions; there was a second rank of virgin priestesses, the Naditu, and several ranks of women performing special services. One of these services was "temple prostitution." In Babylonia, as in Egypt and Phoenicia, the concept of rendering sexual services on a public basis evidently first developed in connection with temples, and intercourse with temple women was considered an act of worship. All fees for such services took the form of offerings to the temples (Henriques, 1962). The women who provided the services were often of the middle and upper classes. Prostitution as a secular service came later. Below the rank of the special-service women was an intermediate service and maintenance class, and finally, the temple slaves. Slavery, like prostitution, was strongly linked with temple service in its earliest forms. There appeared to be room for women from all strata of society in the temple complex.

Women of the upper classes who were not involved in temple-related occupations continued to administer landed estates and were also involved in trade, as we may infer from the number of references to women's contractual rights in the Code of Hammurabi. Generalizations about women being the "property" of men—husbands or fathers—come from literal interpretations of the sections in law codes on marriage and family, with no attention to actual practice or to special stipulations. A description of the life of women in any society today, from tribal to industrial, based exclusively on a reading of law codes, would be most misleading.

According to the legal stipulations of many societies, it appears that a woman must always be under the rule of a father, husband, son, or other male relative. But in fact, property rights of women under special circumstances are nearly always provided for in law. There are two reasons for this flexibility. First, no law can prescribe the personalities and abilities of women and men. If in an individual family the wife has an abundance of talent for the work required by the family enterprise, and the husband does not, then the wife is very likely to be the *de facto* manager of the family business. Second, no law can provide for all the exigencies of family life. There are many circumstances, including widowhood, which leave women with substantial properties to administer and no appropriate male available to assist her. We will see ample evidence in the chapters to come of women taking care of their own households and estates without male assistance.

In the case of Sumerian law, it has been suggested that the items recorded in Hammurabic Code were in fact alterations of previous customary practice. According to this view, provisions that remained unchanged were not repeated. This is one possible explanation for the fact that many areas of customary law are not included in the code. The likelihood has already been mentioned that earlier rights of women to property, and older descent and marriage rules, were abrogated through the creation of the new code. This cannot be documented in the case of the Hammurabic Code, but it can be studied by comparing the Hammurabic provisions with the new provisions of the Middle Assyrian Laws, dated between 1450 and 1250 B.C. The Middle Assyrian Laws are not a code, but a miscellaneous assortment of laws in the character of amendments, nearly all referring to women, on the subject of property rights and offenses to and by women (Driver and Mills, 1935:12). I have not been able to discover a definitive comparison of the Hammurabic and Middle Assyrian laws, but it appears that the second set represented a further limitation on the rights of women.

In general, it appears that women had less personal and sexual freedom than men did, once privatized family life began in the stratified urban societies. Both law and practice confirm a growing double standard from this point on through history, again applied chiefly in strata above the semiskilled working class. Limitations on property holding for women were perhaps due to a combination of the acquired patriarchal pride in the capacity of men to fertilize women and the need for a conflict-resolution device for keeping estates intact. The tendency to treat women as a private fertility bank was kept in check, however, by the institution of the dowry, and women made the utmost use of the courts to protect their access to this dowry—often their only capital.[6]

An area as confusing to the modern reader as the temple hierarchy of women is the palace hierarchy of wives. It is difficult from the records to make operational distinctions about different kinds of wifely status. There were wives who were queens and corulers; wives who were queens and ceremonial figures, but not coregnant; wives who were uncrowned "chief wives" in a cohort of wives; wives who were secondary wives, but with recognized status and privileges; women who were concubines chosen for their beauty, but had no special court status; women who were chosen from the concubine group to enjoy special consort status; and other classes of concubines with differential status and privileges within that minicourt, the harem. Furthermore, there was a certain amount of social mobility in these systems, and wives could move up or down the wife-status ladder.

In an international system of negotiation and alliance by marriage, every important king would have a number of wives, and it would be perfectly clear to everyone at court at any given time what the status and function of each wife above a certain rank was, what particular regional diplomacy she had responsibility for, etc. These marriages would not necessarily be sexual alliances, though they usually were, and the resulting offspring were a part of the international alliance system. Historians often distinguish only between queens and concubines, whereas the real significance of royal marriages lies in the large band of secondary wives, each one brought to court in relation to a specific diplomatic need. These are not called queens except in the case of a very important alliance (or, sometimes, in the case of a love match). Many Babylonian and Assyrian women, and women of surrounding kingdoms all the way to Egypt, entered active court life with well-defined roles within the marriage-alliance system during the era we are describing. They are mentioned so infrequently, however, that it is impossible to describe their activities except through extensive analysis of the papyri exchanged between kingdoms—a task that could only be undertaken by appropriately trained specialists. Egyptian papyri are the richest source for this kind of information.

In addition to court life, temple-related occupations, estate management, and trade, women ran taverns and inns. Houses for sexual services came later in the period, and are associated, Henriques (1962) suggests, with the availability of an increased number of women slaves for use outside the temple-palace complex. Managing houses for sexual services became increasingly profitable for women as cities grew larger, and has remained a lucrative business for women with few means and much ingenuity right up to the twentieth century.[7] Another group of women comprised the professional class: physicians, scribes, musicians, midwives, and healers. Some were associated with the temples, but some were probably independent.

Working-class women and slaves labored in the large textile and craft workshops producing cloth and other materials for export. Such workshops might belong to the palace, a temple, or to a private merchant family. Slaves were also everywhere as domestic servants and sometimes as traders for their masters and mistresses.

While there were no open-space marketplaces in the old cities of Mesopotamia, there were plenty of niches in the narrow alleys of the bazaars. It was here that poor women could earn their pennies as vendors of local products. There were also women—from wealthy families—engaged in the international trade of the times. Babylonia had a premarket economy, utilizing a network of trading posts located on the rivers in port towns, controlled by the temple-palace system. Polanyi calls this "no-risk" administrative trading. Risks there must have been, however, and individual families must have had their own way of figuring profit and loss (Polanyi et al., 1957). Women merchants appear in temple and palace records just often enough throughout this era in the Mediterranean to suggest that there were a number of them. Widowhood has always been a standard route by which women become independent merchants, and many of these women traders may have been widows.

The first Assyrian records begin in 1300 B.C., introducing a long story of slaughter. Shalmaneser I describes how he dealt with the Hittites: he took 14,400 captives, captured nine strongholds and a capital city, leveled 180 cities, and slaughtered all the armies of the Hittites, and their allies the Aramaeans. The *cult of frightfulness,* as historians call it, had begun. Often entire armies and town populations were chopped to pieces so that "the rivers and fields ran red with blood." Conquered peoples who were not slaughtered were systematically resettled in other towns, so that all of Mesopotamia became one vast ethnic mixture. Every conquered town that was not razed to the ground was assimilated into the central Assyrian government administrative system. Power was concentrated in the Assyrian capital as never before in history.

What happened to ordinary women during the cult of frightfulness? There is a long period when there is no mention of women in the histories which are my source. Some women were probably wiped out in the general slaughter. Those who were not killed or deported were probably either enslaved or married to soldier citizens of other towns (figure 6-5). Rarely would families survive intact in the regions of military activity. Military activity, however, was not everywhere, so probably the vast majority of women survived this era as men did, keeping a low profile, paying tribute, and farming or trading as best they could. Since in war-scarred regions most women

Figure 6-5. *Captive Women and Animals Being Led
Away by Assyrian Soldiers, c. 858-824 B.C.*

were left without men, those who escaped the fate of capture and
forced marriage would have been a tough and hardy lot. The wiping
out of the males could happen to both settled agricultural and
nomad groups. It is from this period that we begin to get the tales of
the Amazon bands and kingdoms. Amazons were women from nomadic bands whose men were exterminated, or widowed women
whose towns were burned and who became nomads to survive. The
latter would have learned to defend themselves with weapons previously used chiefly by men. We will discuss these bands of women
later, only taking note now of the setting in which they arose.

The women of the ruling elite fared much better; as members of
the new aristocracy, they, too, had access to the resources that accrued to the increasingly powerful temple-palace-army coalition.
Among men, there was considerable mobility in the post-1300 B.C.
era, as the demand for military genius catapulted ex-slave soldiers
into generalships and sometimes led to one of them being crowned
king, to start a new dynasty. Whether there was a comparable mobility for women we do not know, but it is less likely. The court ladies
probably married the climbers and "civilized" them. Occasionally a
slave girl would become a queen.

One unusual note is sounded in this era of increasing militarism.
During the rule of the Kassites, former nomads who rapidly became
acculturated and who revered the older Sumerian ways, there was a revival in Nippur of an ancient Sumerian tradition of bringing singers

and scribes together for common training. This was in about 1200 B.C. The texts prepared by scribes were traditionally intended for chanting or singing by the Nardu, the professional women chanters mentioned earlier, but the training for writing and for chanting had gotten separated. The Kassites had ties with matrilineal nomadic tribes of the Arabian desert that sometimes had queens. The Kassites also arranged for Arabian princesses to attend the newly revived school for scribes and singers.

In the next century many from the military class of the desert-dwelling Chaldeans entered the Assyrian military service as a kind of state corps, but they kept their desert ties active. This linking with the Arabian desert may have provided some persistent source of matrilineal influence through the succeeding militaristic eras.

The first outstanding Assyrian woman to emerge from centuries of bloody warfare is Queen Sammuramat (late ninth, early eighth century B.C.), who in the legend-making tradition became Semiramis, daughter of a goddess. Queen Sammuramat was the wife of one king and mother of another. A powerful queen while her husband reigned, she vastly extended that power after his death. Memorial stelae and inscriptions testify to her accomplishments and influences, both in monument building and civic and military affairs. There are perhaps more legends about her, says Rogers (1915: 254-258), than about any other figure in Assyrian history. Consistent with the theory of close contact between matrilineal warrior elites from the Arabian desert and the Assyrian rulers (Klimberg, 1949), she is supposed to have led troops in battle.

In the 730s B.C. we find the energetic Tiglath Pileser IV encountering two queens of Arabian tribes in succession as he pushes southward into the Arabian desert. Were the old friendly alliances of the 1200s forgotten? Neither Queen Zabibi nor Queen Samsi was inclined to bend the knee to the Assyrians, and they both seem to have led their troops in battle themselves. Zabibi agreed to pay tribute, Samsi refused—and got away with it. Given the character of the times, this says a lot for the mettle of Arabian queens. They already had a long tradition of autonomy behind them. For whom in Assyria were they role models, I wonder? Perhaps for Queen Naqi'a, also a semilegendary figure sometimes called Nitocris. She was wife of Sennacherib, the able but ruthless king who applied the "final solution" to Babylon by diverting the river Euphrates through it, a simple way to wipe out a population. Naqi'a seems to have been independent-minded, for when her son Esarhaddon became ruler of Assyria, she took leadership in the rebuilding of the flooded

Babylon—a most exemplary task of reconstruction. This same son Esarhaddon befriended the very Arabian tribes Sennacherib had fought, and they became his military allies. He seems to have negotiated for an Assyrian princess to marry into an Arabian tribe as co-ruler, not simply queen consort. How much of a "sisterhood" alliance there was between women of Assyria and women of Arabia is not clear, but it does seem that the Arabian queens had some continuing influence in the land of two rivers for a long time.

Indo-European migrations from the north pressed long and hard on Assyrian borders, and finally Assyria fell in a squeeze play of Medes and Persians. The result was the first world empire. The apparently sudden emergence of obscure tribes of Medes and Persians to establish a world empire is not as remarkable as it appears. It in fact provides a brief case study in advance of the interactions of nomads and settled peoples to be examined in the next chapter. Parsua and Mada were two mountain valleys north of Assyria inhabited in the 800s B.C. by nomadic tribes of horsemen who already had a highly stratified society and were growing rich by raiding Assyria. By the 500s these nomads had become more settled people, but they were still living on their high mountain plateau away from the "softening" influence of the cities of the plains. Cyrus, an ambitious young vassal king of a tribe in the Persian federation, managed to unite under his rule one set of tribes after another—some by conquest, some by alliance. Finally, weak Assyria and Babylonia were absorbed into the new Persian empire, now known as the Achaemenid empire. The fresh nomadic blood of the warrior aristocracy of Cyrus's little kingdom became the new ruling elite.

The women of the warrior elite immediately began to play a major role in the development of the Achaemenid empire. There are frequent references in the history of this period to Atossa, who was the wife of a satrap of Cyrus and was known to promote Zoroastrianism as the state religion of the new empire. Atossa was also the mother of Cyrus's successor, Darius. King Cyrus himself was killed on the battlefield by a woman, Queen Tomyris of the neighboring Massegetai—a people also not far removed from nomadism. Another queen, Artemisia of Halicarnassus, later fought *for* the Persians under Xerxes in the famous battle of Salamis. A series of savage and not so savage queens intervened again and again in the succession of the Persian empire: Queen Pheretime of Cyrene; the queen mother Amnestris, wife of Xerxes; and many others, all duly recorded in Persian annals.

The significance of the Achaemenid empire for our purposes is that it signaled the end of a series of assimilations of peoples, the peoples of the Babylonian and Assyrian kingdoms. The great days of these states were now over, and their women and men settled down in what niches they could find in an entirely new world. To summarize the role of Mesopotamian women when these kingdoms were at their height, one might say that Sammuramat and Naqi'a are notable exemplars of the capacity of women to take leadership in one of the most intensely militaristic societies known to date.

Some of the leading women of the period came from nomadic tribes that had traditions of women rulers, but there were others, whose origins, unfortunately, we can rarely trace. Since only military conquests are recorded, we know nothing of the roles, constructive or otherwise, of the other thousands of elite women of that society. The peasants and the urban poor survived as much as they had done in the pre-1300 B.C. era, with women assuming a greater variety of production roles due to war-induced manpower shortages. How the middle-class women traders fared we have no idea. They would have had to be tough to survive. By the end of this period there would be an enormous increase in the number of slaves in the cities, and every household would have slave attendants. The gradual change in the character of households as slaves became important to the domestic economy would be interesting to trace, but we have no data on the slave-mistress relationship within families before Hellenic times.

In general, this would appear to have been an era of prolonged and slow constriction of social spaces and role opportunities for women. A few women must have survived in public roles in temple and palace enclaves, since we read of the school for priestesses, from 555 to 539 B.C., at the Nin-gal temple at Ur under the priestess Bel-shalti-Nannar, daughter of a king, and it is mentioned that this is a continuation of a school located in the same building since 1400 B.C. Revival of earlier educational practices for Assyrian women and Arabian princesses, and the continuation of a school for women through the holocausts of 1300 to 600 B.C., suggest the durability of well-institutionalized roles and services through rapidly changing times—and the durability of women. These are enclaves, at the most, however. In the public sphere leadership roles, whether in temple or palace or marketplace or battlefield, went to the men who had risen through the military hierarchies of the preceding centuries.

Egypt

While Sumerian women suffered a two-thousand-year attrition of status and role opportunities, Egyptian women held their own to a far greater degree during the same time period. They were not exactly ruling matriarchs, but they did continue to be visible in a wider range of economic, religious, and social roles in Egypt than in any of the other pristine civilizations. Why? We have already noted that goddesses were more firmly entrenched in ancient village Egypt than in the Near East, and also that urbanization never developed in Egypt to the extent that it developed elsewhere. Moving the capital city was a favorite game of the Pharaohs, and kept any one city from accumulating records and power past a given dynasty. Few of the names of Egyptian capitals sound any echoes in the historical record: Hieraconpolis, Thebes, and Memphis we recognize, but not Ith-Taui, Tell el-Amarna, Tanis, or Avaris, the desert capital of the Hyksos rulers. In one sense the mobility of the capital strengthened the position of the Pharaoh, giving him highly privatized personal power that went where he and his divine-consort-sister went. It also left local temple administrators with a freer hand, throughout Egypt. When these administrators were women it gave them a firm grasp on local resources. Another curious fact is that extended family groupings apparently did not develop in Egypt as in Mesopotamian and Indo-European cultures. There are no Egyptian terms for aunt-uncle, only for mother-father, wife-husband, sister-brother, daughter-son. Each household thus became a new household, and there were no Engelian Great Family Communities around which to build power centers (Mumford, 1961: 139). In that context, the practice of sister-brother marriages to keep lines of descent clear becomes more understandable.

Women continued in the same range of roles mentioned in the last chapter, but with an intensification of political activity. While most of this activity was beneath the surface and does not appear in historical documents, from time to time an unusually forceful queen initiated activities which gave new life and energy to the "women's society" at court. The consequences were felt through several generations of women as the role-model effect worked itself out. One of the first women we read about is Tausert, who, as regent queen and mother of Pepi II, ruled under her own name as a Pharaoh in the twenty-third century B.C. She was a "foreigner" and there was much unrest during this century. Palace revolts, revolutions, and throwing out invaders were among the activities that palace women engaged in. We do not know whether palace women were responsible for opening up secret archives to the public in the popular uprising that took place in the period in which Tausert lived, when

> the lower orders had broken into the [temple] precincts ... and captured knowledge that had been withheld from them (Mumford, 1961:100).

We know that palace women did make alliances with the populace and foment revolution in later times.

One of the most interesting periods of women's activity is between 1600 and 1200 B.C. Queen Ahotep, heroine of the liberation movement that threw the occupying Hyksos rulers (ex-Palestinian nomads) out of Egypt between 1580 and 1510 B.C., was herself already a second-generation revolutionary. Her mother, Queen Tetisheri, was the ancestress of a new dynasty and the harbinger of a new age of individualism in the Nile country. Queen Ahotep, the first to be named divine consort in the new-style religious tradition, had entered with her two sisters, Merit-Amon and Sat-Kamose, into a wife-trio relationship with Amenhotep. It was as a member of the wife-trio that she laid the groundwork for throwing out the Hyksos. This was actually accomplished by the daughter of the next generation, Thothmes, with her spouse Amose. The fourth generation in this succession of political dynamite was the famous Hatshepsut (see figure 6-6), the woman who ruled as Pharaoh for twenty years while she kept her power-hungry son-in-law waiting in the wings for his turn. She gave Egypt a rest from military activity and engaged in large-scale works of domestic reconstruction. The angry son-in-law, Tuthmosis III, effectively curbed female power when he got to the throne. He stopped all reconstruction work and turned the country back to military activity. The same power sequence occurred again a hundred years later, though not so dramatically. It started with the Cinderella-queen Tiy, the homely, brilliant commoner who married Amenhotep III and affected two generations of politics after her time, and it continued in the reform activities of her daughter-in-law, the beautiful Queen Nefertiti.

This is the same period in which the Mediterranean marriage-alliance system was at its height. Court women were well informed about international affairs. In order to understand women's roles in this alliance system one must have an adequate picture of the court, the "harem," and marriage practices. It is unfortunate that the term *harem* is generally used to describe any type of arrange-

Figure 6-6. *Hatshepsut (Thebes).*

ment associated with the polygamy of aristocrats. The word comes from the Arabic for sanctuary, holy place, and refers in later Eastern traditions to the women's part of the house. It has no necessary connection with polygamy (Penzer, 1935: 15). Whatever the Egyptians called their women's court, it was certainly not by a word belonging to another and later culture.

When the word *harem* is used in connection with a royal court, the historian means to signify the women's court. In certain times and places in history this court has become an instrument for the complete seclusion—in fact imprisonment—of women. This pathological form of what may have originated as a separate and parallel government of women by women in the temples of the major priestesses should not be mistaken for the whole institution.

At some point in Egyptian history the special women's government in the temples became associated with the palace and with the royal alliance process. After that amalgamation, every military or trade agreement with a foreign power brought into the women's court one or more ladies from the country concerned. When Amenophis III married Gilukheba, the daughter of a Mitanni monarch, the princess brought "persons of her harem, 317 women," with her. The term harem as used by the translator of those records clearly does

not refer to women brought for the Pharaoh's sexual pleasure. It rather refers to the entire retinue from the home court of each newly arriving princess or lady of rank. There was a special administrative bureaucracy that looked after women's-court affairs, including both married men and married women of high rank, living outside the palace. The court provided all kinds of special edu-

Figure 6-7. *Egyptian Women, 18th Dynasty.*

cation and training, and the famous "harem" dancing girls and musicians were only a few among the many women trained there (figure 6-7). Many of these women spoke several languages and engaged in trade as well as political activity.

There is no evidence to my knowledge that the women of the Egyptian women's court were secluded. Rather they were part of an intellectual and cultural elite that administered cultural and political affairs both for their own women's section and for the government as a whole. Many centuries later the royal harem of Siam was vividly described by an Englishwoman (Leonowens, 1953), well after the custom of physical seclusion developed. These descriptions, though belonging to another time and place, give some clue as to the scale of operation of women's courts. In the Siamese harem, women physicians, judges, artists, scholars, and warriors all received the best education the country could give and administered a social and economic and political system including nine thousand women (1953: 11). Only a very small percentage of these women were the wives and concubines of the king. Talented young girls from poor families, both slave and free, could receive the same education as a princess, if a woman administrator decided they could be used in one of the orchestras, choirs, dance troupes, or theater companies of the court. There was always a certain risk of being noticed by the king and taken into the more secluded apartments of the concubines, which was in fact a lifelong imprisonment. It is probable, however, that the majority of women who worked in these settings, even in nineteenth century Siam, lived "normal" lives, going home at night to husbands who lived in the city. The women's-court system lent itself to great abuses as the status of women declined, but a careful study of the women's sections associated with palace complexes in all the great civilizations would probably reveal a stronger women's culture than is generally attributed to that part of royal institutions.

To return to the Egyptian women's court, there is no lack of evidence of women's involvement in politics. From time to time their involvement in domestic conspiracy, "only referred to by allusions, since one was afraid to let such incidents become well-known," surfaces. We have, for example, the report from the Old Kingdom that

> a high official named Uni was called upon, because of his especially trustworthy character, to conduct a secret case against Queen Weretkhetes, whose mistakes were concealed, however. . . . In the Middle Kingdom Instruction of King Ammenemes I, it was conjectured that the assassination of the sovereign was plotted in the harem. Some of the

preserved trial reports tell us about a harem intrigue during the Twentieth Dynasty that took on greater proportions. It was directed against
King Ramses III, who fell victim to this attempt on his life (Wenig,
1970: 38-39).

In the case of this particular intrigue, some conspirators of the
women's court wished to take advantage of a situation of rising
prices, declining food stocks, and the unwelcome presence of a large
number of foreign workers needing to be fed.

> They were led by Tiy [not the Tiy mentioned earlier], a concubine of
> the king, who wanted to install her son Pentawert on the throne, and
> by the chief official of the harem. The reports of the proceedings show
> that they wanted to incite the people to rebel with the help of
> mediators. This is rather unusual, since palace revolutions were general-
> ly limited to a small circle, and the people were not consulted. This
> time, however, they speculated on the people's desire to rise up against
> the king, who was the cause of their misery. The conspirators suc-
> ceeded with their planned murder of the king, but their pretender to
> the throne was defeated by the man who had already been chosen as
> successor, Ramses IV. He then ordered proceedings to be held against the
> insurgents before two special committees of trustworthy persons. . . .
> The unfaithful persons were subsequently punished by cutting off their
> noses and ears, while most of the accused were sentenced to death
> (Wenig, 1970: 38-39).

Sometimes dowager queens tried to circumvent court politics and
make their own international alliances, to keep power in their own
hands. One such queen, Ankhesenamon, tried to get the king of the
Hittites to send her one of his royal sons for a husband so she would
not have to marry the choice of her own court party. The unfortunate prince was murdered by Egyptian nationalists on his way to
the wedding, and she had to marry locally after all.

Both the successes and failures of the politics of the women's
court were kept secret for reasons of state, so we have no way of
knowing how effective this kind of activity was. It was apparently
dangerous. The "harem" could not properly be called the underlife
of Egyptian society, at least not until its later, declining epochs; it
was too much a part of the public arena. The women in it were
trained for international roles, so it is not surprising that they engaged in the activity for which they were trained. The ladies of this
group brought art, literature, music, scholars, and physicians from
their home country with them when they entered a new court. They

also visited one another from country to country. They certainly helped to promote the circulation of the scientific and cultural knowledge of the day.

Elite women did not confine themselves to politics. Administration of temple centers involved training women in a wide variety of skills. The Eighteenth Dynasty represents the high point, according to Drinker (1948), of the development of music by temple women. Large choirs and orchestras were organized, and training and performance in the arts absorbed the energies of gifted women of all classes. Eighteenth Dynasty Egypt sounds in some ways remarkably like nineteenth century Siam.

Among the working class, women worked side by side with men, at similar jobs, as we can see from the wall paintings in tombs. The degree of specialization in Egyptian workshops was tremendous, as reflected in lists of workmen kept by temple scribes.[8] A large force was needed, and every temple city had its temporary camps for workers who labored at temple construction when they were not needed for farming.

The claims on women's labor would foster specialization in domestic services and the serving of food, so there must have been at least as many women innkeepers in the temple towns of Egypt as there were in the cities of Mesopotamia. (The servant girl in figure 6-8 may have been attached to such an inn.) Egyptian women apparently had somewhat greater sexual freedom than the women of Mesopotamia, and there seems to have been less emphasis on professional provision of

Figure 6-8. *Servant Girl with Food Offering, 11th Dynasty.*

sexual services, though this was certainly an important urban enterprise in Egypt, as everywhere. The frequently mentioned presence of a large number of foreign workers, both women and men, living without families, provided both the demand and the supply for organized sexual services.

As in the case of Mesopotamia, we are reminded that there are neighboring cultures with ruling queens that occasionally made themselves felt in Egypt. Ramses II mentions Mysian women fighting on horseback under the leadership of their queen (Diner, 1965). A legendary queen of Cush-Meroe—Nicaula? Kandake? Candace? Queen of Sheba?—was supposed to be trying to influence Egyptian affairs during a time of troubles. These references are vague in the extreme. Another kind of note is sounded by the practice of Cush, during the tenth century when it ruled Egypt, of sending Egyptian women as slaves to Cushite temples. That was a new, and probably crushing, experience for Egyptian women.

Egypt's power gradually petered out in the last millennium B.C. When Ramses III said, "The foot of an Egyptian woman may walk where it pleases her, and no one may deny her," he was already whistling in the dark, both for himself and for women. The time of troubles was by then well under way. Women kept their temple and harem jobs, and the fact that Cleopatra of the Ptolemies could engage as effectively in international affairs as she did in the last century B.C. shows that the political tradition for women was still present. Cleopatra, an Egyptianized Greek with a genius for politics, has had a misleading press; she was less pretty, and far more intelligent, than she is generally given credit for (Harden, 1971: 86).

The whole phenomenon of Alexandria under the Ptolemies offers an interesting case study in the rise of full-fledged urbanization in the context of an old, minimally urbanized civilization. Should Alexandria be considered Egyptian or not, and what part did women play in this great cultural center of the Mediterranean world for the last 300 years B.C.? In a way it was an enclave city unrelated to its Egyptian setting, built by a foreigner—Alexander—for the cosmopolitan elite of his world. The scholars, artists, and scientists who foregathered there, sumptuously fed, elaborately housed, and attentively cared for by Egyptian servants, knew little and cared less about Egypt. The sailors, metallurgists, traders, and assorted wanderers from both barbarian and civilized lands, filling up the inns and taverns, scarcely "saw" Egypt. The farmers, the construction workers, the unskilled workers, the domestic servants, these were Egypt.

There had to be women among the Alexandrian elite—by this time there were women mathematicians and poets in Greek civilization—but there is almost no mention of them until the next millennium. The native Egyptian women, whether part of the service infrastructure or not, performed one major function—they married and educated men of all classes from Greek elites to barbarian craftsmen and traders. Men rarely came to Alexandria with wives. They found them there. Egyptian women who entered into these marriages were free contracting agents and the terms of trade were on their side. There are a number of references in Egyptian documents to these marriages of Egyptian women with foreigners, and also of foreign women to Egyptian men. Their rights are very clearly spelled out. This is almost our only glimpse of Egyptian women of the Alexandrian age. They seem to have walked through that age with some dignity and freedom. Culturally and politically, however, they had no role, except in their own temple culture well outside the Alexandrian sphere.

If pre-Alexandrian Egypt represents the high point of political participation of women in the pristine empires—and in a way it does—the record is hardly overwhelming. A wider spread of jobs for women is not necessarily accompanied by a wider spread of power among women. Women of the middle classes had a better time of it in Egypt than elsewhere—most of the lawsuits in the endless papyri records are about them, showing that they had a lot of rights to protect. In the end, however, they and the women of the elite alike were overshadowed by the priesthood and the army. Egypt never became as militarized as other societies, just as it never became urbanized, so the loss of status for women was more gradual and never went as far as it did elsewhere. None of the foreign powers that have occupied Egypt since the Ptolemies—Rome, Islam, or Britain—have ever fully succeeded in erasing the tradition of an autonomous womanfolk.

Syria and Palestine

The gods of the Phoenicians and the god of the Israelites, peoples living side by side and bounded by desert and sea, are well known to the Westerner brought up on the Old Testament. Competing traditions out of similar nomadic and herding origins produced very different patterns for these two peoples. There were progressive limitations on women's roles in both societies as they became sedentary. One is tempted to think that the women who stayed in the desert had it better; they at least had a long line of queens to point to, while their urban counterparts at the most kept their hands in with political intrigue.

As the Phoenicians grew wealthy through trade, orders of priestesses served Astarte, priests served Melqart, and both were related at the top level to the king. It was as tightly interlocking a network of merchant wealth, religious control, and political power as we will find anywhere, but women of the elite were well integrated into it. The fact that Princess Elissa (or Dido) could take off from Tyre with shiploads of goods, priestesses, and a male retinue to found her own city in 800 B.C. indicates the kind of resources that women could command. Her great-aunt Jezebel, who left Sidon to marry an Israeli king, did not fare nearly so well; she fought the sexist Israeli society all her life and died a courageous death when her side lost in a civil war. In Israel, Jehovah and male priests had the upper hand. Israelite women had no goddess-protector as the Phoenician women did.

What led to the loss of status of the Israeli women? When Sarai set out with her tribe from Ur of the Chaldees in the 1900s B.C., she was setting out from a matrilineal society.9 True, the Israelites were already herders, but the woman's line was clearly recognized. Right through the records of the later Old Testament books, from Judges to Nehemiah, there are the descent listings recording the woman's line, so common in manuscripts of the period. Perhaps the shift toward patriarchy started when the tribes were fighting their way into Canaan; a militaristic orientation works against a high status for women. Certainly the Israelites did not learn to look down on women in Egypt; in fact, Moses was dependent on the women of Pharaoh's family for his very life, for his education, and for his rise to power in the court. His ancestor Joseph married an Egyptian woman.

The memories of women's earlier roles, and a continued status for wise women, prophetesses, and judges, carried on for a long time after settlement in Canaan. Rachel and Leah, descendants of Sarai and wives of Jacob, are called "builders of Israel" in the Book of Ruth (4:11). Deborah was a judge of Israel in the days before Samuel was talked into appointing a king for the Israelites: "And she dwelt under the palm tree of Deborah, between Ramah and Bethel in Mount Ephraim; and the children of Israel came up to her for judgement" (Judges 4:5). When she commanded Barak, one of the tribal leaders, to take an army of ten thousand men to fight the Canaanite Jabon's army under Sisera, he replied:

> If thou wilt go with me, then I will go; but if thou wilt not go with me, then I will not go. And she said, I will surely go with thee: notwithstanding the journey that thou takest shall not be for thine honor; for the Lord shall sell Sisera into the hand of a woman (Judges 4: 7-9).

Not only did Deborah ensure the victory by her presence, but when Sisera fled from the battlefield after defeat, she got the cooperation of Jael, wife of a commander of a tribe supposedly friendly to Sisera's people, in capturing him. Jael completed the battlefield slaughter by calmly inviting Sisera into her tent "for refuge," putting him to sleep, and then driving a stake through his head. Deborah and Jael were clearly part of a sisterhood. Deborah's war song (Judges 5) sings proudly of the victorious battle, and of the sisterhood of Jael and her women. Judith could also have been a member of such a sisterhood. Delilah the Philistine, whose astute work as a spy defeated Samson, was still another, though of a later era. Even after the institution of kingship, women continued to be looked to for prophesy and guidance. The wise woman of Tekoa in 2 Samuel, chapter 14, helps the king out in a tricky diplomatic situation.

In addition to being leaders and advisors, women also managed to establish substantial individual enterprises independently of their husbands. The law of the levirate, providing that a man must marry his deceased brother's widow, is supposed to ensure that every woman is under the protection and rule of a man at all times in her life. The teachings about women as unreliable and lustful creatures give cultural support to the legal doctrines. Yet we find in the Book of Kings (2 Kings 4, 6, and 8) the story of the Shunammite whom the prophet Elisha liked so well that on his journeys he always stopped at her house for bread. She first got her husband's permission to build a special room for Elisha, but that is the last we hear of her husband. When in later years she is warned by Elisha of a famine and leaves the country on his advice for seven years, she manages on her return to get the king to appoint an officer to "restore all that was hers, and all the fruits of the field since the day that she left the land, until now." By this time she is a woman of substance, and we hear no word about the males of her family.

The courage and humor of the women of Israel and Canaan come through again and again. King Saul, who earlier had had all prophetesses, "those with familiar spirits," exiled, becomes fearful before a battle and wants to consult one of the very women he has exiled. She first scolds him for his treatment of her profession, then not only gives him a consultation but also feeds and comforts him before packing him back to court. We have already mentioned Jezebel. When she knew she had lost in a protracted political power struggle (her husband was already dead), she dressed herself in her most regal attire, wore an elegant coiffure and a carefully made-up face, and went to an upper window to watch for her victorious enemy, Jehu. When he came in by the city gate she called out a challenge and a taunt to him from her upper window, before he could give the orders to kill her to the eunuch guards surrounding her (2 Kings 9).

These women were tough, and not always admirable by any

means. In a later round of the same power struggle Jezebel was involved in, Queen Athaliah had all the royal infants murdered when the king died, so she could rule herself (2 Kings 11). Not surprisingly, she was overthrown after a couple of years. Bath-sheba, who looked on with apparent equanimity while King David had her husband killed so he could marry her, saw to it that her son Solomon was crowned king when David was old and helpless in the hands of scheming courtiers.

King Solomon knew how to receive Sheba, a queen of South Arabia, as an equal and with respect. Solomon was an ambitious king, and aspired to an Egyptian-style women's court. Hence his negotiations for women from the Moabites, Amonites, Edomites, Zedonians, and Hittites, as well as for the Pharaoh's daughter. He did not, however, have an adequate political infrastructure to support such negotiations, and he was also continually distracted by his predilection for love matches, which sometimes undermined the strategies of diplomatic marriage alliances. His wives in turn did not have the usual institutional mechanisms at hand for the exercise of power that women in well-established women's courts had. He did however lay the foundation for a political-alliance system for Israel, and his seven hundred wives and princesses and three hundred concubines could be interpreted as a fair start toward an institutionalized harem court. The wives, according to the custom of the time, all brought their gods, goddesses, priests, and priestesses with them, to the great consternation of the conservative Israelites. There was a reaction against the cosmopolitanism of Solomon, and under Ataxerxes, there was a great "putting away of strange wives" (Ezra 9, 10).

It is to the strange gods of the royal wives that we might look for specific political forces contributing to a decline in the status of Israeli women. The royal wives were often priestesses in their own lands. Jehovah already had only male priests, and prophetesses had been exiled. Had army leaders figured that the national strength of the Israelites lay in keeping a pure all-male devotion to the best battle god in the whole area? Jehovah had proved himself over and over. The other gods had done nothing for Israel but cause trouble. Foreign women were dangerous role models for Israelite women, with their political ways and priestess notions. We will see the same scenario played out again a thousand years later, in the Christian church fathers' distrust of pagan women and their priestess tradition. The sexual seduction aspect of this struggle is, I suspect, a male rationalization.

The actual kingdom of Israel only lasted from 1020 to 930 B.C. From then on Jewish communities settled all over the Mediterranean, sometimes by forced displacement, sometimes by voluntary migration. Many of them stayed on in Palestine and were incorporated into the other city-states and empires of the region. Sometimes they showed up in interesting ways in other parts of the Mediterranean world. The Jewish community in Alexandria is spoken of as an important force in the rapid rise of that city as a great cultural center. Queen Esther was the determined heroine of a story of the persecution of the Jews in what was probably Persia, under King Ahasueras, in the high days of Persian power. Ahasueras got angry with his queen, Vashti, because she didn't feel like being shown off to his royal guests on a special occasion. He sent out a call for women to be brought to the palace as a replacement for the recalcitrant Vashti. Esther was an orphan under the protection of her uncle, a Jewish merchant residing in the royal city, and her uncle sent her to the palace, warning her not to reveal that she was a Jewess. She pleased the king so he made her his crowned queen. She was a paragon of docility. Some time later, however, she risked everything to confess her origin when she discovered the king had signed a decree that all Jews should be destroyed as a favor to a scheming courtier. The story had a happy ending, and Queen Esther has become for all time the model of the obedient, submissive wife with a will of iron whose virtue triumphs in the end. Vashti, I am sorry to say, comes off with a totally undeserved bad character.

A study of the different types of female role models that come out of Hebrew tradition would be interesting. The Book of Ruth, which comes considerably before that of Esther, presents another and much subtler set of role models—this time both for men and women. The story of the interactions of Ruth and Boaz presents a picture of the kind of finely tuned mutual adjustment and consideration of the other that comes close to the concept of egalitarianism used in this book, in spite of a setting filled with tribal obligations and the concept of the levirate.

After the dispersion, a new conception of Jehovah as teacher, lover, and guide, one who yearns over his children and over the entire human race, grew in the hearts of the dispersed people alongside the old image of the battle god. The transformation of their own battle-happy heritage into a joyous love for God and creation through the experience of suffering imposed by the Assyrian cult of frightfulness can be seen in the psalms. There the entire gamut of emotions generated by the tribal experience of the Israelites is recorded, from triumphant battle cry to brokenhearted repentance to tender love song. Israelite women could hardly fail to recognize their part in their own history, since it was preserved in the records.

In the end they accepted the new male-dominated priesthood, but we shall never know what struggles the Deborahs among them went through to try to preserve ancient authority. Also we have no idea what their relationships with the alien women and their goddesses were. It is not impossible that the expulsion of foreign wives represented a campaign to break up an alliance of Jewish and gentile women against the Israelite priests and military leaders.[10] What remains today of earlier power is the special role of Jewish women in the remembering and retelling of Jewish history on ritual occasions within the orthodox family. Until the founding of the Jewish state of Israel in the twentieth century, their political roles had been drastically limited for centuries.

The Canaanite neighbors of the bellicose Israelites must have often puzzled over the fuss the latter made over their male god. He hadn't done *that* well by them. The inhabitants of the coastal city-states of Byblos, Beirut, Sidon, and Tyre, all strung out on a hundred-kilometer line along the shores of the Mediterranean, had long since lost any sense of tribal identification. Byblos was a prosperous trading city appearing in Egyptian records as early as 2500 B.C. The city-states evolved slowly, organically, and the rulers and the councils of city elders came from the leading merchant families. It was a socially mobile society, with many rags-to-riches stories. Somewhere around 1500 B.C. the Phoenicians became differentiated from the great mass of Canaanites, but they never developed centralized kingdoms. Always they remained a loose confederation of cooperating city-states. They were good at making money and took a pragmatic approach to life. Solidarity was a result of common residence, not ethnic bonds. Rulers were supposed to see that order was kept so that business could go on, and to "render justice to orphans and widows"—a necessity in a non-clan-oriented society.

The Assyrians were a problem to the Phoenicians. The Assyrians wanted the Phoenician wealth, and the Phoenicians did not want to give it away. Neither did they want to waste their time on bloody wars they were bound to lose, not being warriors. So, sensibly, they bought the Assyrians off each time they could, fighting only when there was no other recourse. One way of controlling the relationship was through negotiation by marriage, and there are a number of records of Phoenician princesses going to Assyria—one whole set of them to marry Ashurbanipal. These princesses probably had their hands full, since this was at the height of the period of Assyrian military activity.

From a variety of evidence we may infer that women were active in trade, as well as in the priesthoods. A common motif in Phoenician ivory carvings is the "woman at the window" (see figure 6-9). It is not possible to tell whether she is goddess, priestess, or citizen, but she is looking out of an upper-story window of a typical Phoenician house. Apart from Jezebel and Elissa, no characterizations of individual Phoenician women come through. Elissa was very enterprising. After she landed at the site of the future Carthage, she is

Figure 6-9. *"Woman at the Window," Assyrian, c. 900 B.C.*

supposed to have bought land from the local Libyans by means of the old "as much land as an oxhide will cover" trick. Cut into thin strips, it will cover quite a lot. The Dido and Aeneas story is pure myth—the timing is all wrong in relation to the Aeneas chronology. It was probably a way of diminishing Elissa's stature as a political figure. Another story goes that, when an "uncouth" neighboring Libyan chieftain asked for her hand, she built a funeral pyre and immolated herself rather than marry him. After everything else she managed, that story is hardly credible, but women founders of cities are bound to have their detractors.

The Phoenicians can be admired—they are real "yankee traders"—but it is hard to love them. The practice of child sacrifice which roused so much loathing in their neighbors has been irrefutably confirmed by archaeological evidence. In the precinct of the goddess Tanit at Carthage, thousands of urns containing the cremated remains of small children, some as much as twelve years old, but mostly under two, and sometimes of birds and small animals as substitute sacrifices, have been found (Harden, 1971: 86).

Evidences of devices to soothe frightened children about to be sacrificed somehow don't help to soften very much our feelings toward the Phoenicians. It is clear that priestesses were equally involved with priests in placing the infants in the dreaded mechanical arms of the hungry deities. Powerful priestly families dominated this society, sometimes for as long as seventeen generations in a single line; priests and priestesses married each other. Sometimes the kings and queens were also of the priesthood, though not always. A hard-boiled merchant state which is also a theocracy and practices child sacrifice is hard to visualize—but it existed.11

The gap between rich and poor widened rapidly after Carthage (Phoenicia West) became wealthy, and the concentrations of power in temple-palace-warehouse soon came to require increased military defense. Carthage became a militarized society, increasingly divorced from the realities of its own poor and on very bad terms with surrounding native Libyans. Perhaps it all started because Elissa did not marry the neighboring chieftain. We all know about the final destruction of Carthage, but it was a sick society long before the confrontation with Rome. The fluidity and mobility of the early mercantile society of the Syrian seaport states did not last, and the women of the elite joined the men in a ruthless exploitation of their own society as well as of their environment. Goddesses are historically rarely gentle, but Tanit, spouse of Moloch, does seem to have been unusually bloodthirsty. What a band of priestesses Tanit must have had!

In this review of Syria and Palestine we have looked at old, settled, merchant city-states that have lost all vestige of attachment to tribal life, and at nomads who settled down and formed a kingdom, only to be dispersed to the world's cities. In the next chapter we will look at nomadic desert tribes who never settled down at all, yet whose fate was closely linked to that of the settlers. The early Israelites, like desert tribes, were ranked societies, and women appear as tribal leaders, prophetesses, and judges in both. In the stratified merchant states women belonged to the priestly elite, and some middle-class women presumably participated in trading and the mobility that trading offers. Of the Phoenician poor we know nothing except that the cities required numerous service workers. As traders, the Phoenicians would be among the first to have widespread use of domestic slaves. The Israelites, under less likely circumstances, also kept women slaves. It is difficult to reconstruct the Phoenician underlife society for women, though it probably existed. For Israelite women, our imagination has more materials to work with.

The description of the day-to-day life of the women of the upper middle class in both Israel and the Syrian city-states that comes to us through the famous passage from Proverbs gives an interesting glimpse into the relative roles of women and men:

> If you can find a truly good wife, she is worth more than precious gems! Her husband can trust her, and she will richly satisfy his needs. She will not hinder him, but help him all her life. She finds wool and flax and busily spins it. She buys imported foods, brought by ship from distant ports. She gets up before dawn to prepare breakfast for her household, and plans the day's work for her servant girls. She goes out to inspect a field, and buys it; with her own hands she plants a vineyard. She is energetic, a hard worker, and watches for bargains. She works far into the night! She sews for the poor, and generously gives to the needy. She has no fear of winter for her household, for she has made warm clothes for all of them. She also upholsters with finest tapestry; her own clothing is beautifully made—a purple gown of pure linen. Her husband is well known, for he sits in the council chamber with the other civic leaders. She makes belted linen garments to sell to the merchants. She is a woman of strength and dignity, and has no fear of old age. When she speaks, her words are wise, and kindness is the rule for everything she says. She watches carefully all that goes on throughout her household, and is never lazy. Her children stand and bless her; so does her husband. He praises her with these words: "There are many fine women in the world, but you are the best of them all!" Charm can be deceptive and beauty doesn't last, but a woman who fears and reverences God shall be greatly praised. Praise her for the many fine things she does. These good deeds of hers shall bring her honor and recognition from even the leaders of the nations (Prov. 31: 10-31, Living Bible translation).

For women there is a clear portrayal of the delicate balance between being anchored to the household and engaging in modest trading enterprises outside the home, characteristic of propertied urban women in all the early civilizations. The extent of a woman's autonomy and authority is revealed. Any sense of mother-child relations is strangely absent in this passage except for the bald statement toward the end that her children will bless her. Perhaps mothering really is a new development in these millennia.

For men, the passage shows an absorption in political roles and very little involvement in productive or domestic activity. Though excluded from political roles, the women of this class appear to have a wider range of activities than do the men. To some degree, this description will hold for propertied women right up to the industrial revolution.

GODDESSES AND AMAZONS IN THE AEGEAN AND GREECE

Crete, the Cheerful Island

In legend and myth Crete is the home of matriarchy, the mother-goddess,[12] and the Eleusinian mysteries. It is also the source of the double-axe cult which became the symbol of all the "Amazonian" kingdoms of the Mediterranean time of troubles. Whether Crete represents a civilization comparable to the pristine civilizations of the Near East is something like the question of whether Egypt ever had true urbanism—it depends on how you define it, and this issue is still debated by scholars. Certainly Crete was an active trading center with protourban communities not unlike those of Sumer in 3200, and by 2000 B.C. it had a flourishing palace economy and a vast international trade.

The Cretans appear to have been a remarkably cheerful and secular people. Woolley describes them as gay, picturesque, humane folk who approached god through dancing and feasting (Hawkes and

Figure 6-10. *Cretan Women in Round Dance with Lyre Player, Late Minoan.*

Woolley, 1963). The archetypal mother-daughter myth comes from Crete—Demeter (De Meter, mother of grain, Ceres in Roman form) in search of her daughter Kore (Gaia or Ge, earth). The basically positive themes of death and rebirth, winter and summer, separation and reunion, which run through these stories, are later overlaid with more somber themes. Zeus, the god in search of power, is also supposed to have been born in Crete, in a cave on Mt. Dikte. His struggle with his father Chronos, which ends with Zeus throwing Chronos into Tatarus, the ancient hell, could be seen as the seal and judgment of the stern patriarchal society placed on the gayer, more casual matriarchy. That overthrow of the matriarchy already represents the Mycenean conquest of Crete. Another version of the stern succession of patriarchy is the Europa and bull story. The bull cult comes to represent male dominance.

The axe symbol, and the cult it represents, is a problem to scholars. The basic single-bladed axe goes back to the Paleolithic, as an all-purpose tool. The double-bladed axe may have been independently invented by several peoples and traveled to Europe with warlike nomads characterized as "battle-axe cultures."[13] The axe of the Cretan axe cult (figure 6-11) is also a double-bladed axe, but it was not used

Figure 6-11. *Double Axes, Middle to Late Minoan.*

as a weapon, unless possibly for child sacrifice, in connection with the archaic harvest rites suggested by the Demeter/Kore story. This makes the Cretans appear somewhat less gay. When prosperity came to Crete, cultic headquarters were apparently located in the snake-goddess shrine in the palace at Knossos. The double-axe symbol carved all over the walls of this shrine gives little information on meanings, however. The axe is never seen in connection with a male god, only with a goddess. The wide distribution of the cultic axe throughout Europe is probably associated with the fact that Cretans were seafarers and traders. It is an interesting fact that the curved double axe was in a later era the battle weapon of the Amazons, the warriors widely recorded in the literature of antiquity.

How many of the Cretan cults actually were mother-goddess cults, and what significance they had at the time, we do not know. That they had immense significance for later peoples, and were the source for later legends about a golden age of matriarchy, we shall see shortly.

Whatever the Cretans believed, they appeared to enjoy life and to love to dance. Their pictures show us this. As Jane Harrison (1912) says, dancing is the vehicle through which many peoples have taught their tribal lore, and learned to separate themselves from and reflect on the experiences they are re-creating through dance. Through dancing, concepts of order, leadership, and religious projections are developed. The Cretans danced their way into culture and civilization, and their dancing figures still delight us today.

There is little evidence of a formal priesthood in this society, though dance leaders may have been priestesses. There are no temples, only minimal shrine sites

Figure 6-12. *Snake Goddess, Middle Minoan.*

and sacred caves. It seems to have been a very egalitarian society, though the representations of the mother-goddess holding the famous double axe may have given rise to later conceptions of an authoritarian matriarchy. The little folded-arms figurines found everywhere are apparently not cultic, but simply figurines to delight the eye.

Knossos was apparently not very impressive as a city—the palace-dominated center and surrounding settlements did not cover more than twelve acres, compared to the Mesopotamian towns that averaged twenty-five acres. The settlements were open; there is no sign of fortification until after the holocaust in 1400 B.C. The Mediterranean triad of wheat, olives, and the vine were all cultivated here, and wine and one-handled cups for drinking spread out in waves from Crete to the entire region. When women were buried, wine vessels and sewing equipment were buried with them. It is doubtful that the Cretans "invented" wine, but they are credited with inventing the dagger and with developing a process of alloying copper to make the metal harder.

We have a very interesting set of contradictory images of the Cretans. On the one hand, there are the cheerful, peaceable people who love to dance. On the other hand, their goddesses' double axe may be dripping with the blood of child sacrifice; and in inventing the dagger the Cretans produced "a military threat which could be answered only by equipping oneself with similar weapons. . . . every man needed a dagger during the bronze age" (Renfrew, 1972: 320). While Crete had a variety of craft specialists attached to the palace culture, Renfrew suggests that the civilization was something between tribe and state—a redistributional chiefdom coordinating economic, religious, and social activities. There appear to have been no "peasant masses" and no private concentrations of wealth. It would be a ranked society on the verge of stratification, perhaps. We have no images of women householders from this society.

The Fall of Crete and the Rise of the Amazons

By 1200 B.C. the whole Cretan phenomenon was over. Homer's pompous heroes had helped to create disorder in the whole Aegean, though they did not do it alone. Even the serious and warlike Myceneans, who took over the island of Crete and its trade, could not cope with the general increase in piracy and unrest. Large-scale population movements in the area finally destroyed the Myceneans too. During the time of troubles many of the inhabitants of Crete left the island and settled elsewhere. Out of this era came the myths of Amazons and matriarchies; Lycians, Carians, Lydians, and

Mysians, all Cretan-related settlers on the coast of Asia Minor, are all supposed to have had similar matriarchal (in fact matrilineal) systems.[14] Herodotus and a host of writers after him wrote of the custom of these people of taking the name of the mother and of property going to daughters. They also write of the absence of formal law. Bachofen, the apostle of the matriarchy theory, says:

> [Women] bore within themselves the law pervading all matter. Justice speaks out of their mouths without pervading self-consciousness and with certainty in the manner of conscience. They are wise by nature, prophetesses proclaiming Fate, Sybil or Themis. Therefore, women were considered inviolable bearers of jurisprudence and sources of prophecy. The battle lines drew apart at their command and they arbitrated the disputes of the nations as sacerdotal umpires; religious foundation on which gynocracy immovably rested (Diner, 1965: 233).

While Bachofen cannot be treated as a scholarly source concerning tribal jurisprudence, the image of the tribal setting for the administration of justice that his passage conveys reminds us of the problems of scale which face matrilineal societies with growing population densities. Sacerdotal umpires are all very well in small communities, but do not serve large city-states or kingdoms very effectively. The Lycians, Lydians, Carians, and Mysians are not mythical peoples. They will be found on maps in all the classical atlases. The Carian Queen Artemisia is a documented historical figure, and did lead both a land army and a naval battle under Xerxes during the Greco-Persian War (Edey, 1974: 50). To describe the capital of matrilineal Lydia as the Paris of Asia Minor (Diner, 1965: 236), exporting finery and horoscopes to the Mediterranean world, may be an exaggeration, but Lydia does seem to have participated in the general Cretan tradition of craft, skill, and beauty. Oddly, there is little mention of craftswomen—mainly of queens, priestesses, and astrologers. Who did the work of production? What the proportions of ruling kings to ruling queens were over a several-hundred-year period in these matrilineal kingdoms I do not know, but it is doubtful that they were ever pure matriarchies. They certainly had substantial kingly rule by the time of the rise of the Greek city-states.

The relatively peaceable movements and activities of the matrilineal societies in the Aegean coincided with other more violent movements of barbarian nomadic tribes and a general period of bloodiness in Mesopotamia. The matrilineal societies may or may not have contributed to the formation of the Amazon bands that appear in classical history. The Black Sea region around the Thermodon

River seems to have been for a time an area of settlement for such women's bands, but these women are usually described as Scythians from the Caucasus. The suggestion that they were nomadic women made husbandless by war is supported by mentions in Greek literature of their being horsewomen and herders living on mare's milk and blood, as many herding peoples do.

That there should have been major pitched battles between women's and men's armies seems a little unlikely. There must, however, have been some armed confrontations, however minor, to account for the widespread myths about these battles and to account for the very large number of sculptures and paintings of "dying Amazons" now

Figure 6-13.
Wounded Amazon.

spread throughout Europe's museums. Figure 6-13 is a reproduction of one of the famous dying-Amazon statues, and figures 6-14 and 6-15 are reproductions from a longer series of some schematic representations of the battle postures in which Amazons are represented in Greek art from 500 B.C. on. The preoccupation of Athenian

Figure 6-14. *Amazons Fighting a Greek.*

Figure 6-15. *Amazons in Battle.*

artists with the theme of women as soldiers is in itself significant, even if there had been no battles. Since it is such a strong Athenian theme, the possibility should not be discounted that a couple of Greeks (probably *not* gods, as storied!) kidnapped a young girl from an Amazon camp and carted her off to Athens, and that angry Amazons followed them to Athens and gave them a good battle before being driven off. We certainly know that women fought in some of the major battles of the Persian wars, though not necessarily as all-women's units. We also know, from much later accounts of Roman soldiers confronting Germanic women warriors in the forests of Europe, that it is unnerving to men to have to fight women in hand-to-hand combat. In other words, there could be a variety of experiences giving rise to the Amazonian theme, not the least of which would be the Spartan practice of giving women essentially warrior-type training.

Athens: New Consciousness and Old
Rigidities in the Greek City-States

The Greek city-states were legion, and to discuss adequately the role of women in them is an impossibility. As Tarn says, the spirit of particularism was the curse of Greece (1961: 66). Each city was insistent on its autonomy, and yet threats from the rest of the Mediterranean continually drove the cities into one type of alliance or another. Their political systems were not complex. They had only one word, *koinon,* to cover every type of association from the village sports team to an intercity league. Some leagues, such as Aetolia, were simply a collection of villages. Aetolia's federal center in 280 B.C. was a temple of Apollo, and its assembly consisted of "every free Aetolian under arms"—male of course. By 220 B.C. so many towns had joined it that it stretched across Greece. Representative government in this context developed to keep the masses out of government and public affairs in the hands of the well-to-do.

Given the tension between particularism and the need for integration into larger wholes both for trade and for military protection, cities developed all kinds of systems for extending rights to residents of other cities. Sometimes a city decreed citizenship en masse to all the inhabitants of another city, other times it gave citizenship selectively, and sometimes it simply put up citizenship for sale.

The three most important institutional devices of the Greek cities from our point of view are the rights of citizenship, the development of free elementary schools, and the development of clubs—religious, occupation-centered, and extended-family associations. They all represent potential public spaces for women. Except in cases of special honoring, women were generally excluded from citizenship probably because citizenship was associated with arms bearing. Macedonia, which had an aristocracy, was different, and we shall see later that the influence of politically active Macedonian princesses was felt in all the Greek states.

Educational institutions were more flexible. In Ionia, Teos, Chios, and Sparta, girls and boys were educated together in elementary school. In the other city-states they were either educated in separate schools or at home. A few women went on to the gymnasia in the four cities named above; we do not know what access women had to the gymnasia in other cities, but we do know that exceptional women found their way to an education. Toward the end of the last millennium B.C. we find that the age of private libraries has begun; Aristotle is considered to have had the first private library on any scale in Greece (Tarn, 1961: 269). Therefore, we may deduce that women could have access to learning in the private spaces of the home.

Religious clubs provided the most important public spaces for women. There were mother-goddess clubs in all the cities of Hellenic culture, both in Greece and Asia. While mother-goddesses were losing out to male gods during this period, even as late as Roman times, Hellenized Lydia had 112 mother-goddess-with-son cult inscriptions out of a total of 237 cult inscriptions examined. Earlier, the proportion of mother-goddess cults would have been larger. Tarn points out how important the mother-goddess was in the Hellenic pantheon:

> Of all the deities of Hellenism, Isis of the Myriad Names was probably the greatest. She was identified with practically every goddess and deified woman of the known world. . . . All civilization was her gift and in her charge. [Furthermore] she was the woman's goddess. Half the human race had been badly off for a friend at the court of Heaven. Athena was uniquely a man's goddess. . . .Isis is the "glory of women" who gives them "equal power with men." "I am Isis" runs her creed, "I am she whom women call goddess. I ordained that women should be loved by men; I brought wife and husband together, and invented the marriage contract. I ordained that women should bear children, and that children should love their parents" (1961: 357-359).

Isis was different from the chtonic goddesses of Catal Huyuk. Something had been happening under the Mediterranean sun. "Her statues portrayed a young matron in modest dress with gentle, benevolent features, crowned with blue lotus or the crescent moon, and sometimes bearing in her arms the babe Horus." In Christian times some of her statues were to be relabeled as Mary, and these are known in Europe today as the Black Virgins (Tarn, 1961: 360). Isis indeed represented new understandings of motherhood and family life; she provides suggestive evidence for a changing conception of parent-child relations.

The religious associations, or "cultic clubs," were the only activity outlet for women in the public arena that could be found in every city-state and kingdom. For the rest, there was enormous variability in the freedom and opportunities allowed to women from state to state. This makes it all the more ironical that it is Athens, where women had perhaps the least freedom of any of the cities, that has magnetized the historical imagination of the West. In Macedonia queens led armies on horseback. In Sparta women wrestled naked in the arena. In Ionia, Teos, Chios, and Sparta they went to school with boys. In Athens, however, women were supposed to stay in the *gynaeceum*, the women's quarters. Yet Athens is our "heritage." Even more, it acted as a magnet to its own times. Women scholars and artists and traders from all the other city-states came to Athens, introducing an intellectual leadership of women that could not have found expression through Athenian culture alone.

Since Athens was the most articulate focal point for Greek culture, much of the discussion in this section will center on the situation of women in Athens. It must be remembered, however, that the context of the Athenian drama was the dynamic interplay of civic, cultural, and economic activities among all the city-states of Greece, and also of Hellenized Asia. Many forces were at work in the consciousness of women and men in the Hellenic world during this last-quarter-of-the-millennium transition period. The relative self-containment of the early civilizations was gone, and the shift toward more complex, internationally linked kingdoms and world empires had to be endured. These empires were beginning to be a major force as the time of troubles sorted itself out, and the Mediterranean reached toward a new equilibrium by the middle of the first millennium B.C. New concepts of social relationships and new ideals of humanness were developing, but the prolonged period of militarization and centralization of power which the Mediterranean people had experienced tended in the main to squeeze women to the sidelines. It was not easy for women and men to explore these new ideas together.

What we see most strongly in the myths and legends about Amazons, about an ancient rule of women, and about mother-goddesses, is a strong undercurrent of male uneasiness. Something is wrong which cannot easily be articulated. The negative husband-wife, mother-son dynamic analyzed by Philip Slater—that of contempt for and fear of the woman by the man, reenforced by the woman's frustration in the face of that contempt and fear—discussed first in chapter 4, would certainly be well under way by now. Thus we have the paradox described by Slater:

> On the one hand one is usually told that the status of women in fifth- and fourth-century Athens achieved some kind of nadir. They were legal nonentities, excluded from political and intellectual life, uneducated, virtually imprisoned in the home, and appeared to be regarded with disdain by the principal male spokesmen whose comments have survived. . . . On the other hand, as Comme points out: "There is, in fact, no literature, no art of any country, in which women are more prominent, more important, more carefully studied and with more interest than in the tragedy, sculpture, and painting of fifth-century Athens" (1968: 4-5).

The explanation of this paradox, says Slater, is that the exclusion of women from political power leads to excessive accumulations of power by women in the home, since power does not follow deference patterns and a sizeable power differential between sexes is not possible. Men facing this enormous accumulation of power at home are indeed miserable and don't know why.

I do not accept the notion of a fixed balance of power between the sexes that will be maintained by overt or covert means—I think social values can induce people (of either sex) to give up large amounts of "power." However, it is true that the possibilities for the exercise of power must be commensurate with perceived opportunity within the total structure. The whole notion of "relative deprivation" is based on perception of opportunity, not actual opportunity. In that sense, Athenian women were suffering from relative deprivation. They had participated to some significant degree in the developments that made the Athenian city-state possible, and now they were pushed into the home and out of the new social space that was to mean so much to the men—the agora. There was a very unfortunate combination of a major new constriction of social space for women and an enlargement of social space for men.

The significance of Aeschylus' treatment of the Orestes legend lies in the attempt to articulate the "unconscious" suppression of women in fifth century B.C. Greece. Put in the stark terms of the replacement of an earlier matriarchy by a patriarchy—"you ran things before—now we will run them"—the play presents the classical dilemma of the power struggle. Someone must win. Orestes has killed his mother to avenge his father, and by matriarchal law that is the unforgivable sin. Apollo advocates a new patriarchal law:

> The mother is not the parent of the child, only the nurse of what she has conceived. The parent is the father, who commits his seed to her, a stranger, to be held with God's help in safe keeping (Aeschylus, 1954: 89).

Athena, the "motherless daughter of Zeus's head, the even daughter, the trembling lightning of her father," has to break the tie since the judges are equally ranged on both sides of the issue:

> The final judgment is a task for me; so for Orestes shall this vote be cast. No mother gave me birth, and in all things save marriage, I, my father's child indeed, with all my heart commend the masculine (Aeschylus, 1954: 91).

The furies (Erinys) respond to this crushing of the matriarchy with a curse:

> Oho ye younger Gods, since ye have trod under foot the laws of old and ancient powers purloined, then we, dishonoured, deadly in displeasure, shall spread poison foul through the land, with damp contagion of rage malignant, bleak and barren, blasting, withering up the earth, mildews on bud and birth abortive. Oh! Venomous pestilence shall

sweep this country with infectious death (Aeschylus, 1954: 93).

The furies later modify the curse, but the damage is done.

The reader will see that I have presented the city-state pattern as the basic pattern of evolution of all societies. In its early stages I have suggested that there is an egalitarianism that stems from a minimum of occupational differentiation, somewhat modified by various ceremonial statutes. Athens fits the early Sumerian pattern nicely, except that in Sumeria women participated more fully in the ceremonial life and had less limitation on their movement. The fact that it was Athens, rather than another Greek city, or a Sumerian one, that was imprinted on the Western mind has had confusing consequences for the understanding of women's roles ever since.

Athens is presented to us as a trick with mirrors. Most historians write as if Athens invented democracy and an incredible new way of life in which individuals participated in the shaping of their personal lives as well as in that of the polity. Yet the same historians assure us that Athens had no place for women but the *gynaeceum,* or the women's quarters in the home. The question is, did Athens have something unique that Sumer did not? If it did, how did women come to be excluded from the "glory that was Greece"?

The answer to the first question is yes, Athens did have something unique: the agora, the public social space in which all transactions mingled—trade, social intercourse, education, the making of laws, and the making of political decisions. The only thing that was not done in the agora was the worship of gods, who were kept up on the hill, in the acropolis, out of the way.

Compare the city plan of Priene in figure 6-16, a city similar to Athens, with that of Arbela (figure 5-4 in chapter 5). There are no public spaces in Arbela. Picture the bustling open space in the heart of cities like Priene and Athens:

> In the agora stood the stoa, the open-sided markets where the philosophers taught; the Boukuterion, where the 500-man council met; the mint; courts; and the Strategion, or military headquarters (Bowra, 1965: 106-107).

The full assembly of the men of Athens had to meet on a neighboring hill, the Pnyx. The agora could not hold them all.

If we contrast the agora as a civic institution with the walled temple-palace compound of a Near Eastern city-state, we see here the conscious re-creation of the concept of public interest. The council of the agricultural village had it—the sense of the civic good

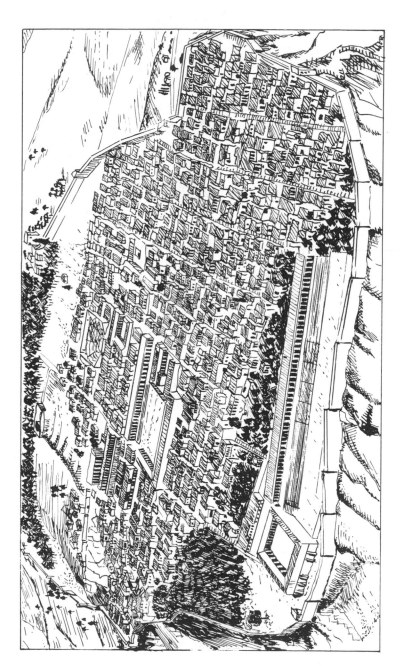

Figure 6-16. *City Plan of Priene, c. 350 B.C.*

extending beyond kinship lines—for these villages were already ethnic mixtures in the posttribal stage. When the civic good was walled up inside the palace-temple compound, however, the consciousness of public interest disappeared. The citizens of Mesopotamian cities could worship in the temples and buy at the bazaars, but they could not enter the trading complexes belonging to palace, temple, or merchant families except as professional traders; they could not enter the palace on government business except as the king's officials.

How was Athens able to break apart the walled secrecy of the Mesopotamian city-state? The answer is not difficult. Athens was small. The average Greek city-state had a population of five thousand. Athens was one of three that had twenty thousand. The city-state of Ur, in contrast, had an estimated population of two hundred and fifty thousand. Greek land was sparse and unfruitful, and with existing technologies could not support a larger population. This environmental poverty was Athens' best resource, leading it to specialize in the productive intellect. The partial sex segregation involved in the development of women's quarters in the households did not lead to the population explosion one might have expected, but rather to a stable city size. This may be due partly to the cultural emphasis on male love relationships, notoriously infertile,[15] and to birth control practices including late marriage, abortion, and infanticide.

Few families reared more than one daughter, and two sons were considered an adequate number (de Mause, 1974: 25). De Mause's emphasis on the severe beatings of children, combined with practices of sexual abuse, can create an unpleasant picture of Greek family life and a particularly unpleasant picture of Greek motherhood. While de Mause's view of high levels of child abuse in Greece may well be correct, I believe that further study of life in the *gynaeceum* will uncover tenderness along with cruelty. It is true, though, that both child-rearing and pedagogical practices do seem to have relied on the rod as the shaper of the child, according to the records generally quoted. If urbanism were unkind to women, it was far worse for children.

In spite of small families, and the abuses inside them, the household and its hearth was important in Greek culture. The geographic isolation of many of the Greek city-states meant that Athens, like the other states, was characterized by an ethnic homogeneity and legacy of preexisting tribal structures that had long since disappeared in the Mesopotamian crossroads. All these features led to an emphasis on the clan-linked household units. The traditions regarding the sacred hearth and sacred clan boundaries come from tribal roots. Kin and tribe were still in the early city-state days meaningful units, and women entered a new kinship group on marriage to become its servant. The daughter of another man's hearth, contracted for and set to serving one's own sacred hearth, could never be fully trusted. She had been born under different gods, and remained in one sense always a stranger.

It is not clear why Athens, the city that developed the most sophisticated public institutions of all the city-states and generated the greatest cultural flowering of Hellas, was also the city that inclined toward the greatest privatization of women's roles. Apparently it applied the ethics of tribalism to women, and the ethics of universalism to men.

The concept of the *oikos* was made to serve both the ethics of tribalism and of universalism. The *oikos* was the household, and served as the basic unit of the *polis,* the city. The father ruled the *oikos* and represented it in the *polis.* The continuation of the male line so that the *oikos* could be continued, in this relatively infertile population, was of crucial importance. Therefore all legal cases relating to the family were classed as public affairs. Any citizen (male) could become involved in these affairs on behalf of the public interest. Under these circumstances, it is all the more striking to find a variety of records that indicate that women, privatized as they were, could and did fight in the courts to protect the freedom of their persons and their property. They were not infrequently successful (O'Faolain and Martines, 1973: 9-25). The confinement to the *gynaeceum* was therefore not complete. The rule that women were not to appear at their own dinner table if there were guests in the house may well have been more honored in the breach than in the observance.[16] The women had a vigorous underlife, and it is this underlife which erupts both tragically and amusingly in Greek theater, Greek literature, and the courtroom.

In fact, the number of women actually confined to the women's quarters must have been rather small, when one stops to consider the categories of women who were free to move about: 1) the older, high-status women; 2) the poor who worked at the same variety of crafts and trades that poor women everywhere work at; 3) the slaves;[17] 4) the foreign born, including women traders; and 5) the hetairae and intellectuals, also frequently foreign born.

Women over sixty performed public ceremonial functions and acted as message bearers for younger women living in seclusion. Poor free women were engaged mainly in retail trade, and seem to have had, if not a monopoly, at least a privileged position in the market place; the soldier's wife plaited and sold garlands; the mother of Euxitheus [a court orator who apologized profusely for having a mother known to work —ed.] sold ribbons at one time, and worked as a wet-nurse at another. . . . All kinds of comestibles were sold by women, both retail and as cafe or inn-keepers (Lacey, 1968: 171).

The innkeepers had the usual bad reputation. Workers in wool were more respected, as were women vase painters. Lacey points out that

it used to be argued that trade was not possible for citizen-women, since the limit of their contractual competence was the value of one medimnos of barley; it has, however, now been shown that this was not a paltry sum, but equivalent in value to more than a poor petty-trader's stock-in-trade, and enough to provide food for a family for several days (1968: 1971).

It is clear that both the poor and some enterprising middle-class women traded. Probably only women of the upper middle and upwardly mobile classes really kept to the confinement practice, not even going shopping. The woman entrepreneur was always wide open to the accusation of being a prostitute—an accusation frequently made against women. Table 6-1 lists occupations open to women in Athens, adapted and expanded from Evelyne Sullerot's *Histoire et Sociologie du Travail Féminin* (1968).

The slaves and some of the foreign-born women who moved about in public were the entertainers, "such as flute-girls and courtesans, who provided the female company at men's dinners and riotous parties" (Lacey, 1968: 172), and the prostitutes:

The successful were able to obtain their freedom, retire and keep brothels or schools to train other courtesans, and we hear of one who acted as a go-between in business deals of men (Lacey, 1968: 172).

Other freed women were wool workers, nurses, and retainers—and "one cobbler."

The fifth group of Greek women who moved freely in public spaces is hard to classify. They were intellectuals—philosophers, mathematicians, physicians. There were poets, and poet-musicians. Some have been coupled with the names of famous men, with circumlocutions—such as "she was said to be the wife of," or "evidently she was the wife of"—used to describe their status. Some were foreign born—from the more sex-egalitarian of the neighboring city-

Table 6-1

Women's Occupational Roles in Athens in the Age of Pericles

I.   Occupations for women slaves (there were an estimated 90,000 women
     slaves in Athens in the fourth century):

     A. Food processing: threshing grain, grinding flour.
     B. Mining: gold and silver mining; separating metal from slag,
         washing metal; transporting ore from underground corridors of
         mines to the surface.
     C. Textile workers: all operations connected with carding, spin-
         ning and weaving carried on by women in workshops--no indica-
         tion whether these were state owned or privately owned.
         Weaving also carried on as cottage industry in private homes.

II. Occupations open to free women:

     A. Agriculture, unspecified except for "field work."
     B. Textile work as above.
     C. Trade: selling of vegetables, processed foods, baked goods,
         other home-manufactured products, unspecified. Selling of
         cloth, garments, headdresses.
     D. Inn-keeping.
     E. Prostitution.
     F. Running schools for courtesans.
     G. Midwifery, nursing.
     H. Music.
     I. Dancing.
     J. Vase painting

III. Occupations specifically forbidden to women:

     A. Medicine (there are records of illegal practice and punishment
         of women practitioners).

IV. Occupations possible but not encouraged:

     A. Scribe; schools for women rare (Sappho's school was an excep-
         tion), but if a woman could write, she was not forbidden to
         exercise her skill.

---

states and elsewhere in the Mediterranean—and some native, but none of them seems to have followed the rules of behavior of the respectable Greek married woman. They are variously referred to as courtesans, hetairae, or high-class prostitutes, in spite of the fact that many of them do not appear to have sold sexual services. They appear to have been a group of women who had an independent status outside the *oikos* system. Some of them were, in fact, married, though most of them were not. It has been difficult for later Western cultures to conceptualize educated, socially productive women standing entirely outside the legal and cultural system of male domination. Yet they were thought highly enough of at the time to be widely written about by their male contemporaries. We know about them mostly through the writings of these male contemporaries, and sometimes through surviving fragments of their own writings.

We will discuss these independent women who participated in the intellectual and public life of Athens in three categories: first, the Pythagoreans, belonging to a group which was "ideologically committed" to the intellectual equality of women; then the poets; and finally those known as hetairae. The Pythagoreans were partly a school, partly a community, and partly a philosophical-mystical "order" in which women were active. A history of women philosophers published in 1765 lists twenty-eight Pythagoreans (Beard, 1946: 321). First and foremost is Theano, who "appears" to have been the wife of Pythagoras,

> devoted to medicine, hygiene, the arts of ethical living, physics and mathematics, a commentator on the art of healing and a writer on virtue in its large Greek meaning (Beard, 1946: 321).

Some of her writings are still extant. There is Perictione, pupil of Pythagoras and author of *Wisdom* and *The Harmony of Women.* Then there is Diotima, priestess of Mantinea and also thought to be a Pythagorean, who taught Socrates and is mentioned by Plato in this regard (she is also thought by some to be only an imaginary person). Schools that were offshoots from Pythagoreanism also had women active in them—sixty-three women are named in a list by Menage.

> Some became heads of philosophic schools, notably Arete of Cyrene who had urged her father Aristippus to set up a school at Cyrene and who conducted it after his death. She was interested in natural science and ethics and like her father she was concerned with a "world in which there would be neither masters nor slaves and all would be as free from worry as Socrates" (Beard, 1946: 326).

Poets are more "believable" as independent females than are philosophers. Sappho was head of a girl's school on the island of Lesbos and one of the more widely renowned poets of her time. In most history books she appears as a lonely mountain peak of women's achievement, but this is because historians have

Figure 6-17. *Sappho Honored by Pupils.*

chosen her as their token woman, and not looked further. Sappho was one of the "nine terrestrial muses" celebrated during what we now call the classical period of Greek culture. The other eight were: Erinna, a pupil of Sappho—called by the ancients the equal of Homer, she died famous at the age of nineteen; Myrus; Myrtis; Corinna of Boetia, Pindar's teacher, who "won five times over him in a poetic competition" (Drinker, 1973: 103); Praxilla of Sicyon, famous for her drinking songs and epics; Telesilla of Argos, writer of political songs and hymns; Nossis; and Anyta. The list, however, leaves out Gorgo, Andromeda, and Danophila, the Pamphylian. These women belong to a much longer list of seventy-six poets of that period, acclaimed as great at the time. It will be noted that where origin is indicated, none of these women is mentioned as an Athenian.

There were at least two outstanding husband-wife teams in the public life of Athens, all philosophers: Crates and his wife Hipparchia, and Leon and his wife Themista, who was called the *solon* ("law-giver") of her time.

Following is a list of the leading hetairae of Athens, and the men they companioned:

Aspasia	—	Pericles
Leontium	—	Epicurus
Danae	—	Epicurus
Glycera	—	Menander
Metaneira	—	Isocrates
Herpyllis	—	Aristotle
Archeanassa	—	Plato
Lais (1)	—	Aristippus
Lais (2)	—	Diogenes
Lais (3)	—	Demosthenes
Phrybe	—	Hyperides

The three Lais are three different women; this was a common name in Greece. We know most about Aspasia of Ionia, often called "the first lady of Athens" and the acknowledged teacher of Socrates. Together with her companion Pericles she created a remarkable civic culture in her lifetime, both through her work as a scholar and as a stateswoman. She supported the education of Athenian housewives and had them included in social occasions whenever possible. She also visited and taught among them herself.

The hetairae from the city-states of Ionia and Aetolia were considered the most brilliant. All hetairae, from whatever city, could attend the Academy and the Lyceum and participate in lectures and discussions on an equal footing with the men. Two of Plato's best-known pupils were Lasthenia of Mantua and Axiothea.

The women scholars from the various Greek city-states who congregated in Athens influenced the entire Mediterranean world for centuries to come, particularly the urban cultures of Alexandria, Constantinople, and Rome, and later the Moslem centers of scholarship. The thread of influence was broken for the Western Christian world with the decline of Rome. With the rediscovery of antiquity in the early Renaissance, numbers of books were written about these lady scholars and poets of Greece. However, little of the original writings of these women survived the various library burnings of Christian and Moslem zealots.

The second revival of interest in women's writings took place in the 1700s and 1800s, with books like G. L. Craik's *The Pursuit of Knowledge under Difficulties, Illustrated by Female Examples*, published in 1847. Such books, unfortunately, can only refer to earlier secondary publications on women scholars and to manuscript fragments of the originals.[18]

Obviously not all hetairae were scholars and leading public figures. Probably the vast majority were in the better-known courtesan tradition of being skilled entertainers with varying degrees of education and cultural interests. One little-known aspect of the hetaira's life in any society in any age is the task of accompanying her companion to war. On the battlefield she is cook, nurse, and sometimes companion-in-arms. In Xenophon's famous account of the "Retreat of the Ten Thousand," that odyssey of human bravery and ingenuity in a leaderless army finding its way home over thousands of miles, he neglects to mention the simple fact that there were actually twenty thousand and more persons in that retreat. The warriors "all had their hetairae, or camp-ladies, the majority of whom were free-born and were attended by slave-women attached to their service" (de Beaumont, 1929: 65). Probably it was the woman slaves of the hetairae who did most of the scouting for food and the pathfinding on the journey home!

We know even less about the political activists, the Lysistratas, than we do about the scholars and the courtesans. We do know, however, that "both in town and country the women knew enough about the other women of their deme[19] to elect a president for the Themophoria" (the annual festival of Demeter and Kore) (Lacey, 1968: 173). In other words, there were functioning deme-wide communication networks for women.

Keeping this array of women in mind, as well as the spoof-item in the laws of Zaleucus, "a free woman may not have more than one girl escorting her unless she is drunk, may not leave the city at night except for adultery" (Lacey, 1968: 228),[20] it is clear that many women did find their own way into the public and nondomestic spaces of Greek society. They had considerably more to do with *creating* Greek culture than is generally recognized. Their male contemporaries admired, praised, and interacted vigorously with them, but were also understandably ambivalent about the role of these women. They were in a plight similar to that of many liberal male university professors today: wanting to recognize the abilities of their women colleagues, but needing reassurance that their own wives would stay at home to keep the established order of things running smoothly. Plato could not properly be called a feminist, in spite of the fact that he did acknowledge women as both his teachers and his students. He was, however, responding in a rather logical fashion to what he saw happening around him when he proposed in *The Republic* that women should have the same education as men, since they also participated in the shaping of society. He had just witnessed the defeat of Athens by Sparta, and Spartan sex egalitarianism was becoming fashionable.

That the reinvention of the concept of free, open, and public decision making in the context of the city-state should be so fraught with difficulties in terms of the participation of women should not surprise us, having seen the difficulties which urbanism presents to the social participation of women in general. The concerns of the Pythagorean women, and of the politically oriented women, all seem to have been in the direction of egalitarianism. Following their own independent paths, and excluded from the usual derivative power base of women of the elite in other societies, they were thinking through the very same questions as the male citizenry.

One might say that the exclusion of women was a "social invention" for dealing with problems of scale, since only half as many people had to be taken into account in decision making. The exclusion of slaves and the foreign born from civic life similarly made the political process more manageable. The doctrine of *included interest,* articulated by Mill senior (J.S. Mill's father), in the nineteenth century (Mill, 1824), began to take shape in the framework of Athenian democracy. The interests of women, children, and slaves were included in the interests of the male head of household. The concept was sufficiently useful to survive for another two thousand years.

The tensions in male-female relationships that underlay this "exclusion through included interest" may have been very ugly. We see the amused and self-confident male view through the literature of the time. One wonders what the Pythagorean women, who wrote on civic problems in manuscripts that no archivists of the time thought worth keeping, were thinking about the exclusion process. They may have had insights about participatory roles for the individual in expanding societies that under other circumstances might have changed the course of political events. They might have contributed to the improvement of the deplorable international relations among the city-states of the Greek League. We can only guess at the intensity of some of the sex-role conflicts that arose in Athens because able women with political ideas were not heard.

This discussion of the Mediterranean world should not close without some brief mention of the role of women in the founding of the first world empires. We have already briefly mentioned Atossa, wife of Darius. It was under Darius and Atossa that the Achaemenian empire was extended all the way to India. The only legal claimant to the throne of Cyrus, Atossa was legally coregnant with Darius. In addition to furthering Zoroastrianism as a replacement for the demonic tribal religion of the Persians, she was considered a great stateswoman and helped develop the political and economic infrastructures that Xerxes was to take over but not be able to maintain.

The Achaemenian empire fell in its turn to the Greeks, who set out to liberate the world from Persian oppression. Philip of Macedonia, who started the crusade for liberation from Persia, died at the very start of his career. His wife Olympia, who was very much a partner in this enterprise, had in the meantime been preparing her son Alexander to take over. She was well known in her own time as an astute and ambitious woman. She was also ruthless and cruel. Many Macedonian women seem to have had a zest for politics.

It has been thought that perhaps Macedonia had a unique tradition of the participation of women, when compared to other Greek states, because such leaders as Olympia, Arsinoe II, and Cleopatra of Egypt, all Macedonians, have played such active and often aggressive roles on the international scene. An interesting study of this question (Macurdy, 1932) brings out no evidence of a traditionally active role for Macedonian women, but pinpoints the introduction of a new and more daring role model into Macedonian history with the marriage of Amyntis III in the late fifth century B.C. to Eurydice, an Illyrian barbarian out of a tradition where "queens fought and hunted like men." Eurydice is famous not only for political activity and ruthlessness on behalf of the throne, but also for having learned to read and write late in life, and for a dedication to humane causes that alternated with her ruthlessness. She evidently set a whole new tone for Macedonian queens, and Olympia appears in that new active role. The historical research on this is not definitive, but if present evidence is confirmed it provides an interesting example of social learning from barbarian traditions on the part of women elites. Certainly the concept of Macedonian princesses as role models for the rest of Hellenic civilization has become part of the historian's lore (Tarn, 1961: 98).

Whatever the source of the new behaviors, Macedonian women were an important part of the international system from Olympia's time onward. The activities of the international women's circle that centered on Athens seem modest by comparison, but both sets of women were trying to find ways to deal with new levels of social interaction and new levels of awareness of the larger world community. One worked from a position of isolation, the other from a privileged position at the hub of the social universe.

THE SIGNIFICANCE OF STRUCTURES OF WORLD EMPIRE: A GLIMPSE OF INDIA AND CHINA

With apologies for the unceremoniously scanty treatment of civilizations that represented half the world's population by 200 B.C., I wish to discuss the issues of scale in empire building, and women's roles in the new empires, with reference to India and China. The time demands involved in the adequate mastery of the history of Asia are insurmountable for the purposes of this book. To ignore half the world seems even worse. What follows should serve as a reminder of the need for making the history of Asia more accessible to the non-specialist scholar.

The drawing of India into a world empire first under Darius of Persia and then under Alexander introduces a brand new problem of scale into human history. The new kinds of resource utilization and resource distribution which this kind of empire building made possible are hardly hinted at in the early period of expansion. The first effects are chiefly felt in the gradual extension of the world trade routes, bringing both China and India into the world trading community. These "new" trade routes were in fact sturdy tracks already beaten firm by nomadic traders for several centuries before Alexander arrived on the scene. Alexander was already following a highway of sorts when he went to India, and much of the credit for the feat of conquest goes to traders, and to the innkeepers and entertainers, women and men, who kept stations open on the trade routes. Alexander's contribution was a firming up of already existing communication and organization patterns that could integrate India with the Mediterranean world, but even so his own empire crumbled rapidly.

Only twenty-seven years later the Mauryan empire was founded in India by another international entrepreneur, Chandragupta, who made extensive use of the trade networks to build up a centralized system of government such as India had never known. Greek women played an important part in Chandragupta's court, as skilled slaves contributing to court culture, as a well-muscled Amazon bodyguard (were these Spartan women?), and as wives of the aristocracy. Chandragupta himself had a Greek wife, though she was secondary wife to his coruling consort, an Indian queen. The Greek Amazons who served both as personal servants and as a bodyguard "armed to the teeth" when the somewhat unpopular monarch rode abroad (Rawlinson, 1916: 47-48) may possibly have served as the prototype for the pattern adopted by Indian kings of using women mercenaries for a standing army.

The significance of Greek women for empire building in India is a topic that might be further explored. We know that some of them came freely over the trade routes as entrepreneurs and entertainers; some of them were imported as slaves; and some of them came as part of the Mediterranean marriage-alliance system. The great unifier of India, Asoka, who came several decades after Chandragupta, must have relied on them for a variety of purposes. Nevertheless, the times of which we write appear to be a period of contracting roles for women, not of expanding ones.

In India, as elsewhere, the growing infrastructure of empire squeezed women out of public roles. Nevertheless, the heritage of the great women philosophers remained in the songs and rituals of the Vedas. The laws of Manu represented the culmination of a concerted effort by the Brahmin caste to replace all earlier traces of matriliny with strong patriarchal structures. These laws prescribed child marriage and eliminated almost all formal education for women. In terms of our thesis of a society needing ever-new techniques of resource utilization as the population expands, it is hard to explain the Indian development. Presumably the work load of Indian society was increasing and it was advantageous to have more hands at work in each household; the sooner a bride entered her new household, the sooner she could be put to work. One way to think of child marriage is as a regressive approach to work-load problems.

Interestingly, the one caste that held out against child marriage and the "diseducation" of women was the Kshatriya, the warrior caste. There were women scholars in this caste longer than in any other. Chandragupta and Kumaradevi, Kshatriyan founders of the Mauryan dynasty, united two separate kingdoms as coregnant king and queen. All royal women received military and administrative training. In pre-Mauryan days, when Alexander attacked India, the Queen of Masaga was one of those on the battlefield directing the defense of her kingdom.

At the close of the first millennium B.C. in India, then, there were highly educated and politically active Kshatriyan women in the public spaces of power; there were lower-caste women doing all the types of maintenance, craft, and trading work they had been doing all along; and there were women of the middle castes confined to the "home workshop." Full purdah, however, came only with Moslem rule, after A.D. 700, and the Brahmin caste never fully succeeded in imposing the new restrictions on its own women; old traditions remained, including traces of old matrilineal customs. The educated Brahmin women developed their own kind of underlife. Further, all these developments are true only for northern India. Southern India had had matrilineal tribal and village patterns from Neolithic times, persisting up to the twentieth century. The Nair, described briefly in chapter 4, is the best-known example today.

In China, the period of warring states was drawing to a close, and the great unifiers of China, first the Chin and then the Han, were at work. This unification process also acted to reduce the range of roles that women could play, while leaving a prominent place for royal women and for the institutions associated with the women's court. In Shang times, for example, we hear of (legendary?) Queen B'iug-Xog of Miwo-Tieng, who contributed ten thousand troops to an expedition against a hostile northern tribe (Wheatley, 1971). When we read of an all-women's army in the state of Chao, this sounds like a product of a woman's court. Battalions of soldiers are described as clad in sable furs, wearing golden rings, and carrying bows painted yellow. Chao also had all-women orchestras, another woman's-court institution (Schafer, 1967: 40). Empress Nee Lu, the widow of the first Han emperor, ruled in her own name after her husband's death, and then again after her son's death. She was evidently powerful, and tried, unsuccessfully, by sending an invading army, to prevent the kingdom of Yueh (Vietnam) from engaging in the iron trade.

While reigning empresses are few and far between, the ladies of the court were as active in Chinese politics as in those of Egypt. The institution of court eunuchs was well developed during the Han period, and a system of alliances between the court eunuchs and the family of the current empress developed which for centuries provided a power base for women of the royal family in Chinese affairs. Another factor which strengthened the position of women in the upper strata was the

> triumph of Confucianism, with its doctrine of the duty of favoring one's own family and relatives. . . . [It] brought about the custom of distributing the highest posts to the family of the empress. All this led to those bloody palace revolutions which recurred so frequently at changes of reign in later times (Needham, 1954: 106).

By Han times, Chinese princesses were being specially groomed for the international diplomatic role they were already performing in relation to the barbarian nomad tribes that were always at the kingdom's gates. When the Han emperor married off a "female relative" to a barbarian king in return for a thousand horses, one suspects that more than horses were at stake.

Buddhism provided another arena for women's activities. In Gautama's lifetime, a substantial education and communication network for women of the middle and upper classes had already been started, and there were thousands of nuns in Buddhist monasteries. Buddhist women's orders will be discussed more fully in the next chapter. In a later power struggle between Buddhists and Confucianists the Confucianists won out, and the monastic avenue to participation in at least quasi-public life was closed to women as the monasteries were liquidated. Trading, however, remained open to women. As in Mesopotamia, great merchant families expanded as China expanded. The widow of a great merchant could herself take over the business when her husband died. Sometimes poor women, starting out as petty traders, could amass considerable wealth. The widow Ching in late Chou times became so wealthy through the sale of cinnabar cakes that the emperor entertained her and built a terrace in her honor (Wheatley, 1971). Every Chinese town had a market quarter. This quarter was not developed to fulfill the functions of the Greek agora, but it had a spaciousness that Near Eastern bazaars did not have. Thus it fulfilled some of those agora functions and was a public space women were free to move about in.

Women's old roles of ruler, shamaness, and ritual leader lessened in importance during Han times, but all these roles filtered into the social organization of the masses and gave the peasant women in China a higher status than in other central empires. Nevertheless, when the central Chinese civil service was instituted, we do not read of women sitting for these examinations—though we know there were women scholars. The woman peasant and the woman trader stayed in touch with reality, while the mandarin class lived in its own insulated world. While matrilineal descent groups gradually lost their distinctive character, peasant activist traditions kept producing women leaders in a history that is pointed to with pride in contemporary China.

Slavery was well established in the Han dynasty, as it was in the Mediterranean world by then. The variety of functions of government slaves reported by Wilbur (1943) gives an interesting glimpse into the range of slave activities and the training levels required for them:

Outdoor Occupations	*Indoor Occupations*
cemetery guard	chamberlain
rancher	entertainer
horse trainer	teacher
game park tender	message chanter
grain transporter	clerk
farmer	accountant
	server

Along with the development of world empires came world religions. A great flowering of new moral teachings, some of which were destined to evolve into world religions, began as early as three centuries before Cyrus of Persia's conquest of Babylonia prepared the way for the first world empire. Prince Parshva of Varanasi taught the first Jain-type doctrine in India in 800 B.C., and Indian princesses abandoned everything to follow his teachings in his lifetime. Confucius, Lao-Tse, Buddha, and the founder of Jainism all began teaching in the sixth century B.C. Mencius was born two hundred years later, and Jesus another two hundred years after that. All of these teachers found women as well as men among the throngs pressing to hear their teachings. The need for a new mental map of the world social order was great.

The eagerness of women disciples for all these teachings is particularly significant in the light of the fact that each religion was working with the problems of conceptualizing new kinds of bonds, new kinds of social and moral unities, beyond family, tribe, and state. The context for this reconceptualization, however, was a rejection of the by-now oppressive bonds of the major urban centers of the known world. Buddhism, Christianity, and, later, Islam, were all in a sense antiurban movements aimed at destruction of the corrupt structures of the old civilizations and rebirth into new charismatic communities. The new, small, egalitarian communities "of the holy spirit" were not, however, retreating into a rural past, but forging new kinds of intercommunity links that were to make it possible for each to spread far beyond its point of origin. Women instinctively found their way to these communities, whether Jainist, Buddhist, Christian, or Moslem, and played similar roles in each of them. Ten thousand years earlier, at the threshold of the agricultural transition, it was the men who had had the "spare time" to reflect on new demands and initiate new levels of social organization, while women were too burdened with their daily work load. Now, toward the close of the first millennium B.C., there were urban middle-class women who had the "spare time" to reflect on new demands and to initiate new ventures. Much of their work in the development of these new communities and of the networks which linked them together has been deleted from the history books. We will see in the next chapter how they began building the new society within the shell of the old, utilizing new concepts of scale. We will also see how they were ruthlessly dismissed from all but a few niches of the new society.

Notes

[1]There is no one-to-one correlation between nomadism and patriarchy, however, as we will see in both this chapter and the next.

[2]The chapter on "Marriage and the Family" in Gideon Sjoberg's *Preindustrial City* (1960) makes it clear that, in relation to marriage arrangements, there is if anything a tighter control over urban than over nonurban woman. It might be said that she trades freedom for ceremonial privileges.

[3]We will find cookshops for the working poor much later in medieval London.

[4]See the interesting theoretical discussion in Goody (1968: 8-13) of the years of the domestic life cycle children spend in their mother's social space. The significance of this for the status of women and the socialization of boys has not received adequate comparative study across societies of different degrees of complexity.

[5]The women's mourning chorus mentioned by Drinker in the following passage may have been lamenting the oppression of their people by newly-arrived nomadic women:

> When the Sumerians and Akkadians were being oppressed by their Gutian conquerors during the third millennium, the women of several towns assembled to mourn their fate. Dividing into two choruses, they gave the lament antiphonally, each group singing, in alternation, appropriate verses (1948: 81-82).

[6]The extent to which monogamy prevailed in the privatized household is not clear. Plurality of spouses in rural areas is associated with the organization of production in agriculture. In the city polygamy is always plurality of *wives,* and is associated with the institution of slavery and affluence, rather than with production. The privatization of the household is a phenomenon independent of the number of wives in the household. The protection of the courts, however, would be less available to other than the senior wife in a polygamous marriage.

[7]It has also been a lucrative business for men. The line separating economic opportunity from economic oppression in the arena of sexual services is not an easy one to draw.

8In mining alone, for example, "there are over 50 different qualities and grades of officials and laborers named in the mining expeditions" (Mumford, 1961: 104).

9The matrilineality of Israeli and Arab tribes is still a matter of dispute among historians. There will be a further discussion of this issue when the matrilineality of the Arab tribes is discussed in the next chapter. In the absence of decisive evidence one way or the other, I am taking the position that the Israeli tribes were originally matrilineal, since this fits my general reading of the history of this period.

10Sheila Johansson (1975) points out that at the time of the Babylonian captivity there are refererences to the Israelite women being denounced by the prophets for returning to the worship of fertility goddesses.

11De Mause (1974: 27) suggests that the practice of child sacrifice, a special form of infanticide, was widespread at this time in the Mediterranean. The Phoenicians may be receiving an undue share of the blame for it because they organized it so efficiently. The Egyptians, the Moabites, and Ammonites, and some Israelites all practiced it, along with Celts, Gauls, and Scandinavians, says de Mause.

12As was said in chapter 3, the female fertility figurines, known from Neolithic times, are not to be considered the mother-goddess proper, source of life and death in all its possible meanings. It is by no means clear that the Cretans can be called originators of the mother goddess, but many legends have it so. See Pomeroy (1975: 13-15) for a discussion of the controversy.

13See chapter 5, pp. 171-172, of this book.

14Again, the existence of this matrilineality is now in dispute among historians.

15Johansson suggests that homosexuality among adult males may have been exaggerated—possibly a fad of the literati (1975). Certainly the Lysistrata plot assumes that males preferred female partners.

16That the confinement was real enough, however, is attested to by the fact that among surviving law court speeches are two "in which the orator brings evidence to prove that a woman who had married and borne children had actually existed" (Lacey, 1968: 168). The seclusion pattern was in some respects similar to that adopted much later by some Moslem societies.

17Freedom of movement for slave women appears to be a contradiction in terms, but in fact mistresses sent slave women on errands to all the places they themselves could not go. This meant that enterprising slave women could get to know the city well and develop some projects of their own on the side.

18Other eighteenth century publications on women writers of antiquity include: *Remains of Greek Poetesses,* n.d., by Johann Christian Wolf (includes 130 to 140 titles); *Greek Female Writers in Prose,* by the same author, published in Hamburg, Germany, in 1735 (contains a 200-page catalogue of women writers from earliest times to the sixth century A.D.); *Historium Mulierum Philosopharum,* n.d., by Menage, about 65 women philosophers, mostly Greek and Pythagorean. Count Leopold Ferri of Padua, who died in 1847, left a library of 32,000 volumes, all by women. Does it still exist? I don't know.

19*Deme* refers to a territorial unit of political organization.

20It should be noted that these laws are said to have been attempts by ridicule to stop ostentation and immorality.

References

Adams, Robert McCormick
  1966 The Evolution of Urban Society: Early Mesopotamia and Prehispanic Mexico. Chicago: Aldine.

Aeschylus
  1954 Eumenides. Tr. by George Thomson. Pp. 69-100 in Charles A. Robinson, Jr. (ed.), An Anthology of Greek Drama. New York: Holt, Rinehart, and Winston.

Beard, Mary R.
  1946 Woman as Force in History: A Study in Traditions and Realities. New York: Macmillan.

Boulding, Elise
  1966 "Japanese women look at society." The Japan Christian Quarterly 32: 19-29.

Bowra, C. M.
  1965 Classical Greece. New York: Time-Life Books.

Craik, G. L.
  1847 The Pursuit of Knowledge Under Difficulties, Illustrated by Female Examples. London: C. Cox.

Darlington, C. D.
  1969 The Evolution of Man and Society. New York: Simon and Schuster.

de Beaumont, Edouard
  1929 The Sword and Womankind. New York: Panurge Press.

de Mause, Lloyd
  1974 "The evolution of childhood." Pp. 1-74 in Lloyd de Mause (ed.), The History of Childhood. New York: Psychohistory Press.

Diner, Helen
  1965 Mothers and Amazons. Tr. by John Philip Lundin. New York: Julian Press. (First published 1932.)

Drinker, Sophie
1948 Music and Women: The Story of Women in Their Relation to Music. New York: Coward-McCann.

Driver, G. R. and John C. Mills
1935 The Assyrian Laws. Oxford: Clarendon Press.

Edey, Maitland
1974 The Sea Traders. New York: Time-Life Books.

Fustel de Coulanges, Numa Denis
1956 The Ancient City: A Study on the Religion, Laws and Institutions of Greece and Rome. Garden City, N. Y.: Doubleday.

Goody, Jack
1968 Introduction. Pp. 1-26 in Jack Goody (ed.), Literacy in Traditional Societies. Cambridge: Cambridge University Press.

Harden, Donald
1971 The Phoenicians. Revised ed. Harmondsworth, England: Penguin.

Harrison, Jane Ellen
1912 Themis: A Study of the Social Origins of the Greek Religion. Cambridge: Cambridge University Press.

Hauser, Philip M. and L. F. Schnore
1965 Study of Urbanization. New York: Wiley.

Hawkes, Jacquetta and Sir Leonard Woolley
1963 Prehistory and the Beginnings of Civilization. History of Mankind, vol. 1. New York: Harper and Row.

Hennecke, Edgar
1963 New Testament Apocrypha. 2 vols. Tr. by M. L. Wilson (ed.). Philadelphia: Westminster Press.

Henriques, Fernando
1962 Prostitution and Society. New York: Grove Press.

Johansson, Sheila
1975 Seattle, Wash.: Historian, personal communication.

Klimberg, H.
1949 Von Frauen des Altertume. Münster, Germany: Aschendorf.

Lacey, W. K.
1968 The Family in Classical Greece. Ithaca, N. Y.: Cornell University Press.

Leonowens, Anna H.
1953 Siamese Harem Life. New York: E. P. Dutton.

Macurdy, Grace H.
1932 Hellenistic Queens: A Study of Woman-Power in Macedonia, Seleucid Syria, and Ptolemaic Egypt. Johns Hopkins University Studies in Archaeology 14, David M. Robinson (ed.). Baltimore: Johns Hopkins Press.

Mill, James
1824 "Article on government." 1824 supplement, Encyclopedia Britannica.

Morris, E. J.
  1974   History of Urban Form: Prehistory to the Renaissance. New York: Wiley.

Mumford, Lewis
  1961   City in History: Its Origins, Its Transformations, and Its Prospects. New York: Harcourt Brace Jovanovich.

Needham, Rodney
  1954   Science and Civilisation in China. Vol. 1. Introductory Orientations. Cambridge: Cambridge University Press.

O'Faolain, Julia and Lauro Martines (eds.)
  1973   Not in God's Image: A History of Women in Europe from the Greeks to the Nineteenth Century. New York: Harper and Row.

Penzer, N. M.
  1935   The Harem: An Account of the Institution. Philadelphia: J. B. Lippincott.

Polanyi, Karl, Conrad M. Arensberg, and Harry Pearson (eds.)
  1957   Trade and Market in the Early Empires: Economies in History and Theory. Glencoe, Ill.: Free Press.

Pomeroy, Sarah B.
  1975   Goddesses, Whores, Wives, and Slaves: Women in Classical Antiquity. New York: Schocken Books.

Rawlinson, H. G.
  1916   Intercourse Between India and the Western World from the Earliest Times to the Fall of Rome. Cambridge: Cambridge University Press.

Renfrew, Colin
  1972   The Emergence of Civilization: The Cyclades and the Aegean in the Third Millennium, B.C. London: Methuen.

Rogers, Robert William
  1915   History of Babylonia and Assyria. Vol. 2. Nashville, Tenn.: Abingdon Press.

Schafer, Edward H., and the Editors of Time-Life Books
  1967   Ancient China. New York: Time-Life Books.

Sjoberg, Gideon
  1960   The Preindustrial City: Past and Present. Glencoe, Ill.: Free Press.

Slater, Philip E.
  1968   The Glory of Hera: Greek Mythology and the Greek Family. Boston: Beacon Press.

Sullerot, Evelyne
  1968   Histoire et Sociologie du Travail Féminin. Paris: Société Nouvelle des Editions Gonthier.

Tarn, W. W.
  1961   Hellenistic Civilization. 3rd ed., revised by Tarn and G. T. Griffith. Cleveland: World. (First published 1927.)

Wach, Joachim
1944 Sociology of Religion. Chicago: University of Chicago Press.

Wenig, Steffan
1970 Women in Egyptian Art. New York: McGraw-Hill.

Wheatley, Paul
1971 Pivot of the Four Quarters: A Preliminary Inquiry Into the Origins and Characters of the Ancient Chinese City. Chicago: Aldine.

Wilbur, C. Martin
1943 Slavery in China during the Former Han Dynasty: 206 B.C.-25 A.D. New York: Russell and Russell.

Wolf, Johann Christian
1735 Greek Female Writers in Prose. Hamburg, Germany.
n.d. Remains of Greek Poetesses.

7
Those Who Dwell in Tents, or The Woman's View from the Road

Human history is written from the perspective of the male city dweller. What does he see of the human landscape, imprisoned within city walls? He is much freer to move about than his wife, but actually both move in very restricted spaces compared to the nomad, man or woman. What does the nomad see? The nomads leave few records, since most of them are nonliterate.[1] Furthermore, they must travel light, and records can become heavy. The wisdom of nomads is not in books, but in their heads. Their libraries are the minds of the gifted scholars they attract, by force or otherwise, to travel with them.

The view from the road is a very different view of history than the view from the city. How different is life for women on the road? And what do they see that their city sisters do not see? Do they share the greater freedom of their men, or is the nomad's caravan a new way of imprisoning women? In this chapter we will be looking at the underside of history in a double sense: we will look at nomads as the swarming underlife that appears when we peek under the solid settlements in the historical landscape; and we will look at the part that nomad women play in this swarming society, in contrast to their stay-at-home city sisters.

279

Who are the nomads? The word comes from the Greek for cattle driving, according to Toynbee. In his well-known treatment of nomads in volume 3 of *A Study of History* (1935), he keeps to that definition, dealing only with herding societies. I propose to broaden that definition and treat as nomads all those who do not live regularly in settled abodes, but move from place to place in pursuit of their livelihood, traveling in complete households. The movement may be a perfectly regular one as between summer and winter pastures, a herding practice known as transhumance. It may be the irregular movement of hunting and gathering peoples through a relatively limited terrain where there are familiar campsites revisited periodically. It may be the movement without destination of the Gypsy, traveling from continent to continent to follow roads without end. It may also be the wandering of the seafarer, though movements of sea peoples tend to be migrations in search of new farmland to settle. The migrant, looking for a place to settle, is not a nomad in our definition. Neither is the fisherman who goes off to sea and returns home at regular intervals. They do not carry their households with them. The term *nomad* for us here represents households more or less continually on the move. Since the woman in settled societies is often bound to her household in ways that the man is not, the situation of women in societies where the very household is on the move will be of particular interest to us.

One could argue that the social organization and patterns of movement of the nomads, for all their fluidity, have provided the true infrastructure of history. Perhaps cities and states are the "debris" and nomadism the actual social development of the human race. In any case, the beginnings of settled agriculture mark the point at which traditions of human adaptation to environments sharply diverge. As pointed out in chapter 3, we were all hunters and gatherers once. After the development of agriculture and the concurrent domestication of animals, there were three options open to human groups: to continue the hunting-gathering life, to settle down on the farm, or to move with the herds, summering in one place and wintering in another. In fact there was a fourth option—to wander from settlement to settlement in pursuit of trade. For women and men alike, the choice between nomadism and settlement implies very different adaptation patterns. The sex-role adaptation itself is rather different in the two life styles, though there are features common to both types of societies, as one would expect.

As a background to the analysis of women's roles in nomadism, it is necessary to say something about the function of nomadism in human history. We tend to think of nomads as marginals—people pushed off to undesirable fringe areas. If this were true we would expect women to be even more marginal. Research on nomadism since the 1930s, however, has made it clear that the transition to a herding way of life, whether it is directly from hunting, or after a period of engaging in settled agriculture, is a choice made by preference. Nomads in every age of history have felt contempt for farmers and city dwellers. At the same time, the farm and the city produce goods useful to the nomads, and so they find various ways to procure these goods. Historically, perhaps as much as 90 percent of all nomad-settler contact has been peaceful, involving exchanges of goods or services between nomads and settlers. (Ahmed, 1973, p. 75ff., and Mohammed, 1973, p. 97ff., confirm the peaceful relations of nomad and settler in contemporary society.)

Herding societies develop characteristics very different from those of settled societies. There is an egalitarianism of steppes and desert that is different from the egalitarianism of the village. At the same time, the taming of horses (after 2500 B.C.) modified nomad egalitarianism. There is a tendency to develop an aristocracy on horseback and a warrior class, at least in areas like the Asian steppes where people can ride great distances at great speeds without any barriers of nature or human habitation to slow them down.[2] (Did horses teach men to become warriors?) This produces a three-layered society: the chief family or families, the people of the tribe, and slaves captured in raids. In less open terrains, or with few horses, nomads remain more peaceable and more egalitarian.

It has been suggested that

> most higher societies with a nobility as leading elite, and therefore, most classical and modern urbanized and industrialized societies, are the result of military conquest or peaceful penetration by nomadic groups (Eberhard, 1967: 279).

In other words, peaceable or warlike, people who come into the city from the steppes or desert come in feeling superior and manage to achieve the ruling positions in societies they penetrate. If it is the view from horseback that has caused all the concentrations of power in successive civilizations, horses have a lot to answer for! Reality, of course, is much more complex than that. It is interesting, however, that stratification may have a basis in the matter-of-fact experience of physical elevation.

The very fact of the distances that nomads cover in their daily lives, year after year, gives them different perceptions of society than people can arrive at who live inside walls and boxes. Seeing any one city or state in the context of other cities, other states, makes it possible for the nomad not only to act as social organizer and living communication network, but also to perceive possibilities of alternative modes of exploiting environmental resources over wide geographical areas.

Nomads have developed a unique set of adaptations to problems of increasing scale of social interaction from the time of the first major human settlements. Some nomads have remained outside the "social order problem" entirely by finding microniches that will seal them off from contact with other populations, using resources not desired by those populations. Within their niches they can have autonomy. This is the hunting and gathering adaptation that has survived all the way into the twentieth century. The more common adaptations involve establishing some sort of relationship with a settled society, while retaining a degree of autonomy and freedom of movement that settled societies do not have. Among themselves, nomads have developed a segmentary model of society (Nelson, 1973: 3-7) that maintains order and communication without hierarchy, diffusing power through the whole social structure. The segmentary model of nomadism is a political, not just an economic, model. Such segmentary tribes may develop a series of beachheads in cities, establishing formal or informal contractual relationships which permit them not only to transport what they need out of the city, but to play leadership roles among the settlers. They may even assist in the federation of formerly separate cities. Their skills of nonhierarchical coordination would be very important in the federation process. Arabs, Turko-Mongolians, and Indo-Europeans have all played such roles, probably from the beginnings of the first pristine civilizations in Egypt and Sumeria.

When tribal federations are very strong, the emphasis shifts away from contractual nomad-settler relations to a highly selective "mining" of the human talent and physical resources of the cities by the nomads. During the period when the steppe empires were at their height, the khans were experts at this kind of mining, incorporating city resources into their own nomadic infrastructure. That this was an infrastructure of no mean proportions can be seen from the fact that when Genghis Khan became khakan at the age of forty-four, he ruled over thirty-one tribes with a population of two million persons. We know this because he had a census taken.

These empires had vast retinues of skilled craftspeople, artists, philosophers, and scientists traveling with them, and had fast transcontinental Eurasian "pony express" systems for information purposes. Their traveling retinue and accompanying knowledge stock and communication systems were the most valuable assets they had.

Nomads also conceive space, possession and boundaries differently than settled people do. The people who dwell in tents are at home everywhere. Everything "belongs" to them. The world is their pasture. Gypsies exemplify this well. They are essentially hunters and gatherers, not herders, and sometimes their gathering is "misperceived" as stealing. They follow the most ancient means of livelihood of the human species.

Both nomads and settlers attribute an independence, an autonomy and freedom, to nomads that settled people do not have. In fact the environmental constraints and physical handicaps of the nomad are often far more severe than those of settled peoples, yet the admiration for and envy of the unconquered fierce ones of history (whether fierce or not, they are thought to be so) is a continuing theme among settled folk, along with the fear and horror that nomads also evoke. The nomads themselves unquestionably feel far freer than city folk. What makes a people feel free is always an interesting question, and it is particularly interesting to note that nomadic women share with the men the feeling of greater freedom. What the bases for this greater feeling of freedom are, we will try to discover in the following pages.

The fact that nomads perceive, move through, and use space differently than settled peoples means that their behavior from time to time has the effect of shifting the political balance of power among settled peoples. Since history records chiefly the doings of kings and generals and battlefield exploits, we are aware of nomad incursions chiefly as bloody events. The long, peaceful periods of interpenetration which eventually bring ex-nomad chieftains to kingship in Mesopotamian cities go unrecorded. The underground developments that undergird power shifts are noted only at moments of dramatic surfacing of new political alignments.

One of the greatest difficulties in studying the nomads has to do with the lack of archaeological remains of a nonbuilding, nonliterate, non-record-keeping society. Because they had no cities, they had no ruins. We only read about them through the eyes of the city dwellers, and then usually only in periods when the nomads are responsible for reducing cities to ruins. This penchant of the nomads for clearing the plains of walls and buildings so there can be more pasture land, a reflection of their feelings about the uselessness of cities, gives us a one-sided view of their activities. In what follows I shall try to reverse the perspective as much as possible and present the nomadic life from the point of view, if not of the nomads themselves, at least of a friendly observer. Our focus will be a double one: on the internal character of the nomadic life and its role structure for women and men, and on the function of the nomads as social organizers who developed a regional approach to resource utilization at a time when city-states had only a rudimentary knowledge of their own local environments.

Historical Overview of Nomadism

If nomadism is indeed the infrastructure of history, as I have suggested, then a look at nomadism between 2000 B.C. and A.D. 1500, from the period of pristine civilization through classical civilization, will give us a better basis for examining sex-role structures than we could otherwise have. The three main types of nomadism appear to be 1) hunting and gathering nomadism, 2) herding nomadism of steppe and desert, and 3) craft and trade nomadism.

Hunting and gathering nomadism is the oldest, with three million years of human experience behind it. Today it represents in one way the most highly evolved approach to resource utilization in submarginal land that we know of. The Kalahari bush people, for example, survive in what is for them comfort under conditions in which other human groups would quickly starve to death. The fact that such societies survive in the twentieth century is a testimony to the skills involved. This is niche nomadism, and depends for its survival on *not* interacting with other forms of social organization and land use.

Herding nomadism of steppe and desert evolved contemporaneously with agriculture. Early farmers with growing herds retreated with their herds to less fertile regions, as the need for food led to the more intensive use of local land. This was the beginning of the competition between the desert and the town. Three major groups are known to us: the Bedouins of the Afro-Arabian steppes, the Turko-Mongolian groups of the Eurasian steppes, and the Indo-Europeans clustered more toward the European side of the Eurasian steppes. Bedouin and Asiatic herding nomadism continue up to the present day, but European herding nomadism has disappeared except in enclaves such as the land of the Lapps in northern Scandinavia. All three of these herding groups had profound effects on the evolution of urban society in the Middle and Far East and in Europe. This was partly through their special relationship with the craft and trading nomads and their superior knowledge of the world's trade routes, and partly through direct involvement with the internal politics of major city-states and kingdoms. It was the long series of negotiations between chiefs and queens of "border tribes" and center cities that provided the nomads with the political skills necessary to organize empires once they had power bases inside the cities. Neither Darius and his partner, Atossa, nor Alexander and his partner, Olympia, would have been able to build their world empires if they had not followed the well-trodden paths of the nomads. Much of the leadership for those empires came from ex-nomad chieftains and princesses. The role of the Celts, the Huns, and the Goths in the development of a fresh new European society on the ruins of the crumbled imperialism of Rome is perhaps a better-known example of this process, though the barbarian invasions of Roman Europe are still apt to be described as a disaster rather than a social blessing. Some contemporary historians are now inclined to describe the barbarians as more humane than the Romans; at the least they were more egalitarian.

The craft and trader nomads are in a special category by themselves: the Gypsies who originated in India and developed a complementary role to that of the Turko-Mongolian hordes, traveling with them and "servicing" their almost craftless societies; the Bedouin peoples who shifted from herding to trading and are best known in history as the intrepid Moslem traders who penetrated everywhere in the Mediterranean world; and the Beaker folk of Europe who brought the products of the Mediterranean civilization to a more backward agricultural Europe. These groups all live on in the twentieth century, most easily recognized in the Gypsy caravans of Europe, the Middle East, Africa, and the Americas.

One other set of peoples, the Vikings, will be included in our overview of nomads, though they are not true nomads at all. The Vikings are exceptions to all nomadic patterns: they moved by sea, while all true nomads hate water; they had behind them thousands of years of settled agriculture in the northlands when they took to the sea; and when they traveled it was always in search of new areas of settlement. For the period between A.D. 600 and 1000, however, they were so constantly on the move—through Russia to Constantinople, along the Atlantic coast of Europe, and across the island-dotted reaches of the northern seas extending all the way to North America —that they performed all the functions of nomadism listed earlier: they were the social organizers of the North Atlantic, with outposts on the Mediterranean; they discovered new environmental resources; and they completely changed the balance of power in Europe. Also, they would have been helpless without the women who traveled with them.

The most visible archaeological traces of all these groups of nomads are the great sets of walls extending from the Roman *limes,* which fortified the Rhine-Danube frontier bounding the western reaches of the "known world," to the Chinese Great Wall bounding the northeastern reaches of the "known world." The walls, of course, were built by the settled peoples to keep the nomads out. They functioned as gates instead, inviting the nomads to destroy barriers and unify ever larger geographical territories.

In general, there was a continual pressure of nomads on settled land because they, like the settlers, were also rapidly expanding populations. Only the hunters and gatherers, who remained on foot, maintained zero population growth. All the other nomads multiplied, and carried their families and possessions in wagons wherever they went. In times of drought, the pressures of herding people on agricultural land would be especially severe. It would be a mistake, however, to see the movements of nomads as only climatically triggered. The nomads came to the cities because they enjoyed them, even while they had contempt for them. The city was a challenge to which the nomad responded. Ibn Khaldun (1969), in *The Muqaddimah,* written in 1377, describes the softening process that went on as one group after another became absorbed in city life and lost both the skills and hardiness of their nomadic heritage. Nevertheless, given the population growth of the nomads left on the steppes and deserts, there was always a fresh supply of nomadic peoples for new leadership in the cities.

Sex Roles and Social Structure among the Nomads

While nomadic societies differ considerably from one another in structure and role patterning, there are some characteristics that are found among nearly all nomads. Before going on to look at individual societies, we will examine some of these general characteristics.

The Family

One of the most widely recognized features of herding societies is their patriarchal structure. The herding mentality and culture has sometimes been blamed for the overthrow of the "Golden Age of Woman" and for her subsequent subjection. Yet, one of the most consistent features of each of the herding societies we will look at—the Arab Bedouin, the Turko-Mongolian, and the Celtic—are persistent traces of matrilineality and of significant public roles for women. There are tribal stories of a time when women remained in their own tents after marriage and received visiting husbands. Tribal genealogists mention the name of the king's mother as well as father in far more instances than we would expect if the mother were of no importance. When the head of a tribal group dies, be it chief, khan, or king, his mother and his widow play a very important part in designating the next ruler. Mothers and wives of chiefs continue to play an important role in nomadic tribal societies in Africa today. While a king or khan usually has more than one wife, there is never any question as to who is the "ruling wife" and plays the chief political role in the tribe.

The man "heads" the family, but when there are plural wives, each wife has her own tent and her own herds. A woman's relationship with her husband has many of the characteristics of a herding partnership, although men do much of the physical tending of the cattle. Women care for goats and sheep and frequently milk the cattle. Among pastoral nomads, only the well-to-do warrior-aristocracy tribes practice polygamy. The average pastoral nomadess and her husband would find partner-wives an economic drain.[3]

The rate of population growth in a nomadic tribe depends on the resources available to the tribe. Tribes with few pack animals and no wagons may keep close to zero population growth, using infanticide as the ultimate means of birth control. Tribes with substantial wagons and draft animals have no problem in transporting children and are less inclined to practice infant exposure, though there may be some attempt to keep down the number of girl babies raised. Girls cannot be used for herding, which is as physically rigorous an occupation as hunting and often requires long absences from camp.

Nomads tend to be sexual puritans, whether Gypsies, Mongols, or Arabs, and punish both women and men for adultery. Marriages are usually arranged, and if there is divorce, there are usually rights to divorce on both sides. Property rights of both sides are protected in divorce.

In general then, within the family there is an egalitarian husband-wife relationship and an economic partnership based partly on individual ownership, partly on shared holdings.

Political Structures

The tribal chief, khan, or king usually has a khatun or queen as co-ruler; the two are usually advised by a council of elders. The council of elders is not a mixed group, but there is usually at least one woman who serves as senior advisor to the council; she has partly the role of political advisor, partly the role of forecaster. Sometimes these roles are separated. The khatun rules until the next khan is designated, and acts as regent during the minority of the next designated ruler, when necessary. In rare cases, as during the height of the Mongol empire, the institution of the harem appears. When it does, it has all the characteristics of a woman's court, with diplomatic retinues in attendance. Women are important as conductors of ceremonials. In some nomadic societies only the women chant and sing, never the men.

We have seen that women of the elite also play important political roles in settled societies. It is difficult to compare the two peoples, since records on nomadic societies are even scarcer than those on settled societies, but political participation of women appears to be more formalized in nomadic societies. Among the Mongols, the khatun *always* rules between khans, as a matter of tribal custom. In most nomadic groups there are traditional spheres of authority allotted to women as corulers, advisors, regents, and participants in the choice of successor rulers, whereas, in general, women of the urban Middle Eastern elite who got into political action had only one formally recognized position to work from: that of priestess. Other activities depended on their own wits, rather than a tradition of participation. As mentioned in chapter 4, there is some evidence that the most outstanding women who appear in the Mesopotamian chronicles are second-generation nomads. When nomadic elites entered cities, the women both activated the traditional priestess roles and generally expanded the sphere of women's political participation in the city.

Economic Roles

There is a sex-based division of labor in nomadic societies, but it is not as rigid as often appears. While men usually follow the herds, sometimes the men do the milking, sometimes the women. If war can be thought of as an economic activity (a type of hunting and gathering), then men are more engaged in fighting than are women. However, since war is often fought as the entire tribe is on the move, the campground becomes the battlefield. The women fight also, and are trained for this. Among the Gypsies, women and men are both craftworkers and traders, but specialize in different products. In general women have more camp-based activities than men do, since women rarely engage in herding or raiding. Camp-based tasks, however, have a different social setting than the home-based tasks of the sedentary woman. Breaking or setting up camp, the woman's task, is a very frequent activity, and is always done in close company with other women. Preparation of food, garments, and containers from wool and skins goes on in the spaces between tents as well as inside. There tends to be women's space versus men's space, rather than private domestic space versus public space. On ceremonial occasions, women's and men's spaces intersect, although there are also all-women's and all-men's ceremonials. The community of women and girls and boys under twelve can be a strongly knit community that can make inputs into the men's community via the woman elder. Nelson (1973: 43, 48-49) is emphatic about the power of nomadic women in policy making and in judging the conduct of men. She also brings out the autonomy the women feel. "What do [men] know about what their women do?" queries one amused informant.

Religion

All types of nomad societies seem to have a deep religious strain, but it is a generalized religious responsiveness that can fit a wide variety of institutional forms. The Mongols were extraordinarily tolerant of all religions, having Nestorian Christians and Catholics, Buddhists, Zoroastrians, and Moslems in their courts. The Gypsies adopt the religion of the country or region they are in at the moment. Their religious fervor is matched only by their openness to highly diverse ways of expressing it. It seems to be particularly the women's job to identify and support the appropriate variety of cults in a given setting, and to "take in" new religions. The underlying faith is shamanistic. The tribal shaman may or may not outrank the prophetess.[4] To the extent that ceremonials reflect the basic belief structures of the society, however, the leading role of women in ceremonials belies the formal prominence of the shaman. The rites of childbirth, of baptism, of marriage, of death, and of the crowning of a king are often women's rites.

The nomadic life, then, does tend to create a man's world and a woman's world, accentuated by the need to provide protected space for childbirth and for children in a camp environment that does not readily allow for protected spaces. Women's participation in the total life of the society, however, is not less—and more probably, greater—than for women in settled societies. The common orientation of both sexes toward the "world as one's backyard," and the common experience of living out of the nomadic equivalent of a suitcase, is probably a more powerful bond between women and men than the separateness of their tasks would indicate.

We will now turn to an examination of the role of women in individual nomadic societies, beginning with a further examination of the hunting and gathering bands already discussed in chapter 3.

Hunters and Gatherers of North America

Our earlier discussion of hunters and gatherers referred to bands in the African and Eurasian regions. Here we will focus on North America. The sheer historical diversity of hunting and gathering cultures in North America is overwhelming. There have been over five hundred languages spoken, some as different from each other as English and Chinese; every type of religious system known to humankind; many types of political organization and descent systems co-existing; over two thousand kinds of plant foods utilized by various groups. Peter Farb's *Man's Rise to Civilization* (1968) makes it possible to conceptualize this diversity of hunting and gathering cultures in such a way that relevant aspects of women's roles can be distilled for the purpose of this study.[5]

First, some background information. Nomads wandered over to Alaska from Siberia, perhaps about 35,000 B.C., during the last ice age.[6] When they found themselves in North America amidst melting snows, they were suddenly exposed to an undreamed-of hunting wealth, and the archaeological record tells us they exterminated all the large mammals from Alaska to Cape Horn, including horses and camels, by about 5000 B.C. This is an incredible example of the mining of environmental resources, only equalled again in the twentieth century by industrial societies. The same hunting to extinction did not take place in Eurasia or Africa, Farb suggests, because bands of humans and the big mammals coexisted from the earliest hominid times. Overhunting took place after the last ice age with the pressure of expanded populations, but never hunting to extinction. Eurasian and African hunters knew their total terrain, and understood the ecological system within which they lived, well enough to move to the herding and breeding of animals when supplies ran low.

When we meet the North American hunter-gatherers in the historical record, they too have achieved familiarity with their environment and learned to utilize it in ecologically sound ways, forced to this by the disappearance of big game. We find three main types of adaptation: the arctic Eskimo culture, the desert culture, and the forest culture. An incipient steppe horseback and herding culture began developing on the Great Plains in the eighteenth century after the Indians acquired horses from the Spaniards, but the conditions created by the invading Europeans were so catastrophic that it was crushed before it could fully develop.

The view of the world from on foot is very different from the view of the world from horseback. Bands moving on foot became familiar with a series of microenvironments across the continent. As in Eurasia, when the big game disappeared, the women's scanning skills once more became primary. The frequency of matriliny in the forest civilizations is possibly a reflection of the importance of women's cooperative efforts in food gathering. In the harsher environment of the arctic and the desert the relationship is simply egalitarian, neither matrilineal nor patrilineal, and bands are very small indeed.

In the arctic each pair of hands is needed to the utmost, and there is a complex system of husband-and-wife-borrowing to ensure that each man who goes out on prolonged hunting trips has a female partner to handle the closely interdependent division of labor necessary to arctic environmental utilization. Women who are pregnant cannot safely make such trips, so the remaining women divide such responsibilities. Since this practice is described for the most part by male anthropologists, it is described as wife-swapping, or wife-borrowing. It would make as much sense to say husband-swapping or husband-borrowing, since the temporary hunting partnerships thus formed are equally necessary to women and men.[7] Much of Eskimo culture can be interpreted as flexible social-bonding arrangements that enable women and men to draw upon helpers from their own and other bands in times of need. Everything depends on this being done as part of mutually agreed upon arrangements within and between bands. What causes jealousy and conflict is when certain individuals begin making unilateral arrangements without full consultation with all the other marital partners involved. The ad hoc man-woman pairings of the Eskimo are public, not private, matters. When treated as private matters they can result in murder.

Under the arctic conditions, there are few "men's spaces" distinct from "women's spaces," little accumulation, and no stratification. Under the circumstances, women are hardly excluded from decision making. The famous nomad-style communication network is seen at its best among the Eskimo. Tell a joke in Alaska and you will hear it next year in Greenland (Farb, 1968: 35). No one to my knowledge has mapped that communication net!

In the desert, the Shoshone with her digging stick lives much as her sister in the Australian desert.[8] These women and their spouses live in a nonstratified leisure society (i.e., they have lots of free, unprogrammed time), moving from site to site in the familiar desert and putting up twig shelters in all their favorite spots. They know where to find the tastiest foods in the sparse land. The same complex elaboration of marriage alliances, combined with small families and much individual freedom, is found in both societies. In the desert there is much more of a separation between women's and men's cultures than in the arctic, since women and men work at hunting and gathering in segregated groups, but decision making involves input from both groups.

The most famous of the forest cultures is the Iroquois, a matrilineal society that initiated the formation of an intertribal league made up of various Iroquois groups and neighboring tribes in A.D. 1450 (Morgan, 1901). The league held together with remarkable skill and adaptiveness during the white man's invasion, but finally disintegrated about 1850. The Iroquois had strong sisterhood institutions. The headwoman of each of the five tribes was responsible for choosing the male sachems who attended the league council meetings. They checked the sachems' behavior and decisions closely. When a sachem did not perform satisfactorily, the sisterhood removed him. This matriliny, however, was related to an already settled mode of existence. The Iroquois had taken up agriculture by the 1400s, and were no longer true nomads. Their village life and social organization might be most comparable to that of the earliest agricultural villages of the Middle East.

The Indians on horseback—Farb (1968) calls them, somewhat unfairly, "make-believe Indians"—on the plains are a consequence of the Spaniards' reintroduction of horses to the continent. In the 1600s Indians began to acquire numbers of horses (through both raiding and breeding), and by 1750 there were Indians on horseback along the eastern slope of the Rockies all the way from Texas to Alberta, and all over the plains. The plains were a melting pot, and the tribal groups that roamed them were all composite tribes, made up of many different ethnic elements. These tribes developed almost overnight the warrior aristocracy we shall see on the Mongolian steppes. It all happened so fast, and the records are so battle-oriented, that it is hard to say much about the women in this "overnight" society. They must have been extraordinarily adaptable, and they certainly had to work hard keeping up with sudden accumulations of goods in the absence of patterns for dealing with such accumulations. If they had been given more time, perhaps a more patterned stratification and reasonable use of accumulated resources would have evolved in this horseback society. Imagine the evolution of these tribes, had not the killing off of all the larger animals occurred by 5000 B.C.: the plains might indeed have been steppe country with a horseback society. In such a scenario, the European invaders would have had a very different kind of native society to reckon with, and North America might look very different today.

As it was, the plains warriors accumulated horses and weapons and power without any clear sense of direction and purpose. There was no time for the slower evolution of new social technologies, adapted social goals. The Indians were crushed by the superior accumulation of horses, weapons, and power of the invaders. There was no time for sisterhood between the independent pioneer women and the independent Indian women to develop.9 That would have been another possible scenario, in a slower-moving play.

North American Indians were not lucky in their adaptations to problems of scale. They wiped out the mammal resources of a new continent before they discovered those animals' worth, and by the time they had created a viable new set of hunting/gathering/agricultural adaptations, they were confronted with a society operating on an entirely different scale, a society that could use the continental resources in totally new ways, and mine them as ruthlessly as the ancient Indians themselves had done. If one is pessimistic, one could imagine a day when only the Shoshone with their desert digging sticks will have the necessary know-how to make a "decent living" from what is left of the continent.

The Bedouin Arabs and the North African Berbers

Now we will move back from the New World to the Old World, where "social time" moved more slowly. We begin by looking at the deserts.

The Bedouins of Arabia, part of a larger Afro-Asian steppe culture that covers all the drier parts of North Africa, live in one of the most unprepossessing—to the outsider—microenvironments that the planet has to offer: the central deserts of their peninsula. Back in 2000 B.C. there was still plenty of space to choose from in that part of the world for settlement. To the contemporary historian, the choice of these deserts seems an improbable one. Therefore, it has been assumed that only those forcefully driven out of more hospitable environments would ever live there. Arabia offers very pleasant places to live along the high, fertile plateaus bordering the Persian Gulf and the Indian Ocean. In the second millennium B.C. it had cosmopolitan trading ports on all three coasts of the peninsula, including the Red Sea side facing Africa. There were land routes to Egypt and a series of trading towns running north to south along the wadis (dry riverbeds), connecting Syria and Mesopotamia with the seaports that led to India and Egypt. These towns, strung out like sculptured beads on a famous old incense-trading track, were an important part of the infrastructure of the earliest trading routes in the ancient world.

But the Bedouins did not live in any of these places, and it is now agreed that they *chose* not to live in these places. They lived in the desert—and continue in the twentieth century to live in the desert— because they love it. It is perhaps by looking at the first Bedouins, the most incomprehensible of all nomads to the comfort-loving city dwellers, that we will get some understanding of the meaning of the nomadic way of life. Sargon II described them as "those who dwell in the desert, who know not governors or overseers, who have never brought tribute to kings." Sennacherib wrote of Adummatu, a place in northern Arabia that keeps turning up in old chronicles, as a place "in the midst of the desert, full of dirt, where there be neither food nor drink." This same Adummatu was, in fact, a nomadic campsite. It was home base for the Arabian queens—the queens of the Aribi that had such long contact with the Assyrians. It was from here that Queens Zabibe and Samsi set forth for battle to avoid paying tribute to Assyria; from here that Queens Iati'e, Te'elhunu, and Tabua defended their autonomy; from nearby Ghassan that Queen Mawiya did the same. It was from here that the Hyksos invaded and ruled Egypt in the 1700s B.C., and that Bedouins, Berbers, and Assyrians launched separate and joint attacks over succeeding centuries until Egypt finally came under Ptolemaic rule. Women warriors were from time to time leaders in these invasions.

In the old silent films of my childhood in the twenties, the women of Arabia were always shown in harems, or being carried, helpless captives, from one harem to the other. This hardly squares with the image of warrior queens at the head of their desert troops. What was the life of these tribes really like, how did women get to be queens, and why are there so many references to them in Assyrian chronicles?

A look at family structure and tribal organization may answer some of these questions. Since the Bedouins and the Israelites are of the same Semitic stock, originating in the same Arabian deserts, the patriarchal structure described for the nomadic Israelites in the last chapter is the same structure found among the Bedouins. The traces of an earlier matrilineal descent system are also present.

In old Arabia (already old in 1000 B.C.), tradition has it that husbands were visitors in the tents of their wives—a desert version of the Nair (Nayar) form of marriage described in chapter 4. Prototypical for this earlier era is the semilegendary Omm Karja, who contracted marriages in more than twenty tribes but sent her husbands home and lived in her own camp surrounded by her children. In those days there were women judges, and a list of these women from ancient times is extant. This information comes from the researches of W. Robertson Smith (1966: 126), who worked on kinship and marriage systems in Arabia in the 1880s, influenced by Bachofen's work on mother-right. Smith's work has been discredited along with Bachofen's, but a reexamination of the data is perhaps in order. Smith, himself, points out that later marriage records are confusing and full of inconsistencies. This is because several different traditions evolved in Arabia, some keeping to the old matrilineal ways, others moving far from them. Every Arabian marriage contract to some extent represented a new negotiation between representatives of different sets of customs. Among the four major marriage patterns described by Smith, there is great variation in the amount of property and power reserved for the woman.

Spencer (1952) uses this variability to argue against the possibility that a matrilineal reckoning ever existed. One of the fascinating aspects of a study of marriage-contract literature for Mediterranean civilizations is how many ways marriage contracts were written. This simply tells us that there has always been a lot more room for bargaining in marriage contracts than social scientists of the structural-functional school of analysis would like to admit.[10] One does not have to postulate any grand evolutionary scheme to suppose that many societies began that bargaining process from a matrilineal descent-reckoning system.

For those who chose the Bedouin way of life, the matrilineal tradition remained much stronger than it did among the settled folk. "She walks with her head held high"—a saying about Tuareg women today—would certainly have been true of the women of the Aribi. In fact, all Bedouins walk with their heads held high. They recognize no authority or social organization not based on kinship structure (Buccellati, 1967: 87). In 2000 B.C., this would have been in marked contrast with their settled fellow-tribes to the south, whose lives in the port cities were already tied up with stratification systems and carefully contracted rights.[11] Such differences in social patterning in an ethnically homogeneous area with no alien tribal infiltrations underlines the significance of the choice of the nomadic as contrasted with the settled existence. Each family roaming the desert is an autonomous unit, and "tribal society is held together by a delicate balance of powers, rather than by strict subordination" (Buccellati, 1967: 88). The nomads who wandered toward Canaan were the same. The Book of Judges reflects the pattern: "In those days there were no kings in Israel; everyone would do what was right in his eyes" (21: 25).

Family units within kin groups formed and re-formed into bands of continually changing composition, and there was no guarantee that common kin ties would prevent the start of blood feuds between bands that got in each other's way. The harshness of the environment, and the fierce clinging to autonomy, meant that tribal federations were of the loosest, and the authority structure was fragile. Yet structure did exist. The roles identifiable in that structure include the *sajjid*, the speaker, one who had moral authority only (this was not a hereditary post, nor were any of the other positions); the *ra'is*, military leader in war; the *hakam*, judge in time of peace; and the *kahin*, priest-diviner. Then there was a *maglis nadwah*, assembly of nobles. The Bedouin would appear to be a ranked, rather than a stratified, society, with nobles holding ceremonial responsibility but not having differential access to resources. Therefore, the term *queen*, applied to the women with whom the Assyrians negotiated, and the term *princesses*, applied to the young women sent to Assyria to school, are misleading. It is the typical bureaucratic response in dealing with a less differentiated society to give rank and titles to those with whom one deals as if there were a counterpart structure to that of one's own society. The colonialist expansion of the West into Africa and Asia from the 1600s on is replete with examples of this. The queens, when leading troops in battle, were acting as *ra'is;* when negotiating with the Assyrians, they would be acting as *sajjid* or *hakam.* Whether they were also members of the assembly of nobles, the *maglis nadwah*, we cannot be sure. We will see many examples in nomadic society of women having special authority roles without counterpart representation in tribal councils. This may be due to the shift from matriliny to patriliny, since men sit on tribal councils as heads of families, rather than simply as men. Women have authority as competent individuals, and also by right of seniority. Men have authority given them by the role structure.

When the Aribi women were acting as tribal leaders in negotiations with the Assyrians, we can be sure that they acted with the same fierce dignity and self-assurance as the men, and won the full respect of those with whom they dealt. In fact, they were probably dealing with their own kin, or persons from tribes well known to them, since we know that some Bedouins began settling in Mesopotamia from earliest times—Sargon, for example, was a second-generation nomad turned settler—and each new Bedouin immigrant in turn played an active role in contact between her newly adopted city and the tribes back home in the desert. Probably the leading temple priestesses in the cities had active contacts with their sister priestesses in the desert; in fact, the Aribi tribes were often referred to as the "confederation of the worshippers of Ishtar." Since each king group worshipped its own goddess, in addition to recognizing Ishtar, the women played the role we shall see in many nomadic societies, that of linking old and new religions and cults.

The old aristocracy of Babylonia and Assyria probably welcomed the arriviste nomad leaders who settled in town, even while they resented them, because they needed help in dealing with the nomads who stayed in the desert. These desert tribes were respected because they were impossible to subdue; the Assyrians, Babylonians, and Persians all tried to restrain them, and all failed. The nomads lived in tent cities that could be moved at a moment's notice. So swift were they in their movements that none of the Mesopotamian troops had a chance at any kind of battle when the Aribi were on their home ground. They could only be defeated if caught off the desert, which happened very rarely. Furthermore, the defeat was highly temporary.

The Bedouin women who dealt so effectively with the Mesopotamian army and palace-temple complex were partly trained for their work by the Assyrians themselves, as we know from the accounts of Arabian princesses going to school in Assyria. This means they were to some extent an elite, and yet all the evidence we have about the desert Bedouins indicates a minimum of stratification and accumulation of wealth. All the women and all the men probably had to work hard to survive in the scanty desert-steppe feeding grounds. It is hard to visualize family life and child care in that setting.

Maysun's poem, at the end of this section, gives a clue as to the feeling of freedom and relatedness to their environment that the women of the desert had. Children probably learned to be self-sufficient at a very early age. Chroniclers of the Assyrian times comment on how healthy the Bedouins were, compared to city dwellers. Probably the infant mortality rate was high, due both to infanticide and early childhood mortality, but the children who survived were sturdy. The diet of cattle blood, meat, and milk seems to be an adequate one for steppe dwellers. The desert steppe is a harsh mother, but will feed a carefully limited population well. Since nonurban women everywhere, nomadic or peasant, develop efficient baby-toting skills, we can assume that the women among the Aribi did not feel confined by their babies. When necessary, they went to battle with their babies on their backs, as nomadic women everywhere have done, including the barbarian women who fought Caesar's troops in Gaul.

Not all of the Bedouins were herders. Some followed the trade routes, and of those, some made their way across the Red Sea to what is now Ethiopia. Once the trail was blazed, both traders and

herders followed it, and the Ethiopian highlands today shelter nomadic tribes that once traveled the Arabian deserts. Due partly to the
nomadic women's tradition of supporting a variety of religious practices, one can find today in Ethiopia three major religious traditions:
Judaic, Christian, and Islamic.

Some of the Berbers who have guarded and used the North
African desert steppes from earliest recorded times and well before
then may well have been Arab Bedouins who made their way across
the land bridge to Egypt, or across the trade routes of the Red Sea.
Other Berbers came up from the Saharan steppes, further south,
during the period when the steppes went from grassland to uninhab-
itable sand, well before 2000 B.C. In ensuing centuries, the Phoenicians, the Romans, and the Moslems had to deal with these Berbers.
Some of the Berbers continued a herding existence. Others were
traders, and others settled on the outskirts of invading civilizations
to provide a buffer between the nomads and the settlers.

The Phoenicians tried to make alliances with the Berbers, without
much success. The Romans built *limes* and fortified settlements, to
keep them out. The Moslems converted them. But no one in three
millennia has succeeded in assimilating them.

> They remained . . . a separate element in the population, with a dif-
> ferent language, social organization and way of life. Even after the con-
> version to Islam, they retained their separate identity, and not infre-
> quently came into conflict with their Arab co-religionists (Oliver, 1968:
> 31).

All the great African empires of the first millennium A.D. depended
on the Berbers for trade and communication skills.

Today, in spite of steamship, railway, and airlines, the Berbers still
to some extent operate their traditional Sahara trade routes. When all
the oil wells have dried up, they will probably still be plying their old
routes.

While the Arab Bedouin and the North African Berber today are
separated by many twentieth century barriers of nation and alliance
systems, there is still a sense in which we can think of the Afro-Asian
steppes as a cultural region. We do not have the word pictures of the
old Arabian tent camps, and of the packing and moving process, that
we have for the later Mongols. We can look, however, at the contemporary desert-dwelling North African Tuareg and Somali nomads who
live on the African Horn, and get something of the flavor of this style
of nomadic life. The Somalis live spread out over several countries
which now abut on the modern state of Somalia, and wherever they

live, from 65 to 85 percent of them are nomads (Silberman, 1959: 560). Modern Somalia has substantial trade in forest products and leather and 90 percent of the world's incense comes from there. There is agriculture in Somalia, of course, but the true nomadic tradition looks down on agriculture. The Somalis do not require vegetables: their main food is milk, and on festive occasions, camel meat. Monteil comments that he has seen sturdy old men—and presumably women!—who have never known any other food than milk (Monteil, 1959: 575). Keeping mobile for these people is important, to prevent both overgrazing and the human diseases that come with too much interhuman contact in that environment.

> Respiratory complaints are rampant and tuberculosis rates would be higher still if people lived in greater proximity for longer periods. It may be merely an instinct that makes Somali women such keen partisans of nomadism—so tragically at times goading their menfolk to fight, as in the massacre of Italians, in Mogadishu in 1947, as symbols of town and sedentary life, but . . . they know that "the first consequence of the transplantation of a nomad group into an agricultural region [in Africa] is an enormous increase in the habitual unrequited work of the women." In Arabia it means, of course, veiling and seclusion (Silberman, 1959: 568).

Why would a woman trade relative health and freedom for agricultural or urban "slavery"? Everything she owns can easily be piled on a couple of camels, and she is the one who decides where the tents shall be erected when camp is moved. She is interested in a politics which will preserve her freedom of movement, and that of her children. A Somali child of five is

> alert, and is not afraid to go thirty miles alone; it knows the genealogy of its clan over 17 generations; and it can milk. All through [her] life the Somali invests in brain rather than brawn. The satisfactions of nomadism are such that senior members of the education department at Hargeisa, "as a good Somali should," return periodically to their herds in the interior (Silberman, 1959: 568).

The desert-dwelling Tuareg are of special interest to us because the status of women is still high among them after centuries of Moslem rule. The Tuareg are a Berber people, and the Berbers have many of the characteristics of the Arab Bedouins. No one is sure what the ethnic origin of the Berbers is. Like the Arab Bedouins, they live in the bleakest part of their country by preference, and they have the same traits of fierce independence and contempt for city dwellers.

The Tuareg women, to whom the proverb about walking with the head high refers, apparently even today take part in tribal councils and have a tradition as warriors. They are also known as preservers of tradition and learning, and

> where the ancient script, which has a similarity to the old Minoan script of Crete, is still used, women are more versed in it than men (Drinker, 1948: 71-72).

Singing at evening tribal gatherings is done by women, not by men; men are the audience. Tuareg women of rank organize and judge sings.

The division of labor among the Tuaregs, with regard to maintenance activities, is determined by the needs of the herds and the scarcity of water. The men must sometimes lead the herds far afield in search of water, and the women remain at the camp doing the typical food preparation, craftwork, and child tending of the nomad society. The path they travel in their moves over any one year is a familiar one, determined by grazing and water resources. Nomadic women must be the best packers in the world, since they do so much of it.

The important role of Tuareg women in ceremonial life is probably a reflection of the amount of time they spend together in camp, able to plan and organize tribal activities. The men, dispersed much of the time, have less opportunity for such planning. As among the Arab Bedouins, the society is ranked, rather than stratified, and few permanent advantages accrue to anyone.

The fact that even today the Tuaregs have traditions (not exercised for some time) of women warriors is an interesting bit of evidence of the persistence of this aspect of cultural history. It should at least be noted that the earliest of the Amazon traditions come from Bedouin country; the European Amazons mentioned in the last chapter were a later tradition. Diner (1965), who draws largely on the writers of antiquity, tells us how the Amazon women, herders and warriors, flourished at the foot of the Atlas Mountains, presumably in the early days of Egyptian glory, "clad in red leather armor, snakeskin shoes, and with python-leather shields" (Diner, 1965: 133). Supposedly they have encountered the mainland survivors of the Atlantis civilization, made an alliance with them, and in general, according to the sources Diner draws on, swarmed over North Africa. She quotes Strabo:

> There have been several generations of belligerent women in Libya. The Gorgons [Amazons] against whom Perseus waged war, were described as a people of great courage (Diner, 1965: 134).

(It should be noted that Libya in Roman times was what is now Morocco, Algeria, and Tunis.) Further, in Diner's own text:

> These tribes were in rebellion against the Atlantean colony. The Amazons, under the stipulations of the new alliance, were asked for help. Thus there came a battle of Amazons against Amazons. Thirty thousand Libyan horsewomen under Myrine delivered a pitched battle to the Gorgons, won the day, and took . . . many prisoners (1965: 134-135).

Later the Amazons under Myrine are supposed to have fought their way through Egypt, Arabia, Syria, and Phrygia. The mention of their being unlucky at sea and of most of the army drowning in the Mediterranean is perhaps the most realistic note in this tale. Nomads do hate the sea. We do not have to subscribe to a major conquest by Amazon women of North Africa and Syria, however, to accept the possibility that there were women's armies among the Berbers.

Given the wide distribution of Amazon legends in different types of steppe countries, it may be that nomadism under certain conditions encourages all-women armies. (To my knowledge, however, similar legends have not arisen among the Turko-Mongolian nomads.) All Amazon legends refer to the women as being herders and as living on cattle blood, meat, and milk. That they would have remained long without men seems unlikely. Even the legends allow for that:

> The Libyan Amazons, who removed their right breasts, had compulsory military service for all girls for a number of years, during which they had to refrain from marriage. After that, they became a part of the reserves and were allowed to reproduce their kind. The women monopolized government and other influential positions . . . lived in a permanent relationship with their sex partners, even though the men led a retiring life, could not hold public office, and had no right to interfere in the government of state or society. Children, who were brought up on mare's milk, were given to the men to rear (Diner, 1965: 136).

While such stories of total role reversals have a certain ideological attraction—for women at least—they fade away under closer scrutiny. The partial role reversal of the women warriors, however, does not. We will find that phenomenon in every century up to and including our own. Since nomads must train their women to fight, for survival's sake, it may be that all-women armies first originated in nomadic societies.

To return to our Bedouin warriors of ancient times, one could say that Queen Zenobia of Palmyra, the northernmost Arab city-state, on the edge of Syria, was the last of the queens in the Bedouin warrior tradition. She herself was probably a Macedonian, and Palmyra was by A.D. 250 well integrated into the settled life of Asia Minor. Nevertheless, it is worth noting that Zenobia defeated the Roman armies and extended her conquests to the Roman provinces of Asia Minor and part of Egypt. This gives some indication of the potentials still alive in the Bedouin tradition at that period. By the time Emperor Aurelian of Rome finally defeated her, she had organized allies from the Persians, the Saracens, the Armenians, and the Syrians. She led her own armies wearing a glittering helmet, but in defeat she bargained for her own safety and is somewhat criticized by historians for ending her days in luxury outside Rome. Had the nomad blood run thin?

Another late example of female Bedouin leadership is the case of La Kahina (The Prophetess), the queen of a tribe in the Aures Mountains who led a confederation of Berber tribes to drive the Moslems back into Tripolitania in the 670s A.D. She was apparently a good military strategist and had some success on the battlefield, but the tribal alliances proved too temporary and fragile. La Kahina did not have the diplomatic skills to deal either with the Moslems or with the groups outside her own immediate tribe. She finished by destroying cities and surrounding plains in an attempt to make the region unattractive to the Moslems, and succeeded only in making herself extremely unattractive to both Moslems and nomads.

Perhaps more typical of the military roles of Bedouin women are the activities of the Lady of Victory cult. The cult's function was to incite patriotism and to lash patriots into ferocious fighting. The Lady of Victory was a woman of high social standing about whom the feminine cult members, likewise of high rank, gathered in the pavilion sacred to the local or tribal deity. There, with war songs which they accompanied on their lutes, they stirred their warriors to martial fervor. Around the Lady of Victory and her retinue the battle raged until it was lost or won. Hind al-Hunud, an enemy of Mohammed, was described as "holding to the heathen practices of Arabia, and as a follower of this cult." Hind herself played the Lady of Victory in a battle with Mohammed's followers, brandishing a sword with great gusto (Beard, 1946: 293-294).

The Bedouin and Berber women certainly played a noteworthy role in Afro-Asian history. They and their men mapped and organized the resources of Arabia and North Africa, providing also a steady stream of leadership into Mesopotamian and Egyptian kingdoms. Their role was however not as prominent as that which their counterparts of the Eurasian steppes were to play. In the end, the harshness of the African steppes led to more of a niche adaptation than an organizing adaptation. Within the limits set by that environment, however, women seem to have shared leadership with men to an extent that we will not find in settled societies. Even though they did not tend the herds as directly as men did, the public spaces of the deserts were their spaces as well as the men's. Everywhere was home.

In A.D. 661 a Bedouin woman named Maysun, probably from one of the fringe tribes bordering on Syria, married the first Umayyad caliph, who had previously been the governor of Syria. Maysun was a poet, and gave voice to the sorrow of every nomad who must leave the open spaces for the closed ones:

> Breeze-flowing tents I prefer
> to ponderous halls
> And desert dress
> to diaphanous veils.
> A crust I'd eat in the awning's shade,
> not rolls,
> And watched by a dog that barks
> not a cat that smiles,
> I'd sleep to the wind's time,
> not to the tambourine.
> A youth's impetuous sword,
> not a husband's wiles,
> Uncouth slim tribesmen I love,
> not corpulent men.
>
> (in Stewart, 1967: 108)

Nomads of the Eurasian Steppes

Moving from the Afro-Asian desert steppes to the grassy steppes of Eurasia puts us in a totally different ecosystem, and a different style of nomadic culture. Grasslands exist in Arabia too, but they are sparser. There are also deserts in Eurasia, but with grasslands plentiful, the steppe dwellers had more horses than did their Afro-Asian counterparts, and more land to move around in. Two great chains of folded mountains created the Eurasian steppes over eons of time: first the T'ien Shan and Altai ranges, and later the Himalaya, shaped an arc within which lies Turkestan and Mongolia. The moister Russian steppes to the west and the drier Iranian steppes to the south complete the total area of steppe terrain, which includes as much as 5 percent of the land surface of the planet. This land is easy to travel over, and roads are not needed. While the mountainous regions create obstacles for movement, over the centuries numerous tribes have beaten tracks over the rougher parts of the terrain. The steppes are the archetypal "trackless wastes."

The desert Arabs of the south threatened only the Egyptian-Syriac-Mesopotamian plain. The nomads of the north, however, ranged over China, India, Asia Minor, and Europe during the last two millennia B.C., and halfway into the second millennium A.D. Genghis Khan for the Mongols, Attila for the Huns, and Tamerlane for the Turks have become the three great symbols of nomad penetration into the civilized world. These nomad incursions are usually treated as interruptions to the serious business of history by barbarians who are sooner or later tamed. Supposedly droughts and internecine war among nomadic tribes bring them tumbling into the plains. The actual history of the movements of steppe populations is much more complex than this theory indicates, and cannot be traced in detail here. For our own purposes in tracking women's roles in successive changes of social structure through the centuries, we need only take note of each of the main nomadic thrusts and how they affected the settled populations and then explore in detail one set of steppe tribes. Since the Mongols have the best documented history, they are the ones we will explore.

In the tangle of tribal groups that have emerged in the Eurasian steppe from time to time, we are conscious of two main groups: those of Iranian stock who move into the western steppes (Scythians and Sarmatians), and the Turko-Mongol peoples of the eastern steppes. What has determined their movements? We have already mentioned the dynamics of the push-pull process. Given the fertility of the land and the ease of transport, with both horses and draft animals available to haul wagons, there was less reason to limit population in the steppes than in the Arabian desert. So populations multiplied, and took the room they needed. Drought would certainly sometimes move whole sets of tribes from one area to another. But movement must also have come from sheer human love of exploration and adventure. The view of the world from the back of a horse is much more likely to feed a thirst for exploration and adventure than the view of the world from on foot.

The earliest steppe dwellers were hunters and gatherers. By 6000 B.C. some herders would be pushing north from the farmlands of the fertile crescent. By 2500 B.C., with the horse, herders would be able to spread over the steppes far more rapidly. The first great federation of nomad tribes that appears in historical chronicles is that of the Hsiung-nu, who first pressed over Chinese borders in the ninth century B.C. The Hsiung-nu were eventually driven out of the eastern steppes and appear several hundred years later at the gates of Europe as the Huns. The Huns and other Turko-Mongolian tribes appear very bloodthirsty when they ram the walls of civilization, but not less so than the Indo-European Scythians and Sarmatians. All had a certain delight in the flowing of blood, including gashing their faces with knives at funerals "so that blood flows with their tears." It was also the general custom to make the skulls of their enemies into drinking cups.

Which of the steppe peoples, the eastern Hunnic Turko-Mongols or the western Scythian-Sarmatians, were the famous Aryan invaders of India? No one knows exactly, but it is now generally considered that the Aryan invasion was a relatively minor incursion resulting in a few steppe bands settling in India. Like so many of these nomadic incursions, the effects on the settled peoples are all out of proportion to the number of nomads involved.

It is interesting to let the historical imagination speculate a bit about those nomadic incursions. From everything we know about the nomad women, they would come in with their men boldly, and move about freely. It is usually said that Indian women lost their high status after the Aryan invasions, in the course of measures adopted to protect Hindu women and to keep "common" women from polluting ritual observances. Could it be that the Aryan women, with their free ways, frightened the Hindus, so that they put constraints on all women in an effort to control the women of the new elites?

There are no records documenting the earlier invasion of India, however, so we must begin with the Hsiung-nu. Their initial thrust resulted in a series of tribal movements in the 200s B.C. that fatally weakened Persia and undid Alexander and Olympia's eastern conquests. The Hellenic world shrank back toward the Mediterranean.

The first Chinese princess, whom we know to have been part of the arduous, centuries-long process of negotiating with the Mongols through the device of the marriage contract, is nameless—she is referred to only as a "Chinese princess or lady-in-waiting." She joined the tent camp of the chief of the Hsiung-nu in 202 B.C., under an agreement entered into by the first emperor of the Han dynasty. Since records are sporadic, we do not read of a second such alliance until 33 B.C.; after that they are frequently mentioned, and both the kings of China and the Mongolian chiefs looked upon the marriage contract between the sons and daughters of the aristocracy of the empire and the aristocracy of the surrounding tribes as a way of ensuring communication between them, and predictability in political relationships. When either side felt very strong, it might refuse such a contract.[12] War usually ensued, and the peace treaty might well be sealed with a marriage contract, after all. Such contracts were the major diplomatic device of that part of the world.

Genghis Khan and his khatun, Borte, were past masters at diplomacy by marriage alliance. We shall focus here on the time of Genghis' ascension to the position of "khan of khans," or khakan, in A.D. 1206, and follow the nomadic empire until it wanes, in the 1400s after Tamerlane. At its greatest extent under Genghis, the khanate reached well into China and Russia, touched the gates of Constantinople, and covered Anatolia and parts of Mesopotamia and northern India. The Persian and Alexandrian empires were postage stamps by comparison.

The evolution of steppe tribes—from loose ad hoc federations and alliances driving out other tribes that were felt to be crowding their space, to well-organized alliance systems under one central administration in the great khanates, having representatives at the royal tent-court from all the states of Europe and Asia and receiving tribute from a vast empire—is one of the most fascinating sequences in human history. The Mongols' genius in surveying all the areas they moved through, in terms of both physical and social resources, and in "mining" the centers of civilization for their best craftworkers and scholars; of alternating threats and raids with alliances and agreements with settled peoples, including matrimonial alliances; and in developing a courier system over an information network that covered all of Europe as well as Asia, is definitely a nomadic-type genius. City dwellers do not make good map makers. When one European army could hardly find its way to the neighboring city-state with which it was at war, Genghis Khan's couriers knew Europe like the backs of their hands.[13]

What would have happened if the women and men who surrounded Genghis' successor, Kublai, had not gotten absorbed by China and essentially abandoned their nomadic commitments? What would a nomad organization of Eurasia have looked like if the nomads had kept their social organization and communication networks, without settling down in cities? Nomads always lost their unique characteristics when they settled in cities, so all their contributions had to be made within the first two generations of settlement. After that they were totally assimilated, and as unable to scan their environment, nomad-style, as any of their city neighbors.

There is real tragedy in the dynamics of the accommodation process.

The horseback warrior nomad of the steppes always begins by hating cities. Cities are excrescences on the beautiful plain, occupying space that could be yielding fodder for the nomad's stock. The people who live in them are not "human." That is why the warrior wreaks such wanton destruction on the cities; they have no use in the nomad's scheme of things. Thus, nomadic women and men fight together to defend common values and to destroy that which stands in the way of those values. There is a touching passage in Grousset's *Empire of the Steppes,* in which a Chinese mandarin who had become an advisor to Genghis Khan is described as unable to control his weeping when the khan destroyed Chinese cities, as he often did. In the setting of Genghis' last campaign in Kansu, the beginning of new social learnings for the Mongols is delineated:

> A Mongol general pointed out to [the khan] that his Chinese subjects would be useless to him, since they were unsuited to warfare, and that therefore he would do better to exterminate them—there were nearly 10 million—so that he might at least make use of the soil as grazing land for the cavalry. Jenghiz Khan appreciated the cogency of this advice, but Ye-lu Ch'u-ts'ai protested. "He explained to the Mongols, to whom any such idea was unknown, the advantages to be gained from fertile soil and hardworking subjects. He made clear that by imposing taxes on land and exacting tribute on merchandise, they might collect 500,000 ounces of silver yearly, 80,000 pieces of silk, and 400,000 sacks of grain." He won his point, and Jenghiz Khan ordered Ye-lu to draw up a system of taxation on these lines (1970: 251).

From that moment on, carnage stopped and infrastructure began; Genghis was known as a just and wise man, and would not kill if he saw alternatives. But the process that began with that teaching on the battlefield ended with Genghis' successor Kublai Khan becoming "soft" in the city and losing those unique nomadic perspectives and energies.

Steppe Social Structure and the Role of Women

Steppe society is more pronouncedly patriarchal than is Bedouin society, probably because it is a more warlike society, and a richer one. The steppe aristocracy consists of

> the aristocracy of the brave (ba'atur) and of chief (noyan) which . . . officer and manage the various social classes: warriors or faithful men who were preeminently free, commoners or plebians, and lastly serfs, who theoretically were of non-Mongol stock. Bonds of personal loyalty,

feudal style, link individuals at different hierarchical levels. The army is tightly organized in a hierarchy with units of tens at the bottom and the Khan at the top, with his own elite bodyguard (Grousset, 1970: 222).

What could the place of women be, in a society organized for battle? To visualize the situation adequately, one must remember that this was a society on the move. Everything the tribe owned was piled on horses and in wagons. As the khanate grew wealthier, large felt tents were sometimes permanently mounted on wagons, so there did not have to be so much breaking and setting up of camp. Anyone who has traveled with household possessions, whether by wagon or in a motor trailer, knows that the skills of "battening down the hatches" so articles do not get battered and destroyed while on the move are crucial. Whether preparing to move, on the move, or setting up a new camp, everyone had to be involved, everyone was busy, everyone was needed. Furthermore, in this society the distinction was not always clear between the "army" and the total tribe. One of the first things Genghis did was organize the wagons as part of the tribal battle formation, with women and children trained to shoot and defend the wagons and the babies. We must infer that women were also trained to fight from horseback, since khatuns sometimes fought by their husbands' sides on the battlefield. Probably only women of the warrior aristocracy received such training.

Nomadic society must generate much more of a sense of shared fate between women and men than either agricultural or urban society does, since both sexes must operate in the same space, under pressure, so much of the time. We will see this later among the Gypsies.

This is not to suggest that there was not also a separation of men's and women's spaces. Raiding, and some of the more substantial battles, may have been conducted at some distance from the tent camp, and herding would take men and boys away from the camp. The major positions of power within army and tribal councils were held by the men. But within the warrior aristocracy, the role of women in the court, their place in determining succession, and their part as both regents and full rulers were so clear-cut that one can infer a strong matrilineal tradition with the possibility that at some time in the past there were tribal "queens" comparable to the Arabian "queens." During the khanate, however, women usually only ruled as "in-betweens."

When a khan died his widow acted as regent until a *kuriltai,* a great council of all the tribes, had been called to elect the successor. In some cases she ruled for several years, and could initiate and supervise military activity during that time. She was also active in the council of elders that was responsible for finding candidates and conducting the election (and, usually, determining its outcome in advance). This, plus the fact that women of the warrior class and the aristocracy owned their own herds and tents, suggests the possibility of an earlier "visiting husband" custom in at least some of the tribes. There are matrilineal tribes today in both China and Tibet, confirming the long-standing presence of this cultural tradition on the steppes.

Because all accounts of the Mongols focus almost exclusively on the battlefields, it is difficult, but not impossible, to sort out information on the role of women. It is clear that the khatun, wife of the khan, was in some sense a coregent who had duties of state. She had a large court of her own. While the khan had other wives, each with her own tents, herds, and attendants, only the khatun could copreside at court with the khan. The company of wives of the khan had some of the characteristics of the Egyptian women's court in that there were women there from the royal families of most of the kingdoms of Europe and Asia. Since each one had her own tents and retinues, the physical space occupied by these women in the royal camp was substantial. Each woman apparently came with her own diplomatic advisor as well as priests, scholars, and the usual array of musicians, servants, and craftspeople. Most of these women from abroad were literate, whereas at the time of Genghis Khan, few of the Mongols were literate. This meant that the women would be maintaining a substantial international correspondence to supplement the khan's courier service.

I have mentioned that negotiation by marriage between the Chinese and the Mongols began to show up in Chinese court records in 202 B.C. Genghis Khan developed this practice to a fine art, not only in his personal marriages, but also in supervising the marriages of the women of his family and of his main chiefs. It used to be that alliances with Chinese princesses were the great goal of international diplomacy. But in Genghis' time, and for several centuries afterward, princesses of the khanate line were a major diplomatic goal for both nomadic and settled societies. This was more true in the Asian than the Mediterranean world, but the alliance structure straddled both.

The life of the princess-diplomats was by no means an austere one. In 626, during the Uigur khanate, one of the first great Mongolian khanates, the Mongols surrounded themselves with the luxury of beautiful brocades, fine food, and both eastern and western music. A Chinese pilgrim of that year wrote:

> The Khan wore a coat of green satin and allowed all his hair to be seen, his brow alone being bound by several turns of a silken fillet ten feet long, of which the ends hung down at the back. He was attended by some two hundred officers wearing brocade coats, all with their hair braided. The rest of the troops consisted of riders mounted on camels or horses; they were clad in furs and fine woolen cloth, and carried long lances, banners, and straight bows. . . . the Khan dwelt in a large tent ornamented with golden flowers that dazzled the eyes. The women, also dressed in brocades, sit on couches near the Khan. The Khatun sits beside the Khan (Grousset, 1970: 94).

Two hundred years later the khans were importing Persian artists and art to their tent court. The pictures produced during this period show the women and men of the khanate aristocracy wearing ceremonial dress, carrying flowers, and accompanied by musicians.

Accounts of khanate courts all agree that the size of the felt-tent camps were impressive, with tents, people, and herds stretching off in every direction as far as eye could see. The khan's tent, forty feet square in A.D. 520, in later days became almost palace size. As mentioned, some of these tents were mounted on wagons, so they did not have to be dismantled when camp was moved. One can imagine the Mongols living in huge covered wagons. Outward symbols of their wealth were confined to portable items like luxurious clothing and tapestries and to large retinues of scholars, musicians, craftspeople, entertainers, and servants.

Court life would appear to have been as cosmopolitan in the felt tents as in the palaces of the Mediterranean and Europe, if not more so. A European visitor was surprised to find fellow Europeans at Mongka Khan's court, including

> a woman from Lorraine called Pacquette, who had been brought from Hungary, and was in the service of one of the prince's Nestorian wives; she herself had married a Russian who was employed as an architect [of tents?]. At the Karakorum court Rubruck also found a Parisian goldsmith named Guillaume Boucher, "whose brother dwelt on the Grand Pont, in Paris." This man was first employed by the Dowager Sorghaqtani and then by Mongka's younger brother Ariq-boga, who was also sympathetic toward Christianity. Rubruck found that at the great court festivals the Nestorian priests were admitted first with their regalia, to bless the grand khan's cup, and were followed by the Muslim clergy and "pagan" monks, that is Buddhists and Taoists. Mongka him-

self sometimes accompanied his Nestorian wife to the services of this
church. "He came, and a gilded bed was brought for him, upon which
he sat with the queen his wife, opposite the altar" (Grousset, 1970: 280).

Since every woman who entered into a marriage alliance with
members of the khanate aristocracy brought her own priests, scholars, and craftworkers, and the khan himself brought talent from all
Europe and Asia, the concentration of talent from a diversity of cultures in the felt-tent courts must have been substantial.

The impression I have of the women of this warrior aristocracy is
that they were unusually direct and forthright by the standards of
urban civilization. While there was a woman's world and a man's
world, the two mingled freely at court. Women spoke up in touchy
political situations, and sang, danced, and toasted at banquets and
ceremonial occasions.

A rare description of a banquet scene on an occasion honoring
Genghis in his prime gives a delightful picture of bands of women
and men of the court spontaneously arising by turn to sing and dance
in front of each person whose name Genghis called out in a toast
(Prawdin, 1940: 88). Spontaneity, gaiety, and a love of singing and
dancing come through in the few descriptions we have of the social
life. These were never "men's only" occasions. Borte, Genghis' wife,
seems to have been a wonderfully independent woman who handled
her husband's rise to power with courage and wisdom, stepping in
when things became too tense. She appears to have been as respected
as he was in councils of state. Oelun, Genghis' mother, may have had
a lot to do with his rise in the first place, by her astute survival operations when all the tribes abandoned her and her young son at the
death of her khan husband. Once after Genghis was khan, when he
started quarreling with one of his younger brothers, Oelun came into
his tent with bared breasts and told him that whereas the other boys
had nursed at only one breast, he, Genghis, had nursed at both and
must never quarrel with the brothers with whom he had shared his
mother's breasts. The quarrel stopped immediately (Grousset, 1970:
218).

Genghis' daughter-in-law, Princess Sorghaqtani, was reputed to be
one of the great Mongol stateswomen, and Genghis turned to her for
advice regularly. She seems to have had a great deal of administrative
responsibility in the expanding khanate. It was due to her that
Nestorianism was the major religion of the court, but she also established schools and temples of all religions and managed to have her
son named khakan in his time.

In the next generation only one, Toragana Khatun, stands out as a major stateswoman. She kept the regency for four years after the death of her husband and built up an alliance structure which included a new Buddhist component, turning over the khanate to her son thereafter. Organa Khatun, a contemporary of Toragana in an associated khanate, ruled under the khakan for nine years during an especially tricky period of khanate politics and also managed to place her own son on the throne in the end. Koquz Khatun, again of the same fast-moving era, is one of the few khatuns mentioned as leading the army on the battlefield jointly with her husband. As powerful champions of Christianity, Koquz and her husband were mourned at their death as the "two stars of the Christian faith." The khakan relied heavily on her advice in affairs of state, and so skillful was her diplomacy that her son was the first to marry into the family of the Byzantine emperors.

Politically active women did not operate as lone wolves. Not only were they part of the central power structure, they could also operate from time to time as a sisterhood, and pounce on an unlucky khan who was pursuing a policy they did not approve of. Genghis Khan was more than once the object of a coordinated attack by his mother and his wife.

Other khatuns led armies in battle: the young widow Mandughai in 1470 took to the battlefield to protect the khanate for her five-year-old son and successfully kept it for him through an eventful twenty-one years. When one of the last khans was killed on the battlefield in 1696, his wife Goldan was by his side and died with him.

Enough has been said to indicate that the women of the aristocracy were active in the political realm, on the battlefield, in connecting the nomads with larger religious networks, and in other ways that helped develop the unique infrastructure of a nomadic society. Prawdin sums up the contribution of women by saying that

> Mongolian history has a good deal to say about notable women; those who, when widowed, were able to save their tribe from decay, by showing superabundant energy and sagacity; those who rode beside their husbands to war and fought boldly; those who were able regents, skilled intriguers and wise counsellors (1940: 287).

While it is true that the patriarchal pattern often seems to require widowhood in order for women to show the full range of their abilities, there seems to be ample evidence that women were active during their husbands' lives as well as after their deaths.

The economic life of the steppe tribes, as indicated earlier, sent men out herding, training horses, and fighting, and by and large kept women closer to the camp, maintaining the physical and social fabric of camp life. While the women of the aristocracy were busy with affairs of state, the commoners worked on basic maintenance. It takes a lot of work to maintain a moving camp in good working order. Several writers comment on how hard nomadic women worked. They were responsible for having their husbands' (and their own) battle gear in battle-ready condition at all times, and the production of food and clothing under camp conditions would take a continuous exercise of ingenuity. Not all the women's time went to maintenance tasks, however. Every woman was mistress of the possessions of her tent (and of her herds, if she had any), so women did a great deal of trading. Women with their own herds surely also learned to train their own horses, as some European Gypsy women do to this day. The skill of animal training is one of the very special skills of the nomads. Toynbee (1935) suggests that it was the basis of the remarkable educational system developed by the Ottoman branch of the Mongols, which trained the Janissaries that kept the Ottoman empire powerful for so long.[14]

Turko-Mongolian nomadic society was full of contradictions. To the extent that it was a highly successful, stratified warrior aristocracy, it partook of the inequalities of settled society that enabled some men and women to command many resources and accomplish a great deal, leaving the rest of the society to work hard on small-scale maintenance activities. To the extent that it was nomadic and developed environmental scanning skills not available to sedentary peoples, it was more flexible and adaptable to new situations. Because it was a society on the move, it was spared the heavy accumulation of possessions, valuing instead people and portable goods like cloth. As the khanate empire grew larger, it was a society that depended on individual skill in the mass setting. The only way camps could move smoothly and efficiently would be for everyone to know how to pack and move at a moment's notice. The only way massive herds of cattle and horses could be handled was with consummate skill in animal training. The scanning and the management skills of nomadic empires at their height were impressive accomplishments. The system could never have worked if women had not been as skilled and flexible as the men were. And children would have had to learn to function in this rapidly moving social environment very early in life; otherwise they would get lost, left behind. Early chroniclers of nomadic movements sometimes describe them in terms of the nomads "piling their women, children and possessions on huge wagons" (Grousset, 1970: 7). This was not at all the case—the women did the piling. In terms of fluidity of roles to meet daily life demands, of command of own property, and of freedom to move in the social spaces of the larger environment, Mongolian women both inside and outside the aristocracy probably had some advantage over city women.

The advantage was not long retained with urbanization. The whole story of the evolution of Moslem society from the early caliphates to the Ottoman empire, dependent on nomad inputs at each stage in its development, is the story of the progressive elimination of women from participation in the central spaces of society as each new Turkish group became assimilated to the urban scene. In assisting with the spread of Islam, nomads promoted the demise of their own way of life. Islam became a city religion, as all scholars from Ibn Khaldun on agree. The men who rose in the early Abbasid caliphate, every one of them of Arabian origin, practically all married out of their own nomad society. The negotiation-by-marriage system worked to exclude the very people—nomadic women—who might have kept Turkish rule more open to the participation of women[15] (Stewart, 1967: 81). Women were very important in preurban Islam, and specifically in promoting the leadership of Mohammed himself. Without the help of his wife Mohammed might never have had his teachings accepted. (Mary Beard [1946] is clear on the importance of women in early Islam.)

Historians are too inclined to blame the dangerous, bloodthirsty nomads for the seclusion of women: settled folk had to put their fragile females in harems and behind veils to protect them from the barbarians, the theory goes. If my interpretation is correct, however, it was the distortion of city social patterns that squeezed women out. The nomadic women who came to the city representing another pattern of participation were not strong enough to fight the forces of urbanized role structures.

Celts, Goths, and Others

We have noticed how important wagons were to the Mongols, minimizing the packing job of the nomadic society and keeping them mobile. Wagons were important to the Celts too—so important that we find a number of ceremonial Celtic burials of the 600s B.C. in which the dead person is laid out on one. One burial in Burgundy is particularly impressive: a young woman of about thirty is laid out on a wagon, and her tomb is filled with rich grave furniture apparently imported from Greece. She could be one of the famous Celtic queens, but we have no way of knowing which one.

No one knows where the Celts came from, or just when they started coming, but it seems reasonable to assume that they started off from the European end of the Eurasian steppes in the late third or early second millennium B.C. As herding and hunting nomads with no particular destination they very slowly drifted westward. By the middle of the second millennium B.C. they were gradually becoming visible in the melange of Central European cultures that included the Battle-Axe, Urnfield, and Beaker peoples, mentioned in chapter 5. The Celts could work metals and they were on horseback, so they began showing the traits of the warrior aristocracy we have already seen on the eastern steppes. They seem to have become a warrior-craftworker society utilizing the sedentary farmers' services for food and working the Mediterranean-European trade routes through central Europe. By 600 B.C. they were spread all over Czechoslovakia, Hungary, Austria, Switzerland, and south Germany, and by 400 B.C. they formed the Celto-Ligurian League.

They were an easygoing people, preferring to live outdoors and steadfastly refusing to build towns. They did build roads, however, or rather wagon tracks. While steppe lands could be used for wagon transport with a minimum of road preparation, not so the forests of Europe. The famous Roman roads, Anne Ross (1970: 78-84) suggests, were simply built over the earlier, carefully laid Celtic wagon trails.

In Roman times the Celts spread out over France and the British Isles, and Ireland today still bears many of the marks of that ancient Celtic culture. Though their free-flowing antiurban ways led to the disappearance of their culture in the face of Roman social organization in Gaul, the Celts' nomadic culture was sufficiently strong to resist urbanization and Romanization in Ireland, Scotland, and Wales. By the time we see them through Caesar's eyes in the memoirs of the Gallic War, they are already partly sedentary, but even then they build *oppida*, essentially hill forts, rather than towns. This enabled them to control surrounding towns and farmlands without settling down. That we are so aware of a Celtic culture today, a culture stemming from a people who did not acquire a system of writing until the fifth century A.D., is a testimony to the extraordinary ethnic and cultural unity of these nomads who once were spread so widely over Europe. Lacking evidence from any but their enemies, the Romans, I can only conclude that their unity depended on the same kind of nomadic communication infrastructure that characterized the nomads of the Eurasian and Afro-Asian steppes. That it did not result in empires is probably due to their live-and-let-live value system—though the Romans thought they were quarrelsome enough.

While they did have a warrior caste, they did not focus their social organization around purposeful military activity. They fought the Romans when they felt crowded by them, but when we see them in Britain relatively secure from further attack, we find a people dedicated to poetry, hunting, feasting, and quarreling, in that order of importance. Graves (1966), who is obviously much attached to the Celts, tells us that it was the function of the poets to determine when it was time to go to war, and when it was time to stop fighting.

While Celtic society was probably more ranked than stratified, since the Celts neither accumulated goods nor developed the degree of hierarchical organization the Mongols had, there seems to have been an aristocracy of warriors and poets. Women were an important part of that aristocracy, and served not only as warrior queens but also as directors of military academies. The most famous and best historically verified Celtic queen is Boudicca. Queen of the Iceni tribe in eastern Britain, she led her troops in battle against terror-stricken Romans:

> She was huge of frame, terrifying of aspect, and with a harsh voice. A great mass of bright red hair fell to her knees: she wore a great twisted golden torc, and a tunic of many colors, over which was a thick mantle fastened by a broach. Now she grasped a spear, to strike fear into all who watched her (Chadwick, 1970: 50).

She and her two daughters fought at the head of the army, and when she was defeated, she committed suicide rather than fall into the hands of the Romans. Suicide in such a situation was common behavior for Celtic women: the Romans had a very bad reputation.

The picture of the fierce Celtic women comes from the Roman writers, of course. As described in Chadwick,

> a whole troop of foreigners would not be able to withstand a single Gaul if he called his wife to his assistance who is usually very strong and with blue eyes; especially when, swelling her neck, gnashing her teeth, and brandishing her sallow arms of enormous size, she begins to strike blows mingled with kicks, as if they were so many missiles sent from the string of a catapult (1970: 50).

As might be expected, there was little love lost between Roman and Celtic women. Two more different conceptions of women's roles could hardly be imagined. The Celtic women were lovers of the outdoors, as were the men. They would never seek a roof as long as there was sky overhead. Meadows were the only carpets they prized, and their banquets would be laid out on boards supported by tree stumps, with the lowing of cattle as background music. A woman's wealth and status, like a man's, was the country's

> soft rains, its vast pasturages, those wandering herds. About this simple commerce there developed a life-mode that was at once dangerous and secure, unconcerned and anxious, reckless and rapacious, unambitious and adventurous, as peaceful and as bloody as the desert (O'Faolain, 1969: 50).

These rough-and-ready people were quarrelsome. It was the custom for men to fight by the dining table before meals, in order to determine who was the bravest man at the table. The bravest got the best cut of meat (Ross, 1970: 54-55). This fighting happened indoors or out, and the women apparently enjoyed it too. An Ulster tale tells of three women who, well in their cups, sang so exuberantly in praise of their respective husbands that the celebrants pulled the house pillars down in their enthusiasm for the songs (Ross, 1970: 92). This was considered a great joke by all, including the women. What could a woman who lived, loved, and raised children in such a setting think of the elegant Roman matron who needed a fine town house as a setting for her social relationships? There is recorded the reply of the Caledonian woman,

> when Julia Augusta, the wife of Serverus, jested with her about the free intercourse of her sex with men in Britain. She replied, "We fulfill the demands of nature in a much better way than do you Roman women, for we consort openly with the best men, whereas you let yourselves be debauched in secret by the vilest" (Chadwick, 1970: 55).

Non-Celts who did not understand the high status of Celtic women could make bad mistakes. There was the native Welsh tribal leader who set out to make an alliance with the leader of the Celtic Brigantes in order to throw out the Romans. It happened that the Celtic leader was only the field commander, and it was his wife, Cartimandua, who was the ruling queen. Since she had already allied herself with the Romans, the luckless would-be rebel soon found himself in chains and delivered to the Romans by the angry queen (Chadwick, 1970: 65). Less serious, but possibly more embarrassing, was the occasion when Celtic warriors were taken prisoner and brought to Rome. When brought before the Emperor Claudius, they

> ignored him and the imperial insignia, and headed straight for the throne of the Empress Agrippina, making their obeisances to her (Diner, 1965: 251).

The free ways in which Celtic women utilized sex come out in stories of Queen Medb, who offered "thigh friendship" to the owner of a bull for the loan of it. She also offered thigh friendships in return for assistance in raids and battles. Apparently all parties, including Medb's husband, considered these deals reasonable (Kinsella, cited in Brennan, 1975: 9).

There are many matrilineal traces among the Celts, and the clearest are among the Picts, a pre-Celtic group with a heavy Celtic overlay:

> The law for succession among the Picts was through the female, and there are grounds for thinking that the bridegroom was usually a visiting prince, and that the marriage arrangement was not regarded as permanent (Chadwick, 1970: 93).

The Venerable Bede notes this in his study of the Pictish kings, discovering no succession through fathers until the ninth century A.D. The ancient system

> involved visiting princes and a system of purely formal marriages, highly organized and intricately provided for. The organization of the royal family seems to have been at times matrilocal as well as matrilineal, but not usually matriarchal (Chadwick, 1970: 118).

I have said that Celtic society was more ranked than stratified, and yet there is among the later Celts, as we shall see among the Vikings, a contempt for the lower classes that does not easily fit into the picture we are apt to hold in our minds of a casual outdoor society. Much later, in the 1500s A.D., we get a picture of an Irish home of the aristocracy that brings together just those improbable traits of casual simplicity and unconscious arrogance that the Irish themselves see as their own characteristics. The great Hugh O'Neill in Ulster is entertaining a visitor, who

> was entertained . . . to a meal and conversation beside fern tables, on fern forms, spread under the canopy of heaven. O'Neill's children were in velvet and gold lace; his bodyguard of beardless boys were stripped to the waist (O'Faolain, 1969: 41).

Houses are dirty, milk is strained through straw, the poor are in rags, and even the great, under their fine cloaks, are naked. In the old battle sagas when casualties are recorded, "we know not the number of peasants and rabble" (O'Faolain, 1969: 42). Liberty these people loved, equality they never bothered about. The family was the only social unit taken seriously. Even here it was not the tight authoritarian family we meet so often in urban settings, but a family within which and outside of which both women and men had great freedom of movement. It was that freedom that made the Roman matrons think Celtic women "loose."

The warrior-queen tradition of Celtic history fits in well with this pattern of freedom for women. Most of these queens, apart from Cartimandua and Boudicca, are semilegendary. Yet the references to them are so frequent, and take so many forms, that I am inclined to think there really was a "Queen Mab" (Maeve, Medb) of Connaught, in western Ireland; a Queen Morrigan, represented as Morgan le Fay in the Arthurian legend; and perhaps a real Queen Badb, turned in legend into the goddess of bat-

tle. They were all fighting queens (Kinsella, 1970). For Medb we even have a description of her position in a battle formation (Ross, 1970: 63). There may also have been a "military academy" for young men and women run by the woman Scathach. There are many references to her institution, and she was apparently a prophetess as well as a military strategist and teacher (Chadwick, 1970: 135-136). The tradition of women warriors survives, in a style reminiscent of the Amazon traditions, in the story of the nine witches of Gloucester, who ap-

Figure 7-1. *Celtic Woman with Neck Ring, Gallo-Roman Period.*

parently lived together in their own military camp. Only after the ninth century A.D.—when the Celts had become settled and acculturated—are there no new references to women warriors in Celtic countries (Chadwick, 1970: 136).

There were also druidesses, and women's festivals that survive today via St. Brigid's festivals, but we know as little of them as we know of the whole mysterious druid tradition. Graves and others mention a famous druid university in Cornwall, but we have no details about it. E. M. White (1924: 30) tells us that there were druidesses of three classes. One class performed temple offices, but lived with their families; one class assisted the druids, and visited their husbands occasionally; one class was a sisterhood living in

seclusion. Some druidesses were members of the Sisterhood of Brighit (goddess of poverty, medicine, and smithies, according to White)
and were responsible for preserving a holy fire.

Anne Ross cites a passage from Tacitus showing the role of the
druidesses in war:

> On the shore stood the opposing army with its dense array of armed
> warriors, while between the ranks dashed women in black attire like the
> Furies, with hair dishevelled, waving brands. All round the Druids, lift-
> ing up their hands to heaven and pouring forth dreadful imprecations,
> scared our soldiers by the unfamiliar sight so that, as if their limbs were
> paralyzed, they stood motionless and exposed to wounds. Then, urged
> by their general's appeal and mutual encouragements not to quail
> before a troop of frenzied women, the Romans bore the standard on-
> wards, smote down all resistance, and wrapped the foe in the flame
> of his own brands (1970: 145).

Beard describes the Cimbrian tribes that swept down from the north
into Rome:

> Among the Cimbrians, priestesses took charge of war captives. Standing
> on ladders which they carried with them to battle, they cut off the
> heads of prisoners, caught the blood in pots, and gave it to their men to
> drink, in the belief that it would double their strength (1946: 288).

Shadows of the earlier tradition of the queen, the priestess, and the
warrioress may be found in the prominent role of women religious[16]
in the formation of the Christian monastic movement in Ireland. St.
Brigid, the Christianized version of the Celtic goddess Brigantia
(Brighit), was used to good advantage by the Christian sisters in the
first centuries A.D.

Oddly, while the women fight, teach, preach, prophesy, and rule,
tradition has it that only the men write poetry. All the great Celtic
historical poems were preserved by the *ollaves,* who had to memorize
150 secret code languages and 350 long traditional histories and romances, besides being versed in philosophy, civil law, music, augury,
divination, medicine, mathematics, geography, universal history,
astronomy, rhetoric, and foreign languages; in addition, *ollaves* had
to be able to extemporize poetry in more than fifty complicated
meters (Graves, 1966: 457). *Ollave* families kept the craft hereditary,
like the priestly families, and I find it hard to believe that there were
not also women *ollaves* whose names were erased from the records.

This brief excursion into Celtic history is mainly to give the flavor
of women's roles in a nomadic tradition that was carried to the heart

of Europe. The brave women of Gaul who fought the Romans were partly Celts, but by Roman times they were also Goths, Visigoths, Vandals, Franks, and Huns. These represented fresh nomadic incursions from the same regions from which the Celts came.

All the accounts we have of these peoples in their first centuries of contact with the Romans involve descriptions of war. Therefore our picture of women is battle-oriented. Because these scenes give a reasonably realistic picture of nomadic women on the battlefield, we can to some extent extrapolate back to the Turko-Mongols and to the Bedouins and the Berbers, allowing for differences in geographical settings and details of tribal culture. It is worth quoting at some length from the passages available to us on women on the battlefield. These are all taken from Beard's work on women in history.

First, in Tacitus' description of the influence of women of the German tribes, he begins

Figure 7-2. *Statue of Epona, Gallo-Roman Period.*

by saying that squadrons or battalions of soldiers were composed of families and clans. Close by them, too, are those who are dearest to them, so that they hear the shrieks of the women, the cries of infants. [Women] are to every man the most sacred witnesses of his bravery—they are the most generous applauders. The soldier brings his wounds to his mother and wife. . . . Tradition says that armies already wavering or giving way have been rallied by women who, with earnest entreaties and bosoms laid bare, have vividly represented the horrors of captivity. . . . [The Germans] even believe that sex has a certain sanctity and prescience, and they do not despise their counsels or make light of their answers. . . . They venerated Aurinia [as divinity], and many other women, but not with servile flatteries or with sham deifications (1946: 289).

Plutarch describes the encounters between the Romans and the barbarous hordes at Aque Sextiae, 102 B.C.:

the fight had been no less fierce with the women than with the men themselves. . . . [The women] charged with swords and axes, and fell upon their opponents uttering a hideous outcry. . . . When summoned to surrender, they killed their children, slaughtered one another, and hanged themselves to trees (1946: 289).

Dio Cassius mentions that the Romans found bodies of women in armor among the corpses of the Marcomanni and Quadi.

Other Roman writers said that several Gothic prisoners proved to be women and among the Varangians, who attacked the Byzantines, women were found wielding arms side by side with their men (1946: 289).

It should be noted that while women are active on the battlefield, and "heard" in tribal councils, there is no trace of a concept of a "rule" by women. Diner does not give the source for her assertion that

when Hannibal marched through Gaul . . . an agreement drawn up between him and the inhabitants stated that any difference of opinion regarding the damage done by his troops in passage and compensations to be paid for it were to be decided exclusively by the supreme council of Gallic women, with no right of appeal from this college of matrons for either party (Diner, 1965: 253).

That the prophetesses in the Germanic tribes had some part in deciding whether or not and when a battle should be attempted is clear. But the role of women in tribal councils, apart from that of being "heard," is far from clear. Matrilineal succession was practiced among all these tribes, almost without exception, and the widely cited Salic law appears to be a late, medieval addition to Germanic practice. What seems in general to have happened as a result of contact between the Romans and the Gallic and Germanic tribes is that the traditional higher status of women in both Gallic and Germanic traditions was gradually whittled away. Inferior-status rules regarding women drive out higher-status rules. The old Wergild laws of compensation for injury, replacing the terrible eye-for-an-eye law with provisions for monetary compensation, originally placed twice as high a value on women as on men, in terms of compensation for injuries wrought. This changed gradually through the Middle Ages (O'Faolain and Martines, 1973: 96-106). Later rules are sometimes confused with earlier rules (Simons, 1968: 84-85).

A tabulation of women's economic roles during the Gallic era puts the matter of women's participation in a more pedestrian perspective (see table 7-1). Unquestionably, the Gallo-Celtic-Germanic tradition gave fuller participation to women in all the affairs of society than the Greco-Roman tradition did. The Gallo-Celtic-Germanic tradition is the tradition of a society on horseback, as compared with the settled Greco-Roman society. We will see in the next chapter how this nomadic tradition of fuller participation of women affected the development of the new Europe out of the old Roman Empire. For centuries to come, two traditions will be in conflict: the freer Gallic tradition, and the more repressive Greco-Roman tradition. The issue is still before us in the twentieth century.

The Vikings

The Vikings were among the more ruthless of the nomads that history has romanticized. After a thousand years of peaceful settled agricultural existence, from the eighth through the tenth centuries A.D. the Vikings became the scourge, not only of Europe, but also of the whole Atlantic from the Faroe Islands to North America, and of Byzantium and Arabia besides—"From the wrath of the Northmen, O Lord, deliver us" was the prayer in every church and monastery in northern France and England in the ninth and tenth centuries.

What shot the Vikings from the Northland's bow? One factor was the overpopulation in the Northland; another, the power vacuum in Europe, caused by doldrums after the Moslem conquests up to the gates of Vienna. Beyond these stimuli, there is always the imponderable of adventurousness and restlessness. The Vikings had a clearly marked aristocracy, bearing some of the marks of the free-and-easy Celtic style, some of the marks of the more elaborate Mongolian style. Society was divided into royalty, landholders (jarls), peasants, and at the bottom, serfs. Jarl and peasant women had high status and enjoyed much freedom. The old Icelandic *Song of Rig,* thought to show Celtic influence (Brøndsted, 1965: 238), reveals in its descriptions of the jarl and his wife sitting at home the upper-class cult of the body shared by Nordics and Celts. The image of the body beautiful becomes a powerful reenforcer of systems of social stratification:

> And the big farmer twisted a bowstring, bent an elmbow, made arrows;
> while the mistress looked at her arms, smoothed her clothes, tightened
> her sleeves. On her breast was a brooch, her shift was blue, her cap
> straight, her train long. Her breast was fair, her brow fairer, and her
> neck whiter than new fallen snow (Brøndsted, 1965: 239).

The serf girl—the farm drudge—looks quite different: "Her legs were

Table 7-1
Women's Roles in Ancient Gaul

I. Occupations Open to both Women and Men

    A. Military

        1. Combatants
        2. Noncombatants providing ammunition, nursing

    B. Construction

        1. Building houses, shelters

    C. Political

        1. Positions on tribal council
        2. Judge for tribal council

    D. Cattle raising

        1. Ownership and supervision of herds
        2. Milking

II. Roles Open Predominantly to Women

    A. Agriculture

    B. Sewing, preparation of skins

III. Role Open Only to Women

    A. Priestess/forecaster

    B. Prospecting

    C. Goldsmith

SOURCE: Evelyne Sullerot (1968).

crooked, her feet dirty, her arms sunburnt, her nose pendulous" (Brøndsted, 1965: 238).

That early racism, and the theme of the ugly troll who lives in dark underground caves in Norse literature, are thought by some to have derived from Stone Age memories of struggles between Neanderthal-type hominids and their fully modern successors, in isolated enclaves in the far North where the Neanderthals lingered on past their time. Whatever the reason for the cast of characters in Norse legends, they have had a long life. The image of the superior Nordic woman striding along in flowing dress, draped with an even more flowing cape, showing her white arms, and wearing at her waist her symbol of authority—the keys of the household—moves through the corridors of time to our own century, breeding both a continued racism and the cult of the superwoman.

There is no doubt that Nordic priestesses dressed in a kind of splendid simplicity that created awe in their time and resonates awe in ours. We can see this from the remains of priestesses and representations of them found in the famous peat bogs of Scandinavia (Glob, 1969: 107, 119, 121-124), and there are many references to the barefoot, gray-haired women in white dresses and fine linen cloaks who accompany warriors, both on land and sea, in the literature of the first millennium A.D.[17] Women, both the wise women of the pagan tradition and Christian women, play an important part in the Icelandic sagas.

The picture we get from the Vinland sagas (1966) is of a sex-egalitarian society forged out of the pioneering experience, though only a few women participated in the life of adventurous voyaging. Navigator, seeress, farmer, and spinner, wise women journeyed everywhere with their brothers. It was their talents of discernment the men relied on, when in doubt, about where to steer, where to land, where to raid, and where to colonize. In the class-conscious society of the Northlands the seeress was a person of great standing, but at sea and in helping found new colonies in Iceland and further west she helped her less prophetically gifted sisters create a new classless society that functioned very differently from the motherland.

These priestesses with the gift of prophecy had an increasingly hard time through the latter part of the first millennium A.D. Many of them had conflicts of loyalty between the old priesthood and the new when Christianity came to be more widely accepted.[18] Their ancient stock of wisdom was often laid aside as Christianity branded it witchcraft.

Our special interest in the Vikings is in their scanning skills that led to the long ocean journeys to Greenland, Iceland, and Vinland (Newfoundland). These long sea journeys were a special challenge to women's skill, since household equipment, seeds, and cattle had to be packed in the longboats—tiny enough for what they carried. Packing a longboat was a lot harder than packing a wagon. Scanning skills at sea are different than scanning skills on land, and women's knowledge of signs and portents and clues about environment resources must have been stretched to the limit on these journeys.

The separation from local peoples that enables one to scan larger horizons is a two-edged device. The Vikings were even more distanced from the populations they encountered than land nomads would be. They inflicted a good deal of mindless cruelty during their raids on settled populations. This raises the question of whether larger perspectives and large-scale scanning skills also contribute to dehumanization. Seeing the larger picture is not an unmixed good, if unaccompanied by a humanizing experience of relationship with that which is seen. The fact that women were such able partners of the Vikings suggests that women are as liable to this dehumanization as men are.

Each of the nomadic societies we have examined thus far has been very vulnerable to destruction by assimilation into settled society once the barrier between the nomad and the settler has broken down. The Mongols, the Bedouins, the Celts, and, after their two-hundred-year fling, the Vikings, only retained their distinctive culture and comparative perspective as long as the settled folk could be thought of as the enemy. The contact which humanized also softened the critical scanning faculties that made these societies so dynamic and interesting. This issue remains perplexing as we look at the Gypsies in the next section. While the suspicion and mistrust between the *gajes* and the *Rom* is deplorable, there is no doubt that Gypsies are in danger of losing many of their special skills, as well as their joy, if they are persuaded to leave the road.

The Gypsies

The Gypsies are both the best loved and most maligned of all nomads. Running away to the Gypsies is a lure for little children that has resulted in some fine pieces of literature on life among the Gypsies in the nineteenth and twentieth centuries. The instinct to take to the road has apparently never quite died out among settled folk.

The prototypical nomads, Gypsies presumably originated in India and pursued the occupations assigned to outcastes by the Laws of Manu—metalsmithing, music, and divining. They are the oldest craft and trading nomads, and with the rise of the Turko-Mongolian empires, attached themselves to the traveling camps of the khans. Historians of the Mongols do not mention them, but other evidence seems to point in this direction. The Mongols themselves had minimal craft skills and had to get their wagon and weapon makers from somewhere. It would be among the herding nomads that the Gypsies would have developed their skills in animal training (Clébert, 1963: 36-39, 129-130, 145).

By the 1100s A.D. we begin to find mention of them in Europe, and by then they were showing all the skills of adaptation to local terrain and customs they have been showing ever since, traveling with "safe-conduct" passes from kings and emperors over lands and across borders that others could not cross (Clébert, 1963: 58). By the early twentieth century they were excellent passport forgers. Persecutions also started soon after their first appearance, and alternations of guaranties of safe conduct and persecution continue to be their lot (Clébert, 1963: 88).

Their mapping skills were equalled by few outside the Gypsy world. In 1596 they were described as having

> the best and most reliable maps on which are marked all the towns, villages, and rivers, the homes of gentry and others, and arrange among themselves a meeting place, with ten days in between at twenty leagues from where they set out. The Captain allocates to each of the oldest men three households to escort there, taking their own short cut, and finding the rendezvous: and for those remaining who are well mounted and armed, he sends them with a good almanac in which are all the fairs of the world, changing accoutrements and horses (Clébert, 1963: 65-66).

1596 sounds extraordinarily like 1976. In spite of intervening wars and the development of ever more rigid national barriers, the Gypsies keep on the move from country to country, knowing no destination except the road itself. The specific composition of any one caravan is ever shifting, yet everyone knows to which *kumpania* they belong. In any caravan everyone also knows who the senior man is, and who the senior woman, though they have no title. Some Gypsies have been lured into settlements, finally giving in to the pressure of authorities who do not know how to deal with peoples on the move. But a significant number of the estimated five million Gypsies in the world today are still on the move. More than four hundred thousand were exterminated by the Nazis for having "impure blood" during the Second World War. It is almost unbelievable that all through the 1930s and '40s, they kept crossing and recrossing boundaries of Western Europe, ignoring all categories such as the Allies, the Axis powers, communism, capitalism, ignoring everything but their own inner mandate to keep moving (Yoors, 1967: 110, 114).

How was this possible? Because the planet really belongs to the Gypsies. They are the people, the *Rom*. All others are barbarians, intruders who clutter up the landscape with settlements. Gypsies have their own private *Rom* space wherever they go, their own language, their own ways. *Gajes*—the non-Gypsies—are utilized as resources, but otherwise ignored.

Some of the traditional traits we have described for other nomadic folk the Gypsies exhibit almost to perfection. In addition to having excellent maps, they have a communication network of taverns around the world for which they carry telephone numbers on tattered scraps of paper. With these they activate the network when they want to reach each other (Yoors, 1967: 110-114). Every *Rom* checks in at the network tavern nearest where he is camping. Until recently largely illiterate, they often have *gajes* write letters for them which are marked "Gypsy mail" and are sent in care of General Delivery to the post offices of the world's major cities, lying in the "Gypsy mailbox" until claimed (Yoors, 1967: 85, 211). When on the road, they leave special Gypsy trail signs, so anyone else coming after them can know who has gone before and where they are headed (Yoors, 1967: 210). "Specific districts, provinces or countries [are] divided into 'hunting territories' or reserved areas 'belonging' to a specific kumpania" (Clébert, 1963: 243). The Gypsies "native" to the area help all comers with the intricacies of local customs and law. Since everyone is on the move, it is not clear how each *kumpania* manages to keep some wagons always on its own hunting territory. Probably they know by Gypsy mail or Gypsy phone when they are needed to help other bands passing through.

By skillful combination of all these resources, Gypsies manage to keep track of each other to an extraordinary degree, and periodically have large tribal gatherings including convocations of the *kris*, the Gypsy judicial council. On such occasions they announce to all the world that they are going to elect a "Gypsy king"—though such an institution does not exist among them—because they have found that this gets them favorable publicity and permission to camp far longer than local police usually allow. Otherwise, Gypsy caravans tend to be hounded across Europe from campsite to campsite. Great pressure in the last few years has led to the establishment of permitted Gypsy camping sites, but even greater pressures exist to make them abandon the road altogether. So far, most of them have resisted.

Women's Roles Among the Gypsies

Like all nomadic tribes, the Gypsies show signs of matriliny, especially in Southern and Eastern Europe (Yoors, 1967: 121-122). Kinship was formerly counted through the mother, but this practice, where it exists, is of minor importance because the father is head of the kinship unit. The father is to the family what the tribal chief is to the tribe, and no other authority figure exists, except in the informal authority of the senior man and the woman elder in each caravan. The tribal chief's role is loose, and he is advised by a council of elders, the old men of the tribe. Every tribe also has a woman elder, who does not actually sit with the tribal council, yet is always consulted by them and carries a great deal of weight among the men as well as among the women. Some scholars believe she is the remnant of an earlier matriarchal system. Since the mother in the family is the equivalent of the woman elder in the tribe, one can say that the family is the microcosm of the tribe.

Since women's and men's spaces and roles are very clearly defined, and there are many taboos surrounding the activities of women, it does not appear on the surface that there is much equality between women and men. Women may not speak at tribal councils. They do not even eat with the men, but send food to the men's circle from the individual family campfires where women sit with their children. Yet from descriptions like Jan Yoors' *The Gypsies* (1967), one realizes that there is a great deal of shared public space between women and men. The campground is one large family space, utilized in various ways by all family members, and everyone lives outdoors on the campground except in inclement weather. Children may be fed by anyone, sleep anywhere. Women and men observe strict monogamy, and young unmarrieds are strictly chaperoned. Oddly, though all Gypsy marriages are arranged by the heads of household in consultation with wives, and the younger generation are scarcely ever consulted, a high value is placed on romantic love. Once a young couple have been joined in matrimony, they proceed to develop a love relationship that has all the emotional commitment of a Western style love relationship, and appears to be more lasting. Divorce is practically unknown. Young people marry early and have many children, which is why there are so many Gypsies in the world today.

Religious ceremonies are devout, but scanty, and take on the forms of the religious community in which they occur. The Gypsies seem to consider all religions as appropriate vehicles for their devotions.

The old herding practices of nomads have developed for the Gypsy men into skill in training and trading horses. When horses disappear, as in the United States, this is translated into dealing in cars. Gypsy men are also famous for the miniature smithies they carry with them. Women bring income into the caravan by telling fortunes, singing, and dancing. Both women and men have become famous circus performers in Europe, as tamers and trainers of wild animals. There are also famous women and men Gypsy musicians. This mixing of traditional sex roles reflects an adaptability of role structure that is not always apparent on the surface.

One has a tremendous impression of the vitality of Gypsy life, and of the vitality of its women and men. The zest with which they sing and dance and talk all night long around campfires, "sleeping it off" in the morning when townsfolk are up and about their business, is surely part of the attraction they have for the children who run off to join them. Why did Wilhelm Bach, oldest son of Johann Sebastian Bach, spend much of his life among the Gypsies (Yoors, 1967: 150)? He was a musician who preferred playing around Gypsy campfires to being choirmaster in Darmstadt. Those who manage to photograph Gypsies in their own setting show happy people, though the *zigeuner* melancholy is as famous as the Jewish melancholy. A photograph in Jean-Paul Clébert's *The Gypsies* (1963) looks startlingly like a photograph of a hippie commune on the move in the 1970s. What the Gypsies have that the hippies do not have is centuries of tradition, puritan sex morals, and a capacity for self-discipline as well as for letting go.

The Gypsies represent an interesting case of nomadism, since in spite of their mapping and environment-exploiting skills, they have not acted as social organizers in the way that the Arab and Turko-Mongol nomads did. Theirs is a niche adaptation, depending on minimum contact with the outside world, and yet their niche is the world itself. The women's lives seem narrow and circumscribed, hemmed in by taboos, lacking the possibility of political participation, yet those who write about Gypsy tribes describe women who apparently feel very free, who have all the "space" they want. The practice of caring for each other's children means that the Gypsy women who are going off to town to dance or tell fortunes never have to worry about child care. The whole camp is a day-care center. One could imagine that they will feel much less free in the future, when they are settled in towns and their children go to local schools, as authorities now dream of. Gone will be the communal arrangements of the campground and the possibility of shared work.

The view from the road seems on the whole to be a liberating one for women, at least from their own point of view. While all nomadic societies have some relatively sharp division between men's and women's spaces, due to the nature of the subsistence activities, nomadic women have shared work spaces among themselves, which settled women do not have, and there are also significant intersections of men's and women's spaces. There is more role fluidity than the formal division of labor leads one to expect. Traces of matriliny are present in all nomads. Women's political roles are important in most nomadic societies, though not among the Gypsies, except through their women elders. The skills that keep a nomadic society functioning smoothly on the road and in the making and breaking of camp, and the skills that enable nomads to scan and utilize their environments in ways that settled peoples often occupying the same general space do not, seem to be the skills that also create the unique social bond that makes nomad society as clearly bounded in social space as settled societies are bounded in physical space.

The skill that neither nomad nor settler has developed is how to relate the two modes of life creatively. If we lose nomadism, we lose a special kind of world-modeling capability that cannot be replaced by the computer.[19] We also lose working examples of nonhierarchical segmented societies that might throw light on problems of societal reorganization from centralized hierarchical modes to decentralist nonhierarchical modes.

If through mistaken goodwill we draw nomads too close to us, we destroy them. As I suggested at the beginning of this chapter, they, not we, may be the laboratory of the future. It is possible that nomadic women, who have special demands made on them to create a balance between scanning skills and nurturance skills as they move their households daily, may have something to teach us about how to move through the world.

Notes

[1]The few sagas that emanate from nomadic cultures do not find their way into our compendiums either as literature or as history. *The Secret History of the Mongols* (Waley, 1963), compiled in the year 1240 by Yuen-chao-pi-shih, or the Celtic *Red Book of Hergest,* or the *Thamudenes,* inscriptions on desert rock left by nomads of the Arabian desert early in the first millennium A.D., are known only to scholars.

[2]The camel has a somewhat similar effect on the desert, but camels move more slowly.

[3]Nelson (1973: 54-55) describes polygamous families living on the Turkish-Syrian border and points out how powerful the senior wife is and how important her role is after widowhood. She is the one who maintains the children and the other wives, controls the land, makes political and economic alliances, arranges work contracts. The widow, in short, acts like and is recognized as a man. Nelson cites Barbara Aswad's data from a study of landowning patrilineages over a period of ten years, showing that nineteen of sixty-eight "heads" of these patrilineages were women.

[4]A recent study of nomadic holy women confirms the possibility that women may be perceived as having greater spiritual and/or healing power than do men and that fierce competition may arise between male and female *marabouts* (Gaudry, in Nelson, 1973: 51-52).

[5]The magnitude of Farb's contribution transcends the limitations of his title and the constraints that the title put on his own thinking. However, the interpretations of women's activities are my own, and should not be ascribed to Farb.

[6]Since science is continuously pushing back dates about human movements, it should be said that this migration may have occurred much earlier.

[7]My somewhat unorthodox discussion of the Eskimo draws on information in David Damas' "The Copper Eskimo" (1972), as well as on Farb (1968).

[8]This description applies to several centuries ago. Today the Shoshone continue a somewhat similar way of life, but it is built around relationships with white settlers. As a niche culture, their way of life has remained more intact than other Indian groups, according to Farb (1968).

9In fact such sisterhood did develop between Indian and pioneer women on the fringes of colonial settlement areas, but it was too little and too late to act as a moderating force in warfare (De Pauw, 1974).

10See the passages on variability in marriage contracts among the Jews of the Cairo Geniza (Goitein, 1967 [vol. 1]: 10, 47-49, 57-59) for an illustration of heterogeneity where one might expect very strictly specified procedures. Egyptian marriage-contract literature shows very great variability, going back to ancient times (Wenig, 1970).

11Moscati characterized these southern towns as "a commercial, fiscal and labour organization, bound to a definite territory. Its members are distributed among various classes, from the noble ruling caste to that of serfs. . . . one may be attached to a tribe by royal decree, that is a group of different origin may be incorporated into the tribe and have equal rights with its existing members" (1959: 115).

12In A.D. 90 the reigning emperor felt strong enough to refuse a princess to the nomad chief of the Indo-Scythians, and successfully stood off the resulting attack. In 565 a northern Chinese king was in such difficult straits that he "humbly" asked for a great khan's daughter in marriage.

13The couriers were called "arrow messengers."

> Every one of these "arrow" messengers was to be regarded as sacred. The highest prince in the land must make room for him to pass when the sound of his horse's bells was heard; and if his mount grew tired, the best available horse had to be supplied. By day and by night these messengers rode across the steppes and the desert, crossing in a few days distances which usually needed weeks to cover. An "arrow" messenger's head and body were bandaged to help him endure his long ride. He rode his steed nearly to death, and slept in the saddle, with the result that nothing could happen throughout the broad land of Mongolia without tidings being promptly conveyed to the Khakan (Prawdin, 1940: 93).

This system was extended in modified form to cover Europe. Riders could make 250 to 300 miles a day.

14It is tempting to develop this animal-training theory of human education further. It must have been a very early form of behaviorism.

15In 1899 Qasim Amin published a book saying that Islam's decline was due to the suppression of women after the days of the prophet.

16The term *women religious* is used to refer to women in religious orders. I am following the usage of the Catholic church here.

17Strabo's passage in his *Geography* is a good example (Glob, 1969: 124).

18The replacement of pagan ritual by the worship of the "White Christ" in Iceland was carried out by women, true to the nomad women's role in introducing new religions (Mowat, 1965: 74).

19I am thinking here about computer-assisted modeling of the world such as the work of Donella and Dennis Meadows, represented in *Limits to Growth* (1972).

References

Ahmed, Abdel Ghaffar M.
1973 "Tribal and sedentary elites: A bridge between two communities." Pp. 75-96 in Cynthia Nelson (ed.), The Desert and the Sown. Berkeley: University of California Press.

Beard, Mary R.
1946 Woman as Force in History: A Study in Traditions and Realities. New York: Macmillan.

Brennan, Peggy
1975 "Analysis of women in Irish history." Unpublished student paper. Boulder: University of Colorado, Department of Sociology.

Brøndsted, Johannes
1965 The Vikings. Tr. by Kalle Skov. Great Britain: Cox and Wyman.

Buccellati, Giorgio
1967 Cities and Nations of Ancient Syria: An Essay on Political Institutions with Special Reference to the Israelite Kingdoms. Rome: Universita di Roma, Instituta di Studi de Vincino Oriente.

Chadwick, Nora
1970 The Celts. London: Cox and Wyman.

Clébert, Jean-Paul
1963 The Gypsies. Tr. by Charles Duff. London: Vista Books, Longacre Press.

Damas, David
1972 "The copper Eskimo." Pp. 3-50 in M. G. Bicchieri (ed.), Hunters and Gatherers Today. New York: Holt, Rinehart and Winston.

Davidson, Basil
1966 The African Kingdoms. New York: Time-Life Books.

De Pauw, Linda Grant
1974 Four Traditions: Women of New York During the American Revolution. Albany: New York State American Revolution Bicentennial Commission.

Diner, Helen
1965 Mothers and Amazons. Tr. by John Philip Lundin. New York: Julian Press. (First published 1932.)

Drinker, Sophie
1948 Music and Women: The Story of Women in Their Relation to Music. New York: Coward-McCann.

Dupire, Marguerite
1963 "The position of women in a pastoral society." Pp. 47-92 in Denise Paulme (ed.), Women of Tropical Africa. Tr. by H. M. Wright. London: Routledge and Kegan Paul.

Eberhard, Wolfram
1967 Settlement and Social Change in Asia. Hong Kong: Hong Kong University Press.

Farb, Peter
1968 Man's Rise to Civilization: As Shown by the Indians of North America From Primeval Times to the Coming of the Industrial State. New York: E. P. Dutton.

Glob, P. V.
1969 The Bog People. Tr. by Rupert Bruce-Mitford. London: Faber and Faber.

Goitein, Solomon D.
1967- A Mediterranean Society: The Jewish Communities of the Arab World
1971 as Portrayed in the Documents of the Cairo Geniza. 2 vols. Berkeley: University of California Press.

Graves, Robert
1966 White Goddess: A Historical Grammar of Poetic Myth. New York: Farrar, Straus, and Giroux.

Grousset, René
1970 The Empire of the Steppes: A History of Central Asia. Tr. by Naomi Walford. New Brunswick, N. J.: Rutgers University Press.

Khaldun, Ibn
1969 The Muqaddimah: An Introduction to History. Tr. by Franz Rosenthal. Ed. and abridged by N. J. Dawood. Princeton, N. J.: Princeton University Press. (Written in 1377.)

Kinsella, Thomas
1970 The Tain. London: Oxford University Press.

Lattimore, Owen
1940 Inner Asian Frontiers of China. Boston: Beacon Press.

Meadows, Donella, Dennis Meadows, et al.
1972 Limits to Growth. New York: Universe Books.

Mohammed, Abbas
1973 "The nomadic and the sedentary: Polar complementaries—Not polar opposites." Pp. 97-112 in Cynthia Nelson (ed.), The Desert and the Sown: Nomads in the Wider Society. Berkeley: University of California Press.

Monteil, Vincent
  1959   "The evolution and settling of the nomads of the Sahara." International
          Social Science Journal 11: 572-585.

Morgan, Lewis Henry
  1901   League of the Ho-De-No Sau-Nee or Iroquois. New Haven, Conn.:
          Human Relations Area Files.

Moscati, Sabatino
  1959   The Semites in Ancient History. Cardiff: University of Wales Press.

Mowat, Farley
  1965   West Viking: The Ancient Norse in Greenland and North America.
          Toronto: McClelland and Stewart.

Nelson, Cynthia (ed.)
  1973   The Desert and the Sown: Nomads in the Wider Society. Berkeley: Uni-
          versity of California Press.

O'Faolain, Julia and Lauro Martines (eds.)
  1973   Not in God's Image: A History of Women in Europe from the Greeks to
          the Nineteenth Century. New York: Harper and Row.

O'Faolain, Sean
  1969   The Irish. London: C. Nicholls.

Oliver, Roland (ed.)
  1968   Dawn of African History. 2nd ed. London: Oxford University Press.

Prawdin, Michael
  1940   The Mongol Empire: Its Rise and Legacy. Tr. by Eden and Cedar Paul.
          London: Allen and Unwin.

Ross, Anne
  1970   Everyday Life of the Pagan Celts. London: B. T. Bottsford.

Silberman, Leo
  1959   "Somali nomads." International Social Science Journal 11: 559-571.

Simons, Gerald
  1968   Barbarian Europe. New York: Time-Life Books.

Smith, W. Robertson
  1966   Kinship and Marriage in Early Arabia. 2nd ed. Ed. by Stanley A. Cook.
          Oosterhout N.B., The Netherlands: Anthropological Publications.

Spencer, Robert F.
  1952   "The Arabian matriarchate: An old controversy." Southwestern Jour-
          nal of Anthropology 8: 478-502.

Stewart, Desmond
  1967   Early Islam. New York: Time-Life Books.

Sullerot, Evelyne
  1968   Histoire et Sociologie du Travail Féminin. Paris: Société Nouvelle des
          Editions Gonthier.

Toynbee, Arnold J.
  1935   A Study of History. Vol. 3. 2nd ed. New York: Oxford University Press.

The Vinland Sagas: The Norse Discovery of America [Groenlendunga Saga and
  Eirik's Saga]
  1966   Tr. by Magnus Magnuson and Herman Polson. New York: New York
     University Press.

Waley, Arthur
  1963   The Secret History of the Mongols, and Other Pieces. New York:
     Barnes and Noble.

Wenig, Steffan
  1970   Women in Egyptian Art. New York: McGraw-Hill.

White, E. M.
  1924   Woman in World History: Her Place in the Great Religions. London:
     Herbert Jenkins.

Yoors, Jan
  1967   The Gypsies. New York: Simon and Schuster.

8
Barbarians, Civilizations, and Women: Rome, Byzantium, and Islam, 200 B.C. to A.D. 100

Times that are supposed to be decisive cutting points in history never, in fact, are, particularly when we are looking at women's roles. These roles rarely show dramatic shifts. In the time period this chapter deals with it *almost* looked as if there would be a dramatic shift. There were great expectations, and one might associate the birth of "futurism" with the onset of the Christian era. But that is not strictly correct, since the idea of a future that is different from the past comes out of all the prophetic religions. With Christianity, however, expectations for the future reached a fever pitch and embraced much of the known world with missionary fervor.

Expectations are one thing. Imaging the future in such a way that images can affect behavior is another. Somewhere between denied expectations and faulty imaging, the alternative future originally set forth by Christianity got lost. The loss was for men as well as for women, but for women the tragedy seems the greater, because the expectations were so much higher.

In this chapter much attention will be given to the developing institutions of Christianity because they are tied up with both the arousing and the crushing of expectancies about alternative ways of life to replace old oppressions. They are also tied up with a special new set of opportunities for women which survived the crushing of expectancies. While this story becomes Eurocentric, events will be examined in the context of happenings in Byzantium and in Islam as well as in Europe.

In the year 200 B.C. the Mediterranean world stood on the threshold of a new kind of society. Many problems of communication, of distribution of resources and organization of large-scale societal interaction, had been solved. During the era of the Roman Republic a new pattern of women's civic affairs began to develop which held some promise for the future. For several hundred years the infrastructures of civic peace developed at least as rapidly as the infrastructure of military might.

If we choose the year 200 B.C. as our dividing line we are highlighting the foot-in-two-worlds role of Rome in the great transition from the oppressions of antiquity to the relatively more open societies of the new Europe. In one sense the Rome of 200 B.C., the "modernized" republic entering on its imperial phase, already represented the new world. In another sense it belonged to the dying world of the first world empires—power reaching into the dark with no understanding of what is being reached for. We take that period here to be our "running start" on the future. The protest movement on behalf of women's rights in Rome which inaugurated the second century B.C. was at least a mild signal of things to come, of reorganized perceptions of social reality (Baldson, 1962: 33-37).

A far more definitive signal of those new perceptions came at the end of the millennium with the appearance of a new teacher in the unlikely small town of Nazareth in the Roman province of Syria. While still a young man, he gathered around him a community of people who bypassed the usual sex-role definitions. Something very remarkable nearly happened. For the first hundred years of the new era, women were everywhere leaving behind old constraints, stepping into the public sphere, and participating in the creation of a new society. The extent of the persecution of these women by Roman authorities was a measure of the extent to which the old world feared the new roles for women. The rate at which women joined the new Christian movement was a measure of the readiness of women for the new life.

As the movement grew larger, it grew more conservative. There were no models for this new kind of participation of women. Might women squeeze men out of their traditional authority roles? Beginning about A.D. 100, but taking another three hundred years to jell completely, a slow process of reviving the earlier domestic role model for women was instituted, and they lost their initial equal status in the new Christian communities.

Yet what had been unleashed could not be stopped. Seeds were sown which took root in even the stoniest soil of stripped-down possibilities for women as social reformers, teachers, scholars, and individuals modeling a new humanness. The new root system also linked with some old root systems—the roles of elite women in the old Mediterranean empires, and of the nomad barbarian women now beginning to settle all along the outer fringes of the Roman Empire in Europe and the Near East. Many different traditions of women's participation intersected over the first thousand years of the new era. By the year A.D. 1000, women had managed to establish themselves securely enough in the niche positions that had been left to them, to be able to participate actively in the postmillennial "second chance" of the late Middle Ages. That is the story of the next chapter.

This chapter is a tale of the hardiness of women, particularly of how they created an entire system of formation and education for children and adults of differing cultures in the very teeth of increasingly barbarous military action. What armies tore down, they rebuilt again and again. The real infrastructures of the first millennium A.D. were created by women in the face of continuous and destructive use of force by men. Male armies converted "barbarians" to Christianity through techniques of slaughter. Women patiently engaged the survivors in the learning-teaching dialogues necessary for the building of new cultures out of old ones. Of course, not all men were destructive, and not all women were constructive. But never before had the difference between the social-learning model of social change and the military-force model been so clear. On the one hand we see the dialogue between different cultures, on the other the forced conformity to one culture. Since history is written largely in terms of the military model, one must search for the evidence of social learnings.

Before launching into a description of women's roles from 200 B.C. to the end of the first millennium, it will be useful to review the situation of the Mediterranean world at the beginning of the period this chapter deals with. The threshold of universalism for human societies was already crossed when Rome moved into position as a major actor on the world scene with the final destruction of Carthage in 202 B.C. All the basic problems of organizing society on a new scale had already been confronted by Darius and Atossa when they embarked on the first major road-building project of the modern world. The Hellenistic empire took over at road building where Persia left off, and we have seen how the Celts had their own wagon tracks in Europe. When Rome began its famous highway network, it was following a well-established communication design. The establishment of local government offices for administration and tax collecting now had a long tradition behind it, and the women and men of the Mediterranean urban elite knew quite a lot about large-scale administration.

By 200 B.C. the art of large-scale warfare had also developed considerable sophistication. The Egyptians were the first to move from a simple massing of soldiers to systematic formations; Sun Tzu wrote the first army manual in 500 B.C. in China; Cyrus developed the first "modern" standing army; and Alexander developed the "phalanx" system.

The first large-scale minting operation was developed under Darius and Atossa, and the Daric was the basic coin for international trade by 500 B.C. The guild system of organization to meet occupational and welfare needs of city dwellers had developed in one form or another in all the major city-states by 200 B.C.

There were universities and libraries in Athens, Alexandria, Taxila (now in Pakistan), and Hien-Yang (China). A tradition of published laws went as far back as Hammurabi of Babylonia, and the Athenian Constitution of 308 B.C. There were several major systems of teachings of universalistic ethics, developed in China, India, and Persia, and universalism had emerged in the most recent Judaic prophetic teachings to replace an earlier tribal religion. The mystery religions of all the major urban centers were adding a new dimension to the religious-ethical world view.

By 200 B.C., the Mediterranean world had already gone through several cult-of-antiquity periods. Ramses II in Egypt had created a major cultural revival as far back as 1290. Nebuchadnezzar developed a passion for archaeology and tried to recreate the ancient Hammurabian kingdom in the late 500s. Following him, Nabu-naid, the last king of the Chaldees, had uncovered what he thought was a thirty-two-thousand-year-old set of records for his forebears. Israel under Josiah in the 600s tried to recreate the Israel of ancient prophecy.

With such a rich past, and such an actively inventive present, the year 200 B.C. was like a gift to the human race. Rome appropriated the gift. She could hardly have missed, in terms of civic achievement. Everything had been set up for her. The women and men of Rome provided the energy and entrepreneurship of the newcomer to the further extension and elaboration of an urban-focused way of life which organized vast hinterlands so that resources could be collected, reworked, and redistributed to meet the needs of the rapidly growing populations of the Mediterranean. If Ferdinand Lot's (1961: 221) interpretation is correct, the Romans were not even innovative in the machinery of state, but used an unworkable city-state mechanism to rule an empire. Roman law was originally the municipal law of

Rome, painfully worked over to apply to the republic of Rome, and never adequate for the empire. What Rome did provide, however, were full-time specialists in law who kept records of new precedents and built up a set of written records in every province, which gave a semblance of order to the empire (Mujeeb, 1960: 110).

The story of the next twelve hundred years is full of ups and downs. The Romans had four "good centuries." By A.D. 200, just at the point when the new small communities of Christians had spread far enough to develop a strong international network of their own, the inadequacies inherent in the Roman village empire plus the pressure of new populations from "barbarian" Europe set in motion a series of interactions that corrupted all the potentials of Romans, tribal barbarians, and Christians alike. Islam's effort, another "new start" on the new society, suffered the same corruption the Roman-Byzantine world suffered, for much the same reasons—though the Moslems were more politically inventive and more tolerant of religious and cultural differences in those they conquered than were the Roman-Byzantine rulers.

Women's Roles: What Went into the Melting Pot

Since in the twentieth century no society is proud of a history of the seclusion of women, historians writing about the period before and after the start of the Christian era are apt to blame some *other* culture for initiating a practice of the seclusion of women from public life. This practice then "contaminates" the historian's own culture. So Sir Steven Runciman, writing of Christian Constantinople, describes the freedom which Byzantium women had, although court ladies did live in specially reserved women's quarters, referred to by the Greek term *gynaeceum:*

> But neither she [the empress] nor the ladies of the court led the secluded lives of Muslim women. They emerged as frequently as they liked (1967: 161).

Ameer Ali writes of women in Islam:

> At the period of the highest blossoming of the Arabian nation, when it held the foremost place in arts and arms, woman was not only on an equality with man but also the object on his part of a chivalrous veneration. Social demoralization, consequent upon political decadence, accentuated the unnerving influence of foreign ideas and foreign customs. "Gradually the noble picture of the free, courageous, independent, self-respecting and therefore respected, Arab matron and maiden disappears

from Moslem society and its place taken by that of secluded ladies"
who copy in their lives and manners the luxury, the inanity and want of
dignity of the inmates of Byzantine or Persian palaces (1899: 755).

A footnote in the Ali paper informs us that

the seclusion of women was common among the Athenians, the ancient
Persians, and apparently the Byzantines. From the latter the Russians
are said to have borrowed their terem (1899: 756).

So the Christians blame the Moslems, and the Moslems the Persians.
But Persian women, as we saw in chapter 6, came into the empire
politics of the Mediterranean world with strong tribal traditions of
women's participation. When the Persians conquered the Greeks, Persian women had nothing but contempt for *gynaeceum*-bound Athenian women.

In all the buck-passing, nobody blames the Romans for the seclusion of women, since their women were already looked upon as
"emancipated." Among the Romans themselves there were those
who blamed the barbarians for the seclusion of women. The Romans,
however, saw only "Romanized" barbarians, and the ways of Gallic
and Germanic tribes of 500 B.C. may have been very different from
the laws recorded by A.D. 500.[1] Also, original tribal traditions dif-
fered, so those using the barbarians as an excuse for the suppression of women tend to quote Saxon, Thuringian, and Lombard law, while those who would look at tribal life as the source of freedom for women tend to quote Burgundian and Visigothic law[2] (see section on Germanic tribal law in O'Faolain, 1969).

Any simple black-and-white picture that puts in any particular quarter the

Figure 8-1. *Scene in Women's Quarters,
Pompeii. Imperial Villa, 1st Century A.D.,
after 3rd Century B.C. Original.*

blame for the growing seclusion of women in the first millennium A.D. is bound to be wrong. We have already noted that the same Athens that produced the *gynaeceum* gave hospitality to women scholars and produced noted public figures among its hetairae. Women scholars who knew Athenian culture played an important role in the Roman-Byzantine empire for a thousand years. We have also noted how, after the barbarian Illyrian woman Eurydice became queen of Macedonia, there developed a whole new tradition of women active in international politics, known as the "Macedonian tradition" (Macurdy, 1927).

If we are to place blame anywhere, we should look at the cultures of the most active trading peoples, since these were the culture spreaders of this era. Greeks and Hebrews were the most active traders in the Mediterranean and Europe from 200 B.C. on. Tavard (1973) suggests that an important influence in making fashionable the seclusion of women in the home was the practice of wealthy Jewish merchants who had homes in each of the major cities of the known world. They drew not only on their own traditions, but also developed further the institution of the *gynaeceum*. Greek and Jewish merchants may well have vied with each other in a Veblenian[3] race to have their wives as conspicuously and expensively secluded as possible. On the other hand, as we will see later in this chapter, a study of the Jewish community in Alexandria toward the end of the millennium indicates a high level of activity of women outside the home, and considerable freedom of movement for them. Anywhere we look, as soon as details are available, the picture of seclusion becomes more ambiguous.

The constraints on women were real enough, but possibly less dramatic than often envisioned. The only way to get an overall view of the multiplicity of cultural patterns is to trace the development of women's roles in each of these traditions over the period under study, and then try to arrive at an overall assessment of the situation of women by the year A.D. 1000.

Women in Pagan Rome

The legends of the founding of Rome, including that of the Romans taking the Sabine women in marriage (the thirty matrilineal clans of ancient Rome?), point to matrilineal origins. The patricians, against whom the plebeians revolted to get constitutional rights for women and men in 451 B.C., were presumably in origin the patriarchs of the thirty "conquered" matrilinies. Most of the accounts of Roman women previous to 200 B.C., however, are accounts of heroic

docility. By 195 B.C. things were different. The Oppian Law, passed
in 215 as a wartime austerity measure, stating that

> no woman might own more than half an ounce of gold, or wear clothes
> of various colors, or ride in a horse-drawn carriage in any town or city
> or within a mile of its confines, except on the occasion of some public
> religious ceremony (Bullough, 1973: 38),

was repealed. Roman women had brought their sisters in from the
countryside in great masses to demonstrate against the law, and there
were lengthy debates in the tribunes. In the now freer political
atmosphere, Roman women increasingly moved about in public,
crowded the court when important trials were going on, attended
senate meetings, and increasingly participated in their husbands'
careers. In addition they conducted large-scale trading enterprises and
had considerable freedom to marry, divorce, remarry, and conduct
their own affairs as they chose. As the empire grew in size and wealth
and its leading citizens were rewarded with gifts of land, women had
increasingly large estates to manage in the countryside (Baldson,
1962: 93). Men were getting nervous about the economic and political power of women. It was argued that women should not accompany their husbands to administrative posts outside Rome because
they would institute a second, secret government (Bullough, 1974:
92). In Asia Minor, according to E. M. White (1924: 287-288),
inscriptions have been found giving evidence of women officials in
the Roman province there, as judges, administrators, priestesses, and
founders of hospitals and orphanages.

The household was the real power base for Roman women, however. Most of their activities were carved out under the "wife-and-
mother" rubric. The Roman matron of affairs managed her home,
her estate, her business affairs, and educated her children, training
them in the international politics of the time.

Not all ladies of the upper classes were civic-minded; the new
wealth of Rome made a gay life possible for those who wanted it.
However, Roman morals continued to be far more straitlaced for
women than for men; riotous banqueting was severely frowned upon
and punished by stringently enforced adultery laws. Since extra-
marital sex was legal for prostitutes, some upper-class women registered as prostitutes to protect themselves (O'Faolain and Martines,
1973: 56). This is only one of many examples of women's use of
laws of prostitution to gain extra freedom of action.

Though I do not know of any specific instances, I can imagine
businesswomen registering as prostitutes in order not to have irrele-

vant laws invoked to hamper their freedom of movement. Is not the following legal opinion suggestive?

> It has been decided that adultery cannot be committed [i.e., there is no such thing as adultery] with women who have charge of any business or shop (O'Faolain and Martines, 1973: 65).

In a similar vein, for women innkeepers and servant girls,

> chastity is required only of those women who are held by the bonds of the law, but those who, because of their mean status in life, are not deemed worthy of the consideration of the laws shall be immune from judicial severity (O'Faolain and Martines, 1973: 65).

I suspect that Roman women were extremely ingenious in obtaining freedom of movement within restrictive laws, and would cheerfully claim menial status or prostitution on behalf of that freedom.

The elitism of Roman society suggested by this legal separation of the matron from all other women, whether freeborn or slave, is important to remember as we move toward the Christian era. The last two hundred years B.C. produced a number of women of substantial wealth and privilege. These were the women who lived in the spacious Roman courtyard-centered homes, who enjoyed the public parks, the forum, the temples, the baths, and who had country houses as well. They had no "political rights," but they knew how to do what they wanted to do. The descendants of these women played an important role in the early Christian community in Rome.

The middle-class women lived with their merchant spouses in apartments above the shops that lined the city streets. They could not afford country houses, and frequented inns and temples instead. The majority of the population of Rome, the three-fourths of the population who were slaves and freed men and women (Goitein, 1967 [vol. 1]: 131), did not, however, frequent these places. They lived in airless, noisy, dusty tenements, six to eight stories high (Nash, 1944). The women worked in all the little shops that crowded the city streets, and they served the well-to-do as dressmakers, hairdressers, midwives, and wet nurses. They kept Rome's inns and they even served as chariot drivers. There was no shortage of jobs for women. In Pompeii there were drinking bars on every street corner and forty bakeries in the town in A.D. 200. Many of the women must have worked in the bathhouses, of which there were a thousand in Rome by A.D. 400 (Nash, 1944).

The selling of sexual services was becoming highly differentiated. At the top of the status scale were the *delicatae* and *famosae*, the

Roman equivalent of the hetairae. Then there were the *meretrices,* the officially registered prostitutes; within this group there were in-numerable special labels for women working in different parts of town and specializing in different types of services. Henriques (1962: 124) speaks of the sense of pride and freedom the women in this pro-fession felt in Rome. The *prostibulae,* the unregistered prostitutes, were another matter. The hardships these poverty-pressed women suf-fered, often with families to support, will be a familiar theme in city life on into the twentieth century.

The situation of slaves was highly varied. On the one hand we read that 25 to 40 percent of them were married; that many lived in their own homes, acquired property, and bought their freedom; that they were as well paid as free labor; that they could be initiated into the mystery cults; that there were many different kinds of political, social, and religious associations of slaves; and that they were a politi-cal force in the city. We read that educated slaves serving as nurses and teachers were often loved and revered by their young charges and given land and wealth when their pupils grew up. Auge, the ex-slave woman of Pompeii who gained wealth and fame may have been one of these. We read of slave women coconspiring with their mistresses in political conspiracies and of their courage in enduring torture when discovered—the slave Epicharis was the heroine of the Pisonian conspiracy. And there was the practice of Delphic manumission, whereby temples could free slaves (Barrow, 1968: 35, 50; Rostovt-zeff, 1945: 13).

On the other hand we know there was widespread industrial slavery, with the use of slaves in factories and mines. And for every story of affection and loyalty between a slave woman and her own-ers, there are other stories of cruelty, bestiality, and sexual exploi-tation on the part of masters and mistresses toward their slaves. In general, however, there appears to have been a general decrease in slavery toward the end of the Roman era. Rostovtzeff (1945) says slave labor was becoming economically less profitable. This was less likely to apply to women, who were domestic slaves.

For the most part, slaves, ex-slaves, and working-class women and men lived in the "other Rome" (E. Morris, 1974: 44), the crowded, dirty city full of violence, sex, and drunkenness. Yet Rome was an egalitarian city from a topographical point of view. The tenement houses of the workers alternated with the enclosed houses of the well-to-do and the apartment houses of the middle classes. "High and low, patricians and plebeian, everywhere rubbed shoulders without coming into conflict" (E. Morris, 1974: 46). To the people who lived there, Rome was probably an exciting place.

By the middle of the second century A.D., with economic decline, Rome had become a "welfare society" and the streets were less fun. There were meal tickets for the plebeians and the poor, child-support payments for families, and festivals and circus games almost every other day. All shops shut at noon so the people could "play." Still, justice was not done, and women and men rioted because they did not get enough bread.

The brutalization displayed at almost daily circus spectacles of an assortment of naked slaves, captives, Christians, and other enemies of the state being torn apart by wild animals or gladiators must have created an odd, anomic state of mind in the average Roman. It certainly affected the women. Wealthy Roman matrons developed passions for gladiators—Eppia, a senator's wife, ran away with one (Auguet, 1972: 165). Women were not just observers of combat, but participants. While most gladiatrices fought privately, enough fought publicly so that finally combats were "forbidden in which women fought in companies with each other, or women with dwarfs" (de Beaumont, 1929: 54).

On the whole, Roman women were well educated. All but the poorest had some kind of schooling. "The poorer ones went to school, the richer stayed at home and had tutors" (O'Faolain and Martines, 1973: 70). In the homes of the well-to-do, the role of the mother as tutor to her children, which I mentioned as developing in Greece, was given considerable public attention. In fact, by A.D. 200 several writings on child development had appeared by Soranus, Galena, and others (de Mause, 1974: 86), and poets include some tender references to children. Lucretius writes of the slow ripening to maturity of the child, and contemplates his own death with sadness:

> No longer will you happily come home
> To a devoted wife, or children dear
> Running for your first kisses, while your heart
> Is filled with sweet unspoken gratitude.
>
> (in de Mause, 1974: 81)

Affection in family life was hardly invented in Roman times—similar passages can be found in Homer, with the warrior longing for his home and little ones—but the theme becomes more frequent in Roman literature, expressed in the context of a concern for child development. While the writings on the subject come from men,[4] they probably would not have appeared if mothering, as well as fathering, had not taken on new dimensions.

The double maternal and tutorial responsibilities of mothers, particularly in the middle and upper classes, set a standard of education for women that led to the tradition of scholarship among Christian women in the succeeding centuries. Wives performed household cult ceremonies together with their husbands. There were also a variety of mystery cults to belong to outside the home. Many of these were now run by men, however, with women taking subordinate roles. The sibylline sisterhood was turning into a brotherhood.

By A.D. 200 Isis temples had spread from Rome to France, Holland, and England. E. M. White tells us that these temples often had husband-wife priest teams, and she suggests that it was the Isis temples in Europe that provided the "black virgin" statues, as Isis worship shifted with the spread of Christianity (1924: 291-293, 315). The nearest equivalent in Rome to the old high priestess roles of the Eastern empires would be the vestal virgins, women of the highest rank, who during the term of their office (averaging thirty years) had a great deal of prestige and power. This power deteriorated as the empire itself deteriorated, especially after A.D. 348.

Figure 8-2. *Young Woman from Pompeii with Stylus and Wax Tablet.*

The institution of the vestal virgins represented the only opportunity for Roman women to hold public office in their own right, and the opportunity appears to have been a dangerous one. The vestals were active in politics, but also vulnerable to accusations of unchastity (which led to the death sentence) when the Senate took offense at their activities. A compilation of all the magistrates of the Roman Republic referred to by name between 509 and 31 B.C. in contemporary annals includes, from 483 on, eighteen vestals (Broughton, 1952). Of these, eleven were accused of misconduct, seven were executed, one hanged herself, and three were acquitted. Of the other seven, five were apparently not politically offensive to the Senate, and two were smart enough to remain politically active without getting denounced.[5] While details are scanty, it appears that most of the vestals denounced for misconduct (incest, unchastity) were really political enemies of the senators who denounced them. The intensity of feeling about vestal activities can be inferred from the fact that two of the vestals finally executed were first tried and acquitted, then retried and condemned.

The political power wielded by women from the second century B.C. followed the typical pattern of operating within elitist structures. The exercise of political power was to a considerable extent for women an underlife activity that they carried out in their capacity as mistress of a household. However, it is easy to be misled by this fact into underestimating the amount of power these women had. The politics of the Republic has to be understood in the context of a relatively small group of consular families whose personal and family lives were totally involved in the life of the Republic. This meant, for example, that every marriage was a policy decision, and we know that women took a very active part in designing the marriage-alliance structures. Women are very conspicuous in the pages of *The Roman Revolution* (Syme, 1939), a history of the Roman Republic. Since women did not have personal names until toward the end of this era, they are referred to only by family name and appear as the sister of X, the wife, daughter, or mother of Y. But nameless though they often are, neither their power nor their independence should be underestimated. Servilia, who was Cato's half-sister, Brutus' mother, and Caesar's mistress, was one of the most powerful persons in Rome, though her name appears in no list of magistrates.

Figure 8-3. *Priestess of Isis, Roman.*

The Romans' own "favorite woman" was Cornelia, the mother of the two Gracchi boys, Tiberius and Gaius. She had married a plebeian by choice over her father's disapproval, and deliberately educated these two sons (out of a total of twelve offspring) to lead a reform movement of the plebeians against the patricians. Both sons died in the ensuing social unrest, but Cornelia remained a major international figure, "visited by men of affairs and men of letters who came from near and far to pay her honor and discuss with her philosophy, letters and the times" (Beard, 1946: 98-99). Ptolemy wanted to share the crown of Egypt with her, but she had her own priorities and refused remarriage. The monument erected to her by the Romans after her death indicates the reverence in which she was held. Helvia, the mother of Seneca, practiced a more emancipated version of the Cornelia tradition, and she taught her son to take the equality of the sexes seriously.[6] The woman Seneca married, Marcia, was another promoter of women's emancipation.

Not too long after Helvia, a tradition of women's participation in the politics of the succession of emperors began. It continued past the fall of Rome into the politics of the Byzantine empire until 1453, the fall of Byzantium, and even then it continued on in the politics of Europe until the time of the French revolution.[7] It is a strange, often brutalizing, tradition in which women fall victim to the depths as well as rise to the heights that empire politics permits.

At the turn of the Christian era Agrippina, wife of Emperor Germanicus (died A.D. 19), set a new place for women in politics, though still in the old heroic Roman woman's style. "She was," says Tacitus, "a greater power in the army than legates and commanders, and she, a woman, had quelled a mutiny which the emperor's authority could not check" (Mozans, 1913: 25). Her daughter Agrippina II, mother of Nero, became Emperor Claudius' wife by persuading him to murder his first wife Messalina. Some writers suggest Agrippina II then had Claudius murdered so she could put Nero on the throne. An astute politician (who used the women's-rights advocate Seneca as her advisor), she was too fond of power for her son's comfort, and in the end he had her murdered. A number of mother-son political partnerships ended in murder. Women who think they are ambitious for their sons often wind up being ambitious for themselves, and disaster usually ensues. The tragedy of this double bind is one of the prices to be paid for underlife politics.

Livia Drusilla, wife of Augustus (Julius Caesar's nephew) and mother of Tiberius, ran into the same trouble that Agrippina II did. She was only exiled and ignored, however, not murdered. Another keen politician, she is sometimes referred to as the "Founder of the Empire" and threaded her way through a complex of intrigue that ended with her success in getting her son Tiberius crowned as emperor.

> At first all public documents were signed by her as well as by Tiberius, and letters on public business were addressed to her as well as to the emperor; and with the exception of her not appearing in person in the

senate or the assemblies of the army and the people, she acted as if she were sovereign (Mozans, 1913: 302).

The Senate was about to heap honors on her when Tiberius decided he had had enough and simply moved his court right out of Rome to get away from her. She lived to be over eighty, a political isolate for the rest of her life. Tiberius would not even visit her on her deathbed.

In the next century Julia Maesa ascended the throne herself and then successively put on the throne each of her daughters-plus-grandson as coregents. Each pair was murdered, until the whole grisly sequence was brought to an end with a successful mother-son combination coming to the throne: Mammaea and her son Alexander, the St. Louis of antiquity. Another harmonious mother-son combination was Victoria and her son Victorinus, during a period of great disorganization when the armies controlled the election of emperors. Her own son and grandson were cut down before Victoria's eyes by angry soldiers, but "in contrition" the army asked her to devise a system of political succession for them, and called her "The Mother of the Camps."

The whole fascinating story of the involvement of women in the politics of pre-Christian Rome is told in several studies and does not need to be given further detail here (Beard, 1946: 301). The transition

Figure 8-4. *Portion of the Frieze of the Ara Pacis Augustae Procession, Gaius Caesar, Julia, and Livia, 13-9 B.C.*

to the Christian era of Rome comes gradually. The wife and daughter of persecuting Emperor Diocletian (late second century) were both Christians and did what they could to soften the persecutions. Helena, the concubine mother of Emperor Constantine (late fourth century), was the first woman to play a direct role in the support of Christianity. It is not clear whether she was born a Christian or converted, but she was both honored by her son and active in the em-

pire, in spite of her equivocal initial social status. Burckhardt says
Constantine was

> said to have been accessible to her counsel always. . . . Purposely
> clothed with official honors, she spent her last years in charitable
> works, pious pilgrimages, and church foundations (1949: 276).

She lived to be over eighty. One of her most memorable contributions to later history was to see the possibility in special sites in the
Holy Land as pilgrimage destinations for Christians. She established
church foundations at a number of such sites. She also offers one of
the rare examples of a happy mother-son relationship in politics.

We have now strayed over the bounds set to this section, which
was intended to cover the women of pagan Rome. As we look back
over the role of the Roman matron we can see the source of the role
model of the "good wife" rediscovered in the Renaissance. Such a
woman served the civic welfare by tending the hearth and educating
her children. All her influence was indirectly exercised. In fact, the
Renaissance version of the Roman matron downplayed the actual
freedom Roman women had—no Roman matron ever went veiled in
public, whereas many women in Renaissance Europe did. The concept of public social space becomes very ambiguous in the Roman
setting, because when the home becomes the training ground for the
empire, the mother's role as teacher is no longer private. This is the
message which the monument to Cornelia, mother of the Gracchis,
conveys. This concept of the public role carried out in the private
spaces of the home is, however, subject to distortions and manipula-
tions. There are no safeguards for women in this position, and
women in the new Christian era rightly rejected it. We will turn now
to the aborted revolution in women's roles which Christianity
initiated.

Women in the First Millennium of the Christian Era

The New Apostolic Communities[8]

One clear message came across to the little communities that banded
together to reflect on the teachings of the executed Nazarene, Jesus,
and to prepare the way for the new society. Humankind was about
to enter a new era which would restore women and men to the condition they were in before the Fall[9]—a situation of perfect love, perfect equality, and perfect justice. For women, this meant most particularly that

the Christian woman is therefore no longer under the curse by which she was made servant to her husband and bound to a chain of painful pregnancies triggered by her desire for him. The Christian woman has become free (Tavard, 1973: 45).

The new era was to come very soon, and Jesus would return to usher it in. This meant there was no reason to carry on with old ways; everyone had to be ready for the new way. Some groups lived together in communes in expectation of the Coming, others continued to live in families. When new partnerships were formed, they were based on a new conception of the woman-man relationship. This new conception was nonsexual and therefore involved celibacy, but did not deny intimate companionship between women and men. The church at Corinth, in particular, tried the experiment of nonsexual common life, with the support of the apostle Paul. Human weakness and the delay in the coming of the new era led to problems.

> If a man has a partner in celibacy and feels that he is not behaving properly towards her, if, that is, his instincts are too strong for him and something must be done, he may do as he pleases; there is nothing wrong in it; let them marry. But if a man is steadfast in his purpose, being under no compulsion, and has complete control of his own choice; and if he has decided in his own mind to preserve his partner in her virginity, he will do well. Thus, he who marries his partner does well, and he who does not will do better (1 Cor. 7: 36-38, as quoted in Tavard, 1973: 32).[10]

It seems at first that Paul was genuinely caught up in a new vision of sex-transcending relationships as a preparation for the new Kingdom. The letter to the Galatians is apparently one of Paul's early ones:

> Before faith came, we were allowed to freedom by the law; we were being looked after till faith was revealed. . . . Now that that time has come we are no longer under that guardian. . . . All baptised in Christ, you have all clothed yourselves in Christ, and there are no more distinctions between Jew and Greek, slave and free, male and female, but all of you are one in Christ Jesus (Gal. 3: 23-28).

In a way, what is being foreshadowed is the concept of the androgynous society, with minimal sex differentiation between women and men. The theme reappears in Christian writings sporadically through the centuries.

But pressures that arose from experiments such as those at Corinth were too much for Paul and the other elders of the early church. Paul, too, was a product of his times. Even in his advice to the Corinthians, he is clearly implying that the decision about maintaining virginity is the man's, not the woman's. How the women of Corinth viewed the situation we do not know. In any case, Paul appears to have given way under pressure. This is one way to explain all the injunctions about women wearing veils in church, being obedient to husbands, etc. Probably a lot more in this vein than Paul himself ever put down was added by later emendation.

The basic issue the church has had to deal with ever since Jesus' time is that *the teaching of the new age has been given*, yet the Coming is continually postponed. Can individuals then live, in the historical present, *as if* the new era had come? On the whole, the church has answered no to this question, but in the first three centuries many people—women, most of all—answered yes.

To understand the meaning of that yes, we must place ourselves first of all back in the towns and villages of the Galilee hill country and look at the kind of people Jesus gathered around him: fisherfolk, artisans, women and men. The "authorized" New Testament lists twelve male disciples. The Gnostic version of the Gospels lists eight men and four women as disciples.[11] J. Morris (1973) (who points out that the number twelve has special symbolic meanings in Judaism) suggests that there were twelve women disciples paralleling the twelve men.[12] In any case, we can be sure that there were more than twelve who moved around with Jesus and prepared to become teachers. We can also be sure that a number of his followers were women, since there are so many references to women in the Gospels.[13]

To these ordinary working folk he taught detachment from conventional family roles, in preparation for the Kingdom:

> The children of this world marry and are given in marriage, but those who are judged worthy of a place in the other world and in the resurrection of the dead do not marry, because they can no longer die (Matt. 22: 30).

As it stands in the Gospels it sounds harsh:

> If someone comes to me, and does not hate his father and his mother and his wife and his children and his brothers and his sisters and even also his wife, he cannot be my disciple. (Matt. 10: 37).

The wording has probably been modified by succeeding generations of male scribes. To his followers the teachings were not a rejection of society, but an affirmation of a new way of living.

Visualize a growing nucleus of women and men living in community and traveling around with Jesus, holding meetings, visiting synagogues, talking with people on the streets. These are working-class people who do not have to observe elaborate social taboos. Jesus himself was very easy and at home with women from all backgrounds, as with men. He was bringing together a new family for a new society, and sex was just not relevant.[14] Nobody was antisex, they were all "beyond" sex. Given that they expected the new dispensation almost momentarily, that was not an unreasonable frame of mind to be in.

It is not difficult to imagine this cheerful band, full of anticipations about the new time. But what kept them going after Jesus' death? The women were the first who were sure they saw him return, then the men also saw him. This shared conviction would greatly intensify the feelings of togetherness of the group. They all flocked to Jerusalem to "see what would happen." It is explicitly mentioned that there were both women and men among the 120 (the number named in the story in Acts 1: 15) who met each day in a second-story apartment in the city. All this built up to a gathering on the fiftieth day after Jesus' death, when people came together with special expectancy. The account in Acts tells us that tongues of fire appeared over the heads of the gathered women and men, and they spoke "with tongues." Peter said a few words at the end of the gathering:

> And it shall come to pass in the last days, saith God, I will pour out of my Spirit upon all flesh: and your sons and your *daughters* shall prophesy. . . . And on my servants and on my *handmaidens* I will pour out, in those days, of my Spirit; and they shall prophesy (Acts 2: 17-18; italics mine).

Think of what it meant for women who had lived the old Judaic pattern of subservience to men to have been part of this group. For them the Age of the Holy Spirit had indeed already started.

It is significant that the Pentecostal experience happened in Jerusalem, where there were merchants from all over the Mediterranean and Near Eastern world:

> Parthians, and Medes, and Elamites, and the dwellers in Mesopotamia, and in Judaea, and Cappadocia, in Pontus, and Asia, Phrygia, and Pamphylia, in Egypt, and in the parts of Libya about Cyrene, and strangers of Rome, Jews and proselytes, Cretes and Arabians (Acts 2: 9-11).

Merchants who had witnessed the event helped spread the news of this unusual occurrence. A number of these were certainly women. We know that there were a number of wealthy widows engaging in trade in the Mediterranean at this time; the presence of some of them at Jerusalem would not be unrelated to the fact that wealthy widows financed so many of the early churches.

The merchant women would have noticed the unusual number of women among the "120" and would have spoken to them afterward. For all their wealth and freedom, these merchant women must have faced many restrictions because of their sex in a male-dominated world. The new teachings would fall on receptive ears.[15]

Women Apostles

Jesus did not start a movement for women, but a movement for humans. It is not surprising, however, that women were especially responsive to his ideas. Trapped in the isolation of a sometimes hostile family, women knew how insecure, unjust, and lonely the world was. It is not surprising that the Pentecostal story ends with the baptism of three thousand persons who decided to remain together, holding all things common and selling their possessions (Acts 2: 44-47). At least half of them must have been women.[16]

They could not all stay around Jerusalem. Some had to keep on with business, to support those who went off to teach. In the end they dispersed to the far corners of the Mediterranean world, individually and in small groups. A look at the map of Paul's journeys shows that he traveled the seacoast all the way from the seaport nearest to Jerusalem over to Rome, founding or visiting churches all the way. He also trekked inland at various points, but he never missed an important seacoast town. Consequently, Paul and his associates converted many merchants. Christianity followed the trade routes, and traders helped spread it. The traders' perspectives on the world would be different from those of laboring folk, so differing interpretations of the teachings began early. What made Christianity so attractive to traders? Perhaps the fact of their own experience of being outsiders, aliens, often discriminated against, in the various countries where they traded.[17]

Traders or laborers, it was the women who had the greatest stake in the new world, and the greatest energy for missionary work. Whenever a new community was founded, the women took the vow of virginity as a matter of course. It was part of the whole liberation phenomenon.

Women did not necessarily feel they needed to be liberated from their husbands, however. A notable wife-husband team in the earliest church community were Priscilla and Aquila. They must have been well-to-do since they had a house on Aventine Hill, which became the first Christian church in Rome. They left for Corinth during the persecutions, and provided a house in Corinth for the church too. Priscilla's name is always mentioned first in the Bible, so it is assumed that she was the more active of the two in the community.

Wife, widow, or single woman, the phenomenon of enthusiastic virginity gave the early church a lot of trouble. It was bad enough when the first groups of women and men apostles were traveling together, like Paul and Thecla, living "beyond sex" and teaching the new social vision. Many of the women cut their hair short and dressed like men to avoid trouble, but if they were caught they faced certain martyrdom for violating both law and custom (Eckenstein, 1935: 72-120). The real trouble began when women from well-to-do pagan families streamed into the new church communities. Objections on the part of the families of the newly liberated women became increasingly vociferous. Thecla herself, of an upper-middle-class family, abandoned a fiancé and marriage plans to join the new sect. Her family and fiancé protested, but did not forbid it. Thousands of young women were thrown in jail, and unknown numbers of them died by fire, sword, and wild beasts, because furious fathers, husbands, and fiancés would rather see them dead than free of the proper duties of every woman.[18] The ferocity of the Roman persecution was not nearly so much because of the teachings about a "new god" as it was because of the practice of women vowing virginity and independence as a prelude to the new era. Think of the loss to the gross national product of the cities of the Roman Empire! Women were removed from the home not only as sex partners and breeders, but as household producers.

It was easiest for the widows. There was no one to forbid their vows, and so the first association to grow up within the burgeoning Christian community of the Mediterranean was the Order of Widows, which flourished all through the second century. Early in the century there were fifteen hundred members of the Order of Widows in Rome, and three thousand in Antioch (J. Morris, 1973: 7). The first churches in Rome and in other major cities, the *domus ecclesia*, were the homes donated by wealthy widows to the local church community.[19] The very earliest assembly places, before Rome became a major center, would be in humbler houses. All the Christian communities mentioned in the Acts of the Apostles are mentioned as meeting in women's houses:

The church in the house of Chloe, in the house of Lydia, in the house
of the mother of Mark, in the house of Nympha, in the house of Priscilla [and her husband Aquila] (J. Morris, 1973: 1).

In Rome by the beginning of the next century another Priscilla, of a
wealthy senatorial family, was to give a catacomb to her Christian
community for the burial of the dead.

Despite the horror they aroused, both the rebellious young women
dressed in men's clothes and the stately widows were in fact very
productive members of society. The wealthier of them provided
housing and resources not only for meeting places, but for schools
and hospitals. Many of the women became healers, and it is noteworthy that a number of Roman women doctors were converted to
Christianity. St. Theodosius, one of the best known, was martyred
in the persecutions under Diocletian. Status was no protection
against being thrown to the lions. Those women already trained as
doctors before conversion helped train others, so the association of
Christianity with the foundation of hospitals and the practice of
healing began very early. There were also herbalists and faith healers.
The fact that the entire spectrum of the healing profession should
find its way into the first Christian circles is an indication of the diversity of backgrounds from which women entered the communities
(Mozans, 1913: 271-272).

The Christian belief in the Resurrection led to a rejection of the
Roman practice of cremation, so women learned embalming. This
was exclusively a woman's occupation from the beginning (Eckenstein, 1935: 97). They also fed the living. As the Roman welfare
system gradually broke down toward the end of the empire, feeding
and helping the poor became one of the major occupations of the
Christian communities.

Meeting together for meals was an important part of cementing
the bonds of community. The earliest communion rituals were freely participated in by everyone, with no distinction as to special authority or status of any individuals. This denial of special priesthood
roles was especially scandalous to their fellow-Romans. It was bad
enough for men, but that the women should participate too!

The very women of the heretics, how bold! who teach, argue, perform
exorcisms, promise cures, baptize. Their ordinations are inconsiderate,
trivial, changeable. . . . Thus today one is a bishop, tomorrow another
(Dietrick, 1897: 42).

In the beginning, Christianity was a challenge to the concept of priesthood as well as to the subjection of women. When specific religious assignments were necessary, they were a dangerous burden rather than a privilege, given the level of persecution in the second and third centuries. There was also a wide variety of beliefs within "the fold," since there was as yet no canon of Christian books. "The majority of Christians worked in scores of perfectly independent cliques, each one of which was fully as 'authoritative' as another" (Dietrick, 1897: 38).

Growth in numbers and increase in respectability eventually combined to produce a formal organization of corporate life and a hierarchy of authority. As the patterns of the larger society took over, men's authority roles became more evident. Also, after the "peace of the church" in 313 there was a great increase in membership. Many women who joined knew nothing of the earlier Pentecostal experience or the commitment to celibacy.

Figure 8-5. *Women Preparing and Shrouding the Body for Burial, 15th Century, A.D.*

They were more likely to accept the traditional authority roles of men (Nugent, 1941). While women retained the role of deaconess for some centuries, they were excluded from the priestly role as soon as it developed. The church fathers consciously referred to priestess roles as being pagan, and unthinkable in a Christian church.

Heretics and Martyrs

The gradual concentration of power within the church did not go

unnoticed by women—or by men. The heresies that developed between A.D. 100 and the Council of Nicea in A.D. 325, when a secular emperor, Constantine, made deviation from church doctrine a
political issue, all had to do with reactions to authoritarianism, sexism, and corruption within the church. Before discussing these issues,
it should be pointed out that the majority of women did *not* pay attention to such matters (nor did men). They found the deaconess
role a busy and fulfilling one, and matters of ecclesiastical hierarchy
seemed remote and uninteresting.

Those who continued to take literally the doctrine of the new era
found themselves at odds with the rest of the community. Marcion, a
rich ship builder born in A.D. 85, whose father had been the head of
the Christian community at Antiope, decided early that Christians in
Rome were falling from the faith. He attracted a group of women
and men who wished to be ready for the Second Coming and not get
led off into marrying and accumulating worldly wealth. In the Mar-
cionian community there was complete equality of women and men,
and women performed baptisms as they had in the earlier days of all
the Christian communities. There was also absolute celibacy. Though
Marcionians were expelled from the Roman church in 144, so powerful was the appeal of this community that Marcionist churches were
still to be found in the Near East until the sixth century (Nigg, 1962:
60-72).

Another perfectionist who wanted to "stay ready" was Montanus,
who also kept to the original tradition of equal participation of
women and men in the church. He began teaching soon after A.D.
155, and many women who saw themselves losing out in the mainstream Christian community joined him. Priscilla and Maximilla were
two famous Montanist prophetesses of the late 200s. Again the rebels
were expelled, in 177, but the Montanist churches lasted for several
more centuries. Nigg (1962: 3-120) recounts the stories of a series of
"heretic" leaders, who all represented a return to primitive Christianity (this was already necessary only one lifetime after the death
of the teacher) and who all attracted women who preferred a rigor-
ously ascetic life and equality in service over soft living in the cities.
(Bishops by then were supposedly condoning women having lovers.)

Perhaps the heresy most powerfully associated with equality
between women and men is the Gnostic heresy.[20] This never
resulted in a sect, but was a philosophical thread that linked the
pagan mystery religions to Christianity and was an important influence on Paul in the early days of his ministry (Nigg, 1962: 26-42).
The Gnostic Gospels give a very prominent place to women, especial-

ly to Mary Magdalene, thus moderating the exclusive emphasis of the mainstream church on Mary, the mother of Jesus. We have already mentioned the Gnostic tradition that there were eight men and four women among the disciples (or parallel sets of twelve). Since many Roman women were already adherents of the mystery religions, it was easy for them to become attracted to Gnostic Christianity both in its mystical aspects and in its recognition of the equality of women and men.

During the first and second centuries, when persecution was at its height, martyrs came from the mainstream and heretic sects alike. Famous among the Montanist martyrs are the Carthagenian Perpetua, the prophetess, and her slave girl Felicitas. Vibia Perpetua was a twenty-one-year-old "matron of good family" nursing a new baby, and her slave Felicitas was pregnant, when they were arrested. Perpetua's firm stand first with her family and then with the authorities, as everyone tried to get her to make the required ritual sacrifice to the emperor to save her life, and the striking visions she recounted make this one of the most vivid and convincing stories in *The Acts of the Martyrs* (Musurillo, 1972: 106-131).[21] Felicitas, weeping with pain during childbirth in the prison, yet calm the next day when facing the lions, is unforgettable. Fifteen-year-old Blandina of Gaul, who was fearless in the arena though her mistress had feared she could not manage the ordeal because she was so young, is another of the more memorable heroines. Then there are the three young women of Thessalonia—Agape, Irene, and Chione—who escaped to the mountains to establish a women's religious community. They were found and brought to trial for not sacrificing to the emperor. The record of their answers is testimony to the keen intellectual capacities of the women who were being attracted to Christianity (Musurillo, 1972: 281-293).

One of the most interesting characters among women of the early church, and one who was not martyred (though she had several narrow escapes), was Thecla, Paul's traveling companion in the ministry. She lived a long, active life for the church, and the site of her final years of retirement in Seleucia became the first monastery for women. The Acts of Thecla is another of the vivid apostolic stories; Thecla's warmth and liveliness as a person come through clearly (Tavard, 1973: 55-56).

These vibrant women were something new under the sun. The men who accepted them as fellow workers were a special breed too. Here was the nucleus of the new society.

The shell of the old world was crumbling. Rome was in decline, but the Second Coming was continually being postponed. Gradually some important changes took place in the rapidly growing church. Now that it was clear that earthly life would be continuing for a while under the old dispensation, family life had to be reevaluated. From the beginning, there had been many husband-wife converts to the new community. Those who had already borne children continued to care for them. Presumably the women who traveled in the ministry left their small children to be cared for by others in the community, as Quaker women did in the seventeenth century. Couples who did not yet have children vowed celibacy. Soon the wisdom of celibacy began to be questioned. Family values were strong in Roman, Jewish, and Greek traditions, and Mary, the mother of Jesus, was increasingly put forth as a role model for women. In place of celibacy came the duty to raise children to make a strong Christian community on earth in preparation for the Second Coming. Christians with pagan partners were urged to fulfill their partners' needs, but not to let this interfere with their prayer life. It was partly over the issue of celibacy that the heretic sects were being expelled from the church.

The Concept of Celibacy

Gradually the idea of two callings evolved. One was the calling to marriage and procreation, to prepare for the Kingdom through the nurture of children. The other was the calling to celibacy, to service outside family life.

The call, or at least the social pressure, to family life is not hard to explain. But the call to celibacy is. The term *call* implies there is a strong inward prompting that leads an individual to make such a choice. That inward prompting, however, may be fostered by such a strong outward pressure that the autonomous act of choice is no longer clear. This tended to happen with celibacy in the Christian church.

Celibacy and eunuchism historically developed together. An aside on eunuchism is necessary here in order to understand the whole phenomenon of celibacy. Whatever the first origins of the practice of castration, Roman history has it that Queen Sammuramat of Assyria (811-808 B.C.) was the first person to castrate men (Penzer, 1935: 125). Since there are frequent references in the Old Testament to eunuchs, the practice must have been well established in Mesopotamia before Queen Sammuramat's time. Its rapid spread through the Near East was due to the fact that it was a useful device for ensuring loyal service to a king or queen. Eunuchs, it was reasoned, would not seek private gain since there could be no offspring to pass rewards on to. Cyrus was the first "modernizer" to make use of this device when he captured Babylonia in 538 B.C. (Penzer, 1935: 137-138). From that time on we find the castration of civil servants in the Persian, Hellenic, Roman, and Byzantine empires.

The single-mindedness-of-service theme would naturally make the institution of eunuchs attractive to religious organizations, and so we find the tradition of eunuch priests established at the Ephesian temple of Artemis.[22] From there the eunuch priest tradition spread to Rome. This is the background of the Christian involvement with castration, which is the most drastic form of celibacy. "There are eunuchs who have made themselves eunuchs for the sake of the kingdom of heaven" (Matt. 19: 12) is the saying of Jesus that, taken literally, has produced a series of sects of eunuchs lasting right up to the 1700s, when the Skoptai sect of Christian eunuchs was rediscovered in Russia (Penzer, 1935: 136). The castration of boys for the papal choir in the Sistine Chapel in Rome was not really religious castration, but rather part of a general secular practice for ensuring male soprano voices.[23] There have been eunuch patriarchs, and possibly eunuch popes. The confusion of castration in the service of a deity with castration as a form of punishment similar to slitting noses, cutting off ears and hands, and putting out eyes, as practiced in Persia and the Byzantine empire and also in Rome itself, makes it particularly difficult to look at this issue objectively. It was widely enough practiced in Rome in the first century A.D. for Emperor Domitian to forbid it entirely. Mohammed also forbade it.

As a form of asceticism, castration is unequivocally condemned today. But the underlying principle of celibacy as a means to single-minded service to the deity remains. As we have seen, it seemed a very natural form of behavior to the first Christians, since the Kingdom was coming soon. When it became a matter of deliberate choice, a way of living in the world, it came to have a different meaning.

For those not already familiar with the best traditions of voluntary celibacy, this may seem like a new form of slavery for women. However, because of the number of other expectations attached to a woman's sex-partner role, freedom from sex can seem like liberation —not just freedom from heterosexual sex, as radical lesbianism advocates, but freedom from all human dependencies as expressed in sexual relations.

The celibacy choice is somewhat easier for women to live with than for men, perhaps mainly because of different social conditionings. One does not read in the writings of holy women about their struggles with tempting visions of beautiful men, though the counter-part struggle is standard fare in the writings of holy men.[24] Today we are very conscious of the pathological elements that may enter into decisions for celibacy, but this should not blind us to the simple fact that in all times there have been "passionate" individuals who chose it freely. They choose it not because they are undersexed, but because they have "another love," a love which spills over to people around them in a way somehow drained of the quality of human sexuality.

A woman may choose celibacy, then, to be free of male domina-tion, or because she loves God, or because it is the only way to get into a desirable career such as those offered by the religious orders for women that began springing up in the third and fourth centuries. Or she might be forced to convent life by a family unwilling to give her a large enough dowry for marriage. Much has been written about all the sex that went on in convents, all the strangled babies, etc., to point up the fraudulent aspects of celibacy for (some? many? most?) of the women so cloistered. Some of the writing is humorous and de-lightful, as in Boccaccio's *Decameron,* some of it angry (McCabe, 1931: 52), some wavering between salaciousness and social commen-tary, as in Aretino's *Dialogues.*

No doubt the full range of human behaviors can be found in con-vents—as elsewhere. It is a pity that women have not had more choices open to them. But for a significant number of women, the convent was not a prison but a place to live and work that provided them with a sense of fulfillment and a freedom of action in the world they could never otherwise have had. Now we will turn to the evolu-tion of that specialist religious role for women, the nun.

Evolution of the Nun's Role

The specialist religious role for women took two forms from the beginning. There were the women who served the churches and cathedrals, and there were the women who lived apart in a life of prayer. The Order of Widows and Virgins belonged to the first type. These women increasingly lived together in small groups, as, for example, those who lived with the widow Dorcas (Acts 9: 36). In the early days, when Christianity was still a "movement," one could say that these women were doing the practical work of building the institutional base for the new society. They worked closely with their brothers in this church activity. In time they were formally recognized and ordained to special service, and became known as canonesses. Some of them continued to live in ordinary apartments near the cathedral, simply making their work at the cathedral the major activity of their lives. Others came to live together in a formal community, developing special vows and a rule for community life to deal with the problems of living together. St. Augustine's sister was the head of one of these houses, and his letter of advice to her about how to handle communal difficulties has often been considered the first "rule" for religious women.25 But the work of canonesses was always "in the world": teaching religion, running schools, caring for the sick, and providing other needed services. They also performed the liturgical services, including choral singing, for the cathedral. Some of them worked entirely outside the church structure, such as the Lady Fabiola, who founded a hospital at Ostia and according to the eulogies at her death revolutionized health care in Rome (Mozans, 1913: 272-273). For the most part, however, health care came to be associated with residential centers and, later, convents.

The other group of religious specialists were the anchoresses or hermits, those who lived in solitude, often in the desert. They were as much a part of the Christian movement in the third century as were their sisters and brothers who worked in the city churches. The journey to the desert was one of the most important developments in the early Christian communities. A small trickle became by the fourth century a stream of thousands of women and men who sought out desert life. At first each one lived in solitude, then small communities were formed, then ever larger ones. In spite of their commitment to physical isolation, they were often in touch with the city; they were trying, in fact, often desperately, to help salvage the vision of the Kingdom which seemed in danger of fading in the midst of the corruption of Rome. They perceived themselves to be undertaking a highly specific task of spiritual reconstruction on behalf of the entire church, through prayer and contemplation. Many of those who chose the desert had been active in the city first, like St. Anthony, who had founded a House of Virgins before deciding in A.D. 280 to go to the desert. (He put the House of Virgins under the leadership of his younger sister before he left.)

A fascinating aspect of the growth of the monastic movement is the number of close brother-sister relationships which emerge in the leadership of the movement. The story of spiritual brother-sister relationsips, i.e., spiritual friendships, is also an interesting one in the movement, but siblings themselves play an important role in the first few generations. This indicates something about the quality of relationship within the families of those who joined the movement.

The warmth and affection between husbands and wives, brothers and sisters, parents and children, in the families of the early Christian communities was to have a profound effect on the monastic movement itself. The family became the model for the monastery.26 Among monks, the abbot was to be father and mother to his flock. Among nuns, the abbess had a similar parenting role. Spiritual guidance was to become that compound of parental tenderness and stern authority that reflects the basic conflict between acceptance of the human and insistence on transformation that characterizes Christianity.

The Monastic Movement

One of the many frustrations in trying to write the underside of history is that the rise of the monastic movement is written almost entirely in terms of men; yet women were equally important in its development. The desert fathers are well recorded; the desert mothers are not. The first women and men to make the journey to the desert were very much a part of the upper classes: wealthy, well educated, experienced in the world, often already in a high position of authority. Later, all sorts of people went, including robbers, outlaws, and thugs. The major movement was into the Egyptian desert, though Syria also housed desert seekers. The problem of sheer numbers as well as of diversity of intention drove the original solitaries to form cenobitic, or communal, living groups.

How does one give a flavor of that life in the desert? It was hot. It was dry. It was uncomfortable. There was little food. People lived in caves, in holes in the ground, in twig shelters. If others came near them, they moved further into the desert to gain more solitude. They gloried in every discomfort. Either discomfort or solitude might seem hard enough by itself. Why both together? To become "new in mind and body" (Lacarrière, 1964: 205-215). This drastic stripping process was the only way "to gain insight into heavenly things," said Cassian (Workman, 1962: 33). It is a measure of the despair these women and men felt about the way society was going that they had to struggle so hard to regain the vision and insight that Jesus had left with them.27

The real impetus for the monastic movement came *after* the official recognition of Christianity by the Roman Empire through Emperor Constantine's Edict of Milan, A.D. 313. This is the point at which Christianity goes from being a persecuted minority to a triumphant, power-wielding majority. The rapidity with which key clerics in Rome adopted all the Roman administrative patterns and incorporated them into the church, keeping both the political and legal infrastructure alive after the "barbarians" took over Rome, alienated many of those who felt a strong commitment to the Christian vision of a new social order. Workman (1962: 6ff.) suggests that the entire monastic movement in its origins should be seen as a protest against the development of a powerful ecclesiastical hierarchy in Rome.28 Women would have even more reason to protest that hierarchy than would men, since it was crowding them out more than it was crowding the men out. Monasteries were alternative societies in a world where alternatives seemed to be disappearing.

When there are choices there are risks, however. It was in the desert that so many monks developed their terrible phobias about women. Nuns stayed on a more even keel, as is delightfully illustrated by the following story:

> A monk ran into a party of handmaids of the Lord on a certain journey. Seeing them he left the road and gave them wide berth. But the Abbess said to him: If you were a perfect monk, you would not even have looked close enough to see that we were women (Merton, 1960: 32).

As more people flocked to the desert, the need for those already there to care for the sick and needy and to provide teaching grew to the point at which certain individuals, like Pachomius, felt called to bring together disciples to live in a community and organize, however simply, their prayer life and their service life. Pachomius had a sister, Mary,

Figure 8-6. *Hermitess in Holy Grotto.*

who initiated the formation of communities for women at Tabbennisi and Tesminé, not far from his settlement. Thalis, a strong-minded woman ascetic, founded twelve convents in Antinoe. Other women joined monasteries already established by men; Shenute headed a desert community of two thousand monks and eighteen hundred nuns. The settlement founded by Thecla near Seleucia, mentioned earlier as possibly the first monastic center, became the center for a group known as Apotactics, which was later declared heretical.

> It included cells for men and for women and was ruled over by a woman
> who is referred to as a woman deacon. It enjoyed a high standing in the
> fourth century (Eckenstein, 1935: 85).

The development of communities did not replace the solitaries. Among the *inclusi*, who lived shut up in caves or cells, were the famous "harlots," like Thais, "the loveliest courtesan in Alexandria," and Pelagia, the beautiful actress of Antioch. Thais appears to have been forced into a sealed cell by a harsh prelate, and the story is not an edifying one, but Pelagia is one of those who chose the new kind of life freely. Here, too, the sexism of the fourth century becomes clear, since Pelagia "passed" as a hermit in a cell on the Mount of Olives and was widely venerated as Pelagius. It was not discovered until her death that she was a woman. The monks would have hidden the information, but it got out (Waddell, 1957: 173ff.). In Syria there were women anchorites like St. Marana and St. Cyriaca, who wore chains for forty-two years as heavy as any human being could bear, for the sake of penance (Lacarrière, 1964: 153).

While pious writings sometimes describe these *inclusi* as weepy milksops, and some may indeed have been so, for the most part these were the fiercest and proudest of women, laying their lives on the line to reconcile vision and reality. How many of them felt they had to renounce femaleness and become like a man to do it, like Pelagia, we shall never know. We do know of Eugenia, the daughter of an Alexandrian prefect, a Greek and Latin scholar whose studies led her to Christianity in the third century and who cut her hair and entered a monastery as a man. Many years later, after she had long served as abbot, her sex was discovered by chance. (Note the portrayal of St. Eugenie in figure 8-7. Accused of rape by the woman to her left, she opens her robe, revealing to the abbot on her right that she could not have committed the crime she is accused of because she is a woman.) Women also lived as men in the desert caves (Eckenstein, 1935: 89-91). More of the desert fathers may have been women than we have dreamed of—discoveries of this kind of "passing" are rare, stories about it rarer still. The early era of fuller participation by women in the religious community was over, it seems, and women were already considered second-class citizens of the Kingdom of Heaven.

Among those who founded communities of religious women in the 300s were St. Augustine's sister and Pachomius' sister, already mentioned; Theobisia, the sister of Gregory of Nyssa; Macrina, the sister of St. Basil; Marcella, the sister of St. Ambrose; Florentine, sister of the two bishops of Seville; and Marguerite, sister of Honoratius.29 In each case we know of them because their brothers wrote about them. How many wom-

Figure 8-7. *St. Eugenie.*

en who did not have famous brothers to memorialize them also founded religious houses? The case of Macrina is particularly interesting because, according to Joan Morris at least, she was the author of the Rule of St. Basil, supposed to be the first formally enunciated monastic rule; her brother took it over from her when he founded his monastery several years after she founded hers (1973: 13-14).

One of the few "quoted" desert mothers is Synclectica, a woman of the Macedonian aristocracy who lived as a recluse near Alexandria and became known as a great teacher, even in her solitude. The quotations I have discovered from her are striking, fiery declarations. She lived to be eighty. Quotations from her are found in Waddell (1957: 68, 85, 95, 110). Abbess Matrona and Abbess Sara are two other mothers quoted in Waddell. Asceticism, solitude, and longevity seem to go together for these early Christians.

Secular and Organizational Leadership of Christian Women

In addition to the women who created their own settings, there were the wealthy Roman matrons of the famous "Aventine Circle" that formed around St. Jerome. Marcella of this circle founded a convent on her own estate. Another group, including the wealthy widow

Paula and her daughter Eustochium, removed with St. Jerome to Jerusalem, where they formed a convent and worked closely with Jerome in one of the earliest spiritual-intellectual partnerships we know of. Paula and Eustochium not only supplied him with all the books he needed for his work, but are said to be themselves the translators of the Psalter ascribed to him and coauthors with him of the Vulgate translation of the Bible. Jerome himself freely acknowledged the partnership, and his great indebtedness to them, in numerous letters and writings, and he dedicated many of his works to them.

Such circles did not exist unchallenged:

> The friendship of Jerome for these ladies led to scandal in later years. In the dedications of his writings it was common for scribes to scratch out their names and substitute "venerable brothers"! (Workman, 1962: 118)

We are not often told so explicitly about the erasing of women from history.[30]

Jerusalem was an exciting place in those days. Melanie the Elder (345-410), one of the richest women in Antioch, became a disciple of a contemporary of Jerome's, Rufinus. She disposed of her Antioch estate, freeing eight thousand slaves (Levy, 1967: 91), and established a convent on the top of the Mount of Olives. Her granddaughter, Melanie the Younger (383-439), was an international figure in intellectual circles, well known at the courts of Rome and Constantinople, but lived as an ascetic. After extensive travels she retired to Palestine to establish two monasteries. There is a biography of her by a priest associate, Geronios.

Ladies of the Roman aristocracy played a very important part in the development of the international networks of the Christian community in the fourth century. We hear a lot about "rich lady tourists" who traveled from monastery to monastery, received by abbots as honored guests (de Carreaux, 1964). Their status as Roman ladies apparently guaranteed them access everywhere. Lady Etheria of Aquitaine was one of the more notable of these. The book she wrote in 385 about her pilgrimage to the Holy Land is a valuable period document (Tavard, 1973: 91; Newton, 1968: 44-48).

All of the women just mentioned lived and worked in the 300s. There was an amazing explosion of interest and activity on the part of the women elite of the Roman Empire during that one century. Many of them, like Melanie the Elder, were women of affairs with substantial financial enterprises to oversee, and they therefore brought a know-how to their participation in the church that reenforced their already high status. These women were founding convents in the very century that Christianity became the official religion of the Roman Empire. The political power that accrued to the church as the old political machinery of the secular empire was falling to pieces also to some extent accrued to the convents. Women had a platform from which to work which they might never otherwise have acquired. Instead of individual women operating each from her own family base within the aristocracy, women built up a network of convents across Europe.[31] They thus developed an independent power which enabled them to retain a substantial measure of autonomy long after the greater equality accorded women in the earlier centuries had been withdrawn by the male power structure.

The battle on the part of women religious to regain the earlier freedom of action began at the close of the next century, in the late 400s. This was the century in which Benedict of Nursia developed a new monastic model balancing spiritual and physical labor. In itself a tremendous "reform" in modifying the excesses of desert asceticism, its function in regard to women religious was somewhat different. It tended to be used as an instrument to urge all religious women into a pattern of seclusion, whether their calling was in that direction or not.

Women of the upper class who wished neither to be active in the world nor to enter a religious order, still had some freedom of choice in the matter, if they were of high enough status. Benedict's sister Scholastica, for example, lived a life of solitary retirement near Benedict's monastery without being either an *inclusi* or in a convent.[32] Scholastica is particularly well known because of her warm lifelong relationship with her brother. How many other women had this kind of freedom we don't know.

The canonesses described earlier had an active vocation of teaching and social service, and retirement from the world was no part of their intention. The freedom of these women, however, was in direct contradiction to the revived social tradition that valued the woman in the home. If women were to continue to be called to the religious life, at least they should be decently secluded in the familistic environment of the convent, and not be intruding on the public space of men. Since many women probably did not have any strong feelings about their religious "life style," it was not hard for religious advisors to guide them into Benedictine convents. Here the emphasis would usually be on prayer and study, with some handwork. They might also teach children inside the convent.

There was no power struggle until after the 900s, when local church authorities tried to control the activities of the independent-minded canonesses in their institutes and to control the royal convents founded by queens and princesses. When bishops confronted women accustomed to wielding authority, the fur began to fly. That story will be told in the next chapter. The pope, it should be noted, supported independent monastic authority for women every time it became an issue. From Rome's perspective an autonomous constituency answerable only to Rome was valuable. Nuns received just as much support from the papacy as monks did in these jurisdictional disputes. It was not until 1874 in Spain that the final blow was struck against the authority of the woman as abbess.

In the meantime, two separate and distinct things were happening within the "women's movement" in the church during the second half of the first millennium A.D. On the one hand, those women who were already inclined toward the scholarly life turned their convents into centers of learning, with fine libraries and high traditions of scholarship. (Daughters of the poor could enter all but the royal convents, but mostly the nuns came from the upper classes.) On the other hand, women who were inclined to a more active involvement in the political life of the new European kingdoms that flourished after the fall of Rome worked with the royal houses of the Goths and the Franks in Christianizing the pagan populations. The scholarly and the activist tradition were not antithetical, but complementary.

The real contrast was not between scholars and activists, but between the women, both religious and secular, and the sword-happy men of the new European kingdoms. The women were working toward a conversion of ways of thinking, social values, and life styles. The men were concerned with consolidating political power, and used forcible conversion to Christianity as a means to that end. The church itself was already committed to interlocking structures of church and state and to the use of political power for its ends. This of course is an oversimplified picture. Many ecclesiastics were concerned with spiritual and social values, and there were certainly women who enthusiastically and ruthlessly used brute force for purely political goals. On balance, however, more women were engaged in a teaching enterprise among the very heterogeneous tribal populations of Europe, and more men were engaged in military action. The first major opportunity for large-scale innovation by the church came about 500, with a solid administrative organization available to it after the fall of Rome. By then, however, the church had reverted to patriarchal domination models for social change.

The Politicization of Christianity: A.D. 500-1000

In A.D. 400 Rome still had two thousand officials in the Prefecture of Gaul (Thrupp, 1967: 130). In 476 Rome "fell," and by the end of the century that infrastructure had crumbled. The medieval historian Lot puts some very complex history very simply by stating that Justinian (reigned 527-565) recaptured the fallen empire and instituted caesaro-papism, or the joint rule of church and state.[33] It seemed clear that the Second Coming was indefinitely postponed, and the church saw the value of Roman law, "adopted it and fitted itself into the framework of ancient legal institutions" (Lot, 1961: 49). The process of adaptation succeeded all too well. Lot describes it thus:

> The church becomes accustomed to employing the secular arm for conversions. It grows impaired and loses its powers of assimilation. Personal propaganda will cease from about the fifth century. Henceforth Christianity will try and obtain recruits only by angling for the confidence of barbarian kings and their courts. Once the ruler has been won over, he is used for imposing the faith on his subjects by gentle or violent pressure. . . . Further the victory was too swift and complete. These herds of Roman and later of barbarian pagans, thrust by consent or force into the bosom of the church, debased and changed Christian feelings (1961: 50).

In A.D. 500 there were the competing kingdoms of the Ostrogoths (Aryan heretics), under Theodoric, and the Franks (pagans), under Clovis. Justinian was laying the groundwork from Constantinople of what was to be the new Holy Roman Empire. By 800 the marriage of church and state was—for a time—complete, with the pope crowning Charlemagne as emperor of this new Christian empire. All Europe had been converted to Christianity except the far north. Yet just a hundred years later Europe was gasping from Moslem attacks from the Mediterranean and Viking attacks from the north. The year 1000, which many of the Christian faithful in Europe devoutly believed would inaugurate the long-postponed Second Coming, was instead an exhausted interlude, with five hundred years of bloody fighting behind, and the Crusades ahead.

The church was not buying any new models of social change. Even the old educational system of pagan Rome, which provided training in literacy for all but the poorest, was nearly gone. All that remained of the vision that was to make a new world was a chain of monasteries and convents across Europe. Nuns and monks were the only teachers left.[34]

Now let us examine the activities of the women religious who provided leadership and continuity during this bleak period. In what was to become a scholar-abbess tradition, Caesaria was one of the first women scholars to found a convent in Europe (at Arles, in the early 500s). Her brother, a cleric, helped write the rule for the new house and seems to have been the more organizationally inclined of the two. He had great reverence for his sister, and writes to her, "I was a lazy youth, you followed learning from the cradle" (Duckett, 1938: 58).

Hilda of Whitby (early 600s) is one of the most interesting women monastics of an era with many outstanding women. Of royal blood, she lived on her own to the age of thirty-four without getting married *or* taking vows, an unusual situation. At thirty-four she evidently decided to enter monastic life, and was almost immediately given the care of the one-year-old daughter of King Oswia, who had promised his daughter to a convent if he should win in battle. (He did.) The estates that went with the royal infant were very extensive, and Hilda built the double monastery of Whitby at the center of these estates. Taking in both nuns and monks, she made it one of the finest centers of scholarship in England. When the highest religious body in Britain convened in council at Whitby, she was a member of the presidency of the council. The secretariat of the council was headquartered at her monastery.

England had many double monasteries ruled by abbesses toward the end of the first millennium. These monastic foundations were sometimes the size of whole counties, including a number of villages and churches. The abbess was the civil as well as the religious ruler of the area, collected taxes and administered justice, and was not under the jurisdiction of the bishop but answered directly to king and pope (J. Morris, 1973: chapt. 5).

Caesaria and Hilda link closely to Roman traditions. In Germany another tradition is tapped, as a long succession of scholar-activist nuns begins with the work of St. Lioba in the mid-700s. The cultural background for Lioba's work in Germany lies in the priestess-prophetess functions of the Germanic tribes. While there is no direct link between the German abbesses and the older prophetesses, Weinhold (1882) may be correct in pointing out the relevance of the earlier tradition. Letters were considered the women's province in many of the "modernizing" tribes in the early Middle Ages, and women of the tribal aristocracies learned to read and write Latin, Greek, and French along with their tribal tongues. The pre-Christian prophetesses themselves are discussed later in this chapter, in the section on women's political roles in the European kingdoms.

St. Lioba was Anglo-Saxon. Orphaned in infancy, she was brought up in a monastery and received her training in England. Greatly revered for her holiness, she became abbess of Tauberbisch of Sheim and may have headed several other convents also. She is described as very beautiful, an outstanding intellect, and an avid reader. She was a favorite political advisor to the princes of Germany.

On the more activist side is the nun Radegunde (died A.D. 587), daughter of the tribal chief of the Thuringians and captured by King Clothair of the Franks as a child. Here we see the independence of the barbarian woman. She was kept at a villa to be educated, tried to escape but did not succeed, and was married to the king against her will at the age of twelve. She proceeded to create an independent life for herself at court, and founded a major religious settlement for women at Poitiers. At court she paid little attention to the king, presiding over her own table as a woman of learning and entertaining visiting scholars. Busy with her own charitable and educational work, she followed her own timetable and was often late for court events, the chronicler tells us. When the king murdered her brother she simply left the court. Subsequently she persuaded a frightened bishop to consecrate her as a deaconess.

Cool-headed in bloody times, Radegunde built a solid fortress-villa to protect her two hundred nuns on the estate at Poitiers. She taught and looked after the nuns and the people settled on her extensive lands. She was also in correspondence with all the kings and queens of Europe and was continually playing the peacemaker role, trying to avert wars; this was a period of many family murders among the royalty she was associated with, so the peacemaking role was not an academic one. A deeply pious woman, she suffered much over the cruelties of her time. She was also a gifted writer and poet. Radegunde is a poignant figure. She literally straddled three worlds: the Germanic prophetess tradition, the Christian monastic tradition, and the new nationalisms of post-Roman Europe. Her anguished writings profoundly convey the gulf between the religious and the nationalist-military vision of the new order in Europe. (For excerpts of Radegunde's writings, see Eckenstein, *Women under Monasticism*, 1896.)

At the very close of the millennium one of the most gifted of women religious writers, Hrotsvitha, continued this Germanic tradition by living close to the heart of the German political arena, at the Convent of Gandersheim. For King Otto she wrote panegyrics. For her nuns she wrote teaching poems and dramas. The dramas make good reading, but will not be found in the standard compendiums of world literature. (For excerpts of Hrotsvitha's work, see Eckenstein, 1896.)

By the 900s there were convents and double monasteries (neighboring religious houses for monks and nuns under a single administration) all over England, Ireland, France, and Germany. Great religious sensitivity, substantial intellectual work, dedicated teaching, and practical political leadership all emerged from the women living quiet but involved lives in these institutions. These were women with knowledge, authority, some resources at their disposal—and a religious vision of the world.

Convent life was not utopia. Many entered convents for reasons of personal convenience with no interest in religious life. When these secular-minded women were wealthy, as they often were, a convent could turn into a great lady's house with a retinue of servants. The character of a monastery depended a good deal on the quality of its abbess. I have picked out the outstanding ones. There were others that were distinguished by nothing so much as their capacity for self-indulgence. Even at their worst, however, these convents provided a place in the world for dowryless women who could not marry.[35] When all possible criticisms have been made of the convent world, the fact remains that many women led spiritually and socially productive lives there.

The convent also provided a base from which women could develop new perspectives on society. It was not just the religious women who developed these perspectives, however. A series of unsung heroines during this entire half-millennium had been coming out of Christian convent schools, marrying pagan kings, and dealing as best they could with extremely turbulent social conditions. Almost the only bit of nonviolent political action going on in this period was the arranging of marriage alliances by popes, bishops, and kings to shore up precarious military alliances.

To do justice to this historical thread, we will go back to A.D. 400 and the declining days of the Roman Empire. At that time, in addition to the women religious, three other sets of "womanpower" stood at the threshold of the new society. First there were the women of the Roman nobility, more Christian than pagan at this point, but still strongly imbued with the traditions of the Roman matron and retaining the political know-how of the women of the Republic. Second there was the "new" Byzantine nobility, stemming from the separation of the eastern and western halves of the empire after Constantine. This nobility was partly from the old Roman nobility, partly from the best families of Greece, and partly from ruling families of tribes at the borders of Byzantium.[36] Third there was the "barbarian" nobility of the Germanic and Gallic tribes now alternately fighting and federating to form kingdoms. The women from each of these three groups played a crucial part in the alliance-formation process out of which the new political entities developed. Additionally, because the story of Islam weaves in and out of the story of Europe and Byzantium, the women of Islam have a part in this story.

Political Roles for Women in the New Empires

The Roman Empire, West and East

From the old Roman nobility, Pulcheria was one of the last and best representatives of empire-building women. Born at the turn of the fifth century, she was the daughter of one emperor (Arcadius), the sister of another (Theodosius II), and ascended the throne of the eastern half of the Roman Empire when she was only fifteen. When when she was only fifteen. When he died she took the throne for a second time, taking a Roman general for a husband (in name only because she was a vowed virgin) to help hold the empire together. For forty years she was an active stateswoman, playing an important part in resolving east-west and church-state conflicts. She laid the groundwork for the Church Council of Chalcedon, which was called to decide whether Rome or Constantinople held ultimate authority. (The council, not surprisingly, failed to achieve concensus.) She was a scholar, trained in medicine and natural science, but also versatile enough to teach her brother horsemanship and military strategy when she undertook his education. She chose for his wife the Athenian Christian scholar Eudocia, to be empress. Although she lived all her life in the public service, she was known as a deeply religious person vowed both to virginity and to service in the world. She was canonized after her death by the Greek Orthodox church.

Placidia did for the western empire what Pulcheria did for the eastern, in the very same time period. Also daughter of one emperor (Theodosius) and sister of another (Honorius), in 414 she married Atawulf, the barbarian invader of Rome, "to help out" in that period of extreme social disorganization, and she married his successor when Atawulf died two years later. In addition she was regent for her son Valentinian III for twenty-five years. Not as good a stateswoman as Pulcheria was, and with nothing like her character, nevertheless the politics of empire was her life and she worked at it with zest.

Placidia's niece Honoria also participated in alliance making with the barbarians. There are various versions of the Honoria-Attila story. The generally accepted version is that Honoria sent a ring to Attila, chief of the Huns, offering her hand in marriage. He came to make good his claim, and at that point Pope Leo came into the negotiations—to try to save Italy from Atilla.[37] Atilla died before negotiations could be concluded. All the women of Placidia's family were involved in the process of establishing marital alliances with barbarians. Placidia's cousin Serena married the Vandal chief Stilicon, who played a key part in the defense of Rome against other barbarian tribes.

Politics, scholarship, and institution building were the areas in which these women of the upper class excelled, and increasingly Constantinople was becoming a center for women scholars. In the late 300s there was already a well-known circle of Christian women scholars there when Eudocia arrived to marry Theodosius. Eudocia became involved in either founding or reorganizing the University of Constantinople (accounts are not clear). She was active in politics, addressed the Senate from time to time, and wrote religious and secular songs. It is thought that she may have initiated the transcription of the Codex Theodosianus, compiled on Theodosius' orders.

We can imagine the consternation in this circle of women scholars when Hypatia, the brilliant pagan mathematician and philosopher, was murdered by some fanatical Christian monks in Alexandria after one of her lectures in A.D. 415. Hypatia is one of the few women scientists that appears in every history of science, and was a major intellectual figure in the transition world of the 400s. She was only thirty when she was murdered.

The continuing contact between Greece and Constantinople is an interesting one. The Greek women we hear of in Byzantium are not the house-bound type; they reflect more the hetairan traditions of Aspasia. One of the best known of these is Olympia. A well-to-do widow at fifteen, she had a long active life as deaconess in the Christian community in Constantinople. The Greek widow Danielis (figure 8-8), several centuries later, represents the continuing nature of the contact between the two societies. She was one of the richest merchants in Greece, and also had a sharp eye for alliances. Befriending the to-be emperor Basil in his early youth, she had him take vows of spiritual brotherhood with her own son. She then regularly visited him over the years and continued the friendship with the emperor's successor. History does not tell us what benefits the widow derived from the relationship, but they were probably substantial.

The role of the empress of Byzantium after the fall of Rome was an interesting one. She became, in fact, the first lady of the Holy Roman Empire. Charlemagne, the backwoods country boy of Europe

Figure 8-8. *Greek Widow Danielis on a Litter Borne by Three Hundred Youths.*

who abortively tried to marry the Byzantine empress Irene in 800, never did succeed in making a Carolingian queen "first lady of the empire" in any comparable way. The Byzantine queens played a more public role in government than had been the practice in the western half of the empire, and participated regularly in regencies, full rulerships, and succession determinations, more on the Mongolian than the Roman pattern.[38] In fact, two of the empresses were Mongol princesses: Justinian I's wife was the khan's sister, took the name Theodora, and was coruler with Justinian; Constantine V married a Khazar princess.

The Byzantine ruling tradition is a strange one, full of cruelty as well as producing some outstanding civic contributions. The beautiful courtesan Theodora, Justinian I's wife and coruler, set a grand style for the empress role with her double enjoyment of politics and institution building. It was she who rallied palace forces to defend a wavering Justinian when angry mobs stood ready to invade the palace and overthrow the government. Besides entering with zest into the theological disputes of the day, she also founded hospitals and convents. The Athenian Irene, Emperor Leo's wife, represents a more aggressive mode. She liked ruling so well that she became coemperor with her son after Leo's death, then had his eyes put out so she could be sole ruler. This is the Irene that Charlemagne tried to marry, but she was deposed and exiled first. By traditional standards she was a good ruler, though ruthless with her enemies. She dealt with complex internal conflicts related to the iconoclasm issue, at the same time skillfully handling the national defense during a series of border wars and rebellions of subject peoples (Naroll et al., 1974: 114-116).

One unusual rule was a triumvirate of mother, daughter, and son, Theodora, Thecla, and Michael. Theodora ruled in her children's minority and had a surprisingly long reign for very troubled times, from 842 to 856. She quieted down the iconoclasm controversy that was a major source of internal bloodshed in that century, and dealt to the apparent satisfaction of her subjects with continuing border unrest and military action. In the next century Emperor Constantine VII chose to turn his rule over to his wife Helena, and it was during Empress Helena's reign that Princess Olga of Russia came to Constantinople to be baptized and to cement Byzantine-Russian relations.

Byzantium is a puzzle. The status of women was high—and not only among the nobility. Byzantine women had better protection of their rights by law in regard to property, divorce rights, and children than did European women of the time. Only the poorest women could not read and write. Women went to the university and there were women doctors and professionals. Guilds were well organized, and women were active in them. At court it was customary for male administrators to have wives with corresponding administrative responsibilities, complete with their own staffs. Ladies of the middle class who were not professionals were often active in religious foundations and hospitals. Constantinople was at the crossroads of the trade world, and Byzantine women traders dealt with Russians, Arabs, Italians, Persians, Central Asiatics, Jews, Egyptians, and occasional emissaries from France or Germany.

In other words, this was a cosmopolitan, cultured society, and a "Christian" one. Yet, the level of interpersonal ferocity in succession politics equals, if it does not exceed, the ferocity of the European barbarians. Every new person on the throne meant hundreds of dead bodies in the city. The practice of punishment by disfigurement meant that people were regularly blinded, castrated, or had hands cut off. Deposed emperors were customarily blinded and had their noses slit. These practices resulted in the increasing brutalization of the society, which all the elaborately constructed law codes could not counteract.

While it must be remembered that Byzantium was fighting for its life against Slavic tribes on one side and Islam on the other, and often against Rome too, so that military action was almost continuous from the eighth century on, I am not sure that this explains the level of internal brutality. Much of the upper-class brutality focused on succession, though the rules for succession seemed to be fairly adequate.

Since succession rules are closely linked to marriage-alliance practices, and therefore involve women in a very intimate way, it may be appropriate to make some observations on succession rules here. The comments will also apply to the European situation, to be examined shortly.

Good succession rules, and intelligent marriage-alliance practices, can only work when universalistic criteria for the best person for the job (whether emperor, empress, or other ruling slot) are applied in making choices from the pool of women and men eligible for the job. Neither in marital-alliance making or in choice of the next ruler would there be only one candidate. There were usually at least two to choose from in selecting an emperor, sometimes up to a dozen— sisters, brothers, sons, daughters, cousins, nephews, even grandchildren. Rules about "the oldest" or "a male" were rarely given priority over the realistic criterion of performance promise. Women could make the critical difference at times of selection crises, by supporting the choice of the best person. When they were driven by personal ambition, they could sabotage the selection process. This is one reason why queens and empresses sometimes appear so diabolical. When they performed universalistically we don't even hear about it, but when they intervened to further their own ambitions, we hear about "petticoat government." In general, the brutalization process worked against an evolving universalism, through a kind of negative resocialization of individuals. Women royalty, therefore, rarely got the kind of training that could help them counteract the existing dynamic of violence.[39] The importance of the monastic movement in this period was that within convents there were schools where women could learn a different perspective on the social order, and observe different behavioral models. Not all the schools were good schools, and not all the pupils were open to this kind of teaching. But it was a possible source of alternatives in a deteriorating society. The importance of that alternative comes clear at certain historic moments, such as when the Ukrainian grand princess Olga, of the recently formed Russian state, came to Constantinople for baptism in A.D. 957. She was very consciously building a new society inside her own country, and chose the resources of the Christian church to help her do it. The alliance structure which she formed between Russia and Byzantium, including a tradition of marriage alliances, was to provide continuity for Byzantine cultural and religious tradition when Byzantium itself was destroyed.

The relationship of Byzantium to the Slavic world, another interesting story, is not gone into here except to say that the same alliance-by-marriage system practiced between Rome and the barbarians of Europe was practiced between Constantinople and the Slavs. With the fall of Constantinople, the tie was continued by Ivan the Great's marriage to the last emperor's niece Sophia, who took on the job of "civilizing" the court at Moscow (to the Russians' great disgust).

Slavs had their own traditions of strong women rulers and women warriors, such as the legends about Princess Libussa who is supposed to have founded the first Bohemian dynasty of Premyslidi (some time before A.D. 800). There are Russian *bylinas* about bold women who carry men off in bags (Halle, 1933: 34). Ukrainian women in particular had a strong tradition of training women as warriors, and a tradition of strong ruling queens (Babiak, 1975, based on translations from Ukrainian history): after Princess Olga came Queen Anna Michailivna (1065), Princess Ivannie Ianka, Queen Polots'ka Predslava (1173), Queen Yaroslavna (1185). These women were all creative diplomats, and most of them were also scholarly historians who contributed to the recordings of the traditions of their people and to the establishment of schools and monasteries where women could be educated. Ianka started the first Ukrainian school for girls. Russia's century of women rulers in the 1700s comes out of this earlier tradition of women rulers.

Before leaving the East and returning to Europe, we will look at the role of women in the rising new world power, Islam, which confronted both Byzantium and Europe toward the end of the first millennium.

Islam[40]

At the start of the seventh century, continuing warfare between Byzantium and Persia had diverted a lot of lucrative trade toward western Arabia, and a new merchant aristocracy was developing that had nothing but contempt for the ways of the majority population of Bedouin nomads. Mohammed, a member of one of the less successful of the urban-based trading groups in Mecca, found at the age of forty that he had a misssion to change the perspectives of the newly powerful merchants. He taught obedience to God and greater justice toward fellow human beings, with particular emphasis on the responsibility of rich merchants for poor nomads. Six hundred years before, Christianity had been born in the countryside and then moved to the city. The religion of Islam, in contrast, started out in the city. Well-to-do merchant women played an important role in both religions. (In Mohammed's case, the first wealthy merchant woman to support him was his own wife, Khadya, who married him in A.D. 580.) Nevertheless, the influence of the nomadic tradition must never be forgotten in evaluating Islam, any more than the influence of the craftworker and fisherpeople traditions must be forgotten in the evaluation of Christianity. Mujeeb tells us that

> a Muslim must regard all men as equal before God. No privilege can be claimed or denied on ground of sex, family, social position, race, language or country. No such distinction is allowed as was made among the Buddhists between the monks and the laymen, or in Christianity between the Church and the laity. Asceticism is forbidden. Historically and socially the novel feature of the Muslim faith is the application of all obligations to all members of the community. This is itself an aspect of the doctrine that life cannot be divided into the spiritual and the worldly, that religion is according to nature and nature consists of both spiritual and material elements (1960: 127).

The extent to which the equality doctrine was applied to women by Mohammed himself and by the men of the Moslem culture that evolved from his teachings is a matter of dispute. As in all religions, there are contradictory references to women. At one time Mohammed said, "The world and all things in it are valuable, but the most valuable thing in the world is a virtuous woman." At another time, "I have not felt any calamity more hurtful to man than woman" (White, 1924: 139). There are some strong references to the equality of women and men in the Koran, but they can be variously interpreted. Because the usual presentations of the status of women in Islam by Westerners is heavily slanted toward almost complete subjection of women, I have chosen to present the more positive side. In practice, the status of women has varied greatly from one Moslem country to another in various periods of history. An overall assessment of the historical status of Moslem women has yet to be rendered.

The Arabic literary traditions must be borne in mind, as well as the sociopolitical aspects of the religious tradition, in considering women's position. In the pre-Islamic era all the great poets had sisters and daughters who were also poets, whose elegies were widely sung. The singing of elegies was a specialty of female professional mourners at funerals (Huart, 1966: 14-15). The poetess tradition continued in Islamic society under the Ummayads. Laila Al-Akhyaliya was a much-loved poetess. Fadl was also a major intellectual figure at the court in Bagdad. Mahbuba, poetess and singer, was a freed harem slave. All these women belong to the eighth century.

It does appear that the doctrine of equality of all persons, referred to above by Mujeeb, was taken seriously by Mohammed in relation to the situation of women. In the course of the new Arabian urbanism, women were already losing their earlier heritage of free participation. Mohammed detailed women's rights of inheritance, administration of property, freedom to choose a partner and to determine conditions of divorce, all of which urban Arabs were taking away from women (O'Faolain and Martines, 1973). One could interpret the history of women in Islam as one long struggle on their part to maintain the rights enunciated by Mohammed in the face of a series of traditions hostile to women's rights in the various Mediterranean countries conquered by the Moslems. Although it appears on the surface that Islam allowed women few rights because of the unilateral right of men to divorce their wives by pronouncing the *talak*, in fact most of women's property rights and the conditions under which divorces were permitted came to be written into the marriage contract. The *ta'lik ad talak* provisions could be taken by any woman into a court of law to protect her rights against unfair treatment, and also in order to compel her husband to divorce her if he violated the provisions. Recent studies of women's property and divorce rights in Morocco (Maher, 1974) and Indonesia (Lev, 1972) indicate that women were able to protect their rights in the traditional rural society. With urbanism it became harder because women became more dependent on men.

The customs of veiling and the harem, from the Moslem point of view, came into Islam from the outside, from the "degenerate" Greeks and Persians. Plural marriages were not eliminated by Mohammed, but in limiting the number of wives permitted a Moslem to four he was setting a higher standard for family relationships than prevailed among the upper classes in Byzantium as well as elsewhere in the Middle East.

The merchant and warrior traditions existed for Arabian women before the rise of Islam, as did the tradition of spiritual leadership. In the lifetime of the prophet, his wife represented the merchant tradition, and his daughter Fatima the tradition of spiritual leadership. In village Islam, women continued to feel very free. As Maher points out, they knew they had control of the means of reproduction: "as sisters, women get men wives. As wives, women get men children" (Maher, 1974: 222). Though Moslem society is a patriarchal one, rural women have apparently always taken a casual attitude toward marriage and kept strong ties with their families of origin, which can be counted on to protect their interests. The high divorce rates associated with that casual attitude have continued from earliest times into the twentieth century. Since most of our information about Moslem women comes from urban settings, where women may be cut off from their matrikin, we have assumed that all Moslem women were as helpless as some urban women have in fact been.

After Mohammed's death, it is not clear what the extent of women's involvement in community life was. Later, after the original tribal welfare state turned into a conquest state, women became involved in succession politics in the caliphate. The pattern is similar to the one already observed in Byzantium and Rome. From 785 on, after the overthrow of the Ummayad caliphate, we hear of the role of the wife of the caliph in matters of succession. The Abbasid caliphate represented in a way the entry of Islam into world politics, and the tradition of alliance by marriage was fully developed under the Abbasids. Persian and Byzantine models were used as models for politics and court life.

Since both Christianity and Islam held ideals of a religious world state, they inevitably collided on all fronts. Shortly after Mohammed's death in 632 his successors overthrew the Sassanids in Persia, and expelled Byzantium from Syria, Egypt, and North Africa. After these military victories, the Moslems advanced to the Atlantic, to the Caucasus, the Oxus, and the Indus without serious opposition. By the time of the reign of Harun-al-Rashid (786-809), Islam was a great and prosperous empire, and by the end of the millennium its cities were centers of knowledge and culture that far outshone any of the cities of Europe—probably even Constantinople (Hazard, 1931). It is hard to know how to characterize this complex civilization, let alone the role of women in it. During the last four centuries of the millennium there were continuous internal strife, consolidations, and successions within the Moslem world. Successions were often attended by bloodbaths as in Persia, Byzantium, and Rome. There was continuous fighting on the borders between Islam and Europe, and between Islam and Byzantium. Yet Islam practiced religious toleration, which Christian Europe did not. Great scholars of all faiths flourished in the major cities of Islam, a thing impossible in the cities of Europe at that time. Islam also allowed a degree of local self-government, which Christian political organization did not provide for. When it came to behavior in war, there was little to choose between the Christians and the Moslems. Christians sometimes massacred civilian populations on the taking of a town, and so did Moslems.

In the midst of all this ferocity, an extraordinary society

developed which was a continuing blend of Arabian nomads and the various urban populations of the Mediterranean world. The nomads were strongest in Syria, and periodically established "reform" governments to do away with urban corruption. Side by side with differing political emphases, came differing religious emphases. As Islamic society became increasingly differentiated and institutionalized, it began to provide the same kinds of niches for alternative ways of life that Christianity provided. One set of niches was the monasteries. The Moslem form of the monastery is the *khanqah,* which potentially gives expression to the same range of socio-economic and spiritual concerns as the Christian monastery. Sufi convents cared for the sick and the poor in much the same way as the Christian convents in Europe did. The Sufi nun Rabi'a is the best-known woman mystic from the Moslem monastic tradition. Stolen into slavery as a child, she was freed as a young woman because of her great purity and love of God, and was widely revered in her own lifetime.

A contemporary of St. Rabi'a, Sukaina, was a granddaughter of Mohammed's daughter Fatima. She was one of the first "role models" in Islamic history for a new urban elite of women, and is supposed to have "invented" the salon. The reunions in her house of poets, scholars, jurists, and other distinguished people of both sexes became the model for similar social gatherings at the residences of other ladies of fashion. Ali laments that while St. Rabi'a's tomb is a pilgrimage center, Sukaina, one of the great women of Islam, no longer has visitors to her tomb. She set a standard of education and culture for Arabian women which has been important ever since, and was *"la dame des dames de son temps"* (Ali, 1899: 758). Women began training in law, theology, and "the traditions" at this time, and leading lady jurists are mentioned up to the fall of Bagdad.

In this same early period a friend of Sukaina's, Umm ul-Banin, was the wife of Al-Walid I, the Ummayad caliph under whom Spain was taken. She is the first queen mentioned as being active in politics, and is said to have

> frequently interfered in affairs of State . . . on the side of justice and humanity. Most of the great works of benefaction introduced by Walid were due to her inspiration (Ali, 1899: 759).

Walid's colleague, the governor of Iraq, complained of petticoat government and advised Walid not to be influenced by her. According to Ali, Walid's response to the complaint was to command the discontented governor to appear before her and receive a lecture!

One of the first women to be involved in the politics of succession was al-Khayzuran, the mother of Harun al-Rashid. Khayzuran engaged in a power struggle with her son Hadi, who succeeded her husband as caliph. When Hadi tried to have her confined in the harem she had her slaves kill him, thus making it possible for her favorite son, Harun, to ascend the throne (Naroll et al., 1974: 122-123). The next interference was less violent. One of Harun's wives, the Arabian Zubayda, competed successfully against another wife, a Persian concubine, to have Zubayda's son declared the next caliph in 792.

Zubayda seems to have been an unusual person, representing that vigorous Arabian strain that keeps erupting into Islamic culture. She built an aqueduct at her own expense in Mecca, rebuilt Alexandretta after it was destroyed by the Greeks, and generally seems to have played the role of "development expert" for Arabian cities.

Women's intervention in politics continued. In 1021 caliph al-Hakim of the Fatimids in Egypt met death—supposedly with the connivance of his sister, the Sitt al-Mulk. This lady, according to the *Cambridge History of Islam* (Holt, 1970), ruled "competently and vigorously" as regent for her sixteen-year-old nephew for six years. In 1045 rule passed to the deceased caliph's mother, a Sudanese slave, who ruled for five years with a council of ministers including her former master, a Persian Jewish banker. One would like to know more details of that story! One of the heroines of Moslem history is Shajar al-Durr. She was the concubine of Sultan al-Malik al-Salih, who died during the hostilities that ensued when King Louis IX came from France to "take Egypt." Shajar concealed the news of the sultan's death and issued orders in his name, holding the army and the kingdom together until his son arrived to take over the rule. Plot and counterplot led one faction to murder the son and proclaim Shajar sultan, but opposition to her was very substantial. The caliph in Bagdad felt insulted at her enthronement since she was a former inmate of his own harem, sent to the deceased sultan as a gift! We are told Shajar was a woman of remarkable ability, who nonetheless needed help in waging war; therefore she appointed a commander-in-chief who became sultan. She continued to stay on top of a seething situation, ruling for seven years before she was finally murdered.

Most queens played quieter roles, but took an active part in promoting colleges and scholarship and making civic improvements. There was a strong tradition of scholarship and learning for women of the upper classes, contrary to the general image Westerners have of women in Islam. Spain is a particularly good example. The account of Moslem Cordova by A. J. Arberry (1967: 175) reveals a cultured society with highly educated women. Education was "perfectly general," with girls and boys attending local elementary schools (except the upper class, who had their own tutors). "Women shared equally with men in the work of pedagogy; not a few became accomplished scholars." Ibn Hazm, as Moslem scholar, testifies that he was educated by women entirely:

> I never sat with men until I was already a youth, and my beard had begun to sprout. Women taught me the Koran, they recited to me much poetry, they trained me in calligraphy (Arberry, 1967: 176).[41]

This passage is particularly interesting because it confirms my earlier suggestion that the effect of boys spending time in the women's quarters of the house could have positive and mutually reenforcing benefits for both women and boys. Cordova, Granada, Seville, and the other towns of Spain all were known for their women scholars and poets, one of whom acted as secretary to the scholarly Hakam II. Waladah (died 1087) was considered one of the best poets of her age. Women lectured at the universities of Cordova and Valencia.

In Egypt, women of rank and learning played important public roles under the Tulunides and the Fatimids. Women, equally with men, could be members of the "House of Science" (Dar ul-Hikmat),

> which combined the characteristics of a scientific institute with those of a masonic lodge, where the esoteric doctrines of the Ismalias were taught (Ali, 1899: 764).

Takia was a famous Egyptian scholar and poet in the reign of Saladin. The tradition of women scholars in Egypt was not destroyed by the advent of Moslem rule.

Yet, individual caliphs did from time to time pass decrees drastically limiting the freedom of women. The fact that Ali Hakem, the "mad caliph," could in the tenth century forbid any woman to appear on the streets on pain of death (White, 1924: 150) indicates considerable vulnerability in their position.

The women we are describing are mostly of the aristocracy. Did middle-class women participate in public life and move about freely? According to Ali, during this period, yes. It would not have been possible for the caliphate to send "both men and women spies into the Byzantine Empire in the guise of merchants, travelers and physicians" if women were not already accustomed to such roles in public in their home society (Naroll et al., 1974: 122). The general practice of purdah came considerably later. The lives of working-class women and slaves would be very much the same in Islam as in Rome, Byzantium, and Europe. Possibly Moslems treated their slaves better than Romans and Europeans did.

Life for Middle-Class Jewish Women in Cairo

Materials on the life of middle-class women in this millennium have been sparse, no matter what part of the world we look at. Owing to a recent study of the documents of the Cairo Geniza from 969 to 1250 we have an unexpected glimpse of the life of the middle-class Jewish woman in this part of the Mediterranean. The documents are a haphazard deposit in the community storage room of the synagogue, consisting of letters, court records, contracts, accounts, and other writings. Not only do they bring the women's underside life to the light, but they bring hope that a further search for these types of records will enable us to learn a lot more about women as householders than we now know.

These middle-class women had female slaves[42] to do their domestic work, a pattern that was surely common among all urban middle-class women of this millennium. The free servant class did not yet exist. From references to slaves in letters, and from frequent references to the freeing of slaves upon the death of the owner, it appears that slaves were often treated as members of the family, or as close friends. Sometimes the slaves were European, but more often they were black.

The Cairo women were involved in many enterprises and handled a good deal of capital, according to the court records. They were money lenders and international traders, and they sometimes had business partners who were gentiles. They were teachers and heads of schools, scholars, and copyists. They were sometimes cantors in the synagogues, in which capacity they would function as singers, marriage counselors, and general social workers for the community. There is also mention of a woman visionary. All girls went to school, sometimes to separate classes, sometimes to classes together with boys. Women spent a good deal of time on community service projects of all kinds. They frequently endowed institutions for relief to the poor in their own names and with their own funds. They headed special financial drives for their synagogues, sometimes to raise money to ransom members of the community who had been captured by pirates. They saw to it that the synagogue warehouse was always stocked with food and clothing for distribution to the poor.

Women were evidently free to make appeals for help and justice to the assembled congregation in the synagogue, and did so frequently and successfully. Although traditional Jewish law was followed, the society appears to have been a surprisingly egalitarian one. This is another evidence that the same law that limits women also protects the rights they do have, if they use it. Two things set Jews apart from other Mediterranean societies in this millennium. One is that they did not practice infanticide. Earlier customs in this regard were effectively stopped long before they were discontinued in other societies. The other is that all girls were educated in regular classes. This equal care for children of both sexes as they were growing up speaks of a special quality of parent-child relations in the Jewish home. We can see in this highly supportive Mediterranean family setting the source for the phenomenon to be observed later in Europe, that Jewish women of the middle class were trained to be doctors and scholars at a time when practically no European women of that class (except nuns) were being educated.

As we turn from Mediterranean to European society, which was undergoing similar strains of diverse populations having to be accommodated in a rapidly secularizing polity, we will see that women's roles may not be so different in the two culture areas as has usually been thought.

European Kingdoms

As Byzantium and Islam were experiencing turbulence in the period we have been discussing, Europe was facing its own storms. The Roman tradition was in some sense broken after 476, and while the church provided some continuity, a whole new set of political units had to be forged out of the remains of the old Roman provinces and the new tribal groups. While these tribal groups had been in touch with Rome for a long time and were by no means nomadic peoples just tumbled out of forest and steppe, the Gothic and Frankish traditions and life styles were substantially different from the Roman, particularly in that they were essentially nonurban.

The development of an urban culture and of usable communication and administrative networks on a scale that could deal with both the old Roman world and the new parts of Europe that had to be integrated into it required considerably more than the skills of the warrior. The women of the ruling families did have some of the requisite skills and played an important part, along with their sisters in religious orders, in organizing and gentling the society.

The old prophetic tribal tradition was still strong in these societies, as I indicated earlier. The great prophetesses and druidesses were not only venerated by their own people but by the Romans. Emperors and generals turned to them for advice. Veleda was a famous prophetess in the reign of Emperor Vespasian. As described by Tacitus, she was of the tribe of Bructeria and lived in a tower on the River Lippe, a tributary of the Rhine. Foreign ambassadors who came to consult with her were not admitted to her presence, but only permitted communication through an intermediary (White, 1924: 31). Albruna prophesied in the time of Tiberius. Ganna and Gambara were the leading prophetesses in the reign of Emperor Domitian (Weinhold, 1882).

Figure 8-9. *Pompeiian Sibyl.*

Because the prophetesses originally wrote and interpreted runes, a tradition of literacy developed among them which we have already noted among the aristocratic women of tribal courts and as a carry-over into the convent culture of Germany in the very early Middle Ages. Druidesses were mentioned in the chapter on nomads. They ranged from women who performed temple offices and lived with their families to a sisterhood dwelling in seclusion (White, 1924: 30). Burckhardt refers to these women somewhat unceremoniously as "the gypsies of the declining ancient world." The stories he tells of the priestesses are interesting:

> Aurelian inquired of a number of them—perhaps a corporation of priestesses—concerning the succession in the Empire, and surely not in jest, for in such a matter jesting was dangerous. Sometimes they uttered their prophecies unsolicited. One bold woman, indifferent to consequences, called to Alexander Severus in the Gallic tongue: "Depart, hope for no victory, do not trust your soldiers!" A Druid landlady in the country of the Tungrii (near Leige) with whom the Subaltern Diocles, later Diocletian, was reckoning his daily board, said to him: "You are too greedy, too stingy." "I will be generous if I ever become Emperor," he replied. "Do not mock," the hostess answered, "you will become Emperor when you have slain a boar" (1949: 69).

The punch line in that particular story, which Burckhardt omits, comes when the subaltern Diocles stabs Aper (*boar* in Latin), the Praetorian Prefect who had murdered the previous emperor, Numerian. This paved the way to his becoming emperor himself, and fulfilled the prophecy of the druidess.

It should not be forgotten that the barbarian queens had this tradition of knowledge and power to draw on. They were accustomed to the exercise of authority. Amalswinthe, daughter of Theodoric, the first barbarian king of Rome, provides a good example of the performance records of these queens. When her father died she served capably as regent of the empire for two years. Having received an excellent Latin education, she devoted a good deal of her energy during her regency to reorganizing the crumbling educational system of the Roman schools.

Amalswinthe stood at the center of a very strong alliance-by-marriage system that her father had worked out between the Visigoths, the Burgundians, the Vandals, and the Thuringians (Brentano, 1964: 49). It was a masterly piece of international negotiation, but Theodoric's successors were not as skilled as he, so there was much blood shed between the various tribes and kingdoms. Amalswinthe herself was strangled by an ungrateful relative she had brought into the alliance system to help rule the country after her father's death.

Contemporaneous with Amalswinthe was Clothilde, the niece of the first Burgundian king. She was married to Clovis, king of the Franks, more or less with the challenging commission to bring about his conversion to Christianity. The Franks were the only really pagan kingdom in Europe—the other tribes and all been converted to Aryan Christianity, which had been declared heretical by the Catholic church. The pope's hand would be much strengthened in dealing with the Aryans if a strong pagan kingdom could be brought directly into the Catholic fold. The entire political future of the church seemed to depend on the success of this maneuver.

Clovis was not an admirable character, and the task did not seem easy, but Clothilde was tough and persistent. She had been through a lot herself, since she had recently escaped into a convent from an uncle who had stabbed her father and strangled her mother. She laid the groundwork for Clovis' believing that God would help him win an important victory, so he converted as a "thank you" to the deity. A mass conversion of his people followed, as expected. St. Gregory's life of Clothilde shows her as a resourceful and determined person (Brentano, 1964: 109-114, 119-120). She knew well the limitations of the mass conversion and did what she could to develop institutions that would help education and Christian service to the Franks. One important step was to found a religious house for royal women, thus providing for a new kind of education and socialization for Frankish women of the upper strata. She became a deaconess, and lived the last years of her life as a nun, founding a variety of useful institutions including hospitals.

Shortly after Clothilde's time we hear that Fredegundis, queen of the Franks, and her son King Chlotar "took possession of Paris and other cities after the barbarian fashion" (Brentano, 1964: 46). This was evidently an unsuccessful attempt by a royal mother to get control of a kingdom for her son. She died shortly thereafter. Another ambitious woman of the Frankish royalty of that generation, Brunihild or Brunechildas, was more successful in the short run, though she was executed in the end by Fredegundis' son Chlotar. For a fifty-year period Brunihild managed to remain a chief actor in the Frankish kingdom, several times serving as regent. It is hard to know what this queen was really like because in one chronicle (Gregory's) she is described as a simple girl. In another (*The Chronicle of Fredegar*, in Brentano, 1964: 135-146), she appears as a bloodthirsty, brutal person responsible for many deaths. An Aryan and unfriendly to Catholic monasticism, she undercut many of the church's power bases in trying to build her own. She may have been a major builder of European roads, as there are roads in northern France and the Low Countries which were known as "Brunehilde's Roads" (Leighton, 1972: 56). She seems to have had a hand in every major appointment in the kingdom throughout her life, except for a couple of interim periods when she was expelled by irate kings. With a passion for ruling, she played the conventional brutal power politics of her day more effectively than most. In the end King Chlotar had her executed rather spectacularly:

Brunechildas was brought before Chlotar, who was boiling with fury
against her. He charged her with the deaths of ten Frankish kings—
namely, Sigebert, Merovech, his father Chilperic, Theudebert and his
son Chlotar, Chlotar's son the other Merovech, Theuderic and Theuderic's three sons who had just perished. She was tormented for three
days with a diversity of tortures, and then on his orders was led through
the ranks on a camel. Finally she was tied by her hair, one arm and one
leg to the tail of an unbroken horse, and she was cut to shreds by its
hoofs at the pace it went (Brentano, 1964: 145).

The seventh century brings another activist queen, with a gentler
style, to the throne of France. Queen Balthild, daughter of Anglo-
Saxon royalty, shared in the typical hair-raising childhood experiences of the times. Captured as a child she was enslaved, but escaped and was befriended by a family of rank. Marrying King Chlod-
wig II, who turned imbecile, she became governing queen of France
for the rest of his lifetime and during the minority of her sons. She
worked against slavery, forbidding the sale of Christians in France,
managed many political reforms, and generally turned a turbulent
kingdom into a peaceful one. She was also a strong supporter of the
monastic movement, founding a monastery herself and helping many
others and also helping link the French and English convent
networks. There was a great expansion of convents during her reign,
and one could say that a whole new educational system was developing for Europe, aided by her efforts. Retiring to a convent when she
left the throne, she had the misfortune to witness the resurgence of
the politics of blood after her peaceful reign.

In Italy we have the same alternation of peacemaking queens and
brutal queens as elsewhere. Queen Rosamund of the Lombards (late
500s) had a reputation for killing off husbands, but the story of how
she got started on her career of crime helps one understand the
socialization for brutality which women experienced: Rosamund's
husband, King Ratchis, had killed her father and made a drinking cup
out of his skull. One day at a banquet he gaily handed her the cup
and ordered her to "drink merrily" with her father (Brentano, 1964:
178).

Given this background of violence, it is the more extraordinary
that we can point to as many peacemakers as we can. In the same
sixth century we find the devout Catholic queen Theodelinda, also of
Lombardy, wife of King Agilulf, devoting her political career to the
negotiation of a treaty for the Lombards and the Italian governor of

Italy with the Roman Empire (then based in Constantinople). She also moderated the effects of the Lombard invasion of Italy and paved the way for the conversion of the Lombards to Catholicism. She was recognized and thanked by Pope Gregory for her work.

Sixth and seventh century England produced a series of devout queens who somewhat gentled the male nobility of a country that was divided into several warring kingdoms. Queen Berhta, wife of Aethelbert of Kent, brought the first Christian ecclesiastic to England after a long period of reversion to paganism. Pope Gregory ordered St. Augustine to go and help her with the work of re-Christianizing England, but Augustine was frightened and turned back before he reached England, begging to be let off (Duckett, 1938). The pope sternly ordered him back and he finally made the trip. The credit for re-Christianizing England usually goes to the frightened Augustine. Rarely is Queen Berhta, the courageous woman who was on the scene all the time and made it possible for Augustine to do his work, even mentioned. (Berhta also converted her own husband.)

Queen Berhta's daughter Aethelburg married King Eadwin of Northumbria and in so doing accepted a commission to avert war between Northumbria and Kent. She brought a Christian cleric with her who baptized her husband; she also founded a double monastery and churches in Northumbria.

Princess Eanswith, also of Kent, refused her commission to marry a heathen king, showing that women were not always helpless pawns in these matters. She devoted her life instead to developing a religious settlement and improving the agricultural practices of the farmers on the estates associated with her monastery. Queen Aethelthrith, or Ethelreda, was the wife of two kings in succession. At the age of thirty she married the second, a fifteen-year-old boy, for reasons of state. She left him shortly afterward to take the veil, founding a monastery at Ely, one of the major English religious foundations. Like St. Hilda (Duckett, 1938: 9), Ethelreda was renowned as a teacher and had many of the leading men of England as her students. She was much loved and there are many legends about her.

The queens of the barbarian kingdoms functioned, as we have seen, as diplomats, peacemakers, founders of educational centers, and Christian missionaries. There is one role which has not been mentioned, and that is the role of administrator of economic affairs. A study by David Herlihy uncovers an interesting part of the work of the Carolingian queens of France, which by extension Herlihy suggests may have been true of the queens in other Germanic traditions. From an essay on the organization of the royal household by Hincmar of Rheims, written in 882:

> The royal treasurer, the "camerarius," is directly under the queen. Moreover, the queen is repsonsible for giving to the knights their yearly gifts, the equivalent of their salaries. This heavy responsibility falls upon the queen in order to free her husband from "domestic or palace solicitude" and to enable him to give all his attention "to the state of the entire kingdom." So too, Agobard of Lyons mentions the Carolingian queens as being in a peculiar way responsible for the "honestas" of the palace (Herlihy, 1962: 102-103).

Evidently, women of the nobility had similar responsibility for the economic administration of the large estates their families held from the king. This seems to be true in Italy and Spain as well as in France (Herlihy, 1962: 103).

When we add economic roles to educational and diplomatic functions, we see that women of the elite carried a heavy share of the administrative responsibility for these kingdoms. The men were left free for military activity. Women generally married between the ages of twelve and fifteen. This means that these difficult diplomatic missions were taken on at very young ages indeed. The fact that at the age of fifteen Pulcheria could rule the Byzantine empire on behalf of her younger brother says a good deal about the maturity, level of education, and purposefulness of royal teen-age girls. Their acceptance of marriage as a diplomatic role and their willingness to undertake unlikely alliances for the sake of public order are worth pondering. On points of principle important to them, they did not compromise. Christian queens did not become pagan to please their husbands. It always went the other way. Furthermore, women could and did refuse marriage alliances they did not wish to undertake, like Eanswith. Their record in founding convents, schools, and hospitals is impressive. On the other hand, their best efforts could be swamped by military action. Like everyone else, female and male, they all lived under the shadow of the sword.

We have been looking at elites. Peasant and working-class women of Europe and the Mediterranean worked much as they did in earlier eras. The pattern did not change very much until the industrial revolution and the advent of factories.

There is some interesting information on the economic roles of middle-class women, thanks to the Herlihy study cited above. In an analysis of European documents between 701 and 1200 dealing with landholdings and transfers of property, Herlihy made the interesting discovery that 1) many men identified themselves in legal documents by their matronymic rather than their patronymic (i.e., as sons of their mothers rather than of their fathers), and 2) women were listed as owners of land more often than expected. Identification through the matronymic for men reached a peak in the eleventh century—8 percent of all identifications in the legal documents studied referred to the mother. To summarize the findings all too briefly, the mother's name was preferred as identification in the following cases: 1) the woman was a freed woman, her husband a serf, and the child's status was determined by the mother; 2) the child was the illegitimate son of a cleric, and therefore took identification through the mother; and 3) the mother was better known in the community than the father was, and therefore a better identifier. This is indirect but interesting evidence of women's economic importance and community status.

The reputation of women as persons of affairs in the community were both cause and effect of the increasing properties accumulating in their hands. In Spain, France, and Germany women held as high as 18 percent of the land, with 12 percent as the overall figure for 1200. This is land specifically listed as the woman's and does not include the land held for "heirs," usually under her administration, which would bring the total of land under women's administration as high as 25 percent in 1100. Wars were of course one of the chief reasons for properties accumulating in the hands of women. General population mobility was another reason; in times of emigration, women (who migrate at lesser rates than men do) always take increased responsibility in the area of out-migration (Herlihy, 1962: 111). Warriors die, emigrants do not return, and women hold on. Did the Crusades "help create a women's world back home"? Poems about women weeping for their lovers in a world emptied of men just might be off the mark (Mancabru, as quoted in Herlihy, 1962: 113). Maybe these were tears of joy.

Most of the foregoing applies to women in families that are landholders. For working-class women, a more typical picture might be that of a woman marrying a local priest and supporting him; out of this she would get living quarters, companionship, children, a certain amount of social status, and he would get economic support. The status of such women in what is technically referred to as a nicholaite family was evidently a problem:

> At Vercelli about 960, married priests ordered to put away their wives answered "that unless they were maintained by the hands of their women they would succumb to hunger and nakedness" (Herlihy, 1962:104).

Herlihy presents similar quotes from Ravenna and Verona and concludes that

> apparently in these nicholaite families, women had assumed economic
> functions of critical importance. The presence of fair numbers of avail-
> able, propertied or at least economically resourceful women may have
> even aggravated the abuse of nicholaiti with the 10th century church,
> as needy clerics sought a relief from their own poverty in advantageous
> liaisons. The sons of priests who use a matronymic were perhaps
> attempting to cover the ignominy of their fathers. But they also give
> illustration of the prominence and repute of their mothers within the
> life of the community (1962: 104).

It would appear that the women of such households might be very well satisfied with their situation. So might the newly freed woman marrying a serf who was ready to move up in the world. More typical than either of the above would be the peasant woman working side by side with her husband on the farm, and the woman artisan working side by side with her husband in town workshops.

Life in the first millennium A.D. in Europe was hard. Neither social class nor sex offered protection against the brutalities and the uncertainties of the age. It has not been possible to give a picture of the emerging political units of Europe in this chapter. Only fragments of the political process have been touched on in describing the activities of women. A good subject for further study, however, would be a careful assessment of the kinds of education and communication infrastructures developed by women as compared to the military-based political structures created by men, in terms of the net contributions of each to the social order. This period is one of attempted consolidation, not of attempted redistribution of social goods, so neither women nor men rate high on efforts for social justice. We find none of the land redistribution legislation that in the previous millennium appeared in Persia, Greece, and Rome. In the next chapter we will see to what extent the consolidations achieved in this period provide the basis for future social reconstruction.

A Note on Religion and the Status of Women in India

Although Buddhism predates both Christianity and Islam, it is useful to include a discussion of women in Indian Buddhism here in order to see the situation of women in these three major religions in comparative perspective. I regret the necessity of omitting a similar discussion on religion and women in China and Japan. Adequate sources are not available to me at this time.

When Gautama Buddha (563-483 B.C.) experienced enlightenment and began teaching, India was just beginning to experience the long series of invasions, beginning with Darius of Persia, which were to be intensified between 200 B.C. and A.D. 300 with the coming first of the Greeks and then of the Scythians and Parthians. In Indian history this was the period of "barbarian invasions." It was a dark time, and the ideal of renunciation taught by the Upanishads, by Gautama Buddha, and by Mahavira, the Jainist teacher, was compelling. The struggle between more activist traditions in India and the ideal of renunciation continued until about A.D. 500, when Buddhism ceased to be a significant religion in India and had already put down roots elsewhere in Asia. Jainism remained as a small but important ascetic religion. The difference between Jainism and Buddhism on the one hand and earlier Hindu teachings on the other are significant in that the two newer religions were oriented to a concept of perfectability rather than to simply escaping from the cosmic cycle of karma. To the extent that Buddhism and Jainism emphasized "becoming" rather than "being," they did not lead to passivity or withdrawal.

The teachings on the possibility of "becoming" attracted Indian women in the 500s B.C. They had been pushed out of earlier participation in Hindu religious rites through Brahminic "reforms." The age of marriage was creeping toward puberty and below, and there was a greatly increased pressure for all women to marry. It is not surprising that there was a great positive response of upper-class women to the teachings of Gautama.[43] The detachment from the responsibilities of family life and the possibilities of individual fulfillment which the teachings offered were welcomed in a society where most options for a woman's personal development were being closed off.

As early as 800 B.C. a few women of the aristrocracy had adopted a special nun-like mode of existence in following the teachings of Prince Parsha of Varanasi. Regular celibate religious orders of monks and nuns who followed Jainist teachings were organized by Mahavira, shortly before Gautama began his teaching (Shanta, 1974). The appeal of Jainism has always been limited because of the extreme degree of asceticism required, but even in the twentieth century it is estimated that there are four thousand Jainist nuns. They are *sadhvis*, contemplatives who make no distinction between the active and the contemplative, between eremitic (solitary) and cenobitic (community) life. Dressed in white, they wander in perpetual pilgrimage, begging, meditating, praying, preaching. They are much sought after by laywomen as counselors.

Buddhist teachings also require self-discipline, but not the extremes of physical self-denial that characterize Jainism. Buddhism therefore spread more widely. Gautama organized men from the very beginning into lay followers and almsmen (monks). It took five years, however, to persuade him to accept women into comparable groups of laywomen and almswomen. Why did it take this long? From the beginning his teachings appeared to be for women and men equally, and he never denied the spiritual capabilities of women. Finally, Ananda, his disciple and a women's advocate, obtained from him an admission that since women could attain *arahanship* (enlightenment) as well as men could, there were no rational grounds for opposing the entry of women into a religious order. Apparently his resistance was simply worn down by repeated deputations of women, and men speaking on women's behalf. What had been the nature of his resistance? It is suggested that, since Gautama was a prince and of the conservative ruling class, he felt it was best not to interfere with the traditional duties of women in the family.[44]

Even after the women's order was established, the rules still required that any woman, no matter of what age and dignity, had to defer to the youngest and rawest monk. Women were not allowed to conduct any important ceremonies on their own, but had to have almsmen come in to do it. And there were numerous other restrictions on what women could do in their order. Unlike monks, they could not simply take on the state of homelessness and live under a tree; they must live together in convents. They could meditate and they could beg, and visit in the homes of lay supporters. During the nonrainy season they could go from convent to convent on prolonged journeys. But there were no daily liturgies, no work with the hands, either craft or farming, no copying of manuscripts—in short, no balanced regime of *orare et labore* as in the Christian monasteries. Nuns were discouraged from reading, with preference given to oral teaching by the monks. Furthermore, there was no emphasis on healing the sick or feeding the poor. The service of the nun to the community was the attainment of *arahanship,* and visiting in the homes of lay supporters. That these services were highly prized by laywomen of the upper classes is amply evidenced by the accounts of the many wealthy lay supporters of the nuns.

There are many beautiful stories of women who gained enlightenment, including courtesans. The most famous courtesans in India at this time were evidently not unlike their sisters in Greece; it appears that many of the "Aspasias" were attracted to Gautama. These were women of wealth and civic standing, sometimes with courts of their own. While they stood outside conventional morality, there is no evidence of social condemnation of the courtesan by Buddha. Gautama welcomed them among his disciples and never said anything about repentance. A courtesan could attain enlightenment while still a courtesan, but if she wanted to *stay* enlightened, she would be expected to adopt celibacy.

Elite women accustomed to authority, whether they remained lay or joined the order, continued to exercise authority. However, most women converts seemed not to have enough to do. They got into mischief, and they sometimes got pregnant (as happened to Christian nuns, also). Women leaders had a clear ceiling placed on their aspirations: "A woman will not become a Buddha, absolutely holy and perfectly enlightened . . . not a universal monarch," said Gautama (Horner, 1930: 291). Gautama often talked about a person becoming "the man in oneself" (Horner, 1930: 358). Evidently he both believed and did not believe that women could have the same spirituality as men. We have seen this ambivalence about women in all the world religions. Indian women might have had more energy for the kind of movements their sisters undertook in Christian monasticism if they had had a greater scope of permitted activity to begin with. In general the social impact of Buddhism, and of the women's movement in Buddhism, seems to have been minimal in India. The poorer classes did not participate, though in theory they could have. Buddhism faded away, and the more rigorous Jainism remained, though for a tiny minority.

In comparing Christian and Buddhist religious orders there are many similarities, but some critical differences. Christianity did not start out as an elite religion, while Buddhism did. The tendency in both societies was for elite women to enter the religious orders. A significant difference between the two types of orders is that Christian monasticism was committed to educating nuns, to providing them with a rich liturgical life as an aid to prayer, and to linking them with the community through social service. Buddhism did not have this orientation. Nuns of both religions were placed under the authority of men and suffered the same kind of second-class citizenship, even while being pronounced "spiritual equals."

The practices of suttee (immolation of widows) and purdah were not current when Buddhism and Jainism entered India. Both practices came into being after the Christian era, and purdah only became widespread after A.D. 1000. The entry of Islam into India at that time was seen by some as a democratizing influence—lower-caste Hindus could raise their status by entering the more egalitarian Moslem community—and by others as a support for the enclosure of women, practiced by the Turkic-Moslem ruling elites then entering India.

While the first millennium A.D. tends to be treated as a bleak time in India's history from the point of view of women, it is questionable whether the situation of Indian women was really any different from that of women in the other societies we have examined. In addition to the wealthy and independent class of courtesans, there were more and more middle-class women traders as property laws for women loosened up after 600 (Horner, 1930: 221). Women also continued to be doctors and teachers. Lower-class women could be dancing girls and musicians, as well as work in the usual range of craft and service occupations.

In the political realm, we have Indian women ascending thrones at least as often as their counterparts farther west. Queen Didda of Kashmir ruled as full sovereign for twenty-two years. Chandragupta and his spouse Kumaradevi (300 B.C.) were corulers. Many women, such as the queen mother of Orissa at the end of the ninth century, assumed regency when their husbands (or sons) died. Queen Nayani-ka headed the Satavahana empire of the Deccan in the second century B.C. The Deccan had a strong tradition of women administrators, with women governors of provinces, queens issuing administrative orders, etc. There were also queens who ruled in wartime and led armies, such as Kurmadevi of Mevad in 1193. Shortly thereafter, Karnavati, a Rajpur queen, led the defense of Chitor after her widowhood; another queen of the same deceased king, Jawahirbai, fought and died at the head of the army.[45] Whether women also participated in the bloody aspects of succession politics I do not know. They probably did, but details are not available.

The surprising thing that emerges from this chapter is how similar women's roles have been in each of the societies studied, given the great cultural, political, and religious differences between them. Threshold points at which great changes seem to be possible appear in retrospect as having signaled only modest changes in the situation of women. Nevertheless, neither is the conventional image of the exclusion of women borne out. While limitations have been placed on them everywhere, we also see that in any particular society women were never excluded as they are generally thought to have been. Trying to write the unwritten parts of the history of this first millennium inevitably makes one aware of enormous knowledge gaps; even so there is evidence enough that every society was teeming with active women for the entire thousand years.

Notes

[1]Hecker (1914) suggests that there are no indications in the law as later codified as to what the original traditions were.

[2]E. L. Hallgren points out that Burgundian and Visigothic laws as we know them were already heavily influenced by Roman law and Christianity (personal communication, 1975).

[3]The reference is to the concept of conspicuous consumption developed by Veblen in his *Theory of the Leisure Class* (1899).

[4]The practice of men selling their children into slavery also continued, however. Carla Slatt draws attention to a clause in the *Twelve Tables:* "If a father sells his son three times let the son be free of his father" (1975: 2).

[5]The following are vestal virgins recorded between 483 and 31 B.C., including date of recording (tabulated from Broughton, 1952)—*Accused of misconduct, executed:* Oppia (483), Minucia (337), Sextilla (273), Tuccia (230), Licinia (123), Aemilia (114), Marcia (114), Caparronia (266); *Accused, acquitted:* Postumia (420), Fabia (73), Licinia (69); *Politically inoffensive:* Perpennia (69), Arruntia (69), Popilla (69), Occia (38), Aemilia (n.d.); *Politically active, "in the clear":* Claudia (143), Fonteia (91).

[6]There is a famous series of letters between Helvia and Seneca (Beard, 1946: 327-328).

[7]In Islam, women played a similar role in the politics of the succession of the caliphate.

[8]Interpretations in this section will be controversial. The theological frame of reference I am drawing on most heavily is that of George Tavard (1973), but conclusions and interpretations are my own.

[9]The technical term is prelapsarian state—i.e., before Eve ate the apple.

[10]Different translations of the Bible are used in different passages in this chapter, as certain translations make the points under discussion clearer than others do.

[11]John, Philip, Peter, Thomas, James, Andrew, Matthew, and Simon; Mary, the mother of Jesus, Mary Magdalene, Martha, and Salome (Eckenstein, 1935: 35-41).

[12]Including Mary, the mother of Jesus; Mary, the wife of Cleophas; Mary Magdalene; Joanna, the wife of Herod's steward Chuza; Susanna, the mother of the sons of Zebedee; Salome; Mary, the mother of James; and Mary, the mother of James the younger and Josef. Morris bases the idea of a parallel set of men and women disciples on a mosaic in the Church of Saint Praxidis: "There is a double circle around the doorway of the chapel of Saint Zeno consisting of the busts of the apostles with Jesus in the center and of the busts of eight women together with Our Lady in the center and two deacons on either side of her" (1973: 114). This does not add up to twelve, but Morris' idea is an interesting one.

[13]Abelard was a strong supporter of the idea that the women followers of Jesus played a more important role than church history has given them. According to Abelard, "because the women of Christ's following showed greater devotion to Him, . . . they were consistently honored and favored more highly than His masculine disciples. Only women had been permitted to minister to Christ, to perform for Him those services of humanity which He Himself had performed for His disciples. More important, women alone had been allowed to perform the 'sacraments,' the anointing of head and feet, by which Christ was made Priest and King" (McLaughlin, 1975: 287-334).

[14]There is a great deal of evidence in the Acts of the Apostles and the Epistles as well as in the Gospels for this traveling together of women and men. Paul mentions this specifically in 1 Cor. 9: 5, and is always sending greetings in his Epistles to his sister-workers.

[15]J. Morris, in speaking of Paul's reliance on women missionaries, mentions Lydia, from the distant town Thyatira, who became a member of the community at Philippi: "She was in the purple dye trade . . . a woman of some wealth. After her conversion to Christianity through the teaching of Paul and Silas, she turned her house into a center for the apostles and the faithful. On one occasion . . . after Paul and Silas had been liberated from a prison at Philippi they went immediately to the house of Lydia and met all the brethren there" (1973: 119).

[16]"At Thessalonika among the Greek converts there were many rich women who joined Paul and Silas. At Borea 'Many Jews became believers, and so did many Greek women from the upper classes and a number of men.'" Also, Paul's reference to Phoebe as "our sister in the ministry of the church at Cenchrae" is considered by some to be a reference to full ministerial roles for women (J. Morris, 1973: 119).

[17]One of the first heretics, the wealthy trader Marcion, taught a doctrine of the Stranger God which suggests very strongly this alienation process (Nigg, 1962: 61-62).

[18]St. Agnes, twelve or thirteen years of age, refused to marry the man her family provided for her and was either beheaded or burned. Her sister Emerenziana, following her example in vowing virginity, was stoned to death. Mothers who publicly took these vows were killed together with their children—Symphorosa with her seven sons, and Felicitas with her seven sons (Eckenstein, 1935: 113-120).

[19]In Dura-Europos (Mesopotamia) a building has been excavated which was first

a private home, then a Christian church. Only its baptismal font makes it recognizable as a church (Lassus, 1967: 10-11).

[20]The Gnostics emphasized the feminine aspect of the Godhead, which helped strengthen the position of women as teachers. Doctrinally, their chief heresy was to differentiate between the heavenly Christ and the earthly Jesus, treating the Resurrection as symbolic only.

[21]These acts have been subjected to careful historical study and chosen as being "historically authentic" (Musurillo, 1972: xi-xii).

[22]There may, of course, have been other sources for this practice in the evolution of the sacrificial rites of the mystery religions.

[23]Though condemned from time to time, this practice was continued, if Penzer (1935) is correct, until the accession of Pope Leo XIII in 1878.

[24]The question of whether women are more or less highly sexed than men is not relevant to this discussion. We are talking about the consequences of socialization, not biology. For a good discussion of the biological issue, see Sherfey (1972).

[25]We do not know the name of Augustine's sister. In fact, there is some question about whom the letter was actually written to, one more evidence of the maddening anonymity of women in history (J. Morris, 1973: 160, n. 3).

[26]I have mentioned earlier the likelihood that new types of family relationships were developing as a result of increased interaction between family members in urban households. Within Christian communities, conditions would be optimal for developing affectionate family life because of the great emphasis on love and mutual support within the community.

[27]Three books on the desert fathers (which include some mention of desert mothers also) make this form of life in the early centuries of Christianity very vivid: Helen Waddell, *Desert Fathers* (1957), Thomas Merton, *The Wisdom of the Desert* (1960), and Jacques Lacarrière, *Men Possessed by God* (1964).

The desert congregations sometimes tended to recreate the problems of Rome. "Abbot Arsenius lived in a cell 32 miles away from his nearest neighbor, and he seldom went out of it. The things he needed were brought there by disciples. But when the desert of Scete where he lived became peopled with hermits, he went away from there weeping and saying: 'Worldly men have ruined Rome and monks have ruined Scete.'" (Merton, 1960: 49).

[28]The movement into the desert and the movement into heretical sects occurred simultaneously. Each group was trying to solve the problem of corruption. The dissenting groups that were active in the cities were expelled, but the desert dwellers, probably because they were not perceived as a threat to the church, were kept in the fold. This is important to the future history of women in the church, because the tolerance of the church for its desert dwellers laid the foundation for the tolerance of the church for a wide variety of activities within the convents and monasteries, the "deserts" of Europe.

[29]There was also at least one husband-wife team, St. Paulinus of Nola and his wife Theresia, who founded a double monastery in Nola after abandoning wealth and position in Rome.

[30]Several other examples of "erasing the traces" are given by Joan Morris. A fresco in the Catacomb of Priscilla in Rome shows a group of women conducting a eucharistic banquet, and the head of the chief celebrant, by all other clues a woman, has been sandpapered down so it is not possible to tell the sex of the celebrant. Presumably this is to conceal that women once celebrated the Eucharist (1973: 7, 8). Another example is the substitution of the word "blessed" for "ordained" in documents referring to the ordination of women, to conceal the earlier practice of ordaining women as abbessés (1973: 19).

[31]For fuller accounts of this network, see Duckett (1938); Eckenstein (1896); J. Morris (1973); and de Carreaux (1964).

[32]There are conflicting accounts of Scholastica's way of life. Sometimes she is described as the founder and head of a convent, but more often as a person living a life of religious retirement.

[33]Another way to put this is that the church entered the vacuum created by the decay of the Roman imperial bureaucracy. The bishops became tax collectors and city defenders, because they were the only ones left to do it (de Carreaux, 1964).

[34]For the Christian world. Pagan priesthoods also continued as teachers.

[35]Convents required dowries also, for operating capital, but it was possible to negotiate more modest amounts for a convent dowry than would be thought proper for a marriage dowry.

[36]The word *Byzantium* is used in these chapters to refer to the eastern half of the old Roman empire, or the Byzantine empire, rather than to the ancient city of Byzantium.

[37]I owe this sorting out of the Honoria-Attila story to E. L. Hallgren, medieval historian at the University of Colorado.

[38]The source for Byzantine history, except when otherwise indicated, is Philip Sherrard, *Byzantium* (1966).

[39]When they did get such training, it often disqualified them from becoming empress. Casia, the ninth century nun and poetess, famed both for piety and literary talent, missed becoming empress because when she was put in the usual bridal line-up for the emperor's inspection she spoke up in an "unladylike" way.

[40]Except where otherwise indicated, the material in this section is taken from the *Cambridge History of Islam* (Holt, 1970); *Atlas of Islamic History* (Hazard, 1931); and "The Influence of Women in Islam" (Ali, 1899).

[41]Another passage in the same Cordova story gives a glimpse into the lives of slave women of the time. It appears that in some houses, at least, they had a status and degree of privacy and autonomy we do not usually associate with the condition of slavery (Arberry, 1967: 172).

[42]Women slaves far outnumber men slaves in the records.

[43]See Horner's *Women under Primitive Buddhism* (1930) and Bode's *Women Leaders of the Buddhist Reformation* (1893) for full descriptions of the first generation of women disciples.

44The importance of the working-class origin of Jesus in the acceptance of women as equals among the disciples cannot be overestimated in considering the early development in Christianity five hundred years later.

45Altekar (1956: 185-190) gives a list of reigning and recent queens of Indian states.

References

Ali, Ameer
  1899 "The influences of women on Islam." The Nineteenth Century Magazine 45 (May): 755-774.

Altckar, A. S.
  1956 The Position of Women in Hindu Civilization. Banaras, India: Motilal Banarsidass.

Arberry, A. J.
  1967 "Muslim Cordoba." Pp. 166-177 in Arnold Toynbee (ed.), Cities of Destiny. New York: McGraw-Hill.

Auguet, Roland
  1972 Cruelty and Civilization: The Roman Games. London: Allen and Unwin.

Babiak, Wira A.
  1975 "The Ukranian woman." Unpublished student paper. Boulder: University of Colorado, Department of Sociology.

Baldson, John Percy Oyvian Dacre
  1962 Roman Women: Their History and Habits. London: Bodley Head.

Barrow, R. H.
  1968 Slavery in the Roman Empire. New York: Barnes and Noble. (Reprint of 1928 edition.)

Beard, Mary R.
  1946 Woman as Force in History: A Study in Traditions and Realities. New York: Macmillan.

Bode, Mabel
  1893   "Women leaders of the Buddhist reformation." Journal of the Royal
          Asiatic Society 25: 517-566.

Brentano, Robert (ed.)
  1964   The Early Middle Ages, 500-1000. New York: Free Press.

Broughton, T. Robert S.
  1952   The Magistrates of the Roman Republic. Vol. 2, 44 B.C.-31 B.C. New
          York: American Philological Association.

Bullough, Vern L.
  1973   The Subordinate Sex: A History of Attitudes Toward Women. Urbana:
          University of Illinois Press.

Burckhardt, Jacob
  1949   The Age of Constantine the Great. Tr. by Moses Hadas. Garden City,
          N.Y.: Pantheon. (First published 1852.)

de Beaumont, Edouard
  1929   The Sword and Womankind. New York: Panurge Press.

de Carreaux, Jean
  1964   Monks and Civilization. Tr. from French. New York: Doubleday.

de Mause, Lloyd
  1974   "The evolution of childhood." Pp. 1-74 in Lloyd de Mause (ed.), The
          History of Childhood. New York: Psychohistory Press.

Dietrick, Ellen Battelle
  1897   Women in the Early Christian Ministry: A Reply to Bishop Doane, and
          Others. Philadelphia: Alfred J. Ferris.

Duckett, Eleanor Shipley
  1938   The Gateway to the Middle Ages: Monasticism. Ann Arbor: University
          of Michigan Press.

Eckenstein, Lina
  1935   The Women of Early Christianity. London: Faith Press.
  1896   Women under Monasticism. Cambridge: Cambridge University Press.

Goitein, Solomon D.
  1967-   A Mediterranean Society: The Jewish Communities of the Arab World
  1971   As Portrayed in the Documents of the Cairo Geniza. 2 vols. Berkeley:
          University of California Press.

Halle, Fannine W.
  1933   Women in Soviet Russia. London: Routledge.

Hallgren, E. L.
  1975   Boulder, Colo.: University of Colorado, Medieval historian, personal
          communication.

Hazard, Harry W.
  1931   Atlas of Islamic History. Princeton, N. J.: Princeton University Press.

Hecker, Eugene A.
  1914   History of Women's Rights. New York: Putnam.

Henriques, Fernando
  1962 Prostitution and Society. New York: Grove Press.

Herlihy, David
  1962 "Land, family, and women in continental Europe, 701-1200." Traditio 18: 89-120.

Holt, P. M. (ed.)
  1970 Cambridge History of Islam. 2 vols. Cambridge: Cambridge University Press.

Horner, Isaline Blew
  1930 Women Under Primitive Buddhism: Laywomen and Almswomen. London: Routledge.

Huart, Clement
  1966 A History of Arabic Literature. Beirut: Khayts.

Lacarriere, Jacques
  1964 Men Possessed by God: The Story of the Desert Monks of Ancient Christendom. Tr. by Roy Monkcom. New York: Doubleday.

Lassus, Jean
  1967 Landmarks of the World's Art: The Early Christian and Byzantine World. London: Paul Hamlyn.

Leighton, Albert C.
  1972 Transport and Communication in Early Medieval Europe, A.D. 500-1100. Newton Abbot, England: David and Charles.

Lev, Daniel S.
  1972 The Islamic Courts in Indonesia: A Study in the Political Bases of Legal Institutions. Berkeley: University of California Press.

Levy, Jean Philippe
  1967 The Economic Life of the Ancient World. Tr. by John G. Biram. Chicago: University of Chicago Press.

Lot, Ferdinand
  1961 The End of the Ancient World and the Beginnings of the Middle Ages. New York: Harper and Row.

Macurdy, Grace
  1927 "Queen Eurydice and the evidence for women power in early Macedonia." American Journal of Philology 48 (July): 201-214.

Maher, Vanessa
  1974 Women and Property in Morocco: Their Changing Relation to the Process of Social Stratification in the Middle Atlas. Cambridge: Cambridge University Press.

McCabe, Joseph
  1931 "How Christianity has treated women." Pp. 49-58 in Samuel D. Schmalhauser and V. F. Calverton (eds.), Woman's Coming of Age. New York: Liveright.

McLaughlin, Mary Martin
  1975 "Peter Abelard and the dignity of women: Twelfth century feminism in

theory and practice." Pp. 287-334 in the Proceedings of the International Symposium of the Centre National de la Récherche Scientifique, July 2-9, 1972. Paris: Centre National de la Récherche Scientifique.

Merton, Thomas
1960   The Wisdom of the Desert: Sayings from the Desert Fathers of the Fourth Century. New York: New Directions.

Morris, E. J.
1974   History of Urban Form: Prehistory to the Renaissance. New York: Wiley.

Morris, Joan
1973   The Lady Was a Bishop. New York: Macmillan.

Mozans, H. J.
1913   Woman in Science. New York: D. Appleton.

Mujeeb, M.
1960   World History: Our Heritage. Bombay: Asia Publishing House.

Musurillo, Herbert
.1972   The Acts of the Christian Martyrs. Oxford: Clarendon Press.

Naroll, Raoul, Vern L. Bullough, and Frada Naroll
1974   Military Deterence in History: A Pilot Cross-Historical Survey. Albany: State University of New York.

Nash, Ernest
1944   Roman Towns. New York: J. J. Augusten.

Newton, Arthur Percival (ed.)
1968   Travel and Travellers of the Middle Ages. New York: Barnes and Noble.

Nigg, Walter
1962   Heretics. New York: Alfred A. Knopf.

Nugent, Sister M. Rosamond, B. S. F.
1941   Portrait of the Consecrated Woman in Greek Christian Literature of the First Four Centuries. Washington, D.C.: Catholic University of America Press.

O'Faolain, Julia and Lauro Martines (eds.)
1973   Not in God's Image: A History of Women in Europe from the Greeks to the Nineteenth Century. New York: Harper and Row.

O'Faolain, Sean
1969   The Irish. London: C. Nicholls.

Penzer, N. M.
1935   The Harem: An Account of the Institution. Philadelphia: J. B. Lippincott.

Rostovtzeff, Mikhail I.
1945   A History of the Ancient World. 2 vols. Revised ed. Norwood, Penna.: Norwood Editions.

Runciman, Steven
   1967   "Christian Constantinople." Pp. 150-165 in Arnold Toynbee (ed.), Cities of Destiny. New York: McGraw-Hill.

Shanta, N.
   1974   "The doctrine and life of Junia." Cisterios Studies 9: 2-3.

Sherfey, Mary Jane
   1972   The Nature and Evolution of Female Sexuality. New York: Random House.

Sherrard, Philip
   1966   Byzantium. New York: Time-Life Books.

Slatt, Carla Diane
   1975   "A study of the effects of Roman law on women." Unpublished student paper. Boulder: University of Colorado, Department of Sociology.

Syme, Ronald
   1939   The Roman Revolution. Oxford: Clarendon Press.

Tavard, George H.
   1973   Woman in Christian Tradition. Notre Dame, Ind.: University of Notre Dame Press.

Thrupp, Sylvia L.
   1967   Early Medieval Society. New York: Appleton-Century-Crofts.

Veblen, Thorstein
   1899   Theory of the Leisure Class. New York: Viking Press.

Waddell, Helen
   1957   The Desert Fathers. Ann Arbor: University of Michigan Press.

Weinhold, Karl
   1882   Die Deutschen Frauen in dem Mittelalter. Wien: Druck und Verlag von Carl Geraed's Sohn.

White, E. M.
   1924   Woman in World History: Her Place in the Great Religions. London: Herbert Jenkins.

Workman, Herbert B.
   1962   The Evolution of the Monastic Ideal from the Earliest Times Down to the Coming of the Friars: A Second Chapter in the History of Christian Renunciation. Boston: Beacon Press. (First published 1913.)

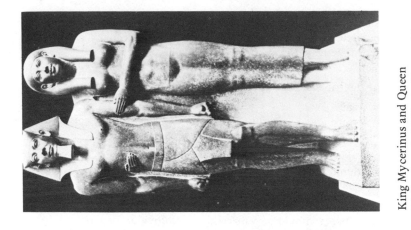

King Mycerinus and Queen Khamerernebti (Hirmer Fotoarchiv München)

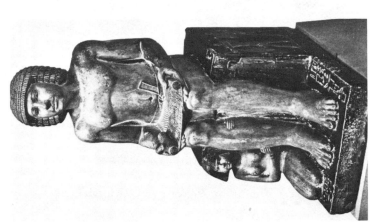

The Inspector of Scribes Sekhema and His Wife (Northampton Museum and Art Gallery)

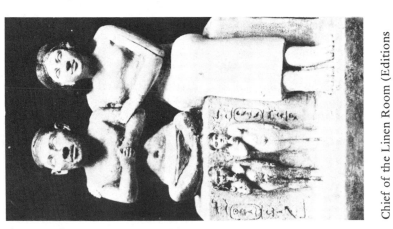

Chief of the Linen Room (Editions d'Art)

The "Phuri Dai" or Old Wise Woman
(Denis Brihat)

Spanish Gypsies (Almasy)

Gypsy Tents and Camps (circa 1960) (Seruzier)

Indian Construction Gang (Josef Breitenbach)

Woman Kazakh Setting Up a Yurt (Museum für Volkekunde)

Woman Picking Hops (Mansell Collection)

Women Harvesters in Norfolk (Colman and Rye Libraries of Local History)

Max Liebermann, *Flax Barn in Laren* (Berlin National Gallery)

Madame de Staël (Culver Pictures)

George Sand (International Museum of Photography)

Rosa Bonheur (Musée du Louvre)

Artemesia Gentileschi, *Self-Portrait* (Royal Collection)

Edmonia Lewis (Eleanor Tufts)

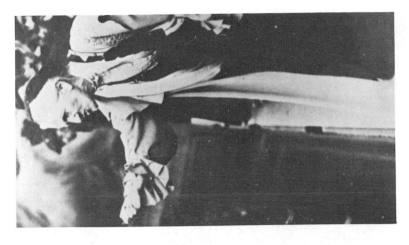

Charlotte Despard (Press Association)

Joan of Arc (Culver Pictures)

Tania (Babylon Brigade)

Deborah

Isabella

Elizabeth I (Lord Brooke, Earl of
Warwick)

Catherine II

Victoria

Hepatia (MIT Press)

Witch of Agnesi (MIT Press)

Harriet Martineau (National Portrait Gallery)

Beatrice Webb (A. Watkins, Inc.)

Sonja Cowin-Kovalevsky (MIT Press)

Madame Curie (Historical Picture Service)

Mothers with Children, Toothill Fields Prison (Culver Pictures)

Women Typesetters

Dahoman Woman Warrior

Vietnamese Woman Learning to Shoot
(Josef Breitenbach)

Goya, *What Courage* (The Hispanic Society of America)

9

Millennialism and New-Old Roles for Women in the Middle Ages: A European Story, A.D. 1000 to 1450

Historical Background

On the rest of the planet it was a night like any other night, but for the common folk of Europe and Byzantium, December 31, 999, was a night of terror. When the church bells rang at midnight, lords and peasants were on their knees, for this was to be the end of the world. For months women and men had been bringing wagon loads of possessions, parcels of land deeds, valuable jewels, and manuscripts, to the monasteries and churches of Christendom. People wanted to be ready and in good standing on Judgment Day.

Christianity had waited its full thousand years for the End of Time, but the pope was not planning on any Second Coming. Rather he was busy planning with Otto III the affairs of the very temporal kingdom of the Holy Roman Empire. He had tried without success to keep the millennialist fervor under control. Popes have a special immunity to millennialism. "Why are those fools awaiting the end of the world?" a later pope was to say when the unassuaged chiliastic[1] fervor erupted again two hundred years later (McGinn, 1971: 30).

On the surface, the first century of the second millennium seemed peaceful enough. In the flood of emotional relief that followed the postponement of Judgment Day, there was an orgy of church build-ing all over Europe, especially in France and Germany. The most visible signs of the fervor lay in the beginnings of the great cathe-drals. "The world was shaking herself, throwing off her old gar-ments, and robing herself in a white mantle of churches" (Baldwin, 1971: 15). Underneath the mantle, battles raged between popes, kings, and emperors competing for legitimacy and power, but the respite was, in a sense, real. The Viking depredations were over. Feudal society, for so long locked in its walled castles, began trickling out into the countryside. The church was strong enough to declare and enforce the Truce of God, spelling out when and where fighting could take place—no fighting was permitted

> from Wednesday evening to Monday morning every week, leaving only three days and two nights per week for . . . private wars. Even these three days were ruled out during Lent, Advent, and the great feasts of Our Lady, the feasts of the Apostles and certain other saints (Nicker-son, 1942: 31).

It was forbidden to charge interest on military loans (a policy worth some consideration in the twentieth century), and soldiers could not fight on land belonging to the church, nor could they attack pil-grims, merchants, women, peasants, cattle, agricultural implements, clerics, or students.

The war-control measures contributed substantially to the condi-tions in which agricultural and craft productivity and trade could develop. New agricultural land was cleared, new towns sprang up on old and new trade routes. Merchant guilds formed, and their spin-offs, craft guilds, multiplied. New monasteries opened to absorb surplus populations. What had been miserable towns in 1000 were flourishing cities by 1350.

Before 1000, what bureaucracies existed had belonged to the church. But by the thirteenth century something new had happened: an amazing multiplication of the number of lay officials throughout Europe. Strayer (1964) calls it one of the most striking phenomena of the thirteenth century:

> In every country the conservatives protested again and again that there were too many officials and in every country the number of officials went right on increasing in spite of protest. . . . The fact that such men [the officials] could brutally disregard the church's rights and still keep their positions must have convinced many people that lay governments were going to be supreme. Finally, with the steady increase in the

number of government jobs a new career was opened up for able men
of all classes. The church could no longer count on securing the services
of the great majority of educated and intelligent men (107-108).

This development represented a significant new power base for the
lay citizenry. As the quotation from Strayer suggests, the new
bureaucracies were for men. Women remained on the underside of
the church bureaucracy, in such posts as were available to them
through the religious orders. The new network of secular officials
had no place at all for women. The absence of women from these
new roles was to have important consequences for women's economic position when the craft guilds began to decline.

In the early Middle Ages, this did not appear to be a problem. We
have already seen in the last chapter that women administered up to
one fifth of the landed estates of Europe. They were also involved in
the growth of the urban centers, as craftworkers in and outside the
guilds and as teachers.
Towns with populations
of ten thousand and un-
der were soon support-
ing schools—some under
the care of local monas-
teries and convents, and
some under the care of
newly prosperous craft
guilds. Cathedral towns
had larger and better-
equipped schools, and
these, along with guild
schools, became the
nurseries of the univer-
sities born in the 1200s.

However, the know-
ledge explosion exclud-
ed women, since only
clerics—men vowed to
the church and to the
priesthood—could enter
these schools. Only in
Italy and Spain, where
universities had a more
ancient organizational

Figure 9-1. *Nuns Working on
Manuscripts, A.D. 1341, Gothic.*

base, did this not apply. The chief role left to women in relation to the new learning through most of Europe was as copyists, since there was a great demand both in the cathedral schools and among the aristocracy for libraries. The fingers of copyists, both women and men, flew to provide manuscripts to meet this demand of newly literate folk.

People were on the move and ideas were on the move. Even while new land was being tilled, cities and feudal armies were filling up with former peasants and serfs who sought to free themselves from bondage to the land. The discontented peasant became the discontented city dweller, for the new towns could not absorb and employ all who came there. *Vagantes,* unemployed clerics, wandered everywhere. So did female vagabonds. Restless Norman war bands also wandered about Europe, spoiling for conquests. They were a problem to Europe, and to the pope.

When a shower of meteorites fell over Europe in the spring of 1095, that was a clear signal from God that the Norman armies should be used in a Crusade. The wide outburst of Christian fervor that followed the declaration of the Crusade was matched only by the parallel outburst of exuberant greed. The Crusades offered something for everyone. Women, men, and children all set out, on foot or on horseback, in rags or in glittering armor.[2] Wave after wave of Crusaders poured out of Europe, in a series of thirty-nine different crusades covering a four-hundred-year period (Hazard, 1931: 36). It all began with the premature setting out of Peter the Hermit in 1096 with thousands of ragtag and bobtail followers, before the regular Crusader knights had assembled. The carnage of that "people's crusade," with gone-wild followers massacring Jews everywhere on the way, was matched only by the tragic Children's Crusade in 1212, which ended in slaughter or enslavement for the entire children's army (Hazard, 1931). The final crusade, 1462-1492, drove the Moslems out of their last European stronghold, Granada. What came from the Crusades? Power and wealth for the few, suffering, enslavement, and death for the many, on both sides of the movable fighting lines. The land reform and social redistribution movements we noted in the empires of antiquity were replaced by land-grab movements. War is a poor teacher. During the last century of Crusades, Europe turned on itself in the Hundred Years War and smothered the last bits of millennialist fervor in its population.

It is not possible to make sense of the years from 1000 to 1450, which include both the High Middle Ages and the later Middle Ages, and the role that women played in those years, without taking account of millennialism, the agony of the Crusades abroad, and the Hundred Years War at home. Wars were not the only problem. Poor agricultural practices and expanding population led to soil exhaustion; there were long cold spells and years of such excessive rainfall that crops could not ripen. The first famine was in 1140, and from 1272 to 1348 there were repeated periods of extreme cold and heavy rainfall, with accompanying famines. When the plague bacillus hit Europe in 1348 from the East, it struck a population already weak from famine and cold. Within the next half-century, the population of Europe dropped by perhaps one-third (various estimates from Ziegler, 1969: 232-239, and Hollingsworth, 1969).

The horror of the plague was not just in the dying, but in the physical agony of the dying and the effect on survivors of seeing dead and dying bodies everywhere. Instead of the millennium there was death. Death from war; death from famine; and, most horribly, death from plague.

It would be easy to go on and on painting the terror of the Middle Ages, but of course we all know that is not the whole story. This is also the age of courtly love, and the era of the cult of the Virgin. The phenomena included under these labels range all the way from absurd swashbuckling chivalry, passionate amours, and convenient if somewhat salacious miracles performed by the Virgin Mary, to the sad and tender love described by Christine de Pisan in the *Book of the Duke of True Lovers* (1966). Boccaccio's *Concerning Famous Women* (1963) falls somewhere in between the extremes. The touching story of the knight who was so lost in prayer in a wayside chapel that he never got to the tournament he was headed for and found afterward that the Virgin had taken his place in the lists and won him great honors (Adams, 1933: 263-264) brings together in one vignette the extremes of medieval sentiments. To confuse things still further, there is the semierotic mysticism found in the popular Tristan and Lancelot legends.

The final blow to the comprehensibility of the Middle Ages comes when one reads the lives of the saints and the mystics side by side with those of the religio-political activists, the chiliasts, and the revolutionaries. The heretics sometimes turn into saints, sometimes into lusty free-livers, and sometimes into petty tyrants who create their own private reigns of terror. The three best-known religious movements of the Middle Ages outside the institutional church—the Cathari, the Beguines/Beghards,[3] and the Brethren of the Free Spirit—all encompassed the full range from sainthood to bestiality. Four popular, yet scholarly, books aimed at trying to interpret this confusing period, by Denis de Rougemont(1956), Jan Huizinga (1924), Henry Adams (1933), and Norman Cohn (1970), all manage resolutions of the conflicting patterns along lines suiting their particular training and perspective. Needless to say, they are all quite different from each other. Although each of these writers must perforce deal with women in their books, none of them is able to move very far from conventional representations of women. It is our buisness to rectify that here.

How was it possible for wars, famines, and plagues to exist side by side with the whole set of phenomena revolving around erotic indulgence on the one hand, religious asceticism and new ideals of service and love on the other, and still make room for utopianism, revolution, and a knowledge explosion? For this period was an axial period in human history, a time when physical, intellectual, and spiritual resources came together in such a way as to put humankind again on the threshold of new developments. It was an age akin to the time of the first emergence of world religions in the closing centuries B.C.

It also led to the rise of the new European universities. In the long interregnum from the fall of Rome to the end of the first millennium A.D., only Italy and Spain kept their ancient schools and Mediterranean-wide knowledge networks intact. From the tenth century on, it was the Moslem universities that represented the great knowledge centers, along with the universities of China and India. With the rebirth of the university in Europe, there was a great busyness with the collection and circulation of manuscripts, the establishment of new libraries, and the gathering together of scholars. By 1445, when guild resistance was overcome and printing presses established, the growing demand for primary schools provided new occupations in teaching for the unemployed army of copyists, both male and female. The thirteenth century in particular was the age of the great schoolmen, the synthesizers of knowledge: Thomas Aquinas, who wrote the summa of theology; Hostiensis, who created the summa of canon law; Vincent of Beauvais, encyclopedist; Roger Bacon, natural philosopher; Albertus Magnus and Duns Scotus, philosophers; Bonaventura, mystic—the names go on, all clerics, and so of course no woman is found in these lists. But we shall make our own list of learned women, for they too participated in the knowledge synthesis.

Alongside the universities, the old guild movement took on new life and new institutional forms in response to the requirements of a new scale of social organization with increased population and a new urbanism. "Brethren and sistren" mingled freely in these guilds until changing economic circumstances forced the "sistren" out.

Finally, as Mujeeb (1960) notes, mysticism flourished everywhere in the world. Why that kind of response, at this particular time? Again, it was a response to the challenge of a changing scale of social organization. When the world religions were first founded, they were small communities of the faithful living relatively close to the traditions of the founder. But

> the idea of the religious world-state among Muslim and Christians expanded the religious community to such dimensions that it became spiritually necessary to organize small units of like-minded people who could live the ideal life for themselves. The monastery, and its Muslim form, the *Khanqah,* appear inevitably as the social, and in many cases, the economic expression of the mystic tendency (Mujeeb, 1960: 153).

Besides the *khanqah,* in which the Sufi devotion to the *Tariqah,* or "Path," was central, there were also the reform movements dedicated to *futuwah,* sometimes translated as "chivalry." In the Middle Ages these were a combination of guild and religious order, and there were as many different movements as there were occupations.[4]

One accompaniment of the mysticism of the Middle Ages was its futurism. The millennium had not come in 1000, but writing in the next century, Joachim de Fiore (1135-1202) expected it in 1200. After his death his writings were used repeatedly to predict the millennium. Putting his finger alternately on the Anti-Christ and on the Savior King, both potential heralds of the millennium, was a favored occupation throughout the Middle Ages. Along with predictions of the millennium came the visions of what the new era would be like. De Fiore painted it as the postbureaucratic age, with all institutional structures of church and state crumbled away. Every revolutionary futurist in the next four centuries was to cite Joachimite writings; the radical Franciscans, especially, espoused Joachimite doctrines. Saint Clare, Saint Francis, and Joachim, the gentlest collection of apocalyptic figures imaginable, guarded the gateway to the new Age of the Holy Spirit.

Yet the flames of the Inquisition eventually roared on the other side of the gateway. By the late 1400s Dominican and Franciscan inquisitor-monks were pushing the futurists—peasants, peddlers, and duchesses—through that gateway as heretics that required burning. The apocalyptics were seen as part of a gigantic world conspiracy of

> wild fanatics who fostered the most subversive and abominable ideas . . . to establish communities and remodel whole territories according to *the programme* (Summers, 1948: xvii).

What was the program?

> . . . the abolition of monarchy, the abolition of private property and of inheritance, the abolition of marriage, the abolition of order, the total abolition of all religion (Summers, 1948: xviii).

The hard-pressed church, guardian of law and order, concluded that there was a "society of witches . . . nothing else than a vast international of anti-social revolutionaries" (Summers, 1948: xxv). At first it was only kings and clerics who believed this. Gradually the frightened bourgeoisie were drawn into the conspiracy view, and finally even peasants turned on each other. What started in 1232 as a program against political sedition ended as mass hysteria in the late 1400s and the 1500s. It was the followers of the gentle Francis and the learned Dominic who unleashed and presided over the fury.

During this entire period there was an underlying shift from land to money as a power base. Society was pressing against its traditional means of subsistence and had to find new resources (Wilkinson, 1973). In the short run, this shift away from feudal toward commercial power structures apparently favored the development of both social equality and spiritual discernment, since reformers, revolutionaries, and mystics alike seemed to flower in this climate. Certainly women flowered, as we shall see. So, very shortly, did the Inquisition. The decline of religious orders and the decline of the workers' orders—i.e., guilds—were only to become evident toward the end of this period. The struggle between the craft and trade guilds over the development of new high-production technologies that pushed wages down for some groups of artisans foreshadowed, toward the end of the Middle Ages, the even more bitter struggle to come, at the dawn of the industrial revolution.

The year 1450 already heralded the modern era. Waterpower and windmills had been developed in the twelfth and thirteenth centuries. All kinds of clockwork mechanisms and precision instruments were available in the fourteenth century. Even the Crusades, the plague, and the economic recession of the fourteenth and first half of the fifteenth centuries could not stem the forward thrust. By 1500 Europe was at take-off and had become the "workshop of the world" (Clough, 1951: 168). The flowering of the Middle Ages was real. It was possible for this to take place side by side with wars, famines, and plagues, in part because medieval society was still primarily a *local* society. While some localities were wiped out by calamity, others were untouched. Wars, even the destructive Hundred Years War, were far more limited in scope than are modern wars. Under feudal law vassals only had to fight forty days a year for their lords, and when forty days were up, a vassal often simply went home, no matter what battle was raging. The lives of most of the women and men of the Christian and Moslem world, as of the Far East, were untouched by war. Crop failures were not as widespread or calamitous as is sometimes pictured (Ladurie, 1971), and even during the worst of the plague, in large areas of the countryside, no one even knew it was going on. However, the women we will be writing about were not village ignoramuses; they understood the character of their times pretty well; they were in touch with the crosscurrents, and responded creatively to them. We will turn now to the character of those responses.

An Overview of Roles of Women in the Middle Ages: Queens, Prophets, Reformers, and Revolutionaries

The Middle Ages are confusing in regard to the status of women. Women had to remain in their own niches inside declining religious bureaucracies while men filled the new secular bureaucracies of the state. The linking of higher education with training for the priesthood effectively barred them from preparing for entry into the new state machinery. Yet in the short run, women religious, particularly the prophetesses, rose to a kind of zenith in social status and public recognition. But when the vogue for prophecy had passed, they went to the stake. There was a gradual economic decline in the women's orders during this period, since they were not organized to participate in the general shift toward a monetized economy. The church itself, moreover, used this economic transition further to limit the autonomy of the women's orders. A parallel development of long-run importance to women was the emergence of secular alternatives for the unmarried. Linked to the craft guild movement, yet separate from it, the Beguine movement outlasted the guilds and gave working women an autonomous niche in urban society which the mixed guilds never provided.

The Crusades, urbanism, and statism are perhaps the major forces affecting women in these centuries. The reemergence of the old prophecy tradition was in one sense, perhaps, an immediate outcome of the year 1000's millennialist fervor; in a larger sense it was a response to continuous social upheaval. The charismatic face of the church could smile on the woman visionary even while the bureaucratic face was trying to clamp down on women's initiatives. The result was almost a reincarnation of the old sibylline sisterhood.

The royal abbeys in particular produced distinguished abbesses

and clairvoyant nuns who advised heads of state. At the same time
the woods of Europe, and more particularly England, were full of
anchoresses who lived ascetic and solitary lives in little hermitages.
These anchoresses often also rendered local services, including healing, and were both revered and feared by local communities as
sources of knowledge closed to others. Many a local functionary had
his own private anchoress-consultant on local affairs. It was a routine
matter for anyone who had a decision to make about affairs of state,
from the local squire to the pope and the emperor, to consult with a
known woman religious before taking any action. This was notably
true from the time of the second Crusade on. (The second Crusade
might never have been launched if Mechthild of Magdeburg had not
taken it as her own particular "cause.") The nun-prophetess, the cult
of the Virgin, and the phenomenon of the rediscovery of the pagan
sibylline books can from one point of view be seen as the revenge
that a society deprived since pagan days of signficant female leadership took on the patriarchal Christian church. This is the way Henry
Adams (1933) puts it, and in a sense he is right, though his conception of female leadership leaves something to be desired. His "Mary-
image" of the female involves an ingenious compound of woman
the inspirer and woman the capricious mistress, leaving out any task-
oriented capacities.

One example of this need to turn to women is found in the recurring Pope Joan legends. The legend of a woman pope, supposed to
have reigned in the 850s A.D., became very popular in the Middle
Ages. It looks as if the original legend was a positive, "pro-woman"
one. By the time medieval chroniclers got through with it, however,
Joan was the dreaded Anti-Christ, to be welcomed as much as feared
because she would usher in the reign of Christ. The medieval mind
never did get its feelings straight about the savior-queen/king versus
the anti-Christ, as to which or both were expected; frequently the
same person is presented both ways. Here is one of the earlier forms
of the Pope Joan legend, given by Martin Polonus in 1282:

> After Leo IV, John Angelus, a native of Metz, reigned two years, five
> months and four days. . . . He died in Rome. He is related to have been
> a female, and, when a girl, to have accompanied her sweetheart in male
> costume to Athens; there she advanced in various sciences, and none
> could be found to equal her. So, after having studied for three years in
> Rome, she had great masters for her pupils and hearers. And when there
> arose a high opinion in the city of her virtue and knowledge, she was
> unanimously elected Pope. But during her papacy she became in the

family way by a familiar. Not knowing the time of birth, as she was on her way from S. Peters to the Lateran she had a painful delivery, between the Coliseum and S. Clements Church, in the street. Having died after, it is said that she was buried on the spot. . . . she [is not] placed in the catalogue of the Holy Pontiffs, not only on account of her sex, but also because of the horribleness of the circumstances (Baring-Gould, 1869: 172-173).

Although scholarship indicates no missing dates in the papal history during which this person could have sat on the throne, the record could have been rewritten. We have already noted some instances of holy men in the history of the church who were accidentally discovered to be holy women. If one or more of the popes of recorded history was actually a woman, we shall never know it![5]

Whatever the merits of Pope Joan, the sibylline sisterhood was certainly being courted. I have already mentioned that the pagan sibylline books were rewritten to help the conversion of the pagans and the Jews to Christianity. The oldest such manuscript known to medieval Europe was the Oracle of Sibilla Tiburtina. Written in the mid-300s A.D., it proclaimed Constantine as the Last World Emperor who would fight the Anti-Christ and usher in the Second Coming. The Last World Emperor theme was too useful to discard, and countless versions of it, under the labels of the sibyls Tiburtina, Samia, and Cumae, were circulated by medieval prophets and prophetesses with various interpretations as to who was meant (Reeves, 1969). Since the prophecies were supposed to have been originally written by women, women had a special role in their interpretation, though most of the interpretive manuscripts that have survived were written by men.

It is hard to sort the wheat from the chaff in looking at these materials. The political pronouncements of well-educated monastic women experienced in political affairs, such as Hildegarde of Bingen, or the imperious but knowledgeable Brigitta of Sweden, cannot be set side by side with those of unstable but charismatic figures such as Prous Boneta, who thought she was the incarnation of the new age, or Manfreda, "candidate" for the papal chair. Unfortunately, however, not even the pronouncements of the scholarly women can be considered reliable. We are well enough aware today that scholarly training does not in itself produce good political judgment. Neither did it in those days. What is important to note is that women were being consulted in matters of public policy, and their judgments were based on the same world view that their male colleagues held. This was "overlife activity," and there was no distinctive "woman's point of view," for good or ill, in the world situation.6

The queens and princesses of the Middle Ages often joined forces with the abbesses both on issues of public affairs and in support of the continuously developing educational and service institutions that convents offered. At least one queen achieved greatness, as we shall see.

A different and quieter leadership role for women is seen in the writings of Mechthild of Magdeburg and other Beguine mystics and in anchoresses like Julian of Norwich. These women were concerned at a very deep level with the interior work of transformation of mind and spirit, yet dealt with the human soul in an allegorical fashion with more or less direct political implications. Some of these women, like Mechthild, addressed directly the corruption of the priesthood and of society. That corruption and the prevalent practice of priests keeping one or more "concubines" or "priestesses" have to be remembered when we read the visions of these women. Ironically, much of their work surfaces in Dante, while they themselves remain unknown. Many passages in the *Divine Comedy* are reminiscent of descriptions of hell and heaven in the writings of these mystics (Kemp-Welch, 1913: 70-82).

It is no accident that Dante lived in Italy, a country that gave an honored place to nonreligious women intellectuals in its universities and its public life throughout the entire Middle Ages. Perhaps his study of the formation of the interior life, *Vita Nuova,* would not seem unique if we were more familiar with his women contemporaries.7 He must have interacted a fair amount with them, and he must also have been familiar with the writings of the Beguine mystics. In fact, either Mechthild of Magdeburg or Mechthild of Hackeborn is supposed to have been the original of his Matilda (Kemp-Welch, 1913). And Dante's Beatrice, both as historical person and as symbol of the inward guide, may also represent something else: the internalized teachings of Dante's women colleagues.

One of the tragic accompaniments of turning to seers, male or female, was the resurgence of the old fear of demonism and sorcery, undercurrent in every society from hunting-gathering bands to sophisticated civilizations. The witchcraft mania did not at all begin by pointing at women. In England two major witchcraft trials, one in 1232 and one in 1324, involved respectively a chief justice and the leading burghers of the town of Coventry. In France in 1308 a bishop was accused of witchcraft, and in 1315 the chamberlain, privy councellor, and chief chamberlain of the king fell under the same accusation. Needless to say, these were political trials aimed at uncovering treason. Most of them were cases of suspected poisoning of a king (Summers, 1948).

From the time of the kings of Israel and before, people in high places were accustomed to calling in soothsayers to forecast futures, and it has always been but a step from asking for forecasts to asking for the means to implement or prevent the predicted outcomes. The forecasters were often also herbalists who knew both healing and poisonous plants. Forecasting, poisoning, and healing thus became in-extricably mixed.[8] High-class witches, or warlocks, tended to be men. But when suspicion started to descend the social ladder, the large group of middle- and lower-class women herbalists and healers began to be caught in the nets. Since these were the traditional medi-cal practitioners for the masses of society, and were generally exclud-ed as women from the possibility of getting formal medical degrees, there was no protection for them if a disgruntled patient or neighbor chose to accuse one of witchcraft.

While it is an oversimplification to say that the witchcraft mania was a plot on the part of male doctors to get rid of their more popu-lar female competition (Ehrenreich and English, 1973), many doctors no doubt enthusiastically took part in the accusation process. By 1460, the date at which the University of Paris made provision for (male) students to matriculate in medicine, witchcraft accusations against women healers were reaching their height.

The social and intellectual environment that fostered this combi-nation of demonism and learning was not friendly to learning for the female. Women scholars did flourish, however, in some protected niches, particularly in the German convents, which had already long traditions of female scholarship. We also find them, surprisingly, at royal courts, and we find them at the Italian universities. This is partly due to the early development of the Renaissance in Italy, partly due to continuing contact with an older tradition of women scholars in Moslem Spain.

It is one of the ironies of history that the rise of the universities and the great mendicant religious orders and the establishment of the Inquisition all happened within a short space of time in the 1200s. Each set of institutions was individually chartered by the pope himself. While none of them set out to victimize women, in fact all three contributed to that process over the next couple of hundred years.

None of the limitations placed on women in this period stifled their creativity as related to one of the major contributions of women not only to the Middle Ages, but to the whole sociocultural development of urban life in the West: the Beguine movement. A religiously oriented laywomen's movement led by upper- and middle-class women who were moving from rural areas to the towns and cities of Europe, it provided autonomy for single women of all classes moving in from the countryside. It created for women a third alternative to the existing ones of marriage or religious seclusion. It also provided a new kind of urban social service network. Responding to the political and economic conditions of the times, it became entangled with numerous heretical movements. Nevertheless, the core of the Beguine movement steered clear of too close an identification movement with the church, the libertines, or the revolutionaries. The movement continues in Europe today. (See pages 445 to 453 in this chapter for a further description of the Beguines.)

One learns only indirectly of the role of women in the many revolutionary and heretical movements. Rodney Hilton, in discussing rural communal movements in Europe in the Middle Ages, comments that

> the majority of [the movements'] supporters were artisans, workers and peasants from the mountain and the plain (and amongst these, as in other heretical sects, a high proportion of women) (1973: 107).

This parenthesis is almost his only mention of women in his entire fascinating study of medieval peasant uprisings. We learn more about them in the urban revolutionary movements, partly because the women leaders in these movements were often from the upper classes. The revolutionary unrest that developed as the craft guilds weakened and the wealthy mercantile guilds became the new oppressors often led to an alliance of idealistic merchants and landholders with oppressed workers. As in the beginning of the Christian era, the houses of women of wealth sheltered many utopian enterprises and charismatic religious sects. Even the flagellants, who scandalized and hypnotized Europe with their bloody public scourgings, were initially solid middle-class women and men concerned with bringing to an end the destructive plagues, wars, and Crusades and with helping the urban poor (Le Goff, 1968).[9]

The religious utopian movements and the more directly political movements were all treated by the authorities as part of a conspiracy involving heresy and witchcraft. Far from being one huge interrelated conspiracy, however, these movements were highly local in orientation. This is one reason why it was easy for women to be active in them. If one wonders how middle- and lower-class women could be attracted to the crudely authoritarian millennialism represented in many of the movements—"Obey me and I will bring you paradise on earth"—it should be remembered that women were already "trained" to obedience by the church, the state, and their husbands and fathers. Some of the movements were indeed frighteningly totalitarian, others astoundingly libertine. However, most women who were prepared to step out of conventional roles entered the Beguines, who represented the great, solid center of the urban social-change movement. We will look at the women in the extremist groups, but also give serious attention to the Beguines.

Outside of the Beguines, the only major social institution available to working-class women was the guild, and we will explore the extent to which women were active in guilds and independent economic enterprises. The Middle Ages represent the peak period of women's guild involvement, and the Renaissance will usher in the long decline in the status of the working woman in Europe.

The context in which the prophesying abbess, the reforming Beguine, and the rebellious peasant women were living out their lives was one in which queens and princesses moved to more overtly political roles than women of the royalty had had before. These noblewomen no longer had the exciting task of taming crude societies for the church—the crudeness was now inherent in the church itself. They headed instead into a protracted balance-of-power game in a new statist-conscious Europe; marriage alliances played the crucial role in keeping the balance. What excitement there was for the female nobility of the Middle Ages lay in games of chivalry and the Crusades. At the same time, the earlier work of supporting convents and the educational and medical activities associated with them continued. In fact, queens and princesses joined forces with abbesses in fighting to keep independent power for the convents in the face of a concerted attack by lower levels of the church bureaucracy and state officials. We will now turn to an examination of individual women in each of the categories we have discussed above, beginning with royal women.[10]

Women of the Aristocracy

The Princesses of England

The skills of elite women in marriage diplomacy were first mentioned in describing women's roles in the ancient empires of the Middle East. The Middle Ages is the first period for which we have the materials to examine the phenomenon in some detail. M. A. E. Green's six-volume study (1850) of the princesses of England from 1035 to 1482 makes it possible to look at diplomatic alliances in a particularly interesting subset of the aristocracy, princesses of the royal blood who did not themselves become queens in their own land. In a way, this is the "underlife" of royalty, though it is the overlife of England in respect to its international alliance system in the Middle Ages.

Table 9-1, which gives data on forty-eight English princesses, shows clearly that the lives of these princesses were totally geared to alliance structures. This was a period of protracted power struggle between European kingdoms, particularly between England and France, and every daughter was worth an army if "deployed" in the right way. Out of forty-eight princesses, three were vowed to convents in infancy or early childhood, and fourteen died before they could be married (of these, three had been betrothed, and the others died in early infancy), leaving thirty to conduct actual diplomacy on behalf of their fathers' kingdoms after marriage.

The amount of time and care given to the betrothal negotiations themselves is indicated by the fact that out of a total of twenty-six betrothals (a subset of the betrothals from table 9-1), only twelve involved negotiations with only one country; three betrothals called for negotiations with two countries; and eleven involved more than two (some almost up to a dozen). The betrothal process began for most princesses between the ages of one and nine. The total number of principalities dealt with was fifteen. The importance of adequate preparation for carrying on diplomacy after marriage can be seen by the fact that five of the princesses were educated in the courts of their husbands-to-be before marriage, and two of the husbands were educated in the English court before marriage (not shown in table 9-1). Many betrothal negotiations involved court appearances for the girls before the age of nine. Age at marriage was as follows:

Age	No. of Princesses
9 or under	2
10-12	4
13-15	9
16-17	5
18-19	4
20 or older	6
Total	30

There can be no doubt about what these princesses were expected to be able to do in addition to providing babies; seventeen of them took active ruling responsibilities. Some, like Joanna, who married David the Bruce, began as early as the age of ten as crowned queen. Philippa, at the age of thirteen, had three countries to rule: Norway, Sweden, and Denmark; her husband didn't like ruling, so he turned the job over to her.

Edward I's daughter Margaret married the Duke of Brabant at age fifteen in what was essentially a trade alliance, and she successfully monitored and increased trade relations between England and Brabant. Some of the princesses participated actively in wars and went along on the Crusades, though most did not enjoy that aspect of ruling. The saddest fate came to Isabella, daughter of Edward II, who left her much-loved husband, de Coucy of France, when war broke out between their two countries, perceiving that her primary loyalties lay with England. This gives an inkling of the tensions these princesses lived under, having diplomatic responsibilities for relations with their native country, immediate responsibility for the government of the countries they married into, and additionally, the responsibilities of motherhood. Babies began to come to most of these women in their teens.

On the whole, they did not live very long. Of the ones who married, a majority died before the age of forty:

Age at Death	*No.*
Teenage	4
20s	2
30s	13
40s	2
50s	3
60s	1
Over 69	1
No info.	4
Total	30

With fourteen the modal age of marriage and thirty-five the modal age of death, most of these women packed a lot of activity into an average twenty-one years of diplomatic married life. Most were active on their own initiative, and most of the actives enjoyed it. The following is a rough coding of their political activity after marriage:

Political Activity	*No.*
Active (with enjoyment)	10
Active (noblesse oblige)	7
Active (disliked)	3
Inactive	9
Unclear	1
Total	30

Those who enjoyed their political activity were generally those who had a talent for it. Those who did their best, but with difficulty, are coded "noblesse oblige." Given the few options open to these

Table 9-1

The Princesses of England from William the Conqueror to Charles I (1035-1482)

	Age at Betrothal	Country of First Marriage Alliance	Age at First Marriage	Age at Birth of First Child	Age at Death	Political Cultural Activities	Level of Activity Code
William the Conqueror							
Caecilia*	Negotiations at birth	--	--	--	--	Convent life	I
Adeliza	Childhood	--	--	--	Childhood	--	--
Matilda	Childhood and teens	Castile	--	--	Teens	--	--
Constance	Late 20s	Brittany	29	?	33	Founded many institutions	A
Adela	13	Blois	18	?	Old age	Active co-ruler, also regent, founded many institutions	A
Henry I							
Mathilda	7	Germany	12	?	?	Very active and very ambitious	A

Stephan

Matilda and Mary   NO INFORMATION

Henry II

Matilda	Many early, final at 9	Saxony	18	19	33	Politically unskilled, but met demands	A,D
Eleanore	Childhood	Castile	9	19	59	Loved political activity, regent, mediator	A
Joanna	Many	Cicily	11	17	36	Loved political activity, participated in Crusades	A

King John

Isabella	Very many	Germany	21	27#	27#	Lived secluded harem existence	I
Eleanore	5	England	15	?	59	Active by choice, poor administrator	A

Henry III

Margaret	Infancy	Scotland	10	18	34	Imprisoned age 10–15, wise, coped well, became loved queen	A,NO

Table 9-1, cont.

	Age at Betrothal	Country of First Marriage Alliance	Age at First Marriage	Age at Birth of First Child	Age at Death	Political Cultural Activities	Level of Activity Code
Beatrice	Three negotiations, 11–16	Brittany	17	20	32	Not independently active, did go on Crusades	Unclear
Katherine		DIED AT AGE 3 1/2					
Edward I							
Eleanora	Many negotiations, childhood, teens	France	27	--	?	Hard life, wars, imprisoned by husband	I
Joanna	Ages 5, 13	Italy	19	?	35	Retiring life	I
Margaret	3	Brabant	15	?	?	Marriage was trade alliance, skillful negotiator	A
Beringaria		DIED IN INFANCY					
Mary*	7	--	--	--	?	Convent life, active as royal nun, many good works	A,NO

				34#	34#		
Elizabeth	Ages 2, 5	Holland	15			Turned out as good politician, unexpected	A,NO
Eleanora		DIED AT AGE 5					
Edward II							
Eleanora	Three negotiations in teens	France	15	16	?	Unskilled, did her best as regent, crowned queen at 10	A,NO
Joanna	8	Scotland	8	—	41	Ruled well in difficulties	A,NO
Edward III							
Isabella	Many negotiations, age 2-15	France	33	—	?	Tragic life, left loved husband when countries at war	I/NO
Joanna	Ages 2, 6, and 13	Spain	17	—	17	Tried hard, life of failures	I
Blanche		DIED AT BIRTH					
Mary	1	Brittany	17	—	17	Died three months after marriage	I
Margaret	Several early negotiations	England	14	—	13	Died shortly after marriage	I

Table 9-1, cont.

	Age at Betrothal	Country of First Marriage Alliance	Age at First Marriage	Age at Birth of First Child	Age at Death	Political Cultural Activities	Level of Activity Code
Henry IV							
Blanche	Many negotiations in teens	Bavaria	13	15	19	Died in third childbirth	I
Philippa	9	Sweden	13	--	37	Active ruler of Norway, Sweden, Denmark; king deferred to her	A
Edward IV							
Mary	Many negotiations	DIED BEFORE MARRIAGE			16	--	I
Cecelia	4	England	20	21	38	Death of Edward IV removed her from all alliance system	I
Margaret		DIED IN INFANCY					
Anne	Negotiations, age 4 to 5	England	22	?	36–37	Obscure, poor health	I
Catherine	Negotiations began at 4	England	16	18	49	Managed estate	I

Name						
Bridget*	--	--	--	23	Religious seclusion	I
Henry VII						
Margaret	6	Scotland	--	18	53	Intense political activity and turmoil, regent of Scotland for a time	AD
Elizabeth		DIED AT AGE 3					
Mary	11	France	18	21	37	Personal political activity, for love, marriage, friends, and relatives	A
Catherine		DIED IN INFANCY					
James I						
Elizabeth	16	Germany	17	17	65	Intense political activity, defender of Protestant cause	A
Sophia		DIED IN INFANCY					
Charles I						
Mary	10	Holland	10	19	50	Active in political sphere	A

Table 9-1, cont.

	Age at Betrothal	Country of First Marriage Alliance	Age at First Marriage	Age at Birth of First Child	Age at Death	Political Cultural Activities	Level of Activity Code
Elizabeth	--	--	--	--	15	Brilliant and intellectual, lived in seclusion after death of father, poor health	I
Anne		DIED IN INFANCY					
Catherine		DIED IN INFANCY					
Henrietta Anne	16	France	17	18	26	Diplomacy between brother Chas. II and brother-in-law Louis; also liked courtly gaity, ballets, etc.	A,NO

Note: Princesses who later became queens of England are excluded.

*Vowed to convent.

Died in first childbirth.

princesses, it is amazing that only three felt actively hostile to their role. The inactives were partly those who died too young to have an activity record, and partly those who had no talent for politics and found a way to live in domestic retirement at court. Two nuns are included in the count. One lived a secluded life, but the other took full responsibility as a royal nun, getting support for enterprises important to her order.

The family and court life of these princesses in early childhood was probably typical of other royal families of Europe of the time. Some fathers, like Edward III, swore they would not sacrifice their daughters' happiness to diplomatic necessity, yet Edward himself was one of the most active marriage negotiators in this set of fathers. He could not avoid dealing with a knotty balance-of-power problem with the only tools he felt he had. Some were equally caught up in the alliance problem and had no more choice than their wives-to-be, so one could hardly say that the system discriminated against women.

What I find of particular interest in pondering the lives of these women is the amount of individuality and autonomy they displayed in a life situation hedged with many restrictions. I have given no details of their political and cultural activities, but they were certainly on the order of the activities a secretary of state of a small nation might undertake today, with the duties of minister of cultural affairs thrown in. One striking feature of their lives is how early they began their public responsibilities. It is almost impossible to imagine ten- to fifteen-year-old girls in Western societies having the necessary training and self-discipline to undertake roles the princesses took for granted. The success of the medieval princesses in their diplomatic roles is all the more remarkable when one considers that nearly every one of them had to make her home in a foreign country and function in a language not her native tongue, with a set of customs alien to her own upbringing. There was no running home to mother. Not a single one of these princesses was considered outstanding in her own time or later. Nonetheless, these women often performed key functions that history ascribes to their less capable husbands, due to the convention of recording history in terms of reigning kings.

Other Princesses and Queens

The story of women in the Middle Ages is often overshadowed by the story of Eleanor of Guienne, or Aquitaine (1122-1202), the richest woman in Europe and the most dominant personality among medieval queens. If the princesses described above represent the underside of the diplomatic marriage system, Eleanor of Aquitaine represents the overside. A woman of towering capabilities and ruler of her own kingdom of Aquitaine in France, she was twice unequally yoked with kings of lesser ability and struggled until the end of her long life to harness her ideas and her political skills to the intractable realities of her situation as queen of a small principality.[11]

Allied to France as the queen of Louis VII at the age of fifteen, she accompanied him to the Holy Land on the Crusade of 1147 and discovered there the exciting intellectual and cultural world of the Mediterranean, unknown to the Europe of her time. She also discovered that she had married a pious, retiring man with no political or cultural interests, and after fifteen years of marriage divorced the king to return to her own kingdom.

Her second marriage at the age of thirty to Henry II of England linked her with a ruler as politically ambitious as she, but without her breadth of intellect and wisdom. Bearing and rearing ten children in her fifty tumultuous years as queen of England, she was often allied with her sons, including the later kings Richard and John, against her husband. In protest against his politics and his very public amours, she determined to return to her own kingdom of Aquitaine. Seized and imprisoned by Henry while in flight, she endured fourteen years of house imprisonment without ever losing her hold on political affairs and successfully defeated Henry's attempts to divorce her and force her into a convent so he could seize her kingdom. She was finally released by her son Richard when Henry died. In her last years she lived quietly and ruled well, serving as regent of England while Richard was away at the Crusades. She died at eighty-three.. Her last signature on a public document read "Eleanor, by the wrath of God, Queen of England."

She shaped much of the culture of her times, as both Kelly and Henry Adams (1933) show. She undertook many institution-building enterprises, educational and religious, including the endowment of Fontrevault, which became one of the major religious houses of Europe. Eleanor was also a notable contributor to the great medieval institution of the Court of Love, which her daughter Mary of Champagne developed further at Troyes. Eleanor might, among other things, be called the Mother of the Century, since she reared and educated a most extraordinary group of sons and daughters who in their turn shaped the institutions of Europe in the next generation. Most notable were Richard, John, Mary, and Leonore. Mary created the rules for the Court of Love and brought together poets and troubadours to set a high cultural standard for this new artistic medium. She supported Chrétien de Troyes as her court poet. Leonore married the king of Spain. The daughter of that union, Blanche of Castile, became one of the great queens of France after marrying Louis VIII at the age of twelve. Queen Blanche served as regent of France twice in her lifetime, saw to the sound management of the country, and produced the son who was to become St. Louis of France.

Another group of royal women, as inconspicuous for the most part as the princesses of England, and totally different in style from the Court of Love queens, are the princesses of Germany, Czechoslovakia, Poland, and Hungary: Matilda, Hedwig, Anna, Agnes, Elizabeth, and, somewhat later, Jadwiga. These were all wives and daughters of kings and all devout Christians who carried on the work of caring for the sick and the poor begun by their royal sisters of the earlier Middle Ages. Two of these royal women are famous: Jadwiga of Poland (1371-1399) and St. Elizabeth of Thüringen (1207-1231).

Jadwiga belongs in the tradition of the heroic Christianizing queens of the earlier Middle Ages. She was betrothed at age seven to the son of the archduke of Austria. When she was crowned queen of Poland at sixteen, she was forced by her subjects to give up a by then unwelcome alliance and marry the boisterous pagan Jagiello of Lithuania. The marriage involved an agreement for the mass conversion of Lithuania. A deeply religious person herself, Jadwiga worked at "taming" Jagiello. She was also a strong political leader, and led her army into the field when border disputes erupted. Her most noteworthy accomplishments were a serious effort to contain the dangerous Order of Teutonic Knights by peaceful negotiation, and the founding of the University of Cracow. The university was to a considerable extent the product of her own personal planning and activity. Working with a committee of duchesses and governors' wives, she studied existing university models at Padua, Bologna, and Paris carefully before deciding on Cracow's format. She died in childbirth at twenty-eight, and is still revered as one of the great rulers and great saints in Polish history (Kellog, 1932).

St. Elizabeth of Thüringen, who lived much more quietly and died even younger than Jadwiga, is nevertheless one of the most written about royal saints of Europe. The daughter of a Hungarian king, Elizabeth was raised in her husband-to-be's court from the age of four, and married at thirteen. She had three chidlren, and the fourth died at birth at the very time that her husband was killed in the Crusades. As a child in her husband-to-be's court, Elizabeth used to walk about the narrow streets of the town outside the castle walls, carrying food to distribute to the poor. Her mother-in-law was unfriendly to her activities, but Elizabeth persisted in works of charity. All through her teens she continued this process of visiting in the families of the poor and nursing the sick. She evidently had a radiant presence. Only twenty when her husband died, she was more or less chased out of the castle by hostile brothers-in-law. She found refuge in the town and continued to work among the poor until she died three years later, at the age of twenty-four (Ancelet-Hustache, 1963; Bordeaux, 1937).

Eleanor, Jadwiga, and St. Elizabeth were very different kinds of persons, but all were in one way typical of royal women: betrothed in childhood, married in the teens, removed from normal personal family supports, finding a way to live an active public life according to their *own pattern,* determined by their own values and interests.

In Byzantium during the early 1100s, the scholar princess Anna Comnena, known as a "pious, learned and passionate" mistress of classical learning, wrote the *Alexiad,* a vivid documentary of the reign of her father, Emperor Alexius I. She was a good historian, and is also supposed to have founded and taught in a medical school in Constantinople. In fact, she was a sad, complaining figure. She had been reared by her father to succeed him as reigning empress, "born to the purple," as she puts it, but circumstances (and a younger brother) intervened and she had to content herself with second-rate status and a second-rate husband. She never accepted this, and her writings are interspersed with personal laments. It is not hard to sympathize with her situation, since her sex-imposed alternative life was a dull one. However, she did exercise her considerable talents to good purpose in her scholarly work. As an eyewitness of the Crusades and the barbarian invasions into Byzantium, she brought more than detached scholarly interest to her writing (Diehl, 1963; Buckler, 1929).

The 1100s in Byzantium witnessed a period of great effort to create alliances by marriage between the Eastern empire and Western Europe. Emperor Manuel married the German princess Bertha of Sulzbach. The unlucky Alexius, who had been betrothed to Agnes of France as a child, was murdered, and Andronicus, who took the throne instead, married Agnes when she was twelve. Constance of Hohenstaufen, daughter of Frederick II, married Emperor John in 1244. Then there was Yolanda of Monterray who married Andronicus II, and Anna of Savoy who married Andronicus III. In each of these cases the lives of the women were lives of stark tragedy, because of the tension and actual warring between Byzantium and Europe during the Crusades. Each woman in turn was totally abandoned to her fate by her European family (Diehl, 1963).

In spite of all the personal and public tragedies that the princesses and queens of the Middle Ages suffered, on the whole they performed remarkably as competent state functionaries. Many of them were women of great individuality and assertiveness, yet they are but infrequently present on the pages of history.

Other Aristocrats

The life of women of the aristocracy outside the royal ruling family was to varying degrees like that of the princesses. Aristocratic women had two major duties: the management of the family estates, and attendance at court. Depending on their temperament and abilities, they could devote themselves to the productivity of the estate, to public works on behalf of the court, or to a life of social activity centering on the Courts of Love and tournament watching. Occasionally groups of more robust ladies, bored with the spectator roles of social life at court, scandalized the local countryside by arriving at tournaments dressed to enter the lists themselves. This kind of activity reached a fever pitch around the time of the black death—perhaps a replay of the restless last days of Rome when women went into the circus as gladiators (Ziegler, 1969: 36). During prolonged absences of the men of a region at Crusades, women sometimes carried on tournaments themselves, dressed as their husbands and jousting under their husbands' names (Reich, 1908: 184).

Women of the aristocracy could also take military training if they chose, and they often did. Among the outstanding aristocratic women warriors of the Middle Ages we find Matilda of Tuscany, who at fifteen rode beside her mother Beatrix and father Godfrey of Lorraine at the head of the Tuscan forces, to repel Norman invaders (Reich, 1908: 174). Spain had several famous women warriors, including, a little later than our period, the "nun-ensign" Dona Catalina de Eraus, who is said to have turned the tide of many a battle by appearing as the soldiers were getting ready to fight (de Beaumont, 1929: 59). Eleanora di Arborea of Sardinia took the field after her brother's murder and successfully suppressed a domestic rebellion, then went on to defeat the king of Aragon in battle (Castellani, 1939: 22). The heroines of the defense of Vienna in 1554 were a three-thousand-woman army which fought in three regiments under Forteguerra, Piccolonimini, and Fausti (Castellani, 1939: 27).

The cavalieressi of Italy were not all of the nobility, but they belong to the tradition of medieval women warriors, to the roman-tic tradition of chivalry. Among them were "the very noble Luzia Stanga"; Margheritona, the courtesan who served as a paid trooper in Count de Gaiazzo's light horse squadron; and the courtesan Mala-testa (de Beaumont, 1929: 57). French women warriors in this period were either duelists who made themselves locally famous in France, or hard-fighting Crusader soldiers who usually died unidentified—and therefore unhonored.

The most famous woman warrior of the Middle Ages was not of the aristocracy at all, but a peasant girl of France. She doesn't belong in this section, but she doesn't belong in any other section of this chapter either. There have been many different historical portrayals of Joan of Lorraine. Common to them all is the picture of a robust peasant girl with mystical leanings who became convinced that she was to "save France." She was not well educated and had neither geographical sense (about where battlegrounds were) nor political understanding, but she had native intelligence and tenacity and man-aged to persuade a relative into introducing her to the local lord who could send her on to the king.

At each step of the way Joan's story seems fantastically unlikely. She learned to ride and gained a smattering of military tactics in her early teens during a period when her own community was overrun by a hostile neighboring army. This is how it was possible for her to han-dle herself creditably on horseback when she later actually rode with an army. The local nobleman of her hometown tried to put Joan off, but finally shipped her away to the king as a political maneuver. The king in turn sent her away with a small retinue of soldiers to placate her, never intending that she should lead an army. Encamped with the main French army, she was completely ignored by the officers. Infuriated, she literally seized an opportunity and rode off with the army *sans* officers on the famous occasion of her first battle. The peasants and the common soldiers already revered her, having heard and believed the story of her mission, so she had no difficulty getting followers en route to battle. When the officers discovered that she had taken off with their men they did the only thing possible—dashed after the army, took over a battle they hadn't intended to fight, and to everyone's surprise won it (Guillemin, 1972; see also Reich, 1908). Joan moved through all this as a charismatic figure who never really understood what she was doing, but did it with a simplicity and faith that makes her come through as "believable" no matter how unfriendly her chronicler. As a historical figure who happens to be a woman, her significance lies in the fact that she acted out a major role in a crucial portion of French national history out of an initial unawareness of the limitations and weaknesses that went with her situation as a woman—and was therefore not constrained in her behavior by those limitations. The awareness of the limitations came to her later and tragically, after her part had been played, as she suffered imprisonment and the Inquisition. But the courage of one who acts as if there are no limitations continues to capture us, centuries later. She evidently did not seem as unusual to her own countrymen as she does to the twentieth century, which suggests that more of a woman warrior tradition that we know of was extant in her time.

Joan did not start a social movement. She was rather a demonstration that a charismatic peasant can have as much as or more impact on society than can a queen. However, while the lonely Joan was playing her part, the Middle Ages were seething with social movements. One significant set of them, known as the "women's movement," developed an interesting alliance between former peasants and the urban middle classes. This is the phenomenon we shall look at next.

The Women's Movement in the Middle Ages: The Beguines

The term *Frauenbewegung* (women's movement) is often used in referring to the activities of upper- and middle-class laywomen who took leadership in promoting the transition to urbanism that began in Europe in the 1100s. It is appropriate to call it a social movement in that it began spontaneously in a number of different locations at the same time, all over the Low Countries. It spread to the rest of Europe very quickly. Colledge calls the *Frauenbewegung*

> that great and victorious revolt of pious women, everywhere in Europe, against the reactionary traditions which would have condemned them in the cloisters as well as in the world to a role of subordination and silence (1961: 7).

It is difficult to give a balanced picture of the movement since some studies treat it primarily as a lay religious movement (McDonnell, 1969), and others as a strictly pragmatic development associated with the women's guilds (Bücher, 1910). Since there was a high background level of religiosity in the Middle Ages, especially for women, even the most pragmatic guild-associated beguinages (a type of women's commune) also had some group religious practices. The guild movement itself had a strong religious component in its ceremonial observances; according to some authorities this developed out of earlier religious associations of workers in the same craft that were similar to, if not actually descendants of, the religious mutual aid associations of Greece and Rome. While the craft guilds became increasingly secular, the Beguines kept more of a religious emphasis. The women who became outstanding in the Beguine movement were in fact religious leaders. These women were also leaders of a movement for social and economic justice and against institutional corruption, however, and this must not be forgotten when we look at the more spiritual aspects of their work. Those who emphasize the religious aspect of the Beguine movement say that it is the women's lay counterpart of the Franciscan and Cistercian movements. However, even the most deeply religious of the Beguines, those known as the ecstatics, sought cloistered life but rarely.

As a social movement Beguinism is unique in that it utilized the old traditions of the all-women's workshops that we discovered in antiquity as a device for establishing autonomous working and living spaces for single women in a postslave society. If the beguinage had some similarity to the workshops run by the matrons of antiquity in the *gynaeceum,* or by the ladies of the manor houses in the Middle Ages (see pp. 481-482 in this chapter), it was also very different because it was not part of a male-headed estate. No men ever had authority roles of any kind in a beguinage. Even more important, the women were free women, neither slaves nor serfs.

The beguinages were started by well-to-do women with property in both countryside and city who built special houses on the edges of cities for unmarried women workers moving into the cities. These larger houses, called beguinages,[12] can be related to two other social models, one earlier, one contemporaneous. One is the *gynaeceum* workshop already mentioned. The other is the *frèrèche,* a kind of extended-family household that was occasionally formed in the fourteenth and fifteenth centuries in rural southern France in response to economic difficulties. The *frèrèche* was a *communeauté familiale* consisting "of brothers sharing their patrimony and their households. . . . sister's husbands and sisters themselves, other relatives, and even strangers, could become incorporated" (Laslett, 1972: 14). Similar familial communities have been found in earlier and later times in Italy, Spain, and Poland, as well as in France, and were usually associated with economic recession. The surplus of women associated with the aftermath of the Crusades, and their concentration in cities where there was a dearth of residences and jobs, could very naturally trigger the formation of *"soeurèches."* Whatever relationship the beguinage might have had conceptually or historically to the *gynae-ceum* and the *frèrêche,* it was nevertheless a remarkable social innovation.

The women who entered into these all-women households took no special vows. They were simply entering into a congenial and practical living arrangement. Working women went on with their former trades; upper-class women stirred by the *Frauenbewegung* left their manor houses to join the working women in their workshops. They gave up fancy clothes, lived on the simplest food, and rose early for prayers before work. Scholars agree that the movement had no place of origin or a single initiator. One group began with a couple of sisters and soon had three hundred women living all crowded together (McDonnell, 1969: 109-110). Groups of three and four expanded to twenty-five and fifty. The rapid expansion was due to the need of increasing numbers of unmarried women workers in the cities to have a place to live and work. Part of the movement thus became almost indistinguishable from women's trade guilds, although religious practices were always maintained. The combination of a surplus of women[13] and substantial urban poverty meant that some of the beguinages functioned in fact as poorhouses, where unpartnered women (and children) could be guaranteed shelter, food, and some work to do.

After the initial period of spontaneous formation of small groups, there was an inevitable second stage of "organizing the movement." Women developed rules about living together, appointed councils of women to administer their affairs, and finally installed a "grand mistress." By this time the church was alarmed, because here were groups of pious women out of control of the church. In the struggle that followed, the women by and large kept cool heads and won recognition as secular institutions with their own rules; in that heresy-conscious age, they needed recognition by the church if they were to go on living together safely. Many Beguines simply "took over" their own religious life, organized their own prayers and rituals, and even heard each other's confessions. They went to church dutifully enough, but did not feel dependent on priests. This kind of autonomy made the priests and the teaching orders, which were ordered by the church to "look after" the women, very uneasy. The women might develop heresies.

The main body of the Beguines was not antichurch, and accepted the idea of being organized into parishes. This meant recognizing the authority of a bishop, but nothing more. After all, everyone lived in parishes, and all parishes were connected to bishoprics. There were localities in which considerable pressure was applied to get Beguines to adopt an enclosed way of life. This they resisted successfully in the Middle Ages, although at a later time beguinages became a kind of secular cloister.[14] During the 1200s and 1300s, the requirements of the Flemish cloth industry were such that the beguinages "were interlaced . . . with guild organization" (McDonnell, 1969: 85).

It is undeniable that many of the Beguines had a strong religious character. They produced a group of mystics whose spiritual classics, predating the famous Rhineland mystics (all men), are of the same literary and spiritual quality as those of their better-know male successors. Here again we tap the worldwide vein of mysticism. Because the Beguine movement was also oriented to the reconstruction of society, it ran schools, hospitals, and workshops for the poor. The Beguine schools were so highly respected that many little girls were sent to them by ambitious parents with no religious interests. Since the little girls usually wanted to become Beguines—a role that must have seemed both glamorous and exciting to girls from conventional homes—an expanding supply of Beguines was assured for several centuries. The outstanding mystics, such as Mechthild, Beatrice, and Hadewijch, all came from worldly backgrounds and were sent to Beguine schools. Each chose to become a Beguine over varying degrees of parental resistance, between the ages of nine and twelve.

All sorts of interesting problems arose in the relationship of these women's groups to the church. The church wanted to control them, but the Dominicans were already overloaded with pastoral work because of the large influx of women into Cistercian convents;[15] many Dominican writings of the time complain of the overload in counseling women. A further overload was created by the fact that the pope continually put whole towns, sometimes whole countries, under papal interdict in the course of power struggles between church and state. An interdict meant that no mass could be said in the affected area. The Beguines, with their independence, could cope with this much better than either nuns or family women, who often felt real terror when the Mass was denied them. The Beguines clearly felt that they could get along without the church when necessary.

It is evident that the Beguine movement was almost perfectly adapted to cope with the economic, social, and religious problems of the times. Within the church, however, the ideology of male dominance won out over the pragmatic usefulness of Beguine independence. The Dominicans forbade women to write their own Psalters (they had been doing just this) and clamped down on the tendency for some beguinages to install their own women preachers and confessors. Finally, in 1274, the pope forbade new religious associations of any kind (though this did not outlaw existing beguinages).

The natural tendency for able women organized in their own living communities to take responsibility for their own lives, both in economic and religious terms, sometimes led these women in unusual directions. It also served to blur the distinctions between Beguines, who generally accepted the ultimate authority of the church, and the heretic movements, which to varying degrees denied that authority. Since being convicted of heresy meant being burned at the stake, this was not an academic issue. What the Beguines had in common with the heretics was a certain independent-mindedness, a general feeling that one's spiritual state did not depend very closely on ministrations by priests, and a high view of the perfectibility of human beings and of the possibility of being "oned" with God. Mystics of all ages have tended to hold these views, yet most of them stay in the bosom of the church.

What determined whether one stayed in the central Beguine fold, or went off with the Albigensians, the Waldensians, the Cathari, the Brethren of the Free Spirit, the Perfecti, or the more violently revolutionary Turlupins and other extremists? In fact, most people of the movements just listed were also loyal to the church, but committed to a more demanding demonstration of Christianity. There were two main forces that separated the heretics from the mainstream. One was a sense of alienation from corrupt society so profound that the individual must participate in destroying that society at any cost. The other was a low threshold of emotional suggestibility that led people to think they had already united with God, that they were already living in the millennium and could do no wrong.[16] The Beguines and the other mainstream groups were institution builders more than protesters. The Beguine movement was particularly important to the European scene because it linked practical problem solving with the development of healthy community life and high religious ideals.

What is definitely not true is that there were a large number of silly, emotional women running around causing problems for the church and for society. Let us look at the women who gave leadership to the Beguine movement.

The first to be associated historically with the movement is Mary d'Oignies. Interestingly, the significance of her role was that she provided leadership to a group of men who then went out and helped create the support within ecclesiastical structures which made it possible for the women's movement to organize outside the religious orders. Mary is particularly interesting because she felt a strong call to preach, yet did not do so. Other women who felt that call and followed it were burned at the stake, as we shall see. The church would not allow such activity. Mary rechanneled her own preaching drive into the teaching of a group of men who became her disciples. She had already raised a family when she felt the call to that life of austerity, devotion, and service—the Beguine "germ" that was to be so contagious. She got permission from her husband to leave home[17] and settle near a small independent "cenobium" (religious commune) —not a regular monastic house, but a group of priests who had felt a call similar to her own—at Oignies. The male counterpart of the Beguine movement was the sprinkling of small groups of clerics in little cenobia around Europe who shared a similar longing for a greater purity of life and more service to the world than the church seemed to require. This was the untapped resource that made it possible for both the Franciscan and Beguine movements to grow so rapidly.

Mary's "circle," as it is referred to, are the men from the Oignies cenobium who responded to her teachings. She trained them to analyze the world the way she did, and to preach eloquently. Some of her students became leading bishops of the day, and they all became promoters of responsibility for women in the church and the community. Since their letters and writings are filled with references to Mary, there is no doubt about the role she played in their work.[18]

Another woman known particularly for her teaching role in relation to clerics was Christine Stemmeln. At the age of ten she had an inner experience that separated her from other children, and at thirteen she ran away from her well-to-do family to the Beguines. She continually embarrassed the Beguines by her religious exaltations, since they were on the whole a practical-minded group of women. She finally found her niche living close to a Dominican center in Cologne, which more or less accepted her as a lay sister and *de facto* spiritual advisor. Like Mary she "trained" men who became prominent supporters of women's activities, and we know about her through her correspondence with Friar Peter of Gothland and through several Dominican biographers including her chaplain Master John. (Christine, incidentally, could not write—all her letters were dictated to willing Dominican brothers—so the Beguine educational system was evidently not effective with her.) The Franciscans detested her and called her the "seductress of Stemmeln." The Dominicans loved her as a holy woman. In other circumstances, she could easily have gone to the stake.

Mary and Christine both came from middle-class families. There were many ordinary village girls—daughters of farmers, millers, and artisans—who were also caught up in religious visioning in the thirteenth century. Ordinarily they remained in their own homes, under the protection of their own families and a friendly local Dominican monastery. Since they were often illiterate, the monks would write down their visions, and these would be passed from hand to hand among "movement" monasteries. Margrete from Ipern and Ludgard von Tonzern are two such relatively unknown local visionaries. This type of working-class piety, protected and revered in local communities, formed a kind of backdrop to the more visible and articulate activities of the women's movement (Weinhold, 1882).

The primary role of leaders like Mary and Christine was to gain support for women among clerics already predisposed to the Beguine approach to life. Most Beguines lived more within a self-contained woman's world, a world which had a place for men, but not too close a relationship with them. Mechthild of Magdeburg and Beatrice of Nazareth represent a generation raised within that women's community, and are outstanding products of that religious culture. They were both sent to school to the Beguines by well-to-do families, and both chose to spend their lives in such communities. Mechthild went into a convent toward the end of her life, and her work will be discussed in the next section on women's religious orders. Beatrice's *Of the Seven Manners of Loving* (Colledge, 1965) is written with the skill and spiritual discernment which comes only to women steeped in religious experience. The same is true for Hadewijch of Antwerp. We know nothing about her except that she appears to have grown up among the Beguines, and her series of letters of spiritual instruction for young Beguines (Colledge, 1965) has become a religious classic. The same clarity of perception and use of language to point to experiences beyond words, so characteristic of Beguine mystics, plus a fresh, spontaneous style, are found in her letters. Knowing more about the lives of these women would not add to the beauty of their writings, but one feels cheated to know so little about them.

With Marguerite of Porété we move into the realm of heresy, or rather, of accusations of heresy. Marguerite was burned at the stake for persisting not only in writing, but in circulating her manuscripts all over France. Even worse, she persisted in preaching in public in Paris. High church dignitaries protected her as long as they could, for they recognized her spiritual gifts. Her independent ways offended too many in the church, however, and the last time she was arrested she had to go to the stake. Mystical writings can easily be misinterpreted by those not prepared for them, and many devotional classics are prefaced by remarks that "this book is not for everyone."[19] Marguerite's book also had such a warning, but what others could write and be revered for, she was burned for.

Apparently someone saved a manuscript at the time when Marguerite's writings were publicly burnt, since Professor Guarnieri has recently identified a medieval manuscript known as *The Mirror of Simple Souls,* ascribed to an obscure medieval writer, as actually being Marguerite's book (Cohn, 1970). Marguerite was not only an activist preacher, she was also a scholar. One of the things that got her in trouble with the Inquisition was a translation she had made of the Bible. Marguerite was a Beguine, but left the residential community of Beguines to engage in a more public life. We do not know what her sisters thought about her activities.

Another Beguine who moved outside the community was Bloemardinne. It is harder to judge her work, since we know about her chiefly through her enemies, who accused her of establishing a cult of libertinism. The fact that her circle of supporters included women of high position and presumably of educated judgment who considered her a saint, and that she was so venerated by the clerics of her own milieu that no one dared bring charges of heresy against her until after her death, suggests that she was in fact a woman of great personal sanctity. It is easy to burn people posthumously.

Another Beguine-type saint who was burnt posthumously was Guglielma of Milan, a Joachimite who founded a sect to inaugurate the Age of the Holy Spirit. She "died in the odour of sanctity" in 1282, but was dug up to be burned when her disciple Manfreda was moved to announce that she, Manfreda, was to usher in the new age as pope. (All her cardinals were to be women.) Manfreda came of a very distinguished Italian family, but it did not save her from the stake (Reeves, 1969: 248). Prous Boneta was associated originally with the Beguines, but had become an independent by the time she was burned for announcing that she was sent to inaugurate the Age of the Holy Spirit (Reeves, 1969: 248).

Most of the women who were burnt are nameless. In our day some of them would be considered harmless Pentecostals, others sensible social reformers. Many of them must have been literate beyond the average, since they were so often accused of producing and circulating new vernacular translations of the Bible. Their other major fault in the eyes of the church, apart from Pentecostalism, was that their meetings were held (out of obvious necessity, once persecution had begun) in secret (McDonnell, 1969: 506-507).

From the fragments of stories that remain, it is hard to tell how politically oriented these women were. Few of them could have been much of a threat either to the church or the state. Jeanne Dabenton, an ex-Beguine, was perhaps more politically minded than most. She seems to have done organizing work among the poor, with a sect known as the Turlupins. She and some companions, women and men, were burned at the stake, presumably for being too effective in arousing the poor (McDonnell, 1969: 500-502; Cohn, 1970: 169).

There seem to have been no women leaders among the obviously totalitarian extremist movements that instituted reigns of terror in some of the German cities, such as the groups led by Matthys and Bockelson (Cohn, 1970: 261-280). This is an indication, I think, of the essentially libertarian approach of the Beguines to individual and social reform. Certainly there were women followers of extremist movements, as there were men followers, but the Beguines should not have to take the blame for extremism, as they are often made to do.

The problem with doing a "big-name" roll call of the Beguines is that it misses what the Beguines were about. Their genius lay in the quality of the local communes. They did have a rich inner life, and a richer sense of the human possibility, than most of the people around them. I wish some record remained of how they educated the children in their charge. Some of the communities clearly bred revolutionaries.

While the Beguines were the secular underlife of the church, they laid the basis for an overlife participation of women in urban society which survived the expulsion of women from guilds; it was the Beguine groundwork that enabled women to retain a foothold in society in the face of the antifeminist elements of the Renaissance and the Enlightenment. We will see the other half of that story when we look at the activities of women in guilds. But first, we will look at what was happening with women within the institutional church itself.

Women Religious in the Middle Ages

Women in the Mainstream Religious Orders[20]

In the last chapter we watched the rise of great women's abbeys as independent power bases from the late seventh century on. By 800, German Saxony was one of the strongest centers of religious women, and the traditions that began in the great convents of Herford, Gandersheim, and Quedlinburg (Essen) flowered in the work of Hrotswitha, described earlier. Hrotswitha was really a transitional figure, belonging both to the earlier days of less demanding monastic scholarship and to the new era of intellectually more sophisticated medieval scholarship. There was a great revival of her work in the 1400s, at the beginning of the Renaissance. Germany continued as the major intellectual center of women's monasticism throughout the Middle Ages. In the 1100s, one hundred new Benedictine convents were established there. French convents spread more slowly, and in England the Danish invasion in the 800s had brought monastic life for women almost to a standstill. By 1100, when convents began to spread again in England, all women prioresses were subject to male abbots, and the new convents had greatly reduced power compared to those that flourished earlier under St. Hilda. Lively nuns made the best of the situation, essentially using the convents as handcraft centers, producing embroidery, tapestries, weaving, manuscripts, and painting.

The eleventh century was a good one for the Benedictine women monastics. Not only did they spread in Germany, but abbeys opened in Bohemia, Poland, Hungary, and the Scandinavian countries. Many of these were royal convents, with a princess abbess who had the right to participate in the coronation of the queen. They often restricted admission to girls of the aristocracy, and abbesses were like peeresses of the realm. Like secular princesses, they were usually betrothed at the age of four to eight, only in this case they were brides of Jesus, not a secular prince. Like the princesses, they often undertook ruling duties at a very young age. Princess Urraca of

Figure 9-2. *"Claricia." Detail, Self-Portrait from a South German Psalter, c. A.D. 1200.*

Aragon became abbess at eleven; many were appointed before the age of twenty. One of the most renowned abbesses of the Middle Ages, Gertrude of Hackeborn, was appointed at the age of nineteen. As in the case of the princesses, one must admire the extent of education, self-discipline, and administrative ability exhibited by the abbesses at very young ages.

In Spain, which had an ancient pre-Benedictine Christian tradition untouched by European developments during the long Moslem rule, Queen Leonore (a daughter of Eleanor of Aquitaine) founded Las Huelges de Burgos on the Cistercian rule. Las Huelges was a true royal abbey, endowed with lands encompassing sixty villages and decreed to be head of all religious houses in Spain. Queen Leonore, who was betrothed to the king of Spain at the age of nine and sent to his court to be brought up, before leaving home had been well trained by her mother for an institution-building role. She gave a lot of attention to the development of Las Huelges. The abbess was the absolute monarch of her sixty villages and could punish clergy for heresy and the king's officials for secular offenses. She also heard confessions. Monks vowed to the hospitals under the abbey's care took their

Figure 9-3. *Nuns Making Cloth, Italian Manuscript, A.D. 1421.*

vows of obedience directly to her. The most famous choir school of Europe developed there. The Spanish royal abbey, with the support both of king and pope, held on to its power longer than any other convent in Europe—right up to the 1800s.

These larger abbeys we have been describing had up to five hundred nuns, including a number who had specialized jobs in addition to their regular work of prayer, devotional reading, liturgical service, and maintenance duties. Besides the dean, cellarer, and wardrobe mistress, there would be the chantress, who directed the choir, composed the music and accompanying poetry, did the work of librarian, and supervised manuscript copying. The infirmarian held another important convent position. She would have special medical training and act as physician, pharmacist, and teacher of the art of healing to other nuns. Every convent had its own medical herb garden which the infirmarian supervised. Some convents ran hospitals and old people's homes, so the infirmarian would have a whole staff of nuns working under her to provide nursing services. Every convent also had to have a magistra, to teach the children who came to the convent. If we add the other administrative and maintenance tasks of treasurer, almoner, portress, and sacristan, there were at least ten specialist jobs in each monastery in addition to that of abbess. As long as Europe remained a land-based economy with a strong barter component, the convents thrived. But with the shift to a monetary economy and the need for cash, abbeys declined rapidly. They were not organized to make that transition effectively, and soon shrank to houses of twenty-five women from an earlier one hundred to five hundred. The aristocracy lasted the longest in the monasteries, since they could bring ample dowries with them. The dowryless working-class women were the first to have to leave; the middle class held on longer. The Beguine movement played an important part in picking up the slack during this transition.

Figure 9-4. *Detail of Scene from Sick Ward at Hotel-Dieu at Beaune, A.D. 1443.*

Abbesses not only had to contend with economic transitions; they had to contend with the determined efforts of bishops to reduce the autonomy of convents. The famous double monasteries of the eighth and ninth centuries, where monks and nuns both served under an abbess, declined in the tenth century under church pressure and were replaced by monasteries with dependent convents attached. Here the nuns "served the monks by copying books and performing other services" (Hilpisch, 1958: 23). It is obvious that nuns did not care much for this situation, because this type of dependent convent also disappeared by 1300. Women simply stopped applying to enter them.

At the same time, new independent religious houses for women were developing. In one form this was a rebirth of the old double monastery, as in the case of the Order of Fontrevault. This order, in which monks served nuns under an abbess, spread all over Europe in the twelfth century, much encouraged by Eleanor of Aquitaine.[21]

Figure 9-5. *Nun and Monk Tilting, from a Gothic Manuscript.*

Other independent religious houses included the Congregation of the Paraclete, Heloise's convent, which established daughter houses around France. St. Sulpice de la Forest did the same, as did the congregation of Santa Anne de'Funari in Italy. This movement represented a renewed declaration of independence of religious women. As usual, the pope supported this. He understood the value of groups of independent women religious answerable only to him.

The struggle between women and men in the church continued throughout the Middle Ages. For every move toward independence of women, there was a new movement toward control by men. The enclosure movement, which had absolutely no basis in the Rule of St. Benedict, but which conformed to prevailing ideas about what was proper for women, kept erupting again and again from the times of the earliest religious houses. Enclosed nuns were never to leave the convent for any reason, nor to be seen by others even inside the convent—hence the use of the grille between nun and visitor in the monastery parlor. Church law moved steadily in this direction from 1100 on, but sensible bishops allowed for exceptions. Strong-minded women religious with a vocation that required contact with the world never accepted enclosure.22

The Cistercian movement was a reform movement of Benedictines who felt a need for more withdrawal from the world, for greater simplicity, a deeper prayer life, and rigorous manual work. It should not be confused with the enclosure movement, which was imposed from without. Cistercianism attracted many nuns as well as monks, and the Cistercian women's houses grew faster than any other order in the 1200s. In fact, the men tried to stop the women from forming houses, because they were obliged to visit them and provide spiritual counsel—and the work load for spiritual counsel was getting too heavy! It is impossible to have a full understanding of the significance of religious orders in the life of medieval women if we do not recognize the differences in types of convents chosen by women: some were scholarly, or liturgical, and "world-oriented" convents; others were secluded, prayer-oriented ones. It is the latter that reflect the new spirituality of the worldwide mystical movements of the Middle Ages. McDonnell (1969: 105) gives a vivid picture of the ardent and prayerful asceticism of women Cistercians.

A third type, the service-oriented convent, did not develop in the Middle Ages,[23] but only after the Reformation. This is why the secular beguinages became so important. Neither the Franciscan nor the Dominican service and teaching orders had the imagination to permit women to serve outside the convent as men served, so those important male religious inventions of the thirteenth century did not open the doors for women in the ways that we might have expected.

Each type of religious house for women produced some outstanding women—outstanding in that their work has been noted by others outside the order. The real work of convents is not a visible work, and may never produce manifestations that others can judge. Therefore in choosing some nuns to discuss in this section, I would like to remind the reader that these few women happened to have special gifts for communication with the world.

The German convents have the longest tradition of autonomy and of scholarship, as we have seen from the previous chapter, so it is not surprising that the most notable scholars and prophetesses should come from there. St. Hildegarde, Abbess of St. Rupert at Bingen (1098-1178), was both scholar and seer. She entered convent life at seven, took vows at fourteen. The most voluminous woman writer of the Middle Ages, though by no means with the literary gifts of Hrotswitha, she was called the "sibyl of the Rhine" and the "marvel of Germany." Her convent, says Mozans,

> became a Mecca for all classes and conditions of men and women. . . .
> Among her correspondents . . . there were simple monks and noble abbots; dukes, kings and queens; archbishops and cardinals and no fewer than four popes (1913: 46).

Three hundred letters remain of this correspondence.

Her own major work consists of six to eight large volumes on theology, scripture, and science. It is not likely that she wrote all this herself. Eckenstein (1896) suggests, for example, that the volume of *Materia Medica* attributed to her was probably prepared under her direction by a group of nuns. Reeves (1969: 281-298) indicates that much of her work was done by dictation and rewritten and polished by her (male) secretaries. This was certainly true of other writers of both sexes, and does not detract from the importance of her work in the history of science. Singer, the science historian, writes of how she related the cosmic and the human:

> The terms macrocosm and microcosm are not employed by her, but in her last great work, the *Liber Divinorum Operum,* she succeeds in most eloquent and able fashion in synthesizing into one great whole, centered around this doctrine, her theological beliefs and her physiological knowledge, together with her conception of the working of the human mind and the structure of the universe (quoted in Saport, 1975: 9).

The natural sciences, astronomy, and medicine, as well as classical learning, theology, and a study of the church fathers, were part of the curriculum for most of these scholar nuns. Still, in our eagerness to admire their skills, we should not overestimate their learning. The standards of the day were not very high, either for men

Figure 9-6. *The Synagogue. Illumination from Hildegard Von Bingen's* Scivias, *A.D. 1165.*

or women. Reeves (1969: 365-387) gives a careful appraisal of this issue.

Much of Hildegarde's fame came from her political prophesying. The tradition of religious prophecy on political matters was, of course, an old one, encompassing the Old Testament prophets, the Revelations in the New Testament, and the German seeresses and the Near Eastern sibyls of the days of the Roman Empire. While it happened that the writings of Joachim de Fiore became the main vehicle for political prophecy in the Middle Ages, many hundreds of scholars were poring over Old and New Testament writings to try to discern the shape of events to come. Hildegarde, a contemporary of de Fiore, was one of these. To say that her prophesying was in the Joachimite style is only to say that she was steeped in the thinking of her times. She brought something more than intellectual curiosity to her search of scriptures, however, and it was her capacity to rework the past and envision the future in a way to which others resonated that made her so important in her time. She was charismatic, with great skill in speaking and writing.

Her most famous public project was mobilizing support for the second crusade, which she did jointly with Bernard of Clairveaux. Bernard himself attributes the main drive to Hildegarde. Her last writing, the *Book of Divine Doings,* included the views of an elder stateswoman (she was eighty when she died) on the future of Europe. Like many seers, she was convinced that she was the chosen mouthpiece of the Lord. Most of her contemporaries apparently agreed with her. In retrospect, the political naiveté of her efforts on behalf of the Crusades leaves some room for doubt about her political judgments. Nevertheless, she must be recognized as one of the thought-leaders of her time. Elizabeth of Schönau was an only slightly less well known scholar nun who also had the gift of political prophecy.

Herrad, Abbess of Hohenburg in Alsace, was another contemporary of Hildegarde and perhaps more noteworthy as a scholar. She prepared a compendium of the current knowledge of the times—the *Hortus Deliciarum,* or *Garden of Delights*—for the education of her nuns. It may be the first encyclopedia of medieval Europe. Only fragments of the original have survived wartime depradations, but they are far-ranging in content and delightful in style. Herrad was an accomplished classical scholar.

In the middle of the next century, a whole group of scholar nuns who were also contemplatives and mystics were based at Helfta, in Saxony. Their abbess was the Gertrude of Hackeborn we noted as having been appointed at the age of nineteen. She developed one of the best monastic libraries in Europe, and maintained that the vitality of spiritual life depended on the well-trained mind. Three books considered religious classics in their time come out of Helfta under Gertrude: Mechthild of Magdeburg's *Flowing Light of the Godhead,* Mechthild of Hackeborn's book on grace, and Gertrude the Great's (not the abbess) *Herald of Divine Love.* Helfta was a Cistercian house, and shows Cistercian spirituality at its best.

Mechthild of Magdeburg (1212-1280) was of the aristocracy, as most of these women were. She first joined the Beguines at the age of twenty-three, and did not enter the Cistercian convent at Helfta until she was nearly sixty. She is therefore not a typical Cistercian. She is, however, the most quoted and discussed member of the Helfta group (Kemp-Welch, 1913). Not one of the more scholarly nuns, she wrote in Low German because Latin was difficult for her. She was well read however, and knew Joachim de Fiore's writings. She had been familiar with court life before becoming a Beguine, and much of her spiritual writing draws on the metaphors of courtly love. The combination of her own keen intellect, her past experience with court life, the accompanying understanding of political realities and feeling of political responsibility, and her own inner mystical drives produced a life full of anguish and tensions. She tried to speak to the public figures of her time and at the same time to provide spiritual guidance for the inward journey of ordinary persons. Since she was not a person of status in the religious world, as Hildegarde was, it was much more dangerous for her to speak out on public issues, but she continued to do so all her life. Her writing has depth and power, and also continuing relevance.

Women in Independent Orders

The independent houses were not as different from the mainstream orders as one might expect. In fact most of them were royal abbeys and reflected the autonomy of queens rather than any new drive toward independence on the part of women. Nevertheless, there had to be initiators, and perhaps the chief significance of these houses lies in the extent of women's entrepreneurship within the church they represent. Starting a new house, and writing one's own rule, takes a great deal of negotiating with church authorities. We would expect, then, that women who found new houses will be women of unusual ability and enterprise. Three outstanding new houses of the Middle Ages did indeed have unusual women associated with them: the Paraclete founded by Heloise of Argenteuil and the Birgittine Order by St. Birgitta of Sweden, and Fontrevault, actually founded by Robert d'Abrissel, was largely piloted by Eleanor of Aquitaine.

The house which Heloise (1100-1164) founded, the Paraclete, is famous as the place that Abelard gave to Heloise so that she might establish her own convent after the Benedictines reclaimed Argenteuil, her convent home after her abortive marriage to Abelard. The Abelard-Heloise story is one of the most often told, and hotly debated, tales of the Middle Ages. The traditional version of the story has contributed much to the crude stereotype of nuns as women languishing for lost lovers. Supposedly, while serving as Heloise's tutor, Abelard fell in love with her and seduced her, then honorably decided to marry her. After their marriage and the birth of a baby, her guardian uncle, in a belated rage at the deceit of Abelard, had him attacked and castrated. Abelard became a monk. Heloise retired to a convent and grieved in silence for twenty years, then suddenly sat down to write a series of passionate love letters to Abelard which he then published (Moncrieff, 1929).

One major reinterpretation of the story appears in *Heloise: Dans l'Histoire et dans la Légende* (Charrier, 1933), based on a reanalysis of Abelard's publications and other documents. In this version, Heloise, convent reared, did indeed come to Paris to live with her guardian uncle, a canon of Notre Dame, and took Paris by storm. Referred to as a second Hypatia, this girl in her early teens knew a number of languages and was widely read both in the classics and theology. She was able to dispute with all the learned masters who taught at the cathedral schools of Chartres and Paris. Mozans (1913) says she was a gifted mathematician. Hurd-Mead (1933) says she studied and taught medicine and practiced it later in her own convent.

According to this interpretation Abelard made love to her as a potential intellectual rival, in hopes of heading off a career that threatened his own. He not only saddled his Hypatia with a baby and marriage, but also was playing around with other women to an extent widely known in Paris at the time. Years later he pieced together parts of letters actually written years before by Heloise, the heartbroken wife suddenly forced into a convent. These pieces are woven into a fabricated whole, and the letters and his autobiography, *Calamities,* were published as a device to bring him some favorable publicity during one of the periods when he was trying to make a comeback in Paris. Passionate love letters from a famous and brilliant nun who had been pining for him for years in a convent? It was a best seller at the time, and has been ever since.

Whatever conclusions one draws about Heloise, there are a variety of sources to look to. There are a number of references to her in contemporary literature, and there is the extraordinary letter Peter the Venerable, abbot of Cluny, wrote to Heloise after Abelard died. Abelard died in disgrace, but under Peter's protection, at a Cluny-administered monastery. The letter is not about Abelard at all, but about Heloise:

> I should have known how large a place of love for you in the Lord I keep in my heart. For truly I do not now first begin to love a person whom I remember that I have loved for a long time. I had not yet completely passed out of adolescence, I had not yet attained young manhood, when the fame, not yet indeed of your religion, but of your distinguished and praiseworthy studies became known to me.
>
> I heard then that a woman, although she was not yet disentangled from the bonds of the world, devoted the highest zeal to literary studies, which is very unusual, and to the pursuit of wisdom, although it was that of the world. . . . you, by your praiseworthy zeal, completely excelled all women, and surpassed almost all men.
>
> Soon . . . you exchanged this devotion to studies for a far better one. Now completely and truly a woman of wisdom you chose the gospel instead of logic, the Apostle in place of physics, Christ instead of Plato, the cloister instead of the Academy (Worthington, 1962: 180).

After more supportive comments about the difficult responsibilities of being an abbess, he finally mentions Abelard. He delicately refers to their earthly marriage many years ago, and their possible reunion in heaven (standard theological doctrine at the time).

Heloise's letters to Peter at this time are brief and to the point and show no signs of a woman who has been languishing in a convent all her life for a lover.

Just how learned and brilliant Heloise actually was we do not know. She may have simply "closed up" after the disastrous initial outcome of her relationship to Abelard. In any case she did marry him, apparently against her will, at eighteen. She also apparently managed to return to Paris to resume her career, leaving her baby in the country. The nature of their relationship after Abelard entered a monastery and ordered Heloise to take the veil is in dispute. In a version friendly to Abelard, McLaughlin (1975a) suggests that the famous love letters were composed jointly by Heloise and Abelard as a kind of moral tale for young nuns. McLaughlin would place much more emphasis on the rest of the Heloise-Abelard correspondence, which deals with the status of nuns in the church, and on

Abelard's authorship of the Paraclete Rule, which is essentially a utopian design for a double-monastery type of community (1975b). She points out that analysis of these writings reveals Abelard to have been one of the strongest promoters of feminism in the medieval church, though he also shared the ambivalence most clerics felt about women. In this interpretation he throws himself heart and soul into a joint venture with Heloise in trying to make the Paraclete the realization of all his ideals about monasticism—ideals rejected by his fellow monks. (He was thrown out of his own monastery because his monks did not like his reforms.)

Certainly Abelard wrote strongly feminist things about women in the early church, some of which have already been quoted in chapter 8. Certainly also he was a self-centered person. Unfortunately none of the treatments of Abelard throws a great deal of light on Heloise: she is thrown into the shadows every time. What was *she* like? Did she deliberately repress great gifts? We know only that she was a good abbess.

The Paraclete became a model of an independent house not tied into the Benedictine network, and also a model of rigorous piety. It was reformist but conservative, and prospered as an order. What else it might have been had Heloise taken her first religious vows freely, and not under orders from a hysterical, castrated husband, we shall never know.

Most of the developments we have been describing in this section took place in the twelfth and thirteenth centuries. By the fourteenth century things were even livelier. The Crusades were still in full swing, the Turks were invading Byzantium, the black death came to Europe, the Hundred Years War was on, and there were insurrections of weavers and other trade guilds all over Europe. One of the last major independent houses was founded at this time, the Order of St. Birgitta of Sweden. Birgitta (1303-1373)[24] was one of the most strong-minded women of a strong-minded century. She married at thirteen and had eight children, all brought up sternly with the rod. (One turned out to be a saint, the holy Katherine, another a black sheep, and we don't know about the rest.)

Already a pious ascetic during her years of motherhood, she took her own private vows at thirty-one when her husband died. At that time she had the first of her famous revelations. She soon moved to Rome where her rapidly developing talents could have better scope. Birgitta was the aristocrats' saint. She founded and patronized orders of knighthood so the Crusaders could fight more devoutly. From her bishop's-palace residence in Rome she issued her *Revelations*—eight thick volumes in all—setting a new tone of aristocratic piety honored more in the breach than in the observance. Every student in the medieval universities of the time had to study these books. They are well written, in the style of a vivid imaging of events in the life of Christ, but they lack other substance. They were enormously popular in those cataclysmic times. She was also a renowned healer—whether by training or psychic gifts is not clear—with major royal cures to her credit. In any case, she played an important part in providing nursing services in Rome during the plague and developed hospital and nursing institutions and orphanages both in Sweden and in Rome.

The order for women she founded in Sweden soon spread over Europe. The Birgittine houses became major cultural centers for European women of the aristocracy, and there were often monks attached to these convents. Birgitta was also active politically, working for a united Europe. Her political prophecies became the policy guides of popes and kings, and she was also active in promoting royal marriage alliances she thought would be beneficial to the peace of Europe. Known as "Christ's secretary" and the "mystic of the North," she was as sure of herself as St. Hildegard, and rather more powerful. She was a politician and an organizer, rather than an intellectual or a mystic, and played an important role in upgrading the quality of the participation of church and aristocracy in the public life of the times.

Catherine of Siena (1347-1380), Birgitta's contemporary, was both her opposite and her counterpart. Catherine was a "daughter of the people," an illiterate who only learned to write three years before her death and who dictated her correspondence to young noblemen who served as her secretaries. Her father was a dyer and her language retained a working-class flavor, which much enhances the spontaneity of her letters. These letters went to prisoners, queens, popes, soldiers, and village folk in trouble. They can be read today in *Saint Catherine of Siena as Seen in Her Letters* (Scudder, 1905). A nun of extreme asceticism who experienced the stigmata and frequent levitations, toward the end of her life she was continually exhausted by overpowering physio-mystical experiences. At the same time she was known as a joyous, gay person—a characteristic notably absent from many in religious orders. She had, as Evelyn Underhill (1961: 173) says, a national destiny. Her destiny was to reform the papacy, and she did in fact complete the task that Birgitta had set for herself, bringing back the pope from his "captivity" in Avignon. She had remarkably sharp political intuitions. She also, with Birgitta, played a major role in the nursing work in Rome during the plague.

Catherine belongs in the tradition of the prophetess-political reformer of the Middle Ages. She also belongs in a rarer company, that company of saints Underhill writes of who breathe another air and have life from another source.

Nuns were unsung heroines of the plague. While Ziegler (1969) mentions that about half the clerics of Europe died as contrasted with a third of the total population—which means many of them must have died through exposure during nursing—he makes no estimate of nuns who died. Yet, frequent but casual mentions of nuns' activities tell us that most of them left the protection of the convents and went into the community to give heroic service during the plague.

Plans to organize pious women as noncelibate missionaries to the Holy Land were mentioned in contemporary writings from time to time. A Pierre Dubois in the mid-1200s published a political utopia, *De Recuperatione Terra Sactae,* recommending that women should be educated and a select group of them sent to marry Crusaders, princes, and statesmen in the Holy Land and to be models to enslaved Turkish womanhood. Some of these women were also to be trained as medical missionaries (Schomanns, 1911). Some efforts were evidently made in this direction, probably most actively by Birgitta, but the project never came to fruition.

The Counterculture Orders

While both the mainstream Benedictine and independent orders provided to some extent an independent power base from which women could participate in the life of their times, these orders were on the whole supportive of the established institutions of society. The gap between the institutional church, often self-serving and corrupt in the face of human need, and the reality of large social injustices led some dissident young people to form groups that would own no property; members would live a life of service and maintain themselves by begging. These became the mendicant orders. Francis of Assisi (1182-1226) is the best known of those who dreamed of a return to the simple apostolic communities of early Christianity. A rich merchant's son with experience in trade, a soldier in Italy's wars, and launcher of a mediation attempt in Egypt between Moslems and Crusaders, he was by no means as naive and unworldly as he has often been presented. He was not a scholar, however, and probably never read Joachim, though his view of the coming of the post-bureaucratic age coincided very much with Joachim's concept of the Age of the Holy Spirit.

Clare (1193-1253) joined Francis very early in his religious adventures. The story of Clare and Francis[25] is very different from the Heloise-Abelard story. Clare came out of the same rich Assisi merchant background that Francis did, and they had known each other as children. As soon as Francis had "permission" to have brothers living together in this new mendicant style, Clare arrived to be included in the order. Her joining was both dramatic and conventional—she is supposed to have fled her home in the middle of the night with Francis' connivance, but she was also put up very quickly at a local convent to avoid scandal. For respectable women to be wandering mendicants at that time was socially impossible; they could only be perceived as vagabonds, and therefore prostitutes. It was questionable enough for men to be doing so. So Francis and Clare compromised by setting up the sister house of Poor Clares, a residential convent vowed to poverty, from which the Clares helped the brothers in ways traditional for women (cooking, mending, making clothes, etc.). The way of life of the Poor Clares did however represent a radical departure from conventional upper-class monasticism, and a real alternative for women who were questioning the social order. Clare built her institution carefully, wrote her own rule, and fought all her life against efforts both of the church and of some of her own nuns to abolish the commitment to poverty. "The Blessing of St. Clare," in the *Legend and Writings of St. Claire* (Franciscan Institute, 1953), is a beautiful document.

An even more radical departure from the relegous convent was the establishment of the Third Order. This provided a Franciscan identity and commitment for both women and men who continued to live in the world and carry out family responsibilities and normal work roles. While Third Order identification has been important in the lives of many distinguished men, it has been even more important for women because it has enabled them to stay in family roles and yet feel an independent commitment outside the family, particularly to social service. It was probably Clare's insistence that made the Third Order open to women as well as men.

Clare was the senior stateswoman of the entire Franciscan Order, male and female. The more one reads about Francis, the more one realizes that he never made a major decision without consulting Clare. They built the order together, suffered together as the bureaucrats took over, and, most movingly, loved God together. Spiritual friendships between women and men which lead to mutual flowering of personalities are perhaps not so rare in real life, but they do not often appear on the pages of history books. When they do, they are frequently falsified. The Clare-Francis story still rings true.

Clare's letters show that she was in correspondence with women in public life, including the circle of devout queens of Eastern Europe mentioned earlier. These women were all Third Order Franciscans, and turned to her for support for their deviant (for royalty) way of life. Her advice deals entirely with the practical and personal religious life—no political pronouncements or prophecies from Clare's pen. Her order continued to grow, however, when others went into decline.

The Independents: Anchoresses[26] and Pilgrims

The highways and byways of England (and to a lesser extent, Europe) in the Middle Ages were dotted with crudely built shacks in each of which lived a hermit or hermitess. There were highway and bridge hermits, ferry hermits and town hermits. Often the town hermit's shack was in a churchyard or at a frequented intersection, where it would be easy for passers-by to leave a penny or two for the recluse. More rarely the shacks were in isolated places in the forests, or the hermit lived in a lighthouse on the coast. No one knows how many women lived this way, but no village was without at least one anchoress. The village herbalist and healer was very often an anchoress. Other anchoresses supported themselves by odd jobs such as weeding the churchyard or sweeping a busy intersection (Judserand, 1890; Sitwell, 1965). In general, anchoresses seem to have been valued people, and were often given a pension by the local village or a higher authority. One fortunate woman got "a penny a day and a robe a year" from the king (Sitwell, 1965: 31).

All kinds of different women chose this way of life, from the well-educated bourgeois to the women of the poorest classes. Sometimes they chose it in their youth, sometimes later in life, after widowhood. Their motivations were as mixed as their backgrounds, though the common features of living in solitude, celibacy, and simplicity gave an at least superficially religious cast to the hermitesses' lives. They were something of a headache to the church, which felt a need to control holiness—hermitesses could not easily be controlled. The most devout of the anchoresses were no problem. They attended church regularly, had an "authorized" spiritual guide, and were sometimes formally recognized and blessed by the church as women who had chosen a special way of life. Rules were written for them by leading religious writers, though they had no obligation to adopt any rules laid down by others. *The Ancrene Rule (The Rule for Anchoresses)*, a medieval classic in itself, suggests the typical problems that troubled the advisors of hermitesses:

> Gossiping, chattering women at the window of the anchorhold, the sin of possessions and notably of anchoresses keeping cattle, scandalous "hospitality," the advisability of appointing an old, grave confessor (Colledge, 1961: 30).

The anchoress movement became a significant spiritual movement that swept England, evolving as an individualistic counterpart to the Beguine movement that swept Europe. Why the hermitage sufficed for English women when beguinages were needed on the continent is not entirely clear. Perhaps the pressure of the rural-urban transition was not as great at this time for women in England as for those on the continent. It may be that both the *gynaeceum* and the *frèrèche* model were absent in England, so that the beguinage idea never developed. Economic independence and a mystical spirituality certainly characterized both groups.

Mother Julian (1343-1416), an anchoress of the church of St. Julian in Norwich, was one of the finest flowers of mysticism not only of the Middle Ages but of any age. Her *Revelations of Divine Love* (Walsh, 1970) is a distillation of the best of the religious imagination, refined and disciplined by years of reflective thought. Both as a spiritual guide and as a theological statement, it belongs with books better known and more widely used (Sitwell, 1960). Far ahead of her contemporaries, and of most present-day theologians, she developed a conception of God as containing the masculine and the feminine, and used both sets of pronouns in referring to the diety. We do not even know whether she was literate; she may have dictated the book to others. Nevertheless, since she was recognized and widely revered in her own day, there is no doubt of the authorship of the *Revelations*.

How close these independent women could come to the appearance of heresy is vividly revealed in the *Book of Margery Kempe*. Margery, a contemporary of Julian, was a successful merchant wife and mother who in later life chose to live as anchoress and pilgrim. She was a colorful character and extremely outspoken. There were some priests who loved and protected her, and others who kept calling her up for heresy trials. In her own account of her confrontation with the Archbishop of York:

> Then the Archbishop said to her: "I have received very bad reports about you. They tell me you are a very wicked woman." And she replied: "Sir, they tell me that you are a wicked man; and if you are as wicked as people say, you will never get to Heaven unless you change whilst you are here" (Colledge, 1961: 301).

When Margery was not at home struggling with the authorities, she was off on pilgrimages. The pilgrimages to Rome and the Holy Land were another aspect of the lay religious movements of the Middle Ages, and were almost a way of life for some women and men.[27] The line between the pilgrim and the vagabond was often difficult to draw, as was the line between the anchoress and the spiritual fraud who made money out of piety. One of the most delightful discoveries about the Middle Ages is how many interstitial, unclassifiable roles were open to women and what fluidity of movement there was between formal roles in the hierarchies of church and state and these self-appointed village helper roles. There was an active underlife, which had many dangers and drawbacks for women, but gave a variety and color to their existence.

How many women there were who remained quietly in the towns, inwardly Julians of Norwich while outwardly conducting conventional household affairs, we can only guess. The Mabel Rich story hints at the religious underlife for the devout medieval housewife. Mabel Rich is a case of an individual woman capturing a historian's fancy and thus being placed on the pages of history. Who first started quoting the passage about Mabel Rich from the writings of her son St. Edmund I don't know, but she is now famous as the widowed tradeswoman who, when she sent off her two boys to the university,

> packed a hairshirt for each of them, which they were to wear occasionally according to their promise to her, to remind them that they must not look for ease and comfort in life, above all must not yield to sensual pleasures, but must be ready to suffer many little troubles voluntarily, in order that they might be able to resist temptation when severer trials came (Walsh, 1970: 327).

Her educational work with her boys, one of whom became archbishop of Canterbury, is worthy of the "Mother of the Gracchi" tradition. For us, what is most interesting about her is that she apparently lived an anchoritic life in the midst of London.

From what we have seen of the Beguines, the women in religious orders, and the anchoresses, we realize that the Middle Ages supported an astonishing variety of life styles for an astonishingly diverse group of religiously oriented women. Table 9-2, from McDannell's (1975) study of Butler's *Lives of the Saints,* shows how diverse were the occupations and backgrounds of holy women recognized by the church. While the majority of these women belonged to the privileged classes, peasants and laboring women made their way to holiness too (table 9-3). While celibacy was strongly associated with sainthood, it was by no means a prerequisite. Sixty-eight percent of

Table 9-2. Occupations of Religious and Laywomen from
Butler's *Lives of the Saints.*

RELIGIOUS (52.7%)		LAITY (47.2%)	
Occupation	Percentage	Occupation	Percentage
Hermit	12	Hermit	10
Abbess	30	Householder	23
Contemplative	16	Third Order	10
Founder of Order	17	Royalty	6
Mystic	2	Laborer-Servant	8
Nursing	2	Prostitute	4
Teaching	5	Unknown	39
Administration	3		
Missionary	2	TOTAL	100
Writer	2		
Monk	2		
Unknown	5		
TOTAL	100		

Source: McDannell (1975: 7).

Table 9-3. Social Class of Religious and Laywomen from
Butler's *Lives of the Saints.*

Class	Percentage
Royalty	36.2
Nobility	36.2
Middle Class	10.1
Working Class	5.8
Peasant	4.3

Source: McDannell (1975: 7).

the women were single, 17 percent widowed, and 15 percent married.
We may note that the church authorities who compiled lists of holy
people did not record as many women's lives as they might have,
since only 18 percent of the saints in Butler's *Lives* are women.

In addition to the many women in the Middle Ages who lived religiously oriented lives, there are several important groups of secular

women that have not yet been considered. One is the women intellectuals and artists, another is the "ordinary" middle-class and working-class women. We will turn to the scholars and artists next.

Women Intellectuals and Artists

The only place in Christian Europe during the Middle Ages where a woman intellectual could choose a scholar's role and stay both single and secular was Italy. Italy stayed in touch with the active intellectual currents of the Moslem world, and read the "lost classics" of the Greco-Roman tradition, while the rest of Europe was struggling along without that stimulation. Moslem and Christian women scholars worked side by side in Italian universities. There were women professors and doctors in many of the major schools in the Moslem world at this time, in Bagdad, Cairo, Kairouan, Cordova, and Toledo, as well as in Constantinople. We have mentioned that in 1083 Anna Comnena founded a new medical school in Constantinople and taught and practiced medicine, in addition to writing history. Even in conservative Persia, where women were very secluded by the thirteenth century, Princess Gevher Nesibe built a famous medical school and hospital in 1206, and Muneccime was a famous lady astronomer at the Seljuk court (Afetinan, 1962: 24).

Salerno, the site of healing springs famous since Augustan times, had the best medical school in Europe at the beginning of the second millennium. A tradition of medical knowledge supposedly dating from the time of Sister Scholastica and St. Benedict fed directly into the university from Monte Cassino, the Benedictine center. One of the most quietly remarkable women of the Middle Ages lived and taught in the eleventh century at the University of Salerno. She wrote a gynecological-obstetrical treatise that served as the major medical reference work for practitioners in Europe for centuries to come. She also raised a family and coauthored medical books with her husband and son. Her name is Trotula, of the noble family of Ruggiero, and she is known in English nursery rhymes as Dame Trot.

In other cultures she might have emerged eventually as the goddess of healing, but in English culture we find her as the sprightly old lady who adds color and humor to children's tales. Only recently has it been verified that her basic manuscript, which was copied and recopied in whole and in excerpt, repeatedly incorporated piecemeal in other medical works, and ascribed to a variety of authors including "a man named Trotulus," was in fact the work of Trotula (see Hurd-Mead, 1933, for a discussion of this). Its original title was

De Morbis Mulierum et Eorum Cura—The Diseases of Women and Their Cure. Another book of hers on *The Compounding of Medicaments* was as famous and widely used as *De Morbis.* The project undertaken jointly with her husband and son, John Platearius Senior and Junior, was an encyclopedia of medicine.

There was evidently a whole group of women doctors at Salerno at the time, but others remained unnamed. The issue of the practice of medicine by women became an increasingly difficult one as the church, male doctors, and universities united to disqualify and penalize women at every opportunity.[28] An interesting tabulation by Muriel Joy Hughes (1943, app. 1) of all the references to women medical practitioners in public records during this period indicates the extent to which women continued to practice even in the face of stiff penalties. Table 9-4 is a brief summary of her tabulations, which reflects only a fraction of actual women practitioners and does not include Italian women associated with schools of medicine. The

Table 9-4. Women Practitioners Mentioned in Public Records in Europe, 1100-1500.

	France	Italy	Germany
Barbers*	22	—	—
Doctors	18	11	15
Surgeons	5	1	—
Empirics**	22	—	—
Midwives	8	5	1
Nurses	12	—	—

Source: Hughes (1943, app. 1).
  *Barbers practiced surgery and other types of healing.
  **An empiric would be a kind of general practitioner.

large number of women listed for France partly reflects the concentration of professionals of all kinds in France in this period and partly is a function of the kinds of records Hughes was able to find.

By the fourteenth century women in France were forbidden to perform surgery, either as "barbers" or as "surgeons." At this point there would have been many experienced women surgeons in France who had traveled with the Crusaders and performed extensive surgery on the battlefields. Bologna was another center renowned

for its women medical scholars, including the legendary Alessandra
Gilani, who was associated with Mondino, the "father of modern anatomy." Alessandra died at nineteen. The French decree against women
surgeons was probably aimed at those groups of highly trained women
who practiced in both France and Italy.

Jewish women doctors were also much in demand in Italy and
France, particularly with prominent clerics, but it was "doubly illegal" for Jewish women to practice medicine. Jacobina Felicie, a
Jewess native of Florence, was evidently the most popular doctor in
Paris. She was brought to court repeatedly and fined for "illegal practice." (There was no way in which she could be legal.) At each trial
she was defended by highly placed clientele. Other women in her
situation included Clarisse of Rouen, Jeanne Converse, and Clarice
Cambriere. The Jewess Sarah of St. Giles conducted a large private
medical school in Montpellier in the 1320s, providing one answer to
where the women got their training.

The very omnipresence of references to prohibitions against
women practitioners serves to underline the important role they
must have played in the health care of the cities of the Middle Ages.
The frequency with which Jewess doctors are mentioned points to a
tradition of educating women in the Italian Jewish subculture akin to
that already noticed in the Cairo Geniza records in the last chapter.
Germany was less hostile to women than was France, and in 1394 fifteen women were licensed to practice medicine in the city of Frankfurt. In the Netherlands Beguines were practicing medicine very
quietly without being troubled by the authorities.

Medicine for women, except in Italy,[29] was an underlife field.
This makes it very difficult to document the extent of the activity.
Hurd-Mead (1933) notes that the group practice of medicine by
whole families was very common in the Middle Ages, so many
women practiced anonymously within "family clinics." The involvement of queens and princesses with nursing and hospitals has been
mentioned from time to time. How much training these women had
is hard to know, but Beatrice of Savoy ordered the preparation of a
medical encyclopedia which she carried with her when she visited her
daughter queens, and Queen Blanche of Castile never traveled without a well-equipped medical kit. She didn't trust local doctors.

Standards of medicine began to decline in the 1500s, and accusations of witchcraft contributed to this general decline and demoral-
ization of the profession. Legal codes in all societies have provided
for the punishment of doctors for malpractice when this can be
demonstrated. Usually there are some safeguards for the doctors, but

in the Middle Ages all safeguards disappeared. "No medical faculty of the sixteenth century would defend any of its pupils against persecutions for heresy" (Hurd-Mead, 1933: 336). Women were hit harder than men, but sex was no guarantee of safety. This tended to push medicine underground, and thus increased the involvement of women in it at the very time that they were also being punished the most heavily for that involvement. The fact that there were so many able women available to carry on practice under all these constraints is due to the apprentice tradition among surgeons, doctors, herbalists, and midwives, which meant that skills were being passed on from generation to generation no matter what was happening in the schools and universities. Hurd-Mead (1933) suggests that the non-school medical knowledge was often superior to that being taught in the schools, since schoolmen were increasingly divorcing themselves from reality. Women had the advantage of being closer to their patients than the schoolmen were, and therefore closer to the medical realities they were dealing with. Nevertheless, this kind of separation left the women in the end very vulnerable to being pushed out of medical practice entirely when the medical sector finally modernized.

While some mother-daughter combinations were found in medicine, in law there seem to have been rather father-daughter combinations. At the University of Bologna, where women shone in law, in the 1300s Novella d'Andrea frequently took her father's place and lectured on canon law. Her predecessor Bettina Gozzadini is described as one of the greats in the field.

In general, women's scholarly and scientific identity has been lost to the men they worked with, no matter how outstanding their work. Thus Tycho Brahe's sister may have been one of the great astronomers of her time, but we will never know about it. She worked side by side with her brother, yet it is only his work we hear of (Mozans, 1913). The same "group practice" in medicine that hid the roles of women doctors from society obtains not only for scholarly and scientific work, but also for artistic work. The Van Eycks' sister Margaretha sacrificed her own artistic fame by painting portions of her brothers' pictures (Waters, 1904). No one knows for sure how much that came out of the Van Eyck studios was Margaretha's.

One remarkable exception to the equivocal underlife existence of women scholars and artists is Christine de Pisan, Italian-born poet, novelist, historian, and writer on contemporary national and international affairs.[30] She grew up at the French court, where her father

Table 9-5

Chronological Table of Works of Christine de Pisan

Date	Work	Description	Code
1389	Triggering Event: Death of husband, requiring de Pisan to support her family		----
1390	First prize-winning ballad		RO/C
1390-99	Cent Ballades	Songs of widowhood, in praise of marriage, love songs	RO/C
1390s	Dits Moraus	Letters of instruction for son	ED
1396	Events: Children leave home; daughter becomes nun at Poissy, son becomes aide in a ducal house		----
1399	Epistre au Dieu d'amour	Attack on Ovid, Roman de la Rose, Jean de Meung, polemics, satire	W PROB
1400	Le Dit du Poissy	Rural pastorale; outing to convent of Poissy, country-side, debate on love	RO/C
1401	Epitre d'Othea à Hector	Historical romance drawing on many sources	RO/H
1401	Debat des Deux Amants	Courtly romance, contemporary and historical	RO/H
1402	Epistre sur le Roman de la Rose	Polemics on woman question	W PROB
1402	Dit de la Rose	"Court of Love," held for serious discussion of woman question	W PO/RO
1403	Chemin de Long Etude	Historical allegory modeled on Dante, uses Cumean Sibyl instead of Vergil	H/PH
1403	Oroison à Nostre Dame	Religious poetry	RE
1403	Dit de la Pastoure	Pastorale—a love story	RO/C
1404	Mutacion de Fortune	Philosophical history of humanity's ups and downs	H/PH
1404	Fais et Bonnes Moeurs de Charles V	Court-commissioned life of King Charles V	H/PO

Date	Work	Description	Code
1404	Livre des Trois Judgments	"Problem" love stories	RO/C
1404	Livre du Duc des Vrais Amans	Courtly romance, contemporary	RO/C
1405	Le Cité des Dames	History of women	W/H
1405	Le Livre des Trois Vertus	Advice to women on public and private affairs	W ED
1406	Lavision Christine	Historical allegory, also a history of France	H/PH
1406	Epistre à Isabeau	Political epistle to the queen about problems of the times	H/M/PO
1407	Le Corps de Policie	Essay on policy, international law	H/M/PO
1409	Livre des Faits d'Armes	Military history, study of military strategy, international law, translations of Vegetius, Frontinius, Valerius Maximus, Honore Bonet, anonymous authors; also original work by Christine	H/M/PO
1409	Sept Pseaulmes Allégories	Religious meditations	RE
1410	Lamentacions sur les Maux de la Guerre Civile	Commentary on political, civil strife in France	H/M/PO
1412–14	Livre de la Paix	Book on nature of state, political duties of princes, need for wisdom, peaceableness	PO/ED
1416	Epistre de Prison de Vie Humaine	Reflections or human conditions in a troubled society	PO/ED
1417–18	Event: Christine leaves Paris, now in acute state of civil conflict, for convent at Poissy		----
1420s	Heures de Contemplation de la Passion	Religious meditations	RE
1429	Poem to Joan of Arc after her victory	Christine probably died shortly after writing this poem	RE

Code: *RO/C* = Romance, Contemporary; *RO/H* = Romance, Historical, *ED* = Education. General; *W PO/RO* = Women, Political Romance; *W PROB* = Women, Problems; *W/H* = Women, History; *W ED* = Women, Education; *H/PH* = History, Allegory, Philosophy; *H/PO* = History, Political; *H/M/PO* = History, Military, International Law, Politics, Public Affairs; *PO/ED* = Political and Moral Education; *RE* = Religion.

Table 9-6

Types of Scholarly and Literary Publications, by Years, of Christine de Pisan

Type	Code	Years	Total
Romance, Contemporary	RO/C	1390, 1390-99, 1400, 1403, 1404, 1404	6
Romance, Historical	RO/H	1401, 1401	2
Education, General	ED	1390 s	1
Women, Political Romance	W PO/RO	1402	1
Women, Problems	W PROB	1399, 1402	2
Women, History	W HIST	1405	1
Women, Education	W/ED	1405	1
History, Allegory, Philosophy	H/PH	1403, 1404, 1406	3
History, Political	H/PO	1404	1
History, Military, International, Law Politics, Public Affairs	H/M/PO	1406, 1407, 1409, 1410	4
Political and Moral	PO/ED	1412-14, 1416	2
Religion	RE	1403, 1409, 1402, 1429	4
		TOTAL.	28

was a distinguished scholar. Through a series of misfortunes she was left widowed with three small children and a mother to support after the death of the men of her family and of the king who had been their patron. In an exceedingly hostile environment, with the men of the court trying to seize what properties still remained to her, she managed to outwit the conspirators and to write poetry successfully for money. Almost overnight she became the most popular literary figure in France.

It is almost hard to believe in Christine de Pisan. She stands head and shoulders above many others of her time in breadth of concerns and range of scholarship. Was she really the author of the works that carried her name? As long as she wrote ballads and romances she was "believable," and universally admired. When she began turning out historical studies and serious works on the major issues of the day, rumors began circulating that her manuscripts were really written by clerics. Scholars are satisfied today that all twenty-eight works listed in table 9-5 are hers. Some of her works were so popular that more copies exist of them than of any other writings of the 1400s. They were very popular in England too, so we can read most of her work in Middle English as well as in medieval French.

A study of tables 9-5 and 9-6 shows that she continued turning out her best-selling romances after beginning her serious work. Her major concerns were 1) the economic plight of widows and the need for education for all women, 2) the political problems of France, 3) the larger questions of historical destiny, and 4) problems of military strategy and international law. Probably attuned to these kinds of questions by her environment at court and her father's tutoring as a child, she was able to utilize the libraries of the palace, the library of the University of Paris (its chancellor, Jean Gershon, was her good friend), and the books her father left her in her explorations of history and contemporary issues. She evidently moved in the kind of overlife spaces usually open only to royal women, and her life and work were a product of unusual opportunities combined with unusual ability.

She is considered by specialists in French literature the best of the "minor writers" of the period. To me she seems something more than that. What is called for is a study of her historical, allegorical, and political works in the context of both the agonizing cross-currents of the Hundred Years War, the French Civil War, the

Figure 9-7. *Christine de Pisan,* La Cité des Dames.

proliferating workers' riots, and the declining position of women as reflected in the activities of the church and the trade guilds. Having grown up in a milieu that separated her completely from the Beguine movement and from the major convent-based intellectual centers, she was nevertheless a kind of distillation in her own person of the women's movement of the Middle Ages. Willard (in Morewedge, 1975) is, I think, right in saying that she was not a feminist, but she had a strong sense of the nature of the social and economic problems that faced women. She not only argued that they should be better educated, she spoke (in the *Livres des Trois Vertus*) to the differing educational needs of princesses, managers of large estates, wives of merchants and artisans in the city, and farmers' wives in the country. Her *City of Women* was the forerunner of many histories of women, the first to be written by a woman. She addressed questions of international relations long before Erasmus. In studying military strategy to see where the destructive potentials of war could be minimized, she anticipated much later approaches.

Christine accepted the court conventions of her environment and was willing to spend a lot of her time both living and writing about a courtly existence that was already considered very old fashioned. When she did get roused about social issues, she dressed her arguments in heavy historical allegories that she knew her audience would love. I suspect that she liked court life, or she could not have written so charmingly about it. Her "courts of love," however, were truly egalitarian, and she reserved most of her biting satire for medieval male chauvinists who placed women on phony pedestals. What she thought in the last years of her life as she watched the crumbling of the society she had loved, we do not know. She stopped political writing and turned toward a more contemplative life, but we don't know how she conceived of her own choice in relation to her times. Her retirement to a convent may have been a conventional choice such as many older women made. But perhaps not. Her ballad celebrating Joan of Arc, written after years of convent silence, tells us she could still hear the world.

Working Life for Women

The Manor

Because of the great diversity of life styles in the Middle Ages it is very difficult to give a coherent account of the physical and social spaces that women moved in as they lived and worked. The manor houses, the homes of the stewards, *maires,* squires, and other gentry below the lords of the castles in the feudal hierarchy in England and on the continent, were an important feature of village life in a society where most people lived in villages. I will therefore begin by describing the life of women in the manor houses.[31] The mistress of the manor worked very hard indeed. She supervised a considerable domestic work force, including many women laborers, in the care of domestic animals and poultry, production of butter and cheese, butchering of livestock for table and market, care of the kitchen garden, food preparation and preservation, spinning, weaving, and sewing. (Originally the word *spinster* referred to female spinners. Later it came to mean an unmarried woman.) Besides these activities she supervised the marketing of everything produced over and above family needs and oversaw storage in the manor warehouses. She was expected to run a school for the village children, teach domestic skills to the dozen or so young women who boarded at the manor, give some supervision to the training of the young men boarders also, and provide nursing and other helping services to the peasants and cottagers associated with the estate. In addition to all of the above, she was responsible for feeding the entire household—which in an average manor house could run between fifteen and thirty people, and in a castle to nearly a hundred. As hostess,

Figure 9-8. *Woman Shearing Sheep, Middle Ages.*

she also had to entertain all guests. When her husband was away at wars or in the city or at court on business, which could be for long periods of time, she had to be able to manage the entire estate, supervising agricultural field work and handling finances. The economic productivity of these estates, as well as the social welfare of the villagers, depended to a considerable extent on the skills of the lady of the manor.

Enterprising women could expand the domestic workshops of the manor houses beyond the usual dozen women and girls. In the towns of northern Europe these manor house ladies sometimes supervised a number of workrooms where women worked at making silk and wool cloth. Such supervision usually entailed maintaining dormitories

Figure 9-9. *Women Preparing Flax Stalks, 16th Century.*

where women "of all conditions and ages" could live, though occasionally workers would come in by the day. These establishments were in fact preindustrial factories (Lacroix, 1926: 667).

The young girls who worked in the manor house workshops married the peasant boys who worked in the fields, and after marriage they carried on a modest replica of the manor house activities at home. Women were usually needed in the fields alongside of husbands at plowing and harvest time, and worked even longer hours than the manor house ladies, at harder manual labor. The girls who did not make it to the manor house for education were the children of cottagers—the squatters who were available for day labor and tried to grow enough food for subsistence from common land in the village. The life of a cottager's wife was very hard indeed, for she did the heaviest of outdoor work as a day laborer with her husband, taking her children along to help in the fields. Nevertheless, she usually had her own garden and was "muscular and well-nourished"; her babies were healthy, and she was of the class of women that the gentry used for wetnurses for their own babies (Clark, 1919: 58). There were small children everywhere in the rural world, and all but the babies were put to tasks of some kind near their mothers.

The work was so physically exhausting that a woman's life expectancy at birth was not much beyond twenty-five years, and shorter than male life expectancy. One effect of the move from the country to the city was the lengthening of the life expectancy of women as compared to men (Herlihy, 1975: 1-22). Bad as city life was, it was easier than rural life for women.

For widows, rural life was hardest of all. They were hemmed in on all sides by feudal obligations that they had to meet if they were to retain their rights to farm, obligations which were hard enough for a husband-wife team to meet. Typical is this description of a village woman in the manor of Frocestor, (1265-1267):

Margery, the widow, holds half a virgate of land which contains 24 acres and she renders 3s. every year at two terms, 12d. at Christmas and 2s.

at Michaelmas. And from Michaelmas to the Feast of St Peter in Chains she must plow half an acre every week, and one day's plowing is worth 3d. And from the Feast of St John the Baptist until August she must perform manual service 3 days every week and the day is worth three farthings. The fourth day she carries on her back to Gloucester or elsewhere at the bailiff's will and that is worth three-halfpence. She shall mow the lord's meadow for at least 4 days and the day is worth 1½d., which is counted as manual service estimated above at three farthings. And she must lift the lord's hay for at least 4 days at her expense, this not being counted as a task, and it is worth altogether 3d. She shall weed 2 days apart from the work due which is worth three-halfpence. And from the Feast of St Peter in Chains until Michaelmas she must perform manual service with a man 5 days a week and the day is worth three-halfpence.

And every second week during the same period she must perform carrying service for one day, this being counted as one day's task.

And furthermore she performs 8 boon works with a man in autumn which is worth altogether 12d. And she gives 2s. 2¼d. for aid. She performs all the untaxed customs [for king and manorial lord]. And she performs a harvest boon work in autumn fed by the master which is worth, apart from the food, a halfpenny. And she must plow one day, fed by the master with half a plow. And she shall give eggs at Easter at will (G. Duby, in O'Faolain and Martines, 1973: 160-161).

Figure 9-10. *Domestic Workshops, Early 15th Century.*
a) Spinning and weaving; b) clothmaking.

In addition to the married women, widows, and young unmarrieds of the villages of Europe, there was another category of partnered women householders. These were the "priestesses," "the concubines who lived with the clergy, . . . a recognized class, notorious for their impertinence" (Reich, 1908: 196), that we already noted in the previous chapter. They continued their much-maligned and economically necessary partnerships through the Middle Ages.

The actual life situation for most couples was a more equal partnership than appears on the surface. Essentially, the woman and the man each had her or his own productive labor in or outside the home and was self-supporting, with both of them contributing resources to a common pool for the care of their children. While some women were associated with their husbands in the latter's enterprises, the women either had additional ones of their own, or contributed to the common enterprise in a way that was distinctive enough that they had independent funds at their own disposal. One of the things Italian peasant women did for money was to sell their hair to the rich ladies of the town (Coulton, 1955: 322). In England, rural women did everything from shearing sheep, to thatching roofs and mixing mortar for village building projects, to whipping dogs out of the church (Clark, 1919: 60-63).

The fact that descent was often traced through women[32] is another evidence of her status. "Even where the exclusion of women continued in theory, it was soon subject in practice to many exceptions" (Bloch, 1961: 201). Whatever rights and properties could be passed on to sons could also be passed on to daughters. The problem of the feudal military obligations attached to land holdings was met by women paying a substitute or sending a male relative. The widespread administration of land by women noted in the early Middle Ages continued.

The great houses of lords and merchants in the cities bore some resemblance to the rural manor house, minus agricultural activities and open spaces. Domestic crafts remained important, often with materials brought in from country estates. The activities of the ladies of the urban manors varied in the extent to which they involved supervision of women's workshops, assisting their husbands in merchandising and keeping accounts, or developing businesses of their own.

One aspect of women's economic roles in the Middle Ages that is easily overlooked is their disposition of property in wills. Wills, as Rosenthal (1972: 17) points out, were a great leveling device between the sexes. The endowment of a benefice enabled a woman to create a new chapel complete with attending clerics who would both "purchase paradise" for herself and her forbears, and provide community services she thought desirable. Interestingly, the prayers so purchased were always for a woman's own parents and forebears, never for those of her husband, nor for their children who in law belonged more to her husband than to herself. An analysis of bequests of spouses shows that 80 percent of all bequests were made independently by husbands and wives, and only 20 percent jointly. Women's wills had a different character than men's. They were longer and more detailed. They gave more attention to alms for the poor, relief of prisoners, dowries for the marriage of poor virtuous girls, and support for anchorites and hermits. It also appears that women were more apt to have libraries than men were, since much attention is given to the details of distribution of women's books in their wills (Rosenthal, 1972: 118).

In short, we see upper-class women controlling the distribution of substantial amounts of capital through their wills, as well as in their daily lives. The organization of the daily work routine was such that women, whether urban or rural, usually had large numbers of workers and servants of both sexes living with them. Tenement housing, providing the dark one-room apartments for city workers, came in the later Middle Ages (Mumford, 1961: 284). When it did develop, it was an expression of a new demand for privacy that did not exist in early European urbanism. Many writers (Thrupp, 1962: 130ff.; Aries, 1962: 391-394; Mumford, 1961: 286) describe a non-family, public style of living as persisting well into the 1600s. People rolled out mats and slept at night wherever they could, preferably in the house of a patron or employer, sometimes in the patron's own bedroom.

As we shall see in looking at guild organization, where there were a number of workers associated with a workshop, there were often dormitories adjacent to the workshop. It is said that Michelangelo

> on occasion slept with his workmen, four to a bed. As late as the seventeenth century, maidservants often slept in trundle beds (rolled under the big bed by day) at the foot of that of their masters and mistresses (Mumford, 1961: 286).

The Guilds

The guild structure of medieval society is one of the most romanticized and least understood aspects of medieval life, in particular in regard to the role of women. There is a persistent myth that women were equal with men in the original guilds, and were gradually pushed out by industrialization. To trace what really happened, we will review the functions of guilds at different stages. The antecedents of guilds in antiquity and their development in medieval times out of religiously-based mutual aid associations of workers in the same trade have already been mentioned. In the early stages, the emphasis was on the family units of association members, so there was good reason for an active participation of women. The brethren and the sistren helped each other's families in marriage, sickness, and death.

The guilds merchant, which were first founded in the late 1100s and continued to flourish for several centuries, were the first associations that brought the trading aspect of craft production into focus. The producers had to sell what they made. People from all kinds of crafts belonged to these early guilds merchant, but with expansion of demand for every kind of product, there was a later differentiation by craft, leading to the development of the craft guilds.

What was the status of women in the guilds merchant? They had membership, as they did in the old mutual aid associations, but they were not members on the same basis as were male artisans. Gross (1890: 66) points out that women, monks, and heads of religious houses were excluded within the guilds from "burgess-ship," as were foreign merchants who received trading privileges in a town through guild membership. In other words, women and clerics were treated as foreigners. They had no voting rights in town affairs, only trading rights. The guilds merchant were for a time so closely linked to local government structures that guild membership created the basis for civic rights. While it was important for women to have trading rights since they were often business partners to their husbands, voting could be taken care of by the head of the household. When widows were heads of households, we find from time to time in the coming centuries that they exercised burgess rights, but on the whole this was rare. When a legal issue was made of it, they were often disqualified. It is probable, though not certain, that the occasional references to women serving on town councils are references to widows.

When craft guilds began developing their own separate organizations women continued to be important in them, both as business partners and workshop helpers. However, the nature of their contribution to the family enterprise gave them a differentiated status in the craft guilds, as it had in the guilds merchant, and the frequent references to the sistren and the brethren have been misinterpreted in regard to the status of women. For example, in a widely quoted passage from her book on English guilds, Toulmin Smith says,

> scarcely five out of 500 were not formed equally of men and women.
> . . . Even where the affairs were managed by a company of priests,
> women were admitted as lay members, and they had many of the same
> duties and claims upon the gilds as men (in Hill, 1896: 47).

But it is clear from a careful reading of specific references to guild operations (Clark, 1919; Pinchbeck, 1930; Renard, 1968; Staley, 1967; Hauser, 1927) that it was the exception for women in the mixed guilds to be trained as apprentices. The fact that they were generally excluded from train-ing for mastery of craft meant that unless as wives they were the business partners of guilds-men their status was highly marginal, and they were allot-ted the more tedious and less skilled tasks. We do find that in the all-women guilds, of which there were fifteen in Paris at the end of the thirteenth century—compared to eighty men's guilds (Renard, 1968: 20)—women were regularly appren-ticed and could go through the system to become guild masters (mistresses). These all-women guilds were generally in the silk, embroidery, millinery, and spe-cial garment trades. The propor-tion of all-women's guilds may have been somewhat higher in France than in England. It is also possible that women were taken as full apprentices more

Figure 9-11. *Woman Apprentice Goldsmith.*

often in the mixed guilds in France than in England. Yet even they were kept as underpaid journeymen (women) and kept from full master status, often by town law, since this status involved burgess rights and military duty (Renard, 1968: 20, 21).[33]

In the ideal-typical fourteenth century craft guild workshop, the guild master and his wife, in village or town, lived in a modest house with workshop attached. There was dormitory space for the live-in apprentices and journeymen, and for the servant girls who helped the mistresses with domestic tasks so that she could be free to help in the shop, where she sold the workshop products over the counter to customers, helped in various ways in the production process itself, and supervised the training of young apprentices in certain parts of the production process. They all lived and ate together as a family. The children of the master began helping in the shop by the time

Figure 9-12a. *Woman Laboratory Assistant, 15th Century.*

Figure 9-12b. *Woman Potter at Kick Wheel, 15th Century.*

they were four years old, and the daughters frequently grew up to marry one of the journeymen, thus eventually becoming wives of guild masters and performing functions similar to those of their mothers. The interpenetration of domestic and workshop roles created considerable fluidity in the patterning of work roles for wife and husband, though the work of the wife was less specialized. There was also an accompanying fluidity in domestic roles. Clark, in describing the situation in the 1600s, gave a description that would be more applicable for the 1200s to 1400s:

> If women were upon the whole more actively engaged in industrial work
> . . . men were much more occupied with domestic affairs. . . . Men in all
> classes gave time and care to the education of their children, and the
> young unmarried men who generally occupied positions as apprentices
> and servants were partly employed over domestic work. . . . a consider-
> able proportion of [domestic work] fell to the share of men (1919: 5).

As the workshop was home for all its members, the guild was the extended family. Guild members helped one another build their houses, and guilds provided dowries for members' daughters who married or entered a convent, and sometimes for girl apprentices. Cultural and social life was centered in the guilds, and the larger ones ran schools for the children of members.[34] Apprenticeship for girls in a mixed guild apparently often meant apprenticeship to a guild master's wife, with privileges of guild membership accompanying the girl's position in the household. Such a young woman, if she married out of the guild, would lose her membership rights. If the wife of a guild master was widowed, she could keep her guild membership if she continued to run the work- shop as a widow, or if she re- married within the guild, but not if she remarried out of the guild. Confirmation of the fact that few widows who ran guild workshops were trained in the craft is found in the frequent references to their dependence on (sometimes unscrupulous) journeymen to continue the business, and in records of law- suits against widows who took in apprentices but were unable to train them.

I believe that the exclusion of the female from the skill train- ing of the guild was responsible for her continued marginal sta- tus. She was auxiliary, if indis- pensable, help to the men of her family in the production pro- cess. The primacy of her

Figure 9-13. *The Carpenter and His Family, A.D. 1500.*

childbearing and home maintenance roles contributed to the auxil- iary nature of her participation in the workshop. This primacy of do- mestic roles was probably minimal in the small workshop, as Clark (1919) suggests. But the idealized picture of complete equality of husband and wife in the home workshop does not stand up well under scrutiny. No matter how helpful she was, the differences in their training kept showing up. In terms of salary, Hauser (1927: 158-160) reports that in rural workshops in fourteenth century

France women's wages were set at three-quarters of the men's wages. By the fifteenth century it was one-half, and by the sixteenth century still less. Hauser was not able to obtain information on wages in urban workshops, but presumed that the same differentials applied there.

From Guild to Factory, and the Long Walk to Work

It was with the expansion of workshop size with increased urbanization that women's marginality became serious. As long as every daughter and female domestic apprentice could anticipate some day being a master's wife, the apprenticeship-journeyman-master system did not work so much against women. The journeyman, who as the name implies traveled around the country to gain additional skills by working in the workshops of other masters, married a guild girl when he was ready to become a master. But over time workshops grew larger. Not only were large numbers of apprentices taken in who stayed on permanently as semiskilled journeymen because they could not accumulate the resources to open their own workshops, but also large numbers of unskilled workers were hired for manual tasks and were never brought into the guild system at all. Powerful trade guilds emerged that employed thousands of laborers who had absolutely no rights as workers. This was particularly true in the cloth industry, which operated large factories in Europe well before the industrial era. The proletariat of the textile guilds were the "blue-nails," the mass of workers who were employed in the manual labor of handling the heavy pieces of cloth ranging from sixty-five to one hundred feet in length, whose fingernails turned blue from the dye-stuffs (Delort, 1973: 336).

This urban proletariat of dependent, unprotected workers began multiplying in the fourteenth century. The idyllic home workshop where workers of every status and sex lived as a family became rarer and rarer. Journeymen, who in an earlier era had stayed bachelor until they could become masters, now were "allowed" to marry, thus acknowledging the permanency of their journeyman status. The women of the artisan class who married the journeymen, and the women of the proletariat who married the blue-nails—and the women who did not marry at all—formed a great body of female laborers in the towns and cities of the Middle Ages. They went out each morning from their one-room tenement apartments as these sprang up in Italy, in Flanders, in Paris, and in London, and they walked to the huge textile workshops built first in the middle of the towns, then on the outskirts when space came to be at a premium. Sometimes it was a long walk to work for the women, just as it was for the men.

Workers lived as near the guild warehouses and factories as they could. Women laborers brought their small children to work with them, giving them tasks that speeded up the mother's productivity. Babies were a problem. Given opiates to keep them quiet, they could be carried to work. Another solution was to give them for the first couple of years to a "baby farmer" who lived outside the town. The mortality rate was high for babies on baby farms, especially for the poorer women's babies since they could pay so little for their keep. Miserable as baby farms were, laboring women had few alternatives. The baby farms were the medieval equivalent of the day care centers, a twenty-four hour version. Another alternative was infanticide, and rates of infanticide continued high throughout the Middle Ages.[35] Children who survived to the age of five or six went out to work on their own or with their mothers.

Because women worked together in large groups in the textile towns, they developed a culture of their own. While the standard of living was low and the work hard, we must remember Herlihy's (1975) point about the lengthening life expectancy for urban women. This Florentine working girl's song (from Staley, 1967: 235) suggests that women had their own ways of controlling an excessive pace of work:

> Monday — Mondayish
> Tuesday — nobody works
> Wednesday — take up the distaff
> Thursday — lay it down again
> Friday — willy-nilly
> Saturday — let us wash our heads
> Sunday — well, that's the festa!

Women with entrepreneurial ability could make fortunes as wine merchants and innkeepers. One woman made a fortune coming into the city every day to sell cabbages from her farm. By order of the city fathers of Florence at her death, the bells of four market churches rang for her from All Saints' Day to Ash Wednesday, and she was buried with pomp in the bishop's tomb (Staley, 1967: 458).

What proportion of the total population lived in towns and cities in the fourteenth century? Estimates range from one-fourth to one-third of the population for England, Italy, France, and Flanders (Clough, 1951; Herlihy, 1975: 1-22). This means that very substantial numbers of women led the kind of working life just described, though often in smaller workshops. Of those who lived in towns and cities, the great majority went out to work each day much as their town and city sisters of the twentieth century do. The proportion who worked by their husbands' sides in home workshops must have been very small. Even in the case of the small village workshop, it was not necessarily adjacent to the house.

The lot of women who were skilled artisans was undeniably easier, since they could employ unskilled women to do their domestic work. There was a wide range of occupations available to the skilled working woman of the Middle Ages. Poll-tax returns, one source of information about working women, give the following picture for Oxford in 1380:

> 37 spinsters, 11 shapesters (tailors), 9 tapsters (innkeepers), 3 sutrices (shoemakers), 3 hucksters, 5 washerwomen, (and also) butchers, brewers, chandlers, ironmongers, netmakers and kepsters (woolcombers); also 148 women domestics (Clark, 1919: 155).

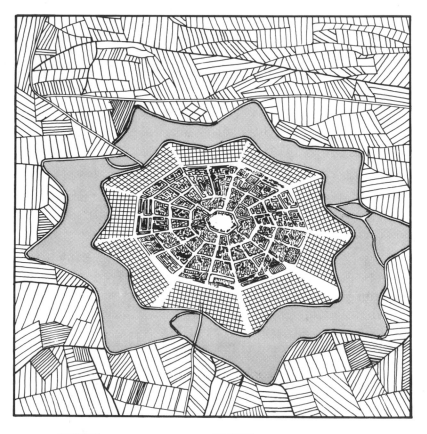

 URBAN    AGRICULTURAL

Figure 9-14. *Drawing of Aerial View of Palma Nova, Italy.*

Figure 9-15. *Peasant Pushing His Wife to Work.*

On the Continent:

> From 1320 to 1500 in Frankfurt 65 lines of work are listed in which only women workers appeared, seventeen in which they predominated, 38 in which men and women were equal, and 81 in which men dominated. In other words, there were no fewer than 201 occupations in which women were engaged (Norrenburg, quoted in McDonnell, 1969: 85).

Women traders also had a broad field of operations. A citizen freeholders' list in London in the early 1400s includes 771 men and 111 women; of the women the majority were single, conducting independent businesses; some were married, with their own business; and some were widows (Thrupp, 1962: 125). English law very specifically protected the rights of married (*femme couverte*) as well as single women to do business and go to law on their own account (Cleveland, 1896: 69-80).

Eileen Power and M. M. Postan (1933) give a lively picture of the women overseas traders of Bristol in the mid 1400s.[36] Seven major women merchants and eight minor women shippers are mentioned, also women merchants operating from Leyden and Bordeaux. Some of them were clearly pillars of the town and subsidizers of major city enterprises. The duchess of York, the mother of Edward IV, is also mentioned as a large-scale overseas trader. Since all this comes from the account of only one town, a complete study of the women merchants of England and the Continent would be a substantial volume.

Cities produced two very different, yet complementary, solutions to survival problems on the part of women. The first was the invention of the beguinages; the second solution was vagabondage. Much has been written about the *vagantes,* the wandering scholars so well described by Helen Waddell (1927). The book about vagabond women has yet to be written. Undoubtedly there are many tales to uncover about the bands of women who traveled about taking in country fairs and festivals of every kind; who trailed around after the king's court (which moved often in those days), always available as entertainers for the king and queen and their courtiers; who sometimes joined the Crusades either on their own or in a knight's party. In addition to all-women bands, many shifting man-woman partnerships were formed as people traveled the court and market routes. Women often teamed up with the *vagantes* (who were really unemployed clerics). Because they had to support themselves, they always showed up on important public occasions, where their services could be required in various ways:

Figure 9-16. *Woman Entertainer, Gothic.*

> In the assembling of the Imperial diet at Frankfurt in 1394 the city was visited by 800 itinerant women, temporarily increasing the adult female population by 25 percent; and at the Church Councils of Constance and Basle their number is said to have been about double this. In such cases these vagabond women had to be organized and controlled. At Basle this duty devolved on the Duke of Saxony. . . . he had the bright idea of taking a census of them, but had to give it up when halfway through as too difficult a task (Wieth-Knudsen, 1928: 223-224).

In the wars between France and England we meet with the vagabond women by the hundreds in the baggage trains of the armies, and they were put in the charge of special bailiffs. The women's bailiff soon became a regular appointment in the armies of the time (Wieth-Knudsen, 1928: 223-224). In military campaigns of any kind it was standard to have one or two thousand women along. Some were regular companions of the soldiers, but many were independent vagabond women. These are described as tough, hardworking women who toiled endlessly at fetching and carrying on the battlefield, at feeding the troops, and nursing the sick. They never refused a chore, were generally self-disciplined and modest, and underneath their toughness, gentle (Ploss, 1964). Probably this women's army corps was not too different in the Middle Ages from the host of women who were along on Xenophon's "March of the 10,000" in antiquity, and they were probably just as much taken for granted.

Other vagabond women worked as laborers in a variety of temporary special-purpose guilds that were formed around a specific undertaking rather than around a craft. Among such special-purpose guilds that took in women workers were cathedral-building guilds and the groups that contracted for trading voyages (Kropotkin, 1972: 153-154).

A smaller class of independent women lived more settled lives and had their own houses in the towns and cities, living under the legal protection (as well as regulation) of the town council. They are frequently referred to in medieval writings as "daughters of joy," and attitudes to them were ambivalent throughout the Middle Ages. The best organized of the residential groups were in effect entertainment guilds, and like all guilds had strict regulations to control the competition. In some towns, as, for example, Geneva and Nuremberg, they had an elected woman leader who represented their interests to the town council (Ploss, 1964: 100). They were always on the lookout for illegal competition, including runaway Beguines who might be looking for work. Like the entertainers of Mediterranean lands described in earlier chapters, they had status and (intermittent) respect in the community and were invited to all public functions of freemen and town councils. When royalty came to town the council sometimes provided the women entertainers with new clothes; one lucky band all got velvet dresses when Emperor Siegmund visited in 1435 (Ploss, 1964: 98). And

> as late as 1516 it was the custom in Zürich for the mayor, the sheriff and the women of the town to dine with the foreign ambassadors who visited the place (Wieth-Knudsen, 1928: 227).

At the French court they were part of the Court of Ribalds. This participation was abolished by a puritanical king, but the ladies soon returned, organized under a new court-appointed officer, the *"dame des filles de joie suivant la cour"* (lady of the daughters of joy following the court). In 1535 Olive Sainte was paid ninety pounds by King

Francis for expenses for herself and the women court followers
(Lacroix, 1926: 733-746). Periodically kings issued stern orders to
tone down the "joy." Orders to wear special clothes, or to wear
special markings on their clothes, were frequently received by these
women. This was part of the branding process that consistently has
dogged the activities of working women who render sexual services.
They were also repeatedly forbidden to wear jewelry and fine
clothes, although this was obviously part of their professional equipment. At worst, very punitive laws were enforced against them, and
for the slightest offenses they were jailed or fined. Typically, it was
the poor among the daughters of joy who suffered the sharp edge
of the law, and sentences such as the following were not infrequently imposed by the courts: hanging, being buried alive, or drowning
by being placed in a cage and lowered into the river. Court records
indicate such sentences were passed because of women's "demerits"
(Lacroix, 1926: 824-831). Those who were only pilloried were
lucky.

Life was dangerous and unpredictable for the lower orders of
daughters of joy, and even for the wealthy and successful ones, life
was not easy. Generally these women were segregated, taxed, and
forced into city-supervised areas. Most appalling, there was a tendency to try to force all unpartnered women into these segregated
houses. A little after this period, in 1493, the following ordinance
was passed in Metz: "All married women living apart from their husbands and girls of evil life shall go to the brothels." Under those circumstances it was risky to leave one's husband, risky to be single,
and risky even to be a widow (Lacroix, 1926: 861). The distinction
between brothel and prison becomes blurred by statutes like this
one: "If any girl has committed a fault and would continue to do
evil," city officials shall commit her to the brothel (Lacroix, 1926:
878).

A problem that we shall meet increasingly from the Middle Ages
on is the habit of the authorities and the middle and upper classes
to treat all poverty-level working women as prostitutes. François
Villon, the vagabond scholar-poet who was hanged in the fifteenth
century after a colorful life as an outlaw, wrote a famous poem to
the women of his circle. Who were they? Not professional daughters
of joy at all, but poor working women—helmet makers, glove makers,
cobblers, sausage makers, rug makers, tapestry makers, hood makers,
and spur makers (Lacroix, 1926: 997-998). A hardy lot, and certainly independent women.

Among the daughters of joy we find poets and ballad makers. The ancient Germanic bardic tradition flowered in delightful and much admired lyric poetry by women in the 1200s and 1300s (Wienhold, 1882).

The word prostitute, used both by Wieth-Knudsen (1928) and by Ploss (1964) to describe these women, is as usual an oversimplification of their status. These historians need not have been so surprised that the "women of the town" in Zürich dined with the ambassador. Zürich has one of the oldest traditions of women in public life in Europe; it is not a tradition of prostitution, but of participation in public affairs. Since public entertainments, carnivals, and fairs were such an important part of town and village life in the Middle Ages, this general delight in public recreation has to be taken into account in assessing the role of women in the entertainment sector of the medieval labor force. Both the vagabond women and the settled entertainment guild women had their places in that sector. What proportion of them were "below the poverty line" for that era it is difficult to estimate, but the evidence from art, song, and story suggests that there were many well-fed women entertainers who enjoyed their way of life. Much of the gaiety that comes through in the descriptions of fairs and street life in medieval cities is due to the colorful styles and behavior of the vagabond women. Their pride, toughness, and sense of humor were also characteristic of medieval working women generally. Their sisters in other craft guilds would not have looked or behaved very differently from the vagabonds.

The term *vagabond* covers a very heterogeneous group of women. Of those who led a more mobile existence, we find at one extreme the wandering saint, on perpetual pilgrimage, and at the other, thieves and murderers. The great bulk of women were somewhere in between—women dislodged from rural life and with no settled niche in urban life. The same was also true of the daughters of joy. Insofar as they were self-organized they set rules and standards for their activities and tried to guard against interlopers. Some of the street fights described were probably between the wandering vagabond women and local entertainment guild members trying to protect their turf.

Prisons and Slavery

Although the term *vagabond* covers a very heterogeneous set of women, as I have pointed out, in general these women tended to be the marginal members of society. They had fewer protections than their more settled counterparts, and along with the poorest of their city sisters, were very vulnerable to being cleared off the streets and the fair grounds and placed in jails. Jails were a new invention of the Middle Ages. Kings and lords had from ancient times had dungeons in which to put away enemies, but the concept of a prison for offenders, linked to the administration of a code of laws, was new in the Middle Ages.[37] At first women and men were imprisoned together, but by the thirteenth century there are references to women's sections in English prisons at York Castle and Maidstone. In 1310 the chancellor of Oxford insisted on a separate women's section in the Oxford prison when the prison became known as a brothel. During this time unlimited alcohol and unlimited sex were available in prisons. By the fourteenth century, separate prisons were being built for women. Punishment won out over sex (Pugh, 1968: 103, 324, 352-353, 357-358).

Women were mostly imprisoned for petty theft. The most helpless of the vagabonds, rural migrants to the city who had not been able to find employment or a niche to live in, and poverty-stricken unmarried mothers were the most likely candidates for imprisonment. Every women's prison was full of babies and small children, not necessarily there with mothers. Four- and five-year-old girls were imprisoned for "theft"—as were boys of the same age.

Jails were used very selectively. When middle- and upper-class persons were imprisoned, they had separate apartments. The poor were the ones who suffered and starved to death, for no town funds were made available for feeding prisoners in the Middle Ages. The poor depended entirely on charity. Mutilation was another punishment frequently used for the poor, and half-starved daughters of joy who were sent back into the streets minus their noses could not have lived very long. The removal of noses, ears, and hands was common punishment in Europe and Byzantium and elsewhere in the Mediterranean in the Middle Ages, for both women and men (Rusche and Kircheimer, 1968: 17).

A more serious danger that lurked for women of the working class was to be kidnapped for the slave trade. The major slave marts of Europe were in Italy, particularly in Venice and Florence. While Italian slave traders dealt primarily in captured Tartars, Circassians, Armenians, Georgians, and Bulgarians, there was also a steady movement of women from the rest of Europe to Italian slave marts.[38] Within Europe itself, after the seventh century, slavery was gradually becoming serfdom, but the evolution took a long time. It is not clear in many texts when the word *slave* means slave and when it means serf, but from the context in which either *slave* or *serf* was used in medieval Europe, it often appears that *de facto* slavery existed, whether it was *de jure* or not. In 1066 William the Conqueror supported the principle of manumission of slaves in England. The mother of Earl Godwin shipped English girls as slaves to Denmark in 1086. In 1102 the London Council passed a resolution forbidding slave trading in England, but little heed was paid to the resolution. Bristol merchants were among the worst offenders, shipping pregnant women as slaves to Ireland. In France and Germany kings began declaring emancipation areas in the 1100s, but final abolition of serfdom in France was in 1779, in Saxony in 1832, in Denmark in 1804, in Hungary after 1850, and in Russia in 1861 (Brownlow, 1969).

Considering the threats that hung over the lives of the poor, the robustness of medieval gaiety had its somber undertones. Yet that gaiety was real enough and has to be remembered when looking at the total picture of women's situation. The nuns, the anchoresses, and the Beguines would have quieter styles, but they too shared the raucous and by our standards often licentious sense of humor of the times, along with the ladies of the merchant houses and the manor houses. Miracle plays about Our Lady became so bawdy that they had to be moved out of the churches and into the squares. But they originated as celebrations in the church, and nuns, Beguines, and artisan women must have enjoyed them as much as anyone. The Virgin's sense of humor is attested to in many a bawdy medieval tale. The "Nun's Tale" in Boccaccio's *Decameron* was taken amiss by no one. This shared sense of humor between women and men had egalitarian aspects to it. When men started to creep away to tell funny stories about sex, it was a sign of something more than emerging puritanism. It was a signal that an important dimension of man-woman relationships had atrophied.

The Economic Situation of Women by the End of the Middle Ages

The idea that the decline of the craft guilds and the decline of the status of women went together, as economic enterprises moved from what Clark calls domestic and family industry to capitalistic industry, is as I have indicated partially true, but it also represents a substantial oversimplification of the actual course of events. What is true is that before the development of greater urban concentrations there was for rural and small town populations a pattern of domestic industry "in which the goods produced are for the exclusive use of the family and are not therefore subject to an exchange or money value." In family industry, "the family becomes the unit for the production of goods to be sold or exchanged" (Clark, 1919: 6). It is also true that in the early stages of the new urbanization the craft guilds continued this unity of capital and labor in a kind of extended family formed on the basis of special craft skills.

The craft guilds were destroyed by the increased volume of trade, both domestic and international, which led to the development of a separate class of traders apart from producers (Renard, 1968). The trade guilds grew into the vast exploitative merchant guilds (quite different from the earlier craft-based guilds merchant) that in the end turned craftworkers into underpaid pieceworkers. The craft guilds belonged to the localist tradition, dealt only with municipal authorities, and had no relationship with the state. The merchant guilds derived their power from the state. The 1563 Elizabethan Statute of Artificers, which established total state control (in theory) over the movement of labor in England, was the natural outgrowth of the ordinances of 1349 and 1351 which forbade laborers to change employers and compelled every unemployed person over twelve to enter the agricultural labor force. This development, aimed at freezing the labor supply generally, in fact only froze women:

> By this Act (the Statute of Laborers) every woman free or bound, under 60, and not carrying on a trade or calling, provided she had no land, and was not in domestic or other service, was liable to be called upon to enter service in the fields or otherwise, and if she refused, she was imprisoned until she complied; whilst all girls who for twelve years had been brought up to follow the plough, were not allowed to enter any other calling, but were forced to continue working in the fields (Cleveland, 1896: 76).

Men continued to move where the jobs were, but village women, more directly burdened with family responsibilities, felt the full force of the compulsion to work in the fields. Beyond that, they also took piecework home, to eke out inadequate wages to maintain home and children. The more women entered into the wage labor market, the more pronounced wage differentials became. Through their relative immobility women had no bargaining power, and so the complaints of wage discrimination began early—and they were found everywhere. The scholars of Toulouse in 1422 paid women grape-pickers half of what they paid the men, who only had to carry the full baskets back to the college cellar. The monks of Paris did the same (Thrupp, 1964: 240-241). The women construction workers who worked side by side with men in building the College of Toulouse were paid far less than the men who did the same kind of labor (Thrupp, 1964: 244). The labor shortage resulting from the black death did not at all affect women's wages, which remained substantially the same on the Continent for nearly a hundred years (E. Perroy, in Thrupp, 1964: 244). Neither did the supposed labor shortages from the black death help the laboring poor in England (Ziegler, 1969: 240-259). Fourteenth century workers, especially women, had to work longer and harder, but were not earning more pay.

This became increasingly true as the large commercial guilds organized workers into specialties, to increase production. As early as the 1200s there were eleven distinct process specialists in that part of the wool industry run by the commercial guilds (Renard, 1968: 80-81). A family carrying out those tasks in a small household could hardly compete, and in the home workshops spinning for merchant houses increasingly replaced the earlier total production process. The division of labor was well developed so early that, as Renard says, mechanization was inevitable, and the wonder is that it didn't happen sooner. The mill as a mechanical source of power had been known from the time of Alexander the Great.

The most exploitative commercial guilds developed in the major trade centers of Italy, which had the advantage of the whole Mediterranean as a trading lake. Simultaneously, the Hanseatic towns, home of the older craft guilds, went into economic decline, since there was no longer a need for the old northern trade route through Russia. But even the Hanseatic guilds had already become fairly large-scale operations, and women's subsidiary roles as auxiliary workers living in dormitory situations or as commuting day laborers already existed before the decline of the Hanse. It is well to remember that the women intellectuals and artists of Italy who flourished in the universities of Bologna and Salerno and in the courts of Florence and Venice were in a way sitting on the backs of their exploited sisters. The Venetian dogaressas, sponsoring the elegant craftwork in lace and gold which their working sisters grew blind to produce, also introduced such forward-looking innovations as bullfights and eunuchs, and they certainly benefitted from the flourishing slave trade. Feminism was not born in Venice.

Spinsters in Italy and elsewhere were a vast reserve labor force so totally controlled by the guilds that on holy days the bishop, instructed by the merchants, would issue a pastoral letter threatening spinsters who wasted wool with ecclesiastical censure and even with excommunication if they repeated the offense (Renard, 1968: 25-26). As the older craft guilds declined, working-class women had increasingly minor roles in production.

The final squeezing out of the sisters from the guilds was a slow process. Long after guilds stopped recognizing other forms of membership and participation of women, they would still permit a widowed woman to carry on her husband's work with guild recognition, even as late as the 1600s (Clark, 1919: 10). Gradually over the next couple of centuries women were confined to a few specialties such as dressmaking, brewing, domestic service, and the street-vending of food. Eventually brewing became a factory operation and women lost control of it (Clark, 1919: 223-228).

While the status of working-class women was declining, the business activities of women merchants were also decreasing. The formerly productive wives of prosperous men of business in the towns of Europe increasingly transferred their activities to more strictly domestic areas, and to social life and "adornment" (Clark, 1919: 38-39). Only women of the upper class, and particularly those who had estates to manage, maintained economically productive roles, and sometimes political roles at court. We see the beginnings of the process that led the legal commentator Blackstone later to write of the "civil death" of the married woman.

The changes that were taking place for women did not represent a sudden shift to a new and lower status. The decline was rather an acceleration of a process that began with primordial urbanization and the rise of an urban laboring class of women in antiquity. With greater population densities, improving techniques of production, and a concentration of wealth in the hands of a merchant class, an acceleration of demand for craft goods simply placed more and more women in preindustrial factory-type workshops. For working-class women, the separation of work from home led to the increased separation of mothers from their children, to baby farming, and to infanticide. At the same time, for middle-class women there was a withdrawal from the worksites and an intensification of mothering and other social roles.

What made the guild master's wife, formerly busy in the work associated with maintaining the workshop-dormitory-school-extended family-merchandising enterprise, opt for a life of lesser mercantile involvement and more leisure? Affluence itself was the crucial factor. She was no longer needed to make the family business run, and few women had the entrepreneurial drive that would keep them in the business after necessity released them. However, it is a mistake to exaggerate the disappearance of her work role. It did not disappear, it diminished.

It would also be a mistake to conclude that these women were choosing leisure per se. The new urban social world was a world that had to be *created*. There were no precedents for the new life patterns of a sizeable and affluent middle-class urban population. Prior to the Renaissance nearly everyone had to work hard, and the higher the status of the women, the more responsibility they had. The secluded, do-nothing middle-class women that we identified during earliest urbanization had always been a tiny sector. Now that sector was rapidly growing. In this new, expanded middle-class world women formerly preoccupied with productive labor were confronted with the new challenges of a world in which social relationships, leisure and reflection, and cultural productivity were suddenly of primary importance. The limitations placed on women in these new spheres because of the secondary nature of their status did not become immediately evident.

The close of the Middle Ages was a period of clashing of opposite tides for middle-class women. On the one hand some were withdrawing from mercantile involvement and exploring the dimensions of a new world of social interaction. On the other hand there were women who were experiencing the moral and intellectual liberation of the dawning Renaissance and wished to participate more fully in the public arenas of society. Meanwhile the lessening economic pressure for the participation of women of the middle class in family business affairs was countered by a tremendous increase in pressure from working-class women for jobs. It was in the midst of these shifting pressures that the gradual limitation of rights to hold property independently, to transact business, and to go to law took place for women. The legal protection for women in equity law remained, but was ignored. Beard (1946: 87-115) has written eloquently about the use of common law to limit women's rights (more specifically, the rights of married women)—a process that began in the late Middle Ages and was to be continued by Blackstone and his successors right up to the twentieth century.

Clark (1919: 303) reminds us that it never occurred to the writers on political philosophy who were developing a new theory of the state as composed of individuals that individuals might be women. It was simply not a question for discussion. If we ask why not, we are back at the concepts of public and private space, of underlife and overlife. Women never had burgess status in the medieval towns. What fluidity there was in the medieval partnership between

Figure 9-17. *Villagers Taking "Law" into Their Own Hands.*

women and men depended on the customs of the common people, and on public opinion; women and men shared in the creation of that custom and opinion. With the growth of cities and large-
scale commercial enterprises, local custom was increasingly replaced
by common law, which despite its plebeian sound was actually the
law of the aristocracy (Clark, 1919: 236). Law is an overlife institution. Custom is not. Women did not participate in the new regula-
tory process whereby aristocratic law was codified, interpreted, and
extended to cover the transactions of an entire population. The all-
important equity law, which was developed to deal with the inadequacies and injustices of the common law, at first protected women
from the consequences of the shift to national codes. But the more
the legal profession specialized and expanded with the expanding
economy, the more it became evident that this new public arena was
a man's world. The famous (mis)statement in 1775 by Blackstone
is a logical outcome of the exclusion of women from the process of
developing interpretations of law in the public arena:

> By marriage, the husband and wife are one person in law; that is, the
> very being or legal existence of the woman is suspended, during the
> marriage, or at least is incorporated and consolidated into that of the
> husband (quoted in Beard, 1946: 89).[39]

All the new clerical and administrative positions associated with
the burgeoning bureaucracy of the state went, as we have already
noted, to men. Many of the able, literate women were inside
convents, while a whole army of wandering unemployed male clerics—

the *vagantes*—were waiting to leap into every job opening. The beguinages, which could have provided literate women for government offices, developed a self-contained world of their own, partly—and understandably—in defense against the indiscriminate witchcraft persecutions. In strictly labor-power terms, there were plenty of literate women to fill some of the new bureaucratic jobs. In terms of functional availability, there were very few.

One could argue that there never was any overt decision to "get the women out," that it all happened by default. On the other hand, given the number of instances in which the church combined with various economic groups from doctors to lawyers to merchant guilds, not only to make pronouncements about the incapacities of women, but often to accomplish the physical liquidation of women through witchcraft and heresy trials, one can hardly say that it all happened without anyone intending it. The exclusion of women was a result of a combination of impersonal and intentional forces.

Once again we see the vulnerability of women because of their underlife roles. Even in the guilds, for all the apparently egalitarian references to the sistren and the brethren, women were relegated to the underlife of supportive and fill-in roles and rarely were apprenticed to master the full range of craft skills. Even if they were, burgess rights were denied them on the basis of the need for all burgesses to be bearers of arms in defense of the city. That same perception of civic duty kept women in secondary status in Greek city-states. The merchant bourgeoisie and the craftsmen had also belonged to the underlife at the beginning of the Middle Ages. They, however, "graduated" from feudal underlife into positions in the overlife structures that enabled them to affect public policy. It was very easy for the brethren to leave their less skilled sistren behind.

In the Middle Ages there were queens and princesses alert to the need to defend the rights of at least some of their sisters. While the social consciousness of women royalty may leave something to be desired, they took responsibility for their sisters in convents, and some responsibility for the urban poor.

The women of the religious orders took responsibility for the education of women of all strata, within limits.

The Beguines and the hermitesses took responsibility for the right of women to remain unmarried and have productive lives in the world outside the convent.

The intellectuals took responsibility for knowledge. Christine de

Pisan particularly spoke for the right to knowledge on the part of women, so they could act responsibly for their families and society.

The vagabonds defended mobility, freedom, and the right of women to have fun.

Who is doing the work of the queens and the princesses today? Of the prophesying and fighting abbesses? Of the Beguines and the hermitesses? Of the scholars and the vagabonds?

The troubadour François Villon was already feeling nostalgic in the middle 1400s, when he wrote his famous ballad:

> Where is the virtuous Heloise . . .
> And Jeanne d'Arc, the good Lorraine . . .
> But where are the snows of yesteryear?

They are around, but they look and sound different. The idea that great women are as evanescent in history as the melting snow is a poetic statement of the fact that women are invisible to each other, as well as to men, as the makers of history. They do not know their own foremothers.

Figure 9-18. *Woman Charging Knight with Shuttle, 13th Century.*

Notes

[1]*Chiliasm* refers to expectations of the end of time, the "last things."

[2]Western accounts of the Crusades do not normally emphasize women's roles. Francesco Gabrieli's *Arab Historians of the Crusades,* however, brings out the fact that there were a number of women soldiers in the Frankish armies, as well as queens with their own all-women's battalions, and that the same phenomenon held for the Moslem side (Gabrieli, 1961: 204).

[3]The Beghards are the male counterpart of the Beguine movement, but they never attained anything like the size and significance of the Beguines. Apart from noting their existence, they will not be further discussed in this chapter.

[4]Comparable developments in Asia include the *Ramanujachary,* which gave a new direction to the *bhakti* movement in India in the 1100s. The latter was a devotional movement that developed in the early Middle Ages as a "defense" against Buddhism and Jainism. In China there was the appearance of Amida Buddhism, and in Tibet the reform of a lax religiosity by the establishment of a new priest-state under the dual rule of a Dalai Lama and a Tashi Lama.

[5]Gibbon thinks that Morozia, born in 880, mistress of Pope Sergius III, mother of Pope John XI, and grandmother of Pope John XII, may have been the source of the Pope Joan myth (Reich, 1908: 194).

[6]In chapter 8, in contrasting the educational and the military approaches to the Christianization of Europe during the early Middle Ages, I spoke of a distinct women's perspective. I may have exaggerated it there, and I may be underestimating it here. In general, the more women are drawn into positions of leadership the more they share the perspective of the men they work with. The underside is a good protector of alternative perspectives.

[7]Barbara Nolan's study of the *Vita Nuova* (1970) makes one aware of the commonality between Dante's work and that of the Beguine mystics, though Nolan herself does not make a point of this.

[8]This mixture comes out particularly in the case histories recorded in *The Devil in Britain and America* by John Ashton (1972).

9See especially "L'Heresie Urbaine et Rurale en l'Italie" [Urban and rural heresy in Italy] , by C. Violante, and "Les Flagellants du Quatorzième Siecle" [Flagellants in the fourteenth century] , by G. S. Zekely, in Le Goff (1968).

10For a stunning pictorial view of the many ways of life for women of the Middle Ages, and one that covers all classes of society, see Harkson (1975).

11The picture of Queen Eleanor as a wealthy, spoiled aristocrat who caused Louis VII's defeat in the Crusades has been so convincingly put forth by so many historians that I had reproduced this version of her in the initial draft of this chapter. I am indebted to E. L. Hallgren and to William Proctor for pointing out that I had erroneously accepted versions of her life as told by "French chauvinist and male chauvinist historians." The rewritten account is based on Amy Kelly's *Eleanor of Aquitaine* (1950), a historical novel based on painstaking historical research.

12The origin of the term is obscure.

13Bücher (Wieth-Knudsen, 1928: 212-213) says that in Frankfurt in 1400 there was a 20 percent surplus of women in relation to the male urban population.

14The Beguines filled a certain niche in society so successfully that they are still functioning today, albeit in a convent-like atmosphere contrary to their original function. Sacheverell Sitwell describes the modern Beguines:

> They are more nun-like than the nuns and are never seen bicycling, driving cars, carrying shopping baskets or ferrying droves of school children across the traffic lights. They dwell in an inaction limpid and perfect of its kind, each Beguinage under the aegis of a Grande Demoiselle, in walled enclosures, sometimes of whitewashed walls, in little gabled houses of brick and stone with green shutters. At Courtnai the Beguinage is a huddle of little steep-roofed houses crowding together as though for company and warmth; while at Bruges and Ghent the houses are grouped together round open grassed spaces (1965: 168-169).

15This influx represented the convent-based wing of the women's movement.

16Since political leaders were often themselves prey to this kind of emotionalism, and could easily rouse it in followers, a now common impression of the chiliastic movements of the Middle Ages is that they were all precursors of Hitlerism. Cohn (1970) gives that view, which seems to me a vast oversimplification.

17A significant aspect of the Beguine movement is that it included, in addition to unmarried women and widows, married women who took more or less permanent leave from their own households.

18Among these men were Jaques de Vitry, John of Vivelles, William of L'Olive, Ivan de Reves, and Theodore of Celles (McDonnell, 1969: 20-58).

19*The Cloud of Unknowing,* for example, one of the most widely read of these classics today, and first published anonymously in Marguerite's time, has such a warning in the introduction.

[20]Except where otherwise indicated, the material in this section is based on Morris, *The Lady Was a Bishop* (1973); Eckenstein, *Women under Monasticism* (1896); and Hilpisch, *History of Benedictine Nuns* (1958). Another book on the subject, discovered too late to utilize here, is Ludlow's *Women's Work in the Church* (1975).

[21]Fontrevault owed its existence and format to the work of one of the most ardently feminist churchmen of the Middle Ages, Robert of Arbrissel (McLaughlin, 1975: 323).

[22]While on the face of it the Enclosure movement was ideological, the same economic problems that weakened the subsistence base of the convents also operated to force enclosure. It was in part a measure to prevent, among upper- and middle-class women, "the return of the professed cloistered daughters to claim their share of the paternal fortunes" (Monica, 1945: 320), since when the coming and going of professed nuns was freer, many changed their minds about convent life and tried to reenter secular life and get regular marriage dowries.

[23]The Franciscan Third Order is a lay order, not conventual.

[24]Sources used here are Montag (1968), and Butkovich (1969, 1972).

[25]The sources for material on St. Clare is *Legend and Writings of St. Claire*, (1953).

[26]The terms *anchoress* and *anchorite* are interchangeable with *hermitess* and *hermit*, referring to women and men living in solitude and not in religious orders.

[27]For a vivid description of life on pilgrimage for a woman, see Monica on Angela de Merici (1945: 135-145); for general descriptions of medieval pilgrimages, see Newton (1968, chapt. 3). See also R. J. Mitchell (1968) on the Jerusalem Pilgrimage of 1458.

[28]Rashdall tells us that "the University of London, after being empowered by royal charter to do all things that could done by any university, was legally advised that it could not grant degrees to women without a fresh charter because no university had ever granted such degrees." He comments, "It had not heard of the women-doctors at Salerno," and footnotes further, "I have been informed by an eminent judge, who was one of the counsel on whose advice the university acted, that a knowledge of this fact would have modified his opinion" (Rashdall, 1936: 460-461).

[29]By the end of the Middle Ages, in the 1400s, there were still famous women professors of medicine in Italy, such as Fedele Cassandra of Venice, who lived to be 102, the mother-daughter team of the Laura Calendas in Naples, and Dorothea Bucca of Bologna.

[30]The following books were utilized in this study of Christine de Pisan: Roy (1884, vols. 2 and 3); Solente (1955); Towner (1969); Varty (1965); Kemp-Welch (1913); de Pisan (1521, 1932, 1966, 1970); and Willard (1975).

[31]For descriptions of life in the manor houses and their urban equivalents, see Holmes (1952); and "Le Managier de Paris," in Power (1963).

[32]For example, Joan sometimes went by her father's name d'Arc, and sometimes by her mother's, Domremy (Bloch, 1961: 138).

[33]We have noted that rural women paid substitutes to fulfill military obligations. This device was apparently never utilized to enable women to achieve burgess status in the towns.

[34]See Walsh, *The Thirteenth, Greatest of Centuries* (1970), for a glowing description of guild life in its idealized form.

[35]"If sex ratios of 150 to 100 (c. A.D. 801) and 172 to 100 (A.D. 1391) are any indication of the extent of the killing of legitimate girls, and if illegitimates were usually killed regardless of sex, the real rate of infanticide could have been substantial in the Middle Ages. . . . As late as 1527, one priest (in Rome) admitted that 'the latrines resound with the cries of children who have been plunged into them' " (de Mause, 1974: 29).

[36]See also A. Abram, "Women Traders in Mediaeval London" (1916). Further information on women's occupations in the Middle Ages can be found in *A History of Technology* (Singer et al., 1956) and *Schaffende Arbeit* (Brandt, 1928).

[37]The first mention of a prison in the English law codes in is Alfred's Code, A.D. 890.

[38]See Origo's "The Domestic Enemy" (1955) for a fuller discussion of the Italian slave trade.

[39]It will be noted that widows and single women do not lose their rights, so the situation was never as bad for them as for their married sisters. For those who want to follow Beard's history of the misinterpretations of women's legal status beginning with Blackstone, a reading of chapters 4-6 in *Woman as a Force in History* (1946) is recommended.

References

Abram, A.
  1916 "Women traders in midiaeval London." Economics Journal 28: 276-285.

Adams, Henry
  1933 Mont-Saint-Michel and Chartres. Boston: Houghton Mifflin. (First published 1905.)

Afetinan, A.
  1962 Emancipation of the Turkish Woman. Paris: UNESCO.

Ancelet-Hustache, Jeanne
  1963 Gold Tried by Fire: St. Elizabeth of Hungary. Tr. by Paul J. Oligny, O. F. M., and Sister Venard O'Donnell, O. S. F. Chicago: Fanciscan Herald Press.

Aries, Philippe
  1962 Centuries of Childhood: A Social History of Family Life. Tr. by Robert Baldick. New York: Alfred A. Knopf.

Ashton, John
  1972 The Devil in Britain and America. Hollywood, Calif.: Newcastle. (Reprint of 1896 edition.)

Baldwin, John
  1971 The Scholastic Culture of the Middle Ages. Lexington, Mass.: D. C. Heath.

Baring-Gould, S.
  1896 Curious Myths of the Middle Ages. Philadelphia: J. B. Lippincott.

Beard, Mary R.
  1946 Woman as Force in History: A Study in Traditions and Realities. New York: Macmillan.

Bloch, Marc
  1961 Feudal Society. Tr. by F. A. Manyon. Chicago: University of Chicago Press.

511

Boccaccio, Giovanni
1963   Concerning Famous Women. Tr. by Guido A. Guarino. New Brunswick, N. J.: Rutgers University Press.

Bordeaux, Henry
1937   Au Pays des Elisabeth. Paris: Librarie Plow.

Bowser, Frederick P.
1974   The African Slave in Colonial Peru: 1524-1650. Stanford, Calif.: Stanford University Press.

Brandt, Paul
1928   Schaffende Arbeit und Bildende Kunst: Vom Mittelalter Bis Zur Gegenwart. Leipzig: Alfred Kroner Verlag.
1927   Schaffende Arbeit und Bildende Kunst im Alterum und Mittelalter. Leipzig: Alfred Kroner Verlag.

Brownlow, W. R.
1969   Lectures on Slavery and Serfdom in Europe. New York: Negro Universities Press. (Reprint of 1892 edition.)

Bücher, Carl
1910   Die Frauenfrage im Mittelalter. Tübingen, Germany.

Buckler, Georgina
1929   Anna Comnea: A Study. London: Oxford University Press.

Butkovich, Anthony
1972   Revelations: St. Birgitta of Sweden. Los Angeles: Ecumenical Foundation of America.
1969   Iconography: St. Birgitta of Sweden. Los Angeles: Ecumenical Foundation of America.

Castellani, Maria
1939   Italian Women Past and Present. Rome: Societa Editrice di Novissima.

Charrier, Charlotte
1933   Heloise: Dans l'Histoire et dans la Légende. Paris: Libraire Ancienne Honore Champion.

Clark, Alice
1919   Working Life of Women in the Seventeenth Century. London: Routledge.

Cleveland, Arthur Rackham
1896   Woman under the English Law. London: Hurst.

Clough, Shepard B.
1951   The Rise and Fall of Civilization: How Economic Development Affects the Culture of Nations. New York: McGraw-Hill.

Cohn, Norman
1970   The Pursuit of the Millennium. New York: Oxford University Press.

Colledge, Eric (ed.)
1965   Medaeval Netherlands Religious Literature. Tr. by Eric Colledge. New York: London House and Maxwell.
1961   The Medaeval Mystics of England. New York: Charles Scribner's Sons.

Coulton, G. G.
   1955   Medieval Panorama. Cleveland: Meridian Books, World.

Delort, Robert
   1973   Life in the Middle Ages. New York: Universe.

de Beaumont, Edouard
   1929   The Sword and Womankind. New York: Panurge Press.

de Mause, Lloyd
   1974   "The evolution of childhood." Pp. 1-74 in Lloyd de Mause (ed.), The History of Childhood. New York: Psychohistory Press.

de Pisan, Christine
   1970   The Epistle of Othea. Ed. by Curt F. Bühler. Tr. by Stephen Scrope. London: Oxford University Press.
   1966   The Book of the Duke of True Lovers. Ed. by Laurence Binyon and Eric R. D. Maclagan. Tr. by Alice Kemp-Welch. New York: Cooper Square.
   1932   The Book of Fayttes of Armes and of Chyuarye. Ed. by A. T. P. Byles. Tr. by William Caxton. London: Oxford University Press.
   1521   Here Beginneth the Boke of the Cyté of Ladyes. Tr. by Brian Anslay. London: H. Pepwell. Film Reproduction: Edwards Brothers, no. 219.

de Rougemont, Denis
   1956   Love in the Western World. New York: Pantheon.

Diehl, Charles
   1963   Byzantine Empresses. New York: Alfred A. Knopf.

Duby, Georges
   1968   Rural Economy and Country Life in the Medieval West. Tr. by C. Posten. London: E. Arnold.

Eckenstein, Lina
   1896   Women under Monasticism. Cambridge: Cambridge University Press.

Ehrenreich, Barbara, and Deirdre English
   1973   Witches, Midwives, and Nurses: A History of Women Healers. 2nd ed. Old Westbury, N. Y.: Feminist Press.

Franciscan Institute (ed.)
   1953   Legend and Writings of St. Claire of Assisi. New York: St. Bonaventure.

Gabrieli, Francesco (ed.)
   1969   Arab Historians of the Crusades. Tr. by E. J. Costello. Berkeley: University of California Press.

Green, Mary Anne Everett
   1850   Lives of the Princesses of England, from the Norman Conquest. London: H. Colburn.

Gross, Charles
   1890   The Guild Merchant. Oxford: Clarendon Press.

Guillemin, Henri
   1972   The True History of Joan of Arc. London: Allen and Unwin.

Hallgren, E. L.
1975   Boulder, Colo.: Medieval historian, University of Colorado, personal communication.

Harksen, Sibylle
1975   Women in the Middle Ages. New York: Abner Schram.

Hauser, Henri
1927   Ouvriers du Temps Passé. Paris: Librairie Felix Alian.

Hazard, Harry W.
1931   Atlas of Islamic History. Princeton, N. J.: Princeton University Press.

Herlihy, David
1975   "Life expectancies for women in medieval society." Pp. 1-22 in Rosemarie Morewedge (ed.), The Role of Women in the Middle Ages. Albany: State University of New York Press.

Hill, Georgiana
1894-   Women in English Life. 2 vols. London: Richard Bentley.
1896

Hilpisch, Stephanus
1958   History of Benedictine Nuns. Tr. by Sr. M. Joanne Muggli. Collegeville, Minn.: St. John's Abbey Press.

Hilton, Rodney
1973   Bond Men Made Free: Medieval Peasant Movements and the English Rising of 1381. London: Temple Smith.

Hollingsworth, Thomas Henry
1969   Historical Demography. Ithaca, N. Y.: Cornell University Press.

Holmes, Urban Tiger, Jr.
1952   Daily Living in the Twelfth Century: Based on the Observation of Alexander Needham in London and Paris. Madison: University of Wisconsin Press.

Hughes, Muriel Joy
1943   Women Healers in Medieval Life and Literature. Morningside Heights, N. Y.: King's Crown Press.

Huizinga, Johan
1924   The Waning of the Middle Ages. New York: St. Martin's Press.

Hurd-Mead, Kate Campbell
1933   A History of Women in Medicine. Haddam, Conn.: Haddam Press.

Judserand, J. J.
1890   English Wayfaring Life in the Middle Ages (14th Century). London: T. Fish Urwin.

Kelly, Amy
1950   Eleanor of Aquitaine and the Four Kings. Cambridge, Mass.: Harvard University Press.

Kellog, Charlotte
1932   Jadwiga: Poland's Great Queen. New York: Macmillan.

Kemp-Welch, Alice
1913   Of Six Medieval Women. London: Macmillan.

Kropotkin, Peter
    1972   Mutual Aid: A Factor of Evolution. Ed. by Paul Avrich. Albany, N. Y.: State University of New York Press.

Lacroix, Paul
    1926   History of Prostitution: Among All the Peoples of the World, from the Most Remote Antiquity to the Present Day. Tr. by Samuel Putnam. New York: Covici-Friede.

Ladurie, Emmound LeRoy
    1971   Times of Feast: Times of Famine. Garden City, N. Y.: Doubleday.

Laslett, Peter (ed.)
    1972   Household and Family in Past Time. Cambridge: Cambridge University Press.

Le Goff, Jacques (ed.)
    1968   Heresies et Sociétés dans l'Europe pre-industriale, 11-18 siècles. Paris: Mouton.

Ludlow, John Malcolm
    1975   Woman's Work in the Church. New York: Strahan. (Reprint of 1866 edition.)

McDannell, M. Coleen
    1975   "An examination of a selection of women saints." Unpublished student paper. Boulder: University of Colorado, Department of Sociology.

McDonnell, Ernst W.
    1969   The Beguines and the Beghards in Medieval Culture. New York: Octagon Books.

McGinn, Bernard
    1971   "The abbot and the doctors: Scholastic reactions to the radical eschatology of Joachim of Fiore." Church History 40: 30-48.

McLaughlin, Mary Martin
    1975a Medieval historian, personal communication, 1975.

    1975b "Peter Abelard and the dignity of women: Twelfth century feminism in theory and practice." Pp. 287 in Proceedings of the International Symposium of the Centre National de la Récherche Scientifique, July 2-9. Paris: Centre National de la Récherche Scientifique.

Mitchell, Rosamund Jocelyn
    1968   The Spring Voyage: The Jerusalem Pilgrimage in 1458. New York: Clarkson N. Potter.

Moncrieff, C. K. Scott (tr.)
    1929   The Letters of Abelard and Heloise. New York: Alfred A. Knopf.

Monica, Sister
    1945   Angela Merici and Her Teaching Idea: 1474-1540. Saint Martin, Ohio: The Ursulines of Brown County.

Montag, Ulrich
    1968   Das Werk der Heilgen Birgitta von Schweven in Ober Deutscher Liberlieferung. München, Germany: C. H. Beck'sche Verlagsbuchhandlung.

Morewedge, Rosemarie Thee (ed.)
  1975   The Role of Women in the Middle Ages. Albany: State University of
         New York Press.

Morris, Joan
  1973   The Lady Was a Bishop. New York: Macmillan.

Mozans, H. J.
  1913   Woman in Science. New York: D. Appleton.

Mujeeb, M.
  1960   World History: Our Heritage. Bombay: Asia Publishing House.

Mumford, Lewis
  1961   City in History: Its Origins, Its Transformation, and Its Prospects. New
         York: Harcourt Brace Jovanovich.

Newton, Arthur Percival (ed.)
  1968   Travel and Travellers of the Middle Ages. New York: Barnes and Noble.

Nickerson, Hoffman
  1942   The Armed Horde: 1793-1939. 2nd ed. New York: Putnam.

Nolan, Barbara
  1970   "The Vita Nuova: Dante's Book of Revelation." Dante Studies 88:
         51-77.

O'Faolain, Julia, and Lauro Martines (eds.)
  1973   Not in God's Image: A History of Women in Europe from the Greeks to
         the Nineteenth Century. New York: Harper and Row.

Origo, Iris
  1955   "The domestic enemy: The eastern slaves in Tuscany in the fourteenth
         and fifteenth centuries." Speculum 30 (July): 321-366.

Perroy, E.
  1964   "Wage labour in France in the later middle ages." Pp. 237-246 in Sylvia
         L. Thrupp (ed.), Change in Medieval Society. New York: Appleton-
         Century-Crofts.

Pinchbeck, Ivy
  1930   Women Workers and the Industrial Revolution: 1750-1850. London:
         Frank Cass.

Ploss, Herman Heinrich, Max Bartels, and Paul Bartels
  1964   Woman in the Sexual Relation. Revised and enlarged by Ferdinand F.
         von Reitzenstein. New York: Medical Press of New York.

Power, Eileen
  1963   Medieval People. 10th ed. New York: Barnes and Noble.

Power, Eileen, and M. M. Postan
  1933   Studies in English Trade in the Fifteenth Century. London: Routledge.

Proctor, Charles
  1975   Personal communication. Department of Letters, Modern Language,
         and Speech, Northern State College, Aberdeen, S.D.

Pugh, Ralph B.
  1968   Imprisonment in Medieval England. Cambridge: Cambridge University
         Press.

Rashdall, Hastings
1936 The Universities of the Middle Ages. Vol. 3. London: Oxford University Press.

Reeves, Marjorie
1969 The Influence of Prophecy in the Later Middle Ages: A Study in Joachimism. Oxford: Clarendon Press.

Reich, Emil
1908 Woman Through the Ages. 2 vols. London: Methuen.

Renard, Georges
1968 Guilds in the Middle Ages. New York: Augustus M. Kelley. (First published 1918.)

Rosenthal, Joel
1972 Purchase of Paradise. Toronto: University of Toronto Press.

Roy, Maurice (ed.)
1884 Oeuvres Poétiques de Christine de Pisan. Paris: Librairie de Firmin Didot et Cie.

Rusche, Georg, and Otto Kirchheimer
1968 Punishment and Social Structure. New York: Russell and Russell.

Saport, Linda
1975 "Scientific achievements of nuns in the middle ages." Unpublished student paper. Boulder: Univeristy of Colorado, Department of Sociology.

Schomanns, Emile
1911 Franzopische Utopisten und Ihr Frauenideal. Berlin: Verlag von Emil Felher.

Scudder, Vida D. (tr., ed.)
1905 Saint Catherine of Sienna as Seen in Her Letters. London: J. M. Dent.

Singer, Charles, E. J. Holmyard, and A. R. Hall
1956 A History of Technology. Vol. 2. New York: Oxford University Press.

Sitwell, Dom Gerard
1960 "Julian of Norwich." Sponsa Regis (September): 12-18.

Sitwell, Sacheverell
1965 Monks, Nuns and Monasteries. New York: Holt, Rinehart and Winston.

Smith, Ernest Gilbrath
1914 St. Clare of Assisi. New York: E. P. Dutton.

Solente, Suzanne
1955 Le Livre de la Mutacion de Fortune par Christine de Pisan. Vol. 3. Paris: Editions A. et J. Picard et Cie.

Staley, Edgcumbe
1967 The Guilds of Florence. New York: Benjamin Blom. (First published 1906).

Strayer, J. R.
1964 "The laicization of French and English society in the thirteenth century." Pp. 103-115 in Sylvia L. Thrupp (ed.), Change in Medieval

Society: Europe North of the Alps, 1050-1500. New York: Appleton-Century-Crofts.

Stuard, Susan Mosher
1975   "Dame Trot." Signs 1: 537-542.

Summers, Rev. Montague (tr).
1948   The Malleus Maleficarum of Heinrich Kramer and James Sprenger. New York: Dover. (First published 1486.)

Thrupp, Sylvia L.
1962   The Merchant Class of Medieval London. Ann Arbor: University of Michigan Press.

Thrupp, Sylvia L. (ed.)
1964   Change in Medieval Society: Europe North of the Alps, 1050-1500. New York: Appleton-Century-Crofts.

Towner, Sister Mary Lewis
1969   Pizan's Lavison-Christine. New York: AMS Press. (Originally a thesis, Catholic University of America, 1932.)

Underhill, Evelyn
1961   Mysticism: A Study in the Nature and Development of Man's Spiritual Consciousness. New York: E. P. Dutton. (First published 1911.)

Varty, Kenneth (ed.)
1965   Christine de Pisan's Ballades, Rondeaux and Virelais: An Anthology. Leicester, England: Leicester University Press.

Waddell, Helen
1927   The Wandering Scholars. London: Constable.

Walsh, James
1970   The Thirteenth: Greatest of Centuries. 12th ed. New York: AMS Press.

Waters, Clara (Erskine) Clement
1904   Women in the Fine Arts. Boston: Houghton Mifflin.

Weinhold, Karl
1882   Die Deutschen Frauen in dem Mittelalter. Wien: Druck und Verlag von Carl Geroed's Sohn.

Wieth-Knudsen, K. A.
1928   Feminism: A Sociological Study of the Woman Question from Ancient Times to the Present Day. Tr. by Arthur G. Chater. London: Constable.

Wilkinson, Richard G.
1973   Poverty and Progress: An Ecological Model of Economic Development. London: Methuen.

Willard, Charity Cannon
1975   "A fifteenth-century view of women's role in medieval society: Christine de Pisan's Livre des Trois Vertus." Pp. 90-120 in Rosemarie Thee Morewedge (ed.), The Roles of Woman in the Middle Ages. Albany: State University of New York Press.

Worthington, Marjorie
1962   The Immortal Lovers: Heloise and Abelard. London: Robert Hale.

Zeigler, Philip
     1969   The Black Death. London: Collins.

Part 3
The Emergence
of Women from
the Renaissance:
1450 to 1900

Introduction

If this were a history in the old style, this would be called "The Four Monarchs." The period 1450 to 1900 in Europe saw the reigns of four outstanding women rulers who not only brought their own countries out of feudalism, but also built the foundations of a new *oecumene,* a Western-based imperial order that was to span all the continents.

The year 1450 also was the occasion of the birth of the Iroquois League, an important political invention in pre-Columbian North America. Since the league was developed by matrilineal tribes it was partly shaped by the women who served as advisors to the male tribal councils. Unlike the queens, these women worked from the underside and remain nameless.[1]

Of the women monarchs, the first was Isabel of Castile, who in the year 1469 moved toward creating a united and imperial Spain by marrying a conservative, provincial-minded neighboring king, Ferdinand of Aragon. A little short of a century later the second monarch, Elizabeth Tudor, stepped from prison to the throne to build a powerful and united England. Still another century later the third monarch, Catherine II, moved to the throne of the czars to preside over the imperial expansion of a new world power, Russia. And finally, in

523

1837, Queen Victoria ascended the British throne to rule for sixty-four years, to give her name to an entire century, to rule over the great imperial era of Britain, and all the while to promote a public image of womankind as domestic and submissive.

It would be perfectly possible for a historian to write the history of the four and one-half centuries in terms of the lives of these four women and the consequences of their reigns, with footnotes now and then on France and the Austrian empire. Such a history would do at least as much justice to the facts as most standard histories do. It would cover the transition of Europe from a land-centered *oecumene* ("imperial order") to a sea-based one. It would cover the incorporation of North America and Russia (culturally speaking) into Europe. It would further cover the annexation of Latin America and parts of Africa and Asia as appendages to Europe. It would cover much of the drama of the Reformation and Counter-Reformation and the rise of the new humanism. Such a four-monarch focus would leave out the Thirty Years War, the American and French revolutions, and the development of modern mass armies. It would leave out the fall of Constantinople and the stream of Greek artist and scholar refugees that fled to Europe rather than live under the Turks. It would leave out the still-expanding Moslem world those refugees left behind. It would also leave out some aspects of the rise of the new international banking system and of the scientific and industrial revolutions. It would include, however, the gradual development of new solutions to the welfare problems that came with increasing urbanization and industrialization. The poor laws of England came to birth under Elizabeth, and were modernized under Victoria. The legislative commission intended to abolish serfdom and deal with the problems of the poor in Russia was set up under Catherine.

Can one justify lumping all these centuries together? We are leaving behind the medieval world in which each continent supported its own kingdoms and empires. The more ambitious rulers tended to push against one another, particularly as between the Moslem and the Christian world, but no one seriously developed imperial policy to deal with the whole known world. The futurists were Joachimites, and dreamt of a universal age of the Holy Spirit, but they had no blueprints—they only waited. These middle centuries of the second millennium that we are now inspecting, however, not only expanded the extent of the known world, they saw the birth of a set of double and contradictory visions: one was of an expansionist imperial world undreamed of even in the heyday of the Roman Empire, and the other was of the nonimperial utopian world community.

Individualism and autonomy were the key concepts of the Renaissance. The very struggle for autonomy inevitably led to a questioning of the limits of autonomy. The struggle was at first a purely European affair. The wars for religious freedom were superseded by wars for national freedom. National freedom then expanded to include the right to annex portions of other continents. At the very time when this movement for "imperial autonomy" reached its zenith in Europe, having stretched from the American Revolution of 1776 to the German, French, Italian, and Austrian revolutions of 1870, an entirely different kind of movement was born: the world peace movement. Eurocentric even today, it nevertheless reached beyond the borders of Euro-North America as rapidly as the new infrastructure fostered by the international exposition movement allowed it to. The great London Exposition of 1851 represented at least the birth pangs of the new world *oecumene.*

If it was the queens who helped build the imperial structures that at first overburdened the world *oecumene,* it was women of all classes who set themselves to breaking down the imperial walls. Women of the upper classes worked within the system. Women of the middle classes worked partly within the system and partly in alliance with their working-class sisters outside the system. The latter were a revolutionary sisterhood whose primary commitments were other than the nation-state system.

At first I intended to close this section with the year 1848. Eighteen forty-eight was quite a year. It witnessed the issuing of the Communist Manifesto from London, the Seneca Falls Declaration of Women's Rights from New York State, and the first International Peace Congress in Brussels. For women in Euro-North America this year symbolized the melting away of long-established internal barriers to action. The previous four centuries had been traumatic for women, and the sense of release was in proportion to the extent of the trauma.

The very fact of that release made it necessary to move with the flood tide of women's activities to the very threshold of the modern world. Thus I close instead with the death of Queen Victoria in 1901, with occasional spill-over references to the political culmination of nineteenth century activities in the enfranchisement of women during World War I. The intellectual and emotional harassment of women characteristic of most of this period began in the Renaissance, with the new "male" humanism. Is it justified to speak of the Renaissance as harassing women? Originally part three of this book was entitled "The Emergence of Women from the Dark

Ages of the Renaissance." Since we do witness a flowering of women's culture in the Renaissance, particularly in Italy but also spreading from there to the rest of Europe, referring to this period as a Dark Age may somewhat overemphasize the male backlash against the education of women and against their ventures into the cultural arena. The mental suffering of many educated women as the backlash developed was, however, great. The sudden and rapid spread of syphilis in Europe beginning in the 1500s compounded the backlash.[2] The syphilis scourge led to viciously punitive regulations aimed entirely at women. These regulations affected many single women, prostitutes or not, and created the atmosphere of horror that still surrounds the label "prostitute."

Reich has written about the "nebulous personality" of the Renaissance woman, complaining that it is "more difficult to visualize a famous woman of the Renaissance, more difficult to grasp her individuality, than in most other periods of which we have knowledge" (1908: 227). The reason is not far to seek. The new interest in the individuality of the human being which lay at the heart of the Renaissance was an interest in the male human being. The entire Renaissance was one long song of rejoicing over this remarkable new male individuality. Since women of the culture could and did read the same things the men were reading, and would themselves be affected by the tremendous intellectual excitement engendered by the new humanist writings, they naturally began wondering where they fitted in. When they raised these questions, the answers were scarcely comforting. Not that answers were lacking. Kelso's *Doctrine for the Lady of the Renaissance* (1956) contains a bibliography of 890 items all written between 1400 and 1600 on the subject of the education of women. With varying degrees of cruelty or refinement they indicate that the purpose of education for women is to make them perfect wives, however unworthy their husbands. Latin and Greek, those foundation stones of all learning in the 1500s, were described as dangerous because they might distract a woman's mind and render her unfit for wifehood. The Dutchman Erasmus, the Englishman Thomas More, and the Spaniard Luis Vives (the latter a tutor to the royal women of England) all held to this view. There was a spectrum of opinion on how much learning a woman's mind could be exposed to without danger, and it is small comfort to know that Erasmus and More were among the most liberal of their time in this regard. More's famous school for his own daughters exemplified the adage that in the country of the blind, the one-eyed man is king.

In Italy there was a special set of niches for women, spaces that had been carefully protected for centuries. They were good niches, and women scholars, scientists, and artists who found life too harsh elsewhere fled to Italy to recover their sense of identity. This process went on right into the 1800s. These niches did not, however, answer to the basic needs of the times.

The only widely read male exponent in the 1500s of the idea that the new humanism applied equally to women and men was Agrippa von Nettesheim (sometimes called Cornelius Agrippa), who said boldly:

> Women and men were equally endowed with the gifts of spirit, reason and the use of words; they were created for the same end, and the sexual differences between them will not confer a different destiny (O'Faolain and Martines, 1973: 184).

The Reformation was no help at all. In fact, it provided another set of reinforcements for the concept of second-class mental and spiritual equipment for women. Luther and Calvin set back at least a hundred years the progress that had been made in the Middle Ages in education for women, largely in convents, by their ideology of destruction of convents and abolition of the roles of monks and nuns. What they substituted for convent education, which had always included some classical learning, was a narrow vocational education that would fit women for their household duties. In fact, the chief argument for teaching women to read at all was to equip them as Sunday school teachers to impart scriptural knowledge to children. Women could have no other use for literacy.

It is painful to move through the literature of the 1500s and 1600s and see how widely the insights of humanism were denied applicability to women. Christine de Pisan's strong voice from the early 1400s was forgotten. I suggest that this period was much worse for women than the medieval period when the church regularly fed them the "woman as the source of all evil" doctrine, because that doctrine was simply part of the cultural furniture of the church. There were many other sources for a different image of women—within the church and outside it—in the Virgin Mary, in the saints, in nuns (especially the prophetess nuns described in chapter 9), and in the many devout women in the Beguine and other movements who lived secure and self-sufficient lives untouched by "Eve" doctrines. The Renaissance, however, created a new situation. There was a rediscovery of the nature of humanness, and there was a group of educated, cultured women in every country who would have every reason to expect to participate in that rediscovery. But their platforms were gone, their niches were gone, and their role models were gone. All they had was the bleak pronouncements that the new discoveries did not apply to them. The abject humility with which many women authors in the next two centuries wrote prefaces to their books apologizing for presuming to write on any subject is a direct outcome of the shock of this exclusion from the Renaissance. We have to realize how universal the male message was in this regard[3] to understand why it took women so long to develop the courage to claim their own nature.

The women who survived the 1500s best were the nonintellectuals. In England they carried on for some time a robust involvement with estate management. Many middle-class women were still involved in merchandising and workshop partnerships, though the number was dwindling. Women of the Elizabethan era knew they had a strong queen, and the general status of women in society was not unaffected. By the time women managers and artisans were shifted out of former occupational statuses, intellectual women had found their tongues and begun the long campaign for their rights. By the 1600s the upper-class women of France had invented their own version of an earlier Moslem, and then Italian, institution: the salon.

The salons were in a way the delayed entry of women into the Renaissance, although it was the Age of Enlightenment they were in fact entering. Renaissance humanism had always been rather self-centered, and never concerned itself, either in Italy or in its trans-alpine forms, with social problems or the situation of the working classes (Hyma, 1930). The salon movement similarly was a narcissistic exercise in the use of human wit. To a degree it was also an exercise in the use of political power from the underside. Little social conscience developed there. To be fair, however, the salons developed more than wit and political maneuvering. Women artists, writers, and musicians flourished in the new environment, and there was a kind of cultural rebirth for many gifted women as a result.

The religious and social ferment involved in the Reformation, the Counter-Reformation, and the dissenting movements outside the Church of England cut across the issues of the new humanism and created another set of hardships for women. These hardships were much more immediate than the deprivation of education resulting from the closing of convents. They stemmed from the political alignments and military obligations on the Continent that went with being a Huguenot or a Catholic. Often, families were divided in their allegiances, and women had to find ways to be loyal to their family obligations without doing violence to their personal beliefs; also, they had to mediate between other family members. On the Continent, there was little that was positive that came out of the feuds, massacres, and continuing wars that lasted from the 1520s until the deportation of the Huguenots from France in 1687. In England, the dissenting sects were not so violently dealt with, and women came to play significant roles in their development. The Quakers, for example, institutionally organized by 1660, were notable for continuing the earlier artisan tradition of the participation of women in the common life. The Quaker group thus became a source of female leadership in England for several centuries to come. The jail terms regularly meted out to them only seemed to whet their appetites for action.

In the eighteenth century women of all classes began to find their bearings in a more urban world. By 1700, 25 percent of the population of England was living in London and the larger towns. It took another century before the same was true in Western Europe (Laslett, 1965).[4] It was a world full of new problems. Increasing population densities since the end of the black death, plus the new trade on the seaways of the world, meant another shift in the scale of social organization. Fuel shortages were already serious in the 1500s as local forests were everywhere depleted, and the 1600s saw the introduction on a large scale of the use of coal and coke (available but little used since the 1100s). Urban housing shortages and lack of sanitation systems to deal with new urban densities were the nightmare problems of the next three centuries.

The 1600s saw the first of the enclosure movements in England—the enclosure of common land for grazing the sheep of the gentry and large landowners. This first enclosure movement worked great hardship on the women and men of the cottager class, leaving them with shrunken subsistence opportunities. The second enclosure movement, extending approximately from 1750 to 1850, had different and more complex effects. By this time there was a population explosion in process, and the countryside was swarming with labor. The second enclosure was associated with a new practice of extensive cultivation of wheat, and at harvest time required massive amounts of labor. A new class of migrant laboring families was created, and led to the phenomenon of the family work gang. By the early 1800s, 50 percent of all rural labor was at least semimigrant, and women and children suffered all the hardships of life in the open even while they "benefited" from ample opportunities for rural employment.

The story of the lot of rural women from the later Middle Ages to the industrial revolution is one of increasing work loads and increasing severity of working conditions. Life was hard for urban women too, but their situation had more social visibility. Middle-class urban women with entrepreneurial abilities, less involved than formerly in economic activity, turned their energies to the development of new approaches to work and housing relief, the education of children, and general aid to the poor. By the 1800s these activities were well organized and were accompanied by the appearance of a large number of women's magazines and women's organizations dealing with these new interests. Within the Catholic church a new set of religious orders had developed enabling women to engage in the active teaching and welfare work denied them during the monastic enclosure movement of the 1500s. The Beguines paved the way for this. Having become "respectable," they were no longer persecuted for "errors in doctrine and moral aberration" and were now chiefly attacked by local guilds as sources of privileged competition. In fact, many beguinages by the beginning of the 1500s operated as urban poorhouses, meeting urgent welfare needs (McDonnell, 1969: 573-574).

The unemployment of women was a new problem. It is hard to know who among working-class women were the worst off, the laboring rural poor, or urban women working in factories for starvation wages. A new unemployed sector was the single gentlewoman, starving in quiet desperation between underpaid governess jobs. Surprising numbers of these "helpless" ladies joined the great stream of migrations to the Americas and later to Australia. The story of these pioneer women on the frontiers of expansionist Europe is the story all over again of the building of new systems of education and welfare under conditions of hardship and savagery,[5] a repeat of the dramas in the days of the old Germanic kingdoms after the fall of Rome.

The voluntary unemployment of women among the middle classes turned many of them toward the "conspicuous consumption" life style characteristic, as we have seen, of a small group of women in every society with any kind of urban center. What was new in the eighteenth and nineteenth centuries was that much larger numbers of women entered this group.

As women left former employments, increasingly restrictive legal interpretations of the rights of married women to engage in business prevailed, particularly in England. Middle- and upper-class women had less and less to do as estate management also shifted into the hands of men. Married women lost control over their property, their persons, their children, and their beliefs.

Since we have no time budgets for women of these centuries we do not know how much "free time" any of them really had. What we can observe from the record is that one fairly visible sector found alternative activities. Among upper-class women the traditional manor house role was never wholly given up, but was gradually transformed into community service roles. Urban middle-class women with energy and initiative followed the manor house pattern. The more problems women took on in dealing with urban and rural misery, the more they realized that the decision-making powers needed to carry out their work were not available to them. Queens or no queens, women as civic beings were invisible in the public spaces of society. The deliberate campaign by women to obtain civic rights did not begin systematically until the 1800s, and it began as a by-product of their other efforts. It was only when they were handicapped in their work for schools, for the poor, for control of conditions of emigration for women, and in their campaigns against slavery and alcoholism—handicapped because of their legal status as females—that they finally were pushed into fighting long-overlooked limitations. The trauma of the Renaissance was over.

This section again centers mainly on Europe, where industrialization, nationalism, and imperialism developed. The settlement of North America is also included, but the whole South American story is left out, as well as that of the other continents. There is little excuse for excluding South America except the inability to master the necessary scholarship. The settlement of Peru and New Granada by Spain, and of Brazil by Portugal, in the 1500s deserves special study because women's roles developed differently there, both the Spanish and the native American roles. The tale of colonialism in South America, Africa, and Asia from the 1500s on, and what it meant for the women who were colonized and the women who were colonizers, will have to wait for another book. Spotty as the presentation of these centuries will be, they do bring us after a fashion to the threshold of the twentieth century with all the discomforts of its imperfectly conceived globalism.

Notes

[1]Nameless, that is, unless the legendary peacemaker queen Genetaska of the Seneca nation was actually a historical character (see "The Peacemaker," in Canfield, 1902: 149-154).

[2]At one time it was thought that the explorers brought syphilis to Europe from the Americas. However, it is now generally considered that the disease was present in Europe all along, and that there was a sudden and unexplained increase in infection rates.

[3]Sheila Johansson (1975) feels I am making too much of a "stream of essays by male authors saying that women shouldn't be highly educated, even [while] they were in fact getting a lot of education in the privileged classes. A few essays never stopped anybody." There may indeed have been, and probably were, many more men supportive of the education of women than the polemic literature implies. There is, nevertheless, such a thing as a climate of opinion. However unrepresentative of a society the creators of that climate are, they leave traces in social thought which to a degree constrain behavior.

[4]By 1800, 20 percent of the population of Western Europe was in towns of over 2500 population. The United States, by contrast, was still predominantly rural, with only 5 percent of its population in urban areas.

[5]The savagery refers to the white man, not the natives. McNeill (1963) in *The Rise of the West* makes it startlingly clear that the success of the expansionism of Europe was due to the superior savagery of the Europeans, who treated natives with a ruthlessness that Indians and blacks were culturally incapable of reciprocating (at least not until it was too late).

References

Canfield, William V.
  1902   The Legends of the Iroquois. Port Washington, N.Y.: Ira J. Freidman

Hyma, Albert
  1930   Erasmus and the Humanists. New York: F. S. Crofts.

Johansson, Sheila
  1975   Seattle, Wash.: Historian, personal communication.

Kelso, Ruth
  1956   Doctrine for the Lady of the Renaissance. Urbana: University of Illinois
         Press.

Laslett, Peter
  1965   The World We Have Lost. London: Methuen.

McDonnell, Ernest W.
  1969   The Beguines and Beghards in Medieval Culture. New York: Octagon
         Books.

McNeill, William H.
  1963   The Rise of the West: A History of the Human Community. Chicago:
         University of Chicago Press.

O'Faolain, Julia, and Lauro Martines (ed.)
  1973   Not in God's Image: A History of Women in Europe from the Greeks to
         the Nineteenth Century. New York: Harper and Row.

Reich, Emil
  1908   Woman Through the Ages. 2 vols. London: Methuen.

10
Queens, Reformers, and Revolutionaries

FROM ISABEL TO ELIZABETH: 1450-1603

The Queens

Each of the great women monarchs in the middle centuries of the second millennium had extraordinary levels of physical energy and moral courage, coupled with high intelligence and human perceptiveness. All lived through their adolescence in great insecurity and fear of their lives. None was "groomed" for queenship, though all knew it was a possibility for them. When finally given a kingdom and a throne, each ruled with a vigor and skill that astounded the men of their courts. They could be tender or ruthless as occasion required. They all looked magnificent on horseback at the head of their armies. They all pursued expansionist policies. What did they "prove" about women? That women could act on prevailing religious and cultural values and political goals as effectively as—or possibly more effectively than—men, given a chance to draw on all the resources a society has to offer. They used the conventional socio-political tools that men used, and more. Their intellectual and social repertoire was a bit wider, perhaps, than that of most ruling men. In no way did they represent a feminine counterculture of nonmilitarism;

535

they worked with the values available to them. This was one of the major reasons for their acceptance by their subjects, and their success. Their legitimacy as rulers derived at least in part from their capacity to wield military power.[1] Even Ashoka, the great peace emperor of India gained legitmacy first through a program of conquest.

Isabel

Isabel of Castile was plunged from a quiet life with a widowed royal mother into hectic court life at the age of eleven by the impeachment of her half-brother the king. The next ruler, her brother Alfonse, kept her close to him during his rule, and when he died in her seventeenth year, she was asked to take the throne. In the years spent by her brother's side she conceived of a mission to unite the petty kingdoms of Spain, and she spent the six years from her seventeenth to her twenty-third year in maneuvers to accomplish this goal. She chose Ferdinand of Aragon as spouse in order to unite their two kingdoms, but she never let him have any regnant power in Castile. The marriage contract, concluded in 1469, was drawn as carefully as any women's rights advocate could draw it in the nineteenth century, protecting all her rights as ruler. This wounded Ferdinand's vanity, but he put up with it. In his younger days Ferdinand never was interested in more than making Aragon strong. Only Isabel had the vision of a united Spain. Isabel was brighter, abler, stronger, and more ambitious than Ferdinand, and it is ironic that the history books tend to portray the reign as Ferdinand's.[2]

Isabel's success lay partly in the fact that she had the physical stamina to live on horseback. She frequently rode all night to be on the spot where something important was happening by morning. She had a miscarriage during one such wild night's ride, and nevertheless directed operations from horseback next morning for the reconquest of invaded territory. She had five children between 1470 and 1485 in spite of her activity level. While she took pride in her reputation as the crusading warrior queen, and personally directed major battles against the Moors as well as supervised the extermination of Jews in Spain and established the Inquisition, her ruthlessness was on behalf of a misguided vision of a "glorious," united, Christian Spain.

Deeply pious, spending much time in prayer, she was always soft-spoken, and never randomly cruel. On the more peaceful side, she built a political system in the towns of Castile that enabled the inhabitants to have both local self-government and an intertown alliance that would create a new consciousness of the larger social entity of Castile and Spain. She used the power of an alliance of burgesses to destroy the older feudal powers of a rapacious nobility, and thereby created a new kind of political community in Spain. She also, of course, subsidized Columbus to open up New Spain for Christianity.

Isabel died in 1504, and Ferdinand spent his remaining years trying to marry off their children in such a way as to make the most of the alliance structures Isabel had created. Much human misery was involved in these negotiations, and in the end they failed in their purpose. Political alliances kept cutting across marriage alliances. Babies died that were supposed to grow up and succeed to the throne. The marriage-alliance system crumbled. It could not withstand the complexity of the emerging new international system. Neither her husband nor her children had Isabel's skills, and the Spain she created did not really survive her, though its shadow and imperial structures seemed powerful for another couple of centuries.

Marguerite of Navarre

The French-born queen of Navarre was a minor queen, born in the year the powerful Isabel supported Columbus in his voyage to the New World. She *was* a "peace queen," acquiring the throne of Navarre by marriage (her second) at the age of thirty-nine. She spent her life as queen in protecting Catholics from Protestants and Protestants from Catholics. She drew the anger of both, inevitably, and charges of heresy, hypocrisy, and deceit. Nevertheless, she followed her own path all her life, and the far-seeing eyes in the kindly but determined face in a lovely painting of her as queen (Bainton, 1973: 12) seem to look far into the future to a very different time.

> Marguerite was a lady of the Renaissance who read Dante in Italian, Plato possibly in Greek, and Luther to a slight degree in German. . . . Pope Paul III marvelled at her saintliness and erudition. She was a poetess of distinction and originality . . . unique in French literature for her recital in verse of the Christian drama of redemption. To find a parallel in any tongue one must turn backwards to Dante and forwards to Milton (Bainton, 1973: 15-16).

Church politicians were always trying to get her on their side and, like Cardinal Pole, found her frustrating "because she was always soaring into the bosom of God" (Bainton, 1973: 29). (The future Queen Elizabeth was to translate Queen Marguerite's *Miroir de l'Ame Pechereuse [Mirror of a Sinful Soul]* into English at the age of ten, and was deeply influenced by it.) Yet she also wrote a Boccaccio-style book, the *Heptameron,* showing once more what a repertoire of styles a talented woman can have. She died at fifty-seven, having witnessed more bloodshed and cruelty than most royalty have to endure, and leaving behind a legacy of local welfare structures in Navarre, a model of peacemaking in the midst of the most virulent hatreds Europe had known, and a daughter, Jeanne D'Albert, who was to be the leader of the Huguenots of the next generation.

Jeanne of Navarre

Jeanne was another peace queen, who on accession to the throne of Navarre at the age of twenty-seven in 1555 publicly announced her adherence to the reformed faith, thus turning her country into a haven for the Huguenots. (Queen Elizabeth of England sent her a message of congratulations for this.) She "is said to be the only sovereign of the sixteenth century who put no one to death for religion" (Bainton, 1973: 43). Whether true or not, it indicates her reputation for tolerance. Like her mother, she led an embattled life as peacemaker and gave a lot of attention to local self-government in her little country.

Other peace queens who maintained the Protestant faith while placed by marriage alliance into Catholic settings, and who displayed great personal heroism throughout their lives, should not go unrecorded here. They were not ruling queens, but they acted as mediators, nursed both sides in wars, and continued to declare publicly their affection and loyalty to family members declared enemies and traitors for religious reasons: Catherine de Bourbon, 1559-1604; Eleanore de Roye, 1535-1564; Charlotte de Bourbon, 1546-1582; Louise de Coligny, 1555-1620 (Bainton, 1973).

These peace queens performed precisely the role that the diplomacy-by-marriage system was invented to further. The human cost to women of that role has always been great, and in the 1500s became almost unbearable. The system was not to die yet—it continued to function until the French Revolution. After that, with monarchy chiefly decorative, the fact that marriage "allied" one royal house with another had less intense political interest. The banker's-daughter alliances that succeeded the royal marriage alliances had a different, though related, signficance.

Catherine de Medici

Catherine de Medici was not a queen in her own right, but served as regent of her principality during the years that Jeanne was queen of Navarre. She was on the other side of the religious struggle, and is considered to be the author of the massacre of St. Bartholomew (which took place just after Queen Jeanne died, in 1572). Yet she was also the architect afterward of peace with the Protestants, and was known equally as a skilled diplomat and a ruthless tactician. She has two major international treaties to her name, and ruled in the style of an Isabel without having the latter's power or charm.

Elizabeth Tudor

Elizabeth's earliest memory was that just before her third birthday her father, Henry VIII, beheaded her mother, Ann Boleyn. Nevertheless she had kind people around her while she was growing up, including her last stepmother, Catherine Parr. (It was for Catherine that Elizabeth translated Marguerite of Navarre's *Miroir*.) Formation of intellect and spirit went hand in hand: Roger Ascham, great humanist scholar, was the tutor who prepared her for ruling. But at twenty-one, when her sister Mary was queen, she was sent to the tower on suspicion of plotting to overthrow her sister. She lived for four years as a prisoner, never knowing from day to day whether she might be executed, but finally she left prison to ascend the throne, having had more time and opportunity than have most rulers to think out a philosophy of life and a plan for ruling. Within her first year she convened parliament and laid the basis for both a firm rule on her part and close collaboration with "her people" through parliament.

Marriage alliances could not serve her as they had served Isabel of Castile. Had she married, it appears that she might have had to give up her throne to her husband:

> Their [her ministers] mood was echoed in the words of the Queen's uncle Lord William Howard, who said, "Whomsoever she shall take, we will have him and serve him to the death" (Luke, 1973).

She utilized marriage negotiations with great skill, however, as an instrument of foreign policy. The royal families of Europe competed for years for the hand—and throne—that she so astutely kept to herself (Hume, 1898; Melancon, 1975).

Elizabeth threaded her way through a series of military alliances that left England much stronger when she died than it had been at her accession, and she left Spain, Armada-less, a second-rate power. She was ruthless in the way Isabel was ruthless when policy required, as in the case of the execution of Mary Queen of Scots and in the putting down of revolts within her realm and in Ireland. Her passion for a united England led to the Act of Supremacy within a year of her accession, and also to the Act of Uniformity. The first act strengthened her own powers, the second outlawed religious nonconformity. Religious dissenters could only weaken England, in her view, and after watching dissenting movements within and without the church culminate in nonconformist demonstrations in London, she pushed the anti-nonconformist legislation of 1593 that in fact made her a persecutor of religous freedom. At the same time, major legislation regarding labor and the poor was undertaken in her reign; the first poor law was passed two years before her death.

Elizabeth certainly accepted no nonsense about limitations of the woman's mind, and it is interesting to note that her women subjects caught the spirit of her independent-mindedness even to the extent of opposing her. Middle-class trading women and working-class women identified themselves strongly with the dissenting religious movements. No monarch was going to tell them how to worship, and they were the main supporters of dissenting priests:

> It was the women who occupied the front line in defense of the preachers, with the sense of emotional engagement hardly exceeded by the suffragettes of three and a half centuries later. . . . When two preachers were sent over London Bridge into exile in the country two or three hundred women feted them with exhortations and goodies. . . . There were more women than men imprisoned in Bridewell in 1569 (Bainton, 1973: 245).

The determined Elizabeth set the pattern for England as "ruler of the waves" in her defeat of the Armada, in her support of high seas adventurer Francis Drake, and in her successful military alliances with the Netherlands. She looked wonderful on horseback in front of her troops, though she did not herself lead them in battle. She presided over and nurtured an economically prosperous era and a great flowering of English culture, to the extent that the age has been named for her. Her critics felt that she had no views of her own, and always did the expedient thing in the immediate situation. Her admirers pointed to the fantastic self-discipline she exercised all her life, the ability to keep her private wishes and needs apart in favor of the good of the realm. There are not many ways to be a successful monarch of a major world power, and for all the depth of piety, extent of learning, and political skill that Elizabeth, like Isabel, had, her ruthlessness inevitably plays a large part in the image that has come down across the centuries.

While in this discussion of queens I have presented the "major queens" as ruthless power figures and the "minor queens" as the peacemakers, it may well be that in the long run the queens of Navarre had more to do with setting viable directions for the future than did Isabel or Elizabeth. Marguerite and Jeanne of Navarre represent new styles of overlife activity, and in a sense symbolize a yet untapped potential for political leadership in nation-state systems —the potential for furthering the self-realization of national communities through creative problem solving instead of through confrontation.

Renaissance Women

Italy

Italy is the country where the term "Renaissance women" has the most meaning. While being put down elsewhere, here women flourished. Perhaps none was more dramatically honored in that era than Tarquinia Molza, who excelled both in poetry and the fine arts, and

> had a rare knowledge of astronomy, and mathematics, Latin, Greek, and Hebrew. So great was the esteem in which she was held that the senate of Rome conferred upon her the singular honor of Roman citizenship, transmissible in perpetuity to her descendents (Potter, in Beard, 1946: 261).

Italian women of the upper classes all through the 1400s and 1500s wrote and orated Latin discourses in their own circles and in public, and exchanged sonnets with their friends of both sexes. They also established Renaissance salons at which they acted as patrons of the arts. The court of King Robert of Anjou in Naples is given credit for being the first Renaissance setting in which women were encouraged not for their "purity" but for their wit. Boccaccio and Petrarch were both frequenters of the court at Naples, and acquired their respect for women's minds there (Tornius, 1929).[3] The Medici salons, on the other hand, did not feature participation of women.

The first great woman salonist is supposed to have been "The Divine Isotta" of Rimini, who died in 1450 (Burckhardt, 1944). Although she was not herself learned, many poets and artists clustered around her court, and she was widely loved. Lucrezia Borgia, the duchess of Ferrara, was another major creator of a cultural center, at the court of Este. Isabella d'Este was such a compelling personality and critic that scholars and artists came to her court from all over Europe for the quality of the cultural life there. She had little money to offer her retinue, for she was relatively poor. By this time women of the Italian nobility were competing with one another to be known for providing the best cultural milieu.

Some of the salons featured courtesans—highly educated middle-class women who "were scholars by day and lovers by night" (Tornius, 1929: 97). There was Madrewa, who could recite Petrarch, Boccaccio, Virgil, Horace, and Ovid. There were Lorentina and Beatrice—when either went to church, she had a whole court of serving men and women, pages, marquises, ambassadors, and dukes in trains (Tornius, 1929: 98). In the Venice of 1509, out of a population of 300,000, there were 11,654 courtesans and some of the finest salons in Italy. Some courtesans ran their own salons, such as Florentine Rullia d'Aragona, a veritable Aspasia. Her home was considered a second Academy, and she concerned herself very much with public affairs. She has been called the "priestess of humanism."

In the 1400s, contrary to trends elsewhere (except in Spain), a humanist school was established in Italy with the same basic curriculum for women and men. Latin was taught as the medium of expression, and Greek as a "foreign language" for development. The Greek system of physical education and classical dancing was taught (Cannon, 1916: 30-31). As might be expected, some of the first publicly recognized women composers came from Italy (Vittoria Alcotti, Francesca Baglioncella, and Orsina Vizzani). And Rome, Florence, Bologna, Venice all had many artists, primarily of the eclectic school. In the early Renaissance period many of the women artists were not known by name, except when they were members of the aristocracy, like Caterine de Vigri, patroness and painter of Ferrara. Canonized, she became "protectress of Academies and Art Institutions" in the Catholic world. Properzia de' Rossi, Bolognese sculptor, who did not have the protection of being of the aristocracy, became so popular with the public that she roused the intense jealousy of her male colleagues. According to Clements they began a crusade against her so that her commissioned work was not mounted on the public building it was prepared for, and she died at forty of "mortification and grief" (Waters, 1904: 300).

In the 1500s the most widely renowned of the Italian artists were Anna Maria Ardoin, poet-artist-musician elected to the Academy of Arcadia; Sophonisba of Cremona (1535-1625), in demand all over Europe as a portrait painter; Lavinia Fontana of Bologna (1552-1614), one of the most prolific and most popular artists of the century;[4] and Catharina van Hemessen (1528-1587), celebrated as a portraitist both in Flanders and Spain. At the very end of this century Artemisia Gentileschi was born (1593-1652), considered by many to be the greatest of Italian women artists. She worked in Rome, Florence, Genoa, Naples, and London and was a primary influence in the development of the Neopolitan School of painting (Tufts, 1974: 59). Favorite poets in the sixteenth century, not only of Italy but of Europe, were Veronica Gambara of Padua and Vittoria Colonna, Michelangelo's great friend.

Spain[5]

Spain also encouraged learning, at least in upper-class women, Queen Isabel herself being very learned. Her companion Beatriz Galindo founded schools, hospitals, and convents all over Spain. Oliva Sabuco de Nantes at the age of twenty-five wrote the seven-volume *Nueva Filosofia* (1587) relating the biology, psychology, and anthropology of the day to medicine and agriculture, starting out with the abrupt statement that "the old science of medicine is in error." Her work reflects mastery of an Arab scholarship unavailable to the rest of Europe. Catalina Mendoza, a scholar with no published works, founded a Jesuit college for women.

The situation of women in Spain in the 1500s is interesting. Convents had high standards of scholarship, and produced musicians and poets as well as scholars. As in Italy, there was an unbroken tradition from earliest times of women attending universities. Such women had contact with both Italian and Arab scholars. The palace schools for the Spanish princesses provided a stimulus to women's education, in that nonroyal women were also admitted to these schools. The women's orders founded schools for lay people as well as training schools for their own orders, so that the Augustinians, Benedictines, Franciscans, Dominicans, Tertians, and Carmelites all contributed to the education of girls in Spain. St. Teresa of Avila's writing skill came partly from her training at the Augustinian convent school in Avila which had a teaching staff of forty nuns.

Northern Europe

The first Renaissance schools outside of Italy and Spain were established by the Brethren of the Common Life. In 1497 in Zanten a lay school for girls both of the nobility and of the "citizen classes" was established under Aldegundis von Horstmar, a directress trained by the Brethren of Common Life. The eighty-four students in this school received a Latin and classical education. The German scholar-abbess tradition produced learned women such as Margaret von Steffel, who wrote lives of St. Bernard and St. Hildegard in verse, and Catherine of Ostheim, who abridged the *Chronicles of Limburg.* The women of the palatinate courts were poets and women of learning. Germany and the Netherlands supported many women artists, chiefly miniaturists and illuminators. One of the most renowned of these was Leonia Teerling of Flanders (1515-1576) who became court painter to the British royal family. In the Netherlands, the Hapsburg Spanish traditions of learning for women were carried on, and culture and scholarship for women somehow survived the hostility of Erasmus and Luther. Visible evidence of this will be seen in the next century, when we observe the milieu out of which Dutch Anne-Marie Schurman emerges to become a world-renowned figure.

France

In France, ladies of the nobility were well educated, and some of them became writers, notably the earlier-mentioned Marguerite of Navarre, but also Anne of Beaujeu and Anne of Brittany. Outside the nobility, there seems to have been an extraordinarily adventurous lot of women in France who did not get the message that the new humanism did not apply to them. There were the poetesses of Lyons, for example, Pernette de Guillet and Louise Labé. Labé is the famous one, the gifted daughter of a Lyons rope maker who could not succeed in being a conventional housewife though she tried. *La Capitaine* Louise dressed as a soldier and tried to help rescue her city from the Spaniards, becoming the town heroine. In the end she was denounced, not for her poetry or for her soldiering, but for her love life.

One of the most significant characters in sixteenth century France in terms of a direct confrontation with Renaissance antifeminism is Marie de Jars de Gournay. Born in 1565 and living to be ninety, she actually spanned two centuries. She discovered Montesquieu, apostle of individualism, before he was generally admired, and made herself his disciple and translator. She was also a promotor of the poet Ronsard. The first of a great company of intrepid spinster intellectuals, she was ridiculed all her life; much was made of the fact that she was plain. She kept cats, which she liked better than people. She chose her own causes, and supported them ardently. Her books on education and public affairs, dedicated to Henry IV and to Marie de Medici, sold well, as did her translations of Virgil, Ovid, Sallust, and Tacitus. Like Christine de Pisan, she could make a living from her writing. She also received well-earned pensions from Marie de Medici, Anne of Austria, and Richelieu. She had a passionate intellectual curiosity, and mastered subjects like alchemy for fun. Her sharp retentive mind fed on everything the Renaissance had to offer, but as a sensitive human being she sometimes lashed out at the society which so scorned women—and she sometimes cast epithets at her enemies. While other women apologized for presuming to write books, Marie published two scathing documents—*Egalité des Hommes et des Femmes,* and *Grief des Dames.* The latter she began with the lines:

> Lucky are you, reader, if you happen not to be of that sex to whom it is forbidden all good things, to whom liberty is denied; to whom almost all virtues are denied; lucky are you if you are one of those who can be wise without its being a crime (Schiff, 1910: 89; translation my own).

In a very modern manner, Marie decried stupidity in either sex, pointed out what women had achieved in antiquity, and said the wonder was not that women had achieved so little, but that they had achieved anything at all given the lack of opportunity for education and development. She even tackled the "bad theology" of the church in its treatment of God as a man, instead of being beyond sex. Twentieth century women owe a lot to Marie de Gournay, though she would not like to be thanked.

England

Returning to those in Elizabeth's England, we find the lady humanists somewhat tame there by comparison with the rest of Europe. The best education for women was found in private families, through tutors. We find three cases of fathers establishing what amounted to special schools for their daughters: Sir Thomas More for daughters Margaret, Cecilia, and Elizabeth (plus a cousin); Sir Anthony Coke for daughters Mildred, Anne, and Catherine; and the Earl of Surrey for daughters Jane, Catherine, and Margaret. (We never hear of mothers running schools for daughters.) The fact that these three "schools" are famous speaks for the general paucity of schools for women. After the closure of the convents in 1546, there were practically none. When secular grammar schools were opened later, they were for boys only. Some of the daughters of the three families mentioned wrote and published, but most of them disappeared into marriage and did not become public figures in any way.

There was considerable home tutoring of women in the upper classes, however, as indicated by references to how well educated women of the Elizabethan era were.[6] This home training sometimes led to a fairly active life for women. Mary Sidney, for example, was taught as a child together with her brother Sir Philip Sidney. In later life she held the only salon I have seen mentioned in England in the 1500s. As Countess Pembroke, she entertained poets and statesmen including Spenser, Ben Jonson, Shakespeare, and John Donne. Lady

Jane Grey, imprisoned and executed at seventeen by the Catholic
Queen Mary for having been made England's nine-day queen by
enthusiastic Protestants, would surely have been a great scholar had
she lived. At fourteen she was corresponding with Swiss theologians,
and was proficient in Latin, Greek, French, and Italian. Stenton's
(1957) book on English women in history describes a number of self-
taught women from this period, and not all were of the nobility.
How many young women of the "lower classes" taught themselves
to read and write, like Anne Prowse, author of a "pious book," we
shall never know. The most colorful characters among Elizabethan
women were not scholars, however. The famous Bess Hardwick, who
exercised control over substantial parts of England through lands and
rights acquired through four marriages, was a thinker who did not get
her ideas from books.

There must have been women artists and musicians in sixteenth
century England, but I have seen no references to them, except for
the 1537 tombstone inscription of an Elizabeth Lucar, who died at
twenty-six and whose grieving husband recounted with eloquence on
stone her skill as artist and musician and scholar.

What this survey of Renaissance women scholars and artists indicates is that, in spite of public denial of the importance of women's
mental capacities, women to a surprising extent acquired and made
creative use of the new learning. Except in Spain and Italy, where
women could attend universities, learning was a special class privilege
of the nobility and the well-to-do, and was fostered privately in
homes and convent schools. It was very much an underlife activity.
Also, it could only exist when tolerated—or encouraged—by men.
The extent of tolerance for learning in women was certainly connected with the highly successful role played by the queens of the
century, both the major and the minor queens. As far as the historical record goes, only one woman in the entire century publicly and
vociferously rebelled against mere tolerance—Marie de Gournay. In
the next century, many more women rebelled.

Religious Women of the Reformation and the Counter-Reformation

Since the Reformation was born in Germany, we think of the stocky
peasant nun Katherine Von Bora, who married the ex-monk Martin
Luther, as the prototype of the new Protestant woman:[7] a strong-
minded materfamilias with many children; one who feeds the poor at

her table, runs the family farm, and generally manages household and family affairs with little or no help from her husband, yet defers to him in all things; a woman with no views on public matters. Actually many Protestant women played precisely this role, but many also took part in community and church affairs in spite of the objections of their men. Katherine Zell, for example, who lived in Strasbourg where the peasant's war struck, was thoroughly involved in community affairs and in caring for refugees, nursing the sick, and effecting reconciliations in town conflicts. She preached in public, even at her own husband's funeral, to the great annoyance of the men of the town. She spoke out courageously and publicly against persecution wherever she found it. Another side of her life is revealed in her publication of a children's hymn book.

Men and women of the Reformation seem to have gone through an alarming number of spouses in a lifetime, an indication of the high death rate of men in war and women in childbirth. Wilbrandis Rosen-blatt, after her first marriage to a tradesman, married three prominent reformers in succession, and it is said that "all her husbands loved her gentleness." Her home was a refugee center throughout her life, and even while living in this storm center she managed to have children by each of her four husbands—ten in all.

Not all Reformation women were of the peasant and working classes. In addition to the peace queens mentioned earlier, many women of the minor nobility became involved in the Reformation controversies, and often defended heretics at great risk to their own lives. Argula von Grumbach was one, Elizabeth of Brandenburg another, and her daughter Elizabeth of Braunschweig a third. They suffered persecution, physical deprivation, and banishment. On the whole their life in Germany was perhaps even harder than the life of the Huguenots in France, although bloodshed was widespread during this period in France.

One of the early heretics among the aristocracy in England was Lady Anne Askew, great-grandmother of Margaret Fell, one of the founders of Quakerism a century later. An attendant at the court of Queen Catherine Parr, Henry VIII's last queen, she developed a reputation for preferring reading the Bible to going to mass. That Henry VIII should have sanctioned proceedings against this young court woman of twenty-five that included being tortured on the rack and burned at the stake for reading the Bible gives a clue to the atmosphere of suspicion and fear generated by the politics of church and state at that time. Anne was a woman of great inner strength, and also a gifted writer. Letters and poems from her last days survive (see Webb, 1867). Her tutor was burnt with her, as having encouraged her wicked practices, and at the stake it was *she* who encouraged and supported *him.*

The Anabaptists had the hardest time of all, partly because they were more extreme in their dissent. They also practiced complete equality of women and men in every respect, including preaching. Both Catholics and Lutherans persecuted them, and they lived hunted lives. We know little about the women except that they could never settle down to normal family life; they were always on the run. Elizabeth Dirks of Holland, an Anabaptist teacher who was imprisoned, tortured, and drowned in a sack, is one of the few we know about from the sixteenth century. That the Anabaptists had staying power in the face of extreme persecution is indicated by the fact that they were still active in the next century. Anna Marie Schurmann, born at the close of this century, became a noted Anabaptist in the next.

The homemaker wife who created a gathering place for members of the religious community was perhaps a special product of the religious struggles associated with the Reformation. It was different in every respect from the salon tradition, which was essentially anti-familial—women held salons on their own, not for or with husbands (with occasional exceptions). Protestantism was in its origin a very familistic religion, and the homemaker wife was always acting on behalf of a husband, present or absent. Partly this was a class difference, not a religious one, since familism is always stronger in the middle than in the upper classes. It was not entirely class, however. In the sixteenth century it was Protestantism that was the more familistic religion, though in the twentieth century we think of Catholicism as the familistic religion. The homemaker-wife role was of course a Catholic one too, and at times it was a very grim role. In Protestant countries Catholic wives and mothers were martyred for trying to bring their children up in the faith, as in the terrible story of Margaret Clitherow of York (Dessain, 1971). This gay but devout young mother of perhaps half a dozen children was ordered crushed to death by the local judge for not attending the Church of England services. She and dozens, perhaps hundreds, like her accepted torture and death rather than give up their faith, though until their time of trial they were strictly domestic persons with no record of public activity. Homemaker heroines are even less likely to make the history books than are women who take community leadership roles. We know about Margaret because she was sainted afterwards by the Catholic church.

In the Catholic tradition the role of the nun has been so striking that there is danger of appearing to ignore or belittle the homemaker. The mass of peasant and artisan women, the middle-class merchant wives, and the scholars and artists we have been describing in the last several chapters were more often than not homemakers in addition to their other roles. If autonomy of nuns has been emphasized, this is not to suggest that married women with all their underlife skills did not also find spheres of autonomy. Particularly during the Reformation and the Counter-Reformation, because of the continuing high levels of conflict and violence that reached into every household, all of the homemakers' creative skills had to be drawn on daily. Peacemaking was not confined to two Protestant queens. Every woman of every faith had peacemaking tasks, though some were more skillful at them than others.

The Counter-Reformation tapped new veins of creativity in Catholic women. While all women to some degree participated in a heightened social sensitivity, women religious played a special part in the developments. The term *Counter-Reformation* is misleading and really should not be used at all; it describes developments that, in the Catholic church, began well before the Reformation, developments that had their own dynamic independent of Protestant activities. It was, of course, these developments that produced Luther. Under different circumstances he might have completed his work inside the Catholic church. That he did not had more to do with political than religious matters.

The Dominicans, Franciscans, Beguines, and Brethren of the Common Life all played their parts in preparing for the new developments within the women's religious orders in the Catholic church. On the one hand was the emphasis on a deep inwardness, already well established by the Beguine mystics, resulting in the 1500s in the development of Illuminism, a devout orthodox movement which nevertheless hovered on the edge of heresy. Illuminati among the nuns were found particularly in Spain, home of Maria de Santo Domingo, Magdalena de la Cruz, and Maria Cazalla. In Italy St. Catherine of Genoa helped organize such illuminati into groups called the Fraternities of Divine Love.

Paralleling this search for inwardness was another development which emphasized teaching and service. Ignatius Loyola, the soldier-founder of the Jesuits who underwent a spectacular conversion after severe wounding and disablement, was the charismatic figure in the movement. Many other forces were also pushing toward a more active service in the world, and women were particularly ready for this. In the next century Mary Ward founded a women's counterpart of the Jesuit order, calling her group Institutes of Mary. It was too radical in conception and was dissolved by the church, but was eventually reconstituted as an accepted teaching order.[8]

Angela Merici's concept of a teaching order, the Ursulines, though less threatening, also met the opposition of church authorities. Angela was a devout and conservative young Italian woman who as a dowryless orphan remained single when her friends married. She lived an austere life of service to friends and neighbors in her hometown of Brescia—a life probably duplicated by unknown thousands of spinster women in Europe whose biographies will never be known. Angela's uniqueness lay in her sense of mission. Fearful of appearing radical or hasty, she pondered her calling for years as she observed the young people of Brescia in the early decades of the 1500s. She watched inflation drive economically pressed families of the Lombard plain into pushing unwilling daughters into convents. She saw what that did to the religious life of the convents as well as to the girls. She watched ignorant teen-age girls milling around the public square with nothing to do, and saw them being swept away by the fads of occult, underground religions that smelled of demonism. She saw the witchcraft hysteria descend on these girls and lead them to the stake for nothing more than adolescent foolishness.

Angela knew that widows and young women with more means than she at their disposal often taught young girls in their own homes.[9] She thought something more was needed than these occasional private-enterprise widow's schools. Finally, by the age of fifty-eight she had gained the support of some of the widows and women of means of Brescia for a bold program of establishing a nonconventional teaching order for women. Women were to take religious vows but live at home, wear no special dress or insignia, and be teachers in the community. A sympathetic bishop supported her idea to the church authorities. Thus the teaching order of the Ursulines, named after the legendary British maiden who emigrated to the Continent with a band of young women in the fifth century, was launched with the blessing of the church in 1537. Social pressures for enclosure soon limited their activities, placing them within convent walls in 1612, but a new principle had been established and was not forgotten. In 1857 the order was able to return to its original vision. In the intervening centuries enclosure did not prevent the Ursulines from teaching in their convent-based schools; eventually they did for the education of girls what the Jesuits did for the education of boys (Daniel-Rops, 1962: 25; Monica, 1945).

This story has been told in some detail because it reflects the strength of the underlife of a less favored class of women—women who rarely appear in history. The self-help culture out of which Angela developed her idea for a teaching order represented a resource of initiative and quiet leadership that in the long run made a greater participation in society possible for women of later generations. Angela's life also suggests that in the 1500s, as in previous centuries, a number of women continued single and independent without being assimilated into the structures of family or church.

St. Teresa of Avila is the towering figure in the spiritual awakening of the sixteenth century. A well-educated, "society-type" convent girl, she underwent powerful religious experiences that awakened her to a very different realization of the human possibility than her own rather conventional religious formation had prepared her for. It says something about the attitude toward women in Spanish society that this woman was able to command the attention of the church in Spain and to carry out reforms that lifted her convents from ordinary "homes for celibate women" to centers of spiritual transformation. It happened that she was a good organizer, an impressive speaker, and had a commanding presence. But what really carried her movement was her depth of religious insight, which stood up under every kind of test a somewhat hostile church could give it.

Teresa was well enough trained in sixteenth century cultural patterns to preface her writings with the "I'm only a poor silly woman" routine, but her writings are among the most widely read devotional literature of the twentieth century.[10] It is sad that Teresa's counterparts have not been easily produced in the Protestant world, with its emphasis on the duties of the housewife. There is nothing in the housewife's role that prevents spiritual transformation except the legitimacy of the *intention* to place God first. The Reformation created a kind of discontinuity that had not existed earlier with regard to attitudes about religious calling in the two worlds of Catholicism and Protestantism. It is all right for Protestant women to be activists, but not contemplatives. One might say that the Reformation was incomplete in Protestantism, in not allowing for the full development of women's spirituality.

Family Life, and the Situation of Middle- and Lower-Class Women

Since the tendency for middle-class women in urban settings to withdraw from involvement in productive activities beyond strictly domestic maintenance begins in the sixteenth century, it is of some interest to look at the typical household size for the century. How many people lived in a household, and what kind of living space did families have? Recent studies (Laslett, 1972) of local records in various parts of Europe indicate the surprising fact that household size has changed very little from the Middle Ages to the present. Apart from the great manor houses of the nobility and the homes of rich merchants, most people lived in families with an average of 4.75 persons per family, plus a servant. These "servants," it turns out, were not servants in the contemporary sense of the word, but rather children of neighboring families in the same parish. Families were in effect training each other's children. Not only were families small, but the age of marriage for women as well as men was beginning to rise. The average age at marriage for European women in the 1500s was about twenty-one, rising in succeeding centuries as high as twenty-five to twenty-eight. Furthermore, multigenerational families were primarily an upper-class phenomenon. Most women were confined to small domestic spaces in small families before marriage, and entered equally small domestic spaces after marriage. Although women certainly had larger households during their childbearing years, high infant death rates and the practice of older couples and widows maintaining separate living quarters created considerable domestic isolation for women as they lost freedom of movement in other spheres.

The great bulk of both rural and urban women of the sixteenth century, and for several centuries to come, lived in crowded quarters. The decline in the live-in dormitory arrangements for apprentices and laborers practiced earlier in urban workshops and manor houses did not create housing pressure at first because there was plenty of housing for a plague-decimated population. With population growing again in the sixteenth century the cottagers of the countryside could build their own little stone houses. In the cities every kind of warehouse and other building was appropriated for family dwellings, soon giving rise to the typical city tenement. Few working-class families had more space than was needed for sleeping and eating. Other activities were carried on elsewhere in the village or town.

Middle-class families had more space, but they too lived in fairly close quarters. Women may have had more time to spend with children, but in the compressed life spaces available there were high tension levels and frequent expressions of physical violence. Partly this may have been a continuation of the "culture of violence" noted from time to time in the relations between parents and children. Pinchbeck and Hewitt note that in the sixteenth century the concept of "breaking the spirit of the child" still prevailed in child rearing (1969: 351). The literature of the time contains many references to brutal child discipline, and the frequency with which mothers beat daughters is particularly noticeable. Daughter beating was often in connection with a child's resistance to parental marriage plans. Even the gentle peace queen Marguerite of Navarre beat her daughter daily for weeks on end to make her agree to a politically designed marriage choice. Lady Jane Grey's mother beat her (Bainton, 1973). Agnes Paston, of the lively Paston family known for its voluminous intrafamily correspondence and numerous lawsuits, beat her daughter so badly that "her head was broke in 2 or 3 places" (O'Faolain and Martines, 1973).[11] It would seem that women of this period were subject to a lot of emotional pressure which they vented by child beating. Putting daughters out to other families as servants was one of the few available means of relieving the strain, but this required reciprocity, in that such a mother must accept someone else's daughter into her home. The disappearance of convents in England and in many places in Europe, and the closing down of other occupational options for women, made marriage arrangements increasingly important and also made marriages harder to achieve.[12] Mothers bore the brunt of these problems in terms of felt pressure to get their daughters out of their small households.

The generally short life expectancy of both women and men—thirty-two at birth in England in 1690, twenty-seven in Breslau in the same year (Laslett, 1965: 62)—contributed to this violence, since there was frequent remarriage of widows and widowers with children from earlier marriages. These children were often regarded as nuisances by their own parent as well as by the new spouse (Pinchbeck and Hewitt, 1969: 12). The idea that children should be happy, and that they would respond to gentleness in a teacher or parent, was somewhat novel when it was espoused by Montaigne in the latter part of the sixteenth century (in his *Essais,* 1960). The anti-whipping movement was slow to develop.

In cities the traditional charitable services provided by church and private charity could not keep up with urban destitution. The phenomenon of vagrant children (orphans, and also, children whose mothers were at work) is increasingly taken note of after 1500. Systems for apprenticing "idle beggars" between the ages of five and fourteen were developed. A very few of these were humane institutions such as the model school established in Ypres in 1525. In England, roundups of "wandering beggars" began taking place, and by 1547 girl children could legally be placed in an enforced apprenticeship until the age of fifteen or marriage (Pinchbeck and Hewitt, 1969: 96), which amounted to *de facto* slavery.

In short, children were in the way. There were no family living spaces adequate for them, and it was difficult to establish enough apprentice and employment opportunities for those who were not kept by their mothers' sides as helpers in field or shop. Girls were even less welcome than were boys because of the burden of providing a marriage dowry.

The effect of limitation of opportunities for women on mother-daughter relations is a subject that needs much more attention. Obviously not all mothers beat their daughters, nor did beatings necessarily lead to bad feelings. Rather, there was apt to be continued expression of affection between mothers and daughters throughout their lives, as in the Paston family.

That women chose to exit from confining extended-family situations and live on their own whenever possible is suggested by the fact that in the 1500s, even with all the housing shortages, 16 percent of all English households in one hundred communities examined by Laslett (1972: 147) were headed by women: 12.9 percent of the heads of household were widows, 1.1 percent single females, and 2.3 percent "unspecified females." While some widows remarried, there are also many references to the joy with which women after widowhood set up their own households, and to the vigor with which they resisted ₀courting by amorous widowers. The extended-family togetherness we nostalgically refer to as part of our golden past simply did not exist in the European heritage, and there is some evidence that it never really existed anywhere, except as an upper-class phenomenon. Laslett concludes that the multigenerational household is the exception in every society.[13]

The 16 percent of women who headed their own households were brave women, because in that century, at the height of the witch-craft persecutions, it was the women living alone who were the most subject to accusations of witchcraft. The majority of the witches were women, and many accusers were clergymen, though at the height of the burnings all kinds of male adventurers got into the act, collecting "bonuses" for every witch they identified.

> Between 1587 and 1593 twenty-two villages in the region of Trier surrendered 368 witches to the bonfires. Two other villages survived the spasm with a female population of one each (O'Faolain and Martines, 1973: 215).

In London a Scotch witch-finder was finally himself imprisoned:

> And upon the gallows he confessed he had been the death of above 220 women in England and Scotland, for the gain of twenty-one shillings

apiece, and beseeched forgiveness. And was executed (O'Faolain and Martines, 1973: 217).

The last "legal" execution of a woman for witchcraft in England took place in 1716, but "witchhunts" continued for another century.

In spite of the pressures on women of confined domestic spaces and witchcraft accusations, there are many evidences that family life "improved" in the sixteenth century.[14] The major contribution of the Reformation to family life was that priests either turned Protestant and took legal wives, or stayed Catholic but stopped having exploited "priestess-concubines" in the parish household. Obviously that practice did not stop overnight, but it could no longer be done overtly as before. Whether there was a net gain for women one cannot be sure—one would have to know what happened to all the "priestesses," and there is no information on this.

Among the poor, legal marriage was a luxury, but peasant and artisan classes were also potential participants in the new familistic culture which began about this time. Contemporary chronicles describe families as playing games together, such as blind man's bluff. In countryside and town there had always been holy days and harvest festivals that provided occasions for community recreation. Processions, dancing, and games were not new in the sixteenth century, but rather as old as community life. What was new was that the family unit now sometimes was also the play unit, though space was too limited for this to happen except among the well-to-do.

In this century the lot of working women became harder, but actual starvation was the exception. Pockets of hunger in Europe and England developed from time to time, but exhaustion and overwork in field, workshop, and preindustrial factory, not simply starvation, were the killers of women, men, and children. Working hours were getting longer. Men were beginning to petition against women being given weaver's work, fearing the competition as employment became scarce (Clark, 1919: 103). In better-off artisan homes, and increasingly in middle-class homes, women became the unpaid domestic servants of their husbands as they left (or lost) their own employment opportunities.

The sixteenth century was a threshold century. The great future surge of urbanization, already beginning to build up, was to be felt increasingly in the next century. By 1600 over seventy-five of the world's great cities had reached the 100,000 population mark (the sociologist Sorokin's estimate in Morris, 1974: 105), and humans faced a new scale of existence.

RISING DISSENT: THE 1600s

The seventeenth century witnessed the rapid development of colonial settlements in the Americas. It was a century of movement, and a century in which women began to become more publicly articulate. The articulation came through a variety of roles, from women as intellectuals, as workers, as religous dissenters, and as overseas migrants. This was the golden age of pamphleteering, and women entered into it with zest, as we note in the 1640 pamphlet published in England, *The Woman's Sharpe Revenge*, by Mary Tattle-Well and Joan Hit-Him-Home, Spinsters, which demolished then-current antifeminist writings. When Bacon said, "Bitter and earnest writings must not be hastily condemned; for men cannot contend coldly, and without affection, about things which they hold dear and precious" (Ward, 1927: xvi-xvii), few were prepared to recognize the right of women also to write earnestly and bitterly; but the boldest of the women took advantage of the new opportunities anyway.

Whether men recognized these rights of expression or not, the battle for women's rights had been joined. There were already strong male voices on behalf of women, such as the anonymous lawyer-author of *The Lawes Resolutions of Womens' Rights* (1632). In this period the first public references to birth control appeared. The condom, first used in England in this century as a protection for men against venereal disease, began to be perceived by women as a protection against pregnancy. In France upper-class women began to express freely their interest in limiting families (one contribution of the salon atmosphere), and by the next century French women had developed a technology of birth control. French birth rates began to reflect this in the 1800s.

Articulate women dissenters and militants were a small minority, but they were there—in Europe, in the Colonial Americas, and also in Asia, though another century was to go by before Europeans felt a sense of sisterhood with Asian women. The dissenting women came from all sectors of society, upper, middle, and working class. They were Catholics, Protestants, and Quakers.

Another significant dissenting group was the bluestockings,[15] who were intellectual women of the upper middle class. Much admired by the progressive men of their day, on the whole they were no threat to anyone except their own more radical sisters. Some, like Marie de Gournay, were feminists, but many bluestockings were actively hostile to the new women's movement. Some showed great skill in privately creating public space in their own homes, through the institution of the salon. While salon tradition originated in the Mediterranean, French women soon made it an institution uniquely their own.

At first, as in Italy, the salon was a mechanism by which women of the aristocracy could extend protection and patronage to artists and intellectuals. The most famous of the *salonières* were both intellectuals in their own right and patrons of intellectual men. Petted and protected by men of their own class, and courted by their protégés, from the feminist perspective they could be seen as a type of degraded courtesan. Rowbotham compares their situation to "that of the mulatto servant in slave society, aspiring only to be a sub-white, and thus enjoying the protection of the whites" (1972: 33). This judgment is unfair to the extent that it underrates the independent intellectual creativity of many *salonières*. However we interpret their social role, they did conform to the humanist tradition of avoiding problems of social justice while exploring intellectual frontiers.

Economic, political, and intellectual life was developing on a new scale in the seventeenth century, and would be fostering new styles of dissent among women. Central to the emerging social order was the male-dominated international banking system. The banks of Hamburg, Amsterdam, and Nuremberg were all founded around 1619, the Bank of Sweden in 1658, and the Bank of England in 1694. (The Paris Bourse was not established until 1724.) Related to the rise of banking was the rise of the merchant adventurers and the establishment of the British, Dutch, and French merchant companies and crown colonies. This was also the century of the Glorious Revolution in England (1688) and of the inglorious Thirty Years War on the Continent. Not only did these developments create new economic and political structures, but they provided the intellectual background for the development of a new set of institutions, the academies. This was the century in which the Académie Française was formed (1635), the French Academy of Science (1658), the English Royal Society (1662), and the Berlin Academy of Science (1700).

In the new style of exclusion of women from economic activities, there were no women in the banks, and few in the colonial enterprises except for the occasional merchant women of England and the Netherlands and the merchant widows who continued their husbands' enterprises. There were no women in the academies either, despite the power of the salons. The scholarly and scientific activities of women developed outside the academies, and for the most part also outside the salons, in private spaces and special niches.

Women in England

Manor House Militants[16]

The civil war brought the manor house aristocracy of English women into new roles. We have described them in earlier chapters as estate managers, teachers, and supervisors of village services. Now we see them as warriors.

Women, more often conservative politically than not, tended to be royalist during the civil war. Since the prevailing trend was anti-royalist, this produced some rather unusual heroines among upper-class women who held family castles while their men were off fighting elsewhere. Lucy Apsley Hutchinson defended Nottingham when besieged, playing double duty as soldier and nurse. The countess of Derby defended Latham House for a whole year in 1643. She tore up all surrender messages and in the end was rescued by royalist troops. Lady Blanche Arundel defended her castle for nine days with twenty-five men against an army of thirteen hundred, refusing to surrender; when her castle fell she and her children were carried off to prison. Lady Mary Bankes held her castle successfully for six weeks, with her daughters, women servants, and five soldiers. The baroness of Offaley, at the age of sixty, successfully defended her castle against two different assaults in 1641.

Anne Howard fought for the royalist cause as a single woman, and had many hair-raising escapes acting as a secret agent. Her autobiography, written after she settled down at thirty-four to become Lady Anne Halkett, gives an idea of how free women of daring could be in that century (Nichols, 1965).[17]

A different kind of manor house militant was Lady Anne Clifford (1590-1675) who was carefully trained by her mother to battle in the courts for the right to own and administer the lands that were supposed to come to her through the will of her father, the earl of Cumberland. Her tutor was the poet-historian Samuel Daniel, and she became one of the best archivists of her era. She fought the courts and the king for twenty-six years for her lands, and must have known *The Lawes Resolutions of Women's Rights* backwards and forwards. Finally at fifty-three she succeeded to her lands. For the last thirty years of her life she ran an almost legendary feudal kingdom in the old style—something no women had done for several centuries in England. While it was a step into the past, it was also a bridge into the future, in that she built model poorhouses on her lands.

Feminist Scholars

Strongly feminist scholars were shaping new ways of thinking about women right through the seventeenth century, in a country that had opened no educational facilities for women since the closing of the convents in the previous century. One of the most dramatic of the feminist scholars was Margaret Lucas, duchess of Newcastle. A popular writer, in 1662 she wrote "Female Orations supposedly made by women who were deliberating on the possibility of combining to make themselves as 'free, happy and famous as men'" in a book of *Orations of Diverse Persons* (Stenton, 1957: 157-158). Crowds used to go to the park in London just to see her ride by in her coach. Then there was Mary Cary, a futurist who predicted the Fifth Monarchy and the millennium. She was widely read and consulted by public figures, almost like a prophetess strayed out of the 1300s. Her millennialist predictions emphasized the role women would play in the new world (Stenton, 1957: 172-175). There were also pamphleteers. The anonymous "Eugenia" attacked a "crude" wedding sermon published by John Sprint in *The Female Advocate* (1699); Lady Chudleigh wrote *The Ladies Defence* in answer to the same sermon. In 1696 an anonymous author produced a cleverly satirical *Essay in Defence of the Female Sex.*

Besides engaging in polemics, a number of thoughtful women were developing proposals for the education of women. Lettice Cary, who died young at midcentury, made such an impression with her proposals for "places of education for gentlewomen, and for the retirement of widows (as Colleges and the Inns of Court and Chancery are for men) in several parts of the Kingdom" (Stenton, 1957: 140) that she continued to be quoted much later in the century. Bathshua Makin and Hannah Woolley both published proposals on the education of women between 1670 and 1675. Both were teachers, writers, and vigorous public figures. Mary Astell, the center of a strong feminist group toward the end of the century, published *A Serious Proposal to the Ladies* (1701) including a proposal for a woman's college. Wealthy women supporters in her circle had actually put up the money for such a college, but Astell was made such fun of for appearing to propose a "nunnery" that they lost heart and retreated. Given the lack of an acceptable pattern for the education of women at the time in England, it was not unreasonable for Astell to propose the monastic model. Her intentions were completely misunderstood by many of her contemporaries. Those who came after understood better, and many of the philanthropic and educational projects begun by women in the next century were inspired by her writings. As a single woman with no income, she had had to make her own way in the world, and had a strictly practical concern for helping single women live independently. She was also a political writer.

Male supporters of the education of women were certainly not absent, as witnessed by Daniel Defoe's proposal for an academy for ladies in *An Essay upon Projects* (1697). The concentration of writings on the education of women at the end of the century indicates a readiness to deal with this long-ignored issue. The militants had made an impression, both on their own sex and on men.

Working-Class Militants

Working-class women were in even more of a fighting mood. They sometimes literally occupied en masse the public spaces that their more educated counterparts wrote about. The civil war hit them hard, ruining their trade, imprisoning their husbands, and generally making life difficult for them. In 1643 peace proposals were before the House of Commons, which that body decided to reject. The citizenesses of London mobilized, and "two or three thousand women, but generally of the meanest sort" (Hill, 1896: 195) presented a petition to parliament. Met with a smooth answer and instructions to go home, they instead stayed and increased in numbers to five thousand women, finally to be dispersed with bullets, swords, and bloodshed.

"The meanest sort" were by no means inarticulate. The year before they had stated in a petition:

> Women are sharers in the common calamities that accompany both Church and Commonwealth, when oppression is exercised over the Church or Kingdoms, wherein they live" (Rowbotham, 1972: 15).

In 1647 the maids of London petitioned parliament for protection against unreasonable working conditions imposed by the "City Dames." In the same year women petitioned for the release of Lilburne, a member of the radical Leveller movement:

> [Women] appear so despicable in your eyes as to be thought unworthy to petition or represent our grievances. . . . Can you imagine us to be so sottish or stupid, as not to perceive or not to be sensible when daily those strong defences of our Peace and Welfare are broken down and trod underfoot by arbitrary power? (Rowbotham, 1972: 17).

In the 1640s a brewer's wife, Anne Stagg, presented a petition on behalf of "Gentlewomen, Tradesmen's wives, and many others of the female sex, all inhabitants of the City of London and the Suburbs thereof" for protection against religious persecution. In 1651 the women were back again, petitioning for relief from imprisonment for debt, with cogent arguments about the oppressive nature of debt imprisonment (Hill, 1896: 199, 200). While men argued that women could not possibly understand the complexities of public affairs, due to weakness of intellect, these tradeswomen showed by word and deed that they understood not only what was going on, but what needed to be done about it.

Nonconformist Women

A whole group of nonconforming sects was emerging in the 1640s out of the Anabaptist traditions of the previous century. In England the nonconformists may well have been drawn from the inhabitants of that one-fifth of all English villages which had never had a resident squire: villages without manor houses.[18] Otherwise it is difficult to account for the extent of self-sufficiency, of self-confident leadership and the total lack of deference patterns, in the behavior of both women and men of those sects. Samuel, writing of a period several centuries later, describes this same lack of dependency and deference in villages where

> no sympathizing ladies made their appearance at the cottage door with words of comfort or exhortation, to bring the poor religion, to correct their spending habits, or to teach them how to work (1975: 157).

These rough and ready artisans, with their wide repertoire of craft skills and strong self-help traditions, were a thorn in the flesh of the local representatives of church and state. They represented a form of participatory democracy alien to the feudal order. They stood for a concept of distributive justice at the opposite pole from that of manor house charity. This egalitarianism was feared wherever it emerged, in England or on the Continent.

Consistent with these egalitarian characteristics, one trait that strongly marked all Anabaptist-inspired groups in the seventeenth century and later was the strong participation of women in every aspect of the life of the group. When Winstanley issued a proclamation for the Diggers and Levellers in 1649—"Why may we not have our heaven here and Heaven hereafter too?"—it was plain that women were included in the "we." Women were equally active with men in taking over "surplus" property and redistributing it to the poor in the Leveller movement, and we will see women leaders pursuing this redistribution theme in the next century in still newer dissenting sects.

Anabaptists, Baptists, Familists (Family of Love), Levellers, and Quakers were all flourishing in the mid-1600s, and they all were noted for the activist women in their midst. When a formal structure for the Society of Friends (Quakers) evolved in 1660 out of many scattered Anabaptist groups, provision was made for separate women's and men's meetings, with separate clerks and funds, though with overlapping agendas.[19]

Militant Quaker women might seem like a contradiction in terms, but only strong and assertive women could hold their own once outside the supportive Quaker circle. Preaching in public was one of the worst things a woman could do in the 1600s, and Quaker women were continually preaching in public—in streets, in fields, wherever they could command an audience. They were in prison a great deal, often publicly whipped and always subject to having their possessions seized. The first structure developed by Quakers was an institution called "Meeting for Sufferings," which organized among other things the care of small children whose mothers were in prison. Child care seems to have been organized to free mothers for social protest even before it was organized to free them for more long-term activities, and with good reason. In 1654,

> Oxford scholars so violently maltreated two Quakeresses who preached
> in the streets that one of them succumbed shortly after. . . . Two years
> later two Quakeresses were placed in the stocks at Evesham by the
> mayor, for visiting some prisoners (Hill, 1894: 247).

The first Quaker woman to preach in London, Ann Downer, evidently fared better. London was more sophisticated than Oxford and the hinterlands.

The homes of women became the first meeting places for Quaker worship, much as the homes of Roman women became the first places for Christian worship. The organizational center for Quakerism was in the home of Margaret Fell, who worked with George Fox in the founding of the Society of Friends.[20] George Fox was a working-class charismatic whose openings (revelations) were very similar to those of the Anabaptists. His doctrine that all could be taught directly by the inner light helped to undermine reverence for traditional university-based learning and authority and encouraged the activist, self-help orientation of an already alienated countryside. Margaret Fell was a remarkable manor house lady who as Fox's coworker built the communications networks of the new society. This phenomenon of women of wealth, education, and social position creating alliances with the artisan class on behalf of revolutionary social change will become increasingly evident from this century on.

Margaret Fell's home, Swarthmore Hall, became (under the eye of a benign and supportive husband, Judge Fell) the world head-quarters of Quakerism. Missions to all continents went out from there, all correspondence and reports were sent there. Margaret Fell was not only the organizer, however; she was also a minister and interpreter of the faith. One of her tracts is entitled *Women's Speaking Justified*. Late in life, after Judge Fell's death, she and George Fox married. They used their marital partnership as an ex-plicit testimony to the possibilities of equality in the husband-wife relationship. Some of Fox's epistles *(Day-Book of Counsel and Com-fort*, 1937) refer to this specifically.

In its beginnings, Quakerism did not create individuality in women, it attracted women who were already autonomous individ-uals. Some of them, like Margaret Fell, came from the manor house tradition, but the bulk of them were artisans and laborers, women who were used to a hard life. Margaret Fell herself raised her own four daughters to be economically self-sufficient. Each daughter had her own business. Three stayed at home unmarried, and managed ventures such as iron smelting and sea trading (Stenton, 1957: 177).

Women as Colonists

A logical action for women who wanted independence was to emi-grate to the Americas or travel as missionaries abroad. The Quaker servant girl Mary Fisher found her way to the court of the Sultan of Turkey and preached to him. (With what consequences we do not know, but she returned to England to tell the tale.) Others traveled to the West Indies and to Russia.

The women who came to North America found the matrilineal societies of the League of the Iroquois in New England. The Native American women, self-assured and with a powerful voice in their own tribal councils (De Pauw, 1974: 4), were strong, hardworking, and kindly. We know they helped the early colonist women with food, and taught them many skills. The openness of their societies, and the warmth of their family life, was such that white children in those first two centuries of settlement who were adopted into Native American families, whether by fortunes of war or for other reasons, rarely wished to return to their own families if later "rescued" (Hallowell, 1972: 200-205). It has been estimated that about 70 per-cent of adults captured by Native Americans preferred not to return to white society (De Pauw, 1974: 4). Native Americans were not similarly attracted to white society, largely because whites made no place for them in their society. Native Americans freely accepted whites as one of themselves; whites could be chiefs, or matrons in the council of mothers, once they had been adopted into a tribe.

The Dutch and the French women who arrived in North America continued to neighbor with the Native American women, learning their languages and trading skills with them. The English women did not. They unfortunately felt antipathy for both Native Americans and blacks (De Pauw, 1974: 9). While there must have been many exceptions to this, racial tensions seem to have developed early.

The authorities in the new colonies understood very well how important women were to the success of the settlements, and women there were not prohibited, as they often had been in Europe, from doing such things as

> speaking for themselves in courts of law, running print shops and news-
> papers, inns and schools, practicing medicine, and supervising planta-
> tions (Scott, 1971: 4).

The Virginia Assembly from the beginning gave land grants to women as well as to men.

In Maryland and New Jersey, as in Virginia, women were given a free hand according to their entrepreneurial abilities. Quaker Elizabeth Haddon persuaded her wealthy English merchant father to let her have the five hundred acres of land he had bought in New Jersey. She studied medicine and agriculture, prayed a lot with her family, and set off to found what became the town of Haddonfield. Alone and single, she built her cabin in the wilderness and not until she had established a successful settlement did she take a husband (Luder, 1973).

In New Amsterdam, Dutch women were crucial to the development of overseas commerce and the Indian trade. The tradition of the wife as business partner, lessening in England, remained strong in the Netherlands and in New Amsterdam. Women learned the Native American languages rapidly, and Dutch women traders competed successfully with French men for the Indian trade. They also acted as interpreters between the colonial government and the Indians.[21] One would like to know more about these "raucous" women traders, as Ryan (1975: 35) calls them, who were evidently as sharp as they were adventurous. One would also like to know what Native American women thought of them! De Pauw (1974) quotes a Frenchman on a Dutch woman trader in 1679:

> This woman, although not of openly godless life, is more wise than
> decent. . . . She is a truly worldly woman . . . and sharp in trading with
> wild people as well as tame ones. . . . She has a husband [who] remains
> at home quietly while she travels over the country to carry on the trad-
> ing. In fine, she is one of the Dutch female-traders who understands the
> business so well (1974: 5).

There was considerable cultural diversity in the colonies from the beginning. Women of all classes crossed the ocean from England, France, the Netherlands, and Spain and Portugal.[22] They came as young single girls, as married women with families, and as widows, alone or with children. Ladies of the manor house class might come to manorial estates of thousands of acres, like the sisters Margaret and Mary Brent of Maryland, or they might arrive with capital to establish commercial empires, like the Dutch widow Philipse, who organized the first transatlantic passenger service from New Amsterdam to Europe. From France great ladies like Mme de Pontrincourt came with their husbands to establish estates in Acadia (later Nova Scotia). Single European women from the rural and urban poor indentured themselves to English farmers in Virginia, Maryland, and Massachusetts, or to Dutch merchants in New Amsterdam. They made their fortunes according to luck and their abilities. Married peasant women sailed with their families to till new soil in New England and New France. "Vagrant" and "criminal" girls aged five and over were shipped, along with boys, to the English and French colonies in lieu of prison or the workhouse.[23]

In short, from Nova Scotia to Virginia, the women and children of Europe were seeking their fortunes, voluntarily or involuntarily, alone or with spouses and offspring. Everywhere they were important in the new economic order. But the early practice of giving women land grants equal to those of men stopped when settlements had "advanced" to the stage of self-government based on participation of male heads of household only.

The vast majority of immigrants to the New World were of rural background; the hard work of field and shop and bearing babies that women had known in the Old World was continued in the new. But hard as the work was, conditions were easier. Food was generally more plentiful, population densities low, and women were able to rear to adulthood nearly all the children they bore. This situation caused a rapid population increase in all the colonies of the Americas. Griffiths points out that there was 50 percent mortality before the age of twenty-one in Europe at this time, contrasted with near zero mortality in the New World (Griffiths, 1973: 14).

Acadia was a kind of "north woods paradise" during this century, oddly untouched by the turbulence in France. Catholics and Huguenots lived there side by side in peace. It was from the beginning a simpler, less urban-oriented society than its neighbor to the south, Massachusetts. The Ursulines, the order founded by Angela Merici the century before, came to Quebec in 1639 to work with the Indians. While their sisters in France had to live in enclosed convents, the Quebec band under the leadership of Sister Marie Guyard de l'Incarnation lived the pioneer life, in close contact with Indian mothers and children. In the midst of all their subsistence and service activities, they mastered the Indian language well enough to compose dictionaries in Algonquin and Iroquois. Their counterparts were doing the same in South America. One wonders whether relations between the English and the Native Americans would have been different if there had been Catholic sisters in puritan New England to speak the language of love that Native American women already knew. French nuns could relate to Native Americans as teachers and friends, Dutch women as traders, but English women had no culturally available role except as neighbor, which they generally rejected.

Mounting persecution of the Huguenots in France, culminating in the revocation of the Edict of Nantes, drove many Protestant families that might otherwise have settled in French Acadia to Massachusetts and Virginia. At its height the persecution in France was so severe that many men were driven to escape alone, leaving women and children behind to devise their own escapes. One such left-behind woman was able to escape by leaving a two-year-old child with a city guard as guarantee of her return—and never returned (Baird, 1885: 102). A teen-age girl escaped in a hogshead (Baird, 108-109). Whenever social upheavals create large numbers of refugees, heroic altruism and selfishness both appear, and neither sex has a monopoly on one trait or the other. One of the heroic figures of the time was the Huguenot princess of Tarente. She did not flee France, but for fourteen years held out in her chateau, where villagers could come to Protestant worship after the church was closed by the authorities. Eventually, most Huguenots had to flee or pretend to renounce their religion. The ingenuity of mothers, widows, and young girls in finding means of escape, and tales of heroism of men in aiding such escapes, are revealed in Baird's (1885) vivid chronicles of the Huguenot migrations.

The women who came to North America were often single and young, but the colonies preferred to have the women of their communities in the married state. Local Dutch and English courts supervised the swift placement of unmarried women and men into households and marriages (Ryan, 1975: 38); widows who wished to stay single had to be tough (Ryan, 1975: 48). Precisely because of the importance of the women to the economic survival of the households, however, the marriages often left more freedom of action to the women than their counterparts enjoyed in Europe.

While women were appreciated as partners, they were mistrusted as intellectuals, particularly in puritan Massachusetts. The poet Anne Bradstreet complained rather gently about this:

> . . . I am obnoxious to each carping tongue
> Who sayes, my hand a needle better fits,
> A poet's pen, all scorne, I should thus wrong.
>
> (in Kraditor, 1968: 29)

Anne Hutchinson, a few years later, gave the Calvinist church fathers an uneasy time with her self-confident heretical doctrines about grace and the role of women in the church. They told her:

> You have stepped out of your place. . . . You have rather been a husband than a wife, and a preacher than a hearer, and a magistrate than a subject, and so you have thought to carry all things in Church and Commonwealth as you would and have not been humbled for it (Rowbotham, 1972: 17).

The occasion of that quotation is in itself a historical vignette that lifts the veil on the superstructure of male dominance in the colonies. One sees underneath the terrible insecurity and fearfulness of men. Anne Hutchinson's teaching and community activities had

> upset Calvinist dogma, political differentiation, and masculine superiority. She was accordingly tried by both civil and religious authority. Pregnant and ill, at one stage while she was being questioned she almost collapsed, but they wouldn't let her sit down. The governor of the colony merely noted tersely in his record of the trial: "Her countenance disclosed some bodily infirmity" (Rowbotham, 1972: 17).

While the male superstructure remained intact, the banished Anne and countless women like her found niches elsewhere, and founded settlements that became refuges for independent thinkers. Nor was the Massachusetts Bay Colony left to itself. Women kept returning there to preach, particularly Quaker women, who were as regularly deported. When death was threatened for any Quaker who returned, Mary Dyer came back one more time to show that human dominance structures had no meaning in her value system. Mary, hanged on Boston Common with three Quaker men, is a continual reminder (now as a statue on that same common) of the moral frailty of a sector of politically dominant Puritan men.

The New World was not a utopia. Since immigrants of both sexes were accustomed to political dominance roles for men, no women sat in the councils of the new village democracies. What public spaces the women occupied in the earliest years when every hand was needed soon became privatized as prosperity made narrower definitions of domestic roles possible.[24] Nevertheless, compared to Europe, it did offer expanded opportunities for women of all classes. Their hands and brains were urgently needed.

Catholic Pioneers in Europe

No pioneer women in the wilds of the Americas had harder times than the sisters in Catholic convents in regions of Europe overrun by the Thirty Years War. Some convents were evacuated and all but demolished half a dozen times or more, the sisters each time returning to rebuild. In the end, some of the convents were permanently abandoned. Another kind of war was made on the nuns when local town councils turned Lutheran and sent Protestant ministers to the convent chapels to preach. The sisters then sat helpless through long heretical sermons, although on occasion they made mass protest exits during such sermons. Sometimes a group of nuns within a convent converted to Lutheranism, and then there would be a tug of war whether the institution was to stay Catholic or become Lutheran.

We have mentioned earlier that many French and German convents were royal convents. When a royal abbess came to be persuaded of the importance of a deeper spiritual life, in accordance with the many spiritual developments taking place within the church during the Counter-Reformation, she sometimes had a hard time persuading her royal sisters to live a more austere and devotionally oriented life. Fellow royalty might see no need for it. Peasant sisters might see it as one more whim of the aristocracy. One particularly dramatic case was in the royal convent of Urspring in Wurtemberg. The abbess, Margaret of Freiburg, wanted to introduce reforms already practiced at a neighboring convent, but suspected there would be resistance to the changes. One day she arrived at her own convent door fortified by nuns from the neighboring convent, some abbots, several preaching friars and a number of noblemen to assist her in case she met opposition from the nuns. Some noblemen of the opposite party also appeared. Under the direction of [a sister] the group of obstinate nuns who refused the reform, had withdrawn into the isolated infirmary in the convent garden and there fortified themselves by barricading the doors with tables, benches, blocks of wood and stones. They themselves occupied the upper floor and appeared at the windows, showing their weapons: stones, sticks, whips and spears. The duchess [backing the abbess] gave her people the command to attack the house. But the noblemen objected, explaining that it would always remain a disgrace, if they fought against women. Besides, they did not wish to make enemies with their equals; after all, these were noblewomen, and nuns too.

The duchess then had the alarm sounded from the nearby bell tower. This brought the common people. The simple townsmen and peasants were prepared to attack and they stormed the house. Those nuns who resisted were bound and put under arrest (Hilpisch, 1958, 52 53).

In the end nuns who didn't want the reform were permitted to leave. Most finally returned and submitted.

As mentioned earlier, the stirrings in the religious orders led in two opposite directions: toward greater devotion in religious seclusion, and toward more activity in the world. Among the activist convents, the royal abbey at Port Royal, France, underwent a complete spiritual revolution under Abbess Mère Angelique. The abbey moved from a swampy backwoods location to Paris, where it had profound and unpredictable effects on the women of the salons and became a meeting place for the major religious figures of the day. It survived embroilment in church politics and the Jansenist controversy for some time, but was finally dispersed. Spirituality does not easily travel from swamps to salons. Mme de Longueville, the Pallas Athena of the salons and of the battlefields of France, was much affected by Port Royal. As a result of that influence, she spent her last days under the strict rule of the Carmelites.

The developments in the activist direction include the work of Mary Ward, the English Catholic mentioned in chapter 9. Her radical ideas survive in a flourishing teaching order today (Evennett, 1968). Jeanne de Chantal, founder of the Visitation Sisters, was a Frenchwoman who raised a family before she responded to the religious call.[25] She conceived, together with her friend and religious director, the mystic St. Francis de Sales, the idea of an order of nuns who would link the contemplative life with the visiting of the poor

and the sick. This would be a kind of *devotia moderna* in action, refusing to make the separation between action and contemplation
that other orders were making. It was an unusual conception, born
of one of the great spiritual friendships in the history of the church.
The order grew rapidly, but the sisters were not given the freedom
of movement that Jeanne had intended. Once again the unreadiness
of the church to deal with autonomy of women was made plain.
Another order founded around this time, the Sisters of Charity of
St. Vincent de Paul, was more successful in retaining freedom of
movement, possibly because its founder, St. Vincent, was a man and
could press more effectively for that freedom for his sisters. Urban
Europe desperately needed the services the sisters were offering,
which made the failure of male church leaders to realize the
appropriateness of the service the more tragic.

Since the Lutheran church did little to promote vocations beyond
wifehood for the women, most of the religious and many of the secular vocational calls which came to devout women of these centuries
tended to be fostered in the Catholic church. Limited though the
opportunities were, the church did provide a special public-private
space within which women's abilities and contributions could
develop.

The Bluestockings and the Salons

The women intellectuals of the sixteenth century were a special
breed, foreshadowing the flowering of women thinkers and activists
in the following century. Since the most visible and famous member
of the sorority in the 1600s was Queen Christina, we will begin with
her.

Queen Christina

Queen Christina (1626-1689) was a bluestocking par excellence, and
though she also wore a crown, she chose not to keep it. Scholars find
her endlessly fascinating.[26] Her father and role model was the empire
builder Gustavus Adolphus. Like the queens Isabel and Elizabeth,
Christina had great physical endurance and could live on horseback
for long stretches of time. As a child, however, she was often ill,
at least partly because of the peculiar coffin-like existence imposed
on her by an emotionally ill mother after her father's death. Brought
up to reign over a Lutheran country, she found her intellectual liberation in Catholic humanism. She had read a lot as a child in her
"coffin," and had examinied the reflections on the human condition
offered by the advanced thinkers of her day. Descartes, whom she

brought to her court for a period, was crucially important in her own life as symbolizing the gift of free will to humankind. Though she fed on many ideas, she was not a deep thinker, and continually frustrated people like Descartes who expected her to be an intellectual giant.

Side by side with this intellectual emancipation there existed in Christina what Stolpe (1966) identifies as the "Pallas Athena complex," typical of certain women of that era who thought of themselves as unique. She conceived of herself as one of the greats in history, along with Cyrus, Alexander, Caesar, and Scipio. She had counterparts among her contemporaries in France: the duchess of Montpensier, who rode to battle with Condé at the head of troops and herself fired cannon in the French religious wars, and Madame de Longueville, Condé's sister, who also rode to battle with him. The role model was entirely male. Christina consciously wished she were a man, and had a horror of her own sex urges.

She abdicated not because she did not want to be queen, but because she found tiny Lutheran Sweden too confining. She abdicated, says Stolpe, because she wanted to get out into the larger world and achieve her true greatness. In support of this he lists the long series of intrigues she engaged in after her flight to Rome to get other (presumably less confining) thrones in Naples and Poland. None of these succeeded, and in the end she had to be satisfied with creating her own court and ruling as an uncrowned queen on the outskirts of Rome. There she created not less than three academies, and supported many musicians, artists, and a theater troupe. In a formal sense she was "religious," making an abdication of conscience because she had converted to Catholicism. In fact, although living in Rome more or less under the protection of the pope, she was essentially a free thinker who turned mystical in her last years.

Christina was a "failed" great queen, but a very successful bluestocking. While she was generally antifeminist and preferred the company of men, this too was a trait of many bluestockings. Typical of the Renaissance humanists, she lacked any social conscience. She scrounged shamelessly all her life to keep up the style of court she felt appropriate to her status. But she also had a great respect for "the other" major woman intellectual of Europe, Anna Marie van Schurman, and visited her in Utrecht on her abdication journey from Sweden to Rome. She was herself an idol of all the bluestockings of her century, and gave them a sense of identity and belongingness in the public sphere of European culture. As Pallas Athena, she could *command* respect, while most of them wheedled it.

The salon, both a stage for gifted women and private launching pad for aspiring and upwardly mobile artists and scholars, was eagerly adopted from Mediterranean traditions when a young Italian woman brought the custom to France. Catherine de Rambouillet was the daughter of Julia Savelli and the marquis de Pisano, ambassador to Philip II and to the Court of Rome; she married the marquis de Rambouillet at age twelve. "It was a happy union of two clever young people with brains far more active than those at the French court" (Reich, 1908: 70). They left court life because it bored them, and created an environment where intelligent and distinguished bourgeoisie who could *not* be received at court could mingle with the more intellectually inclined of the nobility. The salon at the Hôtel Rambouillet first opened at the very beginning of the century, and achieved its height under the marquise's daughter Julie during the years 1629-1648. While it fostered the much ridiculed *précieuses* (a style of cloying preciousness), it both welcomed the "old maid" Marie de Gournay and gave hospitality to Corneille, Boileau, Balzac, Voiture, and Molière. It was the milieu that nurtured the voluble Mme de Sévigné, and made her a woman of letters. De Sévigné addressed remarkably interesting chronicles-of-the-time letters to a remarkably dull daughter—or at least this is how her fellow *salonières* saw it.

While the salon was primarily a man's stage, set by women, it also provided opportunities for clever women. The plain, middle-class spinster novelist Mlle de Scudery could have her own "Saturdays of Sappho" in her simple quarters, and yet be favorably compared to the Rambouillets. While all but the bluestockings looked down on de Scudery, she made lots of money on her novels and held stimulating salons. Salons also helped women play at politics, and aristocratic women like Mlle de Montpensier and Mme de Longueville moved in and out of the salons between military engagements during the fighting of the Fronde, pursuing political intrigues.

Scholars and Artists

Anna Marie van Schurman

Anna Marie van Schurman (1607-1678), the "Sappho of Holland," was the best-known woman of her time in Europe. Her portraits, painted by admirers, hang in museums all over the Continent. In her youth she was a disciple and friend of the older Marie de Gournay. The Holland of her childhood was the crossroads of the world. Refugees streamed there from all the wars of Europe; merchants came there to do business, and scholars came there for new learning. It was a good place for women too. We have already noted the activities of Dutch merchant women in commerce. While the University of Utrecht did not admit women, the town was proud of its lady intellectuals and artists and Anna took the leading place in that circle as a very young woman. She was installed in a special box behind a curtain at the university so she could listen to lectures. Well tutored from earliest childhood, she knew Hebrew, Syriac, Chaldean, Greek, Latin, French, German, and English. She was particularly admired for writing an Ethiopian grammar.

She was a woman of too many gifts. Having promised her father in childhood to remain single and not disperse her gifts, she was in the end unable herself to decide which ones to concentrate on. Until she was twenty-seven, most of her work was in painting, etching (particularly on glass), and music; in this period she was best known as an artist. From twenty-seven to forty-six she was the world-famous scholar, continuously visited and written to by the intellectuals of Europe, and acknowledged senior critic of European literature. As we mentioned, Queen Christina made a pilgrimage to her home. This is the period in which most of her books were written, including one on the education of women. As a disciple of de Gournay, she was a firm and dignified feminist. At forty-six she became a disciple of Labadie, the founder of an Anabaptist sect, and spent the last quarter-century of her life developing a utopian religious community that was visited by Quaker women and men from England. She destroyed many of her scholarly writings after her religious conversion, but kept some of her art work from her earlier days. In the eyes of the world, she was "lost" to an unfortunate religious aberration.

Van Schurman's religious conversion was not like the retirement-to-a-convent pattern we have seen for a number of other intellectual women of medieval and Renaissance times. Rather, it was to a life of difficult activism. She deliberately exposed herself to persecution and poverty by identifying herself with a despised counter-culture sect with a utopian vision. It was only in the very last years that her Anabaptist community was given land and security from persecution. The Quakers who visited it from England found it inspiring. Van Schurman gave more different kinds of things to her century than any person of her time, but she is an embarrassment to the historian of thought. The pattern is too untidy. With the major public spaces of Europe at her disposal, she chose a counterculture life.

The Lowlands, Anna van Schurman's home, was a great center for women artists in the 1600s. Anna and Maria Visscher, the Dutch muses, belonged to van Schurman's circle of dedicated women who etched on glass, wrote poetry, and engaged in a variety of scholarship. Anna Breughel and Judith Leyster were gifted genre painters. Maria van Oosterwyck and Rachel Ruysch were outstanding members of the flower-painting school. There were many family workshops: Gerard Terburg and his sisters Maria and Gezina were outstanding genre painters; Gottfried Schalkers and his sister Maria were equally famous in Europe for their scenes by candlelight. Portraitist Adriana Spilberg married portraitist Eglon van der Neer, and they painted happily ever after.

In England the Dutch styles were popular, and Mary Beale and Anne Carlisle were its chief exponents. In Denmark the daughters of kings Christian IV and V were talented artists along with Anna Crabbe, poet and painter of princes. In Spain, unmarried daughters, sisters, and pupils of famous artists painted side by side with the men of fame. There is no record of their contribution except the general impression that they "helped." In Italy Elisabetta Sirani of Bologna, a prolific painter of religious subjects, whose studio in Bologna became a major tourist attraction, was poisoned (it is thought) by a jealous colleague. All Bologna mourned her early death and the city published a book of sonnets to her.

With the development of opera in the 1600s women immediately gained a public platform as singers in every country. In some countries they composed operas. In 1659 Barbara Strozzi, for example, had an opera performed in Venice. Most women composers in this century wrote religious music: Catterina Assandra, Mararita Cozzoloni, Cornelia Caligari, and Lucrezia Vizzana in Italy; Madelka Bariona in Germany; and Bernarda de Lacerda in Portugal.

It was not a strange thing to see women on the stage in Italy, France, or Spain, either in operas or plays. In England, however, this was not the case for the first half of the century. On January 3, 1661, Pepys wrote in his diary that it was "the first time that ever I saw women come upon the stage" (quoted in Wilson, 1958: 3). The shift came about partly because hard-up theater companies were running out of good young female impersonators, and there were many dowryless daughters of the genteel poor to be had cheaply. They were immediately a great hit. The suddenness of the innovation, and the great pressures immediately put on these women to play real-life courtesan roles they were totally unprepared for, created much social havoc and made it difficult for several centuries for women to go on the stage who did not wish also to adopt a courtesan's way of life (Wilson, 1958: 9-20). Nevertheless, the Restoration Theater provided an opportunity for women to develop a hitherto concealed talent, and there were great women actresses[27] in great and not-so-great plays on the stages of London.

Before the 1600s, most women with a scholarly bent turned to history, theology, and philosophy. In Italy we have noted the possibility for women to be mathematicians and to study the physical and biological sciences, but each case seems like an exception. Many European women in the 1500s developed laboratory skills through the study of alchemy, the forerunner of chemistry, but the references to this are incidental to other information and we cannot identify individual women who made serious contributions to alchemical studies.[28] In the seventeenth century we begin to find a number of reports of women in science. For each woman so identified, we may be sure there were hundreds unreported.

In France, Mme de la Sablière, part of the fashionable salon world, did her best to conceal her studies in astronomy. The word got out, however, and Boileau wrote a cutting satire on the woman who sat up nights studying the stars and ruining her complexion. Her own home was a center for scholars rather than a salon. The baroness de Beausoleil, moving perhaps in different circles, "got away with" doing a major study of French mineral resources—a work widely recognized and used in her own time.

Germany produced women naturalist-explorers of an adventurous turn of mind. Maria Sibylla Merian of Frankfurt studied birds, insects, and plants in Surinam, trained her two daughters to work with her, and published a classic volume on the subject. She might as well be listed among the artists as among the scientists, for her drawings are superb. Science has honored her by giving her name to new botanical discoveries. She was also a member of the Labadist sect that Anna van Schurman joined, and her work in Surinam was done at a Labadist colony there. Josephine Kablick of Bohemia traveled widely to make botanical and paleontological collections for all the major schools, colleges, museums, and learned societies of Europe. She was happily married to a mineralogist, and they managed fifty years of separate but coordinated field work. Amalie Deutsch was another botanical collector, famous for getting specimens from hard to reach places where no botanist had been before; she made many new botanical finds and a number of plants bear her name. She was also happily married, to a fellow botanist.

Maria Kirch of Germany belonged to a hidden matriarchy of

astronomers. Working as her husband Gottfried's astronomer assistant, along with her three sisters-in-law, she discovered a comet which was not named after her because she was a woman; she continued research and publishing after her husband's death. She trained her daughters in astronomy, and for years they did the calculations for the almanac and other publications of the Berlin Academy of Science.

In England Elizabeth Celleor was a noted midwife in the reigns of Charles II and James II who designed a royal hospital and organized a corporation of midwives. She proposed the training and registration of midwives, and there is a document by her dated 1687 on this. She drew suspicion by visiting women prisoners in Newgate before prison visiting was conceived of. Having powerful enemies, she was imprisoned, pilloried, and fined a thousand pounds for supposedly plotting against Charles II.

Reviewing the 1600s we can see a steady increase in the range of thought and activities of women, a gradual emergence from the anti-feminist Renaissance, and a readiness for new fields of action. With some exceptions in the salon world, women were still not taken seriously as thinkers, yet their spheres were steadily widening. The bluestocking phenomenon was complex, and served to launch the greater articulateness of eighteenth century women.

THE CENTURY OF REVOLUTIONS: THE 1700s

I am told that one can provoke uproarious laughter among older-generation English party-goers when conversation lags by solemnly remarking: "Queen Anne is dead." Evidently Queen Anne was considered an absolutely no-news queen. That this joke should have survived into the late twentieth century is remarkable testimony to the enduring invisibility of women as figures in history, and to the enduring attitudes that make that invisibility possible.[29] Queen Anne began her rule in the century that launched the industrial revolution in England, political revolutions in France and North America, and unrest in Russia. The eighteenth was even more a century of queens than the sixteenth—with one English queen and three Russian empresses—though it was also a century of revolution against royalty. It was the century of the turnip-generated revolution in agricultural productivity which abolished the need to keep fields fallow, yet it was also the century of food riots and increasing urban misery. It was a century which invented child-oriented education and yet shipped thousands of children overseas under the Penal Transportation Act of 1717. The steam engine was invented, the labor movement was under way, and Godwin announced in *Political Justice* that people will only have to work one-half hour a day in the society of the future (Brailsford, 1913). The realities of that present, however, were that laboring women were working up to sixteen or eighteen hours a day. Education for girls was still a controversial subject, and discussions on colleges for women were held in hushed tones. If there was progress, it was slow, and women by the middle of the century were showing their impatience in vigorous ways.

The Queens

Queen Anne began her reign in the year of the first daily newspaper in London in 1702. She presided over a union arrangement between England and Scotland (1707); a new set of election laws (1711) that did not exclude women (otherwise qualified under the limited franchise) from voting;[30] an abortive invasion of Canada; and the Schism Act. After her demise, the union with Scotland fell apart and the Act for Preventing Tumults had to be passed—her successor seemed to have trouble keeping things under control. Anne was a quiet queen, but she was not inept. She knew her own mind, and sent other women packing from court if they played politics in a style she did not like.

In Russia, Peter the Great's widow and ex-camp follower Martha presided over Russia for two years, 1725-1727, as Catherine I. Though she was ill-prepared for such responsibilities, she did it "to help out." That brief reign inaugurated a sixty-six-year period of rule by four successive empresses, with three very brief male interregnums. Catherine I was followed by Empress Anne (1730-1740), an inept ruler who left affairs of state in the hands of a foreign favorite (something a goodly number of kings have also done). Ten years of disaster were followed by the rule of two very strong women: Elizabeth, daughter of Peter the Great, and Catherine II.

Elizabeth took over at the age of twenty in a coup that ousted her not very competent aunt, and ruled for twenty-one years. Raised at court and accustomed to public life from the age of two, she was a monarch in the grand style, with lovers and all. Initially a strong, intelligent ruler, she became eratically pious, unpredictably autocratic, and unfortunately lacked her father's imagination (Longworth, 1973). When she died, her daughter-in-law engineered a coup and came to the throne on horseback at the head of her own troops. She arrived no longer encumbered with her politically inept and hostile husband, Grandduke Peter,[31] and ruled from 1762 to 1796 as Catherine II, "the great."

Fighting the power of the nobility and building up a trained and specialized bureaucracy loyal to her, Catherine built the needed infrastructure for the modernization that Peter the Great had introduced. In addition to far-reaching educational reconstruction (Raeff, 1972: 93-111), administrative reform was her great gift to Russia. She also fostered better services for the poor and for the bourgeoisie, and more local elective offices (Dukes, 1967). She did not pursue the emancipation of the serfs very vigorously, after a start in that direction, partly because she was frightened by revolts. Toward the end of her reign she leaned more heavily on the nobility and the landlords. The peasant revolts made her realize what a long-term operation reform would be for a country like Russia. Also, as she got older, she lost her vigor, though to the end she carried on wars with style. She was a widely read woman, and supported Diderot and the Encyclopedia project in Paris when no one else would. She wrote voluminously, and corresponded with Voltaire and many European philosophers. She was much admired in Europe, and generally brought Russia into European society in a way that her predecessor Peter had only dreamt about doing (Raeff, 1972: 21-92).

In mid-reign, Catherine watched with a benevolent eye while Empress Maria Theresa of Austria and the "ruling figure" in France, King Louis XV's mistress Madame de Pompadour, created between them an alliance for their respective countries that reversed a traditional enmity. Whether this diplomacy was really a deal between women, complete with Empress Catherine's blessing, I do not know. Mary Beard (1946: 314-315) suggests that some historians think it was. Catherine also later watched the king and queen of France go to the guillotine, secure in the knowledge that her country was not ready for that kind of revolution. But not too secure. Ruling Russia was a difficult job, and given the possibilities open to a monarch, she did remarkably well. She is the last of the great absolute monarchs among women. After her, all monarchs found increasing limitations put upon their roles by national parliaments. The role she vacated is an unlamented one, but the role was there to be played, and it is to be recorded that women were among those who played it well.

England: Philanthropy versus Radicalism

By 1700 England had been through civil wars and revolution, and "the age of conservatism" was at hand. Women of the aristocracy at

Queen Anne's court were involved with politics, but it was a politics of the elite and of personality. The duchess of Marlborough was exiled from court because of her political preferences—and spent the rest of her life writing about it. Later in the century there was a famous election campaign in Westminster in which the duchess of Devonshire rode up and down the countryside knocking on doors, rather in the style of a twentieth century campaigner, but it was still elite politics. Salon life in England was minimal, but it did exist. According to Hill (1896) it was a dull century for women in that country, and a self-centered one.

But perhaps not so dull after all. Lady Mary Montagu was one of the liveliest women in London, famous for eloping and marrying for love. At the age of twenty-one she wrote an ardent feminist letter to a bishop friend, complaining about being forbidden serious studies as a woman. Later she introduced the practice of vaccination against smallpox into England from Turkey, where she observed its use while her husband was ambassador there (Stenton, 1957: 261). As a woman of learning and wit she gathered the women and men writers of her time at assemblies (English equivalent to salons), but finally gave up on England and fled to Italy to live twenty-three happy years in what was to her a more congenial environment.

Mrs. Thrale, a successful brewer's wife, threw herself with even more zest into creating assemblies—it was the only thing her merchant husband would let her do—and brought promising young women writers like Fanny Burney in contact with other intellectuals like Dr. Johnson. When her husband died she married an Italian opera singer for love (to the horror of all her friends) and became an author. London did not beat the spirit out of everyone.

Besides the ladies who promoted the assemblies were the philanthropists, who were beginning to respond to the problem of an expanding and uncared for population of children of the poor. The famous poor laws of Queen Elizabeth's day, set up to take over community welfare work from the convents, were increasingly useless in dealing with the problems of the laboring poor. Up to a quarter of working-class mothers were heading their own households. The growing number of children in the streets was in part due to the increased availability of food and some decline in infant mortality, and in part due to the fact that the new types of factories could not absorb all the children along with their mothers. The efforts to put children in schools (particularly by the Society for the Propagation of Christian Knowledge), and to educate child factory workers, were from one point of view major developments of the age; from another point of view they were but a drop in the bucket. By 1729 there were sixteen hundred English charity schools (called "the glory of the age") with thirty-four thousand pupils (Pinchbeck and Hewitt, 1969: 291). Yet between 1756 and 1862, ten thousand vagrant children were sent to sea in involuntary merchant service (Pinchbeck and Hewitt, 1969: 105).

The efforts of women like Hannah More, who organized Sunday schools for factory-employed children and then day schools to give vocational training, were important, yet small in relation to need. Hannah More and her associates were careful to provide schooling for girls as well as boys. Since no suitable schoolbooks existed, Hannah More wrote them. This work with the "wild children," as More called them, opened the eyes of educated middle-class women to a whole range of pressing urban problems.

Many manor house ladies moved to the city in this period. Some of them enjoyed a new life of leisure, others became involved in philanthropic work. Other women remained in the country to participate in the agrarian revolution, creating innovations in agricultural methods and products in response to demands for increased food production. Letters from women, describing their work, in the columns of the agricultural journals of the day reveal the extent of women's participation in this process of innovation (Pinchbeck, 1930: 30-32).

In general, middle-class philanthropists were sure of themselves, secure in their position, and able, if they were strong-minded, to accomplish what they set out to do. For the new urban group of upwardly mobile women of the artisan class, and for the moderately educated daughters of poor gentry, things were different. These were women who had to support themselves, and they found nothing but obstacles everywhere. Mary Wollstonecraft (1759-1797), a weaver's daughter who had many hard knocks in trying to support her problem-ridden family, became an articulate spokeswoman for this group. She spent some years trying unsuccessfully to maintain a financially marginal school, and wrote extensively on education. Her book about the education of children, written for parents, was a best seller. In other circumstances, she might have been a brilliant educator. She had a professional apprenticeship with some of the best minds of England in the Samuel Johnson circle. But mostly she had to work at hack articles and translations (from the French and German) to earn a living. She raised a child alone, not by choice, but by victimage.

When she wrote her blast against the oppression of women, *A Vindication of the Rights of Women*, the women of the salons and the philanthropists were horrified. Hannah More had no patience with feminist sentiments, and said sharply "I am sure I have as much liberty as I can make use of" (Flexner, 1972). This was probably true —for her. Mary Wollstonecraft lived in an entirely different world than the philanthropists. Her struggles to make a living made her very aware of the forces operating to hold women back. She was an individual in a society that did not provide for female individualists except among the elite. A radical who identified very strongly with the ideals of the French Revolution—she lived in France during part of it—she wrote *Vindication* out of the shock of her discovery that plans for the new state-directed free educational system for France made no reference to the education of women. A plea for an education for citizenship, and for an equitable social contract for women, the book was originally intended both for France and for England. (See Flexner, 1972, for a further discussion of this. See also the new biography of Wollstonecraft by Tomalin, 1974.) In spite of the circles she moved in, Mary was something of a loner in her own country. Only toward the end of a rather miserable life did she and William Godwin discover each other, as she found her way into a congenial utopian-socialist milieu. She died in childbirth after a brief happy marriage to him.

Vindication was published in 1792. In 1799, the year after Mary died, Mary Anne Radcliffe published *The Female Advocate or an Attempt to Recover the Rights of Women from Male Usurpation*, an incisive work addressed specifically to the problem of single or widowed women in poverty. *Vindication* was primarily for middle-class women, *The Advocate* for the poor. By the next century a more coherent strategy was to develop, but in the 1700s women were generally working in isolation from one another, unaware of the larger picture. Women's roles were still largely privatized.

Women among the Dissenters

The one striking exception to the privatization was the role of women in the dissenting religious sects. The Quaker women's meetings described in the previous chapter continued to train women for community responsibility. Clarkson writes: "The Quaker women, independently of their private, have that which no other body of women have, a public character" (1806: 246). Quaker men have "given to the females of their own society their proper weight in the scale of created beings. Believing them to have adequate capacities, and to be capable of great usefulness, they have admitted them to a share in the administration of almost all the offices which belong to their religious discipline" (1806: 250). Specifically, the women carried out relief work for their own persecuted members and for the poor; went on missionary journeys sometimes for several years at a time, leaving their children in the care of their husbands and the Friends community; preached at recruitment centers against military service; and generally carried on the activities of a dissenting group in a period of rapid social change. Their main concentrations were in England and America.

Three charismatic dissenting sects, all offshoots of Quaker-Anabaptist tradition, and all led by women, became an embarrassment to the increasingly respectable Society of Friends (Holloway, 1966; Armytage, 1961). The first was the Philadelphians, a community founded by the disciples of the visionary millennialist Mrs. Leade in 1696. Mrs. Leade's teachings about the imminent new age were so powerful that many of the utopia-founding movements of the late 1600s and early 1700s were influenced by her. She was also an important influence on the Moravians. Numerous colonists from Europe and England came first to see Mrs. Leade for advice. She wrote many books, some of them dictated after she went blind, and conducted a correspondence reminiscent of the prophetess-abbesses of the Middle Ages. The Philadelphians did not long survive her death at the age of eighty-one, and her writings seem very obscure today, but she spoke a language that was meaningful to the communitarians of her day. Another dissenting sect was led by Jane Wardley. Mother Jane, as she was called, preached with great tremblings and broke into dancing under the power of the holy spirit, so that her group became known as the "shaking Quakers," or Shakers. The Shaker movement really developed under her disciple Ann Lee. Ann emigrated to America as the result of a vision, to organize a network of Shaker communities on the eastern seaboard in the 1770s. These were among the few sex-egalitarian communities of the next century, and that egalitarianism was in part achieved through celibacy. The third Quaker offshoot centered around Joanna Southcott, a less well known prophetess, who in 1802 took a house in Paddington and issued certificates for the millennium—fourteen thousand in all. None of these women acted on the kind of political analysis of production and distribution problems that we find among women leaders in the next century. This is strictly a vision-building era.

The only massing of women in public in this century, apart from millennialist demonstrations, was in connection with the food riots that took place with increasing frequency from 1765 to 1800. Large numbers of bad harvests occurred in that period, and the employment situation became increasingly difficult with displacement of workers by machines. The studies of food riots do not usually focus on women, so we only know by chance the extent to which women were involved. We do know that "housewives" in Essex rioted back in 1709-1710. Since students of food riots have concluded that this is a form of social protest used to deal with other than food issues alone, and is in fact a kind of "strike," we can assume that the Essex housewives had some other issues on their minds besides food shortages, but we are not told what they were (Rudé, 1964).

Food riots seem to have been undertaken by occupational groups, so whenever a guild or occupational group rioted en masse in a district, we can be sure there were women involved. The city riots that took place during this century were more apt to be machinery-smashing than food riots. Again, women would be involved to the extent that their occupational groups supported the riots. At least one-fourth of all rioters must have been women. One-half is a more likely figure. Women would be more motivated to riot than men because their situation, especially that of husbandless women with children to support, would be more desperate. That old problem-word *men* in the historical record conceals the facts.

Women in Field and Factory

The situation of laboring women in this century was very hard, as the references to rioting suggest. In the countryside, women were pushed more and more into competing with men for the heaviest and hardest jobs because of dwindling employment opportunities except at harvest time. The family work gangs, migrant and local, continued. Opportunities for craftwork at home had dwindled substantially, though some village factories, such as pin factories, gave out piecework to be done at home. Cottage industry never totally disappeared, even by the twentieth century, since there were always women willing to add extra hours to their working day at home to increase meager incomes, and there was always some demand for products that could be produced in this way. Women cottagers who could get at land to raise food were lucky; many could not because of the reduced amount of common land. Women who had regular skilled work such as dairying were not much better off than the irregularly employed, because the working conditions were so bad. Working on cheeses that weighed up to 140 pounds destroyed the health of dairymaids and made plowing look like easy work (Pinchbeck, 1930: 13-14).

The hardest hit by unemployment were widows, partnerless

women with children, and young singles. Parish records frequently refer to "vagrant women"; these helpless unemployed women, along with vagrant children, were put in institutions that were increasingly indistinguishable as to whether they were poorhouse, workhouse, or penal institution. In the labor force women got half or less of male earnings, children much less than that.

Many of these women emigrated to the city, but ignorant and ill fed as they were, they had few employment opportunities there. The women already in the cities were being pushed out of occupations they formerly had through pressures from male unemployment—a process that had already been going on for a long time. What apprenticeship and skill-training opportunities they had were similarly dwindling through pressure from male workers. The new immigrants from the countryside took anything they could get, usually odd jobs at starvation wages. If they were lucky they might get jobs as maids to upwardly mobile women who were leaving the labor force, but the latter shrank from taking in rough laboring types of women as domestics.

Shallow-pit mining, working in blast furnaces for twenty-four-hour spells at a time, and other types of industry-related heavy labor gave rise to inhuman working conditions and high casualty rates for women. A hard day's work was not new for women. Rather, the severe suffering of laboring women in the eighteenth and nineteenth centuries was due to the lengthening workday, the low wages, and the complete dependence of poor women on shops for food. The bit of food grown or scrounged in the country, a standby for centuries for the poorest of rural day laborers, was totally unavailable for urban women. It was increasingly so for poor villagers as well. Sixteen- to eighteen-hour workdays left no energy for home or child care, obviously, and contributed further to the problems of the children.

Public exposés of these working conditions began in 1793, but it took another fifty years for governmental notice to be taken. There were easier occupations for women at this time, such as jobs in village smithies and metal shops, making nails, locks, and tools, as well as relatively "light" work in the new industrial textile factories. Even in these factories, however, the work load was heavy and the hours long.

The women most vulnerable of all to the evils of industrialism were the urban employed. Many sold sexual services for food under the grimmest of conditions. Prostitution in this century changed character with the increase in poverty. I have noted earlier that there

was a vast difference between the wealthy courtesan and the under-
employed proletarian prostitute. The development of urban destitution vastly widened that gap, and created the class of streetwalkers
that represent the very bottom of the pit of social suffering for
women. The poorer women were, the more liable they were to be
picked up and imprisoned, and they made up a goodly number of the
ten thousand convicts that were shipped from the Old Bailey alone to
the North American colonies between 1717 and 1775. This practice
of dumping prisoners in the colonies, increasingly protested by the
colonists themselves, was only brought to a halt by the American
Revolution (Rusche and Kirchheimer, 1968: 58).

Yet for all the suffering experienced by workers in England, the
situation led to riots only, not to revolutions. For a revolutionary
situation, we must turn to France.

Revolutions in France

In France the eighteenth century started with the last large-scale
nationwide famine that country was to have. The revolt of peasantry
and proletariat in 1700 against long-continuing persecution of the
Huguenots by the Catholic regime was probably not unrelated to
famine conditions. After an amnesty was declared, warfare and riots
stopped (Whitworth, 1975: 13) and things settled down to relative
quiet. There were periodic epidemics of bread riots in the sixty-three
years between 1725 and 1788, which meant women were out in public laying siege to bakeries or seizing supplies, but these were all
locally inspired, spontaneous occasions, and apparently not linked to
any continuing movement. To understand the regular coupling of
poor harvests with bread riots, one must understand that bread was
the food staple of both the rural and the urban poor and accounted
for 50 percent of their expenditures (Rudé, 1964). Furthermore, the
rural poor were not able to grow grain, or even to bake bread (lack
of fuel for ovens), so they had to buy bread like their city sisters.

In the cities crowds would gather in protest against specific injustices, but again there was no overall program. That five thousand
Parisian women and men would mass in protest in 1721 against the
whipping and putting in stocks of a nobleman's coachman certainly indicates a high level of awareness of social injustice. In 1770 there
was a major riot protesting the rounding up of vagrant children to be
shipped overseas as labor for the colonies (Rudé, 1964: 49), a practice England had been engaging in for some time, apparently unchallenged. The mothers of the "vagrant children," for the most part
poor single or widowed working women, joined in a mass exodus

from their places of work to the ensuing protest demonstrations. For the moment the protest was effective and the children were not deported—but neither was the situation that gave rise to the "vagrancy" remedied. Guilds and artisan groups struck with increasing frequency from 1724 on, and went right on striking through the revolution, but the revolutionary government paid little attention to them. By and large the revolution was not interested in the poor.

It is difficult to estimate the extent of poverty in this century. From 1733 to 1778 incomes were generally rising and more peasants were able to buy small pieces of land. Yet general prosperity rarely reaches the very poor, and working women probably benefited little from chances to buy land. The fact that in 1780 there were seven to eight thousand abandoned babies out of thirty thousand births in Paris does not suggest increasing prosperity for the poor. Neither does the fact that four thousand persons a year were dying in the poorhouses of Paris (Braudel, 1973: 380).

The situation for upper-class and upwardly mobile middle-class women was very different. This was a great period for the salon movement; by the middle of the century these intellectual hothouses were at their height.[32] We do not really know how scholarly or gifted the women who ran the salons were. We do know that they nursed along scholarly and gifted men. Many of the major male writers of the day had *salonières* as critics and editors of their work, and this was general knowledge. Abbé Galiani had Mme d'Epinay; D'Alembert had Mlle d'Espinasse; Voltaire had Mme du Châtelet; and Diderot had Marmontel.

The women were the entrepreneurs of the Encyclopedia project, the first "modern" attempt at assembling knowledge. Much of the work for it was planned in salons, and Mme de Geoffrin's place was famous as the Encyclopedists' headquarters. Mme de Geoffrin was quite a character: she laid out her life plan at twenty, and followed it; before thirty she began dressing like an old woman, "to be beforehand with a difficult period" (Reich, 1908: 124).

Mme de Chatelet was exceptional among the *salonières* in being independently creative, but she chose to hide her brilliance and subordinate herself to Voltaire, with whom she lived for twenty years. She died young. A mathematician, she wrote in the manner of Pascal, prepared commentaries on Newton, and translated Leibniz.

Each *salonière* had her own specialty. You went to Mme Hudson for conversation; to the duchess de Maine for clever entertainment; to the marquise de Lambert, Mme de Tencin, Mme de Geoffrin, and the maréchale de Luxembourg to meet famous people; to Mlle

Pleneuf for music; to the duchess of Gramont for politics; and so on. The only dull place in Paris was the court itself. There one would find a queen, some mistresses of the king, and boredom (so it was said).

The romanticism of Rousseau and the wit of Voltaire, the two dominant century-spanning male intellects, did little to ground these salon women in problems of social justice. Rousseau fostered the worst kind of image of the mental domestication of women:

> To please, to be useful to us, to make us love and esteem them, to edu-
> cate us when young, to take care of us when grown up, to advise, to
> console us, to render our lives easy and agreeable. These are duties of
> women at all times, and what they should be taught in their infancy
> (Rowbotham, 1972: 36).

This passage very straightforwardly tells women to educate men from childhood to oppress them. It was somehow not interpreted that way by the delighted *salonières*. Yet if some of them were very confused bluestockings, there were others who were much involved with the politics of revolution, as we shall see.

The long period of relative prosperity in France came to an end by 1778 with falling prices and unemployment, and strikes and riots increased in frequency and intensity. The issues of the French Revolution are far too complex to be explicated here, but by the '70s all the unsolved issues of the previous century exploded at once for the monarchy. The administrative divisions of France no longer reflected social, economic, and political realities. The fiscal system was an absurdity and the country was bankrupt. The king and queen, and the four thousand families of the Great Nobility who controlled one-fourth of the national budget, were trying to hang onto the old absolute monarchy. The minor nobility and the bankers (who had money) were trying for a limited monarchy. The middle class and the artisans were more or less manipulated by the minor nobility and the bankers, and the poor peasants and unskilled workers (the three million illiterate poor of France) were squeezed out entirely. Women fought hard in the first, second, and third groups during the revolution (and fought against each other too), but in the end all but the nobility and the bankers' daughters were dumped and disqualified from every kind of participation, sharing the lot of the poorest of the men. Whoever "won" the revolution, the women of France lost it.

What was the role of women in the time of the revolution? Starting at the top, Queen Marie Antoinette by the early 1780s was busy mobilizing the resources available to the French monarchy through the alliance Empress Maria Theresa had created back in 1756. Poor Queen Marie—she is not usually thought of as a victim of the social expectation that women should remain quiet and demure, but she was. Her well-meaning husband was a do-nothing, so her efforts came to nothing. By 1792 she was writing to a friend:

> As for myself I could do anything, and appear on horseback were it needed; but that would be furnishing weapons to the king's enemies: throughout all France a cry against the Austrian and the rule of a woman would be raised instantly. By coming forward I should, more-over, reduce the king to a humiliating and inferior position. A queen who, like me, is nothing in her own right—who is not even regent, has but one part to act—to wait the event silently, and prepare to die (Kavanagh, 1893: 94).

She died with dignity. In fact, all the women who went to the guillotine, nobility, middle class, and working class, died with such quiet bravery that Kavanagh (1893) suggests this alone prolonged the Reign of Terror. A few hysterical scenes by women at the scaffold might have shocked the men of the Terror sooner into realizing what they were doing. Only poor old Madame DuBarry, the king's former mistress, gave way to hysterics on the scaffold—embarrassing everyone terribly.

The bankers' daughters went scot-free. They moved right through every phase of the revolution without being touched. Madame de Pompadour was the first banker's daughter to play politics, well before the revolutionary decade. As a young girl she had been adopt-ed by one banker, later married another, and as Louis XV's mistress ruled France (according to one school of historical thought) for the bankers. She was the coarchitect with Maria Theresa of the French-Austrian alliance. Her foreign policy was terrible for France, and her secret police were everywhere. She died before the revolution.

Madame Necker, the wife of a Swiss banker, and her daughter Germaine, who became Madame de Staël, ran salons that brought to-gether bankers, literati, and political leaders in clever conversation in an atmosphere of "liberalism." They closed down their salons in the Reign of Terror, but not their activities. Mme de Staël ran a newspaper chain and survived not only the revolution but also the enmity of Napoleon. Another banker's daughter, Therése de Fontenay, recreated a court atmosphere in her Paris home after the revolution, and was acowledged as "uncrowned queen of Paris." Her friend Rose de Beauharnais, not a banker's daughter but a bourgeois adventuress friend of bankers' daughters, survived the revolution by her wits and then, as Josephine, married Napoleon.

Not all salons were run by bankers' daughters, and not all women of the upper class insulated themselves from concern for the deeper issues of the revolution and from the poverty of the masses. Madame de Condorcet and her husband, one of the few genuine husband-wife teams in the salon world, championed the equality of women and the rights of the working class when very few of their social class were interested in these subjects. Their salon has been called "the command center for thinking Europe." It was the most international of all the salons, anticipating by a century the internationalism of later political movements. Condorcet was the only Frenchman who spoke out strongly in the National Assembly for the political participation of women.[33] He lived in hiding, protected and supported by his wife for the last months of his life, only to be discovered in the end and guillotined. Mme de Condorcet, a former canoness and a pupil of Rousseau, survived and brought up their only child in retirement.

Mme Roland was another woman who did not insulate herself from the issues of the revolution, though she was strictly a "limited monarchy" advocate. An engraver's daughter who married into the upper class, she never moved in salon circles. Because of her own keen interest in the liberal politics of the upper-middle-class-minor-nobility alliance, however, she created a kind of political salon under cover of helping her husband (at one point finance minister to the king) in his work. She appears as a kind of *eminence grise,* for she never spoke in public, hardly spoke even to the political visitors in her own house, and yet was generally recognized in her time as the authoress both of the ideas and of the documents that issued from the gatherings of highly placed political personages that took place in her modest home. She was both hated and admired in her day, and both positive and negative pictures of her have come down to us through the history books. She wrote many letters to political leaders, and both her style and her sentiments today seem sententious. She had courage, however, and went to the guillotine (sedately) for continuing to support the limited-monarchy idea after the revolution had swept past that point.

The heroines of the French Revolution were other kinds of women entirely. Shopworkers, fish vendors, laundresses, seamstresses, journalists, actresses, street women—they were a real medley of lower-middle-class and laboring women. Their participation in the revolution is somewhat unique in the annals of European history, both because they were so visible and well mobilized during certain crucial events, and because they were so completely excluded from all civic participation even before the revolution was over.

Their effectiveness was founded in the preceding decades of experience with bread riots and protest demonstrations. Though each of the previous demonstrations had been spontaneous, the women who participated in them gained a certain sense of the patterning of demonstrations, and of their value, which they could now draw on. Women on the whole succeeded in keeping the price of bread within bounds; because the authorities could not afford to be dealing continually with riots, they sometimes went to great lengths to control the price of bread. The women who were present at the storming of the Bastille were not neophytes. They had been there before.

The decision of women to march to Versailles three months after the storming of the Bastille, and to bring the king to Paris, was also a direct outcome of their previous experience. When bread prices were lowered it was usually done in the name of the king, so in their view the king was the source of rectification of injustice. If he could be brought to Paris to see how bad things were, he would do something about it. Members of the bourgeoisie-minor-nobility alliance were not hungry, so this item was not on their political agenda. But the unemployed women of Paris, and the poorest of the employed, *were* hungry. And their children were hungry. Their slogan reflected their concerns: "Bring back the Baker, and the Baker's wife, and the Baker's little boy, to Paris."

The women who marched to Versailles (it is a fairly long walk—twenty miles) were of all kinds, and historians have described the crowd differently depending on their political sympathies. "Poor but honest" working women led the way. Women like Madelaine ("Louison") Chabray, a seventeen-year-old unemployed sculptress who was now making a living as a flower girl, walked side by side with the market women and porteresses of the city. The unemployed who picked up what pennies they could by prostitution followed. These poverty-stricken women are the ones who have been described as an obscene drunken mob. Well-wishers (and there were many) gave them wine on the road, not thinking what wine would do to malnourished women with empty stomachs. Some of the walkers were reeling by the time they got to Versailles, but the reeling was as much from hiking twenty miles on empty stomachs, as from wine. Louison, the flower girl, was appointed spokesperson. When she stood before the king she was so overcome with emotion and hunger that she fainted. The king picked her up and embraced her, and she came stumbling out crying *"Vive le roi!"* Much fun has been made of this scene, but the women did march back to Paris with grain decrees from the king, and with the Declaration of Rights from the National Assembly. They had used the tactics familiar to them, and they had gotten results.

Théroigne de Mericourt, ex-courtesan and opera singer, was a colorful person with a degree of worldly experience who injected some leadership into the situation at Versailles. Dressed flamboyantly in a huge hat, bright red coat, and with a sword at her side, she protected the massed women from being fired on outside the king's palace by throwing herself on the soldiers and persuading them to desist. It was at this point that people began bringing food to the famished women, so they did not have to march back with empty stomachs. Théroigne led what appeared to be a well-organized crowd of about one hundred fish vendors into the gallery of the National Assembly on a mission to get the assembly to turn its attention to the basic business of bread. An observer of this scene reported that the women seemed to know many of the deputies, and shouted to them by name. Théroigne led the group, and they shouted or stayed quiet at her signal. This vignette (Michelet, 1960: 64) indicates considerable political know-how on the part of some of the worker women.[34]

A postscript to this story of the women's march to Versailles is that after the main body of women had started back to Paris, a small group of women and men broke into the queen's apartment with the intention of seizing her bodily and bringing her back to Paris. The upshot of that incident was that the "Baker and the Baker's wife and the Baker's little boy" did indeed come to Paris, escorted by triumphant crowds of women and men. Thus the women won twice over, in bringing back both the grain decrees and the whole royal family.

Much was hoped for from the National Assembly, in which the third estate for the first time took an active part. Activated women worked to mobilize rural France in support of the assembly, organizing festivals and persuading local village and department officials to write "love letters" to their new government. Urban middle-class women realized increasingly that a more sophisticated type of support of the revolution was required, and Jacobin societies for men and women were formed. The first such "Friends of the Revolution" club was organized by a merchant's widow, a printer, and two surgeons. Sex-integrated fraternal societies of working men and

working women were also formed, and the aristocrats came and lectured to them on the issues of the revolution. Condorcet, Abbé
Fauchet, and a Dutch woman, Mme Palm Aelder, spoke before the
National Assembly on the recognition of the political participation
of women in the revolution, but the assembly turned a deaf ear. A
group of bourgeois women presented a petition:

> You are about to abolish all privileges, abolish also the privileges of the
> male sex. . . . Thirteen million slaves are shamefully dragging the chains
> of thirteen million despots (Sokolnikova, 1969: 147).

The assembly remained deaf.

While Jacobin "Brotherly Societies of the Patriots of Both Sexes"
continued, Olympe de Gouges, an actress and pamphleteer, felt that
a stronger woman's voice was needed. She founded all-women's
societies in 1790 and 1791, and prepared a Declaration of the Rights
of Women. Unfortunately Olympe herself did not have enough political experience—how could women gain political experience in this
Rousseau-mesmerized society? She lost her sense of direction, finally
turning proroyalist out of confusion.

In 1793 another former actress, Claire Lacombe, and a laundress,
Pauline Léon, organized a club specifically for working women, the
Republican Revolutionary Society. Its members were tailoresses,
dishwashers, laundresses, rag-pickers, artisans, and laborers, and the
society quickly allied itself with the "Enraged," a group concentrat-
ing its attention on the food difficulties. Unfortunately there was
considerable political dissension within the Revolutionary Society,
and the radicals who identified with the Enraged came to be in the
minority. In addition, the royalist fishmarket women who felt that
the revolution was ruining their business developed a strong hatred of
the radical women. It was these tough fishmarket women who are supposed to have been the implacable revolutionaries who counted with
such fierce satisfaction the heads that fell into the basket from the
guillotine. In reality, according to Sokolnikova (1969: 176-177),
they were compelled to attend the executions, and only rejoiced
when, during the Reign of Terror, former prominent revolutionaries
took their turn at the guillotine.

In any case, tensions between the radicals and the moderates rose
until finally there was a great free-for-all in the streets of Paris in
October of '73. The minority radicals were caught between the
angry moderate members of their own club and the furious fish-
women. The word having gotten out at dawn that there would be
trouble that day, the market women were well prepared. They let

loose with rotten fruit and vegetables, stones, sticks, and fists, attacking the radicals when they were evicted from their clubroom. The equally hostile men from the neighborhood also joined the fray, and the radical women barely escaped with their lives. The National Assembly self-righteously forbade women to hold any kind of meeting in the future—took away their right to organize, in fact—and that was the end of the role of citizenesses in the revolution. At first the radical women tried to fight the ban, invading the assembly itself to get a hearing, but public opinion was against them, including the public opinion of most women.

The failure of women to become politicized to the point of sustained and effective participation in the activities of the revolution is one of the tragedies of that era. In one sense, the radical women were being more sophisticated than the bulk of their sisters or the National Assembly itself, in that they were trying to promote attention to economic issues that the assembly preferred to ignore. In another sense, they were too unskilled in political analysis to deal with the very issues they were trying to promote. It is painful to read their declarations before the assembly on the occasions when they got a hearing. Olympe de Gouges and Claire Lacombe both sound like bad ham actresses doing a stilted morality play (Sokolnikova, 1969: 155, 165-168, 248-251). Yet the men were speaking in the same style and operating at an even cruder level of analysis.

Where would the women have learned what they needed to know? Two centuries of intellectual exercises in the salons had done little for the capacity of women to engage in economic and political analysis. Except for the bankers' daughters, the women who had the mental training had no sense of the relevance of economic issues. For all the importance of the salon movement in playing nursemaid to the men of the Enlightenment and to the project of the Encyclopedia, with respect to the revolution the *salonières* contributed little.

The position of women during the revolution was further weakened by the attack on the church and its "nationalization," which, as in England earlier, emptied convents and deprived rural and urban areas of convent-rendered education and welfare services. The Goddess of Reason parades in which the prettiest woman of the town was dressed up like Minerva were a poor substitute for what the women had lost.

Nevertheless, there was a long-run gain to women in their exposure to issues which they had not before confronted. Romanticized histories of the revolution obscure this fact. Bemused writers like to feature women like Charlotte Corday, who "killed for peace."[35]

When Robespierre, the architect of the Terror, was finally himself executed, women of every class and sector turned out in a huge carnival of celebration. But after that, there was apparent silence. This suggests a response-level of unthinking emotionalism on the part of women activists that does them an injustice. Thoughtful women among the discredited radicals, in fact, began at this time the long, slow process of thinking out the situation of women and of society that was to bear fruit in the socialist movements of the next century.

Women and Salons in German Lands

The peculiar mixture of romanticism and hothouse intellectualism that characterized the salon movement of France was not confined to France. The palatinate castles on the Rhine also had their salons, though these were to a far greater extent male-organized and male-dominated. The salon in Frederick's castle at Rheimsberg could be taken as typical. There were women present, but as a kind of intellectual adornment. When Frederick became emperor he stopped entertaining even the women-as-adornment idea, and his court became actively antifeminist. His shift in attitude gives a clue as to how dependent on male benevolence the women of the German salons were.

At Darmstadt a group of middle-class women attached to the minor courts of the upper classes developed the extreme of the romantic outlook and life style, which included playing at being shepherds and shepherdesses. Three of these women, intimates of Goethe, were known as the three muses, Psyche, Lila, and Urania. Marck, the man whose home was the salon center for this group, alternated between entering fully into the chorus of Wertherian[36] sighs and making it the butt of his very keen wit. Later, in Weimer, Ann Amelie's salon became the last home of the Minnesinger Court of Love tradition, with Goethe, Herder, Schiller, and Wieland all gathering there. In Berlin Rahel Levin presided over the last of the Goethe salons, 1796-1806, but also lived to introduce another salon of the Heine era, 1819-1833.

The French tradition of display of incisive wit and of intellectual entrepreneurship in bringing together male brilliance of different hues never developed in the same way for German women. There were scholar nuns in the convents, but these were a world apart. Between them and the shepherdesses no middle ground appears in the general intellectual histories of the time. This is probably an artifact of the way the history is written, but also suggests that intellectual entrepreneurship was not valued in German women.

Women Adventurers

Working-class women not only appear in this century as oppressed laborers and as determined demonstrators and rioters, they also appear as adventurers who leave behind the humdrum, edge-of-poverty existence of their sisters to enter armies, navies, and pirate bands. In general their lives were probably not very different from those of the vagabond women of the Middle Ages, but in this period some of them begin appearing as individuals in the historical record, probably because record-keeping systems became better organized (Hargreanes, 1930). The very fact that some of these women caught the fancy of the public suggests that many a working-class woman was a potential adventuress who never made it out of her urban—or rural—captivity.

Christian Ross (1667-1739) served through many battles and was a trooper of the Scot's Greys, a ten-year seasoned soldier, before her sex was discovered. Since army life was the only life she wanted, after her discovery she was allowed to stay on as army cook, and soldier Ross became known as "Mother Ross." How the fighter role was transformed into the nurturant role by a simple act of relabeling would make a fascinating sociological study. Mary Read and Anne Bonney had briefly successful careers as pirates, and their exploits from 1718 to 1720 were widely recounted.

Flora MacDonald is perhaps the most famous of the eighteenth century adventuresses. She was the young Scotswoman who engineered the escape of Bonnie Prince Charlie to France after the rebellion of 1745. In the story of that escape, she moves like a lightning-quick, steely-strong superbrain through and around the laborious maneuvers of the ponderous Scots and English (MacGregor, 1932). Imprisoned after the escape had been successfully carried out, she was released by popular demand and became even in her life a legend. Flora the real-life woman, however, married and bore many children, living a long hard life of poverty after her great adventure. No one thought to draw on her talents in the public sphere again, or history might have been different.

Hannah Snell (1723-1792) was an infantry fighter with English troops in India. Mary Anne Talbot (1778-1808) is one of the puzzles among fighting women. She lived a rough life as a sailor, but always under the whip of an exploiting man. The best known of American women fighters is Mollie Pitcher, who fought in the American Revolution. For all these women, the battlefield, whether on land or sea, was for longer or shorter periods their home and their way of life. Like the women who emigrated to become pioneers, and the women who stayed behind to fight for life in the cities of Europe, they exhibited the basic toughness and resiliency that has been part of the survival equipment of women at the bottom of the social ladder in all periods of history.

Colonists

Most women colonists of North America had less exciting lives than the adventurers, but they too were living through rapid changes. During the eighteenth century the small towns of North America became urban centers—Quebec, Boston, Philadelphia, New York. Commercial agriculture and urbanism developed together, and enterprising women in the colonies as in Europe participated in agricultural and commercial innovation. Eliza Lucas of South Carolina, for example, pioneered the indigo trade. As in Europe, village workshops hummed with the labor of women and children. Ryan notes that "a twelve-year-old girl devised a method of making straw braid for bonnets in 1798 and generated an industry that employed hundreds of women in her hometown of Dedham" (Ryan, 1975: 103). The difference between European and colonist labor was that in the colonies working hours were shorter, and standards of living higher in terms of food and environmental conditions.

For slave women this was not so, and the eighteenth century witnessed a steady increase in the number of women slaves both in the northern and southern colonies. The eighteenth century was also the century of the great slave writers and poets, however. It was not until the nineteenth century that it was forbidden to teach blacks to read and write. Phyllis Wheatley, brought to Boston as a slave from Africa at the age of seven, was taught to read and write by the invalid wife of her owner and became a widely read poet among New Englanders (Bontemps, 1969: 44).

In Boston in this century 10 percent of the merchants advertising locally were women, though many of these were widows carrying on their husbands' businesses. With the shift of emphasis away from subsistence farming, women began to limit family size, in some areas as early as 1700 (Ryan, 1975: 121). Large families were not such an asset in a more commercial economy. The same trend was taking place in France and northern Europe.

A major event of the century for North America was the American Revolution, a war in which matrons of the Iroquois League played an important and little recognized part. Mary Brant, Mohawk head of a society of Six Nations matrons and widow of an important pro-

British chief, was an important force in keeping the western tribes of the Six Nations allied with the British even though the League itself had decided to stay neutral. The minority of tribes that sided with the colonists were influenced by Englishwoman Jerusha Bingham Kirkland, considered a "mother" of the Oneida nation and leader among tribal women (De Pauw, 1974: 17-18). Apparently white women living with the Indians and accepted as "mothers" could intervene diplomatically, and one loyalist white widow thus prevented the Cayuga from making peace with the Continental Congress (De Pauw, 1974: 27). A story of the American Revolution written from the point of view of the Iroquois matrons, and of the white sisters who functioned in their councils, would provide an interesting perspective on that war. With the defeat of the British the Mohawks emigrated to Canada and the other nations moved farther West; "Iroquois matrons retreated with their tribes and never again influenced the mainstream of American history" (De Pauw, 1974: 35).

A little-known fact is that white women became involved in revolutionary terrorist organizations in the period just prior to the revolution. "There were Daughters of Liberty just as there were Sons" (Riegel, quoted in Maine, 1975: 15). "Once, when a group of loyalists disguised as Indians was arrested for robbing . . . and terrorizing the inhabitants, it was found that five of them were women, and three of those were a woman and her two daughters" (Evans, quoted in Maine, 1975: 15).

In general, terrorists apart, white women were not listened to by their men, either in the councils of war or the councils of peace. They performed typical underside roles in spite of Abigail Adams' warning to her Continental Congressman husband John Adams: "If particular care and attention is not paid to the ladies, we are determined to instigate a rebellion, and will not hold ourselves bound by any laws in which we have no voice or representation" (quoted in Ryan, 1975: 85). As after many wars of liberation in which women fought side by side with men, nothing changed for women after the American Revolution. "Neither the Declaration of Independence nor the Constitution of the United States elevated women to the status of political beings" (Ryan, 1975: 85).[37]

The upheavals associated with the aftermath of the revolution brought many women to the Shakers, the Quaker-offshoot sect which under the leadership of Ann Lee traveled from England to America in 1774. Newly independent Americans flocked to this millennialist, celibate sect that preached the essential duality of God as mother and father, and the equality of women. The communitarian organization of the Shaker church after 1788 offered attractive living conditions for proletarian women, and after the great revival in Kentucky in 1799 large numbers of women and men became Shakers (Whitworth, 1975: chapt. 2). The conditions of life that made this and other communitarian sects of the next century attractive to women will be discussed in the next chapter. These movements sparked a continuing commitment to pioneering in the New World.

Women artists and scholars could not flourish easily in these wilderness and pioneer town settings, where hard physical labor was required for survival. For developments in the cultural sphere we must turn to some of the more leisured settings in Europe.

Scholars and Artists

As in earlier periods, Italy continued to produce the outstanding women scholars and scientists of the century. Three extraordinary women were born within eighteen years of each other in Bologna and Milan: Laura Bassi, physicist (1700-1778), Anna Manzolini, anatomist (1716-1774), and Maria Agnesi, mathematician (1718-1799). Bassi, professor of physics at Bologna, was already famous at twenty-one. Her public disputations drew scholars from all over Europe and she was an active public figure in the academic world until her death. Bologna's favorite daughter, with a medal struck in her honor, she was also a very beautiful woman. It is a little surprising to learn that she also had twelve children, an unusually happy family life, was deeply religious, and wrote and published poetry. She did not publish very much in physics—her fame came from her teaching. Holding a professorship of anatomy at Bologna in the same years was Manzolini, noted both for her anatomical discoveries and for her creation of wax anatomical models which were copied and widely used around Europe after her time. Universities and courts all over the Continent tried to lure her away from Bologna, but she would never leave. She was probably aware that she lived in the most nurturant milieu in Europe for women scholars. Why leave it?

Maria Agnesi was a different case altogether. She started out like the others, only more brilliantly, if possible. She gave learned discourses in Latin to the city fathers of Milan at the age of nine, and could work in seven languages in her teens. The work which ensured her fame in mathematics, *Le Instituzioni Analitiche,* was begun when she was twenty, and took her ten years to complete. During that ten years, her absorption in mathematical problems was total. She used

> to bound from her bed during the night while sound asleep and, like a somnambulist, make her way through a long suite of rooms to her study, where she wrote out the solution of the problem and then returned to her bed. The following morning, on returning to her desk, she found to her great surprise that while asleep she had fully solved the problem which had been the subject of her meditations during the day and of her dreams during the night (Mozans, 1913: 144-145).

The opus was an international scientific sensation when published. The French Academy of Science wrote congratulating her on the work (unfortunately they could not elect her to their body because she was a woman). It was translated into French at once, into English somewhat later. She was immediately appointed to the chair of higher mathematics at Bologna. Bassi, Manzolini, and Agnesi would have made a remarkable trio there. But she did not accept the chair. Instead, to the amazement of her contemporaries and even more to the amazement of twentieth century historians, she retired from the world and devoted the rest of her life to the care of the "poor, the sick and the helpless in her native city" (Mozans, 1913: 148). It seems that she had written the *Instituzioni* "primarily for the benefit of one of her brothers who had a taste for mathematics." From the age of thirty, when she finished the magnum opus, to the age of eighty, when she died, she lived a retired life as a single woman in her own home (she did not become a nun), going out to care for the poor. From the moment of her retirement, she cut her ties completely with the scientific world, and never attended a scholarly gathering again.

What was the meaning of that retirement? Catholic scholars have proposed that she be canonized as a saint, though this has never been done. Since she did not take religious vows, she cannot be typed into any "retirement to a convent" pattern. She was in fact very active in social welfare work, and directed a home for the aged poor for the last fifteen years of her life. She never explained her own actions, and legend makers have had a field day. One possible interpretation that I have not seen proposed is that she found the life of the intellectual somewhat hollow. In her own time, with a breadth of social vision, a brilliant mind, and a deeply religious nature, what were her alternatives? No one today can know the full meaning of her choice, but she was as much of a deviant in her own time as she would be in ours. She is one of the few known examples in history of a woman who had the "world," as defined by men, at her disposal, and simply said "No thank you."

Agnesi had a host of sister-mathematicians in the 1700s and 1800s in Italy, including Diamante Medaglia, who wrote on the importance of mathematical training for women as part of their mental development—a very revolutionary concept. In France, a woman chemist important in the historical record of her century is Madame Lavoisier. She was not only a coworker with her chemist husband in his laboratory, doing the drawings for his textbooks, and editing his memoirs on chemistry after his death by guillotine, but she was also a painter, trained by the classicist David. Another century passes by before we hear of another woman in chemistry in France. Émilie du Châtelet, mentioned in the section on salons as Voltaire's companion, was the mathematician who translated Newton's *Principia* into French. She herself wrote *Institutions de Physique,* and also a philosophical work, *Reflections on Happiness.* The *salonières,* who evidently hated the idea of a disciplined scholar in their midst, could not say enough nasty things about her. Among her chief persecutors in the salon world were Mme de Staël and Mme du Deffand.

Catherine Macaulay (1731-1791) was the *first* major English historian to bear the name Macaulay, though Thomas Macaulay of the next century is usually thought of as "the" Macaulay. Her eight-volume *History of England,* considered the best offering of the then-new "radical school of history," was written as a "history of the love of freedom." Catherine was also a lady of high fashion and a *salonière,* achieving in England a kind of recognition that du Châtelet in France neither could nor wanted to achieve. She was a major public figure of her time, and the center of a circle of the most influential politicians of the day. Her forty-sixth birthday was the nearest thing to an Italian-style celebration of a woman ever carried out by the sceptical English male, complete with parades and public jollity. However, her disciples and admirers all melted away when at forty-seven, having been widowed for some years, she married a young man of twenty-one. It was bad enough that she married the young man. What was worse was that this turned out to be a very happy marriage. Fond of America, and a great supporter of the American Revolution, Catherine Macaulay and her new young husband were great friends of George Washington—who was evidently more broad-minded than her British friends.

We don't hear of English women scientists, but Jane Marcet, who took as her task the popularizing of contemporary science for children, began a tradition of rewriting science for the lay person which won great respect from scientists among her own contemporaries and had many imitators in later periods.

In the world of art, as in the world of scholarship, Italy continued in the lead in this century. Waters (1904) says there were no less than forty good women artists in northern Italy in this period, whose works are all to be found in known private collections. Rosalba Carriera of Venice was among the best loved, most renowned and prolific painters of the century. Two others who received a great deal of public recognition were Matilda Festa, professor in the Academy of St. Luke in Rome, and the princess of Parma who was elected to the Academy of Vienna in 1789 (and married the archduke of Austria).

In France there are many names of women artists, but little is known about them. Elizabeth Vigée Le Brun is a notable exception. She was the *salonière* who invented the famous "Greek supper," bringing flair to the serving of small intimate suppers among the aristocracy of art in the salon world. It is an accident that she is more famous for her suppers than for her art, for she was a very popular artist in her day and a member of the French Academy. She painted in the style of Watteau, and her pictures were very much in demand.

In Germany, most women painters were associated with the court and painted for the royal families and for aristocracy. In addition to their work on large canvasses, they were miniaturists, makers of medals, and, increasingly, gem cutters. Susannah Dorsch became famous as a gem cutter. Angelica Kauffman was perhaps the most famous European painter of her time. Born in Switzerland, claimed by the Austrians as their own to the extent of their placing her image on their 100-schilling banknote, having lived and painted many years in both England and Italy, her work was everywhere in demand. During her residence in England, she and her fellow-painter Mary Moser actually became founding members of the British Royal Academy.

Many of the women we have noted were daughters of artists, trained in their fathers' workshops. Countless more women worked unrecognized in family workshops with fathers and brothers.

In music, the 1700s continued the development of the opera, and in England, Italy, France, and Germany women were composing operas as well as symphonies and ballets. Cécile-Louise Chaminade of France, Carlotta Ferrari of Italy, and Emilie Mayer of Germany were the outstanding women composers of the century. Since women of the middle and upper classes were encouraged to cultivate musical skills as part of the "finishing process," women with talent could blossom in the domestic sphere with relative ease. Few were encouraged to work at music seriously, however.

Although the movement was so slight as to be scarcely noticeable, there seems to have been some tendency in this century for women in the rest of Europe who were scholastically or artistically gifted to join their Italian sisters in moving outside the family circle to exercise their gifts. Compared to Italy the movement was slight indeed. It must be seen in the context of the conflicting pressures of 1) a gradual increase in educational opportunities for girls, as well as boys; 2) the final phasing out of the old craft guilds, particularly the women's guilds; 3) a steady increase in the amount of urban housing available; and 4) the rise in importance of the home as a center for child rearing, living, and recreation. We will close this survey of the 1700s with an examination of family life in the century.

Family Life

In the eighteenth century the household as *home base* attained steadily more importance. This new home base was different from the craft workshop of the Middle Ages,[38] and it was only available to the middle and upper classes. The working classes continued to have tiny houses and apartments in which they could do little but eat and sleep.[39] For the middle and upper classes, however, the disappearance of the custom of boarding apprentices and shopworkers, already beginning in the sixteenth century, may have had some kind of effect on the privatization of family interaction. Since we know that household size did not change appreciably over these centuries (Laslett, 1972), we must conclude that apprentices were replaced by domestic servants. Possibly domestics required less interaction with family members than apprentices did. The other change affecting the household was the decline in participation of middle- and upper-artisan-class women in the labor force, either in or out of the home. This gave women free time, the consequences of which were being noted in print by 1799:

> This leisure, however, has one good effect, it makes the mothers better and more wholesome nurses, and induces them to keep themselves and children clean and tight, and contributes greatly to the healthy and good looks universally met with (quoted in Pinchbeck, 1930: 239).

Two parallel developments include an increase in the number of school places generally available to children all over Europe, and the appearance of literature on "child development." De Mause (1974) notes a shift in attitudes regarding discipline by physical punishment in this century, and the beginning of concepts of molding the child by nonphysical means. These developments meant a decrease in compulsory labor force activity for children, and an increase, however slight, in the amount of autonomous space available to children in society.[40] This slight increase in autonomy was accompanied by an increase in the time mothers had for children, in sectors above the working class. It could be argued that women of these classes were now in a position to do more in the mother role than perhaps had been done since the Roman matrons devoted themselves to the education of their children.

How important the differentiation of space in middle-class homes was to this development we cannot be sure. Mumford (1961: 383-384) makes a good deal of the differentiation of household space, as does Aries:

> Domesticity, privacy and isolation were born together: There were no longer beds all over the house. The beds were confined to the bedrooms, which were furnished on either side of the alcove with cupboards and nooks fitted out with new toilette and hygienic equipment. In France and Italy the word chambre began to be used in opposition to the word salle . . . the chambre denoted the room in which one slept, the salle the room in which one received visitors and ate. . . . in England . . . a prefix was added [to "room"] : the dining room, the bedroom, etc. (1962: 399).

It is important to remember that this all applied to a very small sector of the urban population in any European country. For this sector, family life may have developed as a new art of living privately. Certainly this was the period when calling cards were invented, and the institution of receiving hours. Family conversation and family letter writing became an art. If there was in fact a change in the character of family life in the eighteenth century, it was toward an affluence-generated "liberation" for non-task oriented familial interaction. Thus, when it is noted that health and the weather had become major topics of family conversation and correspondence, what is really being noted is that more families had time to talk about the weather, a phenomenon closely tied to individual health and well-being.

As standards of housing improved, even better-off workers' families could afford a separation of sleeping and living quarters, and the family living room became an increasingly general institution. There was development of the arts of indoor recreation and parlor games, and of reading aloud. The family became a *play* group, not just a subsistence enterprise.[41] Quakers are a notable example of this. Clarkson, a contemporary chronicler of Quaker ways, was particularly enthusiastic about their "domestic bliss":

> In consequence of denying themselves the pleasures of the world [they] have been obliged to cherish those which are found in domestic life. . . . The husband and wife are not . . . easily separable. They visit generally together. They are remarked as affectionate. . . . They are long in each others society at a time, and they are more at home than almost any other people (1806: 257-258).

The delights of family life were all very well for Quaker women, who had other spheres of action too. For other women the domestic delights were all there was. One could argue that in general, outside the dissenting sects, the rise of domesticity meant a decline in status and opportunities for women. The focus on the child and the home resulted in progressively more restrictive legislation concerning the right of the woman to make decisions concerning children and property, and produced a peculiar inversion of *de facto* and *de jure* responsibility. As suggested earlier, it may well be that very few women *felt* themselves deprived. They probably felt that the leisure for domesticity and social life represented a far better way of life than had the earlier pressure of work roles. Women's rights were far more an issue for the genteelly poor, the widowed, and the unmarried mothers, and for the philanthropists who saw the relationship between these women's economic plight and their secondary social status.

It is well to remember what crowded spaces most women with families lived in, in order to realize that the "pleasures of domesticity" were a scarce commodity in most households. Whether the household averaged five as in Europe, or six to eight as in colonial North America where fewer children died at birth, most families had to carry out daytime activities within one room. Demos (in Laslett, 1972), reviewing family life in colonial America, asks how these cramped households avoided quarreling all the time. The answer is that they did not. Family and neighborhood quarrelsomeness is very ancient, as court records of antiquity show. Certainly in North America there was a high degree of contentiousness. Demos points out:

> The men and women of these communities went to court again and again, to do battle over land titles, property losses, wayward cattle, rundown fences, unringed pigs—not to mention slander, and witchcraft, and assault and battery (1972: 563).

The reference to witchcraft is particularly illuminating. While witchcraft accusations may have started as primarily political maneuvers for power, by the 1600s many accusations of witchcraft were from women against their own neighbors. I have no frequency counts on this, but many of the accounts in Ashton's *The Devil in Britain and America* (1972) are of such neighbor-to-neighbor accusations. The Salem witchcraft madness of 1692 was initiated by a group of hysterical teenagers acting out the grudges and hostilities against neighbors prevalent in their own families or the families where they were servants (Ryan, 1975: 78-79). By the 1700s these accusations became so totally absurd that no one believed them any more, but they kept on being made right through the eighteenth century.[42]

What triggered the accusations? Unneighborly behavior, such as failing to lend a bit of yeast, figured in more than one story. Social historians often describe the contentment and security of a society in which the women reign as queens over the domestic hearth. As far as I know, no one has investigated the possible relationship between community quarrelsomeness and the extent to which women are confined to this domestic queenship.

This is not to suggest that quarrelsomeness is particularly a feminine trait. I do not know the proportion of male- and female-initiated suits against neighbors to be found in court records over time, but the chances are that men are better represented in such suits than women. Morgan (in Samuel, 1975: 36-37) notes the high level of quarrelsomeness in the English countryside in the eighteenth century, especially under the pressures of harvest time. Both sexes reflected the constraints of confined spaces and a heavy work load. When women became more confined than men were, as seemed to be happening in this century, then we might expect them to feel the consequences of that confinement more keenly, but only to the extent that confinement is felt as deprivation.

If frustration is one accompaniment of a rise in domesticity for women, a rise in the level of unused skill reservoirs is another. The general increase in schooling for women in this century, paralleling the decline in women's labor force participation, left a lot of untapped competence and free time in the social pool. It was this accumulation of competence and free energy which helped produce the explosion of civic activity on the part of women in the next century.

We have seen women moving through three and one-half centuries of eventful developments that have left the status of women less changed than we might have expected. The effect of the developments leading up to the industrial revolution has been to widen the gap between the condition of rich and poor women, even while creating a general rise in societal levels of affluence. Increased leisure and education for the well-to-do have been accompanied by longer working hours for the laboring women. The increase in life expectancy for urban women tells us that rural life was even harder, and at the same time masks the suffering of urban widows, unpartnered mothers, and children. Children of the poor had an especially hard lot, with no choice except being in the labor force from the age of three or four on, or being picked up as vagrants and shipped overseas as labor for the colonies.

The picture is not all dark, for we have seen utopian religious movements coming out of the proletariat. Utopian communities, as such, rarely promoted redefinition of women's roles, only a lessening of their labor. The Anabaptist tradition, however, seems to have freed. women for greater participation in the larger society. Among middle- and upper-class women there was increasing awareness of the meanings of inequality and social injustice, both for the poor and for themselves, although not always where one would expect to find it. Little such awareness was to be found among the women of the French salons. On the other hand, awareness takes many forms, and women's increased productivity as intellectuals, as artists, writers, religious leaders, and social activists, could be seen as manifestations of that awareness. So could the activities of women colonists and adventurers. We have all but seen the last of the great queens, and witnessed the first of the "modern" revolutionaries. In the next chapter we shall see the closing in grand style of the scenario of the queens, and the ascendance of new types of women shaping new scenarios for the twentieth century.

Notes

[1] A number of "peace queens" have been described in previous chapters, but they were consorts, not regnant queens, and sometimes, for brief periods, regents. As far as I know, no major regnant queen in history has pursued an active no-war policy, though some minor ones have, as we shall see in this chapter. The politics of dominance as exercised over the last four thousand years does not readily produce peacemakers at the ruling level.

[2] As, for example, in *Rise of the West* (McNeil, 1963: 579-580). See the *Queens of Old Spain* (Hume, 1906) for the view of Isabel given here.

[3] Discussions of Renaissance women rarely include mention of such traits as business acumen, but Chojnacki (1974: 176-203) makes it clear that they also had a sharp eye for profit and managed considerable business enterprises independently of the men of their families.

[4] Fontana had a portrait medal cast in her honor. Besides having produced 135 documented works, she also had eleven babies (Tufts, 1974: 31-34).

[5] The information on Spain comes from Cannon (1916).

[6] It is very probable that literate women of the middle class opened up their homes for schools for the "displaced girls" of that class, a practice common in Europe for several centuries and referred to in the discussion of Angela de Merici later in this chapter.

[7] Information on Protestant women, unless otherwise indicated, comes from Bainton (1973).

[8] Mary Ward was born in York just the year before St. Margaret Clitherow was martyred, in 1585. She grew up knowing intimately the story of St. Margaret, and in a way the martyred Catholic homemaker was the founder of the Institutes of Mary. The nuns of the order have a very special tradition of veneration for St. Margaret that continues to this day (Dessain, 1971: 109-110).

[9] Sister Monica's biography of St. Angela (1945: 337-338) cites instances of this voluntary establishment of schools by the women of a town in France, Italy, and Geneva for Angela's own time, and one reference dates back to the thirteenth century.

[10]*The Interior Castle* is a major classic of spiritual growth. The three-volume compilation of her complete works (1958) is continuously kept in print. Also, see Elizabeth Hamilton's *The Great Teresa* (1963) for an interesting autobiography.

[11]The records all refer to mothers, not fathers, beating their daughters. Leigh Minturn (1975), on the basis of cross-cultural psychological studies of women's roles, suggests that fathers would never beat daughters; that was the mother's job.

[12]The pressure on mothers to get rid of daughters also existed in the Middle Ages at the height of convent life, and many daughters were beaten half to death by mothers who were trying to force them into convents against their will. There are interesting records of lawsuits of nuns who claim having been forced by parents to take vows (O'Faolain and Martines, 1973: 270-275).

[13]Maher, examining Moroccan society for evidences of the extended-family household, comes to the same conclusion (1974: 70-71).

[14]For further discussion of the problems of women as wives and mothers in this period, see chapter 4 of Laslett (1965).

[15]While the term *bluestocking* was used only in England, the phenomenon is generally identifiable on the Continent.

[16]This section is based on chapter 7 of Georgiana Hill, *Women in English Life* (1896).

[17]Lady Halkett in her *Autobiography* (edited by Nichols, 1965) gives a poignant account of maternal cruelty in describing her youth at home. She was so severely treated by her mother that in desperation she got an uncle to intervene on her behalf. There is no suggestion that Anne was crushed by maternal cruelty —rather she accepted it as part of the conditions of her life.

[18]Laslett (1965: 62) points out the special characteristics of these villages but makes no connection with the dissenting sects. It may be worth exploring.

[19]I attended one of the last of these separate but concurrent women's/men's meetings at an American Yearly Meeting of the Society of Friends in rural Ohio, in 1942, the practice having died out almost everywhere else in Quakerdom before then. I can testify to the impact even in my own youth of seeing women clerks presiding over Meeting for Business and being consulted by the men through the little door set in the partition between the two meetings in the big, old meeting house. There has been discussion among Quakers about whether the separate meetings really fostered the participation of women, or whether they were another way of keeping women out of significant decision making. The dignity and self-assurance that I saw in the rural Ohio women in 1942 suggests that it was not a way of keeping women out.

[20]Among Friends, the term *Quaker* is used interchangeably with the official label, *Society of Friends*.

[21]Governor Peter Stuyvesant used a woman as his interpreter in making the original treaty with the Six Nations in the middle of the century (De Pauw, 1974: 5)

[22]The story of the Spanish women is included, much too briefly, in the third-world overview in chapter 12.

23In 1619 one hundred vagrant London children were shipped to the colonists of Virginia, and a second lot followed the next year. This form of cheap labor became so popular that by 1627 fourteen or fifteen hundred children of both sexes had been sent out (Pinchbeck and Hewitt, 1969: 105-107).

24In addition to Ryan's *Womanhood in America* (1975), there are a number of studies of the varieties of roles performed by women in colonial America which are referred to in the excellent "Women in American Society" by Ann Gordon, Mari Jo Buhle, and Nancy Schrom (1971).

25The story of the day the widow took leave of her husband's family and her fourteen-year-old son to enter the religious life is a famous one. Her son, who did not want her to go, threw himself across the threshold and cried out: "I'm not strong enough to hold you back, but at least it shall be said that you trampled your own child underfoot!" (quoted in Stopp, 1962: 110). The story has been quoted often, sometimes in condemnation of her callousness, sometimes in support of her fortitude.

26Most of my material is drawn from the study by a Swedish scholar, Sven Stolpe (1966), who used new documentation not available to previous writers. See also the biography by Georgina Masson (1968).

27For example, the tragedians Elizabeth Barry and Rebecca Marshall, the comedienne Elinor Leigh, and the irrepressible Nell Gwynn.

28The whole issue of women alchemists needs careful study, since so many different types of roles intersected with the alchemical one. Some women alchemists were primarily prechemists, as suggested in the text. Others were herbalists and healers; some were students of philosophy and religion; and some were practicing ancient druidic and Greco-Egyptian mystery cults, which had enjoyed a "revival" in the fifteenth century. All ran some danger of being accused of witchcraft.

29Mary Astell, at least, did not let the good queen down. She writes of "that Great Queen who has subdu'd the Proud, and made the pretended Invincible more than once fly before her; who has rescu'd an Empire, Reduc'd a Kingdom, Conquered Provinces in as little time almost as one can Travel them, and seems to have Chain'd Victory to her Standard" (Smith, 1916: 246). Furthermore, a historian colleague points out that the last few months of Anne's life, when she was obviously dying, were perhaps the most politically suspenseful in English history. When she died, a coup by the Jacobites (Catholics) was just barely avoided (Susan Armitage, 1975).

30In short, in Queen Anne's reign women held the same franchise as men, could vote, and did.

31Historians disagree as to whether she was personally responsible for his death.

32S. G. Tallentyre calls the salons "forcing-houses of the revolution, the nursery of the Encyclopedia, the antechamber of the Academie" (1926: 1). I would not give them that much credit, but I could be wrong.

33Condorcet is the author of an essay on "The Admission of Women to Civic Rights" (Reich, 1908), which has never received the attention that John Stuart Mill's *Essays on Women* has received.

34To what extent the women of the Camisard movement—a band of male and female prophets who arose during a proletarian-triggered guerrilla war in the Cevennes region between 1702 and 1705—were still active and supplying leadership for the women of Paris I do not know, but this seems to me a possibility that should be investigated.

[35]Corday has been accused of founding the "religion of the poignard," but men have functioned for a long time as political assassins with and without the help of women.

[36]Goethe's *The Sorrows of the Young Werther* became a kind of theme song for this group. Read Tornius (1929) on "Sensibility" to get the flavor of this circle.

[37]Women had sporadic voting rights in the colonies until a few years after the Revolution, when the right of franchise was specifically denied (De Pauw, 1974: 36).

[38]In fact, by 1800 the last of the guilds were gone. Shorter (1973) makes a strong case in *Work and Community in the West* for the relationship between the decline of the guilds and the privatization of the family.

[39]In Italy the poor lived under bridges, on old boats, and in holes in the ground. In winter the men sold themselves as galley slaves for the season (Braudel, 1973: 205).

[40]Pinchbeck and Hewitt (1973) make a strong case for the school as a setting that fostered autonomy and personhood for children in this century. I believe they overstate the case, but nevertheless school was an improvement over existing conditions for the child.

[41]The playing of games is an ancient occupation; no civilization has been without evidence of children's and adult's games. Rabelais' *Gargantua,* published in 1542, included a list of 217 parlor, table, and open-air ganes that his young hero played after dinner. As far as I can tell, however, these games were not played in family groups of adults and children until the eighteenth century (Bakhtin, 1968).

[42]The year 1727 was the last year for the hanging of a woman for witchcraft in England. From then on the judges either dismissed cases or went to some trouble to disprove the charges.

References

Aries, Philippe
1962 Centuries of Childhood: A Social History of Family Life. Tr. by Robert Baldick. New York: Alfred A. Knopf.

Armitage, Susan
1975 Boulder: University of Colorado, Department of History, personal communication.

Armytage, W. H. G.
1961 Heavens Below: Utopian Experiments in England 1560-1960. London: Routledge and Kegan Paul.

Ashton, John
1972 The Devil in Britain and America. Hollywood, Calif.: Newcastle.

Bainton, Roland H.
1973 Women of the Reformation in France and England. Minneapolis, Minn.: Augsburg Publishing House.

Baird, Charles W.
1885 History of the Huguenot Emigration to America. Vol. 2. New York: Dodd Mead.

Bakhtin, Mikhail
1968 "The role of games in Rabelais." Pp. 124-132 in Jacques Ehrmann (ed.), Game, Play, Literature. Boston: Beacon.

Beard, Mary R.
1946 Woman as Force in History: A Study in Traditions and Realities. New York: Macmillan.

Bontemps, Arna (ed.)
1969 Great Slave Narratives. Boston: Beacon.

Brailsford, H. N.
1913 Shelley, Godwin, and Their Circle. New York: Henry Holt.

Braudel, Fernand
1973 Capitalism and Material Life: 1400-1800. Tr. by Mirian Kochan. New York: Harper and Row.

Burckhardt, Jacob
  1944   Civilization of the Renaissance in Italy. Gloucester, Mass.: Peter Smith.

Canfield, William W.
  1902   The Legends of the Iroquois. Port Washington, N. Y.: Ira J. Freidman.

Cannon, Mary Agnes
  1916   The Education of Women During the Renaissance. Washington, D.C.:
         Catholic Education Press.

Chojnacki, Stanley
  1974   "Patrician women in early Renaissance Venice." Studies in the
         Renaissance 21: 176-203.

Clark, Alice
  1919   Working Life of Women in the Seventeenth Century. London:
         Routledge.

Clarkson, Thomas
  1806   A Portraiture of Quakerism. 3 vols. New York: Samuel Stansbury.

Daniel-Rops, Henry
  1962   The Catholic Reformation. Tr. by John Warrington. London: J. M.
         Dent.

de Mause, Lloyd
  1974   "The evolution of childhood." Pp. 1-74 in Lloyd de Mause (ed.), The
         History of Childhood. New York: Psychohistory Press.

Demos, John
  1972   "Demography and psychology in the historical studies of family life."
         Pp. 561-570 in Peter Laslett (ed.), Household and Family in Past Time.
         Cambridge: Cambridge University Press.

De Pauw, Linda Grant
  1974   Four Traditions: Women of New York During the American Revolu-
         tion. Albany, N. Y.: New York State American Revolution Bicenten-
         nial Commission.

Dessain, Mary Joanna
  1971   St. Margaret Clitherow. Slough, England: St. Paul.

Dukes, Paul
  1967   Catherine the Great and the Russian Nobility. London: Cambridge
         University Press.

Ehrmann, Jacques (ed.)
  1968   Game, Play, Literature. Boston: Beacon.

Evennett, H. Outram
  1968   The Spirit of the Counterreformation. Ed. by John Bossy. London:
         Cambridge University Press.

Flexner, Eleanor
  1972   Mary Wollstonecraft: A Biography. New York: Coward, McCann, and
         Goeghegan.

Fox, George
  1937   A Day-Book of Counsel and Comfort: From the Epistles of George Fox.
         Compiled by L. V. Hadgkin. London: Macmillan.

Gordon, Ann D., Mari Jo Buhle, and Nancy E. Schrom
1971 "Women in American society: An historical contribution." Radical America 5: 3-74.

Gordon, Elizabeth Putnam
1924 Women Torch-Bearers: The Story of the Woman's Christian Temperance Union. Evanston, Ill.: National WCTU Publishing House.

Griffiths, Naomi
1973 The Acadians: Creation of a People. Toronto: McGraw-Hill-Ryerson.

Hallowell, A. Irving
1972 "American Indians, white and black: The phenomenon of transculturalization." Pp. 200-224 in Howard Bahr, Bruce Chadwick, and Robert Day (eds.), Native Americans Today: Sociological Perspectives. New York: Harper and Row.

Hamilton, Elizabeth
1963 The Great Teresa. London: Burns and Oates.

Hargreanes, Reginald
1930 Women-at-Arms: Their Famous Exploits Throughout the Ages. London: Hutchinson.

Hill, Georgiana
1896 Women in English Life. Vol. 2. London: Richard Bentley and Son.
1894 Women in English Life. Vol. 1. London: Richard Bentley and Son.

Hilpisch, Stephanus
1958 History of Benedictine Nuns. Tr. by Sr. M. Joanne Muffli. Collegeville, Minn.: St. John's Abbey Press.

Holloway, Mark
1966 Heavens on Earth: Utopian Communities in America 1680-1880. Rev. ed. New York: Dover. (First published 1880.)

Hume, Martin A. S.
1906 Queens of Old Spain. New York: McClure Phillips.
1898 The Courtship of Queen Elizabeth. London: Unwin.

Kavanagh, Julia
1893 Women in France During the Eighteenth Century. 2 vols. New York: Putnam.

Kraditor, Aileen S. (ed.)
1968 Up from the Pedestal. Chicago: Quadrangle Books.

Laslett, Peter
1965 The World We Have Lost. London: Methuen.

Laslett, Peter (ed.)
1972 Household and Family in Past Time. Cambridge: Cambridge University Press.

Longworth, Philip
1973 The Three Empresses: Catherine I, Anne, and Elizabeth of Russia. New York: Holt, Rinehart and Winston.

Luder, Hope Elizabeth
   1973   Women and Quakerism. Pendle Hill Pamphlet 196. Wallingford, Penn.:
          Pendle Hill Publications.

Luke, Mary
   1973   Gloriana: The Years of Elizabeth I. New York: Coward, McCann and
          Geoghegan.

MacGregor, Alexander
   1932   The Life of Flora MacDonald; also, Flora MacDonald in Uist, by
          William Jolly. Stirling, England: E. MacKay.

McNeill, William H.
   1963   The Rise of the West: A History of the Human Community. Chicago:
          University of Chicago Press.

Maher, Vanessa
   1974   Women and Property in Morocco: Their Changing Relation to the Pro-
          cess of Social Stratification in the Middle Atlas. London: Cambridge
          University Press.

Maine, Mary E.
   1975   "Women's political roles in colonial America." Unpublished student
          paper. Boulder: University of Colorado, Department of Sociology.

Masson, Georgina
   1968   Queen Christina. New York: Farrar, Straus and Giroux.

Melancon, Diane
   1975   "A queen as a role model: Elizabeth I of England." Unpublished
          student paper. Boulder: University of Colorado, Department of
          Sociology.

Michelet, Jules
   1960   Les Femmes de la Revolution. Paris: Hachette. (First published 1885.)

Minturn, Leigh
   1975   Boulder: University of Colorado, Department of Psychology, personal
          communication.

Monica, Sister
   1945   Angela Merici and Her Teaching Idea: 1474-1540. Saint Martin, Ohio:
          The Ursulines of Brown County.

Montaigne, Michel de
   1960   Essais. Introduction by Henri Benac. Paris: Hachette.

Morris, E. J.
   1974   History of Urban Form: Prehistory to the Renaissance. New York:
          Wiley.

Mozans, R. J.
   1913   Woman in Science. New York: D. Appleton.

Mumford, Lewis
   1961   City in History: Its Origins, Its Transformations, and Its Prospects. New
          York: Harcourt Brace Jovanovich.

Nichols, John Gough (ed.)
  1965   The Autobiography of Anne Lady Halkett. New York: Johnson Reprint Corporation. (First published 1875.)

O'Faolain, Julia, and Lauro Martines (ed.)
  1973   Not in God's Image: A History of Women in Europe from the Greeks to the Nineteenth Century. New York: Harper and Row.

Pinchbeck, Ivy
  1930   Women Workers and the Industrial Revolution: 1750-1850. London: Frank Cass.

Pinchbeck, Ivy, and Margaret Hewitt
  1973   Children in English Society. Vol. 2. From the Eighteenth Century to the Children Act 1948. London: Routledge and Kegan Paul.
  1969   Children in English Society. Vol. 1. From Tudor Times to the Eighteenth Century. London: Routledge and Kegan Paul.

Raeff, Marc (ed.)
  1972   Catherine the Great: A Profile. New York: Hill and Wang.

Reich, Emil
  1908   Woman Through the Ages. 2 vols. London: Methuen.

Rowbotham, Shiela
  1972   Women, Resistance, and Revolution: A History of Women and Revolution in the Modern World. New York: Pantheon.

Rudé, George
  1964   The Crowd in History, 1730-1884. New York: Wiley.

Rusche, Georg, and Otto Kirchheimer
  1968   Punishment and Social Structure. New York: Russell and Russell. (First published 1939.)

Ryan, Mary P.
  1975   Womanhood in America: From Colonial Times to the Present. New York: New Viewpoints.

Samuel, Raphael
  1975   Village Life and Labor. London: Routledge and Kegan Paul.

Schiff, Mario
  1910   Marie de Gournay: La Fille D'Alliance de Montaigne. Paris: Librarie Honore Champion.

Scott, Anne Firor (ed.)
  1971   The American Woman: Who Was She? Englewood Cliffs, N. J.: Prentice-Hall.

Shorter, Edward (ed.)
  1973   Work and Community in the West. New York: Harper and Row.

Smith, Florence
  1916   Mary Astell: 1666-1739. New York: Columbia University Press.

Sokolnikova, Galina Osipovna
  1969   Nine Women: Drawn from the Epoch of the French Revolution. Tr. by

H. C. Stevens. Freeport, N. Y.: Books for Libraries Press. (Reprint of 1932 edition.)

Stenton, Doris Mary
   1957   The English Woman in History. London: Allen and Unwin.

Stolpe, Sven
   1966   Christina of Sweden. Ed. by Sir Alec Randall. Tr. by Sir Alec Randall and Ruth Mary Bethell. New York: Macmillan.

Stopp, Elisabeth
   1962   Madame de Chantal: Portrait of a Saint. London: Faber and Faber.

Tallentyre, S. G. (Evelyn Hall)
   1926   The Women of the Salons. New York: Putnam.

Teresa of Avila, St.
   1958   The Interior Castle, or The Mansions. Ed. by H. Martin. Naperville, Ill.: Allenson.

Tomalin, Claire
   1974   The Life and Death of Mary Wollstonecraft. New York: Harcourt Brace Jovanovich.

Tornius, Valerian
   1929   Salons: Pictures of Society through Five Centuries. Tr. by Agnes Platt and Lilian Wonderley. New York: Cosmopolitan.

Tufts, Eleanor
   1974   Our Hidden Heritage: Five Centuries of Women Artists. New York: Paddington.

Ward, A. C. (ed.)
   1927   A Miscellany of Tracts and Pamphlets. London: Oxford University Press.

Waters, Clara (Erskine) Clement
   1904   Women in the Fine Arts. Boston: Houghton Mifflin.

Webb, Maria
   1867   The Fells of Swarthmoor Hall and Their Friends. London: F. Kitto.

Whitworth, John McKelvie
   1975   God's Blueprints: A Sociological Study of Three Utopian Sects. London: Routledge and Kegan Paul.

Wilson, John Harold
   1958   All the King's Ladies: Actresses of the Restoration. Chicago: University of Chicago Press.

11
Preparing the Modern World: The 1800s

This is the century of the last strong ruling woman monarch, Victoria. Much of the traditional monarchic power is gone. The salons are gone. The power the great landed families and their women had in the affairs of state is gone. By 1800 the state has passed "to the control of parliament composed of men and elected by men" (Beard, 1946: 317).

Since most of this chapter will be dealing with social change triggered by new types of social movements, perhaps we should begin by discussing the changes triggered by the last major exercise of traditional monarchic power. When Queen Victoria ascended the throne at the age of eighteen in 1837, she had outlived a weak father and entered public life in an atmosphere characterized by the immoralities of her "four wicked uncles." "I will be good," she is supposed to have said when she took the throne. And she was. Although the political significance of royal alliance structures had declined substantially, Queen Victoria created a set of interlocking alliances with almost every royal house in Europe through the judicious marrying off of each of her nine children. She was the matriarch of Europe, every king's mother-in-law, and it has been said that had she still been alive World War I would never have happened. She would simply have told Kaiser Wilhelm, one of her sons-in-law, to stop misbehaving.

Victoria extended the empire on other continents, but kept peace in Europe—give or take a few revolutions over which she had no control. She also maintained an anti-slave trade patrol on the high seas which eventually brought that practice to a halt, though not before another two million slaves had been shipped to the Americas. She kept track of kings and political leaders everywhere through a voluminous correspondence. A strong-minded queen, she made many decisions herself and never let go of the reins even during the years she lived in widow's retirement after the death of her husband, Prince Consort Albert. She happened to choose a husband whose thoughts were in tune with an age yet to come. In designing the first world's fair, the London Exposition of 1851, Prince Albert inaugurated the postcolonial age of internationalism. One might say that Victoria, who became empress of India in 1876, presided over the era of imperial nationalism while Albert opened the door to the successor era of internationalism.

Because she lived for so long, having reigned for sixty-three years when she died, people tended to remember the sorrowing widow and forgot the lively, fun-loving young queen. While her reputation for driving vice underground in England was well deserved, she was far from gloomy. She was gay, and determined. What brought her out of her retirement after Albert's death was a love affair (quite probably platonic) with her highland ghillie John Brown, who appears in her delightful book *Life in the Highlands.* This gave her renewed zest for life and made her decide to take the crown of India. She was the despair of the women of her century, being one of those strong-minded women who could not let anyone else be strong. Her contribution to the suffrage movement at the time that the women's suffrage bill was before parliament in 1870 was the word that

> the Queen is most anxious to enlist everyone who can speak or write to join in checking this mad, wicked folly of "Woman's Rights" with all its attendant horrors, on which her poor feeble sex is bent, forgetting every sense of womanly feeling and propriety. Lady Amberley [an advocate] ought to get a *good whipping* (Langford, 1964: 208).

The fact that women were remarkably active (and remarkably unvictorian, like Victoria herself) all through the Victorian age is evidence that women learned to model themselves on her deeds rather than on her words. It is also evidence that they were clever, because none of the new scripts had parts written for women. The new nationalism was not a salon game, but serious business, carried on by men (Queen Victoria always excepted). Though women contributed energy and personpower for the revolutions of 1848 in Germany, Austria, and Italy, this created no places for them in the new parliaments. Women helped liberate the Latin American colonies beginning with Paraguay and Venezuela in 1811, ending with Brazil and Central America in 1822-1825, but there was no place for them in these parliaments either.

Was there to be any place for women in the overlife of this new world, or were they to remain forever in the underlife, building necessary support structures for men to manipulate and destroy? There is a certain urgency to asking this question at the beginning of the nineteenth century, with so many possibilities coming together for humankind. This is the century in which the modern transport and communication systems developed, with the telegraph, the universal postal union, and the fast steamship making it possible to move about rapidly and make decisions in consultation with on-the-spot "experts" anywhere on the globe. A new international system was emerging, even while the nation-state system was still in the making. Where would women fit in?

The implications have yet to be worked out, in the latter part of the twentieth century, of the trends that began in the nineteenth. In that century alliance structures were formed between aware groups of women and the men who shared their social perceptions, on behalf of common social goals. We will examine these alliance structures, their goals and their possibilities. One major alliance structure was that of middle- and upper-class women with the liberals among industrialists and political leaders. This alliance was to create a new set of welfare institutions to deal with the social problems generated by increasing urbanism and industrialization. In 1801, 26 percent of the population of England lived in cities of five thousand or more (21 percent in cities of ten thousand or more). By 1861, 55 percent of the total population of England lived in urban areas, and by 1891, 72 percent were living in urban districts (Cook, 1951: 115). The employment situation was serious, particularly for proletarian women. Insufficient earnings increasingly had to be supplemented by prostitution.

In the mid-1800s it is estimated that there were between twenty and eighty thousand prostitutes in major cities like London and Paris. The practice of police registration of prostitutes makes it possible for us to see that many women preferred other means of employment when available. In Paris, women were struck from the records when they could demonstrate that they had other employment, and between 1817 and 1827, 1,680 women had their names thus removed. Notations about the employment they entered ranged from laundress to shoemaker to a music mistress in a boarding school (O'Faolain and Martines, 1973: 301). Middle-class prostitutes, at the professional courtesan level, had a very different situation. They lived well and were not entered on police rolls. But the poor lived constantly under the double threat of hunger and police regulation, and so did their children. Increasingly alcohol, the anodyne of poverty, heightened violence levels on the streets and in the homes of the poor.

The tradition out of which middle- and upper-class women allied themselves with men in power to alleviate these problems is that of the aristocracy and of the manor house lady. The women who looked to those traditions, however, were many of them middle-class women who in an earlier generation would have been shopkeepers and skilled workers of various kinds. They shared with their upper-class sisters increased education, exposure to new ideas, and a general restlessness about the limitations of their lives. In a way these women were facing again the situation women faced in the Renaissance. There were new discoveries about the nature of "man" from which they were excluded. The political theories of the seventeenth century led to a conception of the state as an organization of individual men or groups of men, rather than as a commonwealth of families. This led to an emphasis on individual thinking and action. However,

> *none* of the associations which were formed during this period for public purposes, either educational, economic, scientific, or political, include women in their membership (Hill, 1896: 286).

Theories of social evolution referred to men only.

This time, however, women did not accept exclusion. More of them were reading, more of them were traveling, observing, thinking, writing, more of them were going off to pioneer in new lands. Would there finally be a reversal of the situation which had obtained in the first agricultural villages after 12,000 B.C., when women lost out for failing to see the larger scene? In the 1800s men of affairs were overburdened with the tasks of industrialization. More and more it was middle- and upper-class women who were realizing the larger picture. They were developing new approaches to the problems of urban poverty. For the first time middle-class women were in a position to make the kinds of judgments possible earlier only for royal women, and this produced tensions. On the one hand the women were developing their analytic capacities and developing confidence in their own abilities as they got reality-feedback from their efforts. On the other hand they were repeatedly confronted with absurdities: the absurdity of the conventional limitations on their role, the absurdity that men controlled the resources women needed to do their work, and the absurdity that these same men held a definition of women which implied that women could not possibly understand the issues they were dealing with.

In the end, women found that task-oriented cooperative relationships with men in social welfare work could not be carried out as long as women and men were not equal partners in political decision making. The detour which women took on behalf of women's suffrage was in the context of overcoming obstacles to work to be done. It was not at first primarily a consciousness-raising phenomenon. The consciousness raising came as a consequence of the violence of the reactions of the men to the very pragmatic course the women chose. Neither was there any grand theory of history involved, only a simple conviction that the rights of man were also the rights of woman.[1]

The men of the gradualist liberal tradition who allied themselves with the gradualist liberal women reformers were not entirely comfortable with the alliance. They all belonged to the same social class, but there was an uneasiness there, and it has remained to this day. This is why the issue of the need for separate women's organizations, first tried by the Quakers in the 1600s, is still a live one in the twentieth century. The bloodiness of some of the later suffrage battles can only be understood if one perceives the underlying sense of threat to the foundations of the social order felt by men over the issue of equality of women. Since there was no accepted liberal theory of institutional change that could explain new structural relationships between family and society, and between women and men, any change that threatened must be bad. While it may seem absurd to suggest that a *theory* of the role of women in society might have helped the male liberal of the past two centuries, the lack of one made it harder to envisage alternative future male-female relationships.

Socialist societies have a long way to go before women are equal partners with men, but the fact that they have a theory that (imperfectly) accounts for possiblity of equality and an ideology that supports it shows up in a variety of practical ways, including the fact that women are invariably better rerpresented in the political bodies of socialist countries than they are in nonsocialist countries. This will be seen in the last chapter.[2]

A second type of alliance made by women in the nineteenth

century was the alliance of different sectors of middle-class women, and some of their working-class sisters, with middle- and working-class men of the socialist movement to build a classless society. These women were responding to the same set of social problems the reformist women were responding to, but their analysis was different. They had no confidence that a "hidden hand" (with a little help from the reformers) would see to the optimal distribution of goods in a free market, as Adam Smith theorized (*Wealth of Nations,* 1776). Before the mid-century, thinkers like Flora Tristan Moscosa and Louise Michel among women, and Marx and Engels among men, saw a basic block to optimal distribution of goods in the loss of control by the worker over both the instruments and the products of labor. The social relations of production had become pathological through failure to adapt to the changing character of the forces of production. The capitalist system which permitted individual owners of means of production to exploit their workers by appropriating all surplus productivity beyond bare subsistence requirements was an institutional anachronism that created poverty for the masses in the very age in which technological advance made abundance for all possible. The concept of "social relations of production" as developed by Marx and Engels had included the concept of husband-wife relations in the production of children. The first producers whose product was appropriated were mothers, whose children and domestic work were appropriated by fathers in oppressive monogamous family structures. It is interesting that none of the socialist theories of the time (at least to my knowledge) seem to have explored fully the meaning of the social relations of production inside the family in terms of men's responsibility for fathering and domestic maintenance work. Rather, they turned immediately to the liberation of women from family roles through 1) entry into the non-domestic labor force, and 2) the provision of child care and all domestic chores through state facilities. Since it happens that these state facilities tend to be operated by women, not all that much has changed for women. Nowhere is the production of children conceived as a joint process. The "protection of motherhood" theme which was the theme of the nonsocialist women's movement in Europe after mid-century, also lingers in socialist theory. Mothers must be protected in bearing children, protected in their domestic responsibilities, and protected in their right to participate in the labor force, but nowhere is there any mention of fatherhood, or parenthood, or a redefinition of the reproductive process. There is in fact no sociology of reproduction.

As is well known, the Russian socialist state at first thought it could do without the family in the new society. Divorce was available on request, and the state intended to provide public facilities for human maintenance. It turned out that the state was not rich enough to do this. Given the resources available, it was cheaper to get the maintenance work done within individual families by women. And so, while the ideology of state facilities and of the participation of women in the labor force continued, the underlying reality was that most children still had to be cared for outside of state facilities. Within the home women still carried on the traditional tasks of marketing, cooking, laundering, cleaning, and child care, in addition to working outside the home.

The basic issue of the future of private family life in a society that promotes the participation of women in the public sphere will be further examined in the last chapter. The record of the nineteenth century in this matter is that some groups experimented with communes, and there was a certain amount of urban boarding house living,[3] but that in general, family units took individual housing when available, along with the tasks that went with individual housing. The question of permanent versus temporary pairing was hardly an issue in earlier centuries when there were large numbers of unmarried "vagabond" women, and married women were for the most part working partners with their husbands. In the nineteenth century that issue became linked, appropriately, to the phenomenon of increasing numbers of wives isolated in household settings where they had very little to do.

The chief contribution of the socialists to the problem of women's roles was to acknowledge that productive life for women was problematic in the industrial era. Fourier was one of the first to articulate clearly that the status of women could be used as an indicator of the progress of society:

> The change in a historical epoch can always be determined by the progress of women towards freedom, because in the relation of woman to man, of the weak to the strong, the victory of human nature over brutality is most evident. The degree of emancipation of women is the natural measure of general emancipation (quoted in Rowbotham, 1972: 51).

Marxist theory vastly overrated the productivity inherent in technology per se, and assumed that machines would mean abundance of food and material goods for all. It also vastly underrated the difficulty of developing a redistribution system that would regularly redistribute away from the advantaged and toward the disadvantaged at any moment in time. The classless society was supposed to have no distribution problems. The concept of classlessness itself did not take account of the shifting advantage and disadvantage for individuals in various social situations, particularly for women.

The painstaking task of developing figures on women in the labor force, on wage levels, and other relevant data on the conditions of women was all undertaken by socialists: Engels, Marx, and Bebel in Germany, Harriet Martineau and (in the next century) Beatrice Webb in England. We shall see that women came to play an increasingly important role in the science of measurement of states of the social system, and in providing the inputs for social planning and the evaluation of planning outcomes. In the early days of the workers' movement this was not so. Then it was a question of getting first-hand experience in the field, of mobilizing women and men, and getting them to work separately and together. Radical women had to face the same problem reformist women faced—that the alliance with men even of the same class interests was an uneasy one. Not all radical men supported the ideology of the equality of women, and many who supported the ideology did not practice it. The issue of separate radical women's organizations therefore developed very early, and some women worked in segregated organizations, others worked with men. On the whole I have the impression that more radical women stayed in the mainstream radical movement than reformist women stayed in the mainstream reform movements. The alliance process went on whether from separatist or integrated stances, but under difficulties, and with periodic revolts of women against inappropriate male dominance behavior.

Whether separatists or integrationists, reformers or radicals, activist women were in a sense exposed to a more complex set of stimuli in the nineteenth century than men were. This was due to the fact that they entered the public sphere when nationalism was at its height, but in the same century that internationalism was born. While mastering the problems of participation in their own society, they were also seeing these problems in a world context that was completely new. The development of rapid communication and transportation facilities mentioned earlier was one reason for this. The very capitalism that fostered colonialism and the organization of world market networks also fostered an alternative set of perceptions about the world itself. The new internationalism was very different from the old international marriage-alliance system that women aristocrats knew. In this new arena women participated as individuals, although marriage alliances were still to continue.[4]

The very newness of this double exposure to nationalism and internationalism enhanced women's social perceptions in ways that led to an extraordinary flowering of their creativity in the public sphere in the latter part of the century. It also led to sophisticated perceptions of the general social contract that few men of either liberal or radical groups were prepared to accept. Women increasingly understood the character of their underlife position, and were no longer willing to work at the old task of social reconstruction from that position. While much emotionalism went into the women's emancipation movement, it was the underlying analytic clarity of women activists that gave the movement strength and momentum. It is not until the next century, however, that we come to the slow and painful process of rewriting the social contract.

The Revolutionaries and the Workers

The working women of the nineteenth century were not in a very different situation from their eighteenth century sisters, except that there were more of them, towns and cities were more crowded, and sanitation and housing were even more of a problem than before. Women worked in village, town, and city, at an amazing variety of jobs. Appendix 11-1 gives an occupational census for women in England in 1841 which is probably not unrepresentative of the occupations of women elsewhere in Europe, though other countries were not as far along in industrialization. The employment of children also continued through this century. Even by 1901, the reporting of the employment of women is stated in terms of females of age ten and over (Richards, 1974: 350). Appendix 11-2 gives an idea of the range of employments for children outside the cities. If we added city employments and factory work, the list would be much longer.

The working life of proletarian women, as of men, began in early childhood and lasted throughout life. Whether there was time off for childbearing in the working class depended on the level of earnings of a partner, if there was a partner, and of children already born, and on the possibilities of the woman getting piecework to do at home. There were many never-married working women. In England 42 percent of women in the age group twenty through forty were spinsters (Richards, 1974: 349); we shall see that figures were equally high on the Continent. We do not know how many of these women had stable, unregistered partnerships. While schooling facilities for children were steadily increasing, they were not keeping up with the population growth. There was often resistance on the part of parents to putting children in school, even when this option was available,

since their earnings helped out at home. Vagrant children continued
to fill the workhouses throughout this century, and to be shipped
overseas to Australia and Canada to meet various fates.

The disproportion between the number of women seeking jobs
and the jobs available continued to grow. The same phenomenon
that has been noticed in the twentieth century in the third world,
that of a faster contraction of traditional-sector jobs than an expansion of modernizing-sector jobs,[5] was taking place in England over
the eighteenth and nineteenth centuries. As Eric Richards points out,
there was "a clear shrinkage of opportunities in many of the metal
trades and in agriculture after 1815" (1974: 345). Factory opportunities were very limited. Those who did enter factory employment, whether in England or New England, were at least 50 percent
children under fourteen (Richards, 1974: 346). The fact that only
27 percent of factory women were married was not because they did
not wish to go on working, but because factories found it cheaper to
let them go as they grew older and replace them with children. With
traditional employments declining, women swarmed into domestic
services—another phenomenon paralleling the experience of women
in third world countries today. Those who could not get domestic
employment were forced into a variety of pittance-paying odd jobs,
and prostitution. Richards asks where this large surplus army of em-
ployable women came from, and suggests rhetorically but disbeliev-
ingly that they may always have existed (1974: 348). In the view of
history I am giving they certainly always existed, and became visible
only because of the shrinking employment opportunities accompanying industrialization. Their visibility helped the cause of feminism, as numerous publications on the problem attest.[6] Although
exact figures are not available, it is probable that not until World War
II did employment opportunities for women begin to approach the
preindustrialization levels of 1700 (Richards, 1974: 354).

Urban working women bore the brunt of an industrialization that
outpaced every kind of facility for human welfare, and it is among the
urban proletarian women that we find the revolutionaries of the
nineteenth century. In France, these women revolutionaries were the
grandchildren and great-grandchildren of the bread rioters of the
eighteenth century. When Louise Michel broke into the bakeries of
Lyons in 1882 to distribute bread to the unemployed, she was following an old tradition. But the movement she represented was a
different kind of movement. A schoolteacher who had had her baptism in the Paris Commune of 1871, Michel became a leading
exponent of anarchist communism. Her *Memoirs* (1886) and *Le
Monde Nouveau* (1888) show what a long way women have come

from the rhetoric of Olympe de Gouges and Claire Lacombe in the days of the French Revolution. The theme of bread, however, remained a constant. When the women of Paris were faced with endless queuing at the bakeshops during the revolution of 1871, they started remembering "how things were a hundred years ago when the women of Paris had gone to Versailles to carry off the baker and the baker's little boy" (Rowbotham, 1972: 104). In France, men and women fought, and women searched for bread, in 1789, in 1848, in 1871, and in 1882—and countless other times.

The triple responsibility that women faced in each of the revolutionary uprisings had the cumulative effect of radically politicizing one group of French women. The triple role involved 1) helping the men to arm, 2) taking arms themselves, and 3) finding bread for the children, the men, and themselves. In some cases, as in the uprising of the Paris Commune in 1871, they organized nonviolent brigades to disarm the government soldiers.[7] The role they were not permitted was participation in the political decision making of the male revolutionaries. Their very flexibility and capacity for multiple approaches to problem solving made them a threat to the single-minded male leaders. The 1871 Declaration of the Commune, like all previous declarations that were to inaugurate a new society, said not one word about the participation of women.

To present a clear picture of the many aspects of the revolutionary movements of the nineteenth century is an impossible task. There were many separate lines of development, they often crisscrossed, and women were involved in them all. The socialist movement born of the ideas of Saint-Simon, Robert Owen, and Charles Fourier came to encompass two essentially contradictory developments: the cooperative movement, which represented a voluntary effort to improve the condition of the working class, involving cooperation with capitalist structures; and the revolutionary movement, which aimed at destruction of capitalist institutions and their replacement by worker-controlled institutions. Many of the utopian socialist experiments of the 1800s came under the category of cooperation with capitalist structures. Revolutionary socialism, involving replacement of structures, was itself divided into factions. One group tended toward decentralist anarchistic socialism, and emphasized the democracy of the masses, continued participation by the masses in decision making, and continued involvement in the education of the masses. Another group tended toward the conspiratorial elite view, a centralist planning perspective which involved a small group of highly trained persons acting on behalf of the masses.

In general, the mass-participation socialists were committed to internationalism, and opposed the nationalistic tendencies of increasing numbers of socialists in the communist movement after the 1880s. They also tended to oppose all wars. The centralists on the other hand tended to be nationalists, and were more inclined to support national wars as tools for communism. Most of the groups, whether cooperative socialist, or centralist, or decentralist revolutionary socialist, supported equal participation of women in the movement and in society *in theory*. Few did so in practice.

Karl Marx himself played a relatively unimportant role in the evolution of these movements. His 1848 manifesto, as Cole (1953-1960, vol. 2: chapt. 1) points out, was almost unnoticed at the time. The revolutions of 1848 collapsed and the predicted fall of capitalism did not take place. It was "back to the drawing boards." The Paris Commune of 1871 also collapsed, and with it the First International. Back to the drawing boards again. In terms of actual organizing activities, there were whole sets of actors, too numerous to mention here. We will instead pick out some of the women who worked in these movements. Most of these women can be found in the popular chronicles of revolutionary history if one searches carefully for them, but their role has rarely been emphasized except by revolutionary women themselves. Until their role has been more carefully scutinized, I suggest that our understanding of the meaning of the socialist and later communist movements of the nineteenth century cannot be properly understood, nor can their successes and failures.

The women who appear to have stood out in terms of articulateness and leadership all supported the decentralist, democratic, mass education, nonelite approach to revolution. They also represented internationalism, and opposed war. In short, they represented all the features of socialism which lost out in the European communist revolutions of the next century. Had their leadership been more acceptable to the men of the movements, the story of European socialism might have been different.

Flora Tristan Moscosa (1803-1844) is the first representative of women's contribution to revolutionary socialism. She was one of the first to draw up a plan for a worldwide workers' international (*L'Union Ouvrière*, 1843). She not only devised a theoretical underpinning and a practical organizational scheme for the workers' movement, but she also spent her short life in traveling about the world arousing the consciousness of workers and recruiting them for the *internationale*. French born, half Peruvian, she was a revolutionary heroine on both sides of the Atlantic. She was a strong supporter of women's rights, and linked the emancipation of women to the emancipation of the worker. (Her *Emancipation of Women* was published posthumously.) Pretty and talented, she was herself a typical victim of the life situation of the woman worker. The master of her workshop first married and then abused her. After three pregnancies and continual abuse she ran away, was shot by her husband, and yet survived. Divorce was not an option for women at that time. When she entered the socialist movement she gave herself completely to it, and drove herself so hard through writing, traveling, and organizing, that she died, worn out, at forty-one. A laundress coworker cared for her at the end. Exposed to much ridicule, she felt very much alone toward the end of her life. "I have nearly the whole world against me. Men because I demand the emancipation of women, the owners because I demand the emancipation of wage-earners" (Rowbotham, 1972: 55).

Jeanne Deroin was a self-taught working woman who became a schoolteacher and a journalist. She also linked the liberation of women and the liberation of the working class, and together with Pauline Roland worked with a group of trade union men on a plan for the federation of all existing unions—a simpler version of the Tristan Moscosa plan. She was the thinker and organizer for the group. Nevertheless, when she and her male associates were arrested for illegal political association, the court preferred to record her as a prostitute. The political issues were fastened on the men alone. The difficulties of a woman revolutionary working with men is seen in the trial record (O'Faolain and Martines, 1973: 312, 315; Rowbotham, 1972: 110). Apparently, the union men were as eager as the judge for their case to be dissociated from that of Jeanne Deroin. Rowbotham tells us the men begged her before the trial to pretend she knew nothing about the federation she had architected.

Side by side with these more radical women were the "moderates" such as Mme Poutret de Mauchamps. Her form of action was the publishing of a women's rights journal, *Gazette des Femmes* (1836-1838). She took the position that the Constitution of 1830, proclaiming the political emancipation of Frenchmen, had used man generically, "so that the new charter of liberties necessarily included Frenchwomen in its provisions" (Stanton, 1970: 240). Mme de Mauchamps was a good politician. Every issue of the *Gazette* was introduced by a new petition to the king and parliament, making specific requests for reforms in the code relating to women. She always took care to associate prominent public personages with her declarations and petitions. Many decades were to pass before any of them were attended to, but this represented the start of a new kind of women's campaign: well thought out, sophisticated, coolly rational—and insistent.

Mme de Mauchamps' way of working with men caused no problems; she could assume the style of a *salonière* when it suited her. For women like Tristan Moscoa and Deroin, committed to living the revolution as if it were now, things were harder. The women who tried to work with men had to be strong-minded to endure both the disapproval of the public and of their own coworkers. The men who worked in all-women's groups dealt with a smaller segment of the same set of problems—how to increase control over their own lives. Women in government workshops—dressmakers, laundresses, midwives—sought that control by forming associations to increase their pay. Their twelve-hour-plus workdays for low wages were forced by competition with women in prisons and convents who worked for even less. The situation of the women in the workshops is a good illustration of the problems of antagonistic class interests among women's groups. From the upper-middle class came the lady philanthropists convinced that they knew how to improve the lot of poor working women. These same upper classes were helping to support the convents and the beguinages, which had by now in some cases become sweatshop perversions of the earlier cooperative workshops for women.[8] In these shops stunted girls bent over fine embroidery all day in the name of "education."

The women in government workshops suffered the more heavily from this competition because most of them had children to support, and they were often without legal partners. In 1882, one-third of the babies born in Paris were "illegitimate." Not all the mothers of these babies were ready to become political radicals, but some were. They came to increasingly realistic perceptions about the conditions of their lives. They knew that they needed not only higher wages, but also help with child care. Their children needed human care as well as food while their mothers were at work. In 1848, the year of revolutions and declarations, the first petition from women workers for crèches went to a government. Working-class neighborhoods with gardens, reading rooms, and communal dining rooms as well as crèches and a school were proposed. One hundred twenty-five years later, such plans still seem utopian for most working women in any country, north, south, west, or east. We will see later how the need for child care merged with the Froebel kindergarten movement, but in the process moved away from the proletarian women who needed it most, and toward the middle class.

The most important thing about the 1840s movements was that proletarian women were beginning to define their own problems and organize to solve them. Self-educated working women and middle-class teachers and journalists united in associations and in producing journals to provide a forum for their new ideas. *La Voix des Femmes* and *La Politique des Femmes* (later, *L'Opinion des Femmes*) both began as socialist papers, voicing the opinions of dressmakers and midwives as well as of socialist women teachers. The journals became the focus also for organizing women to improve workshop conditions and to discuss other social problems. These clubs frightened men, and not just the conservatives among them either. Who knows what the women might be hatching to disturb the social order? Within the associations, the radicals soon frightened the middle-of-the-roaders, who usually did not have such urgent personal economic problems to deal with.

One arena in which the alliance of middle- and working-class women was very important was that of prostitution. The euphemism *fallen women* used by philanthropists masked an increasingly desperate situation for many of the working poor as well as the unemployed poor. The combination of increased numbers of young women in urban areas and the fact that the age of consent for girls in a country like England was still twelve in the 1870s was a recipe for disaster. The use of children twelve years and younger for prostitution was very widespread. They were there, and they were unemployed. This meant, as Rowbotham (1973: 53) points out, that there were many very young unmarried mothers who had to choose between the prison-like workhouse or the dreary streetwalker's routine, to feed their children. Associations organized to help these young women, often mere children themselves, were somewhat misdirected in their preoccupation with the morality rather than the economics of prostitution. Nevertheless, the efforts of middle-class women did succeed in bringing about a substantial reduction in the white slave traffic in little girls, particularly the international traffic.

An important person in these efforts was Josephine Butler, a courageous British woman who devoted her life to the abolition of government regulation of prostitution, the abolition of the international white slave trade, and a fundamental transformation in the character of institutions for "fallen women." Butler was responsible for the creation of the British and Continental Federation for the Abolition of Government Regulation of Prostitution in 1875, and she fought corrupt police and male class privilege in every country in Europe as well as in England and the United States (Petrie, 1971).

The situation of working women in Paris who lived at margins of subsistence was such that they lived under a reign of terror administered by the dreaded *Police des Moeurs*. The police had an arrest quota to fill each month. Any woman obviously belonging to the working class, or living alone in furnished rooms, could be arrested by the police on no other evidence than their lack of affluence or a partner to protect them and forcibly inspected and licensed. Inevitably many nonprostitutes were picked up in this way. If they refused to submit to registration they were kept in the prison of St. Lazare until they gave in or died. Butler's investigations of such situations are graphically described in Petrie (1971: 155ff.). Her discovery of child abuse in London brothels, and of a regular traffic in children and young girls shipped to the brothels of Europe from London, did not make her popular with "enlightened" British liberal men, many of whom patronized the very institutions she exposed.

The middle level of prostitutes and the well-to-do courtesans were not subject to imprisonment, but their own protection was bought at a price. They shared their earnings liberally with the police, whether in London, Brussels, Paris, or New York. *The Women of New York* (Ellington, 1962) gives some fascinating sketches of women of the New York "underworld." The well-to-do *salonière* types among them gave liberally to charity, particularly for their hard-up sisters in the profession and for children, and seem to have introduced some wider perspectives into an otherwise dull social scene. The poor young prostitutes with younger siblings, aged dependents, and children of their own to support, who walked the streets of New York in the middle 1800s, were the same young girls who walked the streets of Europe. Only the language was different.

Another very vulnerable group in the nineteenth century city was the servants. The habit from slavery days of men considering women household workers as being at their disposal for sexual service continued after slavery. If a servant girl became pregnant there was no recourse when the mistress of the household turned her out. Many prostitutes were forced into the profession via that route, other employment being barred. As soon as other employment was available, women left domestic service in droves and went to the factories. The slave-like character of domestic service made it unattractive when there were alternatives, so the "servant problem" began early. Salmon (1897) gives an interesting description both of the character of domestic service toward the end of the century in the United States and of the efforts of innovative women to organize cooperative housekeeping services to solve the needs created by the exodus of servants. The development of specialized services through women's exchanges and of cooperative housekeeping associations were in the best utopian tradition of the eighteenth century. Some of these ventures were inspired by Edward Bellamy's utopia, *Looking Backward* (1967). There were certainly similar developments in Europe, though I am lacking details on this.

It is impossible to give an adequate description of the overall situation of women in this century because the social climate was so different in each country. In Germany, August Bebel's *Women Under Socialism,* which appeared around 1880, introduced the women's question to a highly resistant German population. The book is a lengthy indictment of the situation of women in the present-day society, brings up the glories of her matriarchal past, and proposes a working partnership between women and men in the future (Bebel, 1971). The objections to the participation of women in society were perhaps stronger in Germany than anywhere else in Europe. The German culture was domestically oriented, and the fact that women made up at least a fifth of the industrial work force was not allowed to intrude on the image of domesticity. Women like Adelheid Popp, who in the 1880s became trade union militants, did not even know there was a women's question when they were young. It was not written about, not discussed.

Yet we find major leaders of the international socialist women's movement coming out of Germany. Bebel's work certainly helped, but the women who were mobilized in Germany and Austria in the 1880s went considerably beyond him in their analysis of the economic situation of women. Clara Zetkin (1857-1933) was a major figure on the European scene after 1890. She was the leader of the women's section of German Social Democracy. After 1892, she edited the journal *Glechheit (Equality),* the voice of socialist feminism for many years. Like her sisters in the movement, she was a strong exponent of the international emphasis of socialism as against nationalistic developments. She and Rosa Luxemburg teamed up again and again to defend internationalism before their more chauvinist (in the original, nationalistic, meaning of the word) male colleagues. She was also a pacifist.[9]

Polish-born Rosa Luxemburg (1871-1918) was a towering figure whose work spanned the close of the nineteenth and the beginning of the twentieth centuries. Not only did she write over seven hundred books, pamphlets, and articles (Whitman, 1970: 16), but she was one of the most skilled educators and organizers in the international socialist movement. She fought against elitism and on behalf of more democratic participation of the masses in revolutionary activity, and was an antinationalist and a pacifist. In short, she represented all the best contributions of women to the concepts of revolutionary action. She did much more than that, however. She rethought the theory of capital accumulation as contained in the second volume of Marx's *Das Kapital,* and produced what Joan Robinson, today's leading woman economist in Britain, suggests was a major theoretical contribution to economics not recognized at the time or since. Robinson says that Luxemburg's work, while incomplete in its analysis, is a "remarkable anticipation" of concepts that were only to be generally understood by economists in the 1930s (Cole, 1953, vol. 3: 517-518). The first volume of her two-volume book, *The Accumulation of Capital,* has just recently been translated into English.

Luxemburg and Zetkin worked closely with their Austrian counterpart, Luisa Kautsky, who was also a writer and editor for the movement. In Russia Alexandra Kollontai was beginning the groundwork of political activity among working-class women which was to result, at the time of the Russian Revolution, in the Zhenodtl, an organized effort to redefine and restructure women's roles in society. Kollontai was a novelist as well as an activist, and a "distinguished official," an ambassador, in the later Bolshevik government. Her novels give sociological insight into the dilemmas of the woman revolutionary.[10]

Krupskaya, who married Lenin and shared his Siberian exile, was one of the few revolutionaries to have a happy personal life. She began teaching classes for workers in her teens, and spent her life building the institutional structures that would strengthen a socialist society: children's homes, nurseries, youth organizations such as the Young Pioneers, and related community facilities (Bohrovskaya, 1940).

Another link in the chain of international women socialists[11] is Angelica Balabonov, Italian feminist socialist and Lenin's wartime secretary (Balabonov, 1938). Zetkin, Kollontai, Kautsky, Balabonov, and Luxemburg all worked together, and their closest English collaborator was Eleanor Marx, daughter of Karl Marx. In addition to working with the women's socialist international, Eleanor Marx was an active trade union organizer, writer, and translator of Ibsen. Her *Woman Question: A Socialist Point of View* brought into focus for English socialists the need to pay attention to the economic basis of women's oppression, and the need for change in the sexual relations between women and men.

The story of the Karl Marx daughters is a sad one, and points up the dilemmas faced by many revolutionary women. Eleanor committed suicide with poison provided for her by her husband, Edward Aveling. Her sister Laura committed suicide jointly with her husband, Paul Lafargue. Their mother Jenny, by being a good German *hausfrau*, had not provided an adequate role model for her revolutionary daughters.[12] Both women had married active socialists and were deeply involved with the movement. Marriage was disastrous for both. Many revolutionary women have given poignant accounts of their desire for love and for children. Some have achieved love, some have achieved children, few have achieved both. Intellectual allegiance to the concept of love without lifetime commitment is at war inside these women with personal needs for continuing relationships. The conflict creates dark threads of tragedy in the lives of many of them. Emma Goldman, Russian emigré and American anarchist, put the hopes and dreams of her generation most beautifully in "Love Among the Free," an essay in her *Anarchism and Other Essays* (1910), suggesting that in some future society, where people have not been misshaped by material conditions, people will be able to give and receive love freely.[13]

While England was very much linked to the international socialist women's movement, it also had its own indigenous revolutionary experience. In that country, working-class women worked side by side with men in the workers' rights movement (the Chartist movement) to a greater extent than happened in other countries. Possibly this was a holdover from earlier traditions of husband-wife cooperation in the guilds. The role of working women in these movements is somewhat overshadowed in the social histories of the time by the tremendous initiatives taken on their behalf by the upper classes.

The Nottingham bread riots of 1812 were led by women, but these preceded the development of a sustained working-women's movement. Visible female leadership in the trade union movement began in the 1830s. In an account of the part that women played in the 1843-1844 strikes in Lancashire, Staffordshire, and Yorkshire, Rowbotham notes:

> It is a singular fact that women were in many instances the directors of the strike—women held their meetings, sent their delegates and drew up their terms—and women accompanied the turnouts in immense numbers, in all their marchings and counter marchings throughout the manufacturing districts. . . . At Halifax these women headed the mob,

on some occasions seizing the soldier's bayonets and turning them aside
with the words "We want not bayonets but bread" (1972: 112).

Since men workers for several centuries had been bending their
efforts to keeping women out of certain trades, women organized to
protect their rights in a dwindling occupational arena. Here alliances
with middle-class women were important. Clergyman's daughter
Emily Faithfull is legendary in English women's history for her success in holding open certain occupational fields for women. Among
other activities, Faithfull opened and successfully ran a printing press
in the teeth of male insistence that this work was too heavy for
women.

The women in the Fabian movement and in the Independent
Labour Party in England during the 1890s and 1900s were one
important group in the cross-class alliance process. Beatrice Webb,
the leading woman Fabian, will be discussed later. Charlotte Wilson,
the Fabian anarchist who was Kropotkin's close collaborator after his
final settlement in England as a refugee in 1886; Katherine St. John
Conway who was a leader of the Independent Labour Party in the
1890s; Emmaline Pankhurst, leading Labour Party suffragette; Maud
Pember Reeves who wrote tracts for the Fabian society; and Annie
Besant who headed the London matchgirls' strike in 1888, all
brought a breadth of perspective, social status, and human energy to
the working-women's cause. Among these women, Annie Besant was
one of the most colorful. She edited *The Link,* a journal that was to
bring together the moderate socialists and the radicals, and was a
major writer and activist in the Fabian movement before she turned
to mysticism and theosophy. (Madame Blavatsky was another prominent socialist-turned-theosophist, and Christabel Pankhurst also later
turned to religion.) Besant supported the Indian nationalist movement in the 1870s before anyone else was ready for that cause. Even
after her shift to mysticism, during her long residence in India, she
was an active Indian nationalist and served in the first Indian government.

A special study of the women who have been secular activists and
also have become mystics and religious leaders would be interesting.
Anna van Schurman is an outstanding example from the seventeenth century; Elise Van Calcar, reformer of women's education in
Holland in the mid-1800s, and then editor of a spiritualist monthly
On the Banks of Two Worlds, is another. Olive Schreiner, British
author of *Women and Labour* (1911), is still another. A member of
the Fabian women's circle, Schreiner studied the conditions of

women in South Africa and in various parts of England and provided a cogent comparative analysis of the situation of the employed woman in society.[14] Yet she is probably better known for her mystical writings. Beatrice Webb, dean of the Fabians, was another person for whom the religious impulse was powerful and basic, as comes out in her autobiographical *Our Partnership* on her life with Sidney Webb (1948: vii).

Side by side with the Fabians were the Tolstoyans, another visionary band with active women members. Still a third approach is represented by a group of women who were active in the Voluntary Cooperative Commonwealth which was intended to interpenetrate the capitalist system and "shame it" to decay: Mary Grover, Mary Boole, Eliza Pickard, Miss Dunn, Nellie Shaw, and Miss S. A. Miller, principal of the Diocesan Training College at Oxford, worked at community experiments and contributed to *The New Order,* a journal reporting on communitarian experiments in America and elsewhere.

The worker-middle-class alliance of women did not survive the turn of the century. The proletarian women of East London embarrassed most of their upper-middle-class sisters, and in the minutes of the East London Federation of suffragettes we find that the mainstream group felt that the East Londoners

> had more faith in what could be done by stirring up working women than was felt at headquarters, where they had most faith in what could be done for the vote by people of means and influence. In other words they said that they were working from the top downward and we from the bottom up (Rowbotham, 1972: 131).

A very different sector of women involved in revolutionary movements in the 1880s and 1890s were the peasant women of Italy and Spain. These were caught up in a revolutionary millennialism that was essentially anarchist, but which in Italy became joined with the communist movement. The peasant women of Italy in particular took a leading part in the development of the peasant leagues, called the *fasci,* and adapted the religious beliefs of centuries to the necessities of political reform:

> "We don't go to church any more," said a peasant woman from Piana dei Greci, "but to the fascio. There we must learn, there we must organize for the conquest of our rights" (Hobsbawm, 1963: 99).

Women and men treated visiting socialist leaders "as though they were bishops . . . throwing themselves on the ground and strewing flowers in their path" (Hobsbawm, 1963: 98). They were not confused about religion, however. They had their own understanding of the conflict between the teachings and the practice of the church.

From an interview with a peasant woman of Palermo:

> How do you stand with your priests?
>
> Jesus was a true Socialist and he wanted precisely what the Fasci are asking for, but the priests do not represent him well, especially when they are usurers. When the Fascio was founded our priests were against it and in the confessional they said that the Socialists are excommunicated. But we answered that they were mistaken, and in June we protested against the war they made upon the Fascio, none of us went to the procession of the Corpus Domini. That was the first time such a thing ever happened.
>
> Do you admit people convicted of crimes to the Fascio?
>
> Yes. But there are only three or four out of thousands and we have accepted them to make them better men, because if they have stolen a bit of grain they have only done so out of poverty. . . . Society should thank us for taking them into the Fascio. We are for mercy, as Christ was (Hobsbawm, 1963: 183).

The woman who spoke these words could not read, but she could think. The movement she was part of was completely wiped out by the military force of an alarmed government before it could reconstruct the rural life of Italy. Danilo Dolci has been able to build on these older traditions in his nonviolent work of reconstructing the peasant society of Sicily (Dolci, 1970) in recent years. His work shows that while militarism may crush movements, it does not crush the social memory.

American women had available neither the revolutionary traditions of French working women, nor the history of bread riots nor peasant anarchist traditions of Europe. Not even the lady-of-the-manor pattern of assistance to the poor was known to them. But the same giant-toothed comb of the industrial revolution that was drawn across the lives of European women left its furrows in the lives of American women too. If the industrial revolution had a beginning in the United States, it began in 1798 when Samuel Slater opened the first American textile factory in Pawtucket, with a labor force of nine children, girls and boys all under the age of twelve (Greenway, 1953: 122). By 1820, half of all textile workers were girls and boys ten years of age and younger, and the other half were young girls from nearby farms. By 1870, 14.7 percent of the female population sixteen years of age and over were in the labor force, and by 1900 the percentage was 20.6 (Scott, 1971: 13). One-quarter of these women were in factories. While they were admitted into a wide variety of occupations (women were reported as employed in all but 9 out of 369 manufacturing and mechanical industries [Scott, 1971: 17]), their working hours, low pay, and (often) heavy family responsibilities[15] made life as hard for them as for women anywhere. Living conditions for women heads of household in Boston, New York, and Philadelphia were as bad as in any European city, and the descriptions of slum housing in Boston in 1849 might well have come from Octavia Hill in London (Ware, 1958: 13).

In the 1830s conditions worsened considerably for working women in the United States. After many farmers were wiped out in the panic of 1837, a new phenomenon developed: a group of women who were part of a permanent mill-dependent labor force. During this era the "Lowell Factory Girls" entered labor and folk-song history. "The Lowell Factory Girl," composed about 1830, was still being sung by a wandering woman minstrel at a Texas cattle fair in the early 1900s (Greenway, 1953: 125). The New England mill town was originally considered an "industrial utopia." The Lowell girls were publishing their own magazine, *The Operatives,* and later, *The Offering.* The first generation of operatives from Lowell produced a poet, an editor, a suffragist, a sculptor, and a labor leader (Josephson, 1949). Lowell was a microcosm of the industrialization process as experienced in all parts of the world, since as working hours lengthened and wages declined, the poets were replaced by pale-faced undernourished daughters of poverty. But the leadership generated in Lowell did not die out. In 1845 the activities of women labor leaders broadened to cover the whole region of New England with the Female Labor Reform Association. By the 1850s women were organizing their own branches within unions organized by men, and drawing up their own demands as in the case of the Shoemaker's Union in 1851.

Already by the 1850s, however, the leadership in the labor movement was almost entirely male. The textile industry labor force became 50 percent male, and the leadership almost 100 percent male. Hence the need for women's branches, or auxiliaries, as they were sometimes called, to articulate the needs of women workers usually not noticed by men. (The term "auxiliary" did not at this time mean "wives of members" as it often does today.)

During the 1890s, when European women were active in the women's socialist international, American women were evolving their own style of participation in the social change movements of the time. The nearest thing to an international elite among American women, the circle around Jane Addams, was not at all socialist. It was rather liberal reformist, in a more conservative sense than its counterpart circles in England.

The working class produced its own women leaders in America. Their names are immortalized, not in the labor histories, but in the protest songs and ballads of the labor movement. In the songs, and in the notes of explanation that accompany them when folklorists record these songs, we see fleetingly the faces of the faceless—the hundreds of thousands of women, with or without partners, who were raising children and working twelve-hour (or longer) days without earning enough in the end to support their families: Ella Mae Wheeler, mother of five and a millhand so talented in song and speech that she was singled out to be shot and killed in a demonstration; Ella May Wiggins, mother of nine, four of whom died of whooping cough because her supervisor would not let her shift from night work to day work at the mill so she could nurse the children through the worst of their coughing spells. She was a talented leader, best known for her song, "The Mill Mother's Lament":

> We leave our homes in the morning,
> We kiss our children good bye
> While we slave for the bosses
> Our children scream and cry.

> And when we draw our money
> Our grocery bills to pay,
> Not a cent to spend for clothing,
> Not a cent to lay away.

> And on that very evening,
> Our little son will say:
> "I need some shoes, Mother,
> And so does sister May."

> How it grieves the heart of a mother,
> You everyone must know,
> But we can't buy for our children
> Our wages are too low.

It is for our little children,
That seem to us so dear,
But for us nor them, dear workers,
The bosses do not care.

But understand, all workers,
Our union they do fear;
Let's stand together, workers,
And have a union here.

(People's Songs Library; from Greenway, 1953: 251-252)

Mother Jones was the best known of all, an active organizer among the miners for fifty years, still organizing strikes at eighty-nine. She died at the age of one hundred. Aunt Molly Jackson was another famous organizer among the miners, trained to union leadership by her father from the age of five. So was Sarah Organ, the most powerful of the women singers. "Which Side Are You On?"—one of the best known of American labor songs—was written by Mrs. Sam Reece after her home had been ransacked by men looking for her labor-organizer husband. All these women could sing as well as organize.

This combination in women of charismatic leadership qualities, organizing abilities, and the gift of song is not unique to the American labor movement, though most easily documented there. Protest ballads are as old as urban concentrations, but most folk singers are not recorded in history. (Remember the Sumerian women who sang to the public assemblies.) There were women singers at fairs back in the earliest Middle Ages, and we have mentioned their contribution to ballad lore at that time. As they moved into factories around the world they certainly lifted their voices in song about their conditions. A study of references to women in ballads through history would provide valuable insight into women's lives as workers.

The women described above did not consider themselves radical, and were very angry when in the 1900s they were increasingly described as "commies." There was an unusual group of women in the Industrial Workers of the World (the IWW): Katie Phar, Elizabeth Gurley Flynn, Vera Moller. John Greenway (1953) calls them amazons. They were young at the end of the last century and did most of their work in the twentieth century. These women were of the same fiber as their European sisters in the international socialist movement. They had some contacts with Europe, but fewer than their male colleagues.

Emma Goldman, an anarchist-socialist and therefore more extreme than the IWW, was part of an even smaller and even more embattled group. Her nickname, "Red Emma," still conjures up images of a horned she-devil, though in fact she was a warm-hearted, sensitive woman with incredible energy (Goldman, 1931).

For all their charisma and organizing ability, women never achieved major leadership in the trade union movement. Where they had it initially, as in the textile industry, they soon lost it (see Maupin, 1974: 5-11). The extra burden of child care and home maintenance that women carried and men were free from partly accounts for this, particularly since many of these women had no men in their homes to help. The greats among the women leaders, however, carried out their organizing in spite of five, nine, or more children (the two Ella Mays, for example).

The trade union movement could never have gotten off the ground without substantial support from women, both those in the factories and the homebound wives. Nevertheless, the prevailing working-class culture, as well as the middle-class culture, was such that women had to accept typical underlife roles just where they should have been operating in the public spaces. The privatization of their union roles was the mirror image of the privatization of their factory jobs. Somehow they were not really in the labor force—working on the assembly line was just another way of standing at the kitchen sink.

In general, radical movements fared considerably less well in the United States than in Europe. At the same time, the United States was a hotbed of experimental communities. While Europe had room for radical thought, it was America that had land to spare for radical experiments. Nordhoff's (1965) study of communistic societies in the United States, which documents eight groups of communities with seventy-two settlements in all, focuses primarily on religiously or humanistically oriented communities,[16] and does not include the Fourier and Owenite and other more politically oriented experiments. Holloway's study (1966) includes another fourteen of the socialist type of utopian communities, plus forty Fourierist phalanxes, all founded in the 1840s. There were probably twice as many experiments as those recorded, and hundreds more that died as gleams in someone's eye. If we add the Mormons, who also were in the utopian community business, we add many hundreds of communities.

What is particularly interesting about these experiments of the

1800s is that two completely different types of utopian ventures were going on simultaneously, drawing on different classes of people. One drew on intellectuals, the other on workers. Women did much better in the working-class communities. The humanists, transcendentalists, and socialists for the most part had very short-lived communities and gave no explicit recognition to women in spite of socialist theory about the role of women.[17] The religious communities that recruited farmers and laborers, many of them immigrants, were longer lasting. Some have persisted into the present. Except for the Shakers, founded by Ann Lee and with a continuing tradition of women's leadership, most were and are led by men. The tradition of women's leadership among the Shakers is not unconnected with their practice of celibacy, which leaves them as free for leadership as men are.

Women thrived in the conservative, working-class, religious utopias because these communities dealt very directly with the hardest problems faced by working women. For single women, this was finding an economically secure niche and a respectable social status. For married women, it was protection from a crushing burden of household responsibilities on top of outside employment. The organization of work, housing, and communal facilities in the seventy-two communes listed by Nordhoff was such that women's working hours were considerably shorter than those of their noncommune sisters, their children were better cared for, and meals were provided with far less effort; except for the Perfectionists, all were monogamous. Whitworth (1975) calls the religious utopias "God's Blueprints," thus emphasizing the dynamism inherent in these experiments.

The polygamous Mormon communities also offered "improved working conditions" and drew women by the thousands because of the attractiveness of economic security and shared work loads. Plural marriage did not put them off—they were more interested in the conditions of life than in the number of cospouses. In some religious communities women sat as elders on the community council, but there was no particular emphasis on political participation of women. Rather, there was an emphasis on sharing the general work load as evenly as possible among all.

In the socialist utopias there seems to have been no equivalent of women elders. Many community entrepreneurs among the socialists obviously had competent, hard-working wives who did a lot of the work of community maintenance, but these wives remain nameless. The only woman's name that surfaces in accounts of the Owenite communities was Marie Louise Duclos Fretageot (Armytage, 1961), a pupil of Pestalozzi who conducted schools in Paris and Philadelphia and then developed the educational system at New Harmony. All references to community schooling seem to indicate that girls were taught traditional women's work. The daughters of utopists frequently married utopists, and continued as wives the role they played as daughters, doing the "dirty work" for communities. Evidently they never caught on to the advantages of celibacy—the secret of the Shakers, who replenished their numbers by adoption and conversion.

In spite of crowding in Europe, there were some communal experiments there too. When these were led by men, women played the usual maintenance role. A few "esoteric," nonsocialist ventures were led by women, however, and are particularly interesting because they were directed to the usually ignored problems of working women. Armytage (1961) calls them esoteric because their leaders were charismatics. There was Mary Ann Girling, who at the age of forty-five had a divine call and founded a community of 160 people (the Abode of Love); many unemployed women were included, and 50 percent of the members were children. Clarissa Rodgers was a Paolo Solerian a century ahead of her time. Her whole community lived in a tower in the countryside where the family needs of working women were cared for. Katherine Tingley in the 1890s founded a Universal Brotherhood Organization. All of these women were hounded by men and their organizations destroyed. Because their practical economic and social programs were put in a cultic context rather than a political one, they are rarely described in the history of social experiments of their time.

One of the few experiments in Europe that succeeded in creating a sex-egalitarian community was the Familistère at Guise, France. It began in the 1850s as a patriarchical community based on a hardware industry. By 1880 it had evolved into a workers' cooperative. It was a "social palace" organized with complete political equality for women in governance, and it provided a range of public and family services for its members. There were similar experiments outside France. In the '60s and '70s young women in Russia organized associations and communes, and Chernychevsky's *What Is To Be Done?* had a great influence in this direction.

> In St. Petersburg workshops and communes appeared. . . . [They were] important in providing homes and shelter for women workers and students who had left parents and husbands. It was believed too that it was necessary to create alternative cultural forms of association before the revolution (Rowbotham, 1972: 124).

The communes not only solved economic problems, but provided educational and support settings for women breaking away from families and traditional modes of life, trying to learn new skills and be self-supporting. Few of these Russian women were working class—they were rather middle and upper class. Many of them converged on the University of Zurich to work out their revolutionary ideas in the context of the study of philosophy, history, and economics. Zurich was one of the few European universities in the 1850s that admitted women.

After the 1850s, the bulk of workers, male and female, moved toward (apparently) simpler goals of better pay. The revolutionaries, committed to more sweeping social changes, became increasingly isolated and operated from increasingly precarious niches in the larger society. One of the few who could offer security and a place to meet for the revolutionaries was Christine Trivulzio (1808-1871), the Milanese princess of Bolgiojose. She was an adventurous soul who became a Parisian emigré after leading an army to defeat against Austria. She ran a St. Simonian salon in Paris.

In the '70s, after the failure of the Paris Commune, there was a period of collapsed morale among the revolutionaries and a feeling of isolation. Out of this situation of "alienation from alienation" the women leaders' continuing commitment to working with the masses was finally picked up again as a way out of the isolation they had experienced. A major campaign was mounted "to go among the people and prepare the revolution." That campaign aroused such fear in the authorities, who thought they had crushed the revolutionaries for good, that a counter-campaign of mass arrest and deportation of revolutionaries ensued. It was this counter-campaign, Cole (1953-1960, vol. 2: 318) suggests, that drove many moderates among the revolutionaries, and particularly those committed to nonviolence, to terrorism, the "propaganda of the deed."

The scenario was not unlike the one to unfold fifty years later in the nationalist movement in India, and in both cases we see women playing key roles in terrorist activity. (See chapter 12 for an account of Indian women terrorists.) There was Sophia Pervoskaya (former aristocrat), who headed the 1881 bombing mission that killed Czar Alexander. She was directly involved in three separate attempts before the one that succeeded. She and her coconspirators of the Narodnaya Volya were publicly hanged (Cole, 1953-1960, vol. 2: 319-321). Vera Figner was arrested in the process of reorganizing the Narodnaya Volya after the hanging of most of its leaders, and survived twenty-one years of imprisonment to be released by the revolution of 1905 (Cole, 1953-1960, vol. 2: 320-321). Vera Zasulich, the anarchist who translated the *Communist Manifesto* into Russian and later became a prominent socialist, shot the chief of the czarist police but was acquitted because of his unpopularity (Cole, 1953-1960, vol. 2: 317-318)!

The resort to terrorism on the part of revolutionaries is one way of entering the public spaces of society after the privatization (and delegitimation) of all other revolutionary activity. Many of those who practiced terrorism were opposed to all war. Even Kropotkin supported the strategic necessity of terrorism at this juncture as the only possible course of *public* action, though he did not personally approve of it. It is of particular interest that women, members of the most privatized sector of all, should be able to perform strategic terrorism competently and with cool heads.

The majority, though by no means all, of the women revolutionaries were aristocrats or of the middle class. The intensity of their struggle was not the less for their privileged background. It is a great cost to a woman to throw away a ready-made identity and put herself on the line for revolution and change, when she has no assurance that the men she is working with will accept her as a comrade. It follows that the women we have been describing were all women of extraordinary caliber. (See *Woman as Revolutionary,* Giffin, 1973, for more about women in these roles.)

Every once in a while the male conspiracy of silence about the importance of women in revolution is broken. Trotsky was one of the few who publicly acknowledged the comradeship so many men shut their eyes to. Here, from his *History of the Russian Revolution,* is a rare passage which gives women a key role in the start of the Russian Revolution:

> In spite of all directives the women textile workers in several factories went on strike, and sent delegates to the metal workers with an appeal for support. . . .
>
> It had not occurred to anyone that it might become the first day of the revolution. . . .
>
> The February revolution was begun from below, overcoming the resistance of its own revolutionary organization, the initiative being taken of their own accord by the women textile workers, among them no doubt many soldiers' wives. The overgrown bread-lines had provided the last stimulus. About 90,000 workers, men and women, were on strike that day. The righting mood expressed itself in demonstrations,

meetings, and encounters with the police. A mass of women, not all of them workers, flocked to the municipal Duma demanding bread. It was like demanding milk from a he-goat. Red banners appeared in different parts of the city, and inscriptions on them showed that the workers wanted bread, but neither autocracy or war. Women's Day passed successfully with enthusiasm and without victims. But what it concealed in itself, no one had even guessed by nightfall (quoted in Rowbotham, 1972: 134).

From bread riots in France in 1620 to bread demonstrations in front of the Russian duma in 1917 is a long way. Women had learned a lot in the meantime.

The Activists and the Middle Class

Middle-class reformers made less dramatic choices than their revolutionary sisters, but did not necessarily lead less dramatic lives. Women's activism of the nineteenth century—middle class or proletarian, radical or reformist—was a new phenomenon on the world scene, and deserves more attention than it has received. In this section we will look at the reformers.

We saw in the eighteenth century the birth of the movement to deal with poverty by working with the poor in terms of their own needs. The nineteenth century witnessed an enormous extension of urban welfare activities on the part of women. Like the radicals, the middle-class women were being more sophisticated about industrialism. We find the science called "political economy"—the forerunner of the later separate sciences of economics, sociology, and political science—being developed and used by women to analyze problems of the industrial society. We also find these same tools being turned to an analysis of the situation of the woman herself.

Ideas about the perfectability of the individual and of society were implemented by increasing attention to education at all levels. If Rousseau's educational theories were something of a setback to women in denying them nondomestic roles in society, Froebel provided a powerful counterforce which released women all over Europe into the schoolroom. Froebel's developmental approach to children and the educational model he developed for the kindergarten began in a traditional all-male context; it was young men he was training to work with children. More memorable perhaps than all the revolutions and declarations of 1848 is the decision Froebel made that year to train women rather than men to work with children. While today we may deplore the fact that women are shunted aside into the role of primary school teacher, this role nearly became one more male specialty. Strategically, training large numbers of young men in child development might have brought about more rapid change in male roles than the women's emancipation movement has achieved, so to a degree it is hard to know whether to celebrate or deplore Froebel's choice. Nevertheless, in the world of the future, primary school teaching will not be a sex-linked role, and in 1848 Froebel's decision to train women instead of men opened up the opportunity for post-elementary education for women in the new teacher-training centers that sprang up everywhere. It also opened up the almost limitless job market in elementary education.

From the point of view of women philanthropists, here was a chance to improve the situation of the poor, and of women of all classes. In addition to opening private model schools, women pushed the governments of Europe in the direction of universal elementary education. They pushed simultaneously for government-sponsored industrial schools to give skill training to workers' children. Since hardly any governments sponsored girls' industrial schools, women founded private associations to support both industrial and normal schools for girls. (See Stanton, 1970, for a country-by-country account of this.) It is not too much to say women's voluntary associations undertook the bulk of the responsibility for agricultural production. In Italy and Sweden the women's associations took note of this and established agricultural training centers for women, thus reversing a centuries-long trend of keeping women as ignorant farmhands rather than as knowledgeable agriculturalists (Stanton, 1970).

The demand for higher education for middle- and upper-class women was an inevitable accompaniment of the educational efforts on behalf of working women. Higher education for women turned out to be a much more controversial issue than elementary or industrial education. Men said publicly and plainly that women were already getting out of hand and would be impossible to manage if they had more education. The famous Edinburgh medical school riots in 1869 after a small group of women had been admitted as students are a clue to the intensity of male fears of competition from professionally trained women. The University of Zurich, which had no sex barriers, became the mecca for women seeking higher education in mid-century. In 1866 the University of Paris, which only permitted women at lectures, abolished differential status between women and men students. Italian universities had no sex barriers. Whatever the country, however, only women of the elite could afford to be students. They also had to be strong enough to withstand general public ridicule. It wasn't until the 1880s that England and other European countries provided regular admission to women at universities. In the meantime women formed associations to establish their own colleges. In the United States this began as early as the 1820s, and in England, in the 1840s. (American male medical students were apparently less insecure than their British counterparts, because they accepted Elizabeth Blackwell as a fellow student as early as 1847. Geneva, New York, opened the first women's medical college in 1865, three years before the Edinburgh riots.)

The very widespread resistance on the part of men to providing anything beyond elementary education for women sharpened the awareness of women about their status in society. On the one hand they were shocked that they were not supposed to thirst for knowledge. On the other hand, they became increasingly aware of the growing band of women on the labor market who, lacking skills, were unable to get employment. The genteel starving spinster looking for a post as governess became a well-marked feature of the social landscape. With domestic craft production removed from the urban middle-class household, families could no longer afford to feed spinster aunts, sisters, and daughters. The spinsters went job hunting, but class feeling kept them out of domestic service and the factory. What were they to do?

New social sensitivities considerably broadened the action agenda of women philanthropists. They turned to the establishment of more intermediate and normal schools for women, and also formed women's employment associations. One set of employment associations specialized in helping women to emigrate overseas.

These activities had a consciousness-raising effect on women of the philanthropic classes. For some this consciousness-raising was channeled toward an identification with problems of poverty, and the energies released went into the formation of associations like the Women's Christian Temperance Union and the Salvation Army. For other women, it led to an identification with the larger world community and the problems of slavery, oppression, and war in far-off colonial territories. The energies released in that direction went into the formation of international antislavery and peace associations. For still others, it led to a specific awareness of the anachronism that the women providing solutions to problems that governments of men were unable to handle were classified legally with children and idiots. This glaring inconsistency built up support for the suffrage movement, which was from the beginning both national and international in scope. Since the newly emerging group of women social scientists were in close alliance with the activists, we will begin by describing the social scientists.

The Social Scientists

The social sciences were still in a formative stage in the 1800s. Political science had developed along certain lines with Hobbes and Locke in the preceding century. The mercantilists of the 1600s and the physiocrats of the 1700s had developed a well-defined, though narrow, approach to a subject which in France was being pursued by people called *économistes*. In England the tradition of political economy as developed by Adam Smith was much broader in scope than the work of the *économistes,* and encompassed significant aspects of political science. It also encompassed what was later to become the discipline of sociology. Adam Smith can equally be called the father of sociology and of modern economics. In the *Wealth of Nations* (1776) and the *Theory of Moral Sentiments* (1759) he mapped the economic and political infrastructure of the modern world and analyzed the dynamics of social interaction.

Women of the 1800s to a significant extent participated in the shaping of the new social science disciplines. Since there were no institutionalized public roles for individuals professing these sciences, there was nothing to bar women from them. The situation in England was particularly fluid. The need for information about the working of social structures was great, so knowledge and competence (even if self-taught, as in the case of women) could gain a hearing. The Social Science Association, founded in London in 1857, played a particularly important role in bringing the expertise of women to the information seekers in the government (Kamm, 1966: 34, 45, 53-54ff., 102ff., 130). Every important issue before parliament was discussed there, on the basis of carefully researched papers prepared by women and men. For women that platform was the more important because they had no other. The association also provided the basis for a working partnership between women social scientists and women activists. The activists also collected data, but in the main relied on their scientist sisters for more basic analyses.

The action research concept was taken for granted by nineteenth century reformers. Thus we find that Mary Carpenter, who worked with children in prisons, gave a paper at the Social Science Association which shaped parliamentary legislation establishing reformatories for juvenile delinquents. Louisa Twining, active in dealing with the plight of workhouse inmates, presented a paper at the association that formed the basis for substantial workhouse reforms. Anne

Jameson's paper on the employment of women, Emily Davies' session on university examinations for women, and Barbara Bodichon's paper on women's suffrage all had direct consequences in parliament or among relevant authorities. (Of course Bodichon did not see quick results—suffrage was long in coming.)

The other women we will be discussing in this section were primarily scientists, but they were usually in close touch with activists. Several of them became major public figures, both nationally and internationally. Because they could offer new kinds of mappings of social systems, their special knowledge was needed for public policy. Here at last was a time of surfacing of the particular kinds of infrastructures that women had worked on for centuries in the special spaces allotted to them. This was not a "family life specialty" that was being offered, but an expertise about the institutional matrix within which family life takes place.

Harriet Martineau (1802-1876), the first major woman social scientist of the century, had a great gift for translating abstract concepts into vivid scenes and stories which stay in the mind of the reader. Not primarily a theorist, she was rather a translator who made the problems of industrial England understandable alike to members of parliament and to factory hands. Martineau had been a timid, unhappy child full of religious fears in her early years; with frail health and early deafness, she might have been just another member of the army of employment-seeking spinster governesses. Her health and timidity precluded teaching, and she tried writing with trepidation. Only the instantaneous success of each of her efforts gave her the courage to recognize her own talents and use them.

What tuned her in to the social problems of her day? It is hard to tell from her autobiography (1877a, 1877b), but at some point her omniverous reading and the finding of a religious home in radical Unitarianism gave her a sense of mission. She had been writing little stories on issues she read about in the newspapers, such as the machine-breaking riots. Her piece on "The Rioters" was such a success that "some hosiers and lace-makers of Derby and Nottingham sent me a request to write a tale on the subject of Wages, which I did, calling it 'The Turn Out.'" This was such a success that from then on she received a steady influx of requests to deal with workers' issues—from the workers themselves. While some of the pieces sounded abstract, like "Principles and Practice," in each case there was a story setting and an underlying analysis of a social problem. After she had been writing these "stories" for several years, a

neighbor lent her Mrs. Marcet's *Conversations on Political Economy.*
She discovered to her amazement that she had been teaching the subject of political economy unaware in her stories about machinery
and wages. It was then that she conceived the plan for what she considered her major work—a series of stories that would provide a complete exposition of political economy in a form that would speak to
the major issues of contemporary British industrial society and deal
squarely with controversial policy problems, including population
control. She undertook the ambitious *Illustration of Political
Economy* (1832, 1833, 1834), convinced that it would ruin her
reputation and destroy all future possibilities for her as a writer, but
knowing that workers wanted it and legislators needed it. The quality of sociological imagination that comes through in Martineau's
stories is suggested by the fact that workers in any category that
became the subject of a story, such as cotton-millhands, inmates of
workhouses, domestic servants, were all convinced that she was one
of them and wrote out of personal experience. Since her works were
also quoted in parliament, no greater audience-reaching capacity has
ever been achieved by a social scientist.

Her powers of observation and comparative analysis of social
structures come out in another, better known work, *Society in
America* (1968), which, like de Tocqueville's *Democracy in America*
(1835-1840), is a major work on American society by a European,
as relevant today as when it was written. Her outspoken support
of abolitionism while in America led to lynch threats that left her
in daily fear for her life for the remainder of her stay in America—
but neither shortened that stay nor softened her outspokenness.

Martineau inevitably became concerned about the situation of
women as a result of her studies. She made cogent observations on
the similarity of the position of the slave and the woman. To call her
a feminist, however, would be to exaggerate a limited aspect of her
work. Her powers of observation and analysis were put at the service
of all disadvantaged groups. She had a capacity for social listening,
and for a creative mirroring-back to people of many conditions, that
made her a unique contributor to the social change movements of
the nineteenth century. All women activists consulted her (except
the ones she refused to see because she thought they were phony—
she was merciless with phonies), and so did leading men of affairs.[18]

Martineau wrote a gently appreciative sketch of the woman
who "taught" her political economy, Mrs. Marcet (Martineau,
1877a: 386-392). Mrs. Marcet was a self-effacing housewife with a
high-powered mental engine that could only be quieted by being

used. Apologetically, she set to writing textbooks on political economy which were adopted in schools all over England. She humbly served social causes whenever social evils were brought to her attention, and would do the "homework" on the problems activists dealt with. There were probably a great many housewifely Mrs. Marcets doing the intellectual homework for the activists in her century.

An unusual wife-husband team who were publishing in political economy toward the end of Harriet Martineau's life were Mary Paley and Alfred Marshall. Alfred Marshall is the great figure in the neo-classical school, but much of his work was written jointly with his wife, and the *Economics of Industry* (1874) bears both their names. Mary Paley Marshall was widely known in the 1880s as the international clearinghouse for the neoclassical school, and after her husband's death she edited all his works.

Other intellectual women who were doing productive scholarly work independently or with male collaborators sometimes did not attach their names to their work for family reasons. In the literary world, we know that women often used male pseudonyms to "protect" their families. An unusual case of unlabeled intellectual partnership involves Harriet Martineau's contemporary, Harriet Taylor (1807-1858). (The two Harriets knew one another, and belonged to the same social circle of Unitarian radicals.) Harriet Taylor was a self-taught political economist who worked as John Stuart Mill's collaborator on his *Principles of Political Economy.* Rossi (1973: 34-41) reports that Harriet's husband, John Taylor, refused permission for her name to appear with Mill's as coauthor of the book. The Rossi study gives the details of the unusual collaboration between Harriet Taylor and John Stuart Mill, which led to their marriage after the death of Taylor's husband. Their long and intimate relationship during the lifetime of her first husband suggests that there were more "open marriages" in the Victorian era than is generally supposed. Taylor and Mill also collaborated on essays on marriage and divorce, and Taylor is the author of "The Enfranchisement of Women." Mill's "The Subjection of Women," written after Taylor's death, was one of the major suffrage documents of the second half of the nineteenth century, and has been translated into many languages.

Close to the intellectuals who coded and analyzed social conditions for the printed page were young women like Octavia Hill, who in the 1870s belonged to the employment-seeking army of middle-class women. While teaching in a school for girls at the edge of a

London slum, she got acquainted with her poor neighbors and discovered living conditions she had never dreamt of. She became a leader in the development of what was then a brand-new concept—the settlement house—and was a founder of the Charity Organization Society in 1869. The women and men who began making their homes in the London slums, some of them university students like Arnold Toynbee, were fired by the idea that the moral philosophy taught at the university should be translated into practice in the new industrial city. They were creating what was later to become the profession of social work.[19] The first "social workers" in Octavia Hill's tenement house organization were specially trained rent collectors. It was their job to help poor women with whatever problems surfaced on rent collection visits, including finding the jobs from which to produce rent money. Hill's equivalent in the United States, working in the very same decades, was Jane Addams.

Beatrice Potter Webb, the first social investigator to develop modern survey research methods, based her life work on what she learned from Octavia Hill and her associates in the London slums. She was not one of those drawn into the labor force by economic need. In her well-to-do home Herbert Spencer, the "father of sociology," had been a frequent visitor when Beatrice was a child; she grew up familiar with the language of "the law of increasing heterogeneity." She had Martineau's intellect and moral determination, and a passion for firsthand investigation of social facts. After completing a history of the cooperative movement she married Sidney Webb. Their union became one of the most productive and affectionate social science partnerships in modern times. Together they documented trade unionism, industrial democracy, and English local government in seven massive volumes.

Sidney and Beatrice had very different abilities, temperaments, and even social philosophies (within the broad framework of socialism), and exerted separate as well as joint leadership roles in the Fabian socialist movement. It was Beatrice who developed for the Fabians the theme of a "national minimum standard of civilized life." Cole (1953-1960, vol. 3: 210) suggests that she was more a sociologist than she was a socialist. She was very critical of economics as it was developing by the late 1800s—a narrow abstract science that ignored noneconomic factors in human behavior. She promoted a general social science that could deal with a broad range of social and economic issues, such as her predecessor Harriet Martineau had practiced. She was also a decentralist concerned wth local and nongovernmental action—seeing the state as one huge consumers' cooperative. One of her major contributions to English society was her work on poor-law reform, which in time led to the abolition of the pauper concept and to the provision of a broad range of social services to the poor. Her book *My Apprenticeship* (1926) is a vivid documentary of the making of a social scientist, and *Our Partnership* (1948) is an autobiographical account of how researchers can affect policy making.

Beatrice Webb occupied the center of the public policy arena in Britain for thirty years, from the 1880s to the 1920s, but she never served the government except in an advisory capacity on government committees. She rejected positions of official power when they were offered her, and also refused the social hostess role that went with her husband's government position. With the privileges of the aristocratic tradition to back her, she remained a completely autonomous person all her life.

The young women trained under people like Octavia Hill and Beatrice Potter Webb should logically have moved into government civil service in the 1890s. Except for poor-law supervision, however, trained women were in general not dealing with women's labor and other issues in government offices until some time after the turn of the century. Instead these women either stayed in the private sector as volunteers or became paid staff of voluntary associations.

Many of Webb's apprentices were fired with an intellectual curiosity which led them to further training, and to a life of scholarship at the London School of Economics and Political Science, which Beatrice herself founded. The university atmosphere in London was very encouraging to women, and with Harriet Martineau and Beatrice Potter Webb as role models, many women took up the study of economics.

Women made particularly distinguished contributions as economic historians, and a significant part of our insight into the complex nature of the economic transition from the Middle Ages to the twentieth century comes from women. Alice Clark and Ivy Pinchbeck focused on the particular role of the woman worker before and during the industrial revolution. Ada Lonfield, Margaret James, Eileen Power, Carus Wilson, and Doris Leech all became specialists on various aspects of economic history. Eileen Power was one of the most prolific, and one of the most versatile of these historians. The American Sylvia Thrupp, who as a young woman studied in this stimulating environment of British historians, carries on that same tradition today as one of America's outstanding social historians.[20]

In France, roughly contemporaneous with Harriet Martineau,

Clemence Augustine Royer published a book on political economy
that led to her sharing a prize with Proudhon. She was a generalist,
publishing studies of Comte's positivism and an attack on the
Laplace theory of the origin of the universe, translating the *Origin of
the Species* into French, and writing her own book, *L'Origine de
l'Homme et des Sociétés*. Her work created many storms, and she
was so controversial that though her election to the French Academy
was often discussed it was never carried out. Renan's praise of her is
probably typical of the attitudes of her day: "She is *almost* a man of
genius" (italics mine). There were a number of women Saint-
Simonians in France at this time, but the references to them are so
brief (and so hostile) that it is hard to tell whether they were trained
économistes or simply enthusiastic advocates of free love.

There must have been many other women doing original social
science work in Europe in the second half of the nineteenth century,
but their work has gone largely unrecorded. A few stand out by the
sheer force of their achievements. One such woman is Concepçion
Arenal, born in 1820 in Spain; she was a self-taught specialist in
"penitentiary science," international law, and public education.
She entered the public arena with an essay on philanthropy that won
the Madrid Academy of Moral and Political Sciences first prize; her
manual on visiting the poor has been translated into five languages;
her essay on law is the only work by a woman ever printed in the
Biblioteca Juridica; and she wrote a two-volume work on *The Social
Question* and two books on women.

Rosalie Olivecrona, a graduate of the first girls' school in Sweden,
also made herself into a generalist social scientist of broad scope. She
helped found a magazine to discuss social questions for women
(1870), did a number of surveys of women's work in Sweden, and
contributed papers at international social science congresses, including studies of the work of women reformers.

In the United States social science also attracted women during
the latter part of the nineteenth century. Only a few are visible in
social history, among them Charlotte Perkins Gilman (1860-1935).
An evolutionist whose main work lay in expounding sociological
theories of social progress (as in *The Man-Made World,* 1911), her
best seller was *Women and Economics,* which, as Rossi (1973: 567)
points out, had much the same impact in her day that psychologist
Betty Friedan's book, *The Feminine Mystique* (1963), had in the
1960s. Gilman addressed herself directly to the situation of the
working woman and the need for institutional change to deal with
the problems of home maintenance and child rearing. As an evolu-

tionist, she saw the reabsorption of women into the economic life of society on the basis of more wholistic roles for both women and men and more equitable support services for both. She also pointed to the effects of socialization processes in maintaining obsolete role structures, and wrote a book *Concerning Children* (1900) that dealt with rearing both girls and boys for autonomy, independence, and greater social responsibility. The story of her life may be found in her autobiography, *The Living of Charlotte Perkins Gilman* (1935).

As in England, American women were beginning to study economics in increasing numbers toward the end of the nineteenth century. Most of their publications are not well known, but Helen Laura Sumner's major work, the *History of Women in Industry in the United States* (1974), has recently been reprinted.

Ida Turnbell, the social historian, had quite an impact on public opinion through her antitrust writings, including the *History of Standard Oil,* and recruited many Americans to socialism through her work. Mary Marcy, editor of the *International Socialist Review,* wrote a best seller that had the same effect—*Letters of a Pork Packer's Stenographer,* based on her own experience in working in a slaughterhouse.

There was a whole group of American intellectual women, half scholars, half activists and reformers, who worked together in the latter part of the nineteenth and through the early twentieth century. Jane Addams (1860-1935) is the best known internationally of these women. She played a special role in the group because of her commitment to linking urban neighborhood reform with the broader question of women in society, and the still broader question of international peace. She belonged to that growing community of international women who helped conceptualize global society at the turn of the century; they saw women's roles in terms of community and world housekeeping. The economists Emily Green Balch of Wellesley and Julia Grace Wales of Wisconsin University, whose work in the early twentieth century on international peace and mediation plans has come down through records of the peace movement, and Sonia Baber, the geography professor whose research on public peace monuments around the world was an early contribution to peace research (Baber, 1948), were her colleagues in the peace movement. *Peace and Bread* is Addams' major theoretical contribution to the linking of the local and the global. Lillian Wald, a founder of the Children's Bureau; Florence Kelley, organizer of the National Consumers' League; Alice Hamilton, founder of the field of industrial medicine; Edith and Grace Abbott, founders of the profession of social work; and Mrs. Warbasse, a founder of the New School for Social Research and organizer of the American Women's Peace Party, all worked with Jane Addams in the development of social services in the United States.

Mary Ellen Richmond, working somewhat outside the Jane Addams circle, was another major figure in the development of social work in the United States. Richmond has disappeared from sociology textbooks because of her social work orientation. A study of her research work as director of the Charity Organization Department of the Russell Sage Foundation shows that she was one of the first American researchers to develop the theory and methodology of indicators to measure states of social welfare (see her *Social Diagnosis*, 1917). She is said to have invented the casework method of teaching (her *What is Social Case Work?*, 1922, was translated into Dutch and French and has had seven reprintings). Her discussion of social policy issues in relation to welfare administration at the time when social work was first becoming a profession could be reprinted as a contribution to current discussions (*Friendly Visiting Among the Poor*, 1903). It can now be seen that she was anticipating many of the problems which have since developed in the profession.[21] Most important of all, she understood the new phenomenon of social activism that was appearing on the turn-of-the-century scene, and perceived that the future of social work lay in the capacity of social workers to operate at the point of intersection with other services and social activities in a community (see "The Interrelationship of Social Movements," in *The Long View*, 1930: 285). *The Long View, Papers and Addresses*, published posthumously, makes excellent reading today.

It is hard to arrive at a balanced discussion of the contributions of women to social history at the turn of the century. There was the Jane Addams circle. There were the radicals. There were the suffragettes. There were also women social scientists who were not part of any circle, and who have dropped out of the social record. The radical thinkers are now being rediscovered and reprinted by various feminist presses.[22] Others are not so lucky. One not-yet-rediscovered thinker is the political scientist Mary Follett, whose *New State* (1920) will sound more relevant to readers in the 1970s than it did to her own contemporaries. Follett saw the significance of what she called the "group organization movement"[23] when it was receiving little attention. Her book spelled out the significance of the increase in voluntary associations and provided a new view of social progress as interpenetration. She developed concepts of the beyond-contract society which are in my view some of the very concepts needed to solve the power and dominance dilemmas discussed in chapter 2 of this book. She was also an early peace researcher. While some of her thinking is obviously limited and outdated, a reprinting of her best work is overdue.

There were other women social scientists who must go unmentioned here for lack of space. A book-length study of women social scientists of the nineteenth and early twentieth centuries is badly needed. It is striking to compare the intellectual climate for women scholars and activists today with the period we have just been discussing, particularly with regard to the interfaces between domestic and international issues. There are few women scholars today working at those interfaces, and most of the activists who concern themselves with them are women who work in organizations founded before 1920. These organizations remain small.

The Philanthropists: England and Europe

In discussing social scientists, I emphasized the collaboration between scholars and activists. The scholars were the theorists, the activists the practitioners, both drawing on a common stock of knowledge of the workings of the social structure. Both groups were concerned with social change. The philanthropists were more often of the upper class, though not uniformly so.

The development of the transport and communication facilities in the nineteenth century that made international collaboration possible had, as already noted, a special effect on women. They acquired new public spheres of action simultaneously in the national and international communities, and each reinforced the other. Thus, we can hardly speak of national philanthropic activity without mentioning the series of international congresses that took place between 1851 and 1893. These were four forums at which elite women for the first time came together from Europe, the Americas, and the Orient (not yet Africa) to scan and compare social landscapes, thereby much enlarging their comprehension of the problems they were dealing with. Only in the twentieth century do "ordinary" middle-class women participate in this kind of international event, and working-class and rural women are still by and large excluded.[24]

The first international exhibition was held in London in 1851, the second and third in Paris, in 1855 and 1867 respectively, and the fourth in Chicago in 1893. The Chicago Exhibition was the first that formally organized a section devoted to the work of women, but the three previous congresses had prepared the groundwork for that.

Princess Christian of Schleswig-Holstein commissioned a report on the philanthropic work of women in England (Burdett-Coutts, 1893) for the Chicago occasion. Mary Kavanaugh Oldham Eagle collected reports from American women for the same occasion (Eagle, 1974). I regret that I do not have similar reports available from other countries. As an overview of activities of interest to the international community of women in 1893, the Burdett-Coutts document in particular gives us some valuable clues to the accomplishments of women philanthropists in the preceding half-century. The woman who compiled the report, Baroness Burdett-Coutts, was the richest woman in England, stayed single all her life, and devoted herself full time to the development and administration of a series of welfare ventures. In 1893, she was certainly the world's leading female philanthropist.

The introduction to the Burdett-Coutts volume on England points out what must have been true for all countries, that much of the philanthropic work carried out in the nineteenth century was not new in substance, but only in form. The antecedents of all these currently urban-centered activities had been carried out in rural areas by the lady of the manor house before industrialization. We observed in a previous chapter that the manor house was a training school for young girls and boys of the village in agriculture, crafts, and domestic skills. The manor house kitchen provided food in times of distress; the manor house chapel, religious services; and the manor house library, reading matter for literate villagers. The manor house tradition was still very much alive in the nineteenth century. In towns and villages there were women carrying on such services as a matter of course, usually under the patronage of the "first lady" of the community. These groups of women were often not dignified by "association" labels, yet did the work formal associations carried out in more urban areas.[25] With urbanism, the shift from individual to collective helping efforts became essential, and the manor house lady modernized and collectivized.

All the English activities discussed here come from the 1893 Burdett-Coutts report, with activities from the rest of Europe added from Stanton (1970). The Stanton essays, though collected at the same time as the Burdett-Coutts report, do not seem to have been collected in connection with the Chicago Exhibition.

Work for Children

In Europe, Catholic religious orders had long provided orphanages and crèches for babies and small children. The Froebel kindergarten movement spread to the Protestant areas of Europe from 1848 on, but was also found in Catholic areas. Froebel Associations for women were widely established. In the larger cities, such as London, these associations not only provided orphanages and crèches, but also developed "houses of industry" which were industrial schools for younger children. They also started special houses for crippled children and children of prisoners. Early (1840) forms of schools for poor children were called "ragged schools"; but this label was soon dropped. In England in the second half of the century a boarding-out program for workhouse children was developed in an attempt to remove children from a crime-breeding atmosphere. Societies for the "prevention of cruelty to animals" were started in several countries beginning in 1824 in England, but societies for the "prevention of cruelty to children" were much later in starting, an interesting commentary on the sensibilities of the 1800s. Women were among the first workers, though not the titular founders, in both.

Work for Women

In England in the 1850s the Friends of Workhouse Girls was formed to follow the careers of workhouse graduates as servants and help them in their adjustment problems. A Society for the Promotion of the Employment of Women was also founded in 1859. In 1856 urban family-style residency centers for working girls began in England, which developed later into the international YWCA with residences for working girls in eighty-one countries. Many independent residence and training centers for working girls developed throughout Europe in the 1880s. The French and the English were the most active in this, since they had the largest cities. In Germany the Lette-Verein and the Alice-Verein (*Verein* means association) were formed about 1866 to further the employment of women. Also nurses' training centers were established. Holland approached the employment issue through associations based on the kindergarten movement, providing training for women to be teachers. In Denmark women concentrated on government legislation to promote the employment of women, and in 1857 achieved significant enabling legislation. Women in Sweden founded a number of institutions to provide services for working girls, and also formed associations to promote rural and village handicrafts. In Italy and Spain women's associations established industrial training centers for girls.

Dutch women at this time were very limited in the activities allowed them, and could only form associations around direct charitable purposes such as aid to "fallen women." (They could not aid "falling" ones, the *rapporteur* for Holland says!) In Russia and Poland in 1880 women's associations as such were not permitted. Women could only work in association with men. During this same period, organized nursing services for the urban poor began to develop in England and elsewhere in Europe. Florence Nightingale was a leader in this movement.

Emigration societies were formed in England about 1850, aimed at regulating emigration so that migrating women would be prepared for employment at the other end. The societies also provided aid and reception services at the destination points. (I have not been able to find out if other countries had emigration societies for women.) This service became important in helping relieve the unemployment of middle-class English women, since many thousands of women were to emigrate to jobs outside of England between 1850 and 1900.

Migrant families, specializing in tunnel, deck, and canal building, known as "navvies" and consisting chiefly of Italians, Norwegians, and English families (about one hundred thousand in 1880), began receiving special services in 1870. It was to be almost a hundred years more before Gypsies were to receive similar attention, in the 1960s.

In this same century Anglican and Protestant sisterhoods for service to the urban poor were formed. The distrust of celibate sisterhoods which were a legacy of Reformation anti-Catholicism had finally been overcome.

Most of the services and institutions described above were organized by local women's associations in each country. There were also some women who traveled around and spread the word, which meant that the model effect operated rapidly when a particularly valuable program, such as the Froebel kindergartens, or services for working girls, was started. An area in which I do not have comparative information from country to country is that of the role of women in improving and innovating in poor-law administration. Judging from publications by the women social reformers mentioned earlier, it is likely that there were women active in this regard in every country in Europe. We know that in England in 1834 women began organizing local volunteer commissions to visit workhouses. The suggestions for improvement they made to local authorities were so useful that by 1853 a regular system of workhouse inspection had been developed based on their recommendations. By 1850 women were publishing a journal on workhouse visiting. This remained an unofficial though recognized activity until 1870, when legislation finally permitted the election of women to the boards of guardians of the poor. It took nearly forty years, in other words, for women's activities on behalf of the poor in workhouses to move from the privatized volunteer space to the public spaces of the local community. In 1875 the acme of public legitimacy was reached when the first woman government inspector of workhouses was appointed.

The Philanthropists: The United States

In the United States, the development of women's activities was not so urban-centered. Until 1900, the United States was still a country of small towns. These small towns were very different from the European villages with their centuries of tradition. Rather, each town had its pioneer memories. Women could recollect the way of life of mothers and grandmothers who had helped clear land and build homes. They remembered the agriculture and domestic crafts that were no longer necessary to the average small-town household by the mid-1800s. There were no manor house models to look to, just a do-it-yourself tradition.

On the East Coast there were the cosmopolitan cities of Boston, Philadelphia, and New York, from which women traveled abroad and engaged in "exotic" intellectual and radical movements. Margaret Fuller (1810-1850), the New England transcendentalist, part of the Brook Farm group and editor of *The Dial,* who finally went abroad to discover new horizons and identify herself with the Italian independence movement, was not comprehensible to the small-town American activist. Neither was Frances Wright (1795-1852), Scotswoman and Owenite identified with the major European movements of her day including women's rights. Wright first traveled to the United States with Lafayette, and later returned to found an Owenite colony, Nashoba, in the swamps of Tennessee. This was to be a utopian community with complete racial and sexual equality. Disease-ridden, it lasted for four sad years, 1825-1829. Wright spent considerable time in the United States trying to organize urban reform on the British model, with a focus on working-class problems. However, because her free thinking shocked the small-town American women, her energy and reform instincts never connected with the perspectives of American "organization" women.

In Europe, the lady of the manor house bridged the rural-urban gap for women. In the United States there were no gap bridgers. Out of the need that gap represented, however, was born a social invention of profound significance for America and for the world community of women: the women's club movement. Neither philanthropic nor suffragette, it rather asserted the right to a social and intellectual identity for women apart from service roles. It was born in New York and first spread to Boston, Philadelphia, and Chicago. It soon took root in small towns across the United States and provided a sphere of autonomy for women and a protected place to develop civic understandings.

Sorosis, the first women's club, was born in New York in 1868. It was created out of the indignation of a group of women journalists who had been denied the right to purchase tickets for a Press Club dinner to hear Charles Dickens speak. "The (male) club" was a very special kind of private public space in American society, and women were completely excluded from the intellectual life that went on in such organizations. After the Dickens affair, the New York women journalists formed their own club, to the jeers of their male colleagues (who said it couldn't last a year). When later condescendingly invited by the Press Club to a tea at which they were only allowed to listen, not speak, they retaliated by inviting the Press Club to a tea at which the men were not allowed to speak. The men got the message, and a historic dinner was jointly sponsored by the two groups, with women and men participating equally in planning and speaking.

There were many efforts to steer women to service activities, but they resisted successfully. They wanted to *think,* observe the social scene, develop perspectives on society. That this was a strongly felt need is best evidenced by the fact that in 1898, when the first history of the women's club movement was written (Croly, 1898), there were already 934 affiliated clubs in forty-two states and the District of Columbia, and affiliates in India, England, Australia, East Africa, Chile, and Mexico. From Sorosis to the nearly thousand-branched Federated Women's Clubs was quite a leap, and it all happened in about twenty-five years.

The clubs took on a great variety of names locally. In Hypatia and Shakespeare clubs, historical and scientific societies, civic clubs, social science associations, village improvement clubs, business and professional women's groups, the members were all ardent generalists, discovering their individual and societal identities in the late nineteenth century. The movement was one of the most impressive self-education ventures in history, and out of it subsequently came many specialized women's professional associations and special-purpose organizations. The suffragette movement was greatly strengthened by it, and the League of Women Voters was one of its many offspring. The federation itself continues today as a generalist organization, and has played an important part in the development of international associations for women. By the 1950s women's clubs were an object of fun in the United States, affectionately but not very flatteringly immortalized in the Helen Hokinson cartoons in the *New Yorker.* That they were a vehicle invented by pioneer society to further the creation of civic culture in the absence of lady of the manor traditions has not been adequately recognized.

The American women who paralleled the work of European women in the settlement house movement, and in protective legislation for women and children in factories, who created reformatories and juvenile courts, and who humanized police stations by introducing police matrons, for the most part sharpened their skills in the women's clubs. A major consequence of the proliferation of clubs for women in the United States was the development of organizing skills. To this day, the American woman's ability to "organize a meetin'" at the drop of a hat awes her European sisters.

Small-town activism at its most creative can be seen in states like Michigan, which played a key role in the operation of the Underground Railway, the pre-Civil War social invention that expedited the movement of escaped slaves from the South to Canada. Laura Haviland, an intrepid Quaker of Michigan, was in her day known as the Superintendent of the Underground Railway.

Haviland is the prototype of the competent American small-town activist, though it should be pointed out that coming from a Quaker tradition she possibly had more encouragement to speak up in public than some of her neighbors. She also had an unusually sharp mind and a quality of Christian faith that carried her serenely through physical dangers most men and women would shrink from. She was not afraid of physical confrontation with furious slave owners, yet she was smart enough to escape from the kidnap traps they set for her. She not only traveled freely through the South where she was Public Enemy Number 1, where there were "WANTED" signs up for her everywhere, she also moved freely through the military bureaucracy once the war was on, in order to clean up scandalous prisons and hospitals and to get malevolent or simply incompetent administrators removed.

Laura Haviland was a self-taught operations research analyst. Her technique was simple, brilliant, and effective. She would collect supplies of clothing and food on her own initiative in Michigan and surrounding states, then travel with her shipment from one army station to another. At each place she presented herself to the commanding officer as one who had supplies to distribute, asking for a letter that would admit her to all the installations under his command. Since supplies were always needed, she always got the letter. In the course of allocating her medical supplies, she would incidentally improve hospital sanitation systems and reorganize ward medical services and administration of supplies. Haviland did all this with one hand while with the other she took the excuse of providing food supplies to clean up the kitchens and teach the cooks how to prepare and serve food properly. She did the same in prisons. When army administrative personnel protested, she had her magic letter from the commanding officer. She could make one shipment of food and clothing from the North carry her through a whole series of battle stations. At every hospital through which she moved with her reforming "magic," she always had time to sit at the bedside of dying soliders.

Her trips to the battle stations did not interfere with her continued superintendence of the Underground Railway, or with running the school she had founded in Michigan for black and white children. If Laura Haviland had not toward the end of her life taken time out to write her autobiography as a device to raise money for the chain of schools she was then organizing, there would be no way of knowing the part she played in the Civil War era. Today a lucky reader may, as I did, come across a crumbling dusty copy of that autobiography (Haviland, 1882) in an old midwest Quaker meetinghouse library. This gentle, iron-willed Quaker lady has a significance beyond her time and place, as an example of how an ingenious woman can preempt public spaces and authority in order to serve the public good, successfully rejecting the underlife spaces allotted her by society.

The reports from which the above accounts of women's activities have been taken were written with pride. They represent substantial achievements, mostly in urban settings. It was in these same urban settings, however, as noted earlier, that the class interests of bourgeois and proletarian women often conflicted. Certainly perceptions of program priorities might conflict. To the extent that the voluntary associations confined themselves to specific services such as identifying employment opportunities, providing skill training, and creating alternatives to the workhouse for women and children, the conflict was minimal. But when the philanthropists were insensitive to the underlying economic issues and focused on morality and life styles, the potential conflict was great. Since poor women were not in a position to argue with their benefactors, the conflict was rarely overt. Many of the social attitudes (particularly of condescension) with which benefactors carried out their activities would be totally unacceptable today. These attitudes were a cultural product of their time, and should not obscure the really remarkable amount of social problem solving that went on in this privatized women's sector. For a whole century women were in effect tutoring male civil servants and government officials in how to deal with social welfare problems.

Religious Philanthropists and Women's Religious Orders

The religious counterpart to the secular developments described above is to be found in the explosion of new teaching and service sisterhoods within the Catholic church, and in new Protestant religious service organizations. It was in this century that the Catholic sisterhoods were finally able to break the cultural barriers within the church that kept earlier efforts to develop missionary teaching and service activities from coming to full fruition.

Counting only those orders which developed branches in the United States, almost five hundred new Catholic women's orders were founded between 1800 and 1899. The tabulation in table 11-1, based on a sample of 116 of these orders, puts this development in the context of the entire history of women religious.

Table 11-1. Date of Founding of a Sample of
116 Women's Religious Orders

pre-1200	2
1200-1399	5
1400-1799	13
1800-1849	28
1850-1899	47
1900+	20
Not ascertainable	1
Total	116

Note: The countries of origin of these orders are: Algeria, Belgium, Brazil, Canada, England, France, Germany, Italy, Mexico, Netherlands, Spain, Switzerland, South Africa, and the United States.
Source: *Guide to the Catholic Sisterhoods in the United States* (McCarthy, 1955). Over three hundred sisterhoods are described in detail.

It is of interest to know to what extent these orders were founded *for* women or *by* women. Since a male religious superior must put through the "founding" request in every case, it is not always easy to tell whether the original initiative came from a church dignitary or a woman. Relying on the way the historian of the order describes the founding, and listing as "founded by women" each order where a woman initiator is mentioned by name, I conclude that of the 116 orders studied, 67 were initiated by women, 44 by men, and 5 are unclear. Man-initiated means that a parish priest or a bishop specifically asked for women to come and organize under his auspices a teaching or social service program. Woman-initiated means that a woman or several women gathered together, decided on a service, then found church backing to do it. Given the prolonged emphasis on enclosure for women, the figure of 67 women-initiated service orders is impressive. While many of the orders began with one specific mission such as conducting an elementary school in a certain parish, by the twentieth century they are nearly all administering a great variety of institutions and services. Their activities can be summarized under the following headings: 1) *teaching and administering schools*—elementary, secondary, college, university, nursing school, normal school; 2) *social service, and administering health and welfare institutions*—orphanages, institutions for the handicapped, homes for unwed mothers, residence homes for working girls, urban settlement houses, schools and community centers for Indians, blacks, Mexican-Americans, centers for juvenile delinquents, hospitals, nursing homes; and 3) *community ministry*—home and community service to categories of people listed above, outside institutional settings. I was not able to find how many countries each order serves, but no order is confined to only one country, and some may serve up to a dozen or more.

Cita-Malard (1964) estimates that there were about one million women in Catholic orders at the time she was writing. Six percent of these orders are contemplatives, the other 94 percent are service orders. That new contemplative orders should continue to be founded in the 1800s is a clue to the continued perception of the relevance of the contemplative life on the part of women in the contemporary world; there are between fifteen hundred and eighteen hundred contemplative convents around the world today. If secular institutes and sisterhoods from Anglican and other Protestant groups and sisterhoods from Buddhist, Moslem, and Hindu traditions were considered together with the Catholic orders, there would probably be over two million women living a life vowed to celibacy, poverty, and service. How many women religious there were in earlier centuries we do not know, but the million figure for the Catholics was probably reached in the nineteenth century. Women religious tend to be long-lived, so many founder-sisters were personally known to the current generation of sisters of their order.

Most of the sisterhoods were founded in Europe at the height of the emigration era, and sisters sailed to new lands right along with the migrant women seeking their fortunes. Whether their destination was North America, Australia, Africa, or Asia, when they landed they had to fend for themselves just as their immigrant job-seeking sisters did. They, too, cleared land and built buildings, but not for themselves. They contributed to the earliest beginnings of schools and hospitals wherever they went. They took their chances with hunger and privation along with everyone else, and sometimes had the added burden of mistrust and persecution. The Catholic church did not always know how to respond to this new brand of pioneering nuns, so different from the quiet cloistered sisters priests were used to—and neither did the Protestant community. The sisters earned the right to teach and nurse and serve by winning the respect and friendship of the communities they came to. Humor, ingenuity, courage, and faith opened doors for them.

In the United States, for example, German sisters emigrated to German settlements in the Midwest and provided a transition educational experience for the children of German immigrants. In fact, every emigrating national group brought its ministers and priests along, and this national enclave effect caused problems at first. Those who held to a strong melting-pot ideology wanted to bypass this transitional period entirely. In the end, the sisterhoods were probably the most effective facilitators of new adjustment. They provided a broader matrix of services than priests and ministers could offer. Their teachings encompassed the nationalisms left behind, the nationalisms entered into, and set them in the context of the more universal sisterhood which the church in its original intention represented.

Some of the most radical developments in the contemporary Catholic church have come from the twentieth century inheritors of these sisterhood traditions. By breaking out of the cloister and away from the motherland the sisters gained many new perspectives at once. Their relative freedom to move about in the new terrains they entered, given their freedom from marital obligations, made them available for innovations that are still being worked out today.

The Protestant sisterhoods soon found their way abroad too. The nineteenth century was the great missionary century. Every church established its "mission field" and sent women and men abroad to teach, to care for the sick, to farm—and to proselytize. The missionary movement was sparked by the dawning internationalism of the century, in which concepts of a family of humankind as a world Christian family played an important part. There were a lot of limitations to that concept. The rhetoric about the little brown brothers (little brown sisters were rarely mentioned) was a rhetoric of condescension. But the missionary travels sparked new learnings both for the missionaries and for those among whom they settled.

The popular image of the nineteenth century missionary is of a narrow-minded preacher dressed in black, traveling with a Bible under his arm to preach fierce sermons to uncomprehending natives. In the first place more than half of the "he's" were "she's." In the second place many of them were of working-class origin themselves and had a more practical approach to relating to "the heathen" than they have been given credit for.

Their endeavors were in part an outcome of a humanitarian impulse to try to undo the harm of the slave trade. Assistance to re-settled colonies of ex-slaves was part of the new missionary thrust. The European government's policy of "Christianity, Commerce, and Colonization" was intended to introduce trading with ex-slaves as "equals," to replace the earlier trading in slaves,[26] and many of the early missionaries were carriers of the new intentions. But the new style of trade did not suit the colonial situation, in which centuries of violence and exploitation had set up quite other expectations. In the end, "merely to keep order," European governments found themselves intervening more and more into the affairs of local peoples. Furthermore, the slave trade was hard to stop, and another two million slaves were shipped across the Atlantic even while the "new" type of European-African relations were being established.

The missionaries were by no means always an arm of these intervening governments. They had their own agendas. While they made many mistakes, and learned the hard way to take account of differing social values, they often gave a type of aid which in the twentieth century we would label intermediate technology. They may in fact have done less harm and more good than twentieth century aid experts.

There is a whole literature on the activities of women missionaries, both Protestant and Catholic, in Africa and Asia and the Americas in the nineteenth century, which deserves special study. The encounter of women of other continents with the missionary women of Europe should properly be written as an encounter between two sets of women's cultures. The scramble to carve up Africa and establish imperial control over Asia was a male enterprise, carried out by the men of Europe with the enforced cooperation of the men of Africa and Asia. Traditional political and trading roles of indigenous women were ignored in the process. It is possible that valuable information on women's activities in colonized areas can be recovered from accounts of women missionaries, who would be far more likely than men to have entered into the women's spaces.

In addition to the church-based missions, there were the broad nondenominational movements such as the YMCA and YWCA, the Salvation Army, and the WCTU. The YWCA addressed itself particularly to the problems of young working women. The Salvation Army and the WCTU worked with everyone, young, old, in families, and particularly with deserted, widowed, and single women with children.

Because these organizations were born in the cities of Europe and North America, when they expanded to Africa and Asia it was in the cities of these continents that they took root. Tokyo, Peking, Bangkok, Delhi, Lagos, and Cape Town were among the first settings where women of the West worked with their third world sisters. Often it was the elites of one society meeting the elites of another, as wives of businessmen and diplomats from Europe brought their organizational habits with them to the third world and entertained their indigenous counterparts in ways they thought appropriate. Nevertheless, it was a beginning. The missionary-trained women doing the everyday work of the YWCA and the WCTU abroad were not elites; they belonged to the middle and upper working classes.

All three of these international movements had in common a twin commitment to spiritual and economic welfare. All three movements emphasized moral purity and practical hard work, all were urban based, and all contributed to some degree to the growing world consciousness of the nineteenth century. The YWCA and the WCTU were for women only; the Salvation Army worked with both women and men. The parts of their programs which twentieth century observers find easiest to understand are those relating to social welfare and the "puritan work ethic." The spiritual welfare concept is to some degree intelligible, but the moral purity concept seems hopelessly out of tune with "liberal" contemporary understandings of human beings. To appreciate the significance of the moral purity concept for organizations working with women one has to remember how vulnerable the 50 percent or so of urban women who lived as singles were to venereal disease. The more men a woman provided sexual services for, the greater the likelihood of her being infected. At the same time the Malthusian problem, which we tend to think was first taken seriously in this century, was in fact taken seriously in the last. It was perfectly obvious that poor single women with children suffered. Contraceptive technology existed, but was largely unavailable to the poor. The Mensinga diaphragm invented in 1870 in Holland was only for the well-to-do. Margaret Sanger had to go to France to find techniques to help urban working women in the United States. Abortions were risky to women's health. Infanticide, the poor women's abortion, was abhorred. The best protection for women was abstention, and the concept of moral purity put the practice of abstention into a context of self-development of the personality and the will. It was not a cramping, inhibiting concept, it was a releasing one. Moral purity was one aspect of a wholistic development of the person, a development which included spiritual and social awareness. Young women trained in the educational programs of missionary reform movements were often able to deal very practically with their own life problems.

The Salvation Army was founded by Catherine Booth and her husband, William (Bolton, 1895). Coming out of the dissenting traditions that encouraged the participation of women, both the Booths were drawn to the revivalist movement and went to London out of a fervent desire to save the poor. The difference between the Booths' and some other evangelical movements was that the Booths shared the way of life of slum people. The Salvation Army centers that dot the world today developed at that time out of the practical need to find food, clothes, shelter, and jobs for the unemployed of the slums. While Salvation Army workers acted on the premise that there were two hungers, they did not confuse physical and spiritual hunger. Their spiritual message was the better heard because they had a practical approach to economic problems: a network of city centers connected to self-supporting agricultural communities. There has always been equality between women and men at all levels of the organization.

The Salvation Army phenomenon could never be explained by practical problem-solving skills alone, however. Catherine Booth in particular had a quality of joyfulness that infected the movement. English folk over fifty who remember bands of Salvation Army lassies singing on the streets remember happy faces. People loved the lassies. In their overseas expansion they have kept to the same practical simplicity of organization, and to the same cheerfulness.

The Women's Christian Temperance Union has many of the qualities of the Salvation Army, although it is an all-women's group, and does more social work and less preaching. An offshoot of an earlier all-male group, it became a national organization in 1873 and an international one in 1891. The WCTU's strength is that it has aimed directly at the problems that face both single and married urban working women—skill training, employment, and decent housing. It has also confronted in a constructive way the associated problems of alcoholism and unwanted babies. Today's more sophisticated generation may smile at the WCTU rhetoric on the evils of alcohol, but urban WCTU centers around the world have provided significant "new start" opportunities for women. They have seen personal problems in social contexts, and local and national welfare problems in the international context. Their literature on the problems of world peace can hold its own with that of the more "intellectual" peace organizations. Their triple program of "temperance, moral purity, and world peace" has taken shape in centers that create environments for young women in which they can reach their full potentials. The WCTU has sections in sixty-one countries, and one of the finest of these is in Japan. The programs for young working women in Tokyo rival or surpass the best urban facilities for women in Europe or North America.

There is a long roster of women who have made the WCTU what it is. In the United States, Frances Willard, its founder, is its best-known member. Her words describe the quality of the organization very well:

> We are a world republic of women—without distinction of race or color—who recognize no sectarianism in religion, no sectionalism in politics, no sex in citizenship. Each of us is as much a part of the world's union as is any other woman; it is our great, growing, beautiful home. The white ribbon includes all reforms; whatever touches humanity, touches us (Gordon, 1924: 69).

It is interesting to speculate on why the two nineteenth century organizations which dealt most directly and honestly with the special problems of poor urban women are looked at with condescension today, while the "fallen woman" rhetoric is still pervasive in middle-class Europe and middle-class America. Most liberal middle-class American women are not comfortable with the idea of sitting in a meeting with a group of prostitutes. Why not? Perhaps because the latter are trying to shift into the public spaces of society issues that the middle class would prefer to keep privatized.

The International Peace Movement

One issue that seriously troubled the suffragette section of the nineteenth century women's movement was that of international peace. All the other social problems that the century's women's organizations dealt with had to do with improving conditions for women, even if they did not directly contribute to her gaining political rights. World peace, however, was problematic, and has remained so for many feminists right up to the present. And yet, as I have suggested, there was a pervasive internationalism in many women's activities. Some women really did feel, even if they would not have put it into just those words, an identification with Frances Willard's "world of community of women."

The double socialization process into national and world public spaces was noticeable as early as 1802, when a young Englishwoman published *A Vision Concerning Peace and War* at the time of the Peace of Amiens between Britain and France (Posthumus-van der Goot, 1961: 11). Between 1816 and 1828 national peace societies were founded in England and America. In 1820 the first all-women's peace societies were active in England, and by the 1830s they were active in America. *An Examination of the Principles Considered to Support the Practices of War,* published by an Englishwoman in 1823, was repeatedly reprinted and translated into French, Dutch, German, Spanish, and Hebrew. A steady stream of publications came from the British women's peace societies in the thirties, with women beginning to sign their names to their writings.

In 1848 the first international peace congress was held in Brussels. One of the most remarkable events of that congress was the unprecedented behavior of the chairman, who addressed the assembled delegates as *"mesdames et messieurs."* The International Anti-Slavery Congress in London several years previously had refused even to seat women. The peace congress seated women, saluted them, and had them speak.

By 1852 the Anglo-American women's peace societies (the Olive Leaf Circles) were issuing the first women's international publication, *Sisterly Voices.* Fredrika Bremer of Sweden proposed an international association of women for peace, and the leaders of this little international community of women were: Bremer, a distinguished writer; two French Saint-Simonians, Elise Grimault and Julie Toussaints; Marie Goegg, a leading humanist of Geneva; Julia Ward Howe of the United States, writer; Priscilla Peckover, English Quaker activist and editor of the journal *Peace and Goodwill;* and Bertha Suttner of Austria, author of a major work on disarmament, *Die Waffen Nieder* (published as *Down With Arms* in 1894). All of them except Peckover worked both with all-women's groups and with mixed groups. Peckover was adamant about keeping men out. She single-handedly built up the first major women's international network, with members in England, France, the Rhineland, Hannover, Rome, Warsaw, Constantinople, Russia, Japan, Polynesia, Portugal, and the United States. The Peckover international network has probably been used by many women's groups since, to the third generation. Suttner was the most public figure of all these women. Her first book was on *The Machine Age,* and her second was the documentary on disarmament. She played a leading role in the Interparliamentary Union, and was responsible for persuading Alfred Nobel to establish the Nobel Peace Prize. An Austrian aristocrat and a powerful and imperious woman, she had been educated in the scholar-aristocrat tradition still extant in Europe. Her biographer Ursula Jorfald tells us how thrilled she was at twelve finally to have a playmate after a solitary childhood; the playmate was versed in Hegel, Fichte, and Kant! (Jorfald, 1962: 7) Suttner brought to the international peace movement both the strengths and the weaknesses of elitist traditions.

By 1900, after a century of activity, there was an International Peace Bureau in Berne (still active in 1975) which coordinated the activities of two hundred different peace societies. Women were active in most of these, and some were all-women's organizations. If we look at women who were attracted to the women's peace movement in the beginning of the twentieth century, many of whom had been active since 1880, we are struck with the extent of their professionalism and commitment to public life (see table 11-2). It was clearly a task-oriented group, directing its attention to problems that today, nearly three-quarters of a century later, still defy definition and precision. It seemed to be a challenge whose time had come, but for lack of specific approaches to meeting the challenge much of this concentrated effort of women has since been diverted from international peace to other problems closer at hand.

The Women's Rights Movement

In my descriptions of women's activities during the nineteenth century, I have made only slight reference to the attitudes and values of the male-dominated societies of which they were a part. For every word or deed I have described as directed to public ends by women in this century, I could reprint pages of male abuse aimed at each

Table 11-2. Occupations of Professional Women in
the 1915 International Peace Movement

Occupation	Number
Doctor	2
Judge	1
Trade Union Movement	3
Lawyer	3
Social Worker	1
Economist	4
International Relations	1
Government Official	2
Member of Parliament	8
Physical Scientist	2
Educator	6
Social Scientist	1
Suffragette, Public Figure	5
Total	39

Source: Bussey and Tims (1965).

word, and at each deed. While in some ways it seems unproductive and unduly depressing to pay too much attention to the barrage of male abuse poured on women through the nineteenth and all preceding centuries, that ongoing phenomenon must be recalled at this time in order to understand the intensity of the women's rights movement when it came into full swing. Women were fighting to throw off legal disabilities that hindered their full command over their own persons, limited their share in societal resources including employment and protection from illness and poverty, and blocked their role in societal decision making. They were also fighting for the right to be treated as adult persons worthy of consideration and respect, rather than as children or idiots vulnerable to any abuse.

Many different currents came together to trigger the women's rights movement in the nineteenth century, and this chapter focuses on some of the less frequently recorded ones. I am suggesting that the sheer amount of frustration built up by the fact of women being active in a wide variety of problem-solving activities, without accompanying political rights and responsibilities, was one force for suffrage. At the same time, it should be pointed out that a number of activist women stayed outside the suffrage struggle, even at its height, because they felt it inappropriate or unnecessary to include suffrage among the causes they worked for. They did not see themselves as part of the victimage system. Among the successful elites, there was often blindness to the class-based nature of their own privilege and freedom, and failure to recognize that others with equal abilities from other classes could not do what they had done.

Since the suffrage movement is the best-documented part of women's history, no attempt will be made here to detail that history. Rather I will point out some cultural differences in origin and program emphasis among different national movements. Each country has dealt better with some of the issues associated with women's rights than with others.

The Anglo-American women's rights movement takes its roots in the stream of thought that can be picked up in Christine de Pisan in the 1400s, in Marie de Jars Gournay in the 1600s, and in Mary Wollstonecraft in the 1700s. In colonial America the thinking of Abigail Adams (C. F. Adams, 1975) and Anne Hutchinson (Abramowitz, 1946: 307-342) belong in the feminist stream, but neither woman wrote for publication, so their ideas never became part of the international women's culture.

One milestone on the road to removal of women's civil and legal disabilities was the publication in England in 1825 of the *Appeal of One Half the Human Race, Women Against the Pretensions of the Other Half, Men to Restrain Them in Political and Thence in Civil and Domestic Slavery,* by William Thompson and Anna Wheeler. His name alone appears as author, but his dedication makes it clear that this was a joint product (Pankhurst, 1954: 26). Anna Wheeler (born 1785) was one of the most advanced thinkers of her time. Victim of a terrible marriage from which she finally escaped with her two surviving daughters, she was for a time the center of a Saint-Simonian circle in France, and close to the young Fourier. Returning to England she worked with Robert Owen in Jeremy Bentham's circle. She and William Thompson are often linked in the records of the cooperative movement, and their friendship of "mutual opinions and ideals" had something of the flavor of the Taylor-Mill friendship of the next generation, described earlier (Pankhurst, 1954: 65-78). The occasion of the *Appeal* was the publication of James Mill's famous "Article on Government" (1824 supplement to the *Encyclopedia Britannica*), which expounded the doctrine of "included interest" for women, stating that women did not need independent political representation because their interests were included in those of their fathers and husbands. The Wheeler-Thompson book dealt not only with the subjection of married women, but with the casually ignored one-fourth of the female population with neither father nor husband.

The Wheeler-Thompson appeal profoundly affected the position of the cooperative movement and the thinking of Marx and Engels, becoming a historical landmark in thought about the position of women in society. The appeal was also incorporated in the original draft of the People's Charter of Rights and Liberties framed by the Chartist movement in 1838. Women began at this time to form associations to promote the Wheeler-Thompson suffrage clause, with Birmingham as the center of the movement. The clause was soon removed from the Chartist declaration as being "premature," but the women's associations stayed alive.

In the preceding decade women had started writing articles advocating votes for women. In 1832 a Yorkshire woman, Mary Smith, petitioned parliament for the right of unmarried women to vote. Four different groups converged in the 1830s to form the first major suffrage movement: 1) the previously mentioned political associations formed in connection with the Chartist declaration; 2) the women's "auxiliaries" in the Anti-Corn Law League, which were giving women direct political experience in lobbying on economic issues; 3) a broad mass of women whose consciousness was raised by the Caroline Norton divorce case, which remained a major public issue from 1836 when it first went to court until 1856 when the Marriage and Divorce Reform Law was passed; and 4) the social scientist-activist alliance engaged in the welfare and education reform movements described in the preceding pages. The Chartist-inspired women's political associations kept issuing leaflets and statements for several decades after their initial proclamation in 1838.

In 1851 the Sheffield Women's Political Association was formed, and in 1865 the Kensington Society, composed of outstanding women leaders, was formed, and began attracting considerable attention. Their first activity was to campaign (successfully) for John Stuart Mill's election to parliament. Next, all the women's political associations mobilized to get signatures for the petition Mill presented to parliament in 1866 for the enfranchisement of women. In 1867 the London National Society for Women's Suffrage was formed. While most people date the British women's movement from that time, there had already been over thirty years of activity on behalf of suffrage.

The famous incident in London in 1840, when American women delegates were refused seats at the International Anti-Slavery

Congress held there, did not play the decisive role in the English suffrage movement that it played in the American movement. It was fury over that event that brought Elizabeth Cady Stanton and Lucretia Mott back to the United States to organize the Seneca Falls Convention of 1848 that launched the American suffrage movement. One reason the antislavery congress incident is not part of the public history of the English movement is that English women already had a fairly high level of activity and awareness at the time. The congress event was not their first shock, and therefore did not have the same dramatic mobilizing effects on them that it had on the Americans.

In the course of the three decades of buildup of the suffrage movement before 1867, two different kinds of emphasis became clear: enfranchisement in order to overcome *economic disadvantage* was the theme of the working-class women, the Chartists, who were suffering severely from economic setbacks during this period; enfranchisement for *political decision making* was the theme of the middle-class women, the suffragettes, who had personally secure situations, but wanted a freer hand to set things straight for society at large. Economic issues were not entirely lacking among the suffragettes—large numbers of unemployed single women seeking nonexistent positions put some added pressure on their suffrage activities—but in the main, the suffrage movement stayed middle class, and trade union women worked for their rights separately. When the suffragettes went radical with the formation of the Women's Social and Political Union in 1903, there was a conscious effort to make an alliance with working-class women, but this only lasted three years. The styles were too different.

For all the class feelings of confidence and superiority with which suffragettes carried on their campaigns, strategically they were not very successful. The sweet reasonableness of the nineteenth century was followed by campaigns of fire and fury in the early twentieth century with women chaining themselves to the gates of parliament. The fire-and-fury period was one of real martyrdom for many English suffragette leaders. Elite women who had always been able to exert authority and control by virtue of their class status were thrown into prison for months at a time, and when they went on hunger strikes they were brutally force-fed. Some women had their health permanently damaged as a result of the force-feeding. This was a new experience for such women, and they might in the end have been politicized in a new way and rediscovered the alliance with their worker sisters, had not the war intervened and set another dynamic in motion.

It is interesting to reflect on the course of the British suffrage movement. Neither reason nor fury got the suffragettes the vote, and many volumes have been written on why a group of women as sophisticated and useful to the national welfare as the British suffragettes could not succeed in their own enfranchisement. In the end it was political convenience that got them the vote—after the war (Pugh, 1974). The suspension of suffragette activity and identification with the war effort on the part of many suffragettes showed that many women were more nationalist than feminist. Those who adhered to international allegiances became pariahs among their former sisters. This split was felt inside the Pankhurst family, England's "First Family" in the suffrage movement. Mother Emmaline and daughter Christobel threw themselves wholeheartedly into the war effort. Daughter Sylvia remained stubbornly socialist and pacifist.[27]

In general the suffragettes stayed a one-issue group, and this meant that they backed away from the very issues that became central to the German and Scandinavian women's rights movements: protection of single women and their illegitimate children, and protection from abusive prostitution-control laws. Josephine Butler was actively disliked by many suffragettes who felt that her campaign for the abolition of police regulation of prostitution deflected attention from feminist issues as they saw them.

While I have used the term Anglo-American for one style of suffrage work, there really was no Anglo-American entity. The American women who came into the women's rights movement were not inexperienced—some of the leaders had participated in the temperance and abolition movements and the moral crusades of the early 1800s—but they were on the whole conservative, small-town activists concerned with the protection of society as they knew it and with a modest extension of their freedom into the political arena.[28] Only a few American suffragettes were interested in international movements. The fact that the American suffrage movement was born out of indignation over the exclusion of American women from an international antislavery congress in London was not calculated to sharpen interest in international activities! The movement's strength lay in the middle classes of the small towns. There were no alliances with working women, and little concern with the protection of single women and illegitimate children. Such phenomena were handled under the category of "fallen women."

There was a link between one wing of the American suffragettes and the peace movement, which led to the formation of the Woman's

Peace party in the early twentieth century. That group was led by the same Addams-Wald-Kelley-Hamilton-type coalition of women leaders noted earlier; they seem to have been a democratic version of England's leading elites. In the end, however, American women, like their English sisters, earned their suffrage in the eyes of men through vigorous support of the war. The pacifist women were as isolated from their sisters in the United States as they had been in England. In terms of outcomes, American women were slightly more successful than their British sisters were. English women over thirty voted by 1918, but not until 1928 could they vote at the same age as men —twenty-one. American women voted by 1920, and everyone over the age of twenty-one was enfranchised at once.

In northern Europe, the vote itself never took center stage in the women's rights movement. Rather, the *Mutterschutz* idea became the overriding goal for the movement. "Protection of motherhood" is not an adequate translation of the concept, which is not directly translatable into Anglo-American values. It has to do with a different approach to the role of women, involving the reform (or, in extreme versions, the abolition) of marriage so that every woman may enter and leave marital relationships freely and at will and may bear children independently of marriage status. The care and responsibility for the welfare of children was not to be linked to marriage. Social security legislation that protects mothers and their children, assures educational and employment opportunities, and guarantees equal pay for equal work was part of the program, as was a reform in sexual ethics. The vote was considered important too, but was not necessarily the top priority in the program.

The *Mutterschutz* concept does not represent a drive to send women back into the home, but a drive to protect women wherever they are, including the factory, and to protect their right to bear children without harassment. Why this focus on the single woman, ignored in most women's rights programs? As in England, about 40 percent of German women of childbearing age were unmarried in the 1880s, and this situation persisted into the 1900s. In 1905, one out of every twelve German babies was born out of wedlock. As Katharine Anthony summarizes it, "Owing to emigration and colonial expansion, industrial accident and war, the women find themselves in the unsought position of the majority" (1915: 85). The result was that half the adult female population were heading a household. Many of these women might wish children even though only temporary unions with men were possible. Many illegitimate children were in fact wanted children, in spite of the opprobrium associated with illegitimacy. Not all, of course. For women who did not wish children, said the women's rightists, abortion must be possible.

Ellen Key, the Swedish feminist, took a rather deviant stand on *Mutterschutz.* She was for the complete abolition of marriage and the return to what she visualized as an original matriarchal system, in which all women would live surrounded by their children and men would support them but have no marriage rights. Public affairs and the vote would be left to men, the lesser beings. This line of thought went so contrary to emerging conceptions of both proletarian and middle-class women that in the end she modified her position and supported suffrage.

Such extremes of the *Mutterschutz* movement sound like a Nazi program for master race eugenics. The main body of the movement, however, kept its eyes unwaveringly on the issues which Anglo-American women's rights movements generally ignored: the plight of the unpartnered woman with children, wanted or unwanted. Only very recently has the "new" women's liberation movement begun to deal with this issue in the United States.

The *Mutterschutz* movement has to be seen side by side with the movement to expand education and employment opportunities for women. This became formally organized on a national basis in Germany in 1865, about the same time that the British women's suffrage movement was formalized. A bimonthly journal, *New Paths,* was started. Legislative reforms for women came slowly, but they did get the vote at the end of the war—paid off, like their sisters everywhere, for loyalty.

None of the high-activity suffrage movements gained the vote before World War I was over. But there were some countries in which suffrage was granted to women *before* the end of World War I: Australia, in 1902; Denmark, 1915; Finland, 1906; Iceland, 1915; New Zealand, 1893; Norway, 1913; and the USSR, 1917 (United Nations, 1964). These dates all refer to the right to vote in national elections on the same basis as the men. Some countries, such as Sweden, had limited municipal suffrage as far back as 1863, so the date of universal suffrage does not reflect previous levels of political involvement of women. Scandinavia and parts of the British Commonwealth did best on early achievement of enfranchisement, but these were not areas of high suffrage activity. Political convenience and chance may have more to do with the date of suffrage than anything else. It was clear from the 1840s on that it had to come, but no known strategy hastened the day of the vote.

Giving women the vote may in some countries have seemed like a power issue, but it was not in fact. When women had the vote they used it conservatively, to support existing power structures. They did not use it to elect women to office, or to promote radical reforms (Duverger, 1955).

Adventurers

Not everyone in the nineteenth century was involved in social movements. The great bulk of women were laboring unadventurously at their places of employment. There was also that other breed of women, the migrants, the adventurers, the pioneers. *New Horizons* (1963), the story of British women's-migration societies, tells harrowing tales of women's adjustments to new life in places as far apart as Canada, New Zealand, Nigeria, Kenya, and Jamaica. The women who organized the migration schemes were as intrepid as the ones who migrated, and often the organizers traveled over the migrant terrain themselves to make sure their planning was being relevant. In the early years the societies had to deal with many genteel ladies who shipped overseas only to return immediately to England because they could not cope with pioneer conditions. Migration organizers soon learned to select for copability.

American women who headed west were another category of migrants. *The Gentle Tamers*[29] (Brown, 1958) describes American pioneer women who built claim shacks to dig for gold, who took land and developed it alone. In 1885 Mary Meegher was the largest rancher on the Pacific slope. Arizona Mary drove a sixteen-yoke ox team and made a fortune. "Charlie" Pankhurst was a stagecoach driver from 1860 to 1879. In 1850, eastern seaboard teachers began the trek westward to open schools. Brown suggests that pioneer women did so well because they had more optimism than men did in the face of hardship, more flexibility, and more physical and psychological endurance at the farthest reaches of suffering on the covered wagon treks. (There were cases where all the men died on a trek, and only the women survived.) All types of women made it: college girls, "fancy women," middle-aged ladies, bloomer girls, teachers, missionaries, ordinary middle-class wives, and tough army women. It is perhaps no accident that the first states to give women the vote at the state level in the United States were the western states. There was no private space-public space issue for women in the west in the middle and late 1800s. The women were simply *present*, wherever there was anything to be done.

Another category of adventurers besides the settler-pioneers are the travelers who traveled for the sake of seeing the world. *Celebrated Women Travellers of the Nineteenth Century* (W. H. D. Adams, 1903) tells us about the princess of Bologna, the radical who ran an expatriot salon in Paris. Her other activities included equipping a two-hundred-horse army and leading it against Austria—to defeat. She went to Turkey to live when she got bored with Paris. Mme Hommaire de Hell wandered over Russia and Turkey, and found a number of European women living "as lonely exiles" in the Crimea. (Some of them may have been happier than she thought.) Fredrika Bremer, the Swedish novelist mentioned earlier as an international peace movement activist, traveled around the world to get background for her novels. Alexandra Tinne of the Hague explored Africa. Ida Pfeiffer was a globe-trotting scientist. Lady Hester Stanhope left high society England to establish a "petty kingdom" in the Lebanon. Lady Brassey sailed around the world in the yacht *Sunbeam* in 1876. The list goes on and on. Some traveled out of curiosity, some as scientists, some to write. Isabella Bird, the Englishwoman who explored the Rocky Mountains in 1878, was one of those who seems to have sought the extremes of hardship for adventure's sake. She is a legend today in Colorado.

Women soldiers flourished in the nineteenth century. The Austrian and Italian armies regularly commissioned women soldiers who saw action, received the highest decorations soldiers could receive, and often married and had children. Augusta Krüger of the Ninth Prussian Regiment was decorated both with the Iron Cross and the Russian Order of St. George, and had the pleasure of seeing her grandson commissioned to her own regiment. In France, Angélique Brulon, sublieutenant of the infantry, was decorated with the Legion of Honor. Dragoon Thérèse Figuer had four horses killed under her in action, but died in her bed at eighty-seven. The American Civil War brought out a whole collection of midwestern "Joan of Arcs," mostly schoolteachers, and sometimes wives who preferred fighting by their husbands' sides to sitting at home: Mary Ellen Wise of the Indiana Volunteers, Mary Hancock of Illinois, Anny Lillybridge and LaBelle Morgan of Michigan, Mary Dennis (a six-foot-two-inch commissioned soldier in a Minnesota regiment), and others.

Lurking behind the midwestern schoolmarm soldiers is the shadowy figure of Anna Ella Carroll, a southern lady of the antebellum aristocracy. She served in Lincoln's "kitchen cabinet" and supposedly formulated the Tennessee River campaign which is considered the decisive action that gave victory to the North in the war (Greenbie, 1940).

Scientists

Records of women scientists became more frequent in this century. Many of them were married and had children, but tended now to practice their science independently rather than in a husband's laboratory. Self-taught Sophie Germain of France, one of the founders of mathematical physics, won a prize from the French National Academy of Science for the solution of an "unsolvable" problem and did a major work on vibrating surfaces in 1816. Mary Somerville, also a self-taught mathematician, wrote *The Mechanism of the Heavens,* which became a University of Cambridge textbook and brought her election to the Royal Astronomical Society and a government pension. (She was also a mother of two who tutored her own children, ran a home famous for hospitality, and was actively writing at her death at the age of ninety-two.) Sonya Kovalevsky of Russia held the chair of higher mathematics at a Swedish university, also won a French National Academy prize for the solution of an "unsolvable" problem, and unfortunately died young while planning her major work. Italy, France, and the United States all produced world-famous women doctors in this century. Mme La Chapelle revolutionized midwifery in France; Maria dalle Bonne, a peasant's daughter, became professor of obstetrics at Bologna; and Elizabeth Blackwell pioneered medical training for women in England and America. Caroline Herschel, astronomer, was the first Englishwoman to receive a government scientific appointment. She discovered eight comets, several nebulae, and received gold medals from all the crowned heads of Europe. She and Somerville were the first two women members of the British Royal Society.

Ida Pfeiffer, Mary Kingsley, Mme Coudreau, and Eleanor Ormerod were all natural scientists who traveled to difficult and dangerous places for exploration and specimen collection. They published widely, were much honored and little paid. Ormerod was perhaps the most exploited, as well as the most bemedaled. She became the "world pest expert" and ran an unpaid international consulting service on how to deal with pests.

The ingenuity of these natural scientists suggests another category of ingenious women, who were not scholars, but inventors. This is as appropriate a place as any to point out the role of women inventors in providing some of the major devices we associate with the industrial revolution. The following passage comes from Russell H. Conwell's *Acres of Diamonds,* written in 1890. He has some startling remarks about who the "real" inventors were in nineteenth century America:

When you say a woman doesn't invent anything, I ask, Who invented the Jacquard loom that wove every stitch you wear? Mrs. Jacquard. The printer's roller, the printing press, were invented by farmers' wives. Who invented the cotton-gin of the South that enriched our country so amazingly? Mrs. General Greene invented the cotton-gin and showed the idea to Mr. Whitney, and he, like a man, seized it. Who was it that invented the sewing-machine? If I would go to school tomorrow and ask your children they would say, "Elias Howe."

He was in the Civil War with me, and often in my tent, and I often heard him say that he worked fourteen years to get up that sewing-machine. But his wife made up her mind one day that they would starve to death if there wasn't something or other invented pretty soon, and so in two hours she invented the sewing machine. Of course he took out the patent in his name. Men always do that. Who was it that invented the mower and the reaper? According to Mr. McCormick's confidential communication, so recently published, it was a West Virginia woman, who, after his father and he had failed altogether in making a reaper and gave it up, took a lot of shears and nailed them together on the edge of a board, with one shaft of each pair loose, and then wired them so that when she pulled the other way, it opened them, and there she had the principle of the mowing-machine. If you look at a mowing-machine, you will see that it is nothing but a lot of shears (quoted in Robins, 1975: 255).

For some reason, it was easier to honor women scientists than women inventors.

The women scientists mentioned above, and many others not mentioned, all made contributions to their respective fields that were widely honored in the international community. In that sense, they were public figures. A few had government appointments, but most of them supported themselves on private incomes or from publications. They lived privatized lives in the sense of rarely having official niches, yet moved in the public arena as far as expectations of their performance went. A good example of the moral and social climate in which they worked can be found in the essay written by the Swedish dramatist Strindberg about Sonya Kovalevsky after she had been appointed to the chair of higher mathematics in Sweden, proving "as decidedly as that two and two make four, what a monstrosity is a woman who is a professor of mathematics, and how unnecessary, injurious and out of place she is" (quoted in Mozans, 1913: 163).

Artists and Writers

The nineteenth century produced so many writers that it becomes impossible to survey them in brief. The Georges—George Sand in France and George Eliot in England—demonstrated something important to women about holding to artistic integrity and personal autonomy under conditions of great public success. This was also the century of the great expressive artists in literature: Jane Austen, Mary Shelley, Elizabeth Barrett Browning, Emily and Charlotte Brontë—and robust Maria Edgeworth. (See Vineta Colby, *The Singular Anomaly* (1971); Ellen Moers, *Literary Women* (1976); and Martha Vicinus (ed.), *Suffer and Be Still* (1972). These sources aren't exhaustive; specialized literary-historical study of women writers of the nineteenth (or any) century is just beginning in earnest.)

Since so much was happening in art, again more than can be conveyed in brief, I will mention only two particularly unusual women artists here. One is the great French animal painter, Rosa Bonheur, daughter of an impoverished Saint-Simonian. She was one of the first painters consciously to assume a women's rights stance and to avoid marriage explicitly in order to maintain her freedom and integrity as an artist. She was also the first woman artist to be named an officer of the French Legion of Honor. She had every honor that the world could bestow, and died with seventy-seven years of extraordinarily productive life behind her. The other artist, Edmonia Lewis, was half native American, half black, raised by her mother as a Chippewa. She went to Oberlin on an Abolition Scholarship, and became a sculptress who won fame in America and Europe for her sculpture work on themes of emancipation of the Negro and on native Chippewa themes. She was last seen working in Rome in 1886, and then disappeared from the record. Both these women were creative in settings of initial poverty and great hardship, unlike the great bulk of women artists mentioned in previous centuries who were born into families of artists and given oils with their mother's milk, so to speak. These two women represent the new woman who chooses her métier independently of family circumstances.

This may be the place to reflect briefly on the women artists we have glanced at from the fifteenth through nineteenth centuries. In spite of the general impression in the twentieth century that there have been no great women artists,[30] the women we have described in each of these centuries achieved great fame in their own lifetime. They were on the whole long-lived; most of them married, but they married late; some of them even had large numbers of children. They were for the most part daughters of artists, and trained by an artist-parent. What was characteristic of all of them (except the early family-workshop painters) was an independence that was hard to come by for women in their time, even for the elite. It is an interesting commentary on the strength of the creative drive in women that some of these artists should have been both biologically and artistically prolific, and so long-lived.

Overview: Women, the Family, and the World

The situation of women in the nineteenth century was one of contrasts. The most rigid expectations of domesticity and obedience stood in confrontation with extraordinary initiatives in mapping and shaping new social realities. It was *not* a century of superwomen. Rather, it was a period in which the talents women had were given freer play because among women an inner confidence was developing. The practical background experience for the new roles had been there for a long time. Georgiana Hill, in her insightful book on Englishwomen, writes:

> It is one of the peculiar characteristics of women that they are able to attend to so many things at one time. Their lives are so usually encumbered with detail that they have acquired the faculty of passing rapidly from one subject to another, added to which their sympathies and their perceptive powers are quicker than those of men, so that they are both stirred to action and able to grasp their object more readily (1896: 233).

This "faculty of passing rapidly from one subject to another" is the only possible explanation of the intellectual productivity of women with heavy responsibilities, and of the social productivity of women who have become involved in many spheres.

A variety of special studies are needed of women's activities in the nineteenth century to get the full picture of the beginning of their entry into the public spaces of society. No one has ever looked at the total social science output of women in this century. When this is done, I believe it will be found that a number of significant conceptual breakthroughs, as well as techniques of observation and measurement, came from women. Much of this is lost in our social histories. No one has looked systematically at the institution building women did to meet the problems of industrial urbanism, nor examined in detail the attendant misery of family living conditions. No one has yet studied adequately the real-life situation of the unpartnered woman in the context of a pervasive social ideology of familism, nor analyzed in adequate historical perspective the structural and behavioral adaptations for survival made by poverty-class women. The ideology of familism has drawn a curtain over many of these adaptations.

Understanding the ideology of familism is essential to an understanding of the century. For all the negative things that can be said about the Victorian age, it did indeed promote family delights for the middle class:

> The prettiest sight in Paris . . . was the crowds of children with their
> parents in the Tuileries or Luxembourg gardens on Sundays or holidays,
> and the extraordinary kindness and attentiveness of both parents. . . . in
> the French family every soul is open to the day (Robertson, 1974: 425).

Similar descriptions could be written for the public parks of any major city of Europe or North America.[31] A new style of family life in which parents and children spend much time together began to receive literary attention. The Taylors of Ongar popularized the idea of reading aloud in the family, and of letting children help in family decision making (Robertson, 1974: 442-443). Mrs. Beeton, author of the bible of home management, *Mrs. Beeton's Cookery and Household Management,* wrote, "It ought to enter into the domestic policy of every parent to make her child feel that home is the happiest place in the world" (Robertson, 1974: 423). This was the era of rich family play life, and *The Girls' Own Book* of 1848 records 130 games to play at home with people of all ages. Families built puppet theaters together, put on shows together, played charades together.

Yet there was family cruelty too. Robertson writes of the two attitudes running in counterpoint through the nineteenth century: "Those who like children against those who do not . . . the Age of Reason confronting the Puritan Ethic" (1974: 422). There were the gentles, like Maria Edgeworth, author of *Practical Education* (1801), who "was once asked how she knew so much about children. 'Why, I don't know,' she said. 'I lie down and let them crawl all over me'" (Robertson, 1974: 420). There were also the stern disciplinarians who believed in total control of the child's mind, like the German doctor Daniel Schreber, who believed that "a well-trained child could be controlled by the eye of the parent, since a good child would not want to behave differently from what the parent wished" (n. 27 in Robertson, 1974: 429). Schreber's son became a famous psychiatric case and was analyzed by Freud.

For all the emphasis on the family, the fact remains that in this century between 40 and 50 percent of women were either single, widowed, or separated in most countries of Europe. Whether they were *once* married is not as important as the fact that, at any given time, this large group of women were unpartnered. Alva Myrdal tells us that as far back as 1750, 35 percent of the population of Sweden was single, and that in the 1860s the average age of marriage for women was 26.92, for men 30.57 years. In the mid-twentieth century, 20 percent of Swedish women never marry (Myrdal, 1945). Where did the idea come from that "everyone" lived in families?

What percent of unmarried women stayed in their parental households we do not know, but among the proletariat few women would have stayed in overcrowded parental households after reaching their teens. Many of them lived as domestic servants, others took rooms or lived in boarding houses. We know that widows often chose to live alone. If we estimate twenty years as the average length of married life in these centuries, widows may have quite a few years alone. Since the unpartnered have never been considered a significant social category, their living circumstances have never been adequately studied. When they are, I believe we are in for some surprises.

A historical picture is beginning to emerge of a society organized "as if": *as if* every household consisted of a husband, wife, and children; *as if* every household must have a woman home at all times; *as if* there were no single women, no illegitimate children; *as if* all productive labor were carried out by men, and all significant civic arrangements created by men.

Reality has always belied the "as if," but it was never challenged. The changes in economic conditions, rising population densities, and particularly the steady growth of urbanism from the seventeenth century on finally brought some women to examine the reality, and to challenge the "as if," the myth of total familism.

By the nineteenth century, many women were no longer willing to support the old fictions of male guardianship of the female, which included the concept of women's intellectual, social, and legal minority. They had knowledge and skills often unavailable to men, talents that were crucial to the task of making urban society workable. Activists began to insist on partnership roles with men and a social, economic, and legal status commensurate with the functions they were performing. The doctrine of "included interest" was exploded forever.

The assertion process for women was slow and painful. They were, and still are, caught in a set of conflicting loyalties and conflicting perceptions of reality. Many are frightened at the thought of having rights instead of protection. Others feel no need for more autonomy than they already have. Counter-feminist movements evolved in the nineteenth century and continue in the twentieth, representing women who are content with traditional patterns and who fear that feminism will destroy the family life they cherish. Women who have lived in private spaces do not see the social whole objectively. It is hard for them to see the broad spectrum of social arrangements that can enhance the lives of women, men, and children, both inside and outside of family households. The absurdity of the privatization of a women's world within the larger society is by no means evident to Western women generally.

In the next chapter we will gain a broader perspective on women's roles in the household and the public sphere by reviewing briefly the developments for women in Africa, Asia, and Latin America over the past millennium. We will see that the problems women face in what is now called the third world are different from first world problems. We will also see that expectations and achievements have been different. This review provides the springboard for a look at the possibilities for women in the twenty-first century, in the last chapter.

Appendix 11-1
Occupations of Women in 1841

	Females 20 yrs and upward	Under 20 yrs		Females 20 yrs and upward	Under 20 yrs
Accoutrement Maker	39	4	Boat and Barge Owner	19	--
Actor (Play)	310	71	Bobbin Maker and Turner	19	10
Agent and Factor (branch not specified)	40		Bonnet Maker	3,331	976
Agricultural Implement Maker	40	18	Bookseller, Bookbinder, Publisher	1,561	458
Anchor Smith and Chain Maker	54	49	Boot and Shoe Maker	8,611	1,953
Artist (Fine Arts)	261	17	Brace and Belt Maker	322	80
Auctioneer, Appraiser and House Agent	37	1	Braid Maker	34	10
Author	15	--	Brass Founder and Moulder	39	4
Baby Linen Dealer and Maker	68	8	Brazier, Brass Finisher, Tinker	100	10
Bacon and Ham Dealer and Factor	23	1	Brewer	172	5
Baker	3,144	79	Brick and Tile Maker	261	169
Banker	7	—	Brick Layer	106	--
Basket Maker	262	51	Broker (branch not specified)	256	3
Bath Keeper and Attendant	77	—	Broker, Furniture	84	5
Bazaar Keeper	26	2	Brush and Broom Maker	535	157
Bead Maker	26	10	Buckle Maker	31	12
Bed and Mattress Maker	90	7	Builder	74	--
Blacking Maker and Dealer	26	4	Burnisher	168	48
Blacksmith	469	--	Butcher	1,047	26
Bleacher (branch not specified)	185	164	Butcher, Pork	85	--
Boat and Barge Builder	19	—	Butter Dealer, Merchant, Factor	39	1
Boat Woman	117	13	Button Dealer and Merchant	13	--

SOURCE: Appendix in Pinchbeck and Hewitt (1969: 317-332).

Note: These dates are from the Occupational Abstract of the Census Returns, 1841 (P.P. 1844, xxvii., pp.31-44). While not altogether accurate, the figures are interesting in showing the distribution of women in industry at this time. The numbers given are for England alone, and trades employing only very few women have for the most part been omitted.

	Females 20 yrs and upward	Under 20 yrs		Females 20 yrs and upward	Under 20 yrs
Button Maker	1,031	607	Dressmaker, Milliner	70,518	18,561
Cabinet Maker and Upholsterer	1,846	181	Dyer, Calenderer, and Scourer	417	74
Cap Maker and Dealer	837	237	Eating House Keeper	173	1
Card Maker	488	362	Embroiderer	593	209
Carpenter and Joiner	389	--	Engine and Machine Maker	45	8
Carpet and Rug Manufacturer	87	158	Engineer and Engine Worker	45	57
Carrier, Carter and Waggoner	464	14	Factory Worker (Manufacturer not specified)	4,338	4,449
Carver and Guilder	68	10	Farmer and Grasser	13,398	--
Cattle and Sheep Dealer and Salesman	13	--	Farmer, Cattle Doctor, and Veterinary Surgeon	78	--
Chair Maker	237	43	Feather Maker, Dealer, Dresser	97	13
Charwoman	18,019	265	File Maker (all branches)	92	31
Chaser	46	3	Fish Monger and Dealer	614	42
Cheesemonger and Factor	115	1	Fisherwoman	277	29
Chemist and Druggist	148	4	Flax and Linen Manufacturer (all branches)	2,746	3,625
Chemist, Manufacturing	11	1	Flour Dealer and Mealman	207	5
Chimney Sweeper	125	--	Flower (artificial) Maker	475	380
China, Earthenware and Glass Dealer	602	84	Fork Maker	32	10
Clerk (Commercial)	137	22	French Polisher	81	23
Clock and Watch Maker	164	21	Fringe Manufacture	207	106
Clothes Dealer and Outfitter	206	11	Furrier	664	134
Coach Maker (all branches)	108	8	Fustian Manufacture	918	354
Coal Labourer Heaver, Porter	184	187	Gardener	841	75
Coal Merchant and Dealer	371	18	Gas Fitter	2	--
Coffee-House Keeper	178	4	Glass and Bottle Manufacture	209	70
Comb Maker	97	33	Glove Maker	4,249	1,600
Cooper	113	6	Glove Manufacture, Silk	106	81
Corn Merchant, Dealer, Factor	114	10	Government Post Office	449	11
Corn Cutter (Chiropodist)	12	--	Greengrocer and Fruiterer	2,629	70
Cotton Manufacturer (all branches)	65,839	49,586	Grocer and Tea Dealer	7,005	127
Cupper and Dentist	23	--	Gun Maker and Gun Smith	67	12
Currier and Leather Seller	140	5	Haberdasher and Hosier	779	109
Cutler	129	30	Hairdresser and Barber	231	15
Die Engraver and Sinker	6	2			
Draper	1,596	377			
Draper, Linen	529	100			

	Females			Females	
	20 yrs and upward	Under 20 yrs		20 yrs and upward	Under 20 yrs
Hatter and Hat			Milk Seller and		
Manufacturer	1,711	544	Cow Keeper	1,622	52
Hawker, Huckster			Miller	410	47
and Pedlar	3,177	214	Millwright	25	3
Hook and Eye Maker	33	34	Miner (branch not		
Hose Manufacturer			specified)	334	364
(all branches)	5,934	2,371	---Copper	903	1,200
Iron Monger	259	9	---Iron	363	36
Jappaner	328	165	---Lead	25	18
Jeweller, Goldsmith			---Tin	68	82
and Silversmith	296	69	Mop Maker	33	4
Keeper, Lunatic			Moulder	12	5
Asylum	157	6	Music Seller and		
Keeper, or Head of			Publisher	33	--
Public Institu-			Musical Instrument		
tion	1,427		Maker	23	--
Knitter	814	274	Musician and		
Labourer	9,398	1,757	Organist	199	51
---Agricultural	26,815	8,447	Muslin Manufacturer	35	11
Lace Agent	15	1	Nail Manufacturer	2,673	1,366
Lace Dealer and			Needle Manufacturer	505	243
Laceman	100	25	Net Maker	106	26
---Manufacturer			Newsagent and Vendor	67	3
(all branches)	14,394	5,651	Nurse	12,476	517
Lamp and Lantern			Nurseryman and		
Maker	10	--	Florist	183	49
Lapidary	21	10	Oil and Colourman	62	9
Laundry Keeper,			Optician	17	--
Washer and			Painter, Plumber		
Mangler	43,497	1,522	and Glazier	349	25
Lead Manufacturer	47	21	Paper Hanger	10	1
Leech Bleeder and			---Manufacturer		
Dealer	51	1	(all branches)	857	370
Librarian	106	3	---Stainer	60	32
Lime Burner	54	7	---Box Maker	42	38
Lint Manufacturer	84	28	Parochial Church and		
Livery Stable			Corporation Officer		
Keeper	107	--	(exclusive of those		
Locksmith and			returned in trade)	359	5
Bell Hanger	35	7	Pastry Cook and		
Lodging and Board-			Confectioner	1,681	158
ing House Keeper	6,073	33	Pattern and Clog		
Maltster	121	5	Maker	65	10
Map Maker and			Pawnbroker	242	14
Publisher	34	5	Pearl Cutter and		
Marine Store Dealer	90	1	Worker	60	41
Mason, Paviour and			Pen Maker and		
Statuary	146	4	Dealer	66	27
Mat Maker	89	7	Pen (Steel) Maker	128	104
Match Maker and			Percussion Cap		
Seller	58	14	Maker	17	8
Mathematical Instru-			Perfumer	86	11
ment Maker	2	--	Pewterer and Pewter		
Medicine Vendor	23	2	Pot Maker	17	1
Merchant	77	--	Pig Dealer and		
Metal Manufacturer	89	74	Merchant	11	1
Midwife	676	--			

	Females 20 yrs and upward	Under 20 yrs		Females 20 yrs and upward	Under 20 yrs
Pin Manufacturer			Silk Manufacturer		
(all branches)	472	356	(all branches)	18,038	11,795
Pipe Maker	343	98	---Mercer	118	--
---Tobacco Maker	18	3	---Merchant	13	1
Plasterer	69	2	Skinner and Skin		
Plater	20	5	Dresser	49	9
Polisher	151	40	Slater	11	--
Porter, Messenger	165	36	Slopmaker and		
Potato Dealer and			Seller	261	39
Merchant	33	--	Small Ware Dealer	92	4
Pottery, China and			Small Ware Manufac-		
Earthenware Manu-			turer (all		
facturer (all			branches)	122	75
branches)	3,843	3,253	Smelter (ore not		
Poulterer and			specified)	118	204
Game Dealer	196	7	Snuffer Maker	16	2
Press Worker	32	32	Spectacle Maker	8	3
Print Seller	36	9	Spinner (branch		
Printer	114	43	not specified)	3,458	1,906
Printer, Copper			Spoon Maker	87	48
Plate	10	2	Spring Maker	16	--
---Cotton and			Stationer	387	30
Calico	239	384	Stay and Corset		
Provision Dealer	217	12	Maker	4,149	666
Pump Maker	17	4	Steel Workers	18	13
Quarrier (branch			Stewardess (ship)	27	2
not specified)	15	4	Stock (Men's) Maker	318	103
---Stone	15	18	Straw Bonnet and		
Quill Cutter	11	4	Hat Maker	6,457	2,021
Quilter and Quilt			---Plait Dealer,		
Maker	92	18	Factor, Merchant	64	19
Rag Cutter Dealer			---Plait Manufacturer		
and Gatherer	446	93	(all branches)	5,686	3,161
Reed Maker	26	8	Stuff Manufacturer		
Register Office			(all branches)	2,028	1,144
(Servants') Keeper	19	--	Sugar Baker, Boiler		
Ribbon Manufacturer	2,394	636	and Refiner	12	--
Roller Maker and			Surgical Instrument		
Turner	114	27	Maker	9	--
Rope and Cord Spinner			Tailor and Breeches		
and Maker	401	85	Maker	5,155	954
Rush Dealer and			Screen Maker	88	75
Manufacturer	21	4	Screw Cutter and		
Sack and Bag Dealer			Maker	279	122
and Maker	187	31	Screw (wood) Maker	22	7
Saddle, Harness and			Seamstress	15,680	2,266
Collar Maker	272	36	Seedsman and Seed		
Sail, Sail Cloth and			Merchant	52	3
Tarpaulin Manufac-			Servant, Domestic	447,606	264,887
turer	99	22	Shawl Manufacturer		
Saleswoman	117	5	(all branches)	107	60
Sand Merchant	37	1	Ship and Smack		
Sawyer	12	--	Owner	48	--
Schoolmistress,			Shopkeeper and		
Governess (see			General Dealer	9,316	266
also Teacher)	27,754	1,499	Shroud Maker	14	4
Scissors Maker	101	47	Sieve Maker	72	24

	Females			Females	
	20 yrs and upward	Under 20 yrs		20 yrs and upward	Under 20 yrs
Tallow and Wax			Typefounder	3	3
Chandler	71	7	Umbrella, Parasol		
Tanner	38	4	and Walking-		
Tape Manufacturer			Stick Maker	423	118
(all branches)	258	131	Undertaker	69	3
Tassel Maker	62	17	Warehouse Woman	567	202
Tavern Keeper, viz.			Weaver (branch		
Beershop Keeper	1,471	15	not specified)	17,728	8,583
Hotel and Inn			Wheelwright	141	5
Keeper	2,941	34	Whip Maker	41	8
Publican and			Whitesmith	23	--
Victualler	5,574	51	Willow Weaver and		
Spirit Merchant	114	4	Worker	56	20
Tea Broker and			Wire Agent and		
Merchant	3	--	Merchant	79	1
Teacher—see also			Wire Drawer and		
Schoolmistress			Maker	9	1
Dancing and			---Worker and		
Gymnastics	60	1	Weaver	88	56
Languages	62	6	Wood Cutter and		
Miscellaneous	36	6	Woodman	61	12
Music and Singing	629	91	---Merchant and		
Thimble Maker	18	11	Dealer	33	--
Thread Manufacturer			Wool, Agent, Mer-		
(all branches)	172	181	chant and Stapler	34	5
Timber Merchant and			Wool (Berlin), Dealer		
Dealer	33	4	and Worker	22	2
Tin Manufacturer			Woollen and Cloth		
(all branches)	125	149	Manufacturer (all		
Tinplate Worker	72	31	branches)	13,196	7,742
Tobacconist and			---Draper	57	3
Tobacco and Snuff			Worsted Dealer and		
Manufacturer (all			Merchant	26	6
branches)	1,683	89	---Manufacturer (all		
Toll Collector	426	20	branches)	6,016	6,126
Tool Dealer and Maker			Yarn Manufacturer		
(all branches)	58	13	(all branches)	118	48
Toy Dealer and Maker	386	76	Yeast Dealer and		
Tray Maker	47	10	Merchant	51	1
Trimming Maker	162	72			
Tripe Dealer and					
Dresser	71	6			
Trunk and Box Maker	226	84			
Truss Maker	22	5			
Turner	74	20			

Appendix 11-2
Employment of Village Children in Nineteenth Century England

acorning	laundry work
bait girls	mangold wurzel pulling
band making	mangold wurzel trimming
bark stripping	manure spreading
bean dropping	net braiding
bean picking	onion peeling
bean tying	osier peeling
binding and stooking	pea picking
bird scaring	pig minding
brickmaking	poaching
cattle minding	rag cutting
cockling	shallot pulling
cow minding	sheep minding
dinner carrying	shrimping
door-to-door selling	singling and thinning root
flax pullers	crop
fruit pickers	stone picking
gang labour	straw plaiting
gloving	turnip pulling
hoeing	turnip singling
hop-picking	vegetable cleaning
hop pole shaving	vegetable pulling
hop tying	walnut bashing
lace making	water drawing
laundry carrying	weeding

SOURCE: Constructed from the index entries under "Children's Employment" (Samuel, 1975: 266-267).

Notes

[1]The men who shared that conviction—Condorcet at the time of the French Revolution, Fourier and William Thompson in the early 1800s, John Stuart Mill, Marx and Engels in the middle 1800s—all went considerably beyond the gradualist evolutionary doctrines of the rights of man in their perspectives on society. They were also more radical than most women reformers.

[2]Whether the quality of male-female relationships is better there is another question.

[3]Read Frances Trollope's horrified account of married couples living in boarding houses in *Domestic Manners of the Americans* (1949: 280-285).

[4]In fact marriage alliances continue to be important to this day both in the international business community and among royalty.

[5]See the discussion of this in Boulding (1972: 13-14); also the detailed analysis in Weller (1968) and Collver and Langlois (1962).

[6]Richards illustrates the "surge of sympathetic writing" with titles like "How to Provide for Superfluous Ladies" and "Why are Women Redundant?" (1974: 350).

[7]Edith Thomas (1966), who was at the barricades of 1944 against the Vichy government, had a very vivid sense of the continuity of women's participation in revolutions and has written a striking account of women's participation in the Paris Commune of 1871.

[8]It would be a great mistake to conclude that this pathological development applied to convents and beguinages generally. They were, however, susceptible to prevailing economic conditions.

[9]See Thönnessen (1973) for more on the women's movement in Germany.

[10]The recent unexpurgated edition of her autobiography (Kollontai, 1971) gives a poignant picture of those dilemmas as we read what she herself censored before publication in 1926.

[11]Other women of that international socialist circle who published on socialism were: Clara Meyer-Weichman, *Mensch en Maatschappij* (1923); Lydie Pissarjevsky,

Socialisme et Féminisme (1910); Ethel Snowdon, *The Woman Socialist* (1907); Marguerite Thibert, *Le Féminisme dans le Socialisme Français 1830-1850* (1926); Lily Gair Wilkinson, *Revolutionary Socialism and the Women's Movement* (1910); Dora Russell, *Hypatia, or Woman and Knowledge* (1925).

12Neither had their father Karl provided a good role model for a revolutionary spouse, since while devoted to his family he also exploited Jenny's housewifeliness.

13There were many ways for a revolutionary to handle the "love" component of life, and some chose Kollontai's approach, putting the revolutionary movement first: "Love, marriage, family, all were secondary, transient matters. They were there, they intertwine with my life over and over again. But as great as was my love for my husband, immediately it transgressed a certain limit in relation to my feminine proneness to make sacrifice, rebellion flared in me anew. I had to go away, I had to break with the man of my choice. . . . It must also be said that not a single one of the men who were close to me has ever had a direction-giving influence on my inclinations, strivings, or my world-view" (Kollontai, 1971: 13). This type of solution is of course not limited to revolutionaries. Gifted women and men of a certain temperament have always chosen this solution.

14It was Olive Schreiner who called the fine lady "the most deadly microbe which can make its appearance on the surface of any social organism" (1911: 81).

15The tradition that factory workers were single girls with nothing to spend their money on but clothes, and only worked until marriage, stems from the early days when farmers' daughters went to the mills for a brief interlude in their lives. Later in the century there were widows and other unpartnered mothers in the factories, and daughters who supported widowed mothers and younger brothers and sisters.

16Five nonreligious communities are mentioned.

17Brook Farm was perhaps a little better than the others, due to its articulate women transcendentalists, Elizabeth Peabody Palmer and Margaret Fuller, and its ardent commitment to the abolition of domestic servitude (meaning, however, domestic servants, not the domestic labor of women).

18A sense of the versatility of Martineau can be gained from reading Alice Rossi's description of her in *The Feminist Papers from Adams to de Beauvoir* (1973: 118-143). Rossi's essay deals with a different set of Martineau's attributes than those discussed here. Two major sociological contributions of Martineau's not mentioned above are her abridged translation of Comte's *Positive Philosophy* (1853) and a treatise on social science methodology, *How to Observe Manners and Morals* (1838).

19See *Women in Social Work* (Walton, 1975) for a more complete account of the development of this profession in England.

20Thrupp is a founder and editor of the journal *Comparative Studies in Society and History*.

21She was not all-wise. She never realized the dimensions of the single-woman head-of-household problem, and tended to treat widows as special cases, therefore not assisting women as a class.

[22]For example, the Feminist Press, Box 334, Old Westbury, New York 11568.

[23]I find it striking that both Mary Ellen Richmond, from the social work perspective, and Mary Follett, from the political science perspective, saw the significance of new patterns of association before these phenomena became general subjects of study.

[24]One notable exception is the Associated Country Women of the World.

[25]That this village manor house service tradition can even today be identified in an old urban area like Birmingham, England, I can testify from personal observation. There is no counterpart institution in the United States, because we never had manor houses.

[26]See Collins, *Europeans in Africa* (1971), for a discussion of this.

[27]Jo Newberry (1975), a Canadian historian working on the life of Catherine Marshall, another suffragette who was actively pacifist, points out that far more women continued to oppose the war throughout its duration than suffragette histories suggest.

[28]See Rossi (1973: 241-281) for an excellent characterization of the American movement.

[29]*Pioneer Mothers of the West* (Frost, 1972) contains similar records.

[30]See, for example, Linda Nochlin's "Why There Are No Famous Women Artists" (1971).

[31]There was one group of women and men in the nineteenth century for whom the ideology of familism was not generally considered relevant: the slaves in the antebellum South. An interesting study of slave family records (Blassingame, 1972: 90) between 1864 and 1866 in the South shows only 13.6 percent unbroken families during that period. Of the 86.3 percent of broken families, 32.4 were broken by the master, 39.9 by death, 3.3 by war, and 10.7 by personal choice. Given the setting for slave family life on plantations, probably worse than the worst rural poverty in England, the 13.6 percent of families that stayed together represent a triumph for the ideals of family partnership.

References

Abramowitz, Isidore
1946   The Great Prisoners. New York: E. P. Dutton.

Adams, Charles Francis (ed.)
1975   Familiar Letters of John Adams and His Wife Abigail Adams During the Revolution. New York: Houghton Mifflin.

Adams, W. H. Davenport
1903   Celebrated Women Travellers of the Nineteenth Century. New York: E. P. Dutton.

Anthony, Katharine
1915   Feminism in Germany and Scandinavia. New York: Henry Holt.

Armytage, W. H. G.
1961   Heavens Below: Utopian Experiments in England, 1560-1960. London: Routledge and Kegan Paul.

Baber, Zonia
1948   Peace Symbols. Philadephia: Women's International League for Peace and Freedom.

Balabanov, Anzhelika
1938   My Life as a Rebel. New York: Harper.

Beard, Mary R.
1946   Woman as Force in History: A Study in Traditions and Realities. New York: Macmillan.

Bebel, August
1971   Women under Socialism. Tr. by Daniel de Leon. New York: Schocken Books. (Reprint of the New York Labor News Press edition of 1904.)

Bellamy, Edward
1967   Looking Backward: 2000-1887. Ed. by John L. Thomas. Cambridge, Mass.: Harvard University Press. (Reprint of 1887 edition.)

Blassingame, John W.
1972   The Slave Community: Plantation Life in the Antebellum South. New York: Oxford University Press.

Bohrovskaya, C.
1940   Lenin and Krupskaya. New York: Workers Library Publishers.

Bolton, Sarah Knowles
1895   Famous Leaders Among Women. New York: T. Y. Crowell.

Boulding, Elise
1972   "Women as role models in industrializing societies: A macrosystem model of socialization for civic competence." Pp. 11-34 in Marvin Sussman and Betty Cogswell (eds.), Cross-National Family Research. Leiden: E. J. Brill.

Brown, Dee
1958   The Gentle Tamers: Women of the Old Wild West. New York: Putnam.

Burdett-Coutts, The Baroness
1893   Woman's Mission. New York: Scribner.

Bussey, Gertrude and Margaret Tims
1965   Women's International League for Peace and Freedom, 1915-1965: A Record of Fifty Years' Work. London: Allen and Unwin.

Cita-Malard, Suzanne
1964   Religious Orders of Women. Tr. by George J. Robinson. New York: Hawthorn.

Colby, Vineta
1971   The Singular Anomaly: Women Novelists of the Nineteenth Century. New York: New York University Press.

Cole, G. D. H.
1953-   A History of Socialist Thought. 5 vols. New York: St. Martin's
1960   Press.

Collins, Robert O.
1971   Europeans in Africa. New York: Alfred A. Knopf.

Collver, Andrew and Eleanor Langlois
1962   "The female labor force in metropolitan areas: An international comparison." Journal of Economic Development and Cultural Change 10: 367-385.

Cook, Robert (ed.)
1951   "The great world cities." Population Bulletin (September).

Croly, J. C.
1898   The History of the Woman's Club Movement in America. New York: Henry G. Allen.

Dolci, Danilo
1970   Report from Palermo. Tr. by P. D. Cummins. New York: Viking Press.

Duverger, Maurice
1955   La Participation des Femmes à la Vie Politique. Paris: UNESCO.

Eagle, Mary Kavanaugh Oldham (ed.)
1974   The Congress of Women, Held in the Woman's Building, World's Columbian Exposition, Chicago, 1893. New York: Arno Press. (Reprint of 1895 edition.)

Ellington, George
  1972   The Women of New York or the Under-World of a Great City. New York: Arno Press. (Reprint of 1869 edition.)

Follett, M. P.
  1920   The New State. New York: Longmans Green.

Friedan, Betty
  1963   The Feminine Mystique. New York: W. W. Norton.

Frost, John
  1972   Pioneer Mothers of the West, or Daring and Heroic Deeds of American Women, Comprising Thrilling Examples of Courage, Fortitude, and Self Sacrifice. New York: Arno Press. (Reprint of 1869 edition.)

Giffin, Frederick C. (ed.)
  1973   Woman as Revolutionary. New York: New American Library, Mentor Books.

Gilman, Charlotte Perkins
  1970   Women and Economics. A Study of the Economic Relations between Men and Women as a Factor in Social Evolution. Ed. by Carl N. Degler. Gloucester, Mass.: Peter Smith.
  1935   The Living of Charlotte Gilman. New York: Appleton-Century.
  1911   The Man-Made World or Our Androcentric Culture. New York: Charlton.
  1900   Concerning Children. Boston: Small, Maynard.

Goldman, Emma
  1931   Living My Life. New York: Alfred A. Knopf.
  1910   Anarchism and Other Essays. New York: Mother Earth.

Gordon, Elizabeth Putnam
  1924   Women Torch-Bearers: The Story of the Woman's Christian Temperance Union. Evanston, Ill.: National WCTU Publishing House.

Greebie, Marjorie Lotta
  1940   My Dear Lady: The Story of Anna Ella Carroll, the Great Unrecognized Member of Lincoln's Cabinet. New York: McGraw-Hill.

Greenway, John
  1953   American Folksongs of Protest. Philadelphia: University of Pennsylvania Press.

Haviland, Laura S.
  1882   A Woman's Life-Work: Labors and Experiences. Cincinnati, Ohio: Walden and Stowe.

Hill, Georgiana
  1896   Women in English Life, Vol. 2. London: Richard Bentley.
  1894   Women in English Life, Vol. 1. London: Richard Bentley.

Hobsbawm, E. J.
  1963   Primitive Rebels: Studies in Archaic Forms of Social Movement in the Nineteenth and Twentieth Centuries. 2nd ed. New York: Praeger.

Holloway, Mark
  1966   Heavens on Earth: Utopian Communities in America, 1680-1880. Rev. ed. New York: Dover.

Jorfald, Ursala
  1962   Bertha Von Suttner: Og Nobels Fredspris. Oslo: Forum Boktrykkeri.

Josephson, Hannah
  1949   Golden Threads: New England's Mill Girls and Magnates: New York:
         Russell and Russell.

Kamm, Josephine
  1966   Rapiers and Battleaxes: The Women's Movement and Its Aftermath.
         London: Allen and Unwin.

Kollontai, Alexandra
  1971   The Autobiography of a Sexually Emancipated Communist Woman. Tr.
         by Salvator Attanasio. New York: Herder and Herder.

Langford, Elizabeth
  1964   Victoria R. I. New York: Harper and Row.

McCarthy, Thomas P., C. S. V.
  1955   Guide to the Catholic Sisterhoods in the United States. 3rd ed. Wash-
         ington, D. C.: Catholic University of America Press.

Martineau, Harriet
  1968   Society in America. Ed. and abr. by Seymour Martin Lipset. Glou-
         cester, Mass.: Peter Smith. (First published 1837.)
  1877a Autobiography. 3 vols. London: Smith Elder.
  1877b Biographical Sketches: 1852-1875. London: Macmillan.
  1838   How to Observe Manners and Morals. London: Charles Knight.
  1832- Illustrations of Political Economy. 9 vols. London: C. Fox.
  1834

Maupin, Joyce
  1974   Working Women and Their Organizations: 150 Years of Struggle.
         Berkeley, Calif.: Union WAGE Educational Committee.

Meyer-Weichman, Clara
  1923   Mensch en Maatschappij [Persons in Society]. Arnhem, Netherlands:
         Loghum, Slaterus and Vesser.

Moers, Ellen
  1976   Literary Women. Garden City, N. Y.: Doubleday.

Mozans, H. J.
  1913   Woman in Science. New York: D. Appleton.

Munro, Irene B. and Winthrop M. Munro
  1942   Handbook for Clubwomen. Clinton, S. C.: Jacobs Press.

Myrdal, Alva
  1945   Nation and Family: The Swedish Experiment in Democratic Family
         and Population Policy. Cambridge, Mass.: MIT Press.

Newberry, Jo
  1975   Edinburgh: University of Edinburgh Institute for Advanced Studies in
         the Humanities. Historian, personal communication.

Nochlin, Linda
  1971   "Why have there been no great women artists?" Art News 69 (Janu-
         ary): 23 25, 32-33, 36-39, 69-71.

Nordhoff, Charles
1965 The Communistic Societies of the United States. New York: Schocken Books. (Reprint of 1875 edition).

O'Faolain, Julia and Lauro Martines (eds.)
1973 Not in God's Image: A History of Women in Europe from the Greeks to the Nineteenth Century. New York: Harper and Row.

Pankhurst, Richard K. P.
1954 William Thompson (1775-1833): Britain's Pioneer Socialist, Feminist and Co-operator. London: Watts.

Petrie, Glen
1971 A Singular Iniquity: The Campaigns of Josephine Butler. New York: Viking Press.

Pinchbeck, Ivy and Margaret Hewitt
1969 Children in English Society. Vol. 1. From Tudor Times to the Eighteenth Century. London: Routledge and Kegan Paul.

Pissarjevsky, Lydie
1910 Socialisme et Féminisme. Paris: Congrès International Permanent Féministe.

Posthumus-van der Goot, W. H.
1961 Vrouwen Vochten Voor de Vrede. Arnhem, Netherlands: Van Loghum Slaterus.

Pugh, Martin D.
1974 "Politicians and the woman's vote, 1914-1918." History 59 (October): 368-374.

Richards, Eric
1974 "Women in the British economy since about 1700: An interpretation." History 59 (October): 337-357.

Richmond, Mary E.
1930 The Long View: Papers and Addresses. New York: Russell Sage.
1925 Child Marriages. New York: Russell Sage.
1922 What is Social Case Work? New York: Russell Sage.
1917 Social Diagnosis. New York: Russell Sage.
1907 The Good Neighbor. Philadelphia: J. B. Lippincott.
1903 Friendly Visiting Among the Poor. New York: Macmillan.

Robertson, Priscilla
1974 "Home as a quest: Middle class childhood in nineteenth century Europe." Pp. 407-431 in Lloyd de Mause (ed.), The History of Childhood. New York: Psychohistory Press.

Robins, Elizabeth
1975 "Ancilla's share." Pp. 250-265 in Mary Cohart (ed.), Unsung Champions of Women. Albuquerque: University of New Mexico Press.

Rossi, Alice S.
1973 The Feminist Papers from Adams to de Beauvoir. New York: Columbia University Press.

Rowbotham, Sheila
  1973   Hidden from History. London: Pluto Press.
  1972   Women, Resistance, and Revolution: A History of Women and Revolution in the Modern World. New York: Pantheon.

Russell, Dora
  1925   Hypatia, or Woman and Knowledge. New York: E. P. Dutton.

Salmon, Lucy Maynard
  1897   Domestic Service. New York: Macmillan.

Samuel, Raphael (ed.)
  1975   Village Life and Labor. London: Routledge and Kegan Paul.

Schreiner, Olive
  1911   Woman and Labour. New York: Frederick A. Stokes.

Scott, Anne Firor (ed.)
  1971   The American Woman: Who Was She? Englewood Cliffs, N. J.: Prentice-Hall.

Scott, G. R.
  1936   History of Prostitution from Antiquity to the Present Day. New York: Greenberg.

Snowdon, Ethel
  1907   The Woman Socialist. London: George Allen.

Stanton, Theodore (ed.)
  1970   The Woman Question in Europe. New York: Source Book Press. (First published 1884.)

Sumner, Helen L.
  1974   History of Women in Industry in the United States. (Report on Conditions of Woman and Child Wage-Earners in the United States, vol. 9; 61st Congress, 2nd Session, Senate Document no. 645, Washington, D. C.) New York: Arno. (Reprint of 1910 edition.)

Thibert, Marguerite
  1926   Le Féminisme dans le Socialisme Français, 1830-1850. Paris: Marcel Gerard.

Thomas, Edith
  1966   The Women Incendiaries. Tr. by James and Starr Atkinson. New York: George Braziller.

Thönnessen, Werner
  1973   The Emancipation of Women: The Rise and Decline of the Women's Movement in German Social Democracy, 1863-1933. Tr. by Joris de Bres. Bristol, England: Pluto Press.

Trollope, Frances
  1949   Domestic Manners of the Americans. Ed. by Donald Smalley. New York: Random House. (First published 1932.)

Tufts, Eleanor
  1974   Our Hidden Heritage: Five Centuries of Women Artists. New York: Paddington Press.

Vicinus, Martha (ed.)
  1975   Women in Social Work. London: Routledge and Kegan Paul.
  1972   Suffer and Be Still: Women in the Victorian Age. Bloomington: University of Indiana Press.

Ware, Norman
  1958   The Industrial Worker: 1840-1860. Magnolia, Mass.: Peter Smith. (First published 1924.)

Webb, Beatrice
  1948   Our Partnership. Ed. by Barbara Drake and Margaret I. Cole. New York: Longmans Green.
  1926   My Apprenticeship. New York: Longmans Green.

Weller, R. H.
  1968   "A historical analysis of female labor force participation in Puerto Rico." Journal of Social and Economic Studies 17 (March): 60-69.

Whitman, Karen
  1970   "Our sister Rosa Luxemburg." Women: A Journal of Liberation 1 (Summer): 16-21.

Whitworth, John McKelvie
  1975   God's Blueprints: A Sociological Study of Three Utopian Sects. London: Routledge and Kegan Paul.

Wilkinson, Lily Gair
  1910   "Revolutionary Socialism and the Women's Movement." Glasgow: Social Labour Party. (Pamphlet circa 1910.)

Women's Migration and Overseas Appointments Society
  1963   New Horizons: A Hundred Years of Women's Migration. London: Her Majesty's Stationery Office.

12

A Historical Note
on the Underside of the
Third World

This history has been far from global in scope. Now it is necessary to take a look, however superficial, into the movement of time as experienced by women of the third world, many of whom live in societies with such ancient traditions that the culture of the European West appears as a hastily constructed hodgepodge by contrast. The feeling of Western women that their history began yesterday is part of a general Western pathology that has had its effect on third world women, and robbed them of their own history. Who did the most harm in the eighteenth and nineteenth centuries: the colonial administrators and merchants who obliterated the indigenous women's traditional positions of responsibility by ignoring them, or their wives who too often served as role models for a life of unproductive glamour in third world countries. Some combination of these two forces erased a considerable part of women's history from public consciousness in the third world. Yet, that is not the whole story. Many Western women who came to Africa and Asia in the nineteenth century as missionaries, as teachers, as feminists, allied with their sisters to create a global women's community that has survived all the disastrous wars of the twentieth century. In order to understand that global community, not well known to the younger women of the West, even after International Women's Year, the historical experience of third world women with "modernization" must be noted.

Islamic modernizers came to north and sub-Saharan Africa, Persia, and India in the eighth to tenth centuries. By the thirteenth century they had spread to much of Southeast Asia, establishing coexistence with Hinduism and Buddhism. By 1450, when Islam had great empires in Persia and India, and had reached the Philippines, the tides were shifting; the first Portuguese boats were reaching Africa, and Christian Europeans were driving the Moslems out of Spain.

Africa

The Portuguese set sail for Africa during a period when several great African kingdoms were at their height. Ancient Axum (Ethiopia) had stayed outside the Moslem world, keeping its Coptic Christian ruling traditions intact. The kingdom of Ghana, already flourishing in the eighth century, had been absorbed by the kingdom of Mali in the thirteenth century, which in turn was absorbed by the kingdom of Songhai in the fifteenth. In the meantime another great kingdom developed in the Lake Chad region, Kanem. The kingdom of Benin and the city-states of Yoruba, the Congo, Kilwa, and Zimbabwe—the forest states that wove together many tribal groupings below the Sudan—also flourished at this time. By 1450, when Prince Henry's navigators arrived, all these kingdoms and other groups of stateless tribes were solidly interpenetrated by Moslem merchants and their ever-present holy men. The merchants had created a network of trade, culture, and mosques linking sub-Saharan Africa with the Islamic world centered on the Mediterranean, and linking states internally on the African continent (Levtzion, 1968). Unlike the North African states of present-day Algeria, Morocco, and Tunisia, which were directly under Moslem rule, these sub-Saharan kingdoms were independent and used Islamic trade and culture as tools for their own internal development. Roland Oliver, writing about "The African Achievement," comments that

> Islam's African fringe can bear comparison with Christendom's northern European fringe at any time up to the late sixteenth century. It was in the seventeenth and eighteenth centuries that Europe, and especially northern Europe, drew ahead (1968: 97).

In terms of the standard of living for the average person,

an easier life was lived in the round houses of Africa than in the cottages of medieval Europe's serfs and free peasants. Certainly the African peasant enjoyed more leisure (1968: 98).

It was in the great concentrations of wealth that Europe and Africa differed. African chiefs never amassed personal wealth in the style of the European nobility. Although they often had plural wives, their life styles remained *relatively* simple.

The slave trade, long practiced in Africa, increased gradually through the activities of Arab and Jewish[1] merchants between the eleventh and sixteenth centuries, but did not reach a substantial volume until the demand from Europe and the Americas developed. The sixteenth century was the turning point. The activities of European Christian "modernizers" resulted in the shipping of one million slaves to Europe in that century. In the seventeenth century, three million, and in the eighteenth century, six million slaves were exported (Collins, 1971: chapt. 2). By the nineteenth century the slave trade slowed.

What was the status of women in the African kingdoms, and what were the relative effects for them of the activities of Moslem and Christian modernizers? First, one has to distinguish between the non-state tribal groups that lived scattered across the whole of Africa, and the kingdoms. The local tribes varied greatly, from stratified chiefdoms with nobility at the top and serfs at the bottom, to acephalous egalitarian bands (see Tuden and Plotnicov, 1970). The latter were perhaps the most victimized by the slave trade, though no one, including sons and daughters of chiefs, was safe from kidnapping by fellow African slavers for the European trade. The small egalitarian bands will not be further discussed because this type of structure has already been examined in this work in several other settings. The occupation patterns specific to African women, however, have not been examined elsewhere. The reader is referred to the Appendix of this chapter for a glimpse into the great variety of occupational roles of tribal African women.

The stratified chiefdoms had varying degrees of matrilineality. There was usually a hierarchy of women in ruling positions paralleling those of men. The mother, wife, and sister of the chief, and a council of matrons, usually played an important role in each society. The tribal organization was often such that women administered the affairs of women, including economic affairs, and also had a general input into overall tribal business. In the Great Lakes kingdoms the sister of the chief, or *kabaka,* was also a *kabaka,* as was his mother, and they shared the rule. There were women as well as men in the priesthood. Sometimes the corulership turned into primary ruler-ship for a woman, as in the eastern Transvaal. In the nineteenth century there were three successive reigning queens in one Transvaal tribe, Mujaji I, II, and III. Mujaji I, an outstanding ruler, set a regular fashion of ruling queens in neighboring tribes.

It is not clear how often women succeeded to the primary chief's role. There are legends of various queens that filter through the history of the major "slaving" centuries:

> In the Niger and Chad regions and in Hausa territory, women founded cities, led migrations, conquered kingdoms. Songhai groups still remember the names of celebrated ancestresses who governed them: in Katsina, Queen Amina became famous during the first half of the fifteenth century through her widespread conquests. She extended her influence as far as the Nupe, built many cities, received tribute from powerful chiefs, and is still held to have been responsible for introducing the kola nut to the region. In a neighboring state, south of Zaria, another woman called Bazao-Turunku appears in the tradition at the head of a group of warriors who established themselves in a town, the ruins of which are still extant. In the myths concerning the establishment of the So in North Cameroon it was also often a woman who chose the site of a city, held the insignia of power, or governed the district (Lebeuf, 1963: 94-95).

One famous warrior queen well documented in history was Queen Nzinga (1582-1663) of the Mbundu peoples in what is now Angola. She successfully defended her people from the Portuguese for years. In spite of a life of continuous hardship, she lived to the ripe old age of eighty-two (Sweetman, 1971). Legends of women founders of states are found among patrilineal as well as matrilineal tribes. The Congo, Cameroons, and Transvaal tribes mentioned above are all patrilineal. It is less surprising to find women as founders of states in matrilineal West Africa, as in the small states of Mampong, Wenchi, and Juaben.

There are also traditions of all-women's armies. The king of Dahomey's well-muscled women warriors, and the system of parallel women and men officials in his court, seem to be a later version of an ancient tradition: Sir Richard Burton witnessed an attack by the king on a neighboring principality, and reports that the women's army was better disciplined and fought better than the men's army, though neither performed very creditably (R. Burton, 1966: 254-267).

Lebeuf provides ample documentation of very widespread political participation of women in the political life of traditional Africa. The participation varied greatly according to whether the society was primarily kin-structured or class-based, and according to the economic base of the society, but nearly always the historical participation patterns have been better defined than present political roles for women.[2] As Lebeuf says,

> there are no valid historical grounds for explaining the present lack of interest in political matters so often found among African women as being a heritage of the past (1963: 96).

Since there are so many Africas, it is difficult to make meaningful statements in a summary as condensed as this one. The vast majority of Africa's population through the centuries has been rural. What proportion have practiced agriculture and what proportion have been nomadic is not clear, but the settlement of nomadic peoples has been going on for a long time. Up to 75 percent of the population of certain countries like Somalia remain seminomadic today. We have already seen that in nomadic societies women are freer than in settled societies.[3] Yet according to Germaine Tillion it was the urbanization of former nomads that was responsible for the extremes of veiling and seclusion of women in North Africa, as the men tried to protect their women from the dangerous environment of the city: "The Bedouin-become-bourgeois, deprived of the protection of the vast desert emptinesses and the unconditional support of his cousin-brothers, falls back on all the artifices and means that come to his mind: iron bars on windows, complicated locks, mean dogs, eunuchs . . . and the veil" (quoted in Gordon, 1968: 8).

The nomad woman, and the farm woman with her digging stick, retained substantial independence. Although marriage was nearly universal, marriage and dowry practices were such that women usually supported themselves and their children after marriage, with the dowry serving as "venture capital" for the trading activities associated with farming. The woman-as-economic-partner model applied whether marriages were monogamous or polygamous. While women of Moslem North Africa were restricted in their movements, working-class women had to work, whatever the religious or political ideology. In some areas the poorest women worked veiled in the fields, but they worked.

The women of sub-Saharan Africa largely moved in the same spaces of society as men, though their political roles tended to be of a subsidiary character. In West Africa, and to a lesser extent elsewhere, the marketing roles of women developed apace with pre-European

Moslem-stimulated urbanization. The traditional prerogative of women to sell surplus produce from their land, and to sell the products of home craftwork, led to larger-scale ventures as urban densities increased. In West Africa women administered the market system, and the proto-legal systems associated with it. European colonial administrators eventually came to forbid administrative market roles to women, because they were considered inappropriate for the female sex by European standards.

Among the Africans with the longest contact with Europeans were the Akans, who traded successively with Portuguese, Dutch, English, French, Danish, and Swedish merchants on the coast of what is now Ghana. A class of wealthy Africans, women and men, developed out of this trade. (African men quickly adapted to the trader role earlier associated with women, once they discovered how lucrative it was.) These wealthy Africans sent their children to the schools built by the Christian missionaries who followed the European traders as the Moslem holy men had followed the Arab traders. The Christian schools educated both sexes. This is one of the rare instances where traditional African values coincided with a set of congruent European values, in this case values carried by feminist Christian missionaries. The resulting African professional class, strongly marked by European culture, from the beginning included African women. This created a new class of women, distinct both from the traditional African and the traditional European. These women were the primary initiators of coco farming. They also became successful businesswomen in the new international trading arena, and successful professionals. In various ways women's traditional roles translated into modern ones, though always in the face of resistance from European men and Europeanized African men. The most Western-oriented women might face the greatest status deprivations, pushed to accept dependent roles by virtue of their adoption of Western life styles as the wives of professional men (Oppong, 1974: 118). The less Westernized ones succeeded in expanding their commercial domain. The Nigerian Omu Okwei, the "merchant queen" of Ossonari (1872-1943), is an example of the success women could obtain who did not permit themselves to be placed in dependent Western-style sex roles. Omu Okwei amassed a large fortune and was elected the last market queen of Ossonari, chairwoman of the Council of Mothers (Ekejiuba, 1967). During her lifetime, however, the supervision of markets was transferred from the Council of Mothers to the city council under the pressure of the British.

A culture as rich in active roles for women as the African market culture does not simply disappear in the face of an alien intrusion. The women's councils kept on meeting, and when the occupying colonial government appeared to threaten their economic welfare, as in the case of the famous taxation issue in Owerri Province of Nigeria in 1929, the women's council network could bring thousands of women to the colonial administrative headquarters for demonstrations. Sylvia Leith-Ross' study of Ibo women gives a sensitive picture both of the 1929 uprising of women and of the women's councils as they carried on their traditional responsibilities in the face of increasing European constraints. In describing a council meeting she refers to "that curious sense one so often had among Ibo women of private and independent lives, an existence of their own lived quite apart from home and husband and children" (1939: 118), which she finds herself powerless to understand in spite of the common bond of sex. If an empathic Britishwoman could not understand it, we must not be surprised that European men could not understand it. She also mentions the large number of women who lived alone, whether married or widowed, and finds it difficult to understand that this is taken for granted by African women, who simply assume that women living alone can manage their own lives (1939: 94).

Rural women in all parts of Africa were having serious problems by the end of the nineteenth century that they did not have two hundred years before. Soil depletion, deforestation, and the introduction of cash cropping laid heavy additional work burdens on women. They had to work harder to grow food, walk further for fuel, and carry more water for the larger cash-crop fields that were increasingly managed by men, making the profits unavailable to the women (Boulding, 1975; White, Bradley, and White, 1972; and Boserup, 1970). At the same time economic conditions were pushing the men to worksites far away, to cities, to mines, to plantations, making them unavailable for any kind of help on the farm. The separation of rural and urban women's associations has meant that only recently are these problems being tackled on a scale that may bring some relief.

Today the women's councils are taking a new lease on life as women realize these councils are a useful tool in dealing with their economic problems. At the same time, since these councils in no way parallel the modern male governing councils in function, women also are seeking and gaining positions in male political bodies at every level. Some aberrant things are happening in the process, however. Thus, we find the shadow of the *kabaka* pattern without the accompanying legitimacy of supporting community consensus, in the tendency of rulers to place their wives, sisters, and daughters in positions of political power in a "dynastic family" approach that is neither traditional nor modern. The "Kenyatta dynasty" in Kenya and the "Bandareika dynasty" in Sri Lanka have both placed a number of women in positions of family-derived power. This pattern enhances the position of elite women at the expense of the participation of other classes of society. On the other hand, it does also utilize available skills. Active leadership by wives of traditional leaders is another commonly found pattern, and it provides a more direct link between traditional and modern practices. An example of this type of leadership at its best, one of many such examples, is that of Mrs. Anna Angwafo of West Cameroon. The daughter of a priest and the wife of a *fon* (traditional ruler), she has become a key agent in rural development programs in West Cameroon (Matheson, 1970).

The trading women in African towns may be the most effective modernizers in Africa. They are translating a whole range of traditional women's associations into modern organizations that provide them with capital, social insurance, and outlets for their social and religious needs (Little, 1973). A variety of women's cooperatives handle both rural and urban needs. Links between rural and urban women's associations are still weak, but urban women have discovered how to link their traditional organizations with the international world of the women's NGOs (transnational nongovernmental associations), thus tapping both economic and political opportunities in a wider arena.

North Africa has a substantially different character and racial composition from the rest of Africa. Algeria, Morocco, and Tunisia are the sites of the trading cities of ancient Phoenicia, a terrain well worked over by all the trading civilizations of the Mediterranean for at least a millennium before Roman times, and then ruled by Rome after the defeat of Carthage. Egypt and the kingdoms of the Sudan and Axum (Ethiopia) belong to the most ancient of civilizations. By the time Moslem rule came to North Africa these societies were already experienced in many types of political and economic organization.

Because the North African coast has been the scene of so many migrations and conquests, almost every kind of tradition of the participation of women has at one time or another been found there. The Berber tradition contains many variations from tribe to tribe, and these include the possibility of women rising to power and influence as magicians, saints, and mystics. The Berber Kabyles still have shrines to their holy women Lalla Imma Tifellut, Lalla Tawritt, Lalla

Imma Mr'ita, Lalla Imma Wachaa, and Lalla Imma Mimen (Gordon, 1968: 10). All-women's religious orders arose in this context. Berber women of the Aures and Shawia women had a great deal of freedom, and a Shawia woman, widowed or divorced, could adopt a special position as *azriya* (free woman), which enabled her to live independently more or less as a courtesan. The Tuareg were the freest of all; women were the writers, musicians, and administrators of community wealth. Nail women have been professional prostitutes in the cities of the Sahara for centuries, and were women of wealth, dignity, and status before European tourists came on the scene.

The interaction of tribal and urban ways, while it may have intensified the Moslem practices of seclusion beyond what obtained elsewhere, as Tillion (in Gordon, 1968) suggests, also brought powerful women into the politics of Islam. Queens and princesses thread their way through the politics of the North as well as in sub-Saharan Africa. Nevertheless, as the veil spread everywhere, middle-class urban women were increasingly secluded. The gradual elaboration of more extreme seclusion practices in parts of the Moslem world after the eleventh century, coinciding with a period of economic development and prosperity, led to an urban purdah culture for the middle and upper classes, in North Africa and elsewhere. Purdah foreshadowed the withdrawal of women from the labor force that industrialization brought about much later for Western women of the same classes.[4]

Nevertheless, women's communication networks brought news of the world into their underlife spaces. Elizabeth Cooper (1915), writing at the beginning of this century, describes what a strong women's culture can develop even under the most confining conditions. It is clear that there was a great deal of visiting between houses. Pilgrimages to the tombs of saints, going to the women's section of the local mosque, frequent visits to the baths, trips to market on special days for women, and going on all-women's expeditions to nearby parks or woods, all provided additional opportunities for communication.

The fact that women played a crucial part in the liberation struggles of a number of countries with strong seclusionary practices indicates that women do participate in the ongoing life of a society, even from purdah. The underlife is strong. The two Algerian revolutionary heroines, Djamila Bouhired and Djamila Boupacha, were not mutants. They were only more articulate representatives of thousands of women who became coolheaded terrorists carrying bombs under their *burkas*, women who withstood torture without a

word when caught, women who identified completely with the cause
of liberation. Repeated raping did not break them. They were tough
(see the account of Algerian women in the revolution in Gordon,
1968). The fact that after the revolution women were forced back
into purdah indicates that it takes extraordinary physical and moral
energy to overleap the barriers to public participation, and that such
energy cannot be easily sustained after a revolution. During a revolution participation is made easy by the men of a society because they
need their women on the battlefield. Afterward, doors that were
opened for women may be shut again.

West Asia

In West Asia, the heartland of Islam, there are traditions of male-
female economic partnership as strong as those of any African
country, side by side with the practice of seclusion of women.
From 981 to 1278 there were a series of decrees progressively
limiting women's public appearances and dictating how they could
dress. In 1030, Abbasid Qadir b'Ullah banned women from public
ceremonies. Nevertheless, there was a great variety in the patterning
of women's life from one country to another depending on the mix
of pre-Islamic traditions and the character of the Moslem colonial
occupiers. The Turks retained some of the earlier freedom for
women from their nomadic days. The princesses of the Seljuk Turks
in the tenth to thirteenth centuries built hospitals and schools in the
tradition of urban princesses everywhere (Afetinan, 1962: 23). The
tombs of the princesses may be visited on pilgrimage today. Upper-
class women were ladies of learning, like Muneccime Hatun, a lady
astronomer at the Seljuk court.

The sixteenth century Mongol invasions were hard on the succeeding Ottoman Empire (1299-1918) and contributed to the seclusion
practices which increasingly affected the status of Turkish women.
Middle-class families copied upper-class practices of having separate
women's quarters in the homes. It was stylish, and it was safer.
Queens remained active, however. Bibi Khanam, Tamerlane's queen,
did much to rebuild what her Mongol husband ruthlessly destroyed,
and her tomb at Samarkand was still an object of veneration at the
beginning of this century. Gouhan Shad, the wife of Timur's son and
successor, was also of Bibi's caliber, and many of the mosques and
colleges destroyed by the Mongols were restored with her help
(Ali, 1899: 766). Such women were in no way secluded from the
realities of their societies.

Segregation was hardest for middle-class women. Working-class women continued to go about their traditional labor. One new occupation for women was that of vaccinator. The practice of vaccination against smallpox spread to England when Lady Montagu reported it in her travel letters. There was also a class of trading women, in the Mediterranean woman-merchant tradition. Among the upper classes, there were writers, poets, and musicians: Zeynep Hatun (d. 1474); Fahrinusa Mihri Hatun (d. 1522); and a series of women in a great lyric tradition, the Divan, that lasted until the mid-nineteenth century. Some of these women lived in Dervish convents that may have paralleled the convents of Europe as centers for gifted women, though in the West little is known about them.

The status of women was not high in the Ottoman court, however, and the royal harem was filled with slave concubines. No sultan raised any woman in his harem to the status of queen between 1403 and 1541. At that date the Russian slave Roxelana persuaded the sultan to marry her and received the title "Sultan Valide." Roxelana began what Penzer calls "the rule of women" in the empire, and he suggests that for the next one hundred-fifty years women had the major political power. One such woman ruler, Safieh, is supposed to have corresponded with Catherine de Medici to keep the Turks from war with Venice (Penzer, 1935: 187).

The freedom of women in Constantinople, much envied by women elsewhere in the Moslem world in the nineteenth century (Ali, 1899: 773), is hard to relate to the practice of rigid purdah, and is one more evidence that women found ways to be active in spite of sequestration customs. The fact, mentioned before, that boys were reared in the women's quarters at least until the age of seven meant that women had a chance to train boys to respect them, and that boys saw women as autonomous actors in the harem world, the only world the boys knew, during their most formative years. An account of the education of boys in the Ottoman Empire in 1604 mentions that boys stayed in the harem until they were eleven, though a male tutor came in from outside for their fifth to eleventh years. Eleven years is a long time to live in the women's world (Penzer, 1935: 128). It was essentially through their harem tutelage of boy rulers that women seized political power in the period ushered in by Roxelana.

European colonization of some West Asian countries on the one hand spurred an intensification of purdah practices to protect native women from Westerners, and on the other hand set countercurrents in motion as women missionaries from Europe arrived to open schools for Asian girls. An indigenous reform movement in many

Asian countries also began in the mid-nineteenth century. Attention focused on cases like the Constantinople factory girls with working hours from 4 a.m. to 8 p.m.—a replication of the European story (M. E. Burton, 1918: 46). This reform movement also involved providing schools for women. Turkey began a major program for women in 1869. Many extraordinary women entered public life in the latter part of the nineteenth century, demonstrating once again what a high level of readiness can exist in a purdah society. Among many distinguished women, one of the best known and most widely read outside Turkey is Halide Edib, fighter in the revolution, active in international diplomacy, leader in developing a national education system for women, social philosopher, innovator of social services, and novelist. The *Memoirs* (Edib, 1926) of this outstanding "peace heroine" of the turbulent turn of the century make moving reading. She describes reading bloody martial histories of her people as a child and wondering what children did in those times. Did they go out to play? The roster of activist women visionaries like Edib is far longer than we shall ever know.

There is a series of photographs in Woodsmall (1960) of the women leaders who have been active since the turn of the century in Turkey and other West Asian countries. Looking at those intent, self-confident faces it would be hard to believe that these are women who have emerged from centuries of purdah, if we did not know that purdah involves an active underlife.[5] The bathhouse alone probably fomented more than one revolution.

Persia, traditionally one of the more seclusionary of the West Asian societies, has its share of stories of women's activism. In 1861 government officials were profiteering from a famine, keeping food prices astronomically high. The word went out through the women's networks and thousands of women came out of seclusion to surround the carriage of the shah when he was returning from a hunting trip one day, to demand action in the food crisis. The thoroughly startled shah promised to meet the demands the women made—and did (Cooper, 1915: 35-36). Another story that lifts the tip of the purdah veil to give a glimpse of the life underneath comes from 1911, when Russia threatened Persia's sovereignty in an ultimatum to the National Assembly. Three hundred veiled women marched out from the harems of Teheran to the assembly and demanded admittance. They confronted the president,

> tore aside their veils, and confessed their decision to kill their own
> husbands and sons and add their own bodies to the sacrifice, if the

deputies should waver in their duty to uphold the liberty and dignity
of the Persian people and nation (M. E. Burton, 1918: 171).

Many of the women held pistols under their skirts or in the folds of
their sleeves, says Burton.

Persia was also the scene of the persecution of thousands of
women followers of the sect of Baha Ullah in the same century.
Cooper tells the story of one fragile-looking woman who was forced
to witness the beheading of her fourteen-year-old son, and then had
the son's head thrown in her lap by the executioner. After holding
the head for a long moment in prayer, the mother flung it back to
the executioner, saying "I do not take back what I give my God"
(Cooper, 1915: 37). Women who lived in purdah were not necessarily sheltered, not necessarily timid, and certainly not necessarily
ignorant.

India, like Turkey, developed a rigidly seclusionary set of institutions that overlaid ancient traditions of public participation of
women in society. The freer Vedic traditions were not totally abrogated by the Laws of Manu, composed in the early centuries A.D.,
nor were the laws in themselves entirely destructive toward women.
As Romila Tharpar says, the laws were originally written to preserve
some of the finer values of Hindu society, and "the rigid application
of ill-digested ideas, taken from this book, led to the emergence of a
society which . . . ended up by becoming a minor hell for some of its
members" (Tharpar, 1963: 473). The customs of child marriage and
suttee, self-immolation of the widow on her husband's funeral pyre,
became some of the features of this "minor hell." If anything, the
modernizing elite of Islam which took over in the 800s somewhat
improved the status of women, in that Islam provided property rights
for women which they had not had before. On the other hand they
also introduced purdah (the women's quarters are called *zenana* in
India) which added to Indian women's other disabilities the handicap of total sequestration for some castes.

That elite women suffered relatively little from the sequestration
is suggested by the activities in the early 1600s of the Persian woman
Mehr un-Nissa. She came as a refugee to the court of the Mongol
emperor Akbar in India with her parents and after many adventures
married Akbar's successor, Jehangir. Known in history as Nur Jehan,
Mehr un-Nissa was the virtual ruler of India, and was responsible for
reforms including the forbidding of some Hindu practices of mutilation (Akbar, her father-in-law, had forbidden *suttee*). Ali describes
a number of daughters and wives of emperors who were gifted in

the arts, as political leaders, and who lived active public lives (1899: 770-772).

Although India had several sets of colonizers through the centuries, each imposing their own patterns, the Indian working-class woman labored changelessly, with a veil handy to pull over her face if men were nearby. Working women crushed stones for road making, labored in the rice fields, tended the silkworms, and later worked long hours in the textile factories. Children worked with their mothers, in field and factory. After 1600 the last wave of occupiers, the British, steadily encroached on the country, laying a London-based administrative system on the ancient empire they did not understand. Maharanis and maharajas kept what control they could. Warrior Maratha princesses rode against the British with their armies, but to no avail. The eighteenth century saw a succession of very able Maratha queens: Tarabai of Kolhapur, Anubai of Ichalkaranji, twenty-four-year-old Ahalyabai (Altekar, 1956: 189).

> An Anglo Indian officer of long standing had observed to J. S. Mill that if a Hindu principality was vigilantly and economically governed, if order was preserved without oppression, if cultivation was extending and people prosperous, in three cases out of four he found it to be under a woman's rule (Altekar, 1956: 189).

Indian girls of the upper classes had always been tutored at home. When Christian mission schools for girls were started by the British, an indigenous schooling movement also developed that gave Indian girls education without the background pressure of conversion. This movement spread rapidly across India, and many home-tutored Indian ladies found an outlet for their talents as teachers. By the 1800s schools and new types of social services of every kind were being formed at a very rapid rate, as world-wide stirrings of women and men were translated into Indian needs. The unsuccessful revolt of 1857 was followed by the formation of the Indian National Congress in 1885, events which brought women increasingly into public life. There were violent and nonviolent branches of the independence movement, and women were active in both. By the 1930s the nonviolent movement was clearly identified with Gandhi. He is given credit for "mobilizing the women of India" since they played such an active role in his *satyagraha* campaigns. They often were in the very front row in protest demonstrations, and were shot down by the British on more than one occasion. While Gandhi deserves full credit for recognizing the part that women could play and encouraging this, more account should be taken of the readiness of the women themselves. Gandhi did not simply "drag the women folk of India from their kitchens into the public life of India" (Guba, 1973: 18), he provided an opportunity for women to carry their concerns from the underlife to the overlife of society.

The women who chose the terrorist route had no protective spokesmen, only their own commitment. Like their European, African, and Asian sisters who chose that route, they were coolheaded. The district magistrate of Comilla was assassinated by two young women, and there were numerous other attacks by women including one on the governor of Bengal in the senate hall of Calcutta, and a second on the same governor on the polo grounds in Darjeeling (Guba, 1973: 22). Many women went underground to continue their activities, unhindered by the jail terms regularly meted out to Gandhi and his followers. Among those who went underground were some who are still leaders of the radical wing of the women's movement in India today, like Asaf Ali. She belongs to that generation of older women revolutionaries found on all continents, trained in the demanding turn-of-the-century struggles, and still working at a pace that few younger women could manage.

When Gandhi went to jail in 1939 in the civil disobedience involving breaking the salt laws, Sarojini Naidu took the leadership of the movement. Poet Sarojini, "the nightingale of India," was one of the four women presidents of the Indian National Congress. Annie Besant, the English labor leader turned mystic who settled in India, was the first, in 1917; Naidu was the second, in 1925; Nellie Sengupta was the third, in 1933; and Indira Gandhi the fourth, in 1959. (She became prime minister in the late 1960s.) Women have served as state governors, as foreign ambassadors to major powers, as ministers in the national cabinet, as justices of the supreme court, and generally have had a distinguished record of public service. Some of them have combined government service with a long record of revolutionary activity and international work in the peace movement. Sushila Nayar, Gandhi's disciple as a teenager and his physician as a young woman, served later as minister of health for independent India, and as international vice-president of the Women's International League for Peace and Freedom. A special combination of gentleness and toughness, and a commanding physical presence, characterized all these women.

Some of the women associated with Gandhi, such as Kamaladehvi, came from the matrilineal societies of South India, where even today women are more active and visible than elsewhere. Kamaladehvi, a national leader in the promotion of craft enterprises in the Gandhian tradition, reminisces about her grandmother who used to hold a salon every afternoon for the intellectual enlightenment of the men of the community. The women of her family were traditionally educated at home; and Kamaladehvi grew up taking women's dignity and civic responsibility for granted (Kamaladehvi, 1974).

Another important and not yet evaluated contribution to the general activism of Indian women is coming from the tribal sector, which, in a category referred to as "the scheduled tribes, the scheduled castes, and other backward classes," represents about 25 percent of India's population (Pritam Singh, 1974). The tribal women, who have much more personal freedom than other Indian women do, are considered "immoral and backward." Their freer, more outspoken ways often cause havoc when they enter the university, as they are being encouraged to do at present. University administrators are sometimes hard pressed to know how to deal with them. Most middle-class women's organizations in India see them as a problem, not a resource.[6]

Another set of traditional castes that are now insisting on recognition in modern India are the castes whose traditional occupation has been prostitution. The Nautch women, courtesans traditionally under the special protection of the ruling class, and temple dancing girls all had an accepted social status. These women were well educated and had a great deal of personal freedom. In 1961, when the Allahabad city police tried to close down houses of prostitution, the prostitutes petitioned the higher court, stating that

> prostitution was their traditional occupation, that the order of the lower court to evict them from their ancestral homes was against the fundamental rights of citizens guaranteed by the Constitution of India (Thomas, 1964: 380).

In emphasizing the activist women of India there is a danger of making the abandonment of purdah seem too easy. Cora Vreede-De Stuers' study of Moslem women in Northern India, *Parda* (1968), brings out both the strength and the helplessness of women bound by the system, and also points to its value as an affirmation of cultural autonomy. The concept of "*zenana* modernization" which she uses describes a wholly different concept of modernization than Westerners are accustomed to.

Another perspective on the purdah issue relates to the feelings of psychological security that seclusion and the veil afford. Taking the step of leaving the secluded quarters, and even more, of taking off the veil, may be physically agonizing for women. It appears that the equivalent effort for the average American middle-class woman would be to walk down the street stark naked. Socialization to seclusion is powerful and lifelong, and cannot easily be abandoned. The level of effort expended and the sheer physical courage displayed by women in leaving purdah should command our profound respect.[7] The not infrequent use of dark glasses by women of the Middle East who have left purdah suggests that a similar practice among some "emancipated" Euro-American women may have common psychological roots.

When English women began coming to India in the 1800s on the wave of the new consciousness about world problems and women's problems, they first found allies among the educated Indian elite and then gradually also among middle-class women who had already left purdah, or were about to. The Indian suffrage movement was already well equipped to tackle the complex legislative work required to remove the numerous restrictions on women by the time the European allies arrived. The new international organizations the European women brought to India, the YWCA, the WCTU, and others, provided an additional set of tools for Indian women. They were particularly useful for middle- and working-class urban girls in the labor force. Residence and training centers sprang up in many places, linking with the larger enterprise of teacher training and establishing a national education for women.

Yet one must be realistic, and recognize that in the midst of all this activity, traditional attitudes toward the relative importance of girl and boy babies still operate today to reduce the life chances of Indian baby girls. They are not as important as their brothers, and it is the mothers who enforce these differential values. In figure 12-1 we find a picture of a young, alert-looking Indian mother and her older son holding two-year-old twins on their laps. The twin on the left is a girl, on the right, a boy. "The difference in their condition is entirely due to the fact that the boy was nursed first and fed first, his sister getting what was left over. Even here in the clinic, the mother (and the brother) . . . are lavishing their attention on the crying baby, while the apathetic little girl is scarcely noticed" (UNICEF News, 1973).

This is one of the background realities that must be kept in mind as we turn to the all-important involvement of Indian women in world affairs. Hunger at home must be dealt with, yet it is also true that the international participation of women is crucial to the future of the world. The high level of readiness of Indian women to enter international affairs is an important aspect of twentieth century life.

Figure 12-1. *Indian Mother with Twins: A Girl and a Boy*

Some of the leading women figures on the world stage in this century have been Indian: Vijaya Lakshmi Pandit, Indian ambassador to both the United States and the Soviet Union and active in many international organizations, was president of the United Nations General Assembly in its eighth session; Rajkumari Amrit Kaur, former minister of health of India, was president of the World Health Organization; Mrs. Lakshmi Menon, at one time deputy minister of external affairs for India, was former chief of the United Nations Section on the Status of Women. These women, with countless others, gave leadership to the formation of the All-India Women's Conference and the mobilization of many thousands of women into community activity. Among the many examples of this mobilization activity is Tara Bai, former president of a women's college, who has served on the planning boards of many of India's welfare ventures, and has developed with the help of a group of women volunteers a series of experimental children's villages for homeless children to be extended over as much of India as possible. A second example is a group of Delhi women, both professional educators and community volunteers, who have developed a program of schools on trucks that visit the construction sites all over Delhi where children of the migrant construction workers live and work with their parents. This is the first time education has ever reached the children of these workers, and the plan is to be extended.

Because of the sheer size of India, the basic organizational work for any activity of national scope takes a skill, toughness, and endurance unimaginable to the average woman activist of the West. Whatever history's final judgment on Indira Gandhi will be, her decisive rule in a turbulent time for India is another notable example of that toughness.

China

China is giant India's giant sister, with even more massive problems of scale to cope with. The mutually antagonistic traditions of Confucianism and Taoism have created the same ambiguity about the status of women in China that the Vedic tradition versus the Laws of Manu created in India. The elitist tradition of Confucianism placed women in a position of semislavery with the rule of "thrice-obeying" (*san tsung*), which in practice meant lifelong sequestration within doors, and lifelong obedience to men, successively to father, husband, and son. The folk tradition of Taoism on the other hand encouraged the participation of women in community life. China has a long history of secret societies among the peasantry, associated with Taoism, and women have been accepted in these societies as members and as leaders. Some of the women leaders of the twentieth century revolution in China came directly out of these societies. Another source of strong women's leadership in China has come from the nomadic tribes, which from China's earliest existence have alternated periods of peaceful coexistence with episodes of war and conquest. The roles of Mongol women were described in chapter 7. China probably has the same proportion of tribal population as India has, up to 25 percent. Over the centuries these peoples have provided a pool of potential women activists. China, like India, still tends to think of its tribal population as "backward," and regards the tribal women as needing emancipation.

Since Confucianism was the belief system of the ruling elite and Taoism the belief system of the peasants, the participation of women stemmed more from peasant than elite traditions. Ancient China was matrilineal. The shamaness and leadership traditions of women were apparently buried in the folk culture, there to stay alive for centuries. I do not have the historical materials for verification of the dates when women's leadership went underground into the folk culture, but reigning empresses in the early centuries A.D. have been noted. The status of women went up and down through the centuries depending on the extent of order or anarchy, war or peace. By the end of the first millennium during the Sung dynasty, there was a period of reform decrees giving greater freedom to women, only to be followed by the Chin dynasty, during which all reformers were abolished and foot binding began. Foot binding was practiced by the middle and upper classes, and as long as the practice was confined to women who had no need to labor, the suffering involved was "minimal." When lower-class families, ambitious to marry a daughter into the middle class, began binding the feet of their girls in hopes of snaring better husbands for them, the full extent of the cruelty of the practice became evident. Few of these girls succeeded in "marrying up," and there are many pitiful accounts of women laborers tottering on stumps in the fields of China, even women drawing canal barges, stumbling along on bound feet. The suffering of working-class women in China was more severe than anywhere else in the world, partly because of the tendency of foot binding to penetrate into working-class culture.

In spite of, or perhaps because of these widespread atrocities, there seems to have been a women's movement among women of the lower gentry and upper peasantry from the Ming dynasty (1368-1644) on, accompanied by widespread literacy:

> In the sixteenth century widespread female literacy provoked men for the first time to perceive not the equality of women but their comparability, and to ask just how, given these obvious talents, they differed from men. These questions once articulated during the late Ming, continued to worry writers during the Ch'ing (Handlin, as quoted in Wolf and Witke, 1975: 16).

Women of the lower gentry became increasingly active during the Ch'ing dynasty (1644-1911). Not allowed into the clan schools giving special training for the mandarinate, they nevertheless were taught in small family classes for girls only. By the 1880s they were being reached by the same influences and movements, somewhat differently channeled, that women in the rest of Asia and Africa were experiencing. The birth of the modern women's movement in China may be associated with the 1898 reform movement, which from the beginning linked the "woman question" with nationalism (Rankin, in Wolf and Witke, 1975).

It is not easy to explain the strength of the women's movement in China in the 1920s except by postulating some kind of interaction in previous centuries between women in the peasant movements, women of the lower gentry, and women of the upper gentry. In the case of upper-gentry women, their husbands were government officials in the mandarin system and by the rules of the imperial bureaucracy were not allowed to serve in their home districts. This meant that the wife of such an official, remaining behind in the clan home, would through most of her adult life be in charge of a large household of hundreds of persons, counting relatives, children, servants, slaves, and concubines (Ayscough, 1937). Her household was closely linked with other households in possibly hundreds of other villages within the clan organization. Thus no amount of formal edicts about women being concerned with the indoors only (as stated in the *Record of Rites,* Ayscough, 1937: 54) could keep women with that extent of responsibility from being extremely knowledgeable about clan and district affairs and very probably about national affairs.

Women of the lower gentry probably were the schoolteachers for the girls in the households of the upper gentry, as well as the counselors and helpers to the women of the peasantry. This counselor-helper role is a traditional role for the lower gentry in China, and might be something like the lady-of-the-manor-house role we noted in England. Yung-Teh Chow's *Social Mobility in China* (1966) makes clear how some of the male lower gentry assisted the peasantry during the revolution, but scarcely mentions the women of the lower gentry. A study of such women is overdue.

Women who could play go-between roles, either from the upper peasantry or the lower gentry to the peasantry, would include nuns from the Buddhist and Taoist orders, who did a great deal of house to house visiting and teaching as part of their religious role; female professors of divination, professors of spiritual manifestations, and praying women (probably terms for various types of shamanesses); marriage go-betweens; herbalists; and midwives. "In a learned Chinese tome is written:'Whoever has these mischief-makers about his home is sure to meet trouble'" (Ayscough, 1937: 87). This reference suggests that the activities of these more mobile women did not go unnoticed by men.

When Ch'iu Chin, China's "first woman revolutionary," began lecturing against foot binding and started a girls' school in about 1900, she was "standing on the shoulders of giants"[8]—the hundreds of thousands of Chinese women, peasants and gentry, who through the centuries had nourished a vision of women's participation in society. She was a member of a secret revolutionary organization of both men and women, in the old tradition, and trained in sword play. She was also the first woman to join Sun Yat Sen's party, formed in 1904, and did much of the organizing work for it. She set up a headquarters in Shanghai for all the secret societies committed to revolution, and was at one time injured by an explosion while supervising the assembly of a bomb. In 1906 she started the *Chinese Women's Journal* to rally women to the revolution. She formed a people's army in the same year, using the secret societies as military contingents. This mother of two young children was beheaded by the Manchu in 1907, at the age of thirty-three, after extreme torture during which she uttered no word but wrote out seven characters as a "confession": "Autumn rain and autumn wind sadden us."

The roster of women revolutionaries in China since 1907 is so immense that there is no possibility of conveying in a few words what has gone on in the past three-quarters of a century. By 1925, when Anna Louise Strong visited China, there were already mass organizations of women. One federation of groups was organized under the women's branch of the Kuomintang, Sun Yat Sen's then revolutionary organization; another set was organized within the trade union movement; and the third (and smallest) was organized under the political department of the army. These were in addition to organizations of women and men together. In 1927 there were "nearly a million and a half women in over ten provinces . . . in some kind of organization under the leadership of the Kuomintang" (Strong, 1965: 103). How many women were organized into unions it is hard to estimate, but Strong addressed fifteen hundred union women in Canton in 1925. Four hundred noncombatant young women propagandists traveled with the army:

> Our work is to organize the women. For this we go into the homes and markets, wherever women are to be found, and talk with them. When we have talked enough, we organize a local women's union and leave it to handle affairs in that district (Strong, 1965: 104).

A study of the work of Helen Foster Snow (1967) on the participation of women in the revolution and in the establishment of the People's Republic of China gives some support to the hypothesis that women from the upper and lower gentry, peasant women, and tribal women shared leadership in the movement. The upper gentry could be represented by Soong Chingling, widow of Sun Yat Sen, "the nearest to a saint that any action has produced since Joan of Arc" (1967: 120) and the first woman Marxist in China. She was one of the famous Soong sisters. Her sisters Mayling and Eling joined the nationalist cause, Mayling as the wife of Chiang Kai Shek and Eling as wife of a conservative Chinese industrialist. All three were ordained to unusual activist roles, though in different causes, and have the double distinction of being directly descended from a sixteenth century imperial chancellor of Emperor Chung Chen and of coming from Hainan Island. Hainan is a Hakka tribal stronghold, and the sisters are supposed to have inherited some Hakka blood from their father, Charlie Soong. The Hakka tribal traditions are strong on the participation of women, and Soong *père* thus provided the hybrid vigor of tribal traditions for his daughters.

Ts'ai Ting-Li, communist leader in the area of the first Chinese soviet, could stand for the lower gentry. Her family were small land-lords and her mother was oppressed by her father's family in typical feudal manner:

> My earliest memory is of her reading to me many works of old fiction dealing with the suffering of people. . . . From her I received my own understanding of the problems of people other than myself and a tendency toward Christian humanitarianism (Wales, 1952: 200).

In 1926, at seventeen, Ts'ai Ting-Li went to Hailufeng to do "wom-en's work"—helping organize the Hailufeng Women's Peasant Union, the first all-women's union in China. She spent her life organizing women at the village level. She remarks how hard it is for intellec-tuals, whether men or women, to endure the physical hardship of the life of the peasant, and how often the peasants had to help and protect them (see Ting-Li's autobiography as recounted in Wales, 1951).

K'ang K'e-ching, a military commander known as the "Red Amazon," represents the peasantry. She was given away at birth in 1912, for her fisherfolk parents had no food. She joined the village women's peasant union at fourteen and became the communist youth inspector in a district of ten villages at the age of fifteen, though she was illiterate. At sixteen she joined the Red Army, and taught herself to read and write by reading billboards and studying slogans while on the march.

The role of tribal women in the revolution is suggested by the fact that Kwangtung Province, the land of the Hakkas, was the home of the T'aip'ing rebellion of 1852-1865; the home of the first soviet, or-ganized in 1927; and the home of Sun Yat Sen and of Soong Ching-ling. Some Chinese are proud of the Hakka tradition and of Hakka women, who did much of the work involved in setting up the first soviet. It was in the Hakka setting that the basis for the alliance of women peasantry and gentry was formed.

From the early 1920s on, intensive work was done among the

women of China by leaders from all classes. Tsai Chang, from the leading "great family" of old China and therefore top gentry, coordinated these efforts so that in the spring of 1949 the All-China Democratic Women's Federation was formed, "possibly the largest single mass organization and the most active one ever formed in the history of mankind" (Snow, 1967: 230). By 1956 it had seventy-six million women members, while the Chinese Communist party had less than eleven million members.

This federation was almost like a state within a state. It undertook the reform of marriage law and the liberation of slave women before the new communist state was established. It held courts, passed judgments, and opened training centers for women. When the new government was formed in Peking in the fall of 1949, members of the federation helped write the new constitution. Tsai Chang and two other women leaders sat on the presidium which formed the new government. When the People's Congress met in 1954, women constituted 14 percent of the membership elected by popular vote. In northern China some districts reported 40 percent of the elected officials to be women. Some women were heads of the town governments.   (Peking had a woman deputy mayor in the 1960s.) Land redistribution was a key part of the women's program, and the fact that land was assigned to *individuals,* women and men, may be the key to the success of the new society. Women for the first time had their share of control over significant productive resources.

The development of industrial cooperatives in China in 1938, well before the revolution, was largely the work of the Soong sisters (and, apparently, Helen Foster Snow). It was the success of that earlier movement, says Snow, that laid the groundwork for the rapid formation across China of cooperatives in every factory and workshop, establishing a pattern of local control that saved China from Soviet-style centralism. The agricultural commune was also a priority for the women's movement, and its great success in increasing productivity was only matched by its success in providing family and community services that enabled women to work and children to be well and healthy. Like land redistribution, the commune principle was basic to the liberation of women. It dealt with them as individuals, paid them as individuals, and treated the children of the community as a collective responsibility (Snow, 1967: 24-33, 168).

The Chinese women did not do this alone. One set of helps consisted of the vast complex of Christian missions administered from Western countries. For all their limitations, these missions brought to China concerned Western women who contributed substantially to the development of schooling for Chinese women. Margaret Burton's *Women Workers of the Orient,* written for the Central Committee on the United Study of Foreign Missions during World War I, shows both the strengths and weaknesses of the Western contribution. It was a plea for the continuation of the labors of peace in the spirit of women's internationalism of that era: "The world's to build anew—not Europe, nor America, nor Asia, but the *world*" (1918: 228).

The international women's movement was also active in China. When the Chinese Women's Federation was formed in 1949, the WCTU and the YWCA were affiliates. Chinese women were themselves internationally minded. In December 1949 the Women's Federation had the first "Bandung idea," and called a conference of the women of Asia. Delegates came to Peking from India, Burma, Indonesia, Iran, Israel, Korea, Lebanon, Malaya, Mongolia, Siam, Syria, Vietnam, the Soviet Union, and the Philippines. "Sororal" delegates appeared unofficially from Great Britain, Algeria, Cuba, Czechoslovakia, France, Holland, the Ivory Coast, and Madagascar (Snow, 1967: 22-23). The lone visitor from the United States was Eslanda Robeson, wife of the singer Paul Robeson.

With the increasing isolation of China from Western-based internationalism, largely through the influence of the United States, Chinese women had few international contacts outside the third world except through the socialist Women's International Democratic Federation. Western radical women were able to stay in touch with China through this organization and by various means of their own devising. Now that contacts are easier, a broader range of Western women are coming in touch again with Chinese women. The pattern of contact is different, but a few Western women like the American Anna Louise Strong, who edited *Letter from Peking* until she died at the close of the last decade, have helped to bridge the gap between the old and the new.

The women's movement in China had a setback after the first rush of progress. The inevitable male reaction set in. What is happening in the seventies, particularly to the role of women in the inner circles of power, is not clear at this writing. The beautifully produced magazine which was the voice of Chinese women to the women of the world, *Women of China,* stopped publication in 1966, and it has not yet been resumed. Knowing the history of the women's effort in China, however, and the strength of the local networks involved in the commune form of production, it seems unlikely that the old patriarchal system could ever fully reassert itself.[9]

There are many Asian countries that have not been touched on in this section, but space makes a further survey impossible. I particularly regret leaving out Japan, from which I have so many happy personal memories of the women's movement, and Indonesia, where women participated so actively in the independence movement in ways that paralleled the activities of Indian women. I regret most of all leaving out the remarkable story of the women of Vietnam, who have stayed courageously international throughout the entire tragedy of Western involvement in Indochina. The freer lives of the women of Burma, Thailand, Laos, and Cambodia, first glimpsed through Barbara Ward's *Women in the New Asia* (1963), must also go unrecorded. Because the flavor of life is so different in Asia, it will take another world history of women, one focused on Asia, to do justice to developments that have been sketched so briefly here.

Latin America

Studies of the status of women in Latin America, both before the arrival of the Spanish in 1500 and afterward, are urgently needed. Particularly needed are studies written from the Latin perspective. When North Americans write about Latin America—even women about women—a distortion effect seems to take over.[10] As Sylvia Leith-Ross (1939) recognized when she was among the Ibo, there are cultural differences which the "feminine bond" alone cannot cross. Because Latin American culture is also "American," and therefore supposedly close to North American culture, relatively few social scientists from the North discover and admit the profound gulf. Nora Scott Kinzer's honest description of that gulf in "Sexist Sociology" (1974) comes as a fresh wind into the pretensions of cross-cultural understanding.

General histories of pre-Hispanic Latin America indicate that the Incan and Aztec empires of Peru and Mexico were highly stratified societies with temple-palace complexes not unlike those of Egypt and Sumer. Robert Adams has in fact made a careful study of the similarities and differences between Mesopotamia and Mexico (Adams, 1966). Royal women were important in public rituals of ruling, and the Incas practiced brother-sister marriage in the manner of the Pharaohs. Women's temples governed by priestesses provided education and convent life for girls who came for brief periods or for a lifetime. There were various categories of priestesses and virgins, some with a special relationship to the ruler, as a part of his harem (Diffie, 1945: 176). Associated with the temples were large textile workshops with women workers, again on the pattern of Egypt. In the Incan empire these workshops ranged in size from five hundred women at Caxa to fifteen hundred women at Cuzco (Wittfogel, 1957). Women and men of the lower classes were ranged in a hierarchy of peasants, serfs, and slaves.

In areas not directly ruled by one of the native empires (the Incan hegemony reached from present Ecuador to Chile), tribal life was of a more egalitarian nature. Two glimpses of such tribes from early Spanish accounts show a relatively fluid division of labor, with weaving and pottery engaged in by women and men, depending on the region. Women were active in the markets. A chronicler comments that "the women were the ones who knew most about everything" (Diffie, 1945: 122, 129).

The Spanish arrived in Latin America a century before northern Europeans settled in North America. Although the conquistadores did not bring women with them in the initial invasions, colonists arrived in family groups with women as early as 1502. By 1530 the first of the women religious had arrived—Franciscan tertiaries who opened schools for girls. There was a feeling at first that it was not appropriate to have women from the enclosed orders in the new country, but by 1550 they were also establishing convents in the New World. By the end of the seventeenth century there were eighty or more convents from the various Spanish and Portuguese orders. The convents conducted schools for girls, and at first accepted all women equally, Spanish, Native American, African, slave, and free. Later they were compelled by the authorities to be selective and segregate their pupils.

Since the sixteenth century was a time of high culture in the Spanish convents, we can assume that some of these convents were centers of scholarship and culture in the New World. A hint of this is found in the story of Sor Juana Inez de la Cruz (1651-1695), sometimes called the first Latin American feminist. According to some accounts, she disguised herself as a boy in order to enter school in Mexico City as a child (Montoya, 1975). She entered a Jeronimite convent at eighteen and won renown as a painter, composer, scientist, mathematician, dramatist, poet, and theologian before she died at forty-four. Herbert (1965) ranks her with Leonardo da Vinci, Roger Bacon, and Newton as a scientist. A great synthesizer as well as creator of knowledge, she wrote in Latin, Portuguese, and Aztec as well as Spanish, and assembled a library of four thousand volumes, possibly the largest collection in the Americas at the time. De la Cruz's collected works (1951), available in Spanish, include *La Respuesta,* her spiritual autobiography. At the peak of her productivity, she was commanded by her religious superiors to stop writing and to dismantle her library, an order which she accepted as part of the discipline of the religious life. The ban was lifted eventually, but she died soon after, before she could return to her mental labors.

While Spanish and Portuguese settlers mixed freely with Indians and blacks in both concubinage and marriage, there was also a very clear-cut class society based on largely absentee ownership of haciendas and a nonworking Spanish upper class. While the indigenous peoples were badly exploited, as were the blacks imported as slaves, they were also protected by the missionary orders of priests in a way that did not happen in North America. This was partly because of the bull of Pope Alexander VI in 1493, which conferred on the Spanish and the Portuguese the right to evangelize the territories of the New World according to the line of demarcation he established. Alexander gave the crown the responsibility for "the preaching and diffusion of the Catholic Faith, so that Indians might be educated and live in peace and order" (Philip II, quoted in Houtart and Pin, 1965: 4). Blacks were also declared to be "sons of Adam," so that both Native Americans and blacks were treated as humans with souls to save. This modified their oppression, enabling enterprising urban Native Americans and blacks to obtain freedom and middle-class status.

Bowser provides examples of this from colonial Peru. Margareta, a slave freed by Diego de Almajio on his death, became a successful businesswoman who founded a convent in her former master's name and lent money to the Spanish Crown to defeat its enemies in a civil war (Bowser, 1974: chapt. 9). The general Spanish reluctance to engage in manual labor gave slaves ample opportunity to apprentice into all kinds of skilled crafts, and also to open their own businesses. By the seventeenth century some of them had already become a comfortable middle-class sector of Peruvian society. Spanish, Native American, and African artisans all took each other in as apprentices, male and female. Free black women were particularly successful with large inns and bakeries.

Deep religious sentiments were more common among Native American and black women than among men. Probably the nuns who taught and worked among the women touched their lives more intimately than the monks ever touched the lives of the men of a community. Many women of the poorer classes bequeathed whatever they had to the church.

When Inca-descended Cecilia Tupac Amaru and her brother José led the 1780 Indian revolt against the Spanish, Cecilia must have had women followers. That story has yet to be fully written. The rebellion was unsuccessful, and Cecilia died soon after being captured, whipped, and exiled. Apparently, many women served both on the battlefields and as spies and messengers in Argentina, Colombia, Mexico, Peru, and Brazil during the wars of independence in the early 1800s (Jaquette, 1973: 344-353). Gertrudis Bocanegra, a mestiza born in 1765, organized an underground army of women during the 1810 war of independence in Mexico. Taken prisoner by the government, she was tortured and publicly executed in 1817. Her particular contribution to Mexican society was the organization of schools for Native American children (Montoya, 1975). Juana Azurduy is one of the most famous of these heroines, and fought by her husband's side with her own Amazon corps for the independence of what is now Bolivia. Juana Robles was the slave-heroine of Argentinian independence. Women revolutionaries played many different kinds of roles, and each had her own style. Isolated examples of battlefield heroism, and the more general, total-commitment revolutionary activity of Flora Tristan Moscosa, the half-Peruvian Frenchwoman who spent some time in Peru on behalf of the workers' international, represent the two extremes of revolutionary style.

Tristan Moscosa felt very alienated from the Peruvian *salonières* she found on her visit, and denounced these women as not living in the real world. The nineteenth century *veladas,* or salons, of Lima, Santiago, and Buenes Aires were widely criticized in their own time and since. It is not clear that they were as totally insulated from pressing social problems as they have been accused of being. According to Chaney (1973: 333-334), the *veladas* of Lima in the 1870s and '80s were feminist and dealt with social-justice issues including the situation of the Native American. Many prominent *velada* women were widows or had remained unmarried, as was true of many of the first university women. One reason they have been so much criticized is that they made a place for themselves outside the familistic structures of Spanish-American society.

It will have to be left to the scholars of Latin American history to begin presenting the underside so that we have a better picture of women in that history. A reading of the articles in Pescatello's *Female and Male in Latin America* (1973) suggests that there is a lot of demythologizing to do before the underside becomes clear. On the one hand there is the conventional picture of the machismo culture, with the women as submissive, dependent creatures who live out their lives in male-dominated cultures. On the other hand there is the picture of marianismo, the other side of the machismo coin, which suggests that it is the female after all who is dominant. From the marianismo perspective the macho males are perpetual children, and must be protected and cared for by women who strive for an ideal characterized by "semidivinity, moral superiority and spiritual strength. This spiritual strength engenders abnegation, that is, an indefinite capacity for humility and sacrifice" (Stevens, 1973: 94). According to the marianismo doctrine, Latin American women are ruthless with their daughters and daughters-in-law to ensure continuance of this ideal of sacrificial moral superiority.

Both machismo and marianismo exist in some form in almost every culture on every continent, distorted remnants of ancient myths. They represent some failure in social maturity with their deliberately maintained distortion of both the male and the female personality in the interests of maintaining a mutual dependency that might be maintained in healthier, more fulfilling ways. Whether Latin American culture represents some unique embodiment of these machismo-marianismo tendencies I very much doubt. Evelyn Stevens sees these culture traits as originating in the southern European, Middle Eastern, and North African honor and shame cultures, and states that "the fully developed syndrome occurs only in Latin America" (1973: 91). I suspect rather that the peculiar distorting mirror that keeps northerners from accurately seeing Latin social roles and values gives the machismo-marianismo syndrome a prominence it does not properly deserve.

It is clear that there has been a long history of both political and professional activity on the part of Latin American women. The world feminist movement of the 1880s reached women who had already fought the independence battles their other third world sisters were just beginning to fight. Many writers on economic development have commented on how Latin America seems to be out of rhythm with the world development clock. It started "take-off" in the 1850s, and remains "at take-off" today. Many things have been invoked to account for this, including the church and the hacienda culture. Domination from the North is rarely included in the standard list of explanations. Before this century is out, some new patterns may emerge in spite of efforts from the North to keep Latin America as its feudal domain.

Latin American feminism is an intact tradition. Maria Alvarado in Peru and Amanda Labarca in Chile appeared to be carrying on lonely feminist battles in the early part of this century, but the work of mobilization continues. There is a radical network covering the continent, which as yet has few spokeswomen to the outside world. The liberal wing of the women's movement is as important as the radical wing, and its voice is heard through the Latin American women who are active in the world of women's international non-governmental organizations. The alliance of women of North and South America is a frustrating one, as the League of Women Voters discovered during its program of developing women's centers in certain Latin American countries in recent years. Reports of that project make it clear that the women of the two cultures are speaking different conceptual languages, responding to different aspects of reality. When the Latin American women speak, they are not "heard."

The first Inter-American Congress of Women held in Havana in 1923 used the theme of social motherhood in approaching the problem of women's roles in public life—the extension of women's family role to the community. This is not a special Latino device, stemming from a macho culture, but the lever with which women on every continent have pried themselves loose from privatized roles. As recently as 1965 Margaret Mead and other women, myself included, were speaking to International Cooperation Year audiences of women on the theme of "women as the world's housekeepers," trying to persuade them that the work of opposing militarism and building a peaceful world was but a logical extension of their housewifely roles. This was shortly before the women's liberation movement began. Few American women activists would use that language today.

Time moves faster than it used to. We have to tune in to all the nuances of the social motherhood theme at the same time that we tune into the Tanias of the guerrilla movements in Latin America and elsewhere. Tania, Argentinian-born Tamara Bunke, was "called" to the revolutionary role in her early teens when her family was living in East Germany. After some years of training to be a guerrilla, training which required keen intelligence, great self-discipline, and much travel in Europe and Latin America, she was in the end trapped and killed in a police ambush with Che Guevara in Bolivia. Her diary and letters (Rojas and Calderón, 1971) reveal a great compassion and warmth—traits that do not belong to the guerrilla stereotype. Here is a poem she wrote in April 1966 while waiting for an underground contact somewhere in Latin America:

To Leave a Memory

So I must leave, like flowers that wilt?
Will my name one day be forgotten
And nothing of me remain on the earth?
At least, flowers and song.
How, then, must my heart behave?
Is it in vain that we live, that we appear on the earth?

(in Rojas and Calderón, 1971: 178)

Some women revolutionaries work and live essentially alone, like Tania; others are familistic. There have been many cases of the imprisonment of the wives of guerrilla leaders, from Peru to Chile, and it is usually, though not always, clear that the women were active revolutionary partners. Cuban revolutionaries tend to be familistic. Jaquette (1973) points out that the three women most important in the Cuban revolution, Haydee Santamaria, Celia Sanchez, and Vilma Espin, were all "closely linked to important male leaders," Fidel Castro, Raul Castro, and Armando Davalos (346-347). There have been revolutionaries who were nuns (Sister Maurina Borgha de Silviera) and revolutionaries who were beauty queens (Rogelia Cruz Martinez). They come from every walk of life. The women revolutionaries of Latin America are perhaps more aware than their middle-class sisters of the realities of everyday life for the masses that keep young girls working in the fields and caring for their younger brothers and sisters, at an age when more fortunate teenage girls are in school (figure 12-2). We must freely recognize that women terrorists belong to the women's movement, whatever century or continent they are found in, and that they play a special role in the speeded-up currents of change in the twentieth century.

* * * *

This rapid survey of centuries of development of women's history in Africa, Asia, and Latin America, while full of gaps, provides some basis for bringing the reader to women's present moment in history as a prelude to the future. There is no continent on which women do not have an ancient history of working for society from the underside, no continent on which women have not also at times walked freely in the public spaces, and no continent where they have been spared the vicissitudes of alternating recognition and oppression by the male society in which they lived. Wherever a people have accumulated wealth we have seen the emergence of classes. We have seen that women at the top have had the freedom of that wealth, and that women at the bottom have had the "freedom of poverty"—the freedom to labor for bread, whether as artisans, prostitutes, or slaves. In every stratum of these multi-tiered societies we have seen children. At the top, little girls of five are decked out to marry kings and sit on thrones; at the bottom, fingers of tiny toddlers are put to simple tasks that lighten, however little, their mothers' labor; in the middle, small daughters are "playing house," trying out every nuance of the role their sheltered mothers play.

The feminist movements that have crept across the continents in the past century and a quarter have not been oriented toward the self-assured women at the top, nor toward the laborers at the bottom, nor toward the little girls at every level who strain so hard to learn the lessons of their class. They have been for middle-class women, for the gropers on the underside, equally insulated from both their upper-class and laboring sisters. Now the gropers are emerging, and feminism has taken to the public spaces of the present.

Figure 12-2. *Bolivian Girl Working in Field While Caring for Her Baby Sister.*

Appendix 12-1
Traditional Occupations of Women in Africa

(adapted from Chart 1, p. 38, of Boulding, 1969)

I. <u>Professional, Technical, and Related Worker</u>

Midwife; Assistant Midwife
Dispenser of Traditional Herbs and Healing Rituals
Magician, Witch, Sorcerer
Priestess
Holy Woman

II. <u>Clerical Worker</u>

Scribe
Record-keeper (non-literate), General
Record-keeper for Women's Credit Associations

III. <u>Commerce and Sales Worker</u>

Broker
Export Merchant
Market Vendor: agricultural and craft products
Pawnbroker
Peddler
Resale Tradeswoman
Home Shopkeeper

IV. <u>Agricultural Worker</u>

V. <u>Transport and Communications Worker</u>

"Talking Newspaper"
Village News-Singer
Carrier of Water, Wood, Charcoal
General Load Carrier

VI. <u>Laborer</u>

Construction-related Transport: Transporter of Stones,
    Water, Sand
Hard-Panner of Road-filling Materials
Tin Miner
Construction of houses, public buildings
Road Building
Bridge Building

VII. Craft and Home Industry Worker

Producers of:

Baskets	Light Furniture
Brooms	Mattresses
Carpets, Rugs	Metal Work
Ceramic Objects	Pillows
Charcoal	Pottery
Cloth (Hand Weaving, Dying, etc.)	Raffia Work
	Saddlecloths
Clothing	Straw Mats
Decorative Needlework	Tents
Domestic Tools	Whitewash
Embroidery	Wicker Chairs
Fibre Sponges	Repair work in connection
Leather Work (Purses, Shoes, Belts, etc.)	with all of above

Food Preparer of Ready-to-Eat Food and Drink

VIII. Service, Sport, and Recreation Worker

Dancer, Entertainer
Domestic Service
Ear-piercer
Hairdresser
Laundress
Marriage Broker
Praise Singer
Prostitute
Singer for Family Festivities
Ritual Leader
Teacher and Planner of Rituals

IX. Administrative and Executive Positions

Clan Chief
Paramount Chief
Head of Market Organization
Member of Council of Women
Head of Women's Secret Organization
Head of Trading, Credit Association
Head of Women's Cooperative
Head of Women's Social Organization

Notes

[1]The fact that Jewish as well as Arab merchants engaged in the slave trade is not always mentioned in histories of the period (Shirley Nuss, 1974).

[2]See Judith Van Allen's "'Sitting on a Man': Colonialism and the Lost Institutions of Igbo Women" (1972) for a vivid if poignant description of traditional devices for the control of men by women.

[3]Freedom must be understood in a relative sense. The recently publicized practices of female circumcision and infibulation in some nomadic and sedentary populations in Africa hardly seem consonant with "freedom." These practices apparently cause a high mortality rate for women, both in the prepubertal period when the operations are performed and in childbirth because scar tissue prevents the needed dilation of the cervix during labor. Women, however, are socialized to support these practices and help carry them out. Dangerous bodily operations performed for a variety of religious and cultural reasons can be found in all societies in all social conditions. Surgical breast-building is a contemporary United States practice that belongs in this tradition.

[4]One of the fascinating things about purdah is how women themselves develop its extreme forms as a status symbol. See Papanek's "Purdah: Separate Worlds, and Symbolic Shelter" (1971) for an interesting analysis of this and other aspects of purdah This pursuit of seclusion by urban Moslem women is very like the pursuit of the domestic role by many middle-class Western women in the nineteenth and twentieth centuries. Purdah is more extreme, of course, creating odd role reversals between mother and child: "The purdah-observing mother may become dependent on her young child when outside the home. The veil hampers her vision and movement so that she may ask the child to lead her" (White, 1975: 27).

[5]See Cynthia Nelson's "Public and Private Politics: Women in the Middle Eastern World" (1974: 551-563) for a discussion of present-day underlife politics.

[6]These comments on tribal women are based on notes taken during discussions with leading members of women's organizations on a visit to India in 1974, and represent my view, not theirs.

744

[7]At the same time, it is true that the term seclusion can be misleading, in that the *zenana* may be a crowded, noisy, even raucous place. Elizabeth Cooper describes a scene in the *zenana* of an Indian lady during a dinner party. In addition to large numbers of women guests, there were about fifty servants and slaves all running around apparently at random. The mistress would direct them from wherever she was in a loud shrill voice. Cooper asked her Indian friend

> if Indian ladies generally had such loud voices and commanding tone, and she laughed and said, "Well, if they have not to begin with they soon acquire them. . . . It takes a strong-minded woman, and one with no mean executive ability, to keep peace and harmony in an Eastern zenana" (1915: 176).

Purdah provides a variety of training for women, some of which is useful in public life.

[8]A reference to Newton's epigram, "If I have seen farther, it is by standing on the shoulders of giants," delightfully pursued by Robert Merton in a book by that title (1965).

[9]A selection of readings from the Chinese press on the women's movement in China from 1949 to 1973 is available in Croll (1974).

[10]This ethnocentrism operates when North Americans and Europeans are writing about any culture not their own; it is not uniquely operative in relation to Latin America.

References

Adams, Robert McCormick
1966   The Evolution of Urban Society: Early Mesopotamia and Prehispanic Mexico. Chicago: Aldine.

Afetinan, A.
1962   Emancipation of the Turkish Woman. Paris: UNESCO.

Ali, Ameer
1899   "The influence of women in Islam." The Nineteenth Century Magazine 45 (May): 755-774.

Altekar, A. S.
1956   The Position of Women in Hindu Civilization. Banaras, India: Motilal Banarsidass.

Ayscough, Florence
1937   Chinese Women: Yesterday and Today. New York: Houghton Mifflin.

Boserup, Ester
1970   Woman's Role in Economic Development. New York: St. Martin's Press.

Boulding, Elise
1975   "Women, bread and babies: Directing aid to fifth world farmers." A Background Paper for the Conference: The World Food and Population Crisis: A role for the Private Sector. Dallas, Texas, April.
1969   "The Effects of Industrialization on the Participation of Women in Society." Ph.D. dissertation, University of Michigan.

Bowser, Frederick P.
1974   The African Slave in Colonial Peru: 1524-1650. Stanford, Calif.: Stanford University Press.

Burton, Margaret E.
1918   Women Workers of the Orient. West Medford, Mass.: Central Committee on the United Study of Foreign Missions.

Burton, Sir Richard
1966   A Mission to Gelele: King of Dahome. Ed. by C. W. Newbury. New York: Praeger.

Chaney, Elsa M.
1973   "Old and new feminists in Latin America: The case of Peru and Chile." Journal of Marriage and the Family 35 (May): 331-343.

Chow, Yung-Teh
1966   Social Mobility in China: Status Careers among the Gentry in a Chinese Community. New York: Atherton.

Collins, Robert O.
1971   Europeans in Africa. New York: Alfred A. Knopf.

Cooper, Elizabeth
1915   The Harim and the Purdah: Studies of Oriental Women. New York: Century.

Croll, Elizabeth
1974   The Women's Movement in China: A Selection of Readings, 1949-1973. Nottingham, England: Anglo-Chinese Educational Institute.

de la Cruz, Sor Juana Ines
1951   Obras Completas de Sor Juana Ines de la Cruz. Ed. by Alfonso Mendez Plancarte. Mexico and Buenos Aires: Fondo de Cultura Economica.

Diffie, Bailey W.
1945   Latin-American Civilization: Colonial Period. Harrisburg, Penna.: Stackpole.

Edib, Halide
1926   Memoirs of Halide Edib. New York: Century.

Ekejiuba, Felicia
1967   "Omu Okwei, the merchant queen of Ossomari: A biographical sketch." Journal of the Historical Society of Nigeria 3 (June): 633-646.

Gordon, David C.
1968 Women of Algeria: An Essay on Change. Cambridge, Mass.: Harvard University Press.

Guba, Arun Chandra
1973 "Gandhian technique of revolution" (mimeo).

Herbert, Beda
1965 "The nun who knew everything." Capuchin Annual (Dublin): 157-162.

Houtart, François, and Emile Pin
1965 The Church and the Latin American Revolution. Tr. by Gilbert Barth. New York: Sheed and Ward.

Jaquette, Jane E.
1973 "Women in revolutionary movements in Latin America." Journal of Marriage and the Family 35 (May): 344-354.

Journal of Marriage and the Family
1973 Special Section on "Women in Latin America," 35 (May): 295-354.

Kamaladehvi
1974 Uaranasi, India. Personal interview.

Kinzer, Nora Scott
1974 "Sexist sociology." The Center Magazine (May/June): 48-59.

Lebeuf, Annie
1963 "The role of women in the political organization of African societies." Pp. 93-107 in Denise Paulme (ed.), Women in Tropical Africa. Berkeley: University of California Press.

Leith-Ross, Sylvia
1939 African Women: A Study of the Ibo of Nigeria. London: Routledge and Kegan Paul.

Levtzion, Nehemia
1968 Muslims and Chiefs in West Africa: A Study of Islam in the Middle Volta Basin in the Pre-Colonial Period. Oxford: Clarendon Press.

Little, Kenneth
1973 African Women in Towns. Cambridge: Cambridge University Press.

Matheson, Alastair
1970 "A job for national importance." UNICEF News 65 (May): 8-10.

Merton, Robert K.
1965 On the Shoulders of Giants: A Shandean Postscript. New York: Free Press.

Montoya, David G.
1975 "Perspectives of women in Mexico." Unpublished student paper. Boulder: University of Colorado, Department of Sociology.

Nelson, Cynthia
1974 "Public and private politics: Women in the Middle Eastern world." American Ethnologist 1: 551-563.

Nuss, Shirley A.
1974 "Roots of the Middle East crisis: The Jewish question and Zionism." Boulder: University of Colorado, Department of Sociology (mimeo).

Oliver, Roland
    1968   "The African achievement." Pp. 96-103 in Roland Oliver (ed.), Dawn
            of African History. 2nd ed. London: Oxford University Press.

Oppong, Christine
    1974   Marriage among a Matrilineal Elite: A Family Study of Ghanaian Senior
            Civil Servants. Cambridge Studies in Social Anthropology, no. 8. Cam-
            bridge: Cambridge University Press.

Papanek, Hannah
    1971   "Purdah in Pakistan: Seclusion and modern occupations for women."
            Journal of Marriage and the Family 33: 517-530.

Paulme, Denise (ed.)
    1963   Women of Tropical Africa. Tr. by H. M. Wright. London: Routledge
            and Kegan Paul.

Penzer, N. M.
    1935   The Harem: An Account of the Institution. Philadelphia: J. B. Lippin-
            cott.

Pescatello, Ann (ed.)
    1973   Female and Male in Latin America: Essays. Pittsburgh: University of
            Pittsburgh Press.

Rojas, Marta, and Merta Rodriquez Calderón (eds.)
    1971   Tania: The Unforgettable Guerrilla. New York: Random House.

Singh, Pritam
    1974   Varanasi, India. Personal communication.

Snow, Helen Foster
    1967   Women in Modern China. The Hague: Mouton.

Stevens, Evelyn P.
    1973   "Marianismo: The other face of machismo in Latin America." Pp.
            89-102 in Ann Pescatello (ed.), Female and Male in Latin America:
            Essays. Pittsburgh: University of Pittsburgh Press.

Strong, Anne Louise
    1965   China's Millions. Peking: New World Press.

Sweetman, David
    1971   Queen Nzinga: The Woman Who Saved Her People. London: Longman.

Tharpar, Romila
    1963   "The history of female emancipation in southern Asia." Pp. 473-499
            in Barbara Ward (ed.), Women in the New Asia. Paris: UNESCO.

Thomas, P.
    1970   Social Stratification in Africa. New York: Free Press.

Tuden, Arthur, and Leonard Plotnicov (eds.)
    1964   Indian Women Through the Ages. Bombay: Asia Publishing House.

UNICEF News
    1973   "Third World Women." 76-17.

Van Allen, Judith
    1972   " 'Sitting on a man': Colonialism and the lost institutions of Igbo
            women." Canadian Journal of African Studies 6: 165-182.

Vreede-De Stuers, Cora
  1968   Parda: A Study of Muslim Women's Life in Northern India. Atlantic Highlands, N. J.: Humanities Press.

Wales, Nym
  1952   Red Dust: Autobiographies of Chinese Communists. Stanford: Stanford University Press.

Ward, Barbara E. (ed.)
  1963   Women in the New Asia: The Changing Social Roles of Men and Women in South and South-East Asia. Paris: UNESCO.

White, Elizabeth Herrick
  1975   "Women's Status in an Islamic Society: The Problems of Purdah." Ph.D. Dissertation, University of Denver.

White, Gilbert, David J. Bradley, and Anne U. White
  1972   Drawers of Water: Domestic Water Use in East Africa. Chicago: University of Chicago Press.

Wittfogel, Karl August
  1957   Oriental Despotism: A Comparative Study of Total Power. New Haven: Yale University Press.

Wolf, Margery, and Roxane Witke (eds.)
  1975   Women in Chinese Society. Stanford: Stanford University Press.

Woods, Dorothea E.
  1974   "The teen-age girl: Her problems and prospects." UNICEF News 79: 16-19.

Woodsmall, Ruth Frances
  1960   Women and the New East: Washington, D. C.: Middle East Institute.

Part 4
Epilogue

13

Prologue to the Future

The Twentieth Century in Euro-North America

While tracing the paths of the third world out of ancient pasts into the present, we left Euro-North America behind. In 1920 European and North American women were emerging from World War I with the vote. Some had it well before the war, others got it later, but the decade of the flaming twenties has a special significance in the history of the underside quite apart from the suffrage issue because of the flamboyant visibility of a few women during the era of the short-skirted, leggy flapper. On the serious side, a greater proportion of women were receiving Ph.D.s at American universities at that time than at any time since.[1] Women scholars were publishing with all the major presses of Europe and the United States. The women from the warring countries who had met at the Hague in 1915 were preparing documents for use in the drafting of the Covenant of the new League of Nations (Bussey and Tims, 1965). Women entered the arena of international politics with zest. By comparison, in the labor movement, this was a time of relative decline, as women felt the backlash against their efforts at self-assertion in the early part of the century beginning with the Triangle Shirtwaist factory strike in 1911 (Maupin, 1974).

753

The contrast between the women of the first quarter-century and women of this last quarter-century of the 1900s comes out interestingly in a study comparing samples of women listed in the 1915 and 1973 *Who's Who of American Women* (Krelle et al., 1975). Allowing for differences due to the fact that the 1915 volume was the first women's *Who's Who* published, and that by 1973 there was a well-developed system for identifying and including women, the comparison is nevertheless illuminating. Both populations represent the most educated sector of their respective societies. Between 1915 and 1973 there is a shift in the character of their activities; the category "writers" (authors, poets, journalists, editors) shrinks from 33 percent to 12 percent, and the category "educators" from 26 percent to 20 percent. There is more specialization in 1973, and there are more women in the paid labor force. The number of career-type activities by individual women ranged from 0 to 46 in 1915, and 0 to 25 in 1973. The picture is the same for noncareer activities. In 1915, 17 percent of the women were reported as having six to ten separate civic and volunteer responsibilities, and in 1973 there were 10 percent of women with that number of community roles. A subjective impression, not verifiable except through further analysis, is that the typical professional woman of 1915 was engaged in more outside activities than the typical professional woman of 1973. More of them stayed single—38 percent in 1915 as compared with 30 percent in 1973.

Certainly there was a tremendous sense of the opening up of new horizons in the first quarter of this century. By the twenties, idealists everywhere looked to the new social experiments in Russia. Radical innovations in education, in child care, and in the nature of the marriage contract, permitting easy dissolution and recombination of households, were taking place there. This was also the age of the back-to-nature movements in Europe which took thousands of young people away from the cities and into the mountains. The depression cut bleakly into all these movements. Women were pushed out of the labor force, membership fell off drastically in many women's organizations, never to regain the level of the twenties, and the Hitler youth movement lured young people down from the mountains into Nazism. The mountains had not been a good training ground for political life. Some of the women who served as administrators of concentration camps during World War II had been part of the 1920s back-to-nature movement.[2] One of the many tragedies of World War II was the number of young people who died as soldiers or victims who had been pupils in the International School in

Geneva, a school founded by idealistic parents in the International Labour Office in 1925 to educate their children as world citizens.[3]

There was a death struggle in Europe between the forces of liberalism and the forces of totalitarianism. The European women's movement was at the heart of this struggle. Many movement women were killed, decimating a group that could ill afford to lose members. The story of that struggle has yet to be fully written. It exists in fragments in the records of participating organizations, in private correspondence, and in the heads of an older generation of women activists.[4] Germaine Tillion is the only woman underground agent to my knowledge who both survived and recorded a concentration camp experience as a social scientist and a human being. In *Ravensbruck* (Tillion, 1975) she describes the human bonds and networks women constructed to protect each other from torture and death.

Another group of women who fought the forces of totalitarianism and war were found within the personalist movement of the Catholic church. Revolutionaries committed to social and personal transformation, they gave strong leadership to social action projects among the urban poor in Europe. Three great Catholic women radicals, all born before 1900, spent the last quarter-century bringing the European spiritual revolution of the thirties to North America—Russian-born Baroness Catherine de Hueck Doherty, Russian-born Helen Iswolsky, and American-born Dorothy Day. All three were institution builders for an alternative society—radical activists, writers, saints, and mystics who were equally at home in palaces, slums, and jails. Close friends with separate callings, they supported one another in a powerful and little-recorded change movement countering the regressive militarism of the middle decades of this century.

In a sense World War II never ended, for the cold war flared quickly after the cessation of hostilities in Europe. The involvements in Korea and Indochina added fuel to cold war flames. It is no wonder that young women born after 1940 cannot easily imagine how promising the world looked to women beginning their careers in the twenties. The women of the twenties were world shapers. The women of the forties, while they entered the labor force in large numbers as war workers, were already beginning the psychological retreat into the home so graphically described by Betty Friedan (1963). The fifties were quiet, timid years for many women. But in some of the countries that had suffered most from the war, in the Soviet Union, Poland, Japan, the women picked themselves up from their exhaustion and terror and engaged in reconstruction and outreach in those timid fifties. The luxury of retreat was not for them. I wish I could devote another chapter to the stories of how women went about that reconstruction. How, for example, Russian mothers buried their thousands of babies who died of malnutrition—how they then went back to work and to school, to play their part in every arena of a society so recently feudal. A major international initiative by women after the end of the war came from the women of the Soviet Union, in the founding of the Women's International Democratic Federation (WIDF). It was intended to bridge the gap between socialist and nonsocialist countries, and is still trying to do this. The cold war greatly limited the organization's effectiveness, particularly since women of both the West and the East by and large "supported" the cold war.

I wish I could write about Polish women too—about how the prewar Society of the Friends of Children rose from the ashes of the destruction of Warsaw and began to clear safe underground and aboveground spaces for the surviving children they found in the ruins; and how women whose bodies were severely crippled from medical experimentation in concentration camps used their minds and hands to turn out Europe's most beautiful children's books. The tremendous surge of effort to make a good environment for children developed a momentum that carried women into many other activities and linked with an old Polish tradition of intellectual women taking public responsibility. The Liga Kobiet, the Polish Women's League, operated at the same high level of political sophistication as the European women's groups of the early twenties. Among other things, it was actively supporting the new postwar peace research movement in its earliest stages. The charm, dignity, and intellectual incisiveness of these women left a deep impression on visitors from outside in the early sixties (Boulding, 1963).

One "old" Western organization that consistently and carefully responded to the reaching out of the socialist women was the Women's International League for Peace and Freedom (WILPF), reduced in membership though it was. Contact with its members in socialist countries had been lost during the war. Disarmament, the joint goal of both the WILPF and the WIDF, seems farther off than ever in the 1970s.[5]

After the timid fifties, the sixties was the decade when social activism broke out again in the United States and in Europe. Because a new age must have new movements, the sixties saw the birth of a new international women's peace organization, Women Strike for Peace, in response to the threat to life from the fallout from nuclear testing. Many new national women's peace organizations were also born at this time in Euro-North America. Most of them, like Women Strike for Peace, operated in an ad hoc fashion and maintained continuity with difficulty. Not surprisingly, many of those who helped found the new Women Strike for Peace were experienced movement women from the Women's International League (Boulding, 1965). When Dagmar Wilson, the charismatic young illustrator of children's books, who first led Women Strike, explained to an early gathering of women in 1962 that the present international crisis was a fire requiring that we all don fire-fighter's hats and run to put it out, oldtimers from the Women's International League smiled. They knew that such fires were not quickly put out.

None of the sixties movements were really new. The commune movement had several antecedents in the 1920s, '30s, and '40s. Among the most recent antecedents in the United States were the communities founded by World War II conscientious objectors and their wives. During the war itself some of these wives lived in rural communes near their husbands' camps, sharing child care while they struggled to support themselves.6 It was very natural to move from that experience to subsistence agricultural communities after the war. None of these women and men wanted to return to the old society. They wanted to make a new one. Although many of them were reabsorbed into suburbia, the process was never total. They brought up their children to "the sound of a different drummer." Many of these children in turn now live in communes such as the "Life Centers," a loosely organized network known as the Movement for a New Society.7

Perhaps the timid fifties were not so timid after all. The women turned full-time homemakers were breeding a set of revolutionaries who powered the antiwar movement, the civil rights movement, the black liberation movement, and finally, in the very late sixties, the women's liberation movement. (The Chicano and Native American liberation movements have their own dynamic, not traceable to the middle-class homemakers of the fifties.) There have been a number of studies of the family life and parent-child relations experienced by student protesters in the sixties.8 Sometimes these are a bit patronizing about the parents who "talked liberal and lived conservative." Given the social forces bearing down on them, one could argue that women were acting in the only way open to them, outwardly conforming but planting the seeds for change in their children. The ones who remained activist and nonconforming have been as much criticized in the literature as their quieter sisters (for being cold, distant mothers who were so busy with social reform that they neglected their children). Both types of critique are beside the mark.

One product of the "quiet mothers" was the SDS, the Students for a Democratic Society. This organization was formed partly from the earlier Student League for Industrial Democracy, and partly out of the immediacy of the trial by fire of the sheltered young middle-class women and men who had police dogs set at their throats as they worked at voter registration of blacks in the south.[9]

The first voices in the "new" women's liberation movement came from the young women SDSers such as Casey Hayden, Tom Hayden's recent wife. They had been through what the men had been through. Not surprisingly, they protested the fact that they were subsequently considered most useful to the organization in the work of running the mimeograph machine and preparing coffee for the men. Both the SDS and women's liberation have gone through many stages since then. The repeated experience of violence has its own effect. There was much public brutality toward young people, white and black, male and female, on the part of persons in authority—not only the police—in the sixties. Some young people who at that time came to feel that counterviolence was the only possible weapon have rediscovered nonviolence. Others have not. Women will be found in both groups. Not too surprisingly, violence in social movements is usually associated with authoritarianism toward women, so violent movements cannot long hold women once they realize that the instruments of struggle are also the bonds that hold them in captivity.

The radical lesbian movement was a logical outgrowth of the experience of radical women with male authoritarianism. In other social climates, celibacy has been women's best escape from male domination. In the sexuality-focused culture of the affluent West this was an unlikely solution for most women. Lesbianism retained sex without supporting sexism.

Unlikely as celibacy may seem in our time, it is also a fact that women's religious orders are still attracting radical visionary young women. One Franciscan order recently celebrated its one hundredth anniversary by spending a year in a futures-invention process intended to free members for new roles (Boulding, 1974). The revolutionary movements of Latin America have led to martyrdom for both North and Latin American sisters.

A recent round-the-world survey of "living saints" (*Time*, December 29. 1975: 47-56) includes some extraordinary twentieth century samples of an ancient breed: Albanian-born Mother Teresa, sixty-five-year-old founder of the Calcutta-based Missionaries of Charity, who care for the destitute and dying in places one might think even God had forgotten; Annie Skau, the six-foot-five-inch-tall Norwegian evangelical nurse who went to China in 1938 and who still works in Hong Kong today, with declining strength but undimmed fervor; Yaeko Ibuka, the seventy-eight-year-old angel of a leprosarium near Mount Fuji where she has lived and worked since girlhood; Schwester Selma Mayer, a ninety-two-year-old German-born nurse who went to Jerusalem in 1916 and has worked in hospitals there ever since. Another "living saint" (not in the *Time* article) is the Austrian-born octogenarian Dr. Anna Dengel, who pioneered in medical work among Indian women in purdah in the early years of this century and founded the Medical Mission Sisters, who have been carrying on highly innovative medical work since the 1920s.

Not all nuns are innovators, but at one level or another they represent a commitment to change, if only in the inward recesses of the human spirit. The anchoress way of life also persists, followed today by women in Canada, the United States, Europe, and Asia who have chosen solitude and contemplation, interwoven in various degrees with service and contact with the world. Nuns and former nuns have their own national and international networks, one of which operates from the Center of Concern in Washington, D. C. The ministry is attracting more and more women in the 1970s, and each decade between now and the year 2000 will see a further crumbling of the institutional barriers to the ordaining of women.[10]

Young women radicals of every kind, both violent and nonviolent, have all in their own way worked at the old problem of forming alliances with the proletariat. It has not been easy. Perhaps we are a less class-oriented society now than in lady-of-the-manor-house days, but suburbia has created as much of a barrier to shared life across socioeconomic statuses as wealth and breeding ever did. Other barriers are giving way, however, and new liberation movements have brought new activists into society's overlife. Women in prisons, always the most vulnerable poverty-level sector of any society, have begun to organize, and to call attention to a life situation untouched by the theories and institutions of penal reform. They have been helped by women activists on the outside, such as Jessica Mitford (1973) and Kathryn Burkhart (1973), whose books have lifted the curtain on sufferings long concealed. Most of all they have helped themselves, in rediscovering themselves as persons.

Prostitutes have also begun to organize, both nationally and internationally. Always before, other women—and sometimes men—were their advocates. Now they are their own advocates for the human right to practice their occupation without legal hindrance. The International Abolitionists Federation brings together professionals and concerned citizens who seek to decriminalize prostitution. Members of this association, including American prostitutes, were meeting at UNESCO in Paris in October of 1975, as this chapter was being completed, to discuss decriminalization of their profession.

In the spring of 1975, a clampdown of French police on the prostitutes of Lyons led to a two-week occupation of the fifteenth century St. Nizier's church by the women, who issued a statement declaring that "police harassment must stop . . . and the country's ten thousand full-time *filles de joie* should be officially recognized as 'workers whose profession depends on the sexual needs of part of society'" (*Newsweek,* June 23, 1975: 42). The women were asking for the right to pay into pension funds to obtain social security benefits. The parish priest at St. Nizier's was reported to have given a sermon to the group on the redemption of Mary Magdalene.

By the end of the first week the strikes had spread to a chapel in the center of Paris, to a church in Marseilles, and to a church annex in Grenoble. Prostitutes in the Riviera resorts of Cannes and Nice went on solidarity strikes over the weekend, refraining from "their customary sidewalk beats."

It is possible that prostitution will be decriminalized in the near future in those countries such as the United States that still make it a criminal offense. Awareness of the issues is increasing among women; the era when only men write the history of prostitution is over. In the United States, Pauline Tabor's *Memoirs* of her life as a madam (1971) and Margo St. James' work as an organizer, speaker, and publisher of the newspaper *Coyote* reveal professional prostitutes as sensitive, gifted people with extraordinary humor and resourcefulness. St. James (1975) makes the point that many prostitutes spend more time as counselors, rendering listening and helping services to men, than they do in sexual services.[11]

Women's movements in the twentieth century encompass the entire range of human experience. It is almost beyond us to grasp their richness and complexity, but it is crucial that we try. Everyone can make up their own roster of women's movements, but that roster should start with the third world women described in the previous chapter, since numerically they represent by far the largest and strongest groups in the twentieth century. When the roster moves to Euro-North America, the whole range of movements must be included, from the prostitutes, prisoners, and radical feminists to the women in religious orders, with the great bulk of women civic workers and community volunteers, and moderate feminist organizations like the National Organization of Women, in between.[12]

Since much has been written and is being written about all of these movements, further description of them here is not necessary. The intention in this section has been to show how each of these movements has its roots in the past. Our concern now is with the future. The past is our resource, our tool, as we move into the future and make it what we want it to be.

Locating the Benchmarks, 1975

What will women make of the future? We have looked at the social maintenance, salvage, and repair work women have done since the beginning of urban civilization. Working mainly from the underside, the vast majority of them have continued to breed and rear children, hold households together, labor at economically productive work, and manage a grassroots level of redistribution of goods and services that has somehow held the polity together. All this they have done with and often without the aid of men. In every age and climate they have also managed improbable outbursts of artistic and social creativity.

On the whole the human story has been a grim tale of wars of conquests, with peaceful interludes. The last time things looked really promising for the human race was perhaps around 1900, when it seemed that science and technology could save us. In 1975, we see that the physical environment of the planet is deteriorating, both in terms of air, water, soil, and forest cover; we see major cities at the breakdown point, unable to render properly the services on which urban dwellers depend for their very existence; we see the threat of nuclear annihilation more serious than ever after two decades of disarmament efforts. We realize that science and technology cannot save us, at least not as currently administered by men. The design for disaster we currently face was not planned by women. They are absent from nearly all the decision-making bodies that have brought us where we are.

Recognition of the Role of Women by the United Nations

We are indeed at threshold now, in every way. The old-style women monarchs and ladies of the manor house are no more. The internationalists of the early part of the century are long past retirement, or dead. A new generation of women began to take hold in international affairs at the United Nations level when the idea of a UN

International Cooperation Year was initiated. It was conceived by women, developed by women,[13] and lost in the maws of international officialdom because women had yet not enough expertise to make concrete programs work. It was intended to create an internal network of women working for peace at the community level. As symbolic of women's intentions it was important, and it was a beginning.

When the Stockholm Conference on the Environment was held, women were better prepared. The tribune device had evolved as a way of getting nongovernmental voices heard during intergovernmental deliberations. Women, and dissenting men, used the tribune as a kind of counter-conference that brought out agenda issues not discussed in the main conference. The World Conference associated with International Population Year saw women even better prepared, both in the tribune and the main conference. This time many came as professionals with documentation on population problems taking account of women's long-ignored role in family planning. At the World Food Conference in Rome they came similarly prepared. At each conference it became increasingly clear that the failure of male professionals, administrators, and planners to recognize the most elementary facts about women's part in the entire complex of productive processes from childbearing to agriculture to industry and back to feeding families was leading to disastrous planning and policy errors. Since no technical aid programs were being directed at women, half of the human race stood outside the entire so-called development process.

When International Women's Year was finally approved as a result of mounting pressures, no one had any illusions about a great "turnaround" in world policy. But it was an opportunity to state the case women had been building up for the previous ten years to male policy makers at home and in the United Nations. What happened in Mexico City itself is of minor importance. The continual building of the case for women in policy making is of major importance. In that sense International Women's Year represents, if not a "turnaround," at least a tipping point in the sense Jessie Bernard describes (1975): a critical proportion of a relevant population is moving in a new direction, and there is no going back to a *status quo ante*. The evaluation by Helvi Sipila, the first woman assistant secretary general to the United Nations and the secretary general for International Women's Year, makes this clear:

1. *Never before* have women and men representing 133 governments, 31 intergovernmental, and 113 non-governmental organizations and 7

liberation movements, come together to deal with problems of women. . . .

2. *Never before* have 891 women represented 131 governments at any conference of the United Nations. . . .

3. *Never before* have there been so many high ranking women present at and participating in the U.N. session. . . .

4. *Never before* have so many Heads of States and governments sent messages to a Conference expressing their particular support to its goals and objectives. . . .

5. *Never before* have so many women been in the front pages of the newspapers. . . .

6. *Never before* has the world seen so much data collected and analyzed. . . .

7. *Never before* has a U.N. Conference attracted the mass media and the non-governmental circles to such an extent—with over 1500 representatives of the mass media covering it and over 5000 persons participating in the parallel activities. . . .

8. *Never before* has there been such a world-wide mobilization of human and material resources . . . (reported in WIN, 1975).

The World Plan of Action prepared for International Women's Year is an important priority-setting document. The triple themes for IWY of equality, development, and peace summarize well the three basic concerns of the world women's movement. In this sense, IWY was not the product of the previous ten years, but of the previous one hundred and more years.

The resolution introduced at Mexico City on "The Integration of Women in the Development Process as Equal Partners with Men" is reproduced here because it gives a clue to the kinds of specific implementations which will have to be made, and will be made, in order to institutionalize the participation of women so that we do not return to the underside of history:

The World Conference of the International Women's Year . . .

1. *Recommends* that all organs of the United Nations development system, specialized agencies, and other international technical and financial assistance programmes and agencies

a) give special attention to those development undertakings which integrate women in the development process;

b) incorporate in their development assistance plans, programme and sector analyses and programme documents an impact statement of how such proposed programmes will affect women as participants and beneficiaries, in consultation with the United Nations Commission on the Status of Women;

c) establish review and appraisal systems, as well as research to serve in the design, implementation and evaluation of programmes and to provide a means of measuring progress in the integration of women in the development process;

d) ensure that all women are included on an equitable basis with men on all levels of decision-making which govern the planning and implementation of these programmes, keeping in mind the principle of geographical distribution;

2. *Invites* all Member Governments and private organizations engaged in development programmes to adopt the above recommendations in their programming processes.

Note: This Resolution was UNANIMOUSLY adopted (reported in WIN, 1975).

A hint about the future comes from Enrique Penalosa, secretary general of International Habitat Year, the next major UN project. In a significant address to the International Women's Year Conference he stated:

HABITAT, if it is to succeed, must be part of a *re-evaluation of all the systems* and structures of our social and economic organization. It must be seen as a continuation of a process of analysis on an intergovernmental and global scale which is exemplified by the conference at *Stockholm on the human environment, Bucharest on population growth, Rome on food supply* and this meeting in *Mexico on the role of women.*
. . . in the expert opinion that will influence the documentation and the proceedings of the HABITAT conference, I see assumptions of so-called normality which completely ignore the present condition and the future potential of women in society. For example, *who decides the length of a normal workday?*
. . . And, *who decides that all kinds of work must be done in a plant or factory of business,* usually a long way from home and children. *And who decides in the planning of a community* that businesses, shops, schools and day care centres should be separated by such distances as to require hours a day on public transport or automobile? These are the kinds of questions that should be raised at the *HABITAT conference.* But it is only fair to warn you that they may not be raised
. . . due to the largely male dominated profession of planning. . . . The themes of HABITAT are no more nor less than the issues of *how we*

should organize our future societies. . . .

For this reason . . . governments and the women's organizations of the world should insist that *relevant points are raised in terms of the rights of women* in the planning, construction and management of the human settlements in all parts of the world (reported in WIN, 1975).

One specific outcome of International Women's Year is the convening of an advisory committee in February 1976 by Helvi Sipila to plan for the establishment of the International Institute on Research and Training for the Advancement of Women. It is intended that this new institute will engage in research and data collection both for monitoring the situation of women and for making policy recommendations that will further the participation of women in all sectors of society. It may also develop training programs. This initiative is a hopeful sign that the momentum built up during International Women's Year will continue, and that new opportunities for women will steadily increase.

Before discussing future directions for women's activities an assessment of the participation of women at present, in occupational, training, and decision-making sectors is necessary to provide a baseline for evaluating future developments.

Current Data on the Position of Women

To begin with, we will examine a series of figures from the most recent available United Nations data on women's family roles, occupations, educational levels, and public statuses, for the world as a whole and for its major regions.[14] None of the data to follow are reported by countries, only by regions, with a world mean included for each figure. To let readers know what countries are included in each region, table 13-1 provides a list of those countries. If any readers are furtively peeking ahead to see if individual figures are given for "important" countries like the United States, they will not find them. Nation-state units will not be considered significant in this analysis. There are two "we's" offered in these tables: the regional "we" and the world "we." For a fuller understanding of these "we's," table 13-2 provides a world economic and nutritional profile. It shows that extremes of national wealth and poverty exist in each of the world's regions.[15] The world means are given at the bottom of the table. Our per capita income in the world family is $631 per year, our caloric intake 2,443 calories per day, our protein 66.6 grams per day. This is *our* "standard of living."

Now let us turn to the world "we" of women. Table 13-3 shows how

Table 13-1
Listings of Countries Included in Each Region

Africa

Algeria	Equatorial	Malagasy	Sierra Leone
Angola	Guinea	Republic	Somalia
Botswana	Ethiopia	Mauritius	Sudan
Burundi	Gabon	Mali	Swaziland
Central	Gambia	Malawi	Togo
African	Guinea-Bissau	Morocco	Tunisia
Republic	Ghana	Mozambique	Uganda
Chad	Guinea	Namibia	Upper Volta
Cameroon	Ivory Coast	Nigeria	Tanzania,
Congo, Peoples	Kenya	Niger	United
Republic of	Liberia	Rhodesia	Republic of
Dahomy	Libya	Rwanda	Zambia
Egypt	Lesotho	South Africa	Zaire
	Mauritania	Senegal	

North America

Barbados	Dominican	Haiti	Panama
Bahamas	Republic	Honduras	Puerto Rico
Canada	El Salvador	Jamaica	Trinidad
Costa Rica	Grenada	Mexico	and Tabago
Cuba	Guatemala	Nicaragua	United States
			of America

South America

Argentina	Chile	Guyana	Uruguay
Bolivia	Colombia	Paraguay	Venezuela
Brazil	Ecuador	Peru	

West Asia

Bahrain	Jordan	Saudi Arabia	Yemen
Cyprus	Kuwait	Syria	Yemen, Peoples
Iran	Lebanon	Turkey	Democratic
Iraq	Oman	United Arab	Republic
Israel	Qatar	Emirates	

Asia

Afganistan	Japan	Maldives	Taiwan
Bhutan	Khmer	Malaysia	Thailand
Bangladesh	Korea,	Mongolia	Vietnam,
Burma	Democratic	Nepal	Democratic
China, Peoples	Peoples	Pakistan	Republic
Republic of	Republic	Philippines	of North
Hong Kong	Korea, Republic	Ryukyu Islands	Vietnam,
India	of South	Singapore	Republic
Indonesia	Laos	Sri Lanka	of South

Europe

Albania	Germany,	Italy	San Marino
Andorra	Democratic	Liechtenstein	Spain
Austria	Republic, East	Luxembourg	Sweden
Belgium	Germany,	Malta	Switzerland
Bulgaria	Federal	Monaco	United Kingdom
Czechoslovakia	Republic, West	Norway	of Great
Denmark	Greece	Netherlands	Britain
Finland	Hungary	Poland	U.S.S.R.
France	Iceland	Portugal	Vatican City
	Ireland	Romania	Yugoslavia

Oceania

Australia	Nauru	New Guinea	Western
Fiji	New Zealand	Tonga	Samoa

Table 13-2

World Economic and Nutritional Profile, by Region and with World Means (1968 Figures)

	GNP in Dollars Per Capita			Calories Consumed Per Capita Per Day			Protein Consumed, Grams Per Capita Per Day		
	Low	High	Mean	Low	High	Mean	Low	High	Mean
Africa	$ 50 (Brunei)	$ 1020 (Libya)	$ 191	1760 (Tanzania)	2835 (Egypt)	2190	32.7 (Zaire)	32.4 (Egypt)	57.7
Americas	70 (Haiti)	3980 (U.S.)	737	1760 (Bolivia)	3210 (U.S.)	2404	45.8 (Bolivia)	101.7 (Argentina)	63.2
Asia	60 (Bhutan)	3541 (Kuwait)	495.5	1780 (Indonesia)	2390 (Israel)	2232	40.1 (Indonesia)	92.9 (Mongolia)	60.7
Australasia	130 (Western Samoa)	2070 (Australia)	801	--*	3380 (New Zealand)	--	--*	108.4 (New Zealand)	--
Europe	400 (Albania)	2620 (Sweden)	1339	2370 (Albania)	3450 (Ireland)	3045	71.3 (Albania)	103.0 (France)	87.8
World	50 (Brunei) (also Upper Volta and Malawi)	3980 (U.S.)	631	1760 (Bolivia and Tanzania)	3450 (Ireland)	2443	32.7 (Zaire)	108.4 (New Zealand)	66.6

SOURCE: Global Data Bank, Institute of Behavioral Science, University of Colorado, Boulder.

*Information not available for 13 of 15 units of Australasia.

many of us age fifteen and over are unpartnered, by categories of single, widowed, and divorced or separated, and also the total percentage unpartnered. Many of the women who make up the singles category will later be married, but the significance of this table lies in the fact that at any one point in time, one-quarter of the world's women are single, with regional variations from 17 to 38 percent. At any one time, 11 percent of the world's women are widowed, and 3 percent are divorced or separated. In total, 39 percent of adult women are unpartnered at any one time, varying from only 29 percent in West Asia to 49 percent in North America. It is not possible at present to report how many of these unpartnered women have dependents, children or other relatives to care for, but it is clear from a variety of other evidence that a substantial number of them do have such dependents. Since in this century women are tending to live longer than men (see table 13-3), and life expectancy gaps are widening (data not shown here) we can expect even more unpartnered women in the future. Household size, the last entry in table 13-3, while certainly inadequately reported, appears surprisingly stable over regions. The two stabilities, the percentage of unpartnered women and household size, suggest that for all the variation in cultural patterns the dimensions of household responsibility of women may not vary very much around the world. These stabilities also suggest the importance of reorienting economic and social policy toward women as individuals rather than as dependents in male-headed households.

Given the responsibilities women have, how much specialist training are they given? Table 13-4 gives the proportions of women in advanced degree programs in several fields. We see that women share equally with men in higher training in the field of education. This is to be expected since women everywhere comprise the majority of teachers in the world's elementary schools. Beyond that category, the proportion of women receiving advanced training drops rapidly for all other fields, from one-twentieth to one-quarter of what is available. The fact that they are almost as likely as men to emigrate to another country to seek better opportunities is interesting in light of the limited education they are given. Women are nearly one-half of the immigrants to North America. Some of these women migrate in families, but many migrants are single.

Turning to table 13-5, we see how women are distributed among different occupational categories. The relatively high percentage of women in the professional-technical fields is a reflection of the high number of women in the teaching profession. Many of the women

Table 13-3

Unpartnered Women, Life Expectancy and Household Size

	Africa	Asia West	Asia	Europe	N. Amer	S. Amer	Oceania	World
Proportion Women 15 Years of Age and Over Who are Single	15	16	22	21	37	35	25	25
Proportion Women 15 Years of Age and Over Who are Widowed	12	12	13	14	09	07	09	11
Proportion Women 15 Years of Age and Over Who are Divorced/Separated	06	01	02	03	03	02	03	03
TOTAL	34	29	39	38	49	47	37	39
Life Expectancy for Women	42	54	55	73	61	59	66	59
Ratio of Life Expectancy of Women to That of Total Population	1.02	1.00	1.01	1.04	1.00	1.00		1.02
Household Size	4.5	5.9	4.9	3.3	5.0	5.0	5.9	4.9

SOURCE: Boulding, Nuss, Carson, and Greenstein (1976).

Note: Life expectancy is the average number of years of life which would remain for males and females at age zero if they continued to be subjected to the same mortality conditions existing in 1968. Average size household is the ratio of the population in households to the total number of households. Proportion refers to women as a proportion of all those in each age category.

Table 13-4
Women's Education and Emigration

	Africa	Asia West	Asia	Europe	N. Amer	S. Amer	Oceania	World
Proportion Women Educated at Third Level in Education	28	44	50	56	65	61	46	50
Proportion Women Educated at Third Level in Law	11	16	11	21	10	21	10	15
Proportion Women Educated at Third Level in Social Science	18	24	23	29	29	37	18	26
Proportion Women Educated at Third Level in Engineering	05	04	02	08	04	04	01	04
Proportion Women Educated at Third Level in Agriculture	15	05	09	13	10	06	05	09
Proportion Women Who are Emigrants	44	44	43	47	46	46	42	45

SOURCE: Boulding, Nuss, Carson, and Greenstein (1976).

Note: Third-level education includes full-time and part-time students in all degree-granting and non-degree-granting institutions of higher education of all types (such as universities, teacher-training colleges, technical colleges, etc.), both public and private. *Long-term emigrants* are defined as residents intending to remain abroad for a period of more than one year. *Proportion* refers to women as a proportion of all those educated in the category named.

Table 13-5

Economically Active Women by Occupational Category

	Africa	Asia West	Asia	Europe	N. Amer	S. Amer	Oceania	World
Proportion Women Who are Professional-Technical Workers	27	31	30	42	47	50	—	38
Proportion Women Who are Administrative-Managerial Workers	06	09	07	19	15	09	10	11
Proportion Women Who are Clerical Workers	21	13	18	49	43	30	32	30
Proportion Women Who are Sales Workers	25	06	30	46	41	29	32	30
Proportion Women Who are Service Workers	31	19	38	65	62	64	53	48
Proportion Women Who are Agricultural Workers	18*	23*	35*	30	13	07*	11*	20
Proportion Women Who are Transportation Workers	08	09	24	18	17	21	08	15

SOURCE: Boulding, Nuss, Carson, and Greenstein (1976).

Note: *Proportion* refers to women as proportion of total labor force in that occupational category.

so categorized are elementary school teachers. The next category, administrative-managerial, is more revealing. Eleven percent of the world's administrators are women, with a low of 6 percent and a high of 19 percent. Other studies indicate that when women do hold administrative positions it is at the lower echelons. This will become clearly evident when we look at women's employment in the United Nations. In short, they are not functioning at planning and decision-making levels. Clerical, sales, and service occupations, as we would expect, claim much larger shares of women's labor everywhere in the world, though less in the purdah-keeping countries of West Asia. The figures on agriculture, asterisked, are far too low for these regions, and have more to do with the failure to count women's work than with the reality of agricultural production. I have left the figures in because they are "official," but each asterisked figure should be much higher than it is. (Possibly the same is true for the European and North American figures, but I am less certain there.) Eighty to 90 percent of women are farmers in some African countries (see Boulding, 1975a).

Finally, in table 13-6, we see how women are distributed in different economic sectors. These figures represent all women associated with that sector as a proportion of the total labor force in that sector. That would include associated clerical work, etc., and does not necessarily mean, for example, that all women included under mining are miners. It is nevertheless interesting to note how many women are associated with mining in Asia, Europe, and North America. Apart from agriculture (again incorrect), trade, commerce, and service occupy women the most around the world.

I have not included figures on women listed as unpaid family labor, although this is reported for many countries, because nearly all women not in the recorded labor force are in fact in the unpaid family labor category. As we have seen from our historical materials, the great majority of women at any time are in the labor force, whether counted or not. Conceptualization of that labor force, and adequate provisions for counting it, must improve drastically before we will have reasonably accurate information on women's work.

Male planners are at a double handicap because they do not know the size of the female work force, and have no firsthand experience that would enable them to make corrections for false or misleading data.[16]

The development of programs to increase productivity in any sector, agricultural or industrial, is meaningless without a knowledge of the requirements for increasing the productivity of the

Table 13-6

Economically Active Women by Industrial Category

	Africa	Asia West	Asia	Europe	N. Amer	S. Amer	Oceania	World
Proportion Women in Agriculture	21	21	36	23	13	12	11	21
Proportion Women in Mining	03	06	14	05	12	07	03	08
Proportion Women in Manufacturing	18	15	31	25	31	28	14	24
Proportion Women in Utility and Sanitation	04	06	08	13	09	07	05	07
Proportion Women in Construction	01	01	07	06	03	03	03	03
Proportion Women in Trade	19	07	31	44	38	27	03	28
Proportion Women in Transportation	04	02	06	15	08	05	08	07
Proportion Women in Finance, Social Services	25	15	29	50	54	55	58	41

SOURCE: Boulding, Nuss, Carson, and Greenstein (1976).

Note: Proportion refers to women as proportion of total labor force active in that industrial category.

female part of that work force. This requires examination of the level of domestic services and available child care, and of the quality of the equipment used by women in their work. In any sector, whether agricultural, industrial, or in home workshops, women work with far more obsolete equipment than men, as Boserup (1970) among others has pointed out. Less well trained, less well equipped, with responsibilities for childbearing and child rearing that men do not have, and working for smaller cash incomes than men receive, the wonder is how women do manage to be such productive members of the labor force in every society.[17]

How well do women do in elected positions in their respective countries? Since election figures by sex for the parliaments of the world are not systematically collected, it is impossible to give overall figures on this. In 1966 I compiled such data for seventeen countries at various levels of industrialization, along with estimates on the recency of industrialization. I made the interesting discovery (table 13-7) that the most recently and rapidly industrialized countries had the largest number of women in parliament, between 10 and 29 percent. All the "old industrial" countries, except Sweden, had fewer than 7 percent of women in parliament. In general it does not appear that the old democracies of Euro-North America are strongly associated with the political participation of women. The newer socialist countries are so associated, and to what extent this is attributable to labor force needs and to what extent to political ideology is still being debated outside the socialist world.

Even in countries where women are most represented in the elected bodies of government, they are still not represented at any level according to their actual numbers, and are almost completely absent from the highest levels of government. At the nation-state level, then, women have very limited opportunities for administration and decision making.[18]

Given the tradition of international activity of women, how well do they fare in the new set of international positions they helped create through their work in Europe during and after World War I? Particularly, how well do they fare in the United Nations today? Table 13-8 gives that information for 1973. If we compare the regional and world figures for professional women in table 13-5 with the figures for professional women in the United Nations in table 13-8, we see that they are very poorly represented indeed at the United Nations.[19]

Women who have the training and the desire to participate in the international arena have one outlet left to them outside the business,

Table 13-7

Percentage of Women in Parliament and Recency

of Industrialization

Country	Women in Parliament		Recency of Industrialization*
	%	Rank	
Over 10% in Parliament			
USSR	29	1	recent, rapid
GDR	25	2	recent, rapid
Hungary	18	3.5	recent, rapid
China (PR)	18	3.5	recent, early stages
Rumania	17	4.5	recent, rapid
Bulgaria	17	4.5	recent, rapid
Finland	12	8	recent, rapid
Sweden	12	8	"old industrial"
Poland	12	8	recent, rapid
Indonesia	10	10	recent, early stages
Under 10% in Parliament			
GFR	7	11	"old industrial"
Italy	4	12.5	recent, rapid
Japan	3.5	12.5	recent, rapid
UK	3	14	"old industrial"
USA	2	16	"old industrial"
France	2	16	"old industrial"
Cambodia	2	16	incipient industrialization

SOURCE: Adapted from Boulding (1966).

*These categories are based on stages as defined in Russet et al., *World Handbook of Political and Social Indicators* (1964), on the basis of GNP per capita, percentage urban, percentage adult literacy, percentage in higher education, inhabitants per physician, number of radios, percentage voting, and expenditure of central government. Our interest here, however, is *not* in stages of development but in relative rapidity of change.

professional, and United Nations world: the women's international nongovernmental organizations (NGOs) they have themselves created.20 The activities described in chapters 11 and 12 did indeed result in a number of such women's NGOs being formed. They have been important social problem-solving institutions available to women in the twentieth century. Table 13-9 gives the founding date for each organization. The reader may be interested in comparing this table with the discussion of women's international activities in chapter 11. Religious and educational organizations represent the first wave of women's international organizing activity, international relations the second, and professional and sports organizations the third. Each represents a different set of capabilities on the world scene.

Table 13-8

Number of Women on the Professional Staff
of the United Nations and Related Agencies

Organization	Number of Women at Various Professional Levels			Percentage of women on total profes- sional staff
	Top Level (D-2)*	Transition Levels (D-1, P-5)	Lower Levels (P-4 to P-1)	
United Nations	3	33	421	21.7
UNICEF	–	2	23	12.0
UNDP	–	5	42	9.5
ILO	–	4	117	18.9
FAO	–	3	184	4.6
UNESCO	–	21	238	14.8
WHO	–	11	376	21.5
IBRD	–	4	99	6.9
IMF	1	13	89	16.6
ICAO	–	–	20	9.0
UPU	–	–	2	2.9
ITU	–	–	17	11.8
WMO	–	–	9	7.8
IMCO	–	–	6	14.2
GATT	–	2	22	27.2
IAEA	–	1	39	11.6

SOURCE: Adapted from Szalai (1973, Table 11).
*Two top levels of appointment are missing from the table; there is no woman deputy director general, and there is now one assistant secretary general, Helvi Sipila.

Table 13-9

Founding Dates for Women's NGOs and Number of Section Memberships

Organization Category	1880–1901	1900–1915	1916–1930	1931–1945	1946–1970
Religious	WYWCA (81) WWCTU (50)	GB (40) ICJW (34) IULCW (9) SJIA (12) WUCWO (82)		WFMW (20)	IFMW (27)
International Relations		*IAW (45) *ICSDW (34) WILPF (21)	ACWW (67) PPSAWA (14) WIZO (51)	WIDF (97)	AAWC (35) EUW (12) FAWA (11)
Professional	ICN (74)	IFHE (63)	ICM (42) IFBPW (52) IFUW (56) IFWLC (39) MWIA (37) NNF (5) ODI (12) SIA (48) ZI (44)	IFWL (68) WAWE (11)	LAWHPJ (22) ICWES (11) IUWA (32) PAMWA (13) WEGN (12)
Educational	GFWC (50) ICW (64)	IALC (13)	AI (12) IIW (42) WAGGGS (101)		WMM (46)
Sports			IFWHA (34)		IAPESGW (58) IWCC (8)

SOURCE: Compiled in Boulding (1975b) from *Yearbook of International Organizations, 1973* and *Yearbook of International Organizations, 1974* (Brussels: Union of International Associations, 1973 and 1974). Complete names of organizations are listed in table 13-10.

*The original name for IAW was International Women's Suffrage Alliance, and the original name for ICSDW was International Socialist Women's Secretariat.

Some of the oldest organizations have the largest number of national branches, suggesting how difficult it is to build a new international network from scratch. Most of those founded since 1946 have fewer than thirty-five sections. Table 13-10 shows the average size of the transnational networks for each category of organization.

Table 13-10

Key to Initials of Women's NGOs

Initials	Organization Name
AAWC	All African Women's Conference
ACWW	Associated Country Women of the World
AI	Altrusa International
EUW	European Union of Women
FAWA	Federation of Asian Women's Associations
GB	Girls' Brigade
GFWC	General Federation of Women's Clubs
IA	International Association of Lyceum Clubs
IAPESGW	International Association of Physical Education and Sports for Women
IAW	International Alliance of Women
LAWHPJ	International Association of Women and Home Page Journalists
ICJW	International Council of Jewish Women
ICM	International Confederation of Midwives
ICN	International Council of Nurses
ICSDW	International Council of Social Democratic Women
ICW	International Council of Women
ICWES	International Conference of Women Engineers and Scientists
IFBPW	International Federation of Business and Professional Women
IFHE	International Federation for Home Economics
IFMW	International Federation of Mazdaznan Women
IFWHA	International Federation of Women Hockey Associations
IFWL	International Federation of Women Lawyers
IFWLC	International Federation of Women in Legal Careers
IFUW	International Federation of University Women
IIW	International Inner Wheel
IULCW	International Union of Liberal Christian Women
IUWA	International Union of Women Architects
IWCA	International Women's Cricket Association
MWIA	Medical Women's International Association
NNF	Northern Nurses Federation
ODI	Open Door International
PAMWA	Pan-American Medical Women's Alliance
PPSAWA	Pan Pacific and Southeast Asia Women's Association
SIA	Soroptimist International Association
SJIA	St. Joan's International Alliance
WAGGGS	World Association of Girl Guides and Girl Scouts
WAWE	World Association of Women Executives
WEGN	West European Group of Nurses
WFMW	World Federation of Methodist Women
WIDF	Women's International Democratic Federation
WILPF	Women's International League for Peace and Freedom
WIZO	Women's International Zionist Organization
WMM	World Movement of Mothers
WUCWO	World Union of Catholic Women's Organizations
WWCTU	World Women's Christian Temperance Union
WYWCA	World Young Women's Christian Association
ZI	Zonta International

Table 13-11a.

Categories and Mean Number of Sections of Women's NGOs

Organization Category	N	Percent	Number of Sections
Religious	9	20	39.0
International Relations	10	21	38.7
Professional	18	38	35.6
Educational	7	15	46.8
Sports	3	6	33.3
All	47	100	38.4

Table 13-11b.

Distribution of Organizational Strength of Women's NGOs by Region

Region	Countries and Territories		All NGO Branches		Mean Number Branches Per Country
	N	%	N	%	
Africa	56	26	349	19.3	7.4
Americas	50	23	461	25.5	9.8
Asia	46	21	334	18.5	7.1
Australasia	27	12.5	89	5.0	1.9
Europe	37	17	574	31.8	12.2
WORLD	216	99.5*	1807	100.1*	8.4

SOURCE: Compiled by Boulding (1975b), from *Yearbook of International Organizations, 1973* and *Yearbook of International Organizations, 1974* (Brussels: Union of International Associations, 1973 and 1974). Additional information for Africa from "Contemporary African Women," in Volume 6, *Special Bibliographic Series,* African Bibliographic Center (New York: Negro Universities Press, 1969).

*Errors due to rounding.

There is not much variation, except that the educational organizations seem to have the largest number of sections. (The General Federation of Women's Clubs was one of the first of the women's international organizations, and spread the fastest.) Table 13-11 looks at the same information a little differently, showing how the total number of national branches of NGOs, regardless of organizational type, are distributed in various regions. Africa, with the largest number of countries and territories to be served, has the fewest sections. Europe, with the smallest number of countries, has the most. The majority of these NGOs were of course initiated in Europe.

The women's NGOs work valiantly with small budgets, dealing with large problems. If they were to be judged according to the distribution of their organizational resources in relation to world need, they would get poor marks. They are least well represented where they are most needed. Their resources do not lie in their fiscal budgets, however, but in the quality of women they attract to their work, and in the alliances they can create across class, race, ethnic, and national boundaries. In a way, they represent a beachhead on a new continent, the continent of transnationalism. As new standards develop for world conduct, so also will better techniques for sharing resources emerge. As yet the world "we" of women is a shaky concept, International Women's Year notwithstanding.

The problem of creating a new world with the human materials from the old is a recurring one. What would be the use of implementing the one-third rule now being suggested—that one-third of every organizational body of every kind should be women[21]—if these women respond in ways determined by the old society? Have not women and men been shaped by the same culture? Yes and no. Here the underside becomes a special resource. It is society's free fantasy space, its visioning space, its bonding space. It is a space in which minds can learn to grapple with complexities that are destroying the overside. The underside space will not be useful to women or men, however, if women are not trained to use it on the overside.

Creating Futures

There are few women authors in my futures library. (Margaret Mead is one of the great futurists of this century, but is not ordinarily described as such.) The creative imagining work of women does not easily fit into the mold of the professional futurist.[22] We are more likely to encounter it in science fiction[23] than in the "serious" work of spelling out futures. This is nonsense, of course, because every woman with responsibility for a household is a practicing futurist. Families have traditionally depended on the capacity of mothers to hold in their minds the differently rhythmed developments of each person in a household as they age at their various rates through childhood, adolescence, middle years, and old age. Every family is a constellation of ever changing individuals, and is itself moving through successive stages of a family cycle, each stage with its own social, economic, and political requirements. Families would be in constant chaos if women did not have a grasp of futures and were not able to live mentally ahead of those around them. In fact all human beings have that capacity. Women develop it to a special degree because they have been given a larger share of the responsibility for family well-being.

Practical futurism is a way of describing not only women's family activities, but the entire range of women's activism of the past two centuries. Women have worked into the time spaces of the near tomorrow to rearrange it in terms of perceived needs of social groups not well served today. From time to time women have appeared whose minds leaped far into the future, who saw different social constellations entirely. Annie Jiagge, justice of the Supreme Court of Ghana, is such a person. Soong Chingling of China was such a person. So was Madame Pandit of India, Halide Edib of Turkey, Beatrice Webb of England, Rosa Luxemburg of Poland, Eugenie Cotton of France, Dolores Jimenez y Muro of Mexico, and Eleanor Roosevelt of the United States. Of course there have been women futurists, only they have not been called by that label. And because they have appeared so far removed from the life of ordinary women, the gulf between their visioning and the private daydreaming of women who would like to see the world a better place has appeared immense. Yet futurism is only private daydreaming turned public. It is social daydreaming.

If the phenomenon of the underlife is a chance detour in the evolutionary process as suggested in chapter 2, a detour that "drifted" toward the absurd sex-role imbalance we note today, how is the evolutionary process to be redirected? Serious consideration of this postulate of evolutionary detour is not likely as long as the general conviction holds in the West that evolution has somehow been "working for us." This is a comforting myth, suggesting that a minimum of human effort is required. If we are in fact on a detour that is leading to a dead end, overlife decision makers will resist the perception of this as long as possible.

Redirection is far from hopeless, in my view, for we are not as far off the track as might appear. The underlife situation of women has not damaged the human potential, only held it in check. While the underlife has always meant compulsory privatization, it has not always led to victimage. The "best and the brightest" have often shot through into the overlife, no matter what their class or ethnic origin.

The underlife-overlife dichotomy has appeared to support a male-dominance view of history, and yet we have seen many ways in which the social and cognitive skills from the underlife crosscut over-life activities. This applies in community conflict resolution and in international alliances, both dependent on the bonding skills of the women who were married into the conflict, so to speak. Simplistic models of male dominance do not seem useful. The politics of sex, as so passionately delineated by Kate Millet (1970), are often not relevant in the determination of what women's roles will be in a given situation.

Nevertheless the underlife phenomenon has supported differential opportunity structures for women and men for some millennia. The twentieth century profile of that differentiation has been shown in the previous section of this chapter. Some historical eras have been better than others for women, but no class-stratified society has given equal opportunity to women within its stratification structures. The fact that the structures of inequality have done so little damage over the centuries to women's capacities to perform over the whole range of human ability could be taken as a positive indication that changing those structures may not be so difficult after all. If social evolution has not been working for us, neither has it been working against us. It has stayed neutral, maintaining the capacities of women of the species because there was no other option, if the capacities of the species itself were to be maintained.

The chief reason for optimism regarding the future status of women in society as the year 1976 opens is that the old structures simply are not working any more. A good indication of this is that the major theme of social movements today, whether conservative, middle-of-the-road, or radical, is "the struggle for survival." Survival is a theme that has brought the human race through many struggles in the past, but hardly seems appropriate to an age with the knowledge and resources of this one. In other space-time continua, life has surely done better than that.

Survival is not the goal, however often stated. Dig underneath the rhetoric and one finds a conception of potential, of something as yet unfulfilled. *That* is why we go on.

Even for survival, let alone continued growth in humanness, structural changes are required. The basic organizational principle on which the entire set of civilizational enterprises of the past eight thousand years, at least, have been founded, that of hierarchical organization, has played itself out. A planet of four billion people cannot manage with organizational principles that evolved when human aggregates were only counted in hundreds of thousands. It is in fact astounding how well they worked and for how long. The ancient universalistic bureaucracy of China, the mandarin system, in which only the best minds rose to the top and governed the empire; the expanded city-state model the Romans used to govern their empire; the janissary system of the Ottomans which put ruling entirely in the hands of the best trained and the most competent, combined with a millet system for local self-government of ethnic minorities; the Cesaro-papism that merged bureaucracies of the old Roman state and the new Christian church in Byzantium and its successor, Russia; all these have sufficed in their time.[24]

No organizational innovation has touched the basic principle of hierarchical organization in a century that has seen the development of a new science of organization. The twentieth century has witnessed the rise of schools of business management and of public administration, and of a tradition of empirical studies of the organization of work that brings every principle of mechanical efficiency and human motivation into play. (See Rosabeth Moss Kanter's "Women and the Structure of Organizations," 1975, for a good survey of these innovations.) Nevertheless, though organizational research has emphasized better information processing, varied communication patterns, more feedback systems, and the moving of the locus of decision making as far down the hierarchical structure as possible, the underlying structural principle has remained intact. By the same token, the structural bases for inequalities of participation by women in all such organizations have also remained intact.

The hierarchical principle is based on the assumption that the higher one climbs, the better the view, and the better the capacity to plan and design the future for the social entity in question. Anarcho-decentralists have always questioned this, but their voices went unheard as long as hierarchy worked reasonably well. Today we face "design problems" for which no perch is high enough to ensure a view of the larger picture. NASA has worked out a new nonhierarchical technique called "matrix management" to deal with the unimaginable complexities of their space missions. Schon (1970) calls it the solar system model, the solution to modern large-scale systems requiring maximum flexibility. The solar system model is also the solution for transnational movement activities (Judge, 1971).

Many of today's enterprises are beyond planning in the conventional hierarchical mode: space missions, the administration of large cities, coordination of global projects of all kinds. In the United States, the most social-systems-design-oriented country with the most highly trained design capabilities in the world, system after system under federal administration is displaying increasingly faulty delivery capabilities: nursing homes for the elderly, food stamp plans for the poor, school lunch programs for the young, and on ad infinitum.

What sectors of society are best equipped to replace hierarchy with decentralist structures based on nonhierarchical communication? Women. Their underlife experience ideally equips them for this, and promotes fresh approaches to situations where present system designs do not work. Here are some examples:

The plight of the cities. Women community analysts are needed who can help in the block by block self-reorganization of a city to discover the resources for mutual aid that exists in the families, in the communes, and among the live-alones of each neighborhood. Towns and villages as well as cities need this type of help.

The plight of the schools. Women community analysts also trained as educators are needed who can assist teachers and administrators in the dismantling of ineffectual classroom-based teaching. These women would help reorganize education around a use of schools as headquarters only, available for "the three Rs" and other special skills programs as needed. They would help develop a community apprenticeship program for children, in a placement network so well constructed that every adult in the community would come into relationship with children of different ages each year in a teaching role. The development and coordination of this apprenticeship network, to which every citizen of the community would belong both as potential apprentice and as potential teacher, would require skills of mapping community terrains that many women have to a greater degree than men because of their underlife experience. This reorganization of schools would solve a variety of problems for children, school administrators, for the penal system (which would also have its share of apprentices), and for the community as a whole. It would reduce social autism, generalized violence, and community distrust. This system would be more easily initiated in smaller towns, but should eventually extend to the large cities too. Apprenticeships, needless to say, would be designed for a crossing of all economic, ethnic, and racial barriers, both for teachers and apprentices. It becomes an individualized alternative to busing. There would be no special apprenticeships reserved for the poor.

Alternative energy programs. Public utilities need women who can work on a variety of locally feasible alternative energy packages to be offered to homes and community enterprises. Research will be directed not only to the energy packages themselves, but to relevant daily energy-utilization habits and to promising approaches to a change of habits.

Industry. Industrial enterprises need women who can assist in designing nonhierarchical communication and control structures utilizing a cooperative organization of work that is maximally flexible in the face of a changing resource base for the industry. Patterns developed in England, Scandinavia, China, and elsewhere may be useful.

Foreign policy. The departments of state and the military commands of every society need women who can develop alternative systems analyses that will introduce new criteria for decision making in relation to total ecosystems on the planet, and a more reality-based analysis of decision consequences. They also need women to design new concepts and institutional structures for nonmilitary conflict management, and to train personnel for nonviolent conflict-management roles.

There are men in every society who have the skills required for the above assignments. The intent is not to suggest that the world should be run by women, but to show the relevance of underside skills in a society where the old underside-overside dichotomy is leading to disastrous consequences. The women who enter these jobs will not simply be dashing from kitchens to public spaces. Reconstruction is difficult work, and will require the use of that vast reservoir of trained female minds now kept at clerical and minor administrative levels. The women described in the latter part of this book are all examples of the character of that reservoir. In order for women not to recreate what men have wrought, they will need continually to draw on their underside experience.

The research frontiers that must be tackled in order to make a decentralist world work are immense. There must be development of adequate communication, travel, and problem-solving technologies to avoid the traps of neofeudalism and pressures toward reactionary small-town conformity, in a society where neighborhood self-help is an important value. Obviously women and men will be working together on those research frontiers, as they will everywhere else.

Large-scale systems research is probably the area that women are least inclined to, the area for which the underside seems a particularly inadequate preparation, and also the area where women are most badly needed. Because the world is one ecosystem, interrelationships, both physical and social, must be studied at the planetary level. It is easy to lose one's grounding in reality, however, when studying global systems. This can lead to serious errors in judgment, as military decision makers demonstrate daily.

One of the major challenges that lie immediately ahead for women is to develop a training sequence for people who must work with large-scale systems, a sequence that utilizes those skills of environmental scanning and of taking feedback from the immediate environment that every person first develops in the family and neighborhood setting. A graduated sequence would involve taking feedback from ever-larger environmental systems, with repeated returns to primary feedback systems. This is necessary to help people gain "grounded" perceptions of global reality. Another set of educational inventions is needed to train the capacity for nonlinear, metaphoric thinking to supplement linear thinking, particularly for use in working with complex systems which cannot be grasped linearly.

There is nothing inherent in global thinking that is antithetical to decentralism. The decentralist world does not represent a retreat from responsibility for global welfare, but a new approach to it. Because women have not entered the world-order and global-modeling fields to any great extent, they have not had the opportunity to try to spell out the institutional structures of this decentralist world. This spelling out will certainly be coming in the next decades.[25]

Women's grounding in the underside is a tremendous advantage for work in all the research frontiers mentioned. The questions they will bring to the research process will be different from overside questions, and their reality-testing procedures will stem from different life experiences.

The ways of using the underlife experience of women that I have been describing will result in the obliteration of the underside-overside dichotomy, and will make knowledge and skills relevant to the creation of a human, decentralist society available to everyone. What will happen to family life in the course of localization? Will localization be a new device for trapping women? Certainly in the past, small-town life has been much more confining to women than to men. The key to the reconstructed society I visualize is in the apprenticeship system that replaces the present excessively classroom-oriented educational system. Girls and boys will both be apprenticed to nursery schools, child care centers, and homes with small babies in them. Whatever set of skills one sex learns, the other will also learn. Once parenting ceases to be viewed as an exclusively female function, then the responsibilities resulting from childbearing will be equally shared in whatever type of household is formed.

While the male-female partnership as a core feature of household formation has proved remarkably durable over millennia, it has always been but one of several ways to organize households. It will probably never account for the living patterns of more than 50 percent of adult women and men at any one time in the future, nor has it probably in the past. Communes under various labels, whether consisting of all women, of all men, or of couples in more or less stable partnerships, have also proved remarkably durable as alternative patterns for households though the specific communal forms change. Some are religious, some are secular. This last quarter of the twentieth century is once again an active period for communal experiments, so we will certainly be seeing new communal forms evolving in the future. (See for example Kanter's study, *Communes*, 1973.) The solitary life has also had recurring attraction for people in either a secular or a religious mode.

The significance of all these household patterns is that they will exist in a neighborhood context interpenetrated by a community-wide apprenticeship system. Children will be scattered throughout the community as part of the daily routine, and involvement with children will be part of every adult's role. Child abuse will be greatly reduced when one relatively small sector of the population, young mothers, no longer feels crushed by a totalistic type of responsibility for a child that dehumanizes both child and adult. There will be child care centers, but because so many parts of the community are involved in them, they will not contribute to the sterile age-segregation which day care centers now support, as part of the kindergarten-through-twelfth-grade system. The concept of age interpenetration draws on the best of past human experience, when children spent much more time in adult life spaces, engaged in socially meaningful activity; it leaves out the worst aspects of that experience, which were excessive and harmful child labor and little opportunity for new learnings, creativity, and play. One of the anomalies of the child's role in industrial society is the absurd stigma of illegitimacy for children born to unpartnered women. This type of labeling will disappear as all societies return to practices once universal in tribal society, the legitimation of a child's existence through the recognition of the birth itself (United Nations, 1971). Womb implantation will be possible for the men who desire it. The number of people who change partners in a lifetime, like the percentage unpartnered at any one time, is another one of the stabilities that is not likely to change. In the United States, where the divorce rate has been rising rapidly, the average duration of marriage has remained the same (table 8 in Commission on Population Growth, 1972: 256). What has changed is length of life, encouraging consideration of more partnerships.

With the shift from a high-energy-budget life style to a low-energy-budget life style that will be coming in the next twenty-five years, Western countries will develop their own intermediate technologies. These will be different from those developed in the third world, but will also involve more emphasis on labor-intensive rather than capital-intensive productive activities, including community food-raising ventures (Wade, 1975). This will counteract any possible regressive inclination to shift women out of the labor force with a decline in certain industrial activities. In addition to changing production patterns, many new types of jobs will emerge from the new network approach to community health, education, and welfare. A whole new set of skills will be required to create and maintain the networks.

Advanced technology will not disappear. Communication and transportation technology will increase in importance, to enable local communities to hold discussions via neighborhood video screens with other communities in any part of the world. There will be much traveling between "sister communities" on different continents. A few cities on every continent will remain major world capitals, but very differently organized and administered than at present.

In my projection of the future I have suggested nothing the least bit radical. I have assumed that shifting to a smaller scale of organization for many aspects of daily life, and developing a more intensive utilization of the human resources of both sexes and all ages and ethnic and racial backgrounds in local communities, will also stimulate the fuller development of all individuals and shift us gradually away from the evolutionary detour of a sex-segregated division of labor. On the whole, people like continuity as well as change, and need other people to care about them, whether they are young or old. That is why both family-type and commune-type households are likely to continue into the future. Both sets of patterns can provide stability and caring over time, particularly in a supportive community environment. The loneliness and alienation of suburbia has no place in the future I am describing; neither do the extreme marital tensions that arise from that alienation. When women have an autonomous sense of their own being, having a husband will not oppress them, living alone will not oppress them, having children will not oppress them, having a job will not oppress them. They will move from one pattern to another, as men will, when the time seems right for it. Since there will be no public spaces marked for white men only, women and minorities will be fully involved in the work of shaping the new society.

The utopia I have been describing is from a first-world perspective. The second-world, or socialist, perspective would be somewhat different, but perhaps not so very different. In the future I envision, development experts, business investors, and military advisors (whether first or second world) will no longer make the harmful if sometimes well-meant interventions in the third world that have resulted in so many disasters in the past for countries receiving aid. The new type of training in global ecosystem analysis will help prevent this type of intervention. The sheer fact of removal of the outside pressures generated by first- and second-world military and development aid will give breathing space to countries that have been forced into dependency syndromes. A reexamination of internal resources, both physical and cultural, will lead to patterns of reorganization that neither Western-style socialism nor Western-style capitalism could have predicted. This is already happening in China, of course. Resource sharing among the three worlds will continue, but the terms of sharing will be different. The use to which resources will be put will also be different. Population spiraling will come under control rather rapidly as new variants of Gandhi-style indigenous village-development plans, such as were initiated in India before that country decided on Western-style industrialization, start to take hold (Gandhi, 1962; Narayan, 1970). The oil-rich third world may be the last to shift to decentralism and intermediate technology. At first resisting the new ecological analyses, in time oil-exporting countries will come to see the value of new types of national life styles, different from the ones they had been preparing for. Norway, the latest country to become an oil exporter, will be one of the first to choose the new low-energy life style, and will be instrumental in changing the thinking of other oil-exporting countries.

In the future world I have been describing, women are *people.* How do we get from here to there? When are school systems going to begin hiring women to reconstruct community education? When are cities going to begin hiring women to reconstruct neighborhoods and develop new kinds of community services? When is the military-industrial complex going to let women teach them how to conceptualize the planet differently?

Part of the answer is: when women are themselves ready to begin doing these things. Nothing I have described in my image of the future for the West is not already being done somewhere, on however small a scale, but it is not often being initiated by women. Their underlife training inhibits them from using their own skills of imagining and innovating. There are parts of the world where that is not true, parts of the world where women already feel the autonomy I am imagining for Western women in the future. For Americans, North and South, there is an alternative model for women close at hand, in the Native American communities. Many of the tribal communities have been destroyed by internal colonialism, and "chiefs" chosen and supported by United States government officials have replaced indigenous patterns of leadership in many areas. Nevertheless, these decades are witnessing a resurgence of awareness of tribal traditions and a readiness to create new intertribal traditions that may point the way to new life for once-dying Native American nations. It doesn't take many encounters with women tribal leaders who have the quiet confidence of centuries of traditional knowledge behind them to realize that here are a set of teachers for European-stock American women right in our midst. Where does their serenity and self-confidence come from? What do they "know"? Only they can tell us, and they are busy. They are busy with their own problems of injustice, with problems of broken treaties, with their task of creating a world network of indigenous peoples. They haven't much time for us, and they don't necessarily think the problems of white or black women's "liberation" are very important, embedded as these are in a way of life rejected by Native Americans. A combination of humility and good sense should make it possible for non-indigenous American women to learn from Native American women. (See American Indian Treaty Council Information Center, 1975.)

Another place to look for role models is in black Africa. African women have many problems, at least as many as Native American women. But where does that inner serenity, that quiet sureness, that sense of a life apart that Sylvia Leith-Ross described (in chapter 12), come from? What do they "know"?

Another place to look, of course, is China. How could oppressed Chinese women organize a nation containing one-third of the world's population? How did they manage a women's organization reaching into every nook and cranny of China? How were they able to write new family laws that provided for their own liberation from feudalism, and see to it that they were enforced? How were they able to design a land distribution scheme that gave land to women for the first time in China's history, and see to it that it was enforced? How were they able to design a commune system that has reshaped economic and social life for a third of the world's population? We know there have been setbacks, and that the old China still lives inside the new. But how did they manage to achieve as much as they did? Where does *their* serenity, *their* sureness, come from?

Every part of the world has teachers for women. These women of quiet self-confidence, with knowledge, with strength, are everywhere. Their skin is all colors, their language all languages, their religion all religions. Euro America has them too.

This is a time for the rest of us, especially middle-class Western women, to "go to school" to those of our sisters who have the unacknowledged skills, the confidence, the serenity, and the knowledge required for creative social change. Not because other solutions from other traditions are necessarily better, not because women elsewhere are smarter. No, underlife structures exist everywhere and have confined most women. We have walked through ten thousand years of such structures in this book. We have also discovered how strong women are, how steadily and creatively they have built century after century from the underside. This is a time to break through those underside barriers, moving with the strength and confidence our history can give us. We must help each other on every continent. We owe it to each other in that great sisterhood of humanity that stretches out to encompass all women who have ever lived and all women yet to be born.

Appendix 13-1
Women in National Legislative Bodies

Country	Legislative Body	No. of Members	Year	Proportion of Women (percent)
NORTH AND EAST EUROPE				
Finland	Eduskunta	200	1907	10
			1908	13
			1930	6
			1966	17
			1975	22
Sweden	Parliament*	380	1921	1
			1949	7
			1967	14
		350	1975	21
Denmark	Folketing	179	1963	8
			1975	17
Poland	Parliament		1975	15
Bulgaria	Parliament		1975	19
	Council of the People		1975	37
U.S.S.R.	Supreme Soviet		1974	31
			1975	35
	Central Committee	241	1975	2
	Council of Ministers	92	1975	0
	Politburo	22	1975	0
WEST EUROPE, NORTH AMERICA AND OCEANIA				
U. K.	House of Commons	630	1943	4
			1951	3
			1963	4
			1975	4
W. Germany	Bundestag	518	1950	10
			1963	9
			1975	7
Greece	Chamber of Deputies	300	1963	1
			1975	2
U. S.	Congress*	535	1961	4
			1971	2
			1975	3
New Zealand	Parliament	80	1963	5
	House of Representatives	87	1975	5
ASIA				
Japan	House of Representatives	410	1946	10
		467	1968	2
			1970	2

Country	Legislative Body	No. of Members	Year	Proportion of Women (percent)
Philippines	Senate	24	highest in any year	12
	House of Representatives	104	"	6
India	Parliament*	756	1951	3
		767	1975	5
		509	1951	3
			1957	5
		523	1962	6
			1967	5
			1971	4
Bangladesh	Parliament	313	(15 seats reserved for women)	
China (PRC)	Central Committee	74	1956	5
		145	1969	8
		260	1975	14
	Politburo	25	1973	8
		22	1975	5
	Standing Committee of the Politburo	9	1973	0
AFRICA AND MIDDLE EAST				
Israel	Knesseth	120	1948	9
			1973	7
Egypt	National Assembly	350	1975	2
Lebanon	Parliament	99	1973	0**
Syria	Parliament	122	1973	4
Tunisia	Parliament	90	1973	4
Liberia	Congress*	70	1974	7
Sudan	Parliament	250	1973	5
Guinea	National Assembly	–	1975	27
LATIN AMERICA				
Argentina	Legislature*	291	1952	11
			1972	0
			1975	2
Brazil	Legislature	430	1969	2
			1975	1
Chile	Chamber of Deputies	135	1963	4
			1968	9
			1969	7
Colombia	Congress*	232	1963	3
			1969	3
			1975	3
Costa Rica	National Assembly	57	1963	2
			1975	5
El Salvador	National Assembly	54	1963	3
		52	1975	3

Country	Legislative Body	No. of Members	Year	Proportion of Women (percent)
Guatemala	National Assembly	66	1975	2
Mexico	Parliament	238	1963	3
			1975	8
Nicaragua	Legislature*	58	1963	9
		90	1975	6
Panama	National Assembly	505	1975	0
Paraguay	Legislature	90	1975	7

SOURCE: Newland (1975: 39-41).

*Indicates a bicameral legislature.

**Only one woman has ever served in the Lebanese Parliament (*Arab Women*, Report No. 27, Minority Rights Group, 1975: 7).

Notes

1"By 1920 women . . . were receiving roughly 15 percent of the Ph.D.'s. . . . Today women . . . receive about 10 percent of the doctorates" (Graham, 1970).

2Based on a personal communication regarding unpublished study of the backgrounds of Germans associated with the extermination camps (Ernst Winter, 1973).

3Madame Marie-Thérèse Maurette, for many years director of this school, spoke with great emotion about these catastrophes at the 1962 Brussels World Forum of Women (Boulding, 1962).

4Women of that period include Gertrude Baer and Gertrud Woker of Germany; Marguerite Thibert and Eugenie Cotton of France; Johanne Reutz Gjermoe of Norway; Alexandra Kollontai of the Soviet Union; Dolores Ibarruri of Spain; Mme Dombska of Poland; Anna Kethly of Hungary; Anna Schustlerova of Czechoslovakia; Aletta Jacobs of the Netherlands; Ellen Wilkinson and Chrystal MacMillan of England; and many many others. During their lifetimes they carried on the recurring task of reconstruction after war that women have always performed. They were all writers and activists of note. A few are still alive today.

5WILPF and WIDF jointly sponsored a seminar on disarmament at the United Nations as part of the program for International Women's Year, the only occasion during the year when problems of peace and war were officially given priority by women.

6I visited some of these "women's communes" during the war while visiting the camps for conscientious objectors administered by the Quakers, Brethren, and Mennonites. The ruggedness of the living conditions was matched only by the resourcefulness of the women.

7See *Dandelion: Newsletter of the Movement for a New Society*, 4722 Baltimore Avenue, Philadelphia, Pennsylvania 19143.

8See the two issues of the *Journal of Social Issues* devoted to this topic, October 1964 and July 1967; the Block, Haan, and Smith study of activism and apathy in adolescents (1968); the Rosenhan study of the civil rights movement activists (1971); and Robert Lifton's analysis of the role of Japanese mothers in the activism of radical Japanese students in the fifties (1969).

[9]Sale's *SDS* (1974) gives a good description of the formation period, though he describes the men more vividly than he does the women. The New Year's Eve gathering he mentions on page 41 of his book was held in our home in Ann Arbor.

[10]Two women theologians have been particularly articulate in exposing sexism in church structures, doctrine, and practice. Rosemary Reuther in *New Woman, New Earth* (1975), and Mary Daly in *Beyond God the Father* (1973), both look to the church of the future in which the human spirit will be liberated both in its femaleness and its maleness.

[11]It goes without saying that not all prostitutes who have taken to writing about their profession are producing human documents of equally high quality.

[12]Excellent pictures of the contemporary women volunteers, and of workers "inside the system," can be found in Herta Loeser's *Women, Work, and Volunteering* (1974), and Laile Bartlett's *New Work / New Life* (1976).

[13]International Cooperation Year was born in the kitchen of a Kansas mother of two young children, Kathy Menninger, who was thinking one day as she did her chores how millions of mothers around the world were also doing similar chores for their families. Suddenly the idea came to her that the United Nations might declare a year in which ordinary women and men everywhere would be helped to establish links with their counterparts in other countries. It would be a year of thousands of small cooperative international projects, enabling the average person to see everyday acts as part of the building of world community. She immediately telephoned her friend Roger Fisher, professor of international law at Harvard University, to tell him of her idea. He happened at the time to be consulting with the Indian delegation about initiatives they would present to the General Assembly. When he transmitted Kathy Menninger's idea to them they liked it so well that they sponsored a resolution for a United Nations Year for International Cooperation, which was accepted by the General Assembly. Kathy soon became part of a much larger women's network supporting the idea, and the Canadian-based Voice of Women, the Women Strike for Peace, the Women's International League for Peace and Freedom, and the Women's International Democratic Federation all actively participated in preparing international teams and workshops to mount projects for the year. (This account is based on my own experience and observations. Other participants would have other perceptions of the genesis of International Cooperation Year.)

[14]There are many weaknesses and misreportings in the United Nations data on women, beyond the usual problems of coverage that all United Nations data involve. Few countries have good reporting systems on women's activities. As will be noted, I reject outright some of the figures on women in agriculture, for example. However, these figures are, with some exceptions, the best approximations available to the real-life situation of women internationally. (See Boulding, Nuss, Carson, and Greenstein, 1976, for a more complete discussion of the limitations of the data. The data cited here are from a prepublication printout for the handbook; regional categories do not conform with those in the published version.)

[15]For computational reasons, the two Americas are listed together in table 13-2 and the appendix to this chapter. Elsewhere, North and South America are kept separate. The fact that purdah-keeping North Africa is lumped together with

black Africa in all the tables to follow means that participation figures for African women may be lower than they would otherwise be.

16Even in a field like population programs, where knowledge of women's "underlife" resources, values, and behavioral options should be crucial for policy planning, one finds that a recent major review of cultural factors in population programs (Office of International Science, 1974) was undertaken by a research advisory group with less than one-third women. And less than one-third of the scholars interviewed in the course of the survey were women. While the list of scholars interviewed is impressive by conventional standards, their understanding of the dynamics of the life situation of the women who must become involved in taking control of their own reproduction remains at a high level of abstraction. There is a great gap between the understandings developed by field workers in major grassroots surveys like the recent Indonesian study (Ihromi et al., 1973) and policy decisions.

17A comparison of women and men farmers in a county in Ghana shows that when inputs and supporting services are held constant, women produce more food per acre than men do (Moock, 1973).

18Newland's (1975) excellent global review of women in politics contains a good updating of figures on women in legislative bodies, with more countries included. The general picture remains the same. The table from her pamphlet is included as the Appendix to this chapter.

19One problem is that there are no kindergartens at the United Nations. A little kindergarten-level retraining of each United Nations body might be advantageous to the world community, and employ more women in the United Nations organization.

20The vast majority of the three thousand or so NGOs are mixed organizations. Women participate actively in a number of them, but generally at the same lower levels of responsibility assigned to them in other types of mixed bodies.

21This proposal has been made by Ali Mazrui in his essay in the first book of the Preferred Worlds for the 1990's series, *On the Creation of a Just World Order* (Mazrui, 1975).

22See, however, the October 1975 issue of *Futures* (vol. 7, no. 5). It is devoted to the future of women, with four women contributors out of a total of nine authors. The reader may be interested in comparing the futures presented there with the future as projected in this chapter.

23In writers such as Ursula Le Guin (for instance, *The Dispossessed*, 1974).

24Cesaro-papism never developed in the same way in the West since the pope and the Holy Roman Emperor never merged into one person as in Byzantium. The more individualistic style of Western bureaucracies stems from centuries of state-church struggles.

25Donella Meadows, coauthor with Dennis Meadows of *Limits to Growth* (1972), is experimenting with ways to relate localist emphasis to global modeling in her present work at Dartmouth. Schon (1970) and Judge (1971), cited earlier regarding a solar system model of world order, are working in the same direction.

References

African Bibliographical Center
1969 "Contemporary African Women." Vol. 6, Special Bibliographic Series. New York: Negro Universities Press.

American Indian Treaty Council Information Center
1975 Native American Women. New York: American Indian Treaty Council Information Center.

Bartlett, Laile E.
1976 New Work / New Life. New York: Harper and Row.

Bernard, Jessie
1975 Women, Wives, Mothers: Values and Options. Chicago: Aldine.

Block, Jeanne H., Norma Haan, and M. Brewster Smith
1968 "Activism and apathy in contemporary adolescents." Pp. 198-231 in James F. Adams (ed.), Understanding Adolescence: Current Developments in Adolescent Psychology. Boston: Allyn and Bacon.

Boserup, Ester
1970 Woman's Role in Economic Development. New York: St. Martin's Press.

Boulding, Elise
1975a "Women, bread and babies: Directing aid to fifth world farmers," a background paper for a conference on The World Food and Population Crisis: A Role for the Private Sector, Dallas, Texas, April.
1975b "Alternative capabilities for world problem-solving: A comparison of religious and secular non-governmental organizations in the woman's sector," paper prepared for the INTERNET on Religion of the Comparative Interdisciplinary Studies Section, International Studies Association, Washington, D. C., February.
1974 "Futures for Franciscans," paper prepared for the Chapter of Mats, Franciscan Sisters, Centennial Celebration and Futures Convention, August 11-17.
1966 "The road to Parliament for women," paper presented to the International Seminar on the Participation of Women in Public Life," Rome, October.

1965 "Who are these women? Report on research on new women's peace movement." in M. Schwebel (ed.), Behavioral Science and Human Survival. Palo Alto, Calif.: Science and Behavior Books.

1963 "Moscow-Warsaw journal" (mimeo).

1962 "Report to women's groups and educators in the United States on the Brussels conference on 'The Education of Children and Youth in the Spirit of Friendship and Understanding among Peoples,'" November (mimeo).

Boulding, Elise, Shirley A. Nuss, Dorothy Carson, and Michael Greenstein
1976 Women's Global Data Handbook. Beverly Hills, Calif.: Sage Publications.

Burkhart, Kathryn Watterson
1973 Women in Prison. Garden City, N. Y.: Doubleday.

Bussey, Gertrude, and Margaret Tims
1965 Women's International League for Peace and Freedom, 1915-1965: A Record of Fifty Years' Work. London: Allen and Unwin.

Commission on Population Growth
1972 Demographic and Social Aspects of Population Growth. The Commission on Population Growth and the American Future Research Reports.

Daly, Mary
1973 Beyond God the Father: Toward a Philosophy of Women's Liberation. Boston: Beacon.

Friedan, Betty
1963 The Feminine Mystique. New York: W. W. Norton.

Gandhi, M. K.
1962 Village Swaraj. Compiled by H. M. Vyas. Ahmedabad, India: Navajivan Publishing House.

Graham, Patricia Albjerg
1970 "Women in academe." Science 169 (September 25): 1284-1290.

Ihromi, T. O., et al.
1973 The Status of Women and Family Planning in Indonesia. Jakarta: National Training and Research Center.

Judge, Anthony
1971 "Matrix organization and organizational networks." International Associations 3: 154-170.

Kanter, Rosabeth Moss (ed.)
1975 "Women and the structure of organizations: Explorations in theory and behavior." Pp. 34-74 in Marcia Millman and Rosabeth Moss Kanter (eds.), Another Voice: Feminist Perspectives on Social Life and Social Science. Garden City, N. Y.: Doubleday / Anchor.

Krelle, Janet, Jody Zemel, Judy Reynolds, Karen Garcia, Wendy Speziale, Holley Phelps, and Melinda Lopez
1975 "Women's Who's Who in America: A comparative analysis between 1915 and 1973." Unpublished student paper. Boulder: University of Colorado, Department of Sociology.

Le Guin, Ursula K.
  1974   The Dispossessed. New York: Harper and Row.

Lifton, Robert
  1969   History and Human Survival. New York: Random House.

Loeser, Herta
  1974   Women, Work, and Volunteering. Boston: Beacon.

Maupin, Joyce
  1974   Working Women and Their Organizations: 150 Years of Struggle.
         Berkeley, Calif.: Union WAGE Educational Committee.

Mazrui, Ali A.
  1975   "World culture and the search for human consensus." Pp. 1-38 in Saul
         H. Mendlovitz (ed.), On the Creation of a Just World Order: Preferred
         Worlds for the 1990's. New York: Free Press.

Meadows, D. H., and D. L. Meadows, et al.
  1972   Limits to Growth. New York: Universe Books.

Millet, Kate
  1970   Sexual Politics. Garden City, N.Y.: Doubleday.

Mitford, Jessica
  1973   A Kind and Usual Punishment: The Prison Business. New York: Alfred
         A. Knopf.

Moock, Peter Russell
  1973   "Managerial Ability in Small-Farm Production: An Analysis of Maize
         Yields in the Vihiga Division of Kenya." Ph.D. Dissertation, Columbia
         University.

Narayan, Shirman
  1970   Relevance of Gandhian Economics. Ahmedabad, India: Navjivan
         Publishing House.

Newland, Kathleen
  1975   "Women in politics: A global review." Worldwatch paper no. 3. Wash-
         ington, D.C.: Worldwatch Institute.

Office of International Science (American Association for the Advancement of
         Science)
  1974   Culture and Population Change. Washington, D. C.: American Associa-
         tion for the Advancement of Science.

Reuther, Rosemary Radford
  1975   New Women, New Earth: Sexist Ideologies and Human Liberation.
         New York: Seabury.

Rosenhan, David
  1971   "The natural socialization of altruistic autonomy." Pp. 251-268 in J.
         Macauly and L. Berkowitz (eds.), Altruism and Helping Behavior.
         New York: Academic Press.

Russett, Bruce, et al.
  1964   World Handbook of Political and Social Indicators. New Haven: Yale
         University Press.

St. James, Margo
1975 San Francisco, Calif.: COYOTE organizer, personal communication.

Sale, Kirkpatrick
1974 SDS: Ten Years Toward a Revolution. New York: Random House.

Schon, Donald
1970 "BBC Ruth lectures." The Listener (December 3). BBC Publications.

Szalai, Alexander
1973 The Situation of Women in the United Nations. New York: United Nations, UNITAR.

Tabor, Pauline
1971 Pauline's: Memoirs of the Madam on Clay Street. Louisville, Ken.: Touchstone.

Tillion, Germaine
1975 Ravensbruch: An Eyewitness Account of a Women's Concentration Camp. Tr. by Gerald Satterwhite. Garden City, N. Y.: Doubleday/Anchor.

Union of International Associations
1973- Yearbook of International Organizations. Brussels: Union of Inter-
1974 national Associations.

United Nations
1971 "La condition de la mère celibataire en droit et dans la pratique." Report of the Secretary General, Commission on the Status of Women (mimeo).

Wade, Nicholas
1975 "Karl Hess: Technology with a human face." Science 187 (January 31): 332-334.

Winter, Ernst
1973 Transnational Research Center, Schloss Eichbüchl, A-2801 Kätzelsdorf, Austria. Personal communication.

Women's International Network
1975 Women's International Network News. New York: Women's International Network.

References to Figures

Illustrations have been taken from the sources cited below. Contributing artists are indicated by initials: BB, Bonnie Boulding; KH, Kathy Hamilton; HBR, Helen Barchilon Redman.

Figure 1-1. Drawn by KH from a model developed by Elise Boulding.

Figure 3-1. La Ferrassie, Dordogne: engraved stone (after Peyrany); Neanderthal. P. 349 in Alexander Marshack, *The Roots of Civilization*. New York: McGraw-Hill, 1972. Redrawn by HBR.

Figure 3-2. Drawn by HBR.

Figure 3-3. Leroi-Gourhan classification of Ice Age cave-painting symbols. In Marshack (1972: 198).

Figure 3-4a. Laussel, Dordogne: bas-relief; Upper Perigordian. In Marshack (1972: 335). Redrawn by HBR.

Figure 3-4b. Dolní Věstonice, Moravia: fired clay; East Gravettian or Pavlovian. In Marshack (1972: 297). Redrawn by HBR.

Figure 3-4c. Peterfels, Germany: reindeer antler; Upper Magdalenian. In Marshack (1972: 286). Redrawn by HBR.

Figure 3-4d. Calendar bone; Late French Magdalenian. In Marshack (1972: 315). Redrawn by HBR.

Figure 3-4e. Peterfels, Germany: coal pendant; Upper Magdalenian. In Marshack (1972: 284). Redrawn by HBR.

Figure 3-4f. Peterfels, Germany: coal figurine; Upper Magdalenian. In Marshack (1972: 285). Redrawn by HBR.

Figure 3-4g. Dolní Věstonice, Moravia: ivory beads; East Gravettian or Pavlovian. In Marshack (1972: 364). Redrawn by HBR.

Figure 3-4h. Dolní Věstonice, Moravia: ivory pendant; East Gravettian or Pavlovian. In Marshack (1972: 292). Redrawn by HBR.

Figure 3-4i. Le Placard, Charente: carved and engraved antler; Middle Magdalenian. In Marshack (1972: 293). Redrawn by HBR.

Figure 3-4j. Peterfels and Pekamas, Germany: line rendition of sculpted image. In Marshack (1972: 307). Redrawn by HBR.

Figure 3-4k. Line rendition of carved and engraved vulval images; Upper Paleolithic. In Marshack (1972: 297). Redrawn by HBR.

Figure 4-1. P. 228 in Jacquetta Hawkes and Sir Leonard Woolley, *Prehistory and Beginnings of Civilization.* Vol. 1, *History of Mankind.* New York: Harper and Row, 1963. Map by Hallwag Berne.

Figure 4-2a. P. 23 in James Mellaart, *Earliest Civilizations of the Near East.* New York: McGraw-Hill, 1965. Drawing by Gillian Jones after Perrot; redrawn by BB.

Figure 4-2b. From Mellaart (1965: 38). Drawing by Gillian Jones after Stekelis; redrawn by BB.

Figure 4-2c. P. 97 in Jonathan Norton Leonard, *The First Farmers.* New York: Time-Life, 1973. Redrawn by BB.

Figure 4-2d. Plate 52 in Douglas Fraser, *Village Planning in the Primitive World.* New York: George Braziller, 1968.

Figure 4-2e. From Leonard (1973: 105). Redrawn by BB.

Figure 4-2f. Drawing by BB from a description in Leonard (1973: 104).

Figure 4-2g. Drawing by BB from a description in Leonard (1973: 103).

Figure 4-2h. From Mellaart (1965: 292). Drawing by Gerard Bakker; redrawn by BB.

Figure 4–2i. From Mellaart (1965: 122). Drawing by Gillian Jones; redrawn by BB and HBR.

Figure 4-2j. From Leonard (1973: 97). Redrawn by BB.

Figure 4-2k. From Mellaart (1965: 55). Reconstruction painting by Gaynor Chapman; redrawn by BB.

Figure 4-3. Kestner Museum, Hanover: terra cotta; 6th century Boetian. P. 100 in Maria-Gabrielle Wasien, *Sacred Dance: Encounter with the Gods.* New York: Avon Books, 1974. Redrawn by HBR.

Figure 4-4. Musée du Louvre, Paris: stone figurines; archaic Greece. Facing p. 41 in Sophie Drinker, *Music and Women: The Story of Women in Their Relation to Music.* New York: Coward-McCann, 1948. Redrawn by HBR.

Figure 4-5a. Musée du Louvre, Paris: alabaster; c. 1st-2nd century A.D., Parthian. Plate 49 in Erich Neumann, *The Great Mother: An Analysis of the Archetype,* tr. by Ralph Manheim. Princeton, N. J.: Princeton University Press, 1963. Redrawn by HBR.

Figure 4-5b. Collection of Colonel Norman Colville: terra cotta relief; c. 2000 B.C., Larsa Dynasty, Sumerian. In Neumann (1963: plate 126). Redrawn by HBR.

Figure 4-5c. Musée du Louvre, Paris: fragment of ivory box; 13th century B.C., Mycenaean. In Neumann (1963: plate 123). Redrawn by HBR.

Figure 4-5d. Formerly in the Museum für Völkerkunde, Berlin: wood figure; n.d., Belgian Congo. In Neumann (1963: plate 39). Redrawn by HBR.

Figure 4-5e. Musée du Louvre, Paris: stone; Thebes, Boetia. In Neumann (1963: plate 147). Redrawn by HBR.

Figure 4-5f. Victoria and Albert Museum, London: copper casting; 17th-18th century, northern India. In Neumann (1963: plate 66). Redrawn by HBR.

Figure 4-5g. Metropolitan Museum of Art, New York: alabaster sculpture; 14th century, Lower Rhine or Moselle Valley. Facing p. 37 in Carmen Gómez-Moreno, *Medieval Art from Private Collections: A Special Exhibition at the Cloisters, Oct. 30, 1968, through March 30, 1969.* New York: The Metropolitan Museum of Art, 1968. Redrawn by HBR.

Figure 4-6. In Hawkes and Woolley (1963: 297).

Figure 5-1. In Hawkes and Woolley (1963: 248). Map by Hallwag Berne.

Figure 5-2. In Hawkes and Woolley (1963: 249). Map by Hallwag Berne.

Figure 5-3. British Museum, London: woodcut from G. Agricola, *De Re Metallica, 1556.* Facing p. 202 in Julia O'Faolain and Lauro Martines, eds., *Not in God's Image: Women in History from the Greeks to the Victorians.* New York: Harper and Row, 1973.

Figure 5-4. P. 9 in Anthony Edwin James Morris, *History of Urban Form: Prehistory to the Renaissance.* New York: Wiley, 1974. Redrawn by KH.

Figure 5-5. Green slate bas-relief; King's Valley temple, Giza. Plate 47 in K. Lange and M. Hirmer, *Egypt: Architecture, Sculpture, Painting in Three Thousand Years,* 3rd rev. ed. Greenwich, Conn.: Phaidon Publishers, 1961. Redrawn by HBR.

Figure 5-6. Staatliche Museum, Berlin: copper; c. 2040-1700 B.C. In Neumann (1963: plate 38). Redrawn by HBR.

Figure 5-7. Tomb painting; n.d. P. 102 in Lionel Casson, *Daily Life in Ancient Egypt.* New York: American Heritage, 1975. Redrawn by HBR.

Figure 5-8. Florence: limestone; V Dynasty, Egyptian. P. 19 in Paul Brandt, *Schaffende Arbeit und Bildende Kunst.* Leipzig: Alfred Kröner Verlag, 1927. Redrawn by HBR.

Appendix 5-1. P. 173 in Samuel N. Kramer, *Cradle of Civilization* (New York: Time-Life, 1967), and p. 177 in C. M. Bowra, *Classical Greece* (New York: Time-Life, 1965). Adapted by Elise Boulding; graph by KH.

Appendix 5-2. In Morris (1974: 3).

Figure 6-1. Compiled by Elise Boulding; graph by KH.

Figure 6-2. Musée du Louvre, Paris: detail of wall painting; 18th century B.C., Babylonian. P. 283 in André Parrot, *Sumer: The Dawn of Art,* tr. by Stuart Gilbert and James Emmons. New York: Golden Press, 1961. Redrawn by HBR.

Figure 6-3a. Baghdad Museum: limestone head; first half of 3rd millennium B.C., Mesopotamian. In Parrot (1961: 110). Redrawn by HBR.

Figure 6-3b. Baghdad Museum: limestone head; first half of 3rd millennium B.C., Mesopotamian. In Parrot (1961: 110). Redrawn by HBR.

Figure 6-3c. Damascus Museum: gypsum head; first half of 3rd millennium B.C., Mesopotamian. In Parrot (1961: 124). Redrawn by HBR.

Figure 6-4. Aleppo Museum: white stone; c. 2040-1870 B.C., Mesopotamian. P. 162 in Eva Strommenger, *Five Thousand Years of the Art of Mesopotamia,* tr. by Christina Haglund. New York: Harry N. Abrams, 1964. Redrawn by HBR.

Figure 6-5. Detail from right-hand post of the bronze gates of King Shalmaneser III (882-858 B.C.). In Strommenger (1964: 212). Redrawn by HBR.

Figure 6-6. Metropolitan Museum of Art, New York: limestone statue; Thebes. In Lange and Hirmer (1961: plate 127). Redrawn by HBR.

Figure 6-7. Metropolitan Museum of Art, New York: tomb painting; Eighteenth Dynasty, Thebes. In Casson (1975: 3). Redrawn by HBR.

Figure 6-8. Cairo Museum: painted wood; Eleventh Dynasty, Egyptian. P. 39 in Jean Yoyotte, *Treasures of the Pharaohs,* tr. by Robert Allen. Geneva: Skira, 1968. Redrawn by HBR.

Figure 6-9. Metropolitan Museum of Art, New York: ivory plaque; late 9th century B.C., Assyrian. Plate 62 in Donald Harden, *The Phoenicians.* Harmondsworth, Middlesex: Pelican Books, 1971. Redrawn by HBR.

Figure 6-10. Kandia Museum: painted gypsum; late Minoan III. Plate 153 in Helmuth Th. Bossert, *Alt Kreta: Kunst und Kunstgewerbe im Ägäischen Kultrukreise.* Berlin: Verlag Ernst Wasmuth, 1921. Redrawn by HBR.

Figure 6-11a. Musée d'Hérakleion, Crete: casting in schist; late Minoan III. Plate 745 in Christian Zervos, *L'Art de la Crète: Néolithique et Minoenne.* Paris: Editions Cahiers d'Art, 1956. Redrawn by HBR.

Figure 6-11b. Musée d'Hérakleion, Crete: Votive double axes in gold; late Minoan I. In Zervos (1956: plate 623). Redrawn by HBR.

Figure 6-11c. Musée d'Hérakleion, Crete: double hatchet in bronze; middle III-late Minoan I. In Zervos (1956: plate 431). Redrawn by HBR.

Figure 6-12. Museum für Völkerkunde, Berlin: faience; late Minoan III. Plate 130 in Bossert (1921). Redrawn by HBR.

Figure 6-13. Vienna Museum: marble statue; Hellenic. Facing p. 21 in Guy Cadogan Rothery, *The Amazons in Antiquity and Modern Times.* London: Francis Griffiths, 1910. Illustration by Allan Barr.

Figure 6-14. Museo Archeologico, Florence: detail of painted limestone sarcophagus; late 4th century B.C., Tarquinia. P. 108 in Jean Charbonneaux, Roland Martin, and François Villard, *Hellenistic Art: 350-330 B.C.,* tr. by Peter Green. New York: George Braziller, 1973. Redrawn by HBR.

Figure 6-15. Museo Nazionale, Naples: bell crater; n.d. Plate 4 in Erwin Bielefeld, *Amazonomachia: Beitrage zur Geschichte der Motivwanderung in der Alten Kunst.* Halle: Max Niemeyer Verlag, 1951. Redrawn by HBR.

Figure 6-16. City Plan of Priene, c. 350 B.C. In Morris (1974: 29). Redrawn by KH.

Figure 6-17. Archaeological Society, Athens: Attic hydria; c. 450 B.C. Plate 44 in Drinker (1948). Courtesy of G. Routledge and Sons, Ltd. Redrawn by HBR.

Figure 7-1. Vindonissa Museum, Brigg, Switzerland: facing tile; Gallo-Roman period, Aargaul. Plate 201 in Marcel Pobé, *The Art of Roman Gaul: A Thousand Years of Celtic Art and Culture.* Toronto: University of Toronto Press, 1961. Redrawn by HBR.

Figure 7-2. Musée Alesia, Alise-St.-Reine: native stone statue; Gallo-Roman. In Pobé (1961: plate 180). Redrawn by HBR.

Figure 8-1. Imperial Villa, Pompeii: wall painting; 1st century A.D. copy of 3rd century B.C. original. In Carbonneaux, Martin, and Villard (1973: plate 135). Redrawn by HBR.

Figure 8-2. Museo Nazionale, Naples: wall painting; Pompeii. In Casson (1975: 21). Redrawn by HBR.

Figure 8-3. Palermo Museo: sculpture; ancient Roman. Drawn by HBR after a slide in Department of Fine Arts, University of Colorado.

Figure 8-4. Rome: detail of marble freize. Ara Pacis Augustas Procession (13-9 B.C.). Plate 103 in Heinz Kähler, *Rom und seine Welt: Bilder zur Geschichte und Kultur.* Munich: Bayerischer Schulbuch-Verlag, 1958. Redrawn by HBR.

Figure 8-5. Koninklijke Bibliotheek, The Hague: detail of a miniature from the *Hours of Philippe le Bon;* mid-15th century, Flemish. Plate 12 in Joan Evans, *The Flowering of the Middle Ages.* London: Thames and Hudson, 1966. Redrawn by HBR.

Figure 8-6. Pinscoteca, Vatican, Rome: reconstructed view based on panel painting by Emmanuel Tzanphournasis of Crete; 16th century, Byzantine. P. 26 in Philip Sherrard, *Byzantium.* New York: Time-Life, 1966. Redrawn by HBR.

Figure 8-7. La Madeleine, Vezclay: nave capital; Romanesque. Drawn by HBR after a slide in Department of Fine Arts, University of Colorado.

Figure 8-8. Biblioteca Nacional, Madrid: manuscript illumination from *Chronicle of John Scylitzes;* 14th century, Byzantine. In Sherrard (1966: 69). Redrawn by HBR.

Figure 8-9. Pompeii: wall painting. In Casson (1975: 109). Redrawn by HBR.

Figure 9-1. Uffizi Gallery, Florence: detail from St. Humilitas altarpiece, by Pietro Lorenzetti; Gothic, 1341. P. 91 in Jacques Dupont and Cesare Gnudi, *The Great Centuries of Painting: Gothic Painting,* tr. by Stuart Gilbert. Geneva: Skira, 1954. Redrawn by HBR.

Figure 9-2. Walters Art Gallery, Baltimore: illumination detail: South German Psalter, c. 1200. In Karen Petersen and J. J. Wilson, *Women Artists: Recognition and Reappraisal.* New York: Harper and Row, 1976. Redrawn by HBR.

Figure 9-3. Biblioteca Ambrosiana, Milan: Italian manuscript, 1421. P. 209 in Charles Singer et al., editors, *A History of Technology.* Vol. 2. New York: Oxford University Press, 1956. After a photograph by K. F. Rowland.

Figure 9-4. Archives Assistance Publique, Paris: painting; Gothic, 1443. P. 58 in Robert Delort, *Life in the Middle Ages,* tr. by Robert Allen. New York: Universe Books, 1973. Redrawn by HBR.

Figure 9-5. Yale Manuscript f 100 v; Gothic, n.d. Plate 706 in Lilian M. C. Randall, *Images in the Margins of Gothic Manuscripts.* Berkeley: University of California Press, 1966. Redrawn by HBR.

Figure 9-6. *Rupertsberger Kodex:* illumination, 1165. P. 31 in Hildegard von Bingen, *Wisse die Wege: Scivias.* Salzburg: Otto Müller Verlag, 1954. Redrawn by HBR.

Figure 9-7. Bibliothèque Nationale, Paris: miniature by Christine de Pisan; MS Français 607, f 2. In Dupont and Gnudi (1954: 158). Redrawn by HBR.

Figure 9-8. Musée de Cluny, Paris: painting; n.d. P. 11 in Clara and Richard Winston, *Daily Life in the Middle Ages.* New York: American Heritage, 1975. Redrawn by HBR.

Figure 9-9. British Museum, London: woodcut, *Virgiliis Solis;* 16th century. In Singer et al. (1956: 196).

Figure 9-10a. British Museum, London: miniature from *Livre des Femmes Nobles et Renomées;* early 15th century, France. In Evans (1966: 251). Redrawn by HBR.

Figure 9-10b. Miniature from *Tacuinum Sanitatis;* Gothic. In Brandt (1928: 79). Redrawn by HBR.

Figure 9-11. British Museum, London: detail of anonymous engraving; 15th century. In O'Faolain and Martines (1973: 187). Redrawn by HBR.

Figure 9-12a. From M. Puff van Schriek, *Ein gutz nutzlichs Büchlein von den ussgebrenten Wassern* Strasbourg, 1512). In Singer et al. (1956: 752).

Figure 9-12b. From a playing card: 15th century, after E. Hartmann. In Singer et al. (1956: 289).

Figure 9-13. Musée de l'Ecole des Beaux Arts, Paris: from a miniature by Jean Baurdichon; c. 1500. In Singer et al. (1956: 391).

Figure 9-14. In Morris (1974: 118). Redrawn by KH.

Figure 9-15. Bibliothèque Nationale, Paris. In Winston (1975: 17). Redrawn by HBR.

Figure 9-16. Illumination detail; *Rutland Psalter.* In Randall (1966: plate 718). Redrawn by HBR.

Figure 9-17. In Delort (1973: 128). Redrawn by HBR.

Figure 9-18. Bibliothèque Nationale, Paris: Detail from Robert de Borron, *L'Histoire du Graal;* late 13th century, Picard. In Randall (1966: plate 708). Redrawn by HBR.

Figure 12-1. U.S. Committee for UNICEF, School Services. P. 17 in *UNICEF News* 76 (July 1973).

Figure 12-2. ICEF 5061/Tardio. P. 17 in Dorothea E. Woods, "The Teen-Age Girl: Her Problems and Prospects," *UNICEF News* 79 (1974).

Acknowlegments

I would like to thank those who kindly granted permission to reproduce the following illustrations and quotations:

Table 2-2, © 1975 by the President and Fellows of Harvard College. *Figure 3-4,* André Leroi-Gourhan. *Figure 4-1,* © 1963 by UNESCO, reprinted by permission of Harper & Row, Publishers, Inc. *Figure 4-2d,* ORSTOM–Service Central de Documentation. *Figure 4-6,* © by UNESCO, reprinted by permission of Harper & Row, Publishers, Inc. *Figure 5-1,* © UNESCO, reprinted by permission of Harper & Row, Publishers, Inc. *Figure 5-2,* © by UNESCO, reprinted by permission of Harper & Row, Publishers, Inc. *Figure 5-3,* Harper & Row, Publishers, Inc. *Quotation, p. 176,* taken from *The Living Bible,* © 1971 by Tyndale House Publishers, Wheaton, Illinois, used by permission. *Appendix 5-2,* © 1972 by George Godwin Limited. *Quotation, p. 243,* taken from *The Living Bible,* © 1971 by Tyndale House Publishers, Wheaton, Illinois, used by permission. *Quotation, p. 303,* © 1967 by Desmond Stewart, reprinted by permission of Brandt & Brandt. *Figure 9-3,* Imperial Chemical Industries Limited. *Figure 9-9,* Imperial Chemical Industries Limited. *Quotation, pp. 482-483,* reprinted by permission of the University of South Carolina Press, © Edward Arnold (Publishers) Ltd., 1968. *Figure 9-12a,* Imperial Chemical Industries Limited. *Figure 9-12b,* Imperial Chemical Industries Limited. *Figure 9-13,* Imperial Chemical Industries Limited. *Quotation, pp. 640-641,* © 1953 by the University of Pennsylvania Press, used by permission. *Appendix 11-1,* © 1969 by Frank Cass & Co. Ltd. *Figure 12-1,* United States Committee for UNICEF. *Figure 12-2,* United States Committee for UNICEF.

If I have unwittingly infringed copyright in any picture, photograph, or quotation reproduced in this publication, I tender my sincere apologies and will be glad of the opportunity, upon being satisfied as to the owner's title, to pay an appropriate fee as if I had been able to obtain prior permission.

Elise Boulding

Index